Modern Information Processing
From Theory to Applications

Cover figure taken from "Similarity, typicality and fuzzy prototype for numerical data".
M.-J. Lesot, In 6th European Congress on Systems Science; Workshop "Similarity
and resemblance", held in Paris, 2005.

Modern Information Processing
From Theory to Applications

Edited by

Bernadette Bouchon-Meunier
CNRS-UPMC, LIP6
Paris, France

Giulianella Coletti
Department of Mathematics and Informatics
University of Perugia, Italy

Ronald R. Yager
Machine Intelligence Institute, Iona College
New Rochelle, New York, U.S.A.

ELSEVIER

Amsterdam • Boston • Heidelberg • London • New York • Oxford • Paris
San Diego • San Francisco • Singapore • Sydney • Tokyo

Elsevier
Radarweg 29, PO Box 211, 1000 AE Amsterdam, The Netherlands
The Boulevard, Langford Lane, Kidlington, Oxford OX5 1GB, UK

First edition 2006

Copyright © 2006 Elsevier B.V. All rights reserved.

No part of this publication may be reproduced, stored in a retrieval system or transmitted in any form or by any means electronic, mechanical, photocopying, recording or otherwise without the prior written permission of the publisher

Permissions may be sought directly from Elsevier's Science & Technology Rights Department in Oxford, UK: phone (+44) (0) 1865 843830; fax (+44) (0) 1865 853333; e-mail: permissions@elsevier.com. Alternatively you can submit your request online by visiting the Elsevier web site at http://elsevier.com/locate/permissions, and selecting *Obtaining permission to use Elsevier material*

Notice
No responsibility is assumed by the Publisher for any injury and/or damage to persons or property as a matter of products liability, negligence or otherwise, or from any use or operation of any methods, products, instructions or ideas contained in the material herein. Because of rapid advances in the medical sciences, in particular, independent verification of diagnoses and drug dosages should be made

Library of Congress Cataloging-in-Publication Data
A catalog record for this book is available from the Library of Congress

British Library Cataloguing in Publication Data
A catalogue record for this book is available from the British Library

ISBN-13:   978-0-444-52075-3
ISBN-10:   0-444-52075-9

For information on all Elsevier publications
visit our website at books.elsevier.com

Printed and bound in The Netherlands
06 07 08 09 10   10 9 8 7 6 5 4 3 2 1

Foreword

IPMU (Information Processing and Management of Uncertainty in Knowledge-Based Systems) is the brain child of Bernadette Bouchon-Meunier and Ronald Yager. Born in 1986, IPMU has grown steadily in visibility and importance. The growth in importance of IPMU reflects the fact that as we move further into the age of machine intelligence and mechanized decision-making, the issue of how to deal with uncertain information becomes an issue of paramount concern.

The volume "Modern Information Processing: From Theory to Applications," or MIP for short, edited by Bernadette Bouchon-Meunier, Giulianella Coletti and Ronald Yager, and published by Elsevier, is a collection of carefully selected papers drawn from the program of IPMU'04, which was held in Perugia, Italy. Perusing the contents of MIP, one cannot but be greatly impressed by the breadth of coverage and the high quality of contributions. On the theoretical side, one finds papers ranging from belief theory and possibility theory to foundations of uncertainty theory and decision-making with fuzzy ternary relations. On the applied side, we see a broad spectrum of papers extending from cluster analysis, biomedical data classification, and probability and statistics in law, to linguistic hierarchical decision-making, and feature extraction for an electronic nose.

The unusually wide variety of concepts, methods and techniques which are discussed in MIP has an explanation. Unlike most other conferences on uncertainty—conferences which are focused on a narrow range of methodologies, IPMU welcomes all schools of thought. Embracing diversity has always been, and continues to be, the leitmotif of IPMU.

Underlying the issues addressed in MIP there is a basic issue which has a long history of discussion and debate: What is the relationship between probability theory and fuzzy logic?

An extreme view is that expressed by an eminent Bayesian, Professor Dennis Lindley, "...probability is the only sensible description of uncertainty and is adequate for all problems involving uncertainty. All other methods are inadequate...anything that can be done with fuzzy logic, belief functions, upper and lower probabilities, or any other alternative to probability can better be done with probability." The prevalent view within the probability community is more tempered. Broadly, it is that extensions of probability theory to theories of belief, upper and lower probabilities, imprecise probabilities, Bayesian networks and related directions are legitimate, but that insofar as fuzzy logic is concerned, anything that can be done with fuzzy logic can be done equally well or better with probability theory. Outside the probability community, the consensus is that probability theory and fuzzy logic are complimentary rather than competitive. The contents of MIP reflect this consensus.

Until a few years ago, my view coincided with the consensus. (See "Probability Theory and Fuzzy Logic are Complementary rather than Competitive," *Technometrics 37*, 271-276, 1995). Today, it is much more radical. (See "Probability Theory and Fuzzy Logic—A Radical View," *Journal of the American Statistical Association*, Vol. 99, 880-881, 2004). Briefly stated, my view is that foundations of probability theory, call it PT, should be moved from bivalent logic to fuzzy logic, resulting in a fuzzy-logic-based probability theory, PTf, which is much more general and much more powerful than PT. First steps in this direction were outlined in my papers "Toward a Perception-Based Theory of Probabilistic Reasoning with Imprecise Probabilities," *Journal of Statistical Planning and Inference*, Elsevier Science, Vol. 105, 233-264, 2002, and "Toward a Generalized Theory of Uncertainty (GTU)—An Outline," *Information Sciences*, Elsevier, Vol. 172, 1-40, 2005. The gain in power and generality which is achieved by moving from PT to PTf is a concomitant of the fact that in fuzzy logic, FL, everything is, or is allowed to be, a matter of degree, that is, fuzzy. The move from PT to PTf opens the door to computing with fuzzy probabilities, fuzzy events and fuzzy relations. Furthermore, it suggests redefinition of such basic concepts as independence, stationarity and expected value, making such concepts a matter of degree.

Among the consequences of moving from PT to PTf there is one that is of fundamental importance. The armamentarium of FL contains a machinery for computing with words (CW). As a part of PTf, this machinery opens the doors to operating on uncertain information which is expressed in a natural language. The fundamental importance of this capability of PTf derives from the fact that much of human knowledge is expressed in a natural language.

Development of PTf will be a complex and long-drawn process. Perhaps I am excessively optimistic, but my belief is that in coming years IPMU is likely to play an important role in furthering this process.

In conclusion, the organizers of IPMU, the editors, the contributors and the publisher deserve a loud applause. "Modern Information Processing: From Theory to Applications" contributes so much and in so many important ways to enhancement of our ability to deal effectively with uncertainty in all of its manifestations. Uncertainty is an attribute of information. "Modern Information Processing: From Theory to Applications" addresses issues which have a position of centrality in our information-centric world.

Lotfi A. Zadeh
Berkeley, July 12, 2005

Contents

Foreword.. v
L.A. Zadeh

Uncertainty... 1

Entropies, Characterizations, Applications and Some History..................... 3
J. Aczél

Belief function theory on the continuous space with an application to model based classification.. 11
B. Ristic, P.Smets

Independence in conditional possibility theory... 25
G. Coletti, B. Vantaggi

Joint treatment of imprecision and randomness in uncertainty propagation...... 37
C. Baudrit, D. Dubois, D. Guyonnet, H. Fargier

Consistency of probabilistic transformations of belief functions.................. 49
M. Daniel

Randomization and uncertain inference.. 61
H. E. Kyburg, Jr., C. M. Teng

An empirical complexity study for a 2CPA solver....................................... 73
M. Baioletti, A. Capotorti, S. Tulipani

Preferences.. 85

Consistency in preference modelling.. 87
J-L. García-Lapresta, J. Montero

Transitive decomposition of min-transitive fuzzy relations......................... 99
S. Díaz, B. De Baets, S. Montes

Decision making with fuzzy ternary relations... 111
S. Ovchinnikov

New Consistency properties for preference relations................................ 121
F. Chiclana, E. Herrera-Viedma, F. Herrera

Management of uncertainty orderings through ASP.................................. 133
A. Capotorti, A. Formisano

Classification and Data Mining.. **145**

Automating the quality assurance of an on-line knowledge-based classifier by fusing multiple off-line classifiers... 147
P. Bonissone

Qualitative classification with possibilistic decision trees........................... 159
N. Ben Amor, S. Benferhat, Z. Elouedi

Discovery of abstract knowledge from non-atomic attribute values in fuzzy relational databases.. 171
R. A. Angryk, F. E. Petry

Kernel-based outlier preserving clustering with representativity coefficients..... 183
M.J. Lesot

Fuzzy C-medoids clustering models for time-varying data......................... 195
R. Coppi, P. D'Urso, P. Giordani

Improving the K2 algorithm using association rule parameters.................... 207
E. Lamma, F. Riguzzi, S. Storari

Aggregation and Multi-Criteria Decision Making **219**

OWA aggregation on an interval argument.. 221
R. Yager

On bi-capacity-based concordance rules in multicriteria decision making......... 231
A. Rolland

Information Evaluation in fusion: Formalization of informal recommendations. 245
L. Cholvy

Application of uncertainty-based methods to fuse language identification expert decisions............... 255
J. Gutiérrez, J-L Rouas, R. André-Obrécht

Intelligent multiattribute decision support model for medical triage............... 269
F. Burstein, J. San Pedro, L. Churilov, J. Wassertheil,

Interval-based multicriteria decision making............... 281
M. Ceberio, F. Modave

A linguistic hierarchical evaluation model for engineering systems............... 295
L. Martínez, L. G. Pérez, J. Liu, J.-B. Yang, F. Herrera

Knowledge Representation............... **307**

Non monotonic aggregates applying to fuzzy sets in flexible querying............... 309
P. Bosc, L. Liétard

Fuzzy spatial data modeling: an extended bitmap approach............... 321
J. Verstraete, G. De Tré, A. Hallez

Introducing λ-specialization into the fuzzy EER model............... 333
G. Chen, L. Lin, X. Guo

A logical reasoning framework for modelling and merging uncertain semi-structured information............... 345
A. Hunter, W. Liu

Applied Domains............... **357**

Machine learning and the prediction of protein structure: the state of the art... 359
R. Casadio, R. Calabrese, E. Capriotti, M. Compiani, P. Fariselli, P. Marani, L. Montanucci, P. L. Martelli, I. Rossi, G. Tasco

Efficient and robust global amino acid sequence alignment with uncertain evolutionary distance............... 371
M. Troffaes

Classifying biomedical spectra using stochastic feature selection and parallelized multi-layer perceptrons.. 383
N.J. Pizzi, R.L. Somorjai, W. Pedrycz

On the sensitivity of probabilistic networks to reliability characteristics.......... 395
L. C. van der Gaag, S. Renooij

Dominance of recognition of words presented on right or left eye –Comparison of Kanji and Hiragana -... 407
T. Yamanoi, T. Yamazaki, J-L Vercher, E. Sanchez, M. Sugeno

Hand posture recognition with the fuzzy glove... 417
T. Allevard, E. Benoit, L. Foulloy

Image retrieval by composition of regions.. 429
J.F. Omhover, M. Detyniecki

Blind Image restoration from multiple views by IMAP estimation................. 441
M. Discepoli, I. Gerace, R. Pandolfi

A combined feature extraction method for an electronic nose..................... 453
I. Hristozov, B.Iliev, S. Eskiizmirliler

Author Index 467

UNCERTAINTY

Entropies, Characterizations, Applications and Some History

János Aczél

Faculty of Mathematics University of Waterloo
Waterloo, ON N2L 3G1, Canada
e-mail: jdaczel@math.uwaterloo.ca

Abstract

Entropies with useful and/or interesting properties are presented. Characterizations are given, based on such properties and some applications are mentioned. Attention is directed to an example of discovery and rediscovery, and to new applications in utility theory.

1. INTRODUCTION, ENTROPY

Defining new entropies in addition to the classical Shannon entropy seems to be an ongoing industry. I am still convinced, however, of what I wrote in [1]:

"In the best of all possible worlds there is an information measure that originated from an applied problem, has interesting properties (usually attractive, reasonable generalizations of properties of Shannon's entropy or of similar widely used measures), and those characterize it. Less ideal but still acceptable is in my opinion the following situation. Some natural looking weakening or generalization of properties characterizing Shannon type measures are isolated and all measures having these properties are determined. If the properties are indeed intuitive and significant then there is a good chance that the measures thus obtained may have future applications.

But what many authors seem to do is to contrive some generalization of known information measures (usually by sticking parameters almost at random here and there), derive its often not very interesting or natural or even attractive properties and then characterize by several of these properties the 'measures' they have defined in the first place. Not many good or useful results can be expected from this kind of activity."

An earlier version of the present paper appeared in [2]. As there, I express also here my belief that two families of probabilistic entropies (of which Shannon's entropy is a limit case) suffice - in addition to entropies depending on objects other than probabilities. I will define them and state (without proof but with references) some of their properties and characterizations that I consider reasonable, and mention some applications.

Our models will mostly be complete systems of mutually exclusive events $E_1, .., E_n$ (such as the possible outcomes of an experiment), with probabilities $p_1, ..., p_n$, respectively ($\sum_{k=1}^{n} p_k = 1$, $p_k \geq 0$, $k = 1, ..., n$). Entropies are *measures of uncertainty* in or *measures of information* to be gained from such a system (we will mention also entropies for incomplete systems, where $0 < \sum_{k=1}^{n} p_k \leq 1$).

2. SHANNON ENTROPY

The Shannon entropy of a complete system is given (with $0 \log_2 0 := 0$) by

$$H_n(p_1, ..., p_n) = -\sum_{k=1}^{n} p_k \log_2 p_k \qquad (1)$$

($\sum_{k=1}^{n} p_k = 1$, $p_k \geq 0$, $k = 1, ..., n$; $n = 2, 3, ...$).

NOTE 1. If incomplete systems are permitted ($0 < \sum_{k=1}^{n} p_k \leq 1$) then the definition

$$H_n(p_1, ..., p_n) = -\frac{\sum_{k=1}^{n} p_k \log_2 p_k}{\sum_{k=1}^{n} p_k}$$

is used. Here $n = 1$ is also permissible and gives as *entropy of a single event*

$$H_1(p_1) = -\log p_1 \qquad (p_1 > 0).$$

We take here the following 'reasonable' properties of the Shannon entropy. It is

(i) SYMMETRIC: H_n is a symmetric function of its n variables (*invariant* under exchange of p_j and p_k ($j, k = 1, ..., n$)),
(n) NORMALIZED: $H_2(\frac{1}{2}, \frac{1}{2}) = 1$,
(e) EXPANSIBLE: $H_{n+1}(p_1, ..., p_n, 0) = H_n(p_1, ..., p_n)$: enlarging by an event of probability 0 does not change the entropy (expected information),
(c) SMALL FOR SMALL PROBABILITIES: $H_2(1, 0) = 0$, $\lim_{q \to 0} H_2(1 - q, q) = 0$: little information can be expected if one of the events is almost certain (has probability close to 1, thus the other(s) close to 0). Thus H_2 is *continuous* at $(1, 0)$.

Now we get to important properties. We deal with three experiments:
P with outcomes $D_1, ..., D_m$, probabilities $p_j = p(D_j)$ ($j = 1, ..., m$);

Q with outcomes $E_1, ..., E_n$, probabilities $q_k = p(E_k)$ $(k = 1, ..., n)$;
"P and Q", denoted by $P*Q$, with outcomes "D_j and E_k", denoted by $D_j \cap E_k$ having the probabilities $p_{jk} = p(D_j \cap E_k)$ $(j = 1, ..., m; k = 1, ..., n)$.

The respective entropies (information expected from experiments P, Q, $P*Q$) are $H(P)$, $H(Q)$, $H(P*Q)$. The remaining two properties are:

(s) SUBADDITIVITY: $H(P*Q) \leq H(P) + H(Q)$: information expected from two experiments is not greater than the sum of informations expected from the single experiments;

(a) ADDITIVITY: $H(P*Q) = H(P) + H(Q)$ if P and Q are independent, that is, if $p(D_j \cap E_k) = p(D_j)p(E_k)$ $(j = 1, ..., m; k = 1, ..., n)$, or, in words: information expected from two independent experiments equals the sum of informations expected from the single experiments.

The following *characterization theorem* has been proved in [6] (see also [4]).

THEOREM 1. *If and only if H is (i) symmetric, (n) normalized, (e) expansible, (c) small for small probabilities, (s) subadditive and (a) additive, then H is the Shannon entropy.*

NOTE 2. The nonnegativity of the constant multiplier is guaranteed by (s). Without (c) and (n) a nonnegative constant times the *logarithm of the number of events with positive probability* can be added. The latter logarithm is often called *Hartley entropy*.

An older, classical characterization of the Shannon entropy is by

(r) RECURSIVITY:
$H_n(p_1, p_2, p_3, ..., p_n) = H_{n-1}(p_1 + p_2, p_3, ..., p_n) + (p_1 + p_2)H_2(\frac{p_1}{p_1+p_2}, \frac{p_2}{p_1+p_2})$ $(n = 3, 4, ...)$ whenever $p_1 + p_2 > 0$.

Improving a result of D.K. Faddeev [17], Z. Daróczy [13,4] has proved the following.

THEOREM 2 *If and only if H is (i) symmetric, (n) normalized, (c) small for small probabilities, and (r) recursive, then H is the Shannon entropy (1).*

G.T. Didderich [16] weakened conditon (c) to *boundedness* on an interval (square).

3. RÉNYI ENTROPY

The Shannon entropy for positive probabilities is the weighted arithmetic mean (with the probabilities as weights) of the quantities $-\log_2 p_k$ $(k = 1, ..., n)$ which can be considered (see Note 1) entropies of single events. The arithmetic mean is not the only interesting average and the Shannon entropy is not the only interesting entropy.

The Rényi [24,25] (see also [4]) entropy of order α is defined by

$$^\alpha H_n(p_1,...,p_n) = \frac{1}{1-\alpha} \log_2 \sum_{k=1}^n p_k^\alpha \quad (n=2,3,...) \qquad (2)$$

$[p_k > 0 \ (k=1,...,n)$ for sake of simplicity]. Here $\alpha \neq 1$ but $\lim_{\alpha \to 1}(^\alpha H_n(p_1,...,p_n))$ equals the Shannon entropy $\sum_{k=1}^n -p_k \log_2 p_k$.

For further reference we define a straightforward generalization of the weighted arithmetic mean of the entropies $-\log_2 p_k$ of the single events, weighted by p_k ($k=1,...,n$):

$$f^{-1}[H_n(p_1,...,p_n)] = f^{-1}[\sum_{k=1}^n p_k f(-\log_2 p_k)], \qquad (3)$$

where f is continuous and strictly monotonic. Notice that $f^{-1}[\sum_{k=1}^n p_k f(x_k)]$ gives the weighted arithmetic, geometric, exponential, harmonic, and power means when $f(x) = x, \log x, e^x, 1/x, x^c$, respectively.

The Rényi entropies of positive order (including the Shannon entropy as of order 1) have the following characterization ([3], see also [4]).

THEOREM 3. *The weighted quasiarithmetic mean (3) is* **(a)** *additive and* **(c)** *small for small probabilities if and only if it is either the Shannon's entropy (1) or a Rényi entropy (2) of positive (but $\neq 1$) order.*

The Rényi entropies $^\alpha H_n$ ($\alpha \neq 1$) need not be **(s)** subadditive. Rényi entropies have applications to random search problems [24,25], questionnaire theory [8], optimal coding (the greatest lower bounds of the arithmetic or exponential mean codeword lengths are the Shannon and the Rényi entropies, respectively) [11], even to differential geometry [12].

4. HAVRDA-CHARVÁT-DARÓCZY-TSALLIS ENTROPY

In 1988, C. Tsallis [27] introduced the entropy

$$S_n^\alpha(p_1,...,p_n) = \frac{k}{1-\alpha}(\sum_{j=1}^n p_j^\alpha - 1) \quad (n=2,3,...) \qquad (4)$$

(this is an equivalent form, slightly altered for the sake of comparisons below). It has been named "Tsallis entropy" and applied to generalizing Boltzmann-Gibbs statistical mechanics and related fields [27,26]. Characterizations were also supplied, including "the most concise set of axioms" in [26].

Already in 1967, however, J. Havrda and F. Charvát [19] defined the entropy

$$H_n^\alpha(p_1,...,p_n) = \frac{1}{2^{1-\alpha}-1}(\sum_{j=1}^n p_j^\alpha - 1) \quad (n=2,3,...) \qquad (5)$$

that is constant times (4). In 1970 Z. Daróczy [14] (see also [4] where, of course, [19] is quoted) deals with (5), its characterization, and application to channel capacity. This entropy has also been applied among others to classification processes [19], to the theory of questionnaires [8], to pattern recognition and Bayes risk bounds [15]. Notice that $\lim_{\alpha \to 1} H_n^\alpha(p_1, ..., p_n)$ is the Shannon entropy. The entropy (5) (and also (4)) satisfies

($\mathbf{r}^\alpha$) RECURSIVITY OF DEGREE α: For $p_1 + p_2 > 0$,

$$H_n^\alpha(p_1, p_2, p_3, ..., p_n) = H_{n-1}^\alpha(p_1 + p_2, p_3, ..., p_n) +$$
$$+ (p_1 + p_2)^\alpha H_2^\alpha\left(\frac{p_1}{p_1 + p_2}, \frac{p_2}{p_1 + p_2}\right)$$
$$(n = 3, 4, ...).$$

The entropies (5) have the following characterisation [14,4] (and (4) has a similar one).

THEOREM 4. *An entropy (sequence of functions of $p_1, ..., p_n$ ($n = 2, 3, ...$)) is of the form (5) if and only if it is* (i) *symmetric,* (n) *normalized, and* ($\mathbf{r}^\alpha$) *recursive of degree α.*

The entropies (5) are (s) subadditive if $\alpha > 1$. Neither (5) nor (4) need to be additive but they are "pseudoadditive":

$$H^\alpha(P * Q) = H^\alpha(P) + H^\alpha(Q) +$$
$$+ (2^{1-\alpha} - 1) H^\alpha(P) H^\alpha(Q),$$

$$S^\alpha(P * Q) = S^\alpha(P) + S^\alpha(Q) + \frac{1-\alpha}{k} S^\alpha(P) S^\alpha(Q).$$

B. Forte and C.T. Ng ([18]) gave the following characterization of (5) for all α by conditions that do not contain α.

THEOREM 5. *An entropy is of the form (5) if and only if it is* (i) *symmetric,* (n) *normalized, furthermore continuous, and satisfies $H_2(1, 0) = 1$,* **branching**:

$$H_n(p_1, p_2, \ldots, p_n) - H_{n-1}(p_1 + p_2, p_3, \ldots, p_n)$$
$$= J_n(p_1, p_2) \quad (n = 3, 4, ...),$$

and **compositivity**:

$$H_{m+n}[(1-q)p_1, ..., (1-q)p_m, qq_1, ..., qq_n] =$$
$$g[H_m(p_1, ..., p_m), H_n(q_1, ..., q_n), q],$$

where $p_1, ..., p_m, q_1, ..., q_n, q \in]0, 1[$, $\sum_{j=1}^m p_j = \sum_{k=1}^n q_k = 1$.

Notice that the branching property is a generalization of recursivity and of recursivity of degree α. Compositivity is related to weighted quasiarithmeticity (3).

There is a connection between (2) and (5) or between (2) and (4) [though not so simple as between (4) and (5)]: $H_n^\alpha = \frac{1}{2^{1-\alpha}-1}[2^{(1-\alpha)(^\alpha H_n)} - 1]$, $S_n^\alpha = \frac{k}{1-\alpha}[2^{(1-\alpha)(^\alpha H_n)} - 1]$.

5. ENTROPIES CONTAINING OBJECTS OTHER THAN PROBABILITIES

There exists a theory of *information without probability*. We dont go into it here but refer the reader to the survey [20] by J. Kampé de Fériet. But we make short mention of the *mixed theory of information* (see e.g. [5,1]). There entropies, called "inset entropies", *may depend upon the events themselves, not only upon their probabilities*. The events can be considered elements of a ring of subsets of a comprehensive set Ω that contains, with any two subsets also their union ($\cup$) and difference ($\setminus$), therefore also their intersection ($\cap$) and the empty set $\emptyset$. Boolean rings of sets contain Ω itself. By an appropriate generalization of the (**r**) recursivity, one can characterize the simplest inset entropies ([5]):

$$a \sum_{k=1}^n p_k \log p_k + \sum_{k=1}^n p_k h(E_k), \tag{6}$$

where $E_1, ..., E_n$ are elements of the Boolean ring of sets, $p_1, ..., p_n$ are their probabilities, h is an arbitrary real valued function on the Boolean ring, and a is an arbitrary constant.

It has applications, among others, in geographical and economic analysis [9,10], in the fuzzy theory of information and in gas dynamics [1].

An interesting early application (before the mixed theory of information was formally developped) is due to J. R. Meginniss ([22]; cf. [1]). He considers the *second* term in (6) as the *expected gain* in gambling (E_k being the k-th outcome of the gamble, with the gain $h(E_k)$ attached to it). So it is the *first* term that has to be explained. Since the expected gain alone would not motivate gambling (it is almost always nonpositive), he interprets the first term as quantifying the *joy in gambling*. He characterized expression (6) in this interpretation as *utility of a gamble*, and also the one corresponding to (5),

$$b(\sum_{k=1}^n p_k^c - 1) + \sum_{k=1}^n p_k^c h(E_k)$$

($0 < c \neq 1$; see also [7] for characterization of the latter inset entropy under weaker assumptions within the mixed theory of information). R. D. Luce recently initiated with coauthors ([21,23]) a new theory of *entropy-modified linear utility* where, in both of Meginniss ([22])'s expressions, probabilities are replaced by more general weights associated with events. They also characterized these expressions under considerably weaker assumptions than Meginniss ([22]).

We could have spoken about entropies of incomplete systems also in sections 3 and 4, about conditional entropies, entropies of continuous distributions, information measures for several systems (distributions) etc. everywhere. But here we stop.

Acknowledgement This work has been supported in part by Natural Sciences and Engineereing Research Council of Canada grant #OGP0002972.

REFERENCES

1. J. Aczél, "Characterizing Information Measures: Approaching the End of an Era" in *International Conference on Information Processing and Management of Uncertainty in Knowledge-Based Systems. Selected and Extended Contributions*, Lecture Notes in Computer Science, Vol. 286, Springer, Berlin/New York, 1987, pp. 359-384.

2. J. Aczél, "Entropies Old and New (and Both New and Old) and Their Characterizations" in *Bayesian Inference and Maximum Entropy Methods in Science and Engineering*, AIP Conference Proceedings, Vol. 707, American Institute of Technology, Melville, NY, 2004, pp. 119-126.

3. J. Aczél and Z. Daróczy, "Sur la caractérisation axiomatique des entropies d'ordre positf, y comprise l'entropie de Shannon" *C.R. Acad. Sci. Paris* **257**, 1581-1584 (1963).

4. J. Aczél and Z. Daróczy, *On Measures of Information and Their Characterizations*, Mathematics in Science and Engineering, Vol. 115, Academic Press, New York, 1975.

5. J. Aczél and Z. Daróczy, "A Mixed Theory of Information, I: Symmetric, Recursive and Measurable Entropies of Randomized Systems of Events" *RAIRO Informat. Théor.* **12**, 149-155 (1978).

6. J. Aczél, B. Forte and C.T. Ng, "Why the Shannon and Hartley Entropies Are 'Natural'" *Adv. in Appl. Probab.* **6**, 131-146 (1974).

7. J. Aczél and P. Kannappan, "A Mixed Theory of Information, III. Inset Entropies of Degree β", *Inform. and Control* **39**, 315-322 (1978).

8. N.L. Aggarval, Y. Cesari, and C.-F. Picard, "Propriétés de branchement liées aux questionnaires de Campbell et à l'information de Rényi" *C.R. Acad. Sci. Paris* **275A**, 437-440 (1972).

9. D.F. Batten, *Spatial Analysis of Intersecting Economies*, Kluwer, Boston, 1983.

10. M. Batty, "Speculations on an Information Theoretical Approach to Spatial Representation" in *Spatial Representation and Spatial Interaction*, Nijhoft, Leiden/Boston, 1978, pp. 115-147.

11. L.L. Campbell, "A Coding Theorem and Rényi's Entropy" *Inform. and Control* **8**, 423-429 (1965).

12. L.L. Campbell, "The Relation Between Information Theory and the Differential Geometry Approach to Statistics" *Inform. Sci.* **35**, 199-210 (1985).

13. Z. Daróczy, "On the Shannon Measure of Information" (Hungarian) *Magyar Tud. Akad. Mat. Fiz. Oszt. Közl.* **19**, 9-24 (1969) [English translation in *Selected Translations in Mathematical Statistics and Probability,* Vol. 10, Inst.Math.Statist./ Amer.Math.Soc., Providence, RI, 1972, pp. 193-210].

14. Z. Daróczy, "Generalized Information Functions" *Information and Control* **16**, 36-51 (1970).

15. P.A. Devijver, "Entropies of Degree β and the Lower Bound of the Average Error Rate" *Inform. and Control* **34**, 222-226 (1977).

16. G.T. Diderrich, "Local Boundedness and the Shannon Entropy" *Inform. and Control* **36**, 149-161 (1978).

17. D.K. Faddeev, "On the Concept of Entropy of a Finite Probabilistic Scheme" (Russian) *Uspekhi Mat. Nauk* **11**, No. 1(67), 227-231 (1956) [German translation in *Mathematische Forshungsberichte,* No. IV, DVW, Berlin, 1967, pp. 88-90].

18. B. Forte and C.T. Ng, "On a Characterization of the Entropies of Degree β" *Utilitas Math.* **4**, 193-205 (1973)

19. J. Havrda and F. Charvát, "Quantification Method of Classification Processes. Concept of Structural α-Entropy" *Kybernetika (Prague)* **3**, 30-35 (1967).

20. J. Kampé de Fériet, "La théorie géneralisée de l'information et la mesure subjective de l'information" in *Théories de l'information, Actes Rencontres, Marseille-Luminy,* Springer, New York, 1974, pp. 1-35.

21. R.D. Luce, C.T. Ng, A.A.J. Marley, and J.Aczél, "Merging Savage and Shannon: Entropy-Modified Linear Additive Utility", in preparation.

22. J.R. Meginnis, "A New Class of Symmetric Utility Rules for Gambles, Subjective Marginal Probability Functions, and a Generalized Bayes Rule" *Bus. and Econ. Stat. Sec. Proc. Amer. Stat. Assoc.* **1976**, 471-476 (1976).

23. C.T. Ng, R.D. Luce, and A.A.J. Marley, "Utility of Gambling: Extending the Approach of Meginniss", in preparation.

24. A. Rényi, "On Measures of Entropy and Information" in *Proceedings of the 4th Berkeley Symposium on Mathematical Statistics and Probability,* Vol. I, University of California Press, Berkeley, 1961, pp. 547-561.

25. A. Rényi, *Probability Theory,* North Holland/Elsevier, Amsterdam/New York, 1970.

26. H. Suyari, "On the Most Concise Set of Axioms and the Uniqueness Theorem for Tsallis Entropy" *J. Phys. A Math. Gen.* **35**, 10731-10738 (2002).

27. C. Tsallis, "Possible Generalization of Boltzmann-Gibbs Statistics" *J. Statist. Phys.* **52**, no. 1-2, 479-487 (1988).

Belief function theory on the continuous space with an application to model based classification

B. Ristic [a]
and Ph. Smets [b]

[a]ISR Division, DSTO
Edinburgh, Australia
[b]IRIDIA, Université libre de Bruxelles
Bruxelles, Belgium

Abstract

The paper defines belief functions on continuous frames of discernment, where masses generalize into densities. Explicit and manageable solutions can be formulated when densities are only assigned to the intervals of $\mathbb{R}$. When our domain knowledge is represented by the pignistic probability density, then we build the corresponding least committed belief function. The theory is applied to model based classification and the results are compared to the classical Bayesian approach.

Key words: Belief function theory, evidential theory, transferrable belief model, target classification.

1. Introduction

The belief function theory (evidential theory) has been primarily developed for discrete frames of discernment (frames). Following [9],[15], this paper defines belief functions on continuous frames, where belief masses generalize into belief densities. Explicit and manageable solutions can be formulated when densities are assigned only to the intervals on the real axis $\mathbb{R}$, although the theory is conceptually valid for $\mathbb{R}^n$.

When our domain knowledge is partial and represented only by a potential betting behavior on the observation (in the continuous domain), we model it by a pignistic probability density. In this case we can build the least committed belief function among those which correspond to the given one. Then we can apply the usual tools of the belief function theory, such as the Generalised Bayesian theorem, combination rules (e.g. Dempster's rule of combination), etc. The theory is applied to model based target classification and the results are compared to those achieved by the classical Bayesian approach.

We accept that beliefs are quantified by belief functions as described in the transferable belief model (TBM) [14]. Classical material about belief functions and the TBM can be found in Shafer [8] and Smets [11]. In order to simplify our presentation we will first consider the case where the frame is the interval $[0,1] \subset \mathbb{R}$, and there is only a final number of focal sets. Later this will be relaxed to the continuous domain (with an infinite number of focal sets) and the entire real axis $\mathbb{R}$.

2. Belief functions on $\mathbb{R}$

This section presents the extracts from a more thorough study presented in [13]. Consider a nonempty interval on the real axis $\mathbb{R}$, denoted as $[\alpha, \beta] \subseteq \mathbb{R}$, $\alpha < \beta$. Let $\mathcal{I}_{[\alpha,\beta]}$ be a set of closed intervals in $[\alpha, \beta]$. Formally,

$$\mathcal{I}_{[\alpha,\beta]} = \{[x,y] : x \geq \alpha, x \leq y \leq \beta\}.$$

We assume that masses are only alloccated to closed intervals. It implies that for a collection of pairwise disjoint intervals in $\mathcal{I}_{[\alpha,\beta]}$, the belief functions satisfy a special form of additivity. Formally, $\forall A_1, A_2, \ldots, \in \mathcal{I}_{[\alpha,\beta]}$, such that

$$A_{i_1} \cap A_{i_2} = \emptyset, \ i_1, i_2 \in \{1, 2, \ldots\}, i_1 \neq i_2$$

we have:

$$bel^{\mathcal{I}_{[\alpha,\beta]}}\left(\bigcup_{i=1,2,\ldots} A_i\right) = \sum_{i=1,2,\ldots} bel^{\mathcal{I}_{[\alpha,\beta]}}(A_i)$$

2.1. Finite number of focal sets

Let $\mathcal{A}$ be a subset of $\mathcal{I}_{[0,1]}$ consisting of a *finite* number of non-empty intervals on $[0,1]$:

$$\mathcal{A} = \{A_i : A_i \in \mathcal{I}_{[0,1]}; i = 1\ldots, n\} \cup \{\emptyset\}$$

For convenience, use notation $A_0 = \emptyset$. Function $m^{\mathcal{A}} : \mathcal{A} \to [0,1]$ is a basic belief assignment (bba) with the property $\sum_{i=0}^{n} m^{\mathcal{A}}(A_i) = 1$. The A_i's with $m^{\mathcal{A}}(A_i) > 0$ are the focal sets of this bba.

There is a very convenient graphical representation of these intervals: every $A = [a,b]$, such that $a,b \in [0,1]$ and $a \leq b$, corresponds to a single point in the triangle of Figure 1, and vice versa. This triangle is defined as:

$$T_{[0,1]} = \{(x,y) : x,y \in [0,1], x \leq y\}.$$

To each point in the triangle $\mathcal{T}_{[0,1]}$ that corresponds to a focal set of $m^{\mathcal{A}}$, we assign a mass equal to the basic belief mass. Hence $m^{\mathcal{A}}([a,b])$ is assigned to the point $(a,b) \in \mathcal{T}_{[0,1]}$ for every $A \in \mathcal{A}$. When $m^{\mathcal{A}}(\emptyset) = 0$, the result of this assignment is a (discrete) probability distribution function on $\mathcal{T}_{[0,1]}$, i.e. $P\{(x,y) = (a,b)\} = m^{\mathcal{A}}([a,b])$. The convention for axes x and y is adopted as shown in Figure 1. In order to further illustrate this concept, consider the following example.

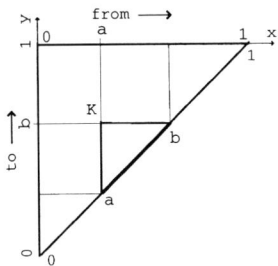

Fig. 1. Point $K = (a,b)$ inside the triangle $\mathcal{T}_{[0,1]}$, uniquely defines the interval $[a,b] \subseteq [0,1]$

2.1.1. Example 1.

Table 1 defines a bba with six focal sets, depicted in Figure 2 inside the triangle $\mathcal{T}_{[0,1]}$. Let $A = [a,b]$ be an interval in $[0,1]$, with $a = 0.2$ and $b = 0.7$. Let us now work out the belief, the commonality and the plausibility functions ($bel^{\mathcal{A}}$, $q^{\mathcal{A}}$ and $pl^{\mathcal{A}}$, respectively) of interval A. The sign × in last three columns of Table 1 indicate the masses to be included in $bel^{\mathcal{A}}(A)$, $q^{\mathcal{A}}(A)$ and $pl^{\mathcal{A}}(A)$.

i	$m^{\mathcal{A}}$	$A_i = [a_i, b_i]$		$bel^{\mathcal{A}}$	$q^{\mathcal{A}}$	$pl^{\mathcal{A}}$
		a_i	b_i			
1	.07	.3	.4	×		×
2	.18	.1	.9		×	×
3	.25	.1	.8		×	×
4	.15	.4	.9			×
5	.05	.4	.5	×		×
6	.30	.8	.9			
total	1.			.12	.43	.70

Table 1
bba defined on $\mathcal{A}$ with six focal sets, and the corresponding belief, commonality and plausibility of $A = [0.2, 0.7]$

$bel^{\mathcal{A}}(A), A = [a,b]$, is the sum of all the masses given to the subsets of A, thus to the non-empty intervals $A_i = [a_i, b_i]$, where $[a_i, b_i] \subseteq [a,b]$, i.e. $a_i \geq a$ and $b_i \leq b$. Graphically, every mass included in $bel^{\mathcal{A}}(A)$ must lie in the shaded triangle of Figure 3.(a) – this triangle contains all (and only) the intervals $[x,y]$ such that

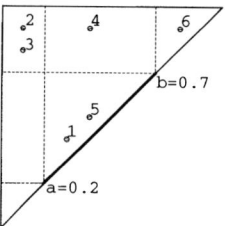

Fig. 2. Graphical representation of the focal set corresponding to Table 1

$x \geq a$ and $y \leq b$. Hence, to compute $bel^A(A)$ one adds up the masses of all the focal sets located in this triangle. In our example $bel^A(A) = 0.12$.

$q^A(A), A = [a, b]$, is defined as the sum of the masses given to the intervals $A_i = [a_i, b_i]$, where $[a, b] \subseteq [a_i, b_i]$, i.e. $a_i \leq a$ and $b_i \geq b$. Graphically, every mass included in $q^A(A)$ must lie in the shaded rectangle of Figure 3.(b) – this rectangle contains all (and only) the intervals $[x, y]$ such that $x \leq a$ and $y \geq b$. Hence to compute $q^A(A)$ one adds up the masses of the focal sets located inside this shaded rectangle. In our example, $q^A(A) = 0.43$.

$pl^A(A), A = [a, b]$, is defined as the sum of the masses given to the intervals $A_i = [a_i, b_i]$, where $[a_i, b_i] \cap [a, b] \neq \emptyset$, i.e. $a \leq b_i$ and $b \geq a_i$. Graphically, every mass included in $pl^A(A)$ must lie in the shaded area of Figure 3.(c) – this area contains all (and only) the intervals $[x, y]$ such that $x \leq b$ and $y \geq a$. Hence to compute $pl^A(A)$ one adds up the masses of the focal sets located inside this shaded area. In our example, $pl^A(A) = 0.70$.

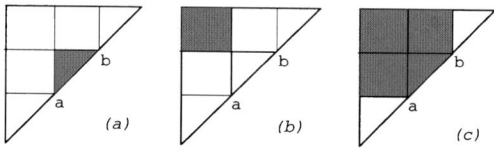

Fig. 3. Graphimathcal representation of (a) belief; (b) commonality; (c) plausibility

The singletons of $\mathcal{I}_{[0,1]}$ are zero-length intervals. If all the focal sets are non-empty intervals (as in our example), we can compute the pignistic probability density function (pdf) over singletons s (where $0 \leq s \leq 1$) as follows [11]:

$$Betf(s) = \sum_{A:s \in A \subset [0,1]} \frac{m^A(A)}{|a^* - a_*| [1 - m^A(\emptyset)]}$$

where $a_* = \inf\{a : a \in A\}$ and $a^* = \sup\{a : a \in A\}$. The computation of pignistic pdf involves the focal sets located in the rectangular area of triangle $\mathcal{T}_{[0,1]}$ defined by $0 \leq x \leq s$ and $s \leq y \leq 1$. In our example, the pignistic pdf of say $s = 0.35$ would involve the focal sets 1, 2 and 3 and would result in: $Betf(0.35) = \frac{0.07}{0.1} + \frac{0.18}{0.8} + \frac{0.25}{0.7} = 1.28$. $Betf$ is a proper probability density function.

2.2. Continuous domain

Next we relax the assumption that the number of focal elements is finite. The finite collection of subintervals $\mathcal{A}$, is now replaced by $\mathcal{I}_{[0,1]}$. Instead of discrete probabilities defined on the triangle $\mathcal{T}_{[0,1]}$, we now assign a probability density over the entire area of $\mathcal{T}_{[0,1]}$. What we described so far essentially will remain valid, except that masses become densities and sums become integrals.

Let $m([a,b])$ be a basic belief density (bbd) (we replace bbm by bbd to enhance that m is now a density). Let $f^{\mathcal{T}_{[0,1]}}(a,b) = m([a,b])$. Then $f^{\mathcal{T}_{[0,1]}}$ is a density function on $\mathcal{T}_{[0,1]}$: $f^{\mathcal{T}_{[0,1]}}: \mathcal{T}_{[0,1]} \to [0,\infty)$ with the property that:

$$\int_{x=0}^{x=1} \int_{y=x}^{y=1} f^{\mathcal{T}_{[0,1]}}(x,y) \, dx \, dy = 1 \tag{1}$$

Normalisation of the basic belief density as in (1) in fact is not necessary. The integral of $f^{\mathcal{T}_{[0,1]}}$ over $\mathcal{T}_{[0,1]}$ may be allowed to result in a value that is less than 1, with the missing belief allocated to the empty set, just as it was done in TBM [11].

Let us now define $bel^{\mathcal{I}_{[0,1]}}$, $pl^{\mathcal{I}_{[0,1]}}$ and $q^{\mathcal{I}_{[0,1]}}$ functions corresponding to $f^{\mathcal{T}_{[0,1]}}$. According to the explanations given so far, these functions will be the integrals of $f^{\mathcal{T}_{[0,1]}}$, with the limits of integration defined by the shaded areas in Figure 3. Thus we have:

$$bel^{\mathcal{I}_{[0,1]}}([a,b]) = \int_{x=a}^{x=b} \int_{y=x}^{y=b} f^{\mathcal{T}_{[0,1]}}(x,y) \, dx \, dy$$

$$pl^{\mathcal{I}_{[0,1]}}([a,b]) = \int_{x=0}^{x=b} \int_{y=\max(a,x)}^{y=1} f^{\mathcal{T}_{[0,1]}}(x,y) \, dx \, dy$$

$$q^{\mathcal{I}_{[0,1]}}([a,b]) = \int_{x=0}^{x=a} \int_{y=b}^{y=1} f^{\mathcal{T}_{[0,1]}}(x,y) \, dx \, dy$$

Using derivative-integral identities one can also write:

$$f^{\mathcal{T}_{[0,1]}}(a,b) = -\frac{\partial^2 \, bel^{\mathcal{I}_{[0,1]}}([a,b])}{\partial a \, \partial b} \tag{2}$$

$$f^{\mathcal{T}_{[0,1]}}(a,b) = -\frac{\partial^2 \, q^{\mathcal{I}_{[0,1]}}([a,b])}{\partial a \, \partial b} \tag{3}$$

The pignistic density function $Betf$ can be derived from $f^{\mathcal{T}_{[0,1]}}(x,y)$ as follows:

$$Betf(a) = \lim_{\epsilon \to 0} \int_{x=0}^{x=a} \int_{y=a+\epsilon}^{y=1} \frac{f^{\mathcal{T}_{[0,1]}}(x,y)}{y-x} \, dx \, dy, \tag{4}$$

for $a \in [0,1]$. We do not put directly $\epsilon = 0$ in (4) in order to avoid division by zero.

2.2.1. Example 2.

Consider the uniform density on $\mathcal{T}_{[0,1]}$, that is

$$f^{\mathcal{T}_{[0,1]}} = 2, \quad \forall x, y \in [0,1], x \leq y$$

Then using (4) we get

$$Betf(a) = -2[(1-a)\log(1-a) + a\log a]$$

for $0 < a < 1$ (see Figure 4).

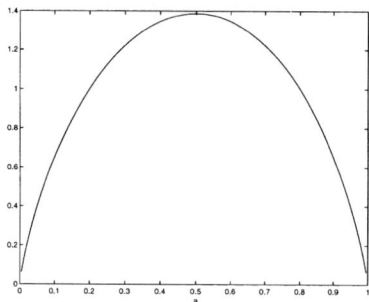

Fig. 4. $Betf(a)$ generated by a uniform density on $\mathcal{T}_{[0,1]}$

2.2.2. Generalisation to $\mathbb{R}$.

So far we have developed belief functions on $\mathcal{I}_{[0,1]}$, as it simplifies the presentation and allows for nice graphical representation in $[0,1]$ interval. However, all concepts directly apply when the frame of discernment is the entire real axis $\mathbb{R}$; one just needs to replace 0 (the lower limit) with $-\infty$ and 1 (the upper limit) with $+\infty$. Thus $[0,1]$ is replaced with $(-\infty, \infty)$. Let us denote by $\mathcal{I}$ the set of intervals on the real axis $\mathbb{R}$ and by $\mathcal{T}$ the set of pairs $(x, y) \in \mathbb{R}^2 : x \leq y$. Then we say that m, bel, q and pl are defined on the Borel sigma algebra generated by $\mathcal{I}$ and f is defined on $\mathcal{T}$.

3. The least committed bbd

Suppose your domain knowledge is partial and based only on some potential betting behaviour, represented by the pignistic density function $Betf(a)$. Since the pignistic transform is many-to-one transform, an infinite number of belief density functions can induce the same $Betf$. These belief funtions are said to be isopignistic. In order to apply the belief function theory (in the continuous domain) one needs to formulate a method of building a belief density (BD) from the pignistic density. The least commitment principle [11],[5] suggests to choose among all iso-pignistic belief densities, the belief density which maximizes the commonality function q. As in the discrete case [12], the q least committed belief density is a consonant belief density. On the real axis $\mathbb{R}$ this means that all focal sets on $\mathcal{I}$ are nested, i.e. can be ordered in such a way that each focal interval is contained by the following one.

We will further concentrate on a unimodal pignistic density with a mode $\mu = \arg\max_a Betf(a)$. The focal sets of the least committed (LC) belief density are intervals $[a, b]$ which satisfy: $Betf(a) = Betf(b)$. Consequently, for every focal interval of the LC-BD, $[a,b]$, we have that $\mu \in [a,b]$. Another very important property of the focal intervals of the LC-BD is that they form a line on the triangle $\mathcal{T}$. This line has the following properties:

- It starts from $(x,y) = (\mu,\mu)$; the plausibility at this point is $pl^{\mathcal{I}}([\mu,\mu]) = 1$.
- For all symmetrical pignistic densities $Betf$ (e.g. normal, Laplace, Cauchy), centered at μ, this is a straight line given by:

$$y = -(x - 2\mu) \qquad -\infty < x \leq \mu$$

Figure 5 shows the line of focal intervals in $\mathcal{T}$ for (a) normal pignistic density with $\mu = 2.5$ and $\sigma = 1$; (b) gamma pignistic density $Betf(s) = s e^{-s}$, $(s > 0)$, with the mode $\mu = 1$.

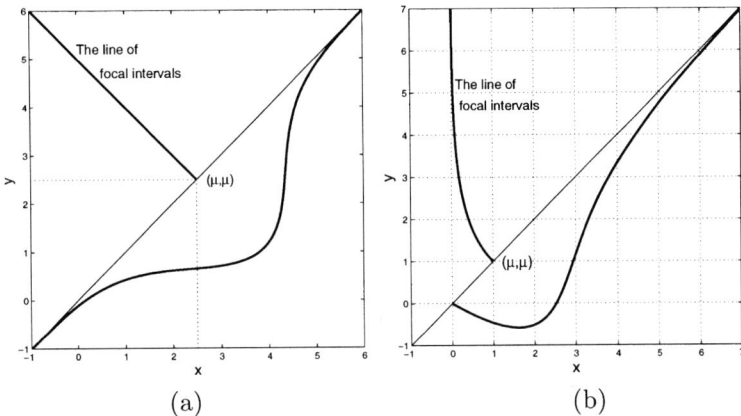

(a)   (b)

Fig. 5. *The focal sets of the LC belief density (solid line in the upper triangle) induced by: (a) normal pignistic density; (b) gamma pignistic density*

The relationship between $Betf$ and any basic belief density in general is expressed by (4). Let us denote the LC bbd (induced by $Bel\, f$) as $\varphi(u)$ where $u \geq 0$. We have seen that the focal sets of this bbd are points on a line in $\mathcal{T}$, and u corresponds to the distance from the point (μ, μ). Due to this specific form of the LC bbd, the relationship between $Betf(s)$ and $\varphi(u)$ has a much simpler form than in (4). If $s \geq \mu$, then

$$Betf(s) = \int_{u=s}^{\infty} \frac{\varphi(u)}{u - \bar{u}} du \qquad (5)$$

where $\bar{u}$ is defined by the property that: $Betf(\bar{u}) = Betf(u)$. Note that $\bar{u}$ is a function of u. By differentiation of (5) we obtain that:

$$\varphi(s) = -(s - \bar{s})\frac{Betf(s)}{ds} \qquad (6)$$

The bbd $\varphi(s)$ is always positive since:
(1) $s \geq \bar{s}$ and
(2) $\frac{dBetf(s)}{ds} < 0$ for $s \geq \mu$.

For model based classification problems, we apply the generalised Bayes theorem [11] which requires to compute the plausibility function from the bbd. Since the LC bbd is a consonant belief function, with the property that its focal sets are the points along a line in $\mathcal{T}$, we can write:

$$pl(x) = \int_x^\infty \varphi(a) \, da \tag{7}$$

$$= -\int_x^\infty (a - \bar{a}) \, [Betf(a)]' \, da \tag{8}$$

The limits of integration in (7) reflect the fact that only the focal intervals with the property $x \leq a \leq \infty$ will have a non-empty intersection with x. Using the differentiation rule: $(uv)' = uv' + uv'$ and the property of our unimodal bbd: $\lim_{x \to \infty} Betf(x) = 0$ we obtain:

$$pl(x) = (x - \bar{x}) \, Betf(x) + \int_x^\infty \left(1 - \frac{d\bar{a}}{da}\right) Betf(a) \, da \tag{9}$$

3.1. Example 3.

Suppose the pignistic density is a normal density, i.e. $Betf(x) = \mathcal{N}(x; \mu, \sigma)$. In order to work out the LC bbd $\varphi(x)$ and its corresponding plausibility $pl(x)$ we make the standard substitution $y = (x - \mu)/\sigma$. In this case $y - \bar{y} = 2y$ and thus $d\bar{y}/dy = -1$. Application of (6) and (9) yields for $y \geq 0$:

$$\varphi(y) = \frac{2y^2}{\sqrt{2\pi}} e^{-y^2/2} \tag{10}$$

$$pl(y) = \frac{2y}{\sqrt{2\pi}} e^{-y^2/2} + \text{erfc}(y/\sqrt{2}) \tag{11}$$

where $\text{erfc}(s) = \frac{2}{\sqrt{\pi}} \int_s^\infty e^{-t^2} dt$. It follows than: $\varphi(x) = \varphi(y)/\sigma$ and $pl(x) = pl(y)$. The two functions are shown in Figure 6 for $\mu = 1$ and $\sigma = 1.5$.

3.2. Example 4.

Let $Betf(x)$ be an exponential density:

$$Betf(x) = \begin{cases} \frac{1}{\theta} e^{-(x-a)/\theta} & x \geq a \\ 0 & x < a \end{cases} \tag{12}$$

Using the substitution $y = (x - a)/\theta$ we note that the LC bbd is a Gamma density: $\varphi(y) = ye^{-y}$ for $y \geq 0$. The plausibility is then $pl(y) = (1 + y)e^{-y}$. As before, $\varphi(x) = \varphi(y)/\theta$ and $pl(x) = pl(y)$.

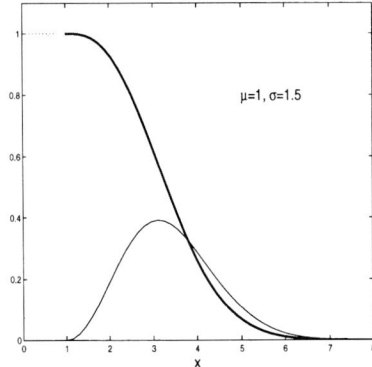

Fig. 6. *The LC bbd $\varphi(x)$ (thin line) and its plausibility $pl(x)$ (thick line), corresponding to $Betf(x) = \mathcal{N}(x; 1, 1.5)$*

4. Application to model-based target classification

In order to demonstrate an application of the theory presented above, let us consider one of the most difficult problems in military air surveillance: correct identification of non-cooperative flying objects in the surveillance volume. In general three groups of target attributes (features) are exploited for identification, those based on target shape, kinematic behaviour and electro-magnetic (EM) emissions [1]. Let us consider a simple example where the aim is to classify targets into one of the three platform categories [7]:
Class 1 - Commercial planes;
Class 2 - Large military aircrafts (such as transporters, bombers);
Class 3 - Light and agile military aircrafts (fighter planes).

4.1. Speed as a target feature

We will assume that the only available target feature is its speed (a kinematic feature obtained from the radar) [2], [16]. The speed profiles for our three classes can be described by Table 2 [2]:

Target class	Min	Max
Commercial (c_1)	560	885
Bomber (c_2)	400	725
Fighter (c_3)	525	950

Table 2
Speed intervals for three air platform categories (in km/h)

First we present target classification using the Bayesian classifier, which is followed by the Belief function classifier.

4.1.1. Bayesian analysis.

In order to apply the Bayesian classifier we must adopt a suitable probability density function of the speed conditioned on the class. Various possibilities are applicable, such the uniform, beta, Gaussian, etc. Let us adopt the Gaussian densities, with the parameters selected in such a way that $P\{s_{\min} < x < s_{\max}\} = 0.99876$, where $[s_{\min}, s_{\max}]$ is the speed interval given in Table 2. Figure 7 shows the distribution of speed feature conditioned on the class. The hypothesis space is defined

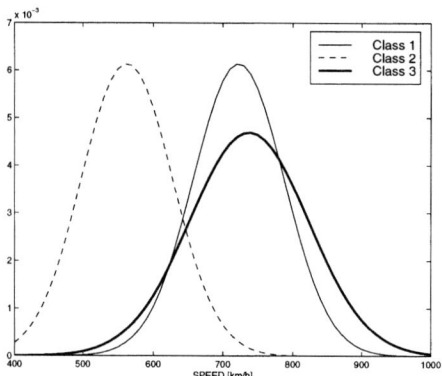

Fig. 7. *Adopted pdf models (Gaussian) of target speed, conditioned on the class*

as $C = \{c_1, c_2, c_3\}$. The Bayesian classifier (assuming the uniform prior for classes) will compute the probability of class c_i ($i = 1, 2, 3$) given feature x as:

$$P\{c_i|x\} = \alpha\, p(x|c_i) \qquad (i = 1, 2, 3) \tag{13}$$

where α is a normalisation constant. Figure 8 displays the class probabilities $P\{c_i|x\}$ computed for a range of speed values $x \in [400, 1000]$ km/h.

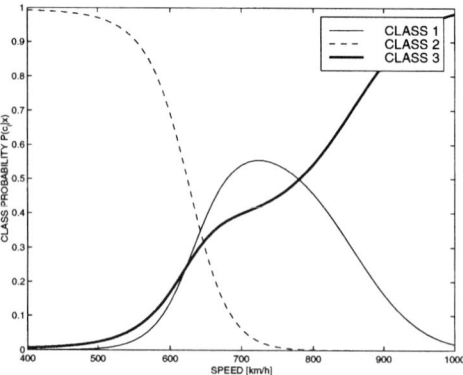

Fig. 8. *Bayesian analysis: class probabilities conditioned on target speed x*

4.1.2. Belief function analysis.

The belief function analysis can start from the very same pdf models adopted for the Bayesian analysis (Figure 7). However, their meaning is different. Since our probabilistic knowledge is very scarce and incomplete (we just know the speed limits for each target class) these models are now considered as pignistic densities of speed x conditioned on class c_i, denoted as $Betf(x|c_i)$. The first step is to build the least committed belief function over the observation space which corresponds to $Betf(x|c_i)$, followed by the application of the Generalised Bayesian Theorem (GBT) [10], [3]. The key here is to compute likelihoods $l(c_i|x) = pl(x|c_i)$, which is done using equation (9). Then the GBT yields for every subset $A \subseteq C$ the following bba:

$$m(A|x) = \prod_{c_i \in A} pl(x|c_i) \prod_{c_i \in \bar{A}} [1 - pl(x|c_i)] \qquad (14)$$

Finally the last step is to apply the pignistic transform to $m(A|x)$ to compute the pignistic class probabilities:

$$BetP\{c_i|x\} = \sum_{A \,:\, c_i \in A} \frac{1}{|A|} \frac{m(A|x)}{[1 - m(\emptyset|x)]} \qquad (15)$$

The resulting pignistic class probabilities are shown in Figure 9, for a range of speed values $x \in [400, 1000]$ km/h.

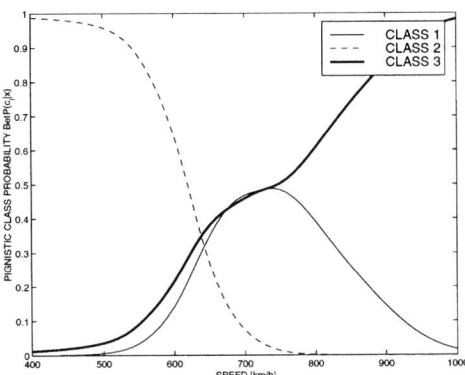

Fig. 9. *Belief function analysis: pignistic class probabilities conditioned on target speed x*

Comparing Figures 8 and 9 one can observe similar performance of both classifiers for speeds less than 650 km/h and greater than 770 km/h. However, in the range [650, 770] km/h, where the pdf of class 1 and 3 overlap, the Bayesian classifier favours class 1, while the Belief classifier is undecided between 1 and 3. We argue that being undecided makes more sense, because the most likely observation of speed, for both class 1 and 3, falls in this region. A similar effect will be illustrated and discussed in the next subsection.

4.2. Acceleration as a target feature

Suppose the only available target feature is its maximum acceleration, denote as a (usually observed during a certain interval of time). Target acceleration can be useful [6] because it is related to target maneuverability. For class 1, the acceleration is rarely higher than $1g$ (where $g = 9.81$ m/s^2 is the gravitation due to gravity), because the acceleration higher than $\pm 1g$ causes sickness in passengers. Targets of class 2 sometimes perform mild evasive manoeuvres but their maximum acceleration (due to their size) is rarely higher than $\pm 4g$. Targets of class 3 are light and agile, with highly trained pilots - the maximum acceleration of modern fighter planes can go up to $\pm 7g$. The steady-state of acceleration, however, for all three classes of targets is *zero*. This is so because a constant velocity flight (i.e. with zero acceleration) ensures the minimum fuel consumption and the least stress for a pilot.

As before, we model the pdf of the feature (maximum acceleration) conditioned on the class, $p(a|c_i)$, $i = 1, 2, 3$. A reasonable model is a zero-mean Gaussian density with three different values of standard deviation, as shown in Figure 10 (the unit of target acceleration is g). Standard deviations of Gaussian densities are adopted as follows: $\sigma_1 = 0.4g$, $\sigma_2 = 1.6g$ and $\sigma_3 = 2.8g$. These values are selected to ensure that $P\{|a| < \gamma\} = 0.99876$, where $\gamma = 1g$, $4g$ and $7g$ for class 1, 2 and 3 respectively.

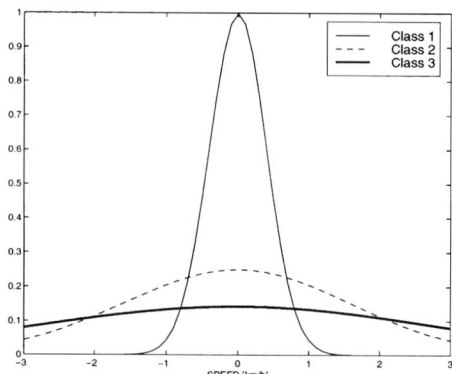

Fig. 10. *Adopted pdf models of target acceleration conditioned on the class*

The classification results (for acceleration values in the interval $[-3g, 3g]$) are shown in Figures 11 for the Bayesian and the belief function classifier, respectively. Observe that for small accelerations ($|a| < 0.25g$), the Bayesian classifier decisively declares a target to be of class 1, while the belief function classifier does not favour any class. Again we argue that for the available prior knowledge about targets and accelerations, being undecided for small accelerations makes more sense: small accelerations are not a distinguishing feature between the classes.

The crux of the belief function analysis is that the LC plausibility $pl(a|c_i)$ is close to 1 if acceleration a approximately equals the mode of $p(a|c_i)$ (see Section 3). Interestingly, a somewhat similar classification result can be obtained in this example using an ad-hoc fudge in the Bayesian classifier, by replacing densities $p(a|c_i)$ with $p(a|c_i)/\max\{p(a|c_i)\}$ [4]. The proposed framework of belief function theory (the least commitment principle, generalised Bayesian theorem, pignistic transform), however, provides a sound theoretical basis for target classification without a need for any fudge.

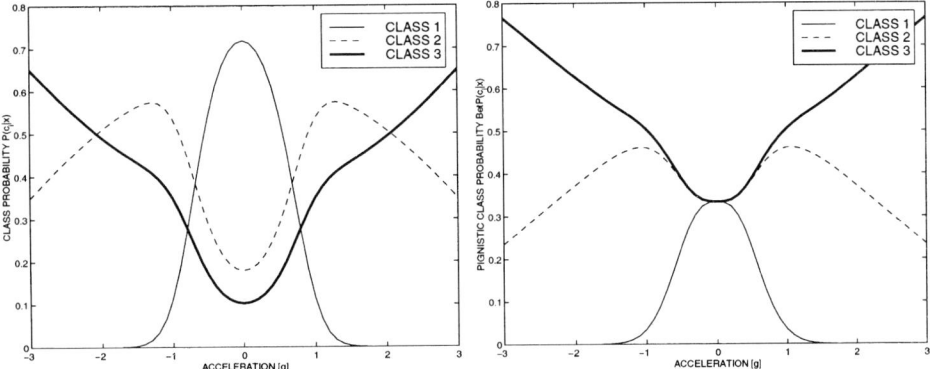

Fig. 11. *Left figure: Bayesian analysis: class probabilities conditioned on acceleration. Right figure: Belief function analysis: class probabilities conditioned on acceleration*

5. Conclusions

The paper presents a theoretical framework of the belief function theory in the continuous domain, where the frame of discernment is the real axis $\mathbb{R}$ (or its segment). When the probabilistic description of observations in the continuous domain is incomplete, we represent it by the pignistic probability density. When the pignistic density is unimodal, the focal sets of the least committed belief function which corresponds to this density, form a line in $\mathbb{R}^2$. This greatly simplifies the relationships between the basic belief density, pignistic density and the plausibility function. The theory has been applied to the model-based target classification, where observations of target speed and acceleration (in the continuous domain) are used as a feature. The classifier based on the belief function theory appears to be very simple to implement and produces results which are arguably more meaningful than those obtained using the Bayesian classifier.

For n-dimensional measurement space (e.g. speed and acceleration considered as a joint measurement) we would need to extend the theory to the case where the frame is $\mathbb{R}^n$. If features are independent, extending the theory to $\mathbb{R}^n$ would be manageable. If features are not independent, a transformation into new independent features would be first required.

References

1. S. Blackman and R. Popoli. *Design and Analysis of Modern Tracking Systems.* Artech House, 1999.
2. A. Caromicoli and T. Kurien. Multitarget identification in airborne surveillance. In *Proc. SPIE*, volume 1098, pages 161–176, 1989.
3. F. Delmotte and P. Smets. Target identification based on the transferable belief model interpretation of Dempster-Shafer model. *IEEE Trans. SMC.* In review.
4. T. Denoeux. Private communication. 2003.
5. D. Dubois and H. Prade. The principle of minimum specificity as a basis for evidential reasoning. In B. Bouchon and R. Yager, editors, *Uncertainty in knowledge-based systems*, pages 75–84. Springer Verlag, 1987.
6. H. Leung and J. Wu. Bayesian and Dempster-Shafer target identification for radard surveillance. *IEEE Trans. Aerospace and Electronic Systems*, 36(2):432–447, 2000.
7. B. Ristic, N. Gordon, and A. Bessell. On target classification using kinematic data. *Information Fusion*, 2003. In Press.
8. G. Shafer. *A mathematic theory of evidence.* Princeton University Press, 1976.
9. P. Smets. *Un modéle mathématico-statistique simulant le processus du diagnostic médical.* PhD thesis, Université libre de Bruxelles, 1978. available through University Microfilm International, 30-32 Mortimer street, London, W1N 7RA, thesis 80-70, 003.
10. P. Smets. Belief functions: the disjunctive rule of combination and the generalized Bayesian theorem. *International Journal of Approximate Reasoning*, 9:1–35, 1993.
11. P. Smets. The transferable belief model for quantified belief representation. In P. Smets, editor, *Quantified Representation of Uncertainty & Imprecission*, volume 1 of *Handbook of Defeasible Reasoning and Uncertainty Mangement Systems*, pages 267–301. Kluwer, Doordrecht, 1998.
12. P. Smets. Quantified epistemic possibility theory seen as a hyper cautious transferable belief model. In *Rencontres Francophones sur la Logique Floue et ses Applications*, pages 343–353. Cépaduès-Éditions, Oct. 2000. http://www.editions-cepadues.fr.
13. P. Smets. Belief functions on real numbers. *International Journal of Approximate Reasoning*, 2005. (Forthcoming).
14. P. Smets and R. Kennes. The transferable belief model. *Artificial Intelligence*, 66:191–234, 1994.
15. T. M. Strat. Continuous belief functions for evidential reasoning. In *Proc. National Conf. Artificial Intelligence*, pages 308–313. Amer. Assoc. Artif. Intelligence (AAAI), Aug. 1984.
16. J. G. Teti, R. P. Gorman, and W. A. Berger. A multifeature decision space approach to radar target identification. *IEEE Aerospace and Electronic Systems*, 32(1):480–487, 1996.

Independence in conditional possibility theory

G. Coletti [a] and B. Vantaggi [b]

[a] Dep. of Matematica e Informatica, Università di Perugia, Perugia, Italy
[b] Dep. of Metodi e Modelli Matematici, Università "La Sapienza" Roma, Italy

Abstract

Starting from a general definition of conditional possibility introduced by Bouchon-Meunier, Coletti, Marsala in [2] we propose a notion of independence, which encompasses the critical situations presented by other independence definitions: for instance we obtain that, in any case, possibility independence implies logical independence. Moreover, we introduce a procedure for checking the consistency of a partial assessment with a conditional possibility.

Key words: conditional possibility, consistency, independence.
2000 MSC: 68T37, 60A05, 28A12

1. Introduction

The notion of conditioning in possibility theory is a problem of long-standing interest, in fact various definitions of conditional possibility have been introduced (see, e.g., [7,9,11,12]) mainly by analogy with kolmogorovian probabilistic case. These definitions have in common the fact that conditional possibility $\Pi(E|H)$ is obtained as a derived concept from joint and marginal possibilities $\Pi(E \wedge H)$ and $\Pi(H)$: it is essentially defined as a solution of the equation

$$\Pi(E \wedge H) = \min\{x, \Pi(H)\}.$$

Note that to have a unique solution for that equation it is not sufficient to reject events with zero possibility, so other particular principles (as, e.g., minimum specifity [9]) have been introduced and they give rise to different definitions of conditional possibility.

Recently in [2] and [3] (following de Finetti conditional probability framework see, e.g., [5,8]) a more general notion of conditional possibility has been introduced, as a primitive concept: the conditional possibility is *directly* defined as a function on a set (with a suitable algebraic structure) of conditional events, in such a way that $\Pi(E|H)$ makes sense for any pair of events E and H, with $H \neq \emptyset$, and it must satisfy *proper axioms*. This concept of conditional possibility generalizes all those given in the literature and avoids any "problematic situation". Starting from this framework a "natural" concept of independence has been introduced.

In the quoted papers a characterization theorem of conditional possibility in terms of a class of unconditional possibility measures has been proved. In Section 2 we give a similar characterization, and by using this, we introduce a procedure for checking the coherence of a partial possibilistic assessment.

Moreover, such characterization allows us to introduce a new notion of independence, which is a formal counterpart of stochastic independence in the framework of coherent conditional probability [5].

A comparison with the classic notions of possibilistic independence [1,6,7,9–11] is presented showing that the controversial aspects have been encompassed in our framework. Actually, the suggested definition is a reinforcement of that one proposed in [2]. The motivation for this reinforcement is related essentially to get some natural implications: as, e.g., possibility independence implies logical independence. This relevant implication can fail in all the other approaches, even if it is very intuitive: in fact *if an event influences "logically" an other one, then, under any uncertainty measure, they must be dependent.*

2. Conditional Possibilities

Definition 1. Let $\mathcal{F} = \mathcal{B} \times \mathcal{H}$ be a set of conditional events $E|H$ such that $\mathcal{B}$ is a Boolean algebra and $\mathcal{H}$ an additive set, with $\mathcal{H} \subset \mathcal{B}$ and $\emptyset \notin \mathcal{H}$. A function $\Pi : \mathcal{F} \to [0,1]$ is a conditional possibility if it satisfies the following properties:
1. $\Pi(E|H) = \Pi(E \wedge H|H)$, for every $E \in \mathcal{B}$ and $H \in \mathcal{H}$;
2. $\Pi(\cdot|H)$ is a possibility measure, for any $H \in \mathcal{H}$;
3. $\Pi(E \wedge F|H) = \min\{\Pi(E|H), \Pi(F|E \wedge H)\}$, for any $H, E \wedge H \in \mathcal{H}$ and $E, F \in \mathcal{B}$.

Condition 3 implies that the conditional possibility $\Pi(\cdot|H)$ *is not singled-out (only) by the possibility of its conditioning event H, but its value is bound to the values of other conditional possibilities* $\Pi(\cdot|E \wedge H)$, for suitable events E.

Definition 2. Let $\mathcal{B}$ be a finite algebra and $\mathcal{C}_o$ the set of atoms in $\mathcal{B}$. The class $\mathcal{P} = \{\Pi_o, ..., \Pi_k\}$ of possibilities defined on $\mathcal{B}$ is said nested if (for $j = 1, ..., k$) the following conditions hold:
- $\Pi_j(C) = \Pi_{j-1}(C)$ if $C \in \mathcal{C}_j \setminus \mathcal{H}_j$ ($j > 0$);
- $\Pi_{j-1}(C) \leq \Pi_j(C) \leq 1$ if $C \in \mathcal{H}_j$ ($j > 0$);
- $\Pi_j(C) = 0$ for all the atoms $C \in \mathcal{C}_o \setminus \mathcal{C}_j$;

- for any $C \in \mathcal{C}_o$ there exists a (unique) $j = 0, ..., k$ such that $\Pi_j(C) = 1$.

where $\mathcal{C}_j = \{C \in \mathcal{C}_{j-1} : \Pi_{j-1}(C) < 1\}$ and

$$\mathcal{H}_j = \{C_i \in \mathcal{C}_j : \nexists C \in \mathcal{C}_o \text{ s.t. } \Pi_{j-1}(C) > \Pi_{j-1}(C_i)\}.$$

Note that $\mathcal{H}_j$ ($j > 0$) is the subset of atoms (of $\mathcal{C}_j$, or better of those atoms with "higher" possibility under Π_{j-1}) which can have possibility equal to 1 under Π_j.

Theorem 1. Let $\mathcal{P} = \{\Pi_o, ..., \Pi_k\}$ be a nested class of possibility on $\mathcal{B}$. Let f be a function defined on $\mathcal{B} \times \mathcal{B}^o$ (with $\mathcal{B}^o = \mathcal{B} \setminus \{\emptyset\}$) into $[0,1]$ such that $f(A, B)$ is solution of all the equations

$$\Pi_\alpha(A \wedge B) = \min\{x, \Pi_\alpha(B)\} \tag{1}$$

$\alpha = 0, ..., j_B$ and $j_B = \max\{j : C \in \mathcal{C}_j, \forall C \subseteq B\}$, and $f(A, B)$ is the unique solution of equation (1) related to j_B.
Then, f is a conditional possibility on $\mathcal{B} \times \mathcal{B}^o$.

Proof: Since $f(A, B)$ is solution of all the equations (1) and it is the unique solution of that related to Π_{j_B}, then $f(A, B) = \Pi_{j_B}(A \wedge B) \geq \Pi_j(A \wedge B)$ with $j < j_B$. The result follows from the proof of implication (b) $\Rightarrow$ (a) of Theorem 2 in [2].

Theorem 2. Let Π be a conditional possibility on $\mathcal{B} \times \mathcal{B}^o$, and $\mathcal{C}_o$ the set of atoms of $\mathcal{B}$. Consider the class of possibilities $\mathcal{P} = \{\Pi_o, ..., \Pi_k\}$ defined on $\mathcal{B}$ as follows:
- $\Pi_o(B) = \Pi(B|\Omega)$ with $B \in \mathcal{B}$;
- for any $j = 1, ..., k$, $\Pi_j(B) = \Pi(B|H^j)$ (with $B \in \mathcal{B}$) where $H^j = \bigvee_{\{C \in \mathcal{C}_j\}} C$ and $\mathcal{C}_j = \{C \in \mathcal{C}_{j-1} : \Pi_{j-1}(C) < 1\}$.
Then, the class $\mathcal{P}$ is a nested class.

Proof: Condition 2 of Definition 1 implies that Π_j's ($j = 0, ..., k$) are possibilities.
If $C \not\subseteq H^1$ (i.e. $\Pi_o(C) = 1$ and $C \in \mathcal{C}_o \setminus \mathcal{C}_1$), then $\Pi_1(C) = \Pi(C|H^1) = 0$.
If $C \in \mathcal{C}_1$ and $\Pi_o(C) < \Pi_o(H^1)$ (i.e. $C \in \mathcal{C}_1 \setminus \mathcal{H}^1$), then

$$\Pi_o(C) = \Pi(C|\Omega) = \Pi(C \wedge H^1|\Omega) = \min\{\Pi(C|H^1), \Pi(H^1|\Omega)\} = \Pi(C|H^1) = \Pi_1(C).$$

While if $C \in \mathcal{H}^1$, it means $\Pi_o(C) = \Pi_o(H^1)$, then $\Pi_o(C) \leq \Pi_1(C) \leq 1$ since

$$\Pi_o(C) = \Pi(C|\Omega) = \min\{\Pi(C|H^1), \Pi(H^1|\Omega)\} \leq \Pi(C|H^1) = \Pi_1(C).$$

Moreover, at least one atom $C \subseteq H^1$ must be such that $\Pi_1(C) = 1$ being $\Pi(\cdot|H^1)$ a possibility. Analogously that conditions hold for Π_j with $j > 1$.

By construction there is j such that $\mathcal{C}_j = \mathcal{H}_j$ (i.e. $\Pi_{j-1}(C) = \Pi_{j-1}(H^j)$ for any $C \in \mathcal{C}_j$), so if $\Pi_j(C) = \Pi(C|H^j) = 1$ for any $C \in \mathcal{C}_j$, then $j = k$; otherwise there is an atom C with $\Pi(C|H^j) < 1$). The procedure continues till H^k is such that all $C \subseteq H^k \in \mathcal{B}^o$ are such that $\Pi(C|H^k) = 1$. Then, the class $\{\Pi_o, ..., \Pi_k\}$ is nested.

Remark 1. Any given conditional possibility on $\mathcal{B} \times \mathcal{B}^o$ generates a unique nested class on $\mathcal{B}$, and vice versa a nested class gives rise to a unique conditional possibility on $\mathcal{B} \times \mathcal{B}^o$. Then, any conditional possibility can be "represented" by means of a suitable class of possibilities instead of just a possibility measure (as noted also in [2,3] by their characterization theorem).

Any class of possibilities on $\mathcal{B}$ is said *agreeing* with a conditional possibility $\Pi(\cdot|\cdot)$ on $\mathcal{B} \times \mathcal{H}$ if it is nested and satisfies condition (1) for any $E|H \in \mathcal{B} \times \mathcal{H}$.

Definition 3. Let π be an assessment on an arbitrary finite set of conditional events $\mathcal{E}$, then π is coherent iff it can be extended on $\mathcal{B} \times \mathcal{B}^o \supset \mathcal{E}$ (with $\mathcal{B}$ a Boolean algebra) as a conditional possibility (Definition 1).

Theorem 3. Let $\mathcal{F} = \{E_1|H_1, ..., E_n|H_n\}$ be a finite set of conditional events, $\mathcal{C}_o$ and $\mathcal{B}$ denote, respectively, the set of atoms and the algebra generated by $\{E_1, H_1, ..., E_n, H_n\}$.
For a real function $\pi : \mathcal{F} \to [0,1]$ the following two statements are equivalent:
a) π is a coherent conditional possibility on $\mathcal{F}$;
b) there exists (at least) a nested class $\mathcal{P} = \{\Pi_o, ..., \Pi_k\}$ of possibilities on $\mathcal{B}$, such that for any $E_i|H_i \in \mathcal{F}$ one has that $\pi(E_i|H_i)$ is solution of all the equations

$$\Pi_\beta(E_i \wedge H_i) = \min\{x, \Pi_\beta(H_i)\} \tag{2}$$

for any β such that $\Pi_\beta(H_i) \leq 1$.

Proof: If π is a coherent conditional possibility on $\mathcal{F}$, then there is a conditional possibility $\hat{\Pi}$ on $\mathcal{B} \times \mathcal{B}^o$ such that its restriction on $\mathcal{F}$ coincides with π, so by Theorem 2 $\hat{\Pi}$ gives rise to a unique nested class $\mathcal{P}$, which is agreeing with π, and so $\pi(E_i|H_i)$ is solution of all the equations (2) for all β such that $\Pi_\beta(H_i) \leq 1$ and it is the unique solution for equation (2) related to the greatest β.
Conversely, b)$\Rightarrow$a): the nested class $\mathcal{P}$ on $\mathcal{B}$ of condition b) generates a unique conditional possibility $\hat{\Pi}$ on $\mathcal{B} \times \mathcal{B}^o$ (see Theorem 1), and $\hat{\Pi}_{|\mathcal{F}} = \pi$.

The previous result implies that the coherence of a given assignment π can be proved by finding a nested class agreeing with it, i.e. checking the compatibility of the following sequence of systems (with $\alpha = 0, ..., k$)

$$S_\alpha = \begin{cases} \max_{C_r \subseteq E_i \wedge H_i} x_r^\alpha = \min\{\Pi(E_i|H_i), \max_{C_r \subseteq H_i} x_r^\alpha\} & \text{if } \max_{C_r \subseteq H_i} x_r^{\alpha-1} < 1 \\ x_r^\alpha \geq x_r^{\alpha-1} & \text{if } C_r \in \mathcal{H}^\alpha \\ x_r^\alpha = x_r^{\alpha-1} & \text{if } C_r \in \mathcal{C}_\alpha \setminus \mathcal{H}^\alpha \\ \max_{C_r \in \mathcal{C}_o} x_r = 1 & \\ x_r^\alpha \geq 0 & \forall C_r \in \mathcal{C}_o \end{cases}$$

where $\mathbf{x}^\alpha$ (with r-th component x_r^α) is solution of the system S_α and $\mathbf{x}_r^{-1} = 0$ for any $C_r \in \mathcal{C}_o$.

Moreover $\mathcal{C}_\alpha = \{C_r : \mathbf{x}_r^\alpha < 1\}$ and $\mathcal{H}^\alpha = \{C_r : C_r \in \mathcal{C}_\alpha, \mathbf{x}_r^{\alpha-1} = \max_{C_j \in \mathcal{C}_\alpha} \mathbf{x}_j^{\alpha-1}\}$.

Actually, the notion of coherence for possibility is that introduced in [3], however from the characterization given through Theorem 3 a procedure for checking the possibilistic coherence of a given assessment arises naturally.

3. Independence

The concept of independence has been discussed in literature [1,6,7,10,9,11] and the main proposals are based on definitions analogous to the classic probabilistic formulations, which present some counter-intuitive aspects (related essentially to logical constraints and 0 or 1 evaluations on possible events). Since these situations have been encompassed in coherent conditional probability setting through the notion of cs-independence [5], we propose a new definition of independence for possibility theory, based on the same idea.

Definition 4. Let π be a coherent conditional possibility on $\mathcal{F}$, and $\mathcal{P}$ an agreeing class for π, then, for every event $H \in \mathcal{B}^o$, the significant-layer of H (denoted as $\circ(H)$) related to $\mathcal{P}$ is defined as the minimum number α such that $\Pi_\alpha(H) = 1$. Moreover, define $\circ(\emptyset) = \infty$.

The significant-layer of a conditional event $E|H \in \mathcal{B} \times \mathcal{B}^o$ is defined as the (positive) number

$$\circ(E|H) = \circ(E \wedge H) - \circ(H). \tag{3}$$

Note that $\circ(E|H) = \infty$ iff $E \wedge H = \emptyset$.

Definition 5. Given a coherent conditional possibility π on a set of conditional events $\mathcal{G}$ containing $\mathcal{D} = \{A^*|B^*, B^*|A^*\}$ (with A^* - analogously B^* - stands for A or A^c), then A is independent of B under π (in symbol $A \perp\!\!\!\perp B \; [\pi]$), if both the following conditions hold:
i. $\pi(A|B) = \pi(A|B^c)$ and $\pi(A^c|B) = \pi(A^c|B^c)$;
ii. there exists an agreeing class $\mathcal{P}$ for the restriction of π to $\mathcal{D}$ such that

$$\circ(A|B) = \circ(A|B^c) \text{ and } \circ(A^c|B) = \circ(A^c|B^c). \tag{4}$$

Actually, the restriction of π on $\mathcal{D}$ admits more than one agreeing class, but as follows from Theorem 4, condition *ii* of Definition 5 either holds for all the agreeing classes for π or holds for none of them.

Theorem 4. Given two logically independent events A and B, and a coherent conditional possibility π defined on $\mathcal{G}$ containing $\mathcal{D} = \{A^*|B^*, B^*|A^*\}$, such that

$$\pi(A|B) = \pi(A|B^c) \text{ and } \pi(A^c|B) = \pi(A^c|B^c).$$

If there exists an agreeing class for $\pi_{|\mathcal{D}}$ such that

$$\circ(A|B) = \circ(A|B^c) \quad \circ(A^c|B) = \circ(A^c|B^c)$$

then this holds true for any other agreeing class for $\pi_{|\mathcal{D}}$.

Proof: One has the following situations:

a. Suppose that $\pi(A|B) = \pi(A^c|B) = 1$, so

$$S_0 = \begin{cases} \Pi_o(A \wedge B) = \min\{1, \Pi_o(B)\} \\ \Pi_o(A \wedge B) = \min\{\pi(B|A), \Pi_o(A)\} \\ \Pi_o(A \wedge B^c) = \min\{1, \Pi_o(B^c)\} \\ \Pi_o(A \wedge B^c) = \min\{\pi(B^c|A), \Pi_o(A)\} \\ \Pi_o(A^c \wedge B) = \min\{1, \Pi_o(B)\} \\ \Pi_o(A^c \wedge B) = \min\{\pi(B|A^c), \Pi_o(A^c)\} \\ \Pi_o(A^c \wedge B^c) = \min\{1, \Pi_o(B^c)\} \\ \Pi_o(A^c \wedge B^c) = \min\{\pi(B^c|A^c), \Pi_o(A^c)\} \end{cases}$$

If $\pi(B|A^c) = \pi(B^c|A^c) = 1$, then $\Pi_o(A^* \wedge B^*) = 1$ and the condition (4) holds. If $\pi(B|A^c) < 1$, then $\Pi_o(A^c \wedge B^c) = 1 = \Pi_o(A \wedge B^c)$, while $\Pi_o(A^c \wedge B) = \Pi(B|A^c) = \Pi_o(B) = \pi(B|A) = \Pi_o(A \wedge B) < 1$. Moreover, the 1st and 5th equations of S_0 admit no unique solution. Hence, $\circ(A^c \wedge B^c) = \circ(A \wedge B^c) = 0$, while solving the system $S_1 = \begin{cases} \Pi_1(A \wedge B) = \min\{1, \Pi_1(B)\} \\ \Pi_1(A^c \wedge B) = \min\{1, \Pi_1(B)\} \end{cases}$

one gets that $\circ(A^c \wedge B) = \circ(A \wedge B) = 1$, so condition (4) holds.

The proof in the case $\pi(B^c|A^c) < 1$ goes along the same line of the above one.

Therefore, any agreeing class for $\pi_{|\mathcal{D}}$ in the case $\pi(A|B) = \pi(A^c|B) = 1$ satisfies condition (4).

b. Suppose that $\pi(A|B) = 0$, then

$$S_0 = \begin{cases} \Pi_o(A \wedge B) = \min\{0, \Pi_o(B)\} \\ \Pi_o(A \wedge B) = \min\{\pi(B|A), \Pi_o(A)\} \\ \Pi_o(A \wedge B^c) = \min\{0, \Pi_o(B^c)\} \\ \Pi_o(A \wedge B^c) = \min\{\pi(B^c|A), \Pi_o(A)\} \\ \Pi_o(A^c \wedge B) = \min\{1, \Pi_o(B)\} \\ \Pi_o(A^c \wedge B) = \min\{\pi(B|A^c), \Pi_o(A^c)\} \\ \Pi_o(A^c \wedge B^c) = \min\{1, \Pi_o(B^c)\} \\ \Pi_o(A^c \wedge B^c) = \min\{\pi(B^c|A^c), \Pi_o(A^c)\} \end{cases}$$

Independence in conditional possibility theory 31

(i) If $\pi(B|A^c) = 0$, then the $1^{st}, 2^{nd}, 4^{th}, 5^{th}$ equations have no unique solution and $\Pi_o(A^c \wedge B^c) = 1$, while $\Pi_o(B) = \Pi_o(A \wedge B^c) = 0$ and

$$S_1 = \begin{cases} \Pi_1(A \wedge B) = \min\{0, \Pi_1(B)\} \\ \Pi_1(A \wedge B) = \min\{\pi(B|A), \Pi_1(A)\} \\ \Pi_1(A \wedge B^c) = \min\{\pi(B^c|A), \Pi_1(A)\} \\ \Pi_1(A^c \wedge B) = \min\{1, \Pi_1(B)\} \end{cases}$$

  i. If also $\pi(B|A) = 0$ one has the following cases:
    - $\Pi_1(A) < 1$, then $\Pi_1(A^c \wedge B) = 1$, $\Pi_1(A \wedge B) = 0$, $\Pi_1(A \wedge B^c) = \Pi_1(A)$. It follows $\Pi_2(A \wedge B) = 0$ and $\Pi_2(A \wedge B^c) = \pi(B^c|A) = 1$. Then, $\circ(A^c|B^c) = 0 = \circ(A^c|B)$ and $\circ(A|B^c) = 2 = \circ(A|B) = \circ(A, B) - \circ(B)$. - $\Pi_1(B) < 1$, then $\Pi_1(A \wedge B^c) = 1$, $\Pi_1(A \wedge B) = 0$, $\Pi_1(A^c \wedge B) = \Pi_1(B)$. Moreover, $\Pi_2(A^c \wedge B) = 1$, $\Pi_2(A \wedge B) = 0$. Therefore, it follows $\circ(A^c|B^c) = 0 = \circ(A^c|B) = 2 - 2$, $\circ(A|B^c) = 1 = \circ(A|B) = 3 - 2$.
    - $\Pi_1(B) = \Pi_1(A) = 1$, then $\Pi_1(A \wedge B^c) = \Pi_1(A^c \wedge B) = 1$ and $\Pi_1(A \wedge B) = 0$, it follows that $\circ(A^c|B^c) = 0 = \circ(A^c|B) = 1 - 1$, $\circ(A|B^c) = 1 = \circ(A|B) = 2 - 1$. Then, condition (4) holds.
  ii. If $0 < \pi(B|A) < 1$, then $\Pi_1(A) = 0$ (only the 1st and 4th equations of S_1 have unique solution) and $\Pi_1(A^c \wedge B) = 1$, and $\Pi_2(A \wedge B) = \pi(B|A) \in (0,1)$, $\Pi_2(A \wedge B^c) = 1$. Then $\circ(A^c|B^c) = 0 = \circ(A^c|B)$, $\circ(A|B^c) = 2 = \circ(A|B) = 3 - 1$, so condition (4) holds.
  iii. If $\pi(B|A) = 1$, then $\Pi_1(A) = 0$ and $\Pi_1(A^c \wedge B) = 1$; $\Pi_2(A \wedge B) = 1$ and $\Pi_2(A \wedge B^c) = \pi(B^c|A)$. Hence, $\circ(A|B^c) = \circ(A \wedge B^c) \geq 2 > \circ(A|B) = 2 - 1$, so condition (4) does not hold.

Hence, for $\pi(B|A) = 1$ there is no nested class agreeing with $\pi_{|_D}$ satisfying (4); while if $\pi(B|A) < 1$, then all the agreeing classes for $\pi_{|_D}$ satisfies (4).

(ii) If $\pi(B|A^c) \in (0,1)$, then one has $\Pi_o(A^c \wedge B^c) = 1, 0 < \Pi_o(A^c \wedge B) < 1$ and $\Pi_o(A) = 0$. Therefore, being S_1

$$\begin{cases} \Pi_1(A \wedge B) = \min\{\pi(B|A), \Pi_1(A)\} \\ \Pi_1(A \wedge B^c) = \min\{\pi(B^c|A), \Pi_1(A)\} \\ \Pi_1(A^c \wedge B) = \min\{1, \Pi_1(B)\} \\ \Pi_1(A) = 0 \end{cases}$$

$\Pi_1(A^c \wedge B) = 1$ and $\Pi_2(A \wedge B) = \pi(B|A)$, $\Pi_2(A \wedge B^c) = \pi(B^c|A)$. Hence, $\circ(A^c|B^c) = 0 = \circ(A^c|B)$, while $\circ(A|B^c) = \circ(A \wedge B^c) = \circ(A|B) = \circ(A \wedge B) - 1$ iff $\pi(B|A) < 1$.

(iii) If $\pi(B|A^c) = \pi(B^c|A^c) = 1$, then only the 2nd and 4th equations of S_0 do not admit unique solution and $\Pi_o(A^c \wedge B^c) = \Pi_o(A^c \wedge B) = 1$, while $\Pi_o(A \wedge B^c) = \Pi_o(A \wedge B) = 0$. Hence, $\circ(A^c|B^c) = \circ(A^c|B) = 0$ and $\circ(A|B^c) = \circ(A, B^c)$, $\circ(A|B) = \circ(A, B)$, so $\circ(A|B^c) = \circ(A|B) = 1$ iff $\pi(B|A) = \pi(B^c|A) = 1$.

(iv) When $\pi(B^c|A^c) < 1$ the proof is analogous to the above cases for $\pi(B|A^c) < 1$ and (4) holds iff $\pi(B^c|A) < 1$ (if $\pi(B^c|A) = 1$ none satisfies (4)).

c. Suppose that $\pi(A|B) = \alpha$ with $\alpha \in (0,1)$ (so $\pi(A^c|B) = 1$), one has the following situations that S_0 is

$$\begin{cases} \Pi_o(A \wedge B) = \min\{\alpha, \Pi_o(B)\} \\ \Pi_o(A \wedge B) = \min\{\pi(B|A), \Pi_o(A)\} \\ \Pi_o(A \wedge B^c) = \min\{\alpha, \Pi_o(B^c)\} \\ \Pi_o(A \wedge B^c) = \min\{\pi(B^c|A), \Pi_o(A)\} \\ \Pi_o(A^c \wedge B) = \min\{1, \Pi_o(B)\} \\ \Pi_o(A^c \wedge B) = \min\{\pi(B|A^c), \Pi_o(A^c)\} \\ \Pi_o(A^c \wedge B^c) = \min\{1, \Pi_o(B^c)\} \\ \Pi_o(A^c \wedge B^c) = \min\{\pi(B^c|A^c), \Pi_o(A^c)\} \end{cases}$$

(i) If $\pi(B|A^c) = \beta < \alpha$, then $\pi(B|A^c) = \Pi_o(B) = \Pi_o(A^c \wedge B) = \Pi_o(A \wedge B) = \beta$ (so $\pi(B^c|A) = 1$) and $\Pi_o(B) = \pi(B|A^c) = \beta$, $\Pi_o(A^c \wedge B^c) = 1$ and $\Pi_o(A \wedge B^c) = \alpha$, so the equations 1, 4 and 5 of S_0 have no unique solution and $\circ(B^c) = \circ(A^c, B^c) = 0$.

From system

$$S_1 = \begin{cases} \Pi_1(A \wedge B) = \min\{\alpha, \Pi_1(B)\} \\ \Pi_1(A \wedge B^c) = \min\{1, \Pi_1(A)\} \\ \Pi_1(A^c \wedge B) = \min\{1, \Pi_1(B)\} \\ \Pi_1(A^c \wedge B) = \beta \\ \Pi_1(A \wedge B) = \beta \end{cases}$$

it follows $\Pi_1(A \wedge B^c) = 1$, and $\Pi_1(A^c \wedge B) = \Pi_1(A \wedge B) = \beta$, then the 1st and 3rd equations of S_1 admit no unique solution and one gets $\Pi_2(A \wedge B) = \alpha$ and $\Pi_2(A^c \wedge B) = 1$.

So $\circ(A^c|B^c) = \circ(A^c|B) = 2-2$, $\circ(A|B^c) = 1 = \circ(A|B) = 3-2$. Then, according to any agreeing class, when $\pi(B|A^c) < \alpha$ condition (4) holds.

(ii) If $\pi(B|A^c) = \alpha$ the proof is similar to the case b. (part 1.), therefore, one has that all the agreeing classes for $\pi_{|\mathcal{D}}$ satisfy condition (4) if $\pi(B|A) < 1$; while if $\pi(B|A) = 1$, then no nested class agreeing with $\pi_{|\mathcal{D}}$ satisfy condition (4).

(iii) If $\alpha < \pi(B|A^c) < 1$ the proof follows along the same line of b. (part 2.), and condition (4) holds iff $\alpha \leq \pi(B|A) < 1$.

(iv) If $\pi(B|A^c) = \pi(B^c|A^c) = 1$, then (analogously to the proof b. 3.) condition (4) is satisfied iff $\pi(B|A) = \pi(B^c|A) = 1$.

(v) When $\pi(B^c|A^c) < 1$ the result can be proved similarly to the previous cases changing the role of B and B^c.

d. The theorem can be proved in the case that $\pi(A^c|B) < 1$ analogously as done in the above case b. and c. changing the role of the event A with that of A^c.

Proposition 1. Under any coherent conditional possibility π, it follows that for any A, the statement $A \perp\!\!\!\perp A$ does not hold.

Proof: Since by the axioms of conditional possibilities we have that $\Pi(A|A) = 1$, while $\Pi(A|A^c) = \Pi(\emptyset|A^c) = 0$, if follows that the condition i of Definition 5 does not hold.

The previous property (irreflexive) is natural, in fact *any event must be dependent on itself.*

Moreover, the notion of *independence should imply the logical independence*, as proved in the result below Definition 5 respects this natural implication.

Proposition 2. Let π be a coherent conditional possibility such that under π the possible event A is independent of B. Then the events A and B are logically independent.

Proof: If $A \perp\!\!\!\perp B\ [\pi]$, then there is an agreeing class $\mathcal{P}$ for π such that $\circ(A \wedge B) - \circ(B) = \circ(A|B) = \circ(A|B^c) = \circ(A \wedge B^c) - \circ(B^c)$, so, being A a possible event, at least one between $\circ(A \wedge B)$ and $\circ(A \wedge B^c)$ must be finite, then both $\circ(A \wedge B)$ and $\circ(A \wedge B^c)$ are finite. From the equality $\circ(A^c|B) = \circ(A^c|B^c)$, it follows $\circ(A^c \wedge B)$ and $\circ(A^c \wedge B^c)$ are finite. This implies that A and B are logically independent.

Remark 2. The independence definitions [1,6,7,9–11] do not imply logical independence; actually this implication is guaranteed by the requirement ii. of Definition 5. We recall that the notion of independence given in [7] implies logical independence *only* for *particular* conditional possibility (known as classical two-valued possibility).

The next theorem characterizes independence for possibilities of two logically independent events in terms of the possibilities $\pi(B|A)$, $\pi(B^c|A)$, $\pi(B|A^c)$, $\pi(B^c|A^c)$ giving up any direct reference to significant-layers.

Theorem 5. Let A and B be two logically independent events. If a coherent conditional possibility π is such that $\pi(A|B) = \pi(A|B^c)$ and $\pi(A^c|B) = \pi(A^c|B^c)$, then $A \perp\!\!\!\perp B$ if and only if one (and only one) of the following conditions holds:
(a) $\pi(A|B) = \pi(A^c|B) = 1$;
(b) $\min\{\pi(A|B), \pi(A^c|B)\} = 0$ and the extension of π to $\pi(B|A), \pi(B^c|A), \pi(B|A^c), \pi(B^c|A^c)$ satisfies one of the following conditions:
 (1) $\pi(B|A^c) < 1$, $\pi(B|A) < 1$,
 (2) $\pi(B^c|A^c) < 1$, $\pi(B^c|A) < 1$,
 (3) $\pi(B|A^c) = \pi(B^c|A^c) = \pi(B|A) = \pi(B^c|A) = 1$;
(c) $\min\{\pi(A|B), \pi(A^c|B)\} = \alpha \in (0,1)$ and the extension of π to $\pi(B|A^c), \pi(B^c|A^c), \pi(B|A), \pi(B^c|A)$, satisfies one of the following conditions:
 (1) $\min\{\pi(B) = \pi(B^c)\} < \alpha$,
 (2) $\alpha \leq \pi(B|A^c) < 1$, $\alpha \leq \pi(B|A) < 1$,

(3) $\alpha \leq \pi(B^c|A^c) < 1$, $\alpha \leq \pi(B^c|A) < 1$,
(4) $\pi(B|A^c) = \pi(B^c|A^c) = \pi(B|A) = \pi(B^c|A) = 1$.

Proof: The proof follows from the proof of Theorem 4. In particular, when $\pi(A|B) = \pi(A^c|B) = 1$ it follows from the case **a**.

If $\pi(A|B) = 0$ it follows from **b**: $\pi(B|A^c) = 0$ from part 1.; $0 < \pi(B|A^c) < 1$ from part 2.; $\pi(B^c|A^c) < 1$ from part 4.; $\pi(B^*|A^*) = 1$ from part 3..

If $\pi(A|B) = \alpha \in (0,1)$ if follows from **c**: when $\pi(B|A^c) < \alpha$ from part 1., when $\alpha \leq \pi(B|A^c) < 1$ from parts 2. and 3., when $\pi(B^*|A^*) = 1$ from part 4.
While the cases when $\pi(B^c|A^c) < \alpha$ (analogously, when $\alpha \leq \pi(B^c|A^c) < 1$) can be proved along the same line of the previous case changing the role of B and B^c.

While the cases $\pi(A^c|B) < 1$ can be proved following the previous cases changing the role of A and A^c.

The validity of the independence statement $A \perp\!\!\!\perp B$, under a given conditional possibility π, does not guarantee the symmetric independence relation $B \perp\!\!\!\perp A$. However, concerning the possible symmetry of the independence we have the following result:

Theorem 6. Let A and B be two possible events. Given a coherent conditional possibility π such that $A \perp\!\!\!\perp B\, [\pi]$, we have:
 (i) if $\pi(A) = \pi(A^c) = 1$, then $B \perp\!\!\!\perp A$;
 (ii) if $\min\{\pi(A), \pi(A^c)\} = \alpha \in (0,1)$ and $\min\{\pi(B), \pi(B^c)\} < \alpha$, then $B \perp\!\!\!\perp A$;
 (iii) if $\min\{\pi(A), \pi(A^c)\} = \alpha < 1$, $\min\{\pi(B), \pi(B^c)\} \geq \alpha$ and $\pi(B|A) = \pi(B|A^c)$, $\pi(B^c|A) = \pi(B^c|A^c)$, then $B \perp\!\!\!\perp A$.

Proof: If $A \perp\!\!\!\perp B$, then it follows:
 (i) when $\pi(A) = \pi(A^c) = 1$, then $\pi(B|A) = \pi(B|A^c)$, since
  $\pi(B|A) = \min\{\pi(B|A), \pi(A)\} = \pi(A \wedge B) = \min\{\pi(A|B), \pi(B)\} = \pi(B) = \pi(A^c \wedge B) = \min\{\pi(B|A^c), \pi(A^c)\} = \pi(B|A^c)$.
  Moreover, going along the same line one has $\pi(B^c|A) = \pi(B^c) = \pi(B^c|A^c)$.
  If $\pi(B) = \pi(B^c) = 1$, then from Theorem 5 (a) it follows $B \perp\!\!\!\perp A\, [\pi]$.
  If $\min\{\pi(B), \pi(B^c)\} = 0$, then, being $\pi(A) = \pi(A^c) = 1$, $B \perp\!\!\!\perp A\, [\pi]$ follows from Theorem 5 (b)(3).
  When $0 < \min\{\pi(B), \pi(B^c)\} < 1$, Theorem 5 (c)(4) implies $B \perp\!\!\!\perp A\, [\pi]$.
 (ii) if $\min\{\pi(A), \pi(A^c)\} = \alpha$ with $0 < \alpha < 1$, and $\pi(B) < \alpha$, then (by the same calculation of step 1) $\pi(B|A) = \pi(B|A^c)$. Moreover, $\pi(B^c|A) = \pi(B^c|A^c) = 1$. Therefore, the statement $B \perp\!\!\!\perp A\, [\pi]$ holds (Theorem 5 (c) (2)).
  When $\pi(B^c) < \alpha$, the proof is analogous to the previous case.
 (iii) Under the conditions of 3. the result follows from Theorem 5 (b) (2) and (c) (2)) when $\pi(B) \geq \alpha$ while from (b) (3) and (c) (3)) when $\pi(B^c) \geq \alpha$.

Corollary 1. Let A and B be two possible events. Under a coherent conditional possibility π, $A \perp\!\!\!\perp B$ and $B \perp\!\!\!\perp A$ hold iff

$$\pi(A|B) = \pi(A|B^c), \qquad \pi(A^c|B) = \pi(A^c|B^c)$$

$$\pi(B|A) = \pi(B|A^c), \qquad \pi(B^c|A) = \pi(B^c|A^c).$$

The following results show the connection between 5 and the other independence notion known in literature.

Proposition 3. If $A \perp\!\!\!\perp B\,[\pi]$, then $\pi(A|B) = \pi(A)$.
Conversely, if $\pi(A|B) = \pi(A)$ and $\pi(A) < \min\{\pi(B^c), \pi(B^c|A)\} < 1$ one has that $A \perp\!\!\!\perp B\,[\pi]$.

Proof: If $A \perp\!\!\!\perp B\,[\pi]$, then by putting $\pi(A|B^*) = \alpha$ it follows that
$\pi(A) = \max\{\pi(A \wedge B), \pi(A \wedge B^c)\} = \max\{\min\{\alpha, \pi(B)\}, \min\{\alpha, \pi(B^c)\}\} = \alpha$.
Conversely, if $\pi(A|B) = \pi(A)$, then $\pi(A \wedge B^c) = \min\{\pi(B^c|A), \pi(A)\} = \pi(A)$ (being $\pi(B^c|A) > \pi(A)$). Moreover $\pi(A \wedge B^c) = \min\{\pi(A|B^c), \pi(B^c)\} = \pi(A|B^c)$ (being $\pi(B^c) > \pi(A)$), so $\pi(A|B) = \pi(A) = \pi(A \wedge B^c) = \pi(A|B^c)$.
Since $\pi(A) < 1$, then $\pi(A^c|B) = \pi(A^c|B^c) = 1$. Moreover, $\pi(B^c) = \pi(B^c|A^c)$, so it follows $A \perp\!\!\!\perp B\,[\pi]$ from Theorem 5 *(b) (2)* and *(c) (3)*.

Proposition 4. If $A \perp\!\!\!\perp B\,[\pi]$, then $\pi(A \wedge B) = \min\{\pi(A), \pi(B)\}$.
Conversely, if $\pi(A \wedge B) = \min\{\pi(A), \pi(B)\}$ and $\pi(A) < \min\{\pi(B^c), \pi(B^c|A)\} < 1$, then the statement $A \perp\!\!\!\perp B\,[\pi]$ holds.

Proof: From Proposition 3 one has that $A \perp\!\!\!\perp B\,[\pi]$ implies that $\pi(A \wedge B) = \min\{\pi(A|B), \pi(B)\} = \min\{\pi(A), \pi(B)\}$.
Conversely, if $\pi(A \wedge B) = \min\{\pi(A), \pi(B)\}$ and $\pi(B) = 1 > \pi(A)$, then $\pi(A|B) = \pi(A)$. Moreover, if $\pi(B^c) > \pi(A)$, then $\pi(A \wedge B^c) = \min\{\pi(A|B^c), \pi(B^c)\} = \pi(A|B^c) \leq \pi(A)$ and $\pi(A \wedge B^c) = \min\{\pi(B^c|A), \pi(A)\} = \pi(A)$, since $\pi(B^c|A) > \pi(A)$, so $\pi(A|B) = \pi(A) = \pi(A|B^c)$ and since $\pi(A) < 1$, one has $\pi(A^c|B) = \pi(A^c) = \pi(A^c|B^c) = 1$.
The statement $A \perp\!\!\!\perp B$ follows from Theorem 5 *(b) (2)* and *(c) (3)*.

In particular the above result allows to compare our independence notion with that given in [2].

4. Conclusion

We propose a notion of independence, which encompasses the critical situations presented by other independence definitions: for instance we obtain that, in any case, possibility independence implies logical independence.

The proposed independence notion can be generalized to conditional independence among random variables, and in a future work we will check the validity of graphoid axioms, which allow to compare this independence models with other uncertainty calculi and which are relevant for graphical models.

References

1. Benferhat, S., Dubois, D., Prade, H., Expressing independence in a possibilistic framework and its application to default reasoning, Proc. 11th Eur. Conf. in Artificial Intelligence, A.Cohn (Ed.), Whiley, New York, 1994, 150-154.
2. Bouchon-Meunier, B., Coletti, G., Marsala, C., Independence and possibilistic conditioning, Annals of Mathematics and Artificial Intelligence, 35, 2002, 107-124.
3. Bouchon-Meunier, B., Coletti, G., Marsala, C., Conditional possibility and necessity. Technologies for Constructing Intelligent Systems, Bouchon-Meunier, Gutierréz-Rions, Magdalena, Yager (Eds.), Springer-Verlag, 2002, 59-71 (Selected papers from IPMU 2000).
4. Coletti, G., Scozzafava, R., From conditional events to conditional measures: a new axiomatic approach, Annals of Mathematics and Artificial Intelligence, 32, 2001, 373-392.
5. Coletti, G., Scozzafava, R., Probabilistic logic in a coherent setting, Trends in logic n.15, Kluwer, Dordrecht/Boston/London, 2002.
6. de Campos, L.M., Huete, J.F., Independence concepts in possibility theory: part I, Fuzzy Sets and Systems, 103, 1999, 127-152.
7. de Cooman, G., Possibility theory III: Possibilistic independence, Int. J. General Systems, 25, 1997, 353-371.
8. de Finetti, B., Sull'impostazione assiomatica del calcolo delle probabilitá, Annali Univ. di Trieste, 19, 1949, 29-81. (English translation in: (1972) Probability, Induction, Statistics. Ch. 5. London Wiley).
9. Dubois, D., Fariñas del Cerro, L., Herzig, A., Prade, H., An ordinal view of independence with application to plausible reasoning, Proc. Uncertainty in Artificial Intelligence, 1994, 195-203.
10. Fonck, P., Conditional independence in possibility theory, Proc. 10th Conf. on Uncertainty in Artificial Intelligence, R. Lopez de Mantaras, D. Poole (Eds.), Morgan and Kaufmann, San Matteo, 1994, 221-226.
11. Hisdal, E., Conditional possibilities independence and noninteraction, Fuzzy Sets and Systems, 1, 1978, 283-297.
12. Zadeh, L.A., Fuzzy sets as a basis for a theory of possibility, Fuzzy Sets and Systems, 1, 1978, 3-28.

Joint Treatment of Imprecision and Randomness in Uncertainty Propagation

C. Baudrit [a] and D. Dubois [a] and D. Guyonnet [b] and H. Fargier [a]

[a]Institut de Recherche en Informatique de Toulouse, Université Paul Sabatier
Toulouse, France
[b]Service Environnement et Procédés, BRGM,
Orléans, France

Abstract

This paper presents and studies in detail a hybrid method of uncertainty propagation for the case where knowledge regarding some parameters of a physical model is represented by probability measures, while others are represented by possibility measures or belief functions.

Keywords: *(Random) Fuzzy Numbers, Probability, Possibility, Belief functions, Dependence.*

1. Introduction

Currently, decisions regarding the management of polluted sites very often rely on the evaluation of risks for man and the environment. Such an evaluation is typically performed with the help of models that simulate the transfer of pollutants from a source to a vulnerable target, for different scenarii of exposure. Due to time and financial constraints, information regarding model parameters is often incomplete. So the knowledge really available on model parameters is often vague. This leads to uncertainty that needs to be accounted for in the decision-making process.

Uncertainty regarding model parameters may have essentially two origins [13]. It may arise from randomness due to natural variability resulting from heterogeneity or stochasticity. Or it may be caused by imprecision due to lack of information resulting, for example, from systematic measurement error or expert opinions. Imprecision and randomness are often confused in risk analysis. It may occur in practice, that some parameters of empirical models can be represented by probability distributions (variability) while others are better represented by possibility distributions (partial ignorance), or by belief functions of Shafer (variability and partial ignorance). Most researchers typically use either one or the other of these modes of uncertainty representation. But fewer have addressed the combination of these different modes of representation (probability, possibility, belief function) in the same computation of risk.

Let $T: \mathbb{R}^n \to \mathbb{R}$ be a function (model) of n arguments x_i ($x = (x_1, ..., x_n)$). The knowledge on parameters x_i can be represented by means of a probability distribution, a possibility distribution or a Dempster-Shafer mass function. The main issue is thus to carry the uncertainty attached to the variables over to $T(x)$ with the least possible loss of initial information. This is uncertainty propagation. Generally, in the evaluation of risks for man and the environment, one tries to estimate $P_{T(X)}((-\infty, e])$, the probability that some pollutant concentrations be less than an absorbed dose limit e for example.

One can distinguish between three important issues [11] [13]: the first is how to represent the available information faithfully [3], the second is how to account for dependencies, correlations between the parameters in the propagation process (linear, non linear monotone dependency, interaction ...). For example the assumption of stochastic independence between parameters can generate too optimistic results [15] [16]. The last issue is the choice of the propagation technique [4] [12].

Kaufmann and Gupta [19] introduced hybrid numbers which simultaneously express imprecision (fuzzy number) and randomness (probability). Ferson and Ginzburg [14] extended the approach of Kaufmann and used hybrid arithmetic to treat risk analysis [17]. We can consider hybrid numbers as random fuzzy numbers, which in fact can be synthetized by means of belief functions (see further on).

In Section 2, we explain the hybrid method [14] [18] in detail. In Section 3, we study the links between the hybrid method and the random set approach [1,4] using the belief functions of Dempster-Shafer [22] to propagate uncertainties. In Section 4, we discuss the postprocessing step proposed by Guyonnet et al. [18]. We propose an alternative postprocessing [2] for the hybrid calculation results taking the form of a random fuzzy interval. We can see it as a way to extract information from the results of the random fuzzy computation for estimating the probability of events such that $(-\infty, e]$ or $[e, +\infty)$. We also present the postprocessing method of Ferson [14] [17] and compare it with our approach. We will compare results of the hybrid method with the random set approach on a synthetic example in Section 5.

2. Joint propagation of fuzzy numbers and probabilities

2.1. *Methodology and discussion*

Let us assume $k < n$ random variables $(X_1, ..., X_k)$ taking values $(x_1, ..., x_k)$ and $n - k$ possibilistic variables $(X_{k+1}, ..., X_n)$ taking values $(x_{k+1}, ..., x_n)$.

We explain in this section how to propagate the uncertainties generated by $(X_i)_{i=1...n}$ through T with the hybrid method. There are two steps (see [18]) that combine a Monte Carlo technique with the extension principle [8]. We first perform a Monte Carlo sampling of the random variables taking into account dependencies (if known) between random variables, thus processing variability (probability). The values thus obtained are then fixed $(X_1 = x_1, ..., X_k = x_k)$ and fuzzy interval analysis is used to estimate T. The knowledge on the value of $T(X)$ becomes a fuzzy subset. Random sampling is resumed and the process is performed in an iterative fashion to obtain a sample $(\pi_1^T, ..., \pi_m^T)$ of fuzzy subsets (see Fig.1). $T(X)$ becomes a fuzzy random variable [20]. In the case where dependencies are

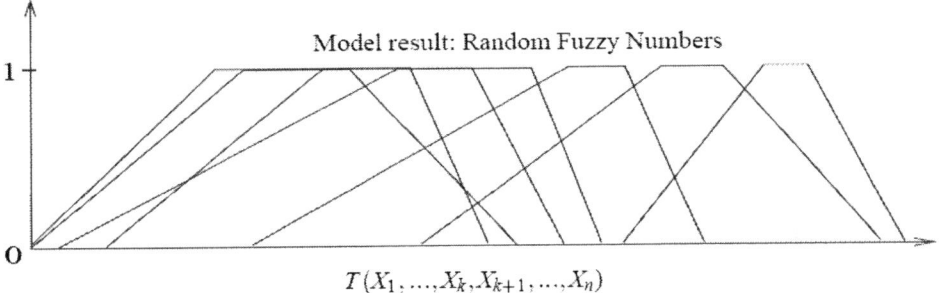

Fig. 1. Results of the "hybrid" method

unknown between random variables, the classical Monte Carlo method presupposes the independence of random variables which has been criticized by Ferson [12]. It is worthwile noticing that within a Monte Carlo approach the rank correlation (non linear monotone dependency) between the random variables [7] can be taken into consideration (if known). Even if we can account for some dependencies between random variables with Monte-Carlo, it is necessary to be aware that the Monte Carlo method cannot account for all forms of dependency.

We must be careful with the extension principle because it also underlies an assumption on possibilistic variables. In fact the presence of imprecision on $X_{k+1}, ..., X_n$ generates two levels of dependencies. The first one is a dependency between information sources attached to variables and the second one is a dependency between variables themselves. The extension principle [8]:$\forall u \in \mathbb{R}$

$$\pi_T(u) = \sup_{x_{k+1},...,x_n, T(x_1,...,x_n)=u} \min(\pi_{k+1}(x_{k+1}), ..., \pi_n(x_n))$$

first assumes strong dependence between information sources pertaining to possibilistic variables, i.e, on the choice of confidence levels or α-cuts induced by these confidence levels [9]. For instance, one expert assigns the same confidence degree to two possibilistic variables A and B. This suggests a strong dependency between the precision of A and the precision of B. However, this form of dependency does not suppose any objective dependence between possibilistic variables themselves. The use of "min" assumes the non-interaction of $X_{k+1}, ..., X_n$, which expresses a lack of knowledge about the links between the values of $X_{k+1}, ..., X_n$ and a lack of commitment as to whether $X_{k+1}, ..., X_n$ are linked or not. The hybrid method also supposes independence between the group of probabilistic and possibilistic variables.

3. Uncertainty propagation in the setting of random sets

Belief functions [22] encompass possibility and probability theory. Let X (resp. Y) be a possibilistic variable. We denote by π^X (resp. π^Y) the possibility distribution of X and $\pi^X_\alpha = \{x | \pi^X(x) \geq \alpha\}$, $\forall \alpha \in [0,1]$, the α-cuts of π^X. Focal elements for X corresponding to α-cuts are denoted $(\pi^X_{\alpha_i})_{i=1...q}$ with $\alpha_q > 0$ and are nested. We denote by $(v^X_i = \alpha_i - \alpha_{i+1})_{i=1...q}$ ($\alpha_{q+1} = 0$), the mass distribution associated to $(\pi^X_{\alpha_i})_{i=1...q}$. Let Z (resp. W) be a discrete random variable with $\Omega_Z = \{z_1,...,z_m\}$ and $p^Z_k = P(Z = z_k)$. Focal elements for Z are singletons $(\{z_k\})_{k=1...m}$ and the mass distribution is equal to $(p^Z_k)_{k=1...m}$ because Z is discrete. We choose a discrete probability for the sake of clarity. Note however that if Z has a continuous density, focal elements can be disjoint intervals obtained by discretization and p^Z_k can be equal to the area under the probability distribution function for each disjoint interval. We thus encode probabilistic and possibilistic variables as belief functions.

We will consider two possiblistic variables X and Y, two probabilistic variables Z and W, and a continuous function T to illustrate the links between the propagation results obtained with the random set approach [1,4] and the hybrid approach. In general, a mass denoted v^T_{ijkl} can be associated to each focal element $T_{ijkl} = T(\pi^X_{\alpha_i}, \pi^Y_{\alpha_j}, \{z_k\}, \{w_l\})$ of $T(X,Y,Z,W)$. We can then compute: $\forall A$ measurable set

$$Pl^T(A) = \sum_{i,j,k,l; A \cap T_{ijkl} \neq \emptyset} v^T_{ijkl} \quad \text{and} \quad Bel^T(A) = \sum_{i,j,k,l; A \subseteq T_{ijkl}} v^T_{ijkl}.$$

With the random set approach [1,4], we suppose independence between focal sets (dubbed "independent random sets" method) and we thus define the mass distribution of $T(X,Y,Z,W)$ by:

$$\forall i,j,k,l \quad v_{ijkl} = v^X_i v^Y_j p^Z_k p^W_l$$

In the case of the hybrid method, the mass distribution v^T_{ijkl} should be defined as follows

$$\forall i,j,k,l; \; i = j \quad v_{ijkl} = v^{X,Y}_i p^Z_k p^W_l$$

$$\forall i,j,k,l; \; i \neq j \quad v_{ijkl} = 0$$

$v^{X,Y}_i$ is the mass associated to the cartesian product of α-cuts $\pi^X_{\alpha_i} \times \pi^Y_{\alpha_i}$. These sets are nested, and this mass function induces a possibility distribution $\pi^{X,Y}$, which is now precisely $\min(\pi^X, \pi^Y)$. This mass $v^{X,Y}_i$ is carried over to each set $T_{iikl} = T(\pi^X_{\alpha_i}, \pi^Y_{\alpha_i}, \{z_k\}, \{w_l\})$. We thus assume a total dependency between focal elements associated to possibilistic variables, and independence between the possibilistic variables and the probabilistic ones. Hence, if we want to estimate $Pl^T(A)$, $\forall A$ measurable set, using the last definition of v_{ijkl}, we have:

$$Pl^T(A) = \sum_{i,k,l; A \cap T_{iikl} \neq \emptyset} v^{X,Y}_i p^Z_k p^W_l = \sum_{k,l} p^Z_k p^W_l \sum_{i, A \cap T_{iikl} \neq \emptyset} v^{X,Y}_i = \sum_{k,l} p^Z_k p^W_l Pl^T_{kl}(A)$$

For each k,l varying from 1 to m, we have $T_{iikl} \subseteq ... \subseteq T_{rrkl} \; \forall i \geq r$. Thus $Pl^T_{kl}(A) = \Pi^T_{kl}(A)$, where Π^T_{kl} are the possibility measures associated to fuzzy numbers π^T_{kl} obtained by the hybrid method. Hence, we obtain:

$$Pl^T(A) = \sum_{k,l} p^Z_k p^W_l \Pi^T_{kl}(A)$$

With a similar reasoning, the same result holds with belief measure Bel^T

$$Bel^T(A) = \sum_{k,l} p_k^Z p_l^W N_{kl}^T(A)$$

Hence, "hybrid" method and "independent random sets" method are special cases of a general random set approach where we respectively suppose total dependency and independence between the focal sets of possibilistic variables (see also Dubois and Prade [9]).

4. Postprocessing of the hybrid method

4.1. The proposal of Guyonnet et al. [18]

Guyonnet et al. [18] propose to synthetise the random fuzzy result into a single fuzzy subset denoted π_d^T. For each α-cut $\pi_{i\alpha}^T=[\underline{a}_{i\alpha}, \overline{a}_{i\alpha}]$ of sample of the random fuzzy subset $(\pi_i^T)_{i=1...m}$ resulting from hybrid method, Guyonnet et al. [18] separately rearrange the left side and the right side of sets in increasing order. The α-cuts $\pi_{d\alpha}^T=[\underline{a}_{d\alpha}, \overline{a}_{d\alpha}]$ of π_d^T are defined such that

$$\underline{a}_{d\alpha} = \sum_{i=1}^{m} \underline{a}_{i\alpha} \delta_{]\frac{i-1}{m},\frac{i}{m}]}(1-d\%) \quad \text{and} \quad \overline{a}_{d\alpha} = \sum_{i=1}^{m} \overline{a}_{i\alpha} \delta_{]\frac{i-1}{m},\frac{i}{m}]}(d\%) \tag{1}$$

where $\delta_{]\frac{i-1}{m},\frac{i}{m}]}(x) = 1$ if $x \in]\frac{i-1}{m},\frac{i}{m}]$, 0 otherwise. Varying $\alpha \in [0,1]$, a fuzzy interval π_d^T is thus built. The standard value $d = 95$ is chosen. That is, they eliminate 5% on the left and on the right side and perform the union of the rest. If such an outlier elimination were not performed, it would come down to computing the idempotent union of the fuzzy outcomes. Starting from this π_d^T, the probability of events such that: $(-\infty,e]$, $]e,+\infty)$, $]e_1,e_2]$ is computed.
However, there are caveats with this postprocessing method. It yields false estimates of $P_{T(X)}([e_1,e_2])$. Indeed the *leftside* $\underline{a}_{i\alpha}$ and *rightside* $\overline{a}_{i\alpha}$ are independently processed, although $\overline{a}_{i\alpha}$ is entirely determined by $\underline{a}_{i\alpha}$ and conversely since α-cuts are generated as a whole. But the most important difficulty is that this method confuses variability and imprecision. It does not account for the probabilities generated by the random variables (the frequency attached to each fuzzy number) and it thus forgets this knowledge. The method thus puts excessive weight on less frequent randomly generated fuzzy numbers (generally located on the extreme right and left parts of the result π_d^T). As a consequence, one may obtain the same fuzzy number π_d^T whether the π_i^T's have large imprecision and small variability as in Fig.2a, or are more precise with a great variability as in Fig.2b.
These drawbacks already appear when combining intervals and probability. For instance, let A, B be two independent random variables and C be an interval such that: $P(A = 1) = P(A = 2) = 0.5$, $P(B = 4) = 1/3$, $P(B = 6) = 2/3$ and $C = [1,2]$. We compute $T = (A+B)/C$. With the hybrid method, we obtain a random interval: $T_1 = [2.5,5]$ with probability $1/6$, $T_2 = [3.5,7]$ with probability $2/6$; $T_3 = [3,6]$ with probability $1/6$ and $T_4 = [4,8]$ with probability $2/6$. Putting $d = 20\%$, with this postprocessing we obtain $T_d = [3,7]$, and we assign to it a mass equal to 1, which is debatable. Indeed we eliminate the knowledge

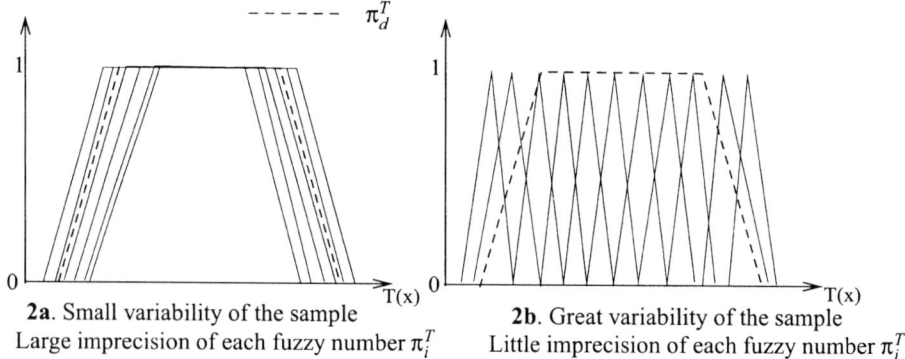

2a. Small variability of the sample
Large imprecision of each fuzzy number π_i^T

2b. Great variability of the sample
Little imprecision of each fuzzy number π_i^T

Fig. 2. The same result π_d^T obtained by the Guyonnet et al. postprocessing on two different fuzzy random variables.

(frequency) brought by A and B, i.e. variability. As can be observed on some examples, the use of π_d^T may put excessive weight on outlier fuzzy values, in the case of precise results with high variability, even if some outliers have been deleted by the threshold d. The postprocessing proposed by Guyonnet et al. is thus debatable. Better alternative postprocessings can separately treat variability and imprecision.

4.2. Measuring variability and imprecision separately

We may wish to define separate indices of variability and imprecision. To evaluate the average imprecision about T, we can estimate an average fuzzy number π_{mean}^T with [20]:

$$\forall z,\ \pi_{mean}^T(z) = \sup_{\frac{1}{m}\sum_{i=1}^m x_i = z} \min(\pi_1^T, \ldots, \pi_m^T)$$

and compute the area under π_{mean}^T. It provides an indicator of the average imprecision of T.

To estimate the variability of T, we can work with a representative value v_i^r of each fuzzy number π_i^T. Then we can estimate a variance V of the form:

$$V = \frac{1}{m}\sum_{i=1}^m v_i^{r2} - \frac{2}{m(m-1)}\sum_{j<i} v_j^r v_i^r$$

where v_i^r is a representative value of π_i^T. If V is small, the variability is small as in Fig.2a for example. As the representative value v_i^r we can choose the middle point of the mean interval [23] also equal to the average of the pignistic probability associated to π_i^T

$$v_i^r = \int_0^1 \frac{(sup\pi_{i\alpha}^T + inf\pi_{i\alpha}^T)}{2} d\alpha$$

V appears only as an indicator of result variability. Other indicators could be defined like the variability of imprecision, the potential variability, etc.

4.3. Computing upper and lower cumulative average distributions.

The use of belief functions [22] enables variability and imprecision to be processed in a common framework. Let $(\pi_i^T)_{i=1...m}$ be the sample of random fuzzy numbers resulting from the hybrid method. Let p_i be the probability associated at fuzzy number π_i^T. We encode each π_i^T with focal elements $(\pi_{i\alpha}^T)_\alpha$ and the mass distribution associated $(v_\alpha p_i)_\alpha$. We obtain a random sampling of intervals $(\pi_{i\alpha}^T)_{i,\alpha}$ with a mass distribution $(v_\alpha p_i)_{i,\alpha}$. Then, we can estimate, $\forall A$ measurable set, $Pl_T(A)$ and $Bel_T(A)$ such that:

$$Pl^T(A) = \sum_{(i,\alpha);\ \pi_{i\alpha}^T \cap A \neq \emptyset} v_\alpha p_i \quad \text{and} \quad Bel^T(A) = \sum_{(i,\alpha);\ \pi_{i\alpha}^T \subseteq A} v_\alpha p_i$$

It is what we named "homogeneous postprocessing". This technique yields:

$$Pl^T(A) = \sum_i p_i \Pi_i^T(A) \quad \text{and} \quad Bel^T(A) = \sum_i p_i N_i^T(A)$$

Value p_i represents the probability to obtain the fuzzy number π_i^T. If the Monte Carlo method yields m distinct fuzzy numbers, then $p_i = (1/m)$ in this case. Let us compare the Guyonnet et al. [18] postprocessing with $Pl^T((-\infty, e])$ and $Bel^T((-\infty, e])$.
With the homogeneous postprocessing, we get $Pl^T((-\infty, t^*]) = 1$, if and only if, $\forall i = 1...m$, $\Pi_i^T((-\infty, t^*]) = 1$. That is $t^* = \max_i\{\inf(core(\pi_i^T))\}$. We also have $Pl^T((-\infty, t_*]) = 0$, if and only if, $\forall i = 1...m$, $\Pi_i^T((-\infty, t_*]) = 0$. That is $t_* = \min_i\{\inf(support(\pi_i^T))\}$. With the Guyonnet et al. method, we build for each α-cut the following intervals: $\pi_{d\alpha}^T = [\underline{a}_{d\alpha}, \overline{a}_{d\alpha}]$ by using equations (1) (see Sec.4.1). We study only the left part, that is upper probability. Note $\underline{a}_{d\alpha} = \overline{F}_\alpha^{-1}(1 - d\%)$ where $\overline{F}_\alpha$ is the upper cumulative distribution function encoded by the probabilities p_i associated to $(\underline{a}_{i\alpha})_i$ and $\overline{F}_\alpha^{-1}(1 - d\%) = \min\{x | \overline{F}_\alpha(x) \geq 1 - d\%\}$. If $d \neq 100\%$, the construction of $\overline{F}_\alpha^{-1}$ will necessarily imply:

$$\text{for} \quad \alpha = 0, \quad \overline{F}_0^{-1}(1 - d\%) \geq t_*$$

$$\text{for} \quad \alpha = 1, \quad \overline{F}_1^{-1}(1 - d\%) \leq t^*$$

Distribution functions $\Pi(-\infty, e]$ induced from π_d^T obtained by Guyonnet et al. (see Sec.4.1) and $Pl(-\infty, e]$ obtained by our average postprocessing are increasing. We can conclude for $d \neq 100\%$ there exists a value t_c such that $\Pi_d^T((-\infty, t_c]) = Pl^T((-\infty, t_c])$ (see Fig.3). A similar reasoning can also conclude it exists a value t_r such that $Bel^T((-\infty, t_r]) = N_d^T((-\infty, t_r])$. Thus we can say that with hybrid postprocessing according to Guyonnet et al. [18], we are more conservative on the right side of t_c and less conservative on the left side of t_c than the homogeneous postprocessing.

4.4. Comparison with Ferson postprocessing method

Ferson [14,17] treats variability and imprecision of random fuzzy numbers separately. In fact, he sets a degree of confidence α and focuses on the upper and lower cumulative probability distributions of the random set obtained by α-cuts $\pi_{i\alpha} = [\underline{a}_{i\alpha}, \overline{a}_{i\alpha}]$ of the fuzzy random variable. Thus, in case of optimism, we use the upper $\overline{F}_1$ and lower $\underline{F}_1$ cumulative distributions at $\alpha = 1$, but in case of pessimism, one uses the upper $\overline{F}_0$ and lower $\underline{F}_0$

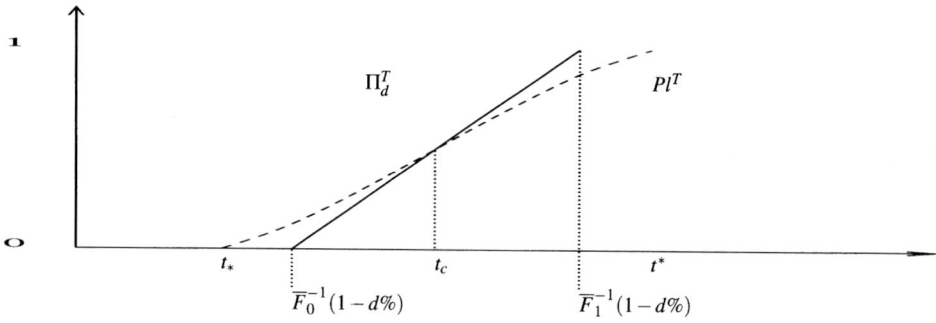

Fig. 3.

cumulative distributions at $\alpha = 0$. We thus obtain two pairs of upper and lower cumulative distributions (see Fig.4). The gap between $\overline{F_\alpha}$ and $\underline{F_\alpha}$ represents the imprecision due to possibilistic variables.

We use the same notations as in Section 4.3 and compare this postprocessing with the previous one. With the homogeneous postprocessing of Section 4.3, we have random intervals $(\pi_{i\alpha}^T)_{i\alpha}$ associated to a mass distribution $(\nu_\alpha p_i)_{i\alpha}$, for all i and all α. With Ferson approach α is fixed and it computes: $\overline{F_\alpha}(x) = \sum_i p_i \Pi_{i\alpha}^T((-\infty, x])$ and $\underline{F_\alpha}(x) = \sum_i p_i N_{i\alpha}^T((-\infty, x])$, where $\Pi_{i\alpha}^T((-\infty, x]) = 1$ if $x \geq \underline{a}_{i\alpha}$ and 0 otherwise, $N_{i\alpha}^T((-\infty, x]) = 1$ if $x > \overline{a}_{i\alpha}$ and 0 otherwise. It is obvious, since $\pi_{i1}^T \subseteq \pi_i^T \subseteq \pi_{i0}^T$, that $\Pi_{i0}^T((-\infty, x]) \geq \Pi_i^T((-\infty, x]) \geq \Pi_{i1}^T((-\infty, x])$ and $N_{i1}^T((-\infty, x]) \geq N_i^T((-\infty, x]) \geq N_{i0}^T((-\infty, x])$. Hence (see Fig.4)

$$\overline{F_1} \leq Pl^T((-\infty, e]) \leq \overline{F_0}$$

and (see Fig.4)

$$\underline{F_0} \leq Bel^T((-\infty, e]) \leq \underline{F_1}$$

. Moreover, we have [10]

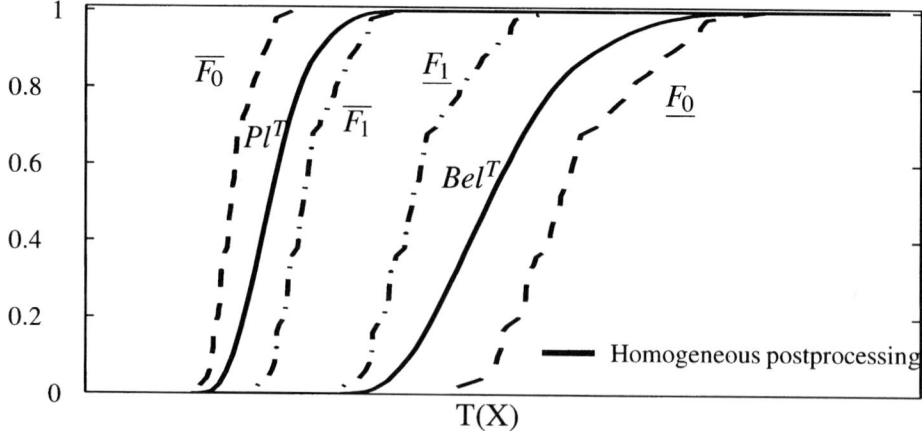

Fig. 4. Postprocessing of Ferson and comparison with our homogeneous postprocessing results.

$$Pl^T((-\infty,e]) = \int_0^1 \overline{F_\alpha}(t)d\alpha \quad \text{and} \quad Bel^T((-\infty,e]) = \int_0^1 \underline{F_\alpha}(t)$$

5. Numerical example

Consider two possibilistic variables A, B (fuzzy numbers such that support(A)=[1,5], core(A)=[2,3]; support(B)=[3,8], core(B)=[4,6]), and one random variable C=Norm(7.5,1). We try to estimate $D = (A+B)/C$. Such a simple expression D may commonly appear in risk assessment calculation. We used the postprocessing method of Guyonnet (dash-

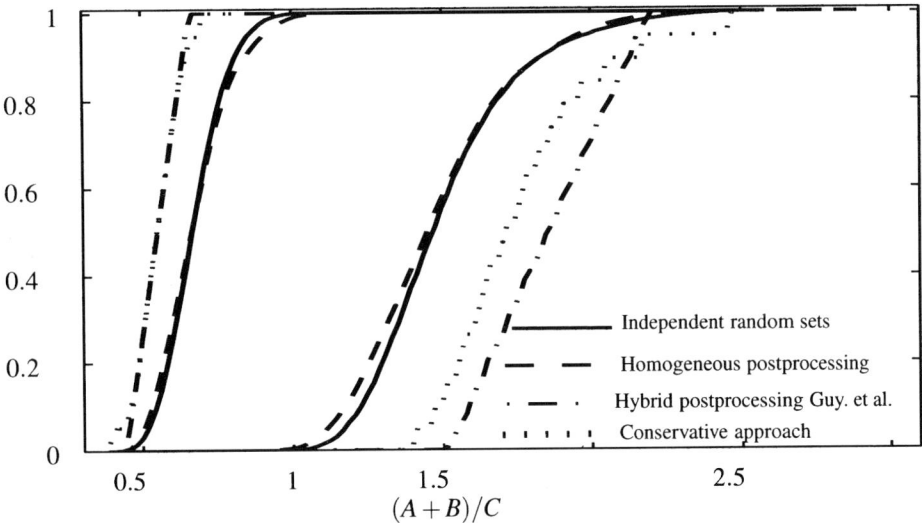

Fig. 5. Comparison of upper and lower cumulative distributions obtained by the random set approach and the postprocessing hybrid methods.

dot lines on Fig.5) and our homogeneous postprocessing methods (dashed lines on Fig.5). We can compare upper and lower distribution functions produced by these techniques on Fig.5 with the Dempster-Shafer (independent random sets) approach of Sec.3 (solid lines on Fig.5) and with a conservative Dempster-Shafer approach (dotted lines on Fig.5) [1,4,5] to estimate upper and lower cumulative distributions of $(A+B)/C$. This conservative approach performs propagation without assuming knowledge on dependencies between variables. For each event of interest, the minimal belief degree (resp. maximal plausibility degree) is computed when varying the joint masses (such as v_{ijkl}^T in Section 3) under the constraints of fixed marginal distributions known for each variable. Dempster-Shafer conservative approach produces an envelope (Bel_{min} dotted line, Pl_{max} dotted line) [5] for all results except for the Guyonnet et al. postprocessing. Indeed, the latter can sometimes be too conservative. It is due to the confusion between variability and imprecision and the fact of not accounting for frequencies (see Sec.4.1). Bel_{min} and Pl_{max} remain the most credible conservative bounds on the cumulative distribution of $(A+B)/C$ in the case where we have no knowledge on dependencies. We can see that our homogeneous postprocessing of the hybrid method (see Sec.4.3) is bracketed by Bel_{min} and Pl_{max}. We thus have for instance with our homogeneous postprocessing: $0.6 \leq P(\frac{A+B}{C} \leq 1.5) \leq 1$. We have no information on $P(\frac{A+B}{C} \leq 1)$ because we only know: $0 \leq P(\frac{A+B}{C} \leq 1) \leq 1$.

6. Conclusion

This paper proposes an approach to jointly propagate probabilistic and possibilistic uncertainty in deterministic mathematical models, and a postprocessing technique based on belief functions that lays bare imprecision and variability of the results separately, and extracts upper and lower cumulative distributions. Our postprocessing method described in Section 4.3 seems to be an adequate approach to treat in a common framework results tainted with both imprecision and variability. The hybrid probabilistic-possibilistic propagation method presupposes that probabilistic variables are independent, while information sources on possibilistic variables are totally dependent, and finally, probabilistic and possibilistic variables are independent of each other. It raises the following question for this method: how to take into consideration dependencies between the possibilistic variables, and between the random and possibilistic variables if such dependencies exist and are known? Accounting for dependence is a very hard problem in the propagation process. Using ideas of rank correlations [7], copulas [21] and the general framework of upper and lower probabilities introduced by Couso et al. [6] we may try to take into consideration some links or dependencies which could exist between possibilistic variables.

Acknowledgements

This work is as part of a collaboration with the French Institutes B.R.G.M, I.R.S.N and I.N.E.R.I.S.

References

1. Baudrit, C., Dubois, D. Comparing Methods for Joint Objective and Subjective Uncertainty Propagation with an example in a risk assessment. *Accepted to Fourth International Symposium on Imprecise Probabilities and Their Applications (ISIPTA'05)*, 2005.
2. Baudrit, C., Guyonnet, D., Dubois, D. Post-processing the hybrid method for addressing uncertainty in risk assessments. technical note accepted to *Journal of Environmental Engineering.*
3. Baudrit, C., Dubois, D., Fargier, H. Practical representation of incomplete probabilistic information. *Advances in Soft Computing:Soft Methods of Probability and Statistics conference, Oviedo*, Springer, 149-156, 2004.

4. Baudrit, C., Dubois, D., Fargier, H. Propagation of Uncertainty involving Imprecision and Randomness. *THIRD EUSFLAT'03, Zittau*, 653-658, 2003.
5. Berleant, D., Goodman-Strauss, C. Bounding results of Arithmetic Operations on Random Variables of Unknown Dependencies using Interval Arithmetic. *Reliable Computation*, 4, 147-165, 1998.
6. Couso, I., Moral, S., Walley, P. A survey of concepts of independence for imprecise probabilities. *Risk Decision and Policy*, 5, 165-180, 2000.
7. Connover, W.J., Iman, R.L. A Distribution-Free Approach to Inducing Rank Correlation Among Input Variables. *Technometric*, 3, 311-334, 1982.
8. Dubois, D., Kerre, E., Mesiar, R., Prade, H. Fuzzy interval analysis. *Fundamentals of Fuzzy Sets*, Dubois,D. Prade,H., Eds: Kluwer, Boston, Mass, 483-581, 2000.
9. Dubois, D., Prade, H. Random sets and Fuzzy Interval Analysis. *Fuzzy Sets and Systems*, 42, 87-101, 1991.
10. Dubois, D., Prade, H. The mean value of a fuzzy number. *Fuzzy Sets & Systems*, 24, 279-300, 1987.
11. Ferson, S., Ginzburg, L., Akcakaya, R. Whereof one cannot speak: when input distributions are unknown. *To appear in Risk Analysis*.
12. Ferson, S. What Monte Carlo methods cannot do. *Human and Ecology Risk Assessment*, 2, 990-1007, 1996.
13. Ferson, S., Ginzburg, L.R. Different methods are needed to propagate ignorance and variability. *Reliability Engineering and Systems Safety*, 54, 133-144, 1996.
14. Ferson, S., Ginzburg, L.R. Hybrid Arithmetic. *Proceedings of ISUMA-NAFIPS'95, IEEE Computer Society Press, Los Alamitos, California*, 619-623, 1995.
15. Burgman, M.A., Ferson, S.Correlation, dependency bounds and extinction risks. *Biological Conservation*, 73, 101-105, 1995.
16. Ferson, S., Long, T.F. Conservative uncertainty propagation in environmental risk assessments. *Environmental Toxicology and Risk Assessment*. ASTM STP 1218, Ed J.S Hughes et al. Am. Soc. for Testing and Materials, Philadelphia, 97-110, 1994
17. Ferson, S. Using fuzzy arithmetic in Monte Carlo simulation of fishery populations. *Management of Exploited Fish, T. Quinn (ed.), Proceedings of the ISMSEFP, Anchorage*, 595-608, 1992.
18. Guyonnet, D., Bourgine, B., Dubois, D., Fargier, H., Côme, B., Chilès, J.P. Hybrid approach for addressing uncertainty in risk assessments. *Journal of Environmental Engineering*, 129, 68-78, 2003.
19. Kaufmann, A., Gupta, M.M. Introduction to Fuzzy Arithmetic: Theory and Applications. *Van Nostrand Reinhold, New York*, 1985.
20. Kruse, R., Meyer, K.D. Statistics with Vague Data. *Reidel, Dordrecht, Netherlands*, 1987.
21. Nelsen, R.B. An Introduction to Copulas. *Lecture Notes in Statistics*, Springer-Verlag, New York, v.139, 1999.
22. Shafer, G. A Mathematical Theory of Evidence. *Princeton University Press*, 1976.
23. Yager, R.R. A procedure for ordering fuzzy subsets of the unit interval. *Information science*, 24, 143-161, 1981.

Consistency of Probabilistic Transformations of Belief Functions

M. Daniel

Institute of Computer Science, Academy of Sciences of the Czech Republic, Prague, Czech Republic

Abstract

Alternative approaches to the widely known pignistic transformation of belief functions are presented and analyzed. The pignistic, cautious, plausibility, proportional and disjunctive probabilistic transformations are examined from the point of view of consistency with upper and lower probabilities and of consistency with combination rules. Several new probabilistic transformations are introduced, analyzed and compared with those above mentioned.

Key words: Belief function, Combination of belief functions, Dempster-Shafer theory, Probabilistic transformation, Probabilization, Pignistic probability, Proportional probabilistic transformations, Belief-plausibility probabilistic transformation, ulb-consistency, combination consistency.
2000 MSC: 68T37, 68T99

1. Introduction

Belief functions are widely used formalisms for uncertainty representation and processing. For combination of beliefs the Dempster's rule of combination is used in the Dempster-Shafer theory. Its strict probabilistic assumptions are rarely fulfilled in real applications and there are even no rare examples where the results of the Dempster's rule are counter-intuitive.

Hence series of modifications of the Dempster's rule were suggested and alternatives approaches were created: e. g. Transferable Belief Model (TBM) using the so called non-normalized Dempster's rule minC combination, see [4], subjective logic with consensus operator [14] and others. Subsequently numerous practical applications were suggested and implemented in a wide range of domains.

What is common for their applications? It is an aim to transform the resulting evidence representation by a general belief function to representation by probability for easier decision making, for resulting beliefs comparison and ordering. Such a probability should be consistent with the original belief function. In fact, we can consider it as a belief function of a special type, so called Bayesian belief function. We call such a transformation as a *probabilistic transformation*.

There exist situations where different probabilistic transformations change the result of decision process because of different order of objects with respect to their final Bayesian belief. The way of probabilistic transformation has very high importance when disjunctive rule of combination is used due to increasing of doubt.

Probabilistic transformations are also important for enabling of interoperability among heterogeneous uncertain reasoning systems, see [1], [2].

Usually only a special case of probabilistic transformation – Pignistic transformation — is used. It was defined in the TBM approach. Some alternatives to pignistic transformation have been very briefly mentioned in 2002, see [3] But no detail comparison has been published till 2003, when 3 papers [1], [2] and [7] concerning this topic have appeared. [2] deals only with classical D-S approach with (normalized) Dempster's rule of combination, it compares pignistic and plausibility probabilistic transformations. While [1] considers a more general field of imprecise probabilities. This contribution summarizes and compares the relevant results from [1], [2] and [7] together with new results on the topic.

Two approaches to consistency of probabilistic transformations ulb-consistency and combination consistency are introduced in Section 3. Various probabilistic transformations from [1,2,7] are presented in the first half of fourth section. They are studied and compared with respect to the defined consistencies. New probabilistic transformations are introduced in the second half of the section. They are analyzed analogically to the previous ones and compared with them. Some of them have appeared to be equivalent to some of the previous ones, the other are brand new, e. g. Prop_{Pl}T and BelPl_T.

2. Preliminaries

2.1. *Basic notions*

Let us first recall some basic notions from the theory of belief functions. Let us consider an n-element frame of discernment $\Omega = \{\omega_1, \omega_2, ...\omega_n\}$. A *basic belief assignment (bba)* is a mapping $m : P(\Omega) \longrightarrow [0, 1]$, such that $\sum_{A \subseteq \Omega} m(A) = 1$, the values of bba are called *basic belief masses (bbm)*. A *belief function (BF)* is a mapping $bel : P(\Omega) \longrightarrow [0, 1]$, $bel(A) = \sum_{\emptyset \neq X \subseteq A} m(X)$, belief function bel uniquely corresponds to bba m and vice-versa. $P(\Omega)$ is often denoted also by 2^Ω. Let us further recall a *plausibility function* $Pl(A) = \sum_{\emptyset \neq A \cap X} m(X)$, and *commonality function* $Q(A) = \sum_{A \subseteq X \subseteq \Omega} m(X)$.

A *focal element* is a subset X of the frame of discernment Ω, such that $m(X) > 0$. If all the focal elements are *singletons* (i. e. one-element subsets of Ω), then we speak about *Bayesian belief function*, it is a probability distribution on Ω in fact. If all the focal elements are either singletons or whole Ω (i. e. $|X| = 1$ or $|X| = |\Omega|$), then we speak about *quasi-Bayesian belief function*, it is something like non-normalized probability distribution.

To underline the cardinality of a frame of discernment we use the left lower indices, e. g. $_nD bel(X)$, $_{3D}m(X)$, $_{2D}BetP(X)$, etc., and we speak about nD BF bel, 3D bba m, 2D pignistic probability, etc.

The *Dempster's conjunctive rule of combination* $\oplus$ is given as $(m_1 \oplus m_2)(A) = \sum_{X \cap Y = A} K m_1(X) m_2(Y)$ for $A \neq \emptyset$, where $K = \frac{1}{1-\kappa}$, $\kappa = \sum_{X \cap Y \emptyset} m_1(X) m_2(Y)$, and $m(\emptyset) = 0$ see [17]; putting $K = 1$ and $m(\emptyset) = \kappa$ we obtain the *non-normalized conjunctive rule of combination* $\odot$, see e. g. [19]. The *disjunctive rule of combination* $\odot$ is given by the formula $(m_1 \odot m_2)(A) = \sum_{X \cup Y = A} m_1(X) m_2(Y)$, [10].

Bayes' rule of probabilities combination is defined as a normalized point-wise multiplication of probabilities of singletons. $(P_1 \otimes P_2)(x) = \frac{P_1(x) P_2(x)}{\sum_{y \in \Omega} P_1(y) P_2(y)}$.

A *consensus operator* $\odot$ is defined 2D BFs on $\Omega = \{\omega_1, \omega_2\}$ as $(m_1 \odot m_2)(\{\omega_i\}) = \frac{m_1(\{\omega_i\}) m_2(\Omega) + m_2(\{\omega_i\}) m_1(\Omega)}{m_1(\Omega) + m_2(\Omega) - m_1(\Omega) m_2(\Omega)}$, $(m_1 \odot m_2)(\Omega) = \frac{m_1(\Omega) m_2(\Omega)}{m_1(\Omega) + m_2(\Omega) - m_1(\Omega) m_2(\Omega)}$, if $m_1(\Omega) + m_2(\Omega) > 0$, and $(m_1 \odot m_2)(\{\omega_i\}) = \frac{m_1(\{\omega_i\}) + m_2(\{\omega_i\})}{2}$, $(m_1 \odot m_2)(\Omega) = 0$ otherwise, for detail see [6], [14].

If we group some elements of Ω_0 to disjoint groups not further distinguishing their members we speak about *coarsening* of Ω_0 to Ω. We have $m(\{X\}) = bel_0(\{X\})$ for $X \in \Omega$ and $m(X) = bel_0(X) - \sum_{\emptyset \neq Y \subset X} m(Y)$ for $X, Y \subseteq \Omega$. On the other hand, when dividing some element(s) of Ω to several disjoint ones, we speak about *refinement* of the frame of discernment, e. g. the above Ω_0 is a refinement of Ω.

2.2. Related algebraic Notions

Let us recall the following from algebraic analyses of belief functions on 2-element frame of discernment, see e. g. [5,6,12,13]. Every 2D BF bel uniquely corresponds to the pair $(m(\omega_1), m(\omega_2))$ due to $_{2D}m(\Omega) = 1 - (_{2D}m(\omega_1) + _{2D}m(\omega_2))$. The set of all 2D BFs is denoted as D_0, the set of all Bayesian 2D BFs, i. e. $m(\omega_1) + m(\omega_2) = 1$ is denoted as G, the set of 2D BFs such that $m(\omega_1) = m(\omega_2)$ is denoted as S and the set where $m(\omega_2) = 0$ as S_1, analogically $m(\omega_1) = 0$ in S_2. For the special belief functions 0 and 0' it holds that $_{2D}0 = (0, 0)$ and $_{2D}0' = (\frac{1}{2}, \frac{1}{2})$. Analogically we can define $_nD0 = (0, 0, ..., 0)$ and $_nD0' = (\frac{1}{n}, \frac{1}{n}, ..., \frac{1}{n}, 0, ..., 0)$, where we have bbm $\frac{1}{n}$ for singletons and 0 for non-singletons.

A *homomorphism* $p : (X, \otimes_1) \longrightarrow (Y, \otimes_2)$ is a mapping which preserves structure, i. e. $p(x \otimes_1 y) = p(x) \otimes_2 p(y)$ for each $x, y \in X$.

We will use the following homomorphisms, see [12,13], [5], and [6]:

$h : (D_0, \oplus) \longrightarrow (G, \oplus), \; h(bel) = bel \oplus 0', \; h(a,b) = (a,b) \oplus (\frac{1}{2}, \frac{1}{2}) = (\frac{1-b}{2-a-b}, \frac{1-a}{2-a-b}),$
$u : (D_0, \odot) \longrightarrow (G, \odot \circ u), \; u(a,b) = (a,b) \odot (\frac{1}{a+b}, \frac{1}{a+b}) = (\frac{a}{a+b}, \frac{b}{a+b}),$
$q : (D_0, \copyright) \longrightarrow (G, \copyright), \; q(bel) = bel \copyright 0', \; q(a,b) = (a,b) \copyright (\frac{1}{2}, \frac{1}{2}) = \ldots = (\frac{1}{2}, \frac{1}{2}),$
$q_0 : (D_0, \copyright) \longrightarrow (S_1 \cup S_2, \copyright \circ q_0),$
$q_0(a,b) = (\frac{a-b}{1-2b}, 0), \text{ if } a \geq b, \; q_0(a,b) = (0, \frac{b-a}{1-2a}), \text{ if } a \leq b.$

3. Probabilistic transformations and their consistencies

Let us consider the following very general definition now. A *Probabilistic transformation* is a mapping $T : Bel_\Omega \longrightarrow ProbDistr_\Omega$. Thus the probabilistic transformation assigns a Bayesian belief function (i. e. probability distribution) to every general one.

Because of different approaches to consistency of probabilistic transformations in literature, see [1,2,7,11], we omit its consistency condition from the general definition. Particular probabilistic transformations will be presented and analyzed in Section 4. We use a terminology such that names of probabilistic transformations (sometimes abbreviated by PT) end with T, while its resulting probabilities with P, e. g. for pignistic probabilistic transformation we use the name BetT while for resulting pignistic probability the name BetP, for a result of transformation of a belief function defined by bbm m, we use $BetT(m) = BetP_m$ (resulting (transformed) probabilities can be abbreviated by TP).

In [1] there is a consistency defined by condition $\underline{P}(X) \leq TP(X)$. If belief function $bel(X)$ is understood as necessity $N(X)$ or lower probability $\underline{P}(X)$ and plausibility $Pl(X)$ as possibility $\Pi(X)$ or upper probability $\overline{P}(X)$ then the condition corresponds to $TP(X) \leq \Pi(X)$, see [11]. Thus there is $bel(X) \leq TP(X) \leq Pl(X) = 1 - bel(\overline{X})$, this consistency criteria is considered also in [7]. Another criterion or condition to probabilistic transformation considered in [1] is similarity based on a distance or an ordering defined on imprecise probabilities. We do not assume any distance or ordering on $P(\Omega)$. Orderings on 2D frames Ω used in [5,6,12,13] are based on homomorphisms of algebras (semigroups) formed by set of all BFs and $\oplus$, $\odot$ resp. $\copyright$ combination rules. Hence similarity criteria based on such orderings should correspond to commutativity of PT with combination of beliefs, see bellow.

In [2] the importance of invariance to combination (especially to $\oplus$) is underlined; i. e. $PT(m_1 \oplus m_2) = PT(m_1) \otimes PT(m_2)$, where $\otimes$ is Bayesian rule of combination. It is possible to show that $\otimes \equiv \oplus \equiv \odot \circ u$ on Bayesian BFs, thus we can rewrite the condition as $PT(m_1 \oplus m_2) = PT(m_1) \oplus PT(m_2)$ and analogically for combination $\copyright$. Hence the condition corresponds to commutativity of probabilistic transformation with the combination rule as it is discussed in [7]. As another principal condition/property is considered keeping of idempotency: $PT(m_i)$ is idempotent with respect to $\oplus$ for all idempotents m_i, i. e. $PT(m_i) \oplus PT(m_i) = PT(m_i)$ if $m_i \oplus m_i = m_i$. This property follows invariance to $\oplus$: $PT(m_i) \oplus PT(m_i) = PT(m_i \oplus m_i) = PT(m_i)$. The other two conditions about the most plausible states, required in [2], deal with limits of infinitely many applications of $\oplus$ to m. Correct using of ⊕ supposes independent beliefs. Because it seems very disputable to have infinitely many mutually independent BFs in real examples, we do not consider such requirements here. [1]

We can summarize the principal consistency requirements [2] as it follows in the next subsections.

3.1. ulb-consistency and p-consistency

Probabilistic transformation PT is *ulb-consistent (upper and lower bound consistent)* if its resulting probability TP satisfies the following consistency condition: $bel(X) \leq TP(X) \leq Pl(X) = 1 - bel(\overline{X})$. Probabilistic transformation PT is *probabilistically consistent (p-consistent)* if $PT(m) = m$ for any Bayesian bba m. In other words Bayesian BFs are fix points of p-consistent PTs. p-consistency is in fact ulb-consistency on Bayesian BFs (i. e. weakening of ulb-consistency) because $bel(X) = Pl(X)$ for Bayesian BFs.

3.2. combination consistency

Probabilistic transformation PT is ⊕-*consistent* if it commutes with the Dempster's rule (with ⊕ combination). Analogically PT is ⊙ or ⓒ-*consistent* if it commutes with ⊙ ∘ u resp. ⓒ combination. Probabilistic transformation PT is $⊕_I$-*consistent* if it keeps ⊕-idempotents, i. e. $PT(m_i) \oplus PT(m_i) = PT(m_i)$ for all m_i such that $m_i \oplus m_i = m_i$. As it was already mentioned that $⊕_I$-consistency is a weaker version of ⊕-consistency. Analogically we define $⊙_I$-*consistency* and $ⓒ_I$-*consistency* weaker versions of ⊙-consistency and ⓒ-consistency, we will discuss $⊙_I$- and ⓒ- consistencies separately in Subsections 4.7 and 4.8.

4. An analysis of probabilistic transformations

4.1. Pignistic transformation

Let us start our analysis of probabilistic transformations with the classical and widely used *pignistic transformation* BetT. BetT corresponds with the principle of insufficient reason, it has been defined (named) and justified by Smets [18] for Transferable Belief Model (TBM), see [18,19], in 1990, and again in 2005, see [20]. Nevertheless the transformation based on the same principle was used by Dubois

---

[1] Moreover it is an open question for a future research whether an infinitely many combination result presents a nature of PT rather than a nature of the combining rule.
[2] A new quite another requirement to probabilistic transformations would be their commutation with refinement/coarsening. Unfortunately none of PTs mentioned in this contribution commutes with R/C hence we are not further interested in this requirement.

& Prade [9] as "equidistribution of the values of bba" and by Williams [22] in 1982 already.

The pignistic transformation $BetT$ projects BF bel given bba m to probability $BetP$ defined on the frame of discernment Ω as follows:
$$BetP(A) = \sum_{A \in X \subseteq \Omega} \frac{1}{|X|} \frac{m(X)}{1 - m(\emptyset)}.$$
It includes normalization and division of bbms assigned to focal elements by their cardinality, non-normalized beliefs as they are used in TMB are supposed. If we works with normalized belief functions only, then we have $m(\emptyset) = 0$ and hence $BetP(A) = \sum_{A \in X \subseteq \Omega} \frac{1}{|X|} m(X)$ for singletons $A \in \Omega$, and $BetP(B) = \sum_{X \subseteq \Omega} \frac{|B \cap X|}{|X|} m(X)$ for non-singletons $B \subseteq \Omega$.

The justification of the pignistic transformation is based on the assumption of the so called *linearity property*: $BetT(\alpha m_1 + (1-\alpha) m_2) = \alpha BetT(m_1) + (1-\alpha) BetT(m_2)$. BetT further satisfies the following 4 assumptions, see [19]. A1: $BetP_m(x)$ depends only on $m(X)$, where $x \in X$, A2: $BetT$ is continuous (or bounded) for each m, A3: anonymity, i. e. renaming of elements of Ω does not modify $BetP$, A4: impossible elements do not change $BetP$.

Assumption A1 is that one which distinguishes BetT from the other probabilistic transformations under the closed world assumption ($m(\emptyset) = 0$), while the other assumptions are fulfilled by all other PTs mentioned in this contribution. On the other hand we have to note here, that A1 is neither fully fulfilled under Smets' open world assumption, where $m(\emptyset) > 0$ is accepted. $BetP_m(x)$ depends on $m(X)$ and on $m(\emptyset)$, where $x \in X$, because normalization adds in fact $\frac{1}{|\Omega|} m(\emptyset)$ to $BetP_m(x)$ for every singleton $x \in \Omega$.

Let us look at pignistic transformation from the point of view of consistencies defined in Section 3 now. The ulb-consistency of BetT simply follows its definition, and obviously also p-consistency. On the other hand BetT is neither ⊕-consistent nor ⊕$_I$-consistent, see [2]. Analogically it is possible show that it is neither ⓒ-consistent nor ⓢ-consistent. Neither ⓒ ∘ $BetT$ commutes with $BetT$ ∘ ⊗ what is different from ⓢ-consistency because ⓒ is not equvivalent to ⊗ for Bayesian BFs.

To complete the discussion on pignistic transformation we have to note that it commutes with averaging of bbas ⓪: $(m_1 ⓪ m_2)(X) = \frac{m_1(X) + m_2(X)}{2}$, $X \subseteq \Omega$, and with any convex combination of beliefs in general, see the linearity property. In other words it holds $BetT(m_1 ⓪ m_2) = BetT(m_1) ⓪ BetT(m_2)$. Similarly for a weighted averaging. Because ⓪ is not associative we do not consider it among the other combination rules and we do not consider commutation with it as a important consistency of probabilistic transformations.

4.2. Cautious and plausibility probabilistic transformations

Another transformation presented in [7] is a *cautious probabilistic transformation* CautT. It is a generalization of the original 2D $CautT(m) = m \oplus 0'$ from [3], which corresponds to Hájek & Valdés results on 2D belief functions from early 90's,

$_{2D}CautP(A) = \frac{1-m(B)}{2-m(A)-m(B)}$. Let us make the following generalization $_{nD}m \oplus _{nD}0'$:

$$CautP(A) = \frac{\sum_{A \in X} m(X)}{n - \sum_{X \subseteq \Omega} |\overline{X}| m(X)}.$$

A *(normalized) plausibility probabilistic transformation* Pl_T, see e. g. [1] or [2], is defined as a normalized plausibility of singletons. Hence we have

$$Pl\_P(A) = \frac{\sum_{A \in X} m(X)}{\sum_{B \in \Omega} \sum_{B \in X} m(X)}.$$

It is possible to show that $CautP(A) \equiv Pl\_P(A)$, see [7], in [1] it is further shown that it is equivalent to Voorbraak's Bayesian transformation (VBT) published in 1989, see [21].

$$VBP(A) = \frac{\sum_{A \in X} m(X)}{\sum_{Y \subseteq \Omega} (m(Y) \cdot |Y|)}.$$

For a demonstration of 2D CautT and Pl_T see Figure 1. $CautT(m)$ we obtain as the intersection of the straight line passing through points $[bel(W), bel(L)]$ and $[1,1]$ with the diagonal (corresponding to Bayesian BFs) while the same $Pl\_T(m)$ we obtain as the intersection of the straight line passing through points $[Pl(W), Pl(L)]$ and $0 = [0,0]$ with the 'Bayesian' diagonal.

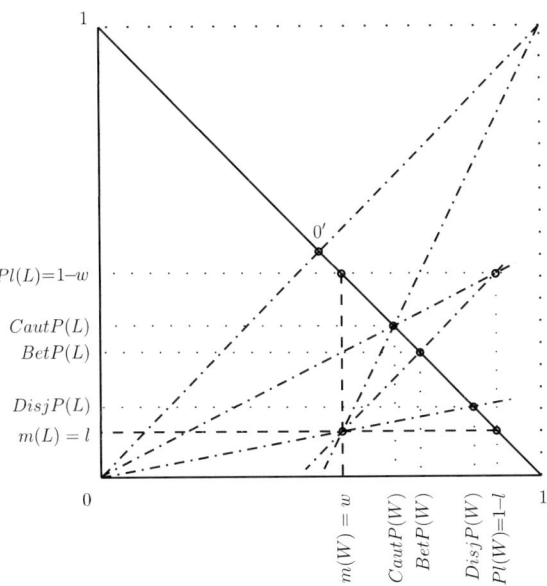

Fig. 1. Probabilistic transformations BetT, Pl_T $\equiv$ CautT, and Bel_T $\equiv$ DisjT ($_{2D}Bel\_T = _{2D}Prop_B T$) on 2D frame $\Omega = \{W, L\}$.

$\oplus$-consistency of Pl_T follows [2], and it corresponds to [7]. From [1] we know that Pl_T is not ulb-consistent. It is ulb-consistent on 2D frames, see [7], but unfortunately ulb-consistency is not fully generalized to nD frames of discernment. On nD we have only ulb-consistency of Pl_T on quasi-Bayesian BFs. The p-consistency of Pl_T follows.

4.3. Disjunctive and belief probabilistic transformations

In [7], there has been presented a *disjunctive probabilistic transformation* DisjT which has been defined on 2D frames so that it commutes with $\operatorname{\bigcirc} \circ u$ on 2D. It is defined by the following formula
$$DisjP(\{A\}) = \frac{m(\{A\})}{m(\{A\}) + m(\Omega - \{A\})}.$$

A *(normalized) belief probabilistic transformation* Bel_T is defined as a normalization of beliefs of singletons, i. e.
$$Bel\_P(A) = \frac{m(A)}{\sum_{X \in \Omega} m(X)}.$$

In the 2D case, it is evident that $Bel\_T \equiv DisjT$ analogically to $CautT \equiv Pl\_T$, moreover $DisjT$ is defined by the same formula as Bel_T in the nD case. For Bel_T see also Figure 1.

It is possible to show that Bel_T commutes with $\operatorname{\bigcirc} \circ u$. Thus it is a generalization of DisjT to general nD frames of discernment. Bel_T is $\operatorname{\bigcirc}$-consistent because of commutation with $\operatorname{\bigcirc} \circ u$. It is not $\oplus$-consistent but it is $\oplus_I$-consistent. Bel_T is not fully ulb-consistent in general. But analogously to Pl_T it is ulb-consistent on nD quasi Bayesian BFs, hence it is also p-consistent on general nD BFs and ulb-consistent on 2D belief functions.

We have to note that DisjT and Bel_T are not defined for 0 and for the cases where $\sum_{X \in \Omega} m(X) = 0$. We can complete their definitions by $Bel\_T(bel) = DisjT(bel) = 0'$ in these cases, but it breaks their $\operatorname{\bigcirc}$-consistency. Further we have to note that Bel_P(A) is significantly sensitive to bbms of singletons.

4.4. Proportional probabilistic transformations

A *proportional transformation*, which consists in taking of belief of singleton A + adding of proportional parts of $m(X)$ for all $X \subseteq \Omega$ containing singleton A, has been defined in [7]. The proportionalization is performed with respect to $bel(B)$ for all singletons B. To underline the way of proportionalization we call this PT as a *proportional belief transformation* $Prop_B T$ now. It is defined as
$$Prop_B P(A) = \sum_{A \in X \subseteq \Omega} \frac{m(A)}{\sum_{B \in X} m(B)} \cdot m(X).$$

If $\sum_{B \in X} m(B) = 0$ then $|X|$ is used instead of it, thus $m(X)$ is reallocated per the same portions among all elements of X in such a case.

Unfortunately, it is similarly to Bel_T significantly sensitive to belief (i. e. to $m(X)$) of singletons. To improve it the *stepwise proportional transformation* has been suggested, where $m(X)$ for $|X| = (n + 1 - i)$, are reallocated in i-th step among $m(X)$ for $|X| = (n - i)$. After $(n - 1)$ steps all the bbm are reallocated among singletons: $m(|X|)$ for $|X| = |n + 1 - n + 1| = 2$ are reallocated among files $|Y| = |n - (n - 1)| = 1$, i. e. among singletons. Unfortunately the result is again significantly sensitive to beliefs of singletons.

To really remove high sensitivity to belief of singletons, let us define a new probabilistic transformation now. We will use proportionalization according to plausibil-

ity instead of belief. A *proportional plausibility probabilistic transformation* $Prop_{Pl}T$ is defined by
$$Prop_{Pl}P(A) = \sum_{A \in X \subseteq \Omega} \frac{Pl(A)}{\sum_{B \in X} Pl(B)} \cdot m(X).$$

Both the proportional transformations $Prop_B T$ and $Prop_{Pl}T$ are ulb-consistent (it follows their definitions) and thus also p-consistent. Unfortunately on the other hand none of them is neither $\oplus$-consistent, $\odot$-consistent, nor $\oplus_I$-consistent in general.

In $Prop_B T$ and $Prop_{Pl}T$ the computations start with $m(A) = bel(A)$ and proportions of other $m(X)$ according to beliefs or plausibilities of included singletons. Analogically we can start with $Pl(A)$ and subtract from it corresponding proportions of beliefs or plausibilities, see Figure 2. Hence we obtain:
$$Prop_{-Pl}P(A) = Pl(A) - (\sum_{B \in \Omega} Pl(B) - 1) \sum_{A \in X \subseteq \Omega} \frac{Pl(A)}{\sum_{B \in X} Pl(B)} \cdot m(X).$$

Analogically to the equivalence $DisjT \equiv Bel\_T$, it is possible to show that $Prob_{-Pl}T \equiv Pl\_T$, hence all the discussion of $Prob_{-Pl}T$ is the same as that of Pl_T.

Let us further define
$$Prop_{-B}P(A) = Pl(A) - (\sum_{B \in \Omega} Pl(B) - 1) \sum_{A \in X \subseteq \Omega} \frac{m(A)}{\sum_{B \in X} m(B)} \cdot m(X). \qquad (*)$$

It works in the 2D case: $_{2D}Prob_{-B}T$ is ulb-consistent, hence also p-consistent. If we define $Prob_{-B}T(0) = 0'$ it is also $\oplus_I$-consistent. But there are cases of nD BFs such that $Prob_{-B}P(A)$ should be < 0 for some A. Thus (*) does not define a probabilistic transformation in general, hence there is no necessity of another discussion of it.

4.5. *Belief-plausibility transformations*

Another brand new *belief-plausibility* transformation $BelPl\_T$ is defined as
$$BelPl\_P(A) = \frac{m(A) + Pl(A)}{\sum_{X \in \Omega} m(X) + \sum_{X \in \Omega} Pl(X)}.$$
BelPl_T is not ulb-consistent, it is only p-consistent in general. Unfortunately it is neither $\oplus$-consistent nor $\oplus_I$-consistent nor $\odot$-consistent.

The analogy of BelPl_T is defined as
$$Pl - Bel\_P(A) = \frac{Pl(A) - m(A)}{\sum_{X \in \Omega} Pl(X) - \sum_{X \in \Omega} m(X)}.$$
Pl-Bel_T is not ulb-consistent, it is not defined for Bayesian BFs, and it is neither $\oplus$-consistent nor $\odot$-consistent.

In this subsection it is necessary to mention also a transformation presented in [1] which is based on $\frac{P(A) + \overline{P}(A)}{2}$. This fraction does not make a probability in general (on the other hand in the 2D case it is equal to $_{2D}BetT$). Hence we have to choose a probability P^* close to it in some way, for detail see [1]. This probability transformation is similarly to BetT ulb-consistent and p-consistent, but not $\oplus$-consistent or $\odot$-consistent.

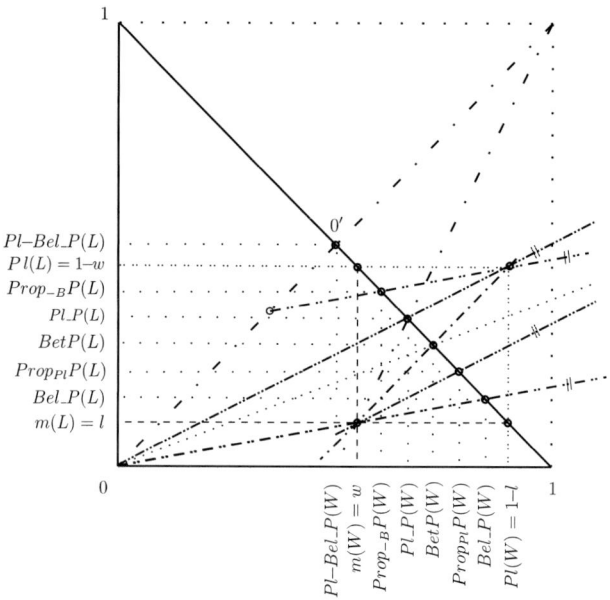

Fig. 2. *Comparison of probabilistic transformations on 2D frame* $\{W, L\}$.

4.6. *Summary of equivalence and equalities of the presented probabilistic transformations*

After presenting of all the PTs we may briefly summarize their relations, see Figure 2. $CautT \equiv Pl\_T \equiv Prop\_{Pl}T \equiv VBT$, $DisjT \equiv Bel\_T$, $_{2D}Prop_BT \equiv {}_{2D}Bel\_T$, $_{2D}BelPl\_T \equiv {}_{2D}BetT$. In the 2D case the following holds, see the figure:
$Pl\_P(X) + Prop_{Pl}P(X) = 2 \cdot BetP(X)$,
$Bel\_P(X) + Prop\_{B}P(X) = 2 \cdot BetP(X)$,
$bel(X) + Pl(X) = 2 \cdot BetP(X)$.
Analogically all equivalent PT can be substituted into the above equalities.

4.7. $\copyright_I$-consistency

Idempotents of $\copyright$ are just beliefs such that $m(A) = 1$ for some $A \subseteq \Omega$, $m(X) = 0$ for $A \neq X \subseteq \Omega$. It is possible to verify that BetT, Pl_T, Prob$_B$T, Prob$_{Pl}$T, Prob$_{-B}$T, and BelPl_T are $\copyright_I$-consistent. For all of them $TP(X) = \frac{1}{|A|}$ if $X \in A$, $TP(X) = 0$ if $X \notin A$. After extension of the definition of Bel_T by these equalities also Bel_T start be $\copyright_I$-consistent.

4.8. $\copyright$-consistency

There is suggested a family of $\copyright$-consistent probabilistic transformations $ConsT(bel) = g(q_0(bel))$ for non-Bayesian BFs, where g is an isomorphism between $S_1 \cup S_2$ and

G, see [7]. If we accept the full definition of consensus operator ⓒ, see [14], also for Bayesian BFs, then we have the only possibility $ConsT_0(bel) = q(bel) = bel$ⓒ$0'$.

$ConsT_0$ maps all non-Bayesian BFs to $0'$ and it is neither p-consistent ($ConsT_0(a, 1-a) = (\frac{a+\frac{1}{2}}{2}, \frac{1-a+\frac{1}{2}}{2}) = (\frac{1}{4} + \frac{a}{2}, \frac{3}{4} - \frac{a}{2})$) nor ⊕-consistent nor ⓒ-consistent nor $⊕_I$-consistent nor ⓒ$_I$-consistent. Moreover the mapping of all non-Bayesian BFs to the only $0'$ is not very intuitive probabilistic transformation. Hence under assumption of full definition of the consensus operator ⓒ see [14], ⓒ-consistency is not a very useful criterion for PT evaluation.

5. Conclusion

Several new probabilistic transformations (PTs) of belief functions (BFs) have been introduced in this paper, Prop$_{Pl}$T and BelPl_T among them. They have been analyzed and compared with PTs from [1], [2], and [7] namely from the point of view of their consistency. For some different approaches to definitions of PTs has been shown that they define the same PT in fact: $CautT \equiv Pl\_T \equiv Prop\_{Pl}T \equiv VBT$, $DisjT \equiv Bel\_T$.

All the investigated PTs (with the exception of $ConsT_0$) are p-consistent wherever they are defined, all of them (with the exception of $ConsT_0$) are ulb-consistent for BFs defined on 2-element frame of discernment. Several ot them are ulb-consistent also in a general nD case: BetT, Prop$_B$T, Prop$_{Pl}$T, BelPl_T.

The only ⊕-consistent PT is Pl_T, and the only ⓒ-consistent PT is Bel_T, it is moreover $⊕_I$-consistent.

Unfortunately none of these PTs is both ulb- and ⊕-consistent of ulb- and ⓒ consistent. For non-existence of such a PT and for other new results about PTs see [8]. Hence in practical applications it is always necessary to carefully consider the reason for which PT should serve and carefully choose which consistency should be preferred.

References

1. Baroni, P., Vicig, P.: Transformations from Imprecise to Precise Probabilities. In: [16], pp. 37– 49.
2. Cobb, B. R., Shenoy, P. P.: A Comparison of Methods for Transforming Belief Functions Models to Probability Models. In: [16], pp. 255 – 266.
3. Daniel, M.: Combination of Belief Functions and Coarsening/Refinement. In: *Proceedings Ninth International conference IPMU*, Université de Savoie, Annecy, Vol. I., 2002, 587 – 594.
4. Daniel, M.: Associativity in combination of belief functions; a derivation of minC combination. *Soft Computing* **7**, 2003, 288–296.
5. Daniel, M.: Algebraic Structures Related to the Combination of Belief Functions. *Scientiae Mathematicae Japonicae* **60**/ 2, 2004, 245–255. *Scientiae Mathematicae Japonicae Online* **10**, 2004, 501–511.

6. Daniel., M.: Algebraic Structures Related to the Consensus Operator for Combining of Beliefs. In: [16] pp. 332 – 344.
7. Daniel., M.: Transformations of Belief Functions to Probabilities. In Vejnarová, J., (ed.), *Proceedings of WUPES 2003 (6th Workshop on Uncertainty Processing)*; VŠE - Oeconomica Publishers, 2003, pp. 77–90.
   Full version: *International Journal of Intelligent Systems* (in print).
8. Daniel., M.: Probabilistic Transformations of Belief Functions. In: Godo, L., (ed.), *ECSQARU 2003; LNAI 3571*, Springer-Verlag, 2005 (in print).
9. Dubois, D., Prade, H.: On several representations of an uncertain body of evidence. In Gupta, M. M., Sanchez, E., (eds.), *Fuzzy Information and Decision Processes* North-Holland, Amsterdam, 1982, 167–181.
10. Dubois, D., Prade, H.: Consonant Approximations of Belief Functions. *International Journal of Approximate Reasoning* **4**, 1990, 419–449.
11. Dubois, D., Prade, H., Sandri S.: On Possibility/Probability Transformations. In Lowen, R., Roubens, M., (eds.), *Fuzzy Logic* Kluwer Academic Publishers, Dordrecht, 1993, 103–112.
12. Hájek, P., Havránek, T., Jiroušek, R.: *Uncertain Information Processing in Expert Systems.* CRC Press, Boca Raton, Florida, 1992.
13. Hájek, P., Valdés, J. J.: Generalized algebraic foundations of uncertainty processing in rule-based expert systems (dempsteroids). *Computers and Artificial Intelligence* **10**, 1991, 29–42.
14. Jøsang, A.: The Consensus Operator for Combining Beliefs. *Artificial Intelligence Journal* **141/1–2**, 2002, 157–170.
15. Lefevre, E., Colot, O., Vannoorenberghe, P.: Belief Functions Combination and Conflict Management. *Information Fusion* **3/2**, 2002, 149–162.
16. Nielsen, T. D., Zhang, N. L., (eds.), *Symbolic and Quantitative Approaches to Reasoning with Uncertainty (ECSQARU 2003); Lecture Notes in Artificial Intelligence 2711*, Springer-Verlag, 2003.
17. Shafer, G.: *A Mathematical Theory of Evidence.* Princeton University Press, Princeton, New Jersey, 1976.
18. Smets, Ph.: Constructing the Pignistic Probability Function in a Context of Uncertainty. In Henrion, M., Schachter, R. D., Kanal, L. N., Lemmer, J. F. (eds.) *Uncertainty in Artificial Intelligence 5*, Amsterdam, North Holland, 1990, 29–39.
19. Smets, Ph., Kennes, R.: The transferable belief model. *Artificial Intelligence* **66**, 1994, 191–234.
20. Smets, Ph.: Decision Making in the TBM: the Necessity of the Pignistic Transformation. *International Journal of Approximative Reasoning* **38**, 2005, 133–147.
21. Voorbraak, F.: A Computationally Efficient Approximation of Dempster-Shafer Theory. *International Journal of Man-Machine Studies* **30**, 1989, 525–536.
22. Williams, P. M.: Discussion of Shafer G. "Belief Functions and Parametric Models". *Journal of Royal Statistical Society* **B44**, 1982, 342 et seq.

Randomization and Uncertain Inference[*]

Henry E. Kyburg, Jr. [a,b] and Choh Man Teng [b]

[a]Philosophy and Computer Science, University of Rochester,
Rochester NY 14627, USA
[b] Institute for Human and Machine Cognition,
40 South Alcaniz Street, Pensacola FL 32502, USA

Abstract

Statistical conclusions must be supported on the basis of a finite amount of experimental data. It would be desirable if our intelligent systems could arrive at warranted conclusions in the same way. One problem is that the validity of an uncertain conclusion is sometimes held to depend not just on the data, but on the provenance of the data. To be specific, in many experiments randomization *is an important part of the protocol, yet precisely the same data could be produced by an experiment in which randomization played no part. From a Bayesian point of view, randomization plays at most a small role. From a classical point of view, randomization is central to ensuring that the long run error rates are controlled as they are claimed to be. We examine this controversy from an AI perspective, and propose that an evidential or epistemic approach to probability allows us to retain the frequency bounds on error, and at the same time allows the data to speak for themselves. Nevertheless randomization can play an important role in the experimental protocol.*

Key words: randomization, probability, frequency, statistics

1. Introduction

In autonomous science, we may be interested in a robot that can be sent to Mars, for example, to collect samples and perform experiments in situ, so that only the

---

[*] Research for this work was supported by the National Science Foundation IIS-0082928, NASA NCC2-1239, NNA04CK88A and ONR N00014-03-1-0516.

interesting results need to be brought back for follow up analysis. Such a robot would have to be able to observe standard experimental protocols for sampling and treatment assignment, as well as perform statistical inference from the outcomes of the experiments, all with little outside guidance.

Suppose the robot is testing a device for detecting the presence of chemical X in rocks under field conditions. The robot takes four rocks with X and four rocks without, and tests them in a certain order on the device in question. The experimental rationale and the resulting inference problem faced by this robot are similar to those in the famous case of Fisher's tea-tasting lady, which we will discuss below.

2. A Rationale for Randomization

2.1. Randomized Treatments

R. A. Fisher's book [2], the first book and still one of the best books on the design of experiments, introduces the idea of randomization and provides a clear rationale for it in the context of significance testing. In the case of the lady who claimed to be able to tell whether the milk or the tea was put into the cup first, the scientist was to test the null hypothesis that the lady would correctly classify the cups in the test "... by pure chance. We have now to examine the physical conditions of the experimental technique needed to justify the assumption that, if discrimination of the kind under test is absent, the result of the experiment will be wholly governed by the laws of chance." We cannot demand that the cups be "exactly alike" for this is a "totally impossible requirement." [2, p. 17] On the other hand, we can, with the help of a randomizing device (in this case, it could be as simple as a well balanced coin) have "a complete guarantee of the validity of the test of significance..." [2, p. 20]

What does Fisher mean by "a complete guarantee of the validity of the test of significance?" He means that the long-run frequency of false rejections of the null hypothesis under test is in fact correctly given by the assumption of random choice. If we grant the lady her claim only on condition that she correctly identify the four cups of eight that were made with the milk first, we run a risk of 1/70 of falsely rejecting the null hypothesis, of granting her claim when in fact she is choosing by chance. There will be differences among the cups: thickness, color, temperature, ...; but if we *randomize*, then *in the long run*, these differences will "cancel out" and the relative frequency with which we mistakenly grant the claim will be 1/70.

In the Neyman-Pearson [6,8,7] approach to the testing of statistical hypotheses, most completely laid out in the important book of Lehmann [5], randomization in the design of experiments plays an even more important role. An example from [5] brings this out. Suppose you are testing a new drug. We measure a particular symptom. We have an experimental group and a control group. The symptom is normally distributed in each population, treated and untreated, with the same variance and possibly different means μ_e and μ_c. We want to test whether $\mu_e = \mu_c$, i.e., whether the drug is without effect.

If we can regard both the experimental group and the control group as random samples from their populations, the hypothesis $\mu_e = \mu_c$ can be tested by a standard t-test. "Unfortunately, under actual experimental conditions, it is frequently not possible to ensure that the patients or other experimental units constitute a random sample from the population of such units. They may be patients in a certain hospital at a given time, or prisoners volunteering for the experiment, and may constitute a haphazard rather than a random sample." [5, p.237] But all is not lost: "Data which could serve as a basis for testing whether or not the treatment has an effect can be obtained through the fundamental device of *randomization*." [5, p. 238]

We assign the patients to the treatment or control groups at random. It follows that *in the long run* each patient, with his particular values of all the variables that affect the magnitude of the symptom in question, would be assigned to the experimental and to the control group with a long run frequency that corresponds to the relative size of the two groups.

"Without randomization, a set of y's which is large relative to the x-values could be explained entirely in terms of the unit effects u_i. However, if these are assigned to the y's at random, they will on the average [in the long run] balance those assigned to the x's. As a consequence, a marked superiority of the second sample [over the control sample] becomes very unlikely under the hypothesis [that $\mu_c = \mu_e$], and must therefore be put down to the effectiveness of the treatment." [5, p. 239].

We have quoted Lehmann at length because it is important to see just how essential randomization is in the classical framework. The whole justification of statistical methods (from a classical point of view) lies in the control of error rates. These are error *rates* and so must have some large (perhaps infinite) class to which to be referred. If we had no knowledge of the long run frequency in those classes, we would have no grounds for accepting a statistical conclusion. It is to generate those classes with the required long run frequencies that randomization is needed.

This is an important point, particularly (but not only) with regard to clinical trials. We shall come back to the role that randomization plays in our inferences from the data provided by experiments.

2.2. Randomized Tests

If we have gone so far, there is one more step that it is natural to take, though Fisher himself never took it. The lady tasting tea examines eight cups of which four are made in each way. If we grant her claim only if her score is perfect, then (given that the treatments are randomized) the guaranteed long run rate at which we will mistakenly grant her claim is $0.014 = 1/70$. That is pretty demanding, and we might consider allowing her to make one mistake. The number of ways in which this can happen is 16; so if we grant her claim when she gets no more than one cup wrong, we run a risk of $0.243 = 17/70$ of making the mistake of falsely crediting her with an ability she does not possess.

The demand that we make a mistake no more than 0.014 of the time seems pretty stringent, since in many psychological experiments a significance level of 10% seems to be acceptable. On the other hand being mistaken almost a quarter of the time seems too sloppy.

Statistics to the rescue! Notice that $0.014*0.625 + 0.243*0.375 = 0.10$. We could construct a test having the right characteristics as follows: take a deck of 8 cards, 3 of which are red. Shuffle it well. Draw a card. If it is red, apply the second test to the lady; if it is not red, apply the first test. In the long run, we will falsely grant her claim just about 10% of the time. Of course it makes no difference when the card is drawn: we may draw it after the lady has performed her test. Even then, if she has failed to find two or more cups, the color of the card is irrelevant; and similarly if she has obtained a perfect score. The only case in which we need a determination of the color of the card is when she has failed to discriminate one cup.

But in the case of informative inference the randomized test seems beside the point. The scientist *knows* which test was applied. He therefore knows exactly which long run sequence his decision to grant the lady's claim belongs to: a sequence characterized by 0.014 frequency of false rejections of the null hypothesis, or a sequence characterized by a 0.243 frequency of false rejections.

The same is true of our robot. It is true that the robot could suppress the information about which test was applied, and just report its results "at the 0.10 level," but this involves the gratuitous throwing away of information.

3. Randomization and AI

One does not have to imagine robots doing our science for us in order to see that inference from samples is central to many forms of AI. Learning theory involves generalizing from the past; data mining and knowledge discovery often involve statistical inference quite directly; it is important to see how far we can go in the automation of statistical inference itself. In this regard common sense is a poor guide; philosophers and statisticians have been applying common sense to these issues for decades and coming up with very little in the way of resolution.

Randomized tests are a staple of classical statistics, and they certainly make sense in some contexts. In quality control of a manufacturing process, for example, it may be that cost considerations dictate that we want to ship cartons with a rate of defectives as great as m/n or more no more than 10% of the time. One inspection rule would lead us to ship imperfect cartons 24% of the time; the next more rigorous rule would cut our rate more than necessary, to 1.4%. Here the deck of cards could be just what the doctor ordered.

Randomization also has a role to play in clinical experiments. If the patients knew who was getting the placebo and who was getting the real stuff, the import of the experiment would be obscured. This might be so even if only the physicians knew, for their attitudes might indirectly communicate this information to the patients. Thus the value of double blind clinical trials.

But once the division is made, once the experiment is run, then, just as in the case of the lady tasting tea, we should take account of whatever it is that we know. Before the test, randomization can ensure that the long run error rate is what we intend it to be. After the test, what we know or come to know may undermine the application of that long run frequency to the particular outcome we have.

That we should take account of the things we do know about — even down to the naming of pets! — is illustrated by an example due to D. Basu [1]. A circus owner needs to transport his elephants from one town to another. He can't afford to weigh all his elephants, but he can weigh one. He proposes to choose one elephant at random (say with the help of a table of random numbers) and multiply the weight of that elephant by the number of his elephants. This procedure is unbiased: the long run expectation of the procedure is exactly the average weight of elephants in the collection. We could not ask for a procedure with better statistical properties, given the size of the sample.

In the execution of the procedure, though, the random procedure happens to pick out an elephant named Jumbo. We then (a) know the name of the elephant, and (b) know that Jumbo's tend to be larger than average elephants.

Randomization is a feature of the experimental protocol, not a feature of the data collected. Exactly the same data can be collected regardless of the procedures of randomization, if any, that led to it. Our AI procedures should respond to the evidence we have, not the evidence we might have had.

4. The Bayesian Slant

Many writers within AI find Bayesianism very appealing, but randomization is hard to defend within the Bayesian framework. There are nevertheless alleged to be some reasons to incorporate randomization into one's tests of hypotheses. Some of these reasons are explored in [3]. Kadane and Seidenfeld examine two kinds of arguments for randomization; it is the second, in which we decide which units to study, or which treatments to assign, that is most directly of concern to us.

We pointed out above, in connection with the randomized test of Lady T.'s ability, that a randomized test would "in the long run" yield a misleading "pass" exactly 10% of the time. "Unfortunately, these arguments are invalid once the researcher ...is made aware of the (ancillary) outcome of the randomization. [Once we know the *actual* order of treatment of the cups,] ...different 'prior' opinions about 'nuisance' factors...can interfere with a shared interpretation of experimental results." [3, p. 335]

Now of course taking account of one's detailed prior opinion about all the aspects of the cups and the ordering of their infusions could be a lengthy and costly endeavor, and would present a formidable AI task. Rubin [9, p.54] points out that "A comparable nonrandomized design would generally be more difficult to execute and analyze because of the need to deal explicitly with all covariates being balanced." There is thus an argument for randomization based on efficiency.

This argument is not bought by Kadane and Seidenfeld: "The details of a study that are omitted should be those that don't matter, those that are suppressible. Here, to the contrary, details are omitted because they do or might matter." [3, p.337] Although on a careful analysis there are a number of arguments for randomization that should be distinguished, Kadane and Seidenfeld find none of them compelling, though they are willing to suppose that randomization can enhance interpersonal communication [3, p. 343].

There is nevertheless something bizarre in a view that encourages us to introspect our beliefs concerning the influence of the thickness of the china on the tendency of the lady to announce "tea first" before we can evaluate the experiment described by Fisher. Compared to the solid long-run frequency support for our assessment of error provided by some sampling or treatment schemes, evaluations that depend on unsupported subjective beliefs seem insubstantial and wraithlike. We *know* that no more than 0.01 of the samples — note the absence of the qualifying "random" — of a population will exhibit a value of X different by more than 10 standard deviations from $\overline{X}$. It has been argued that we should not, *without good reason*, depart from this solid datum.

5. Evidential Probability

Evidential Probability, expounded in detail in [4], provides a framework within which the formal approach of AI can be brought to bear on these practical problems. Evidential probability is interval valued, and thus does not qualify directly as an "interpretation" of the probability calculus. The intervals, however, are based on what we know of relative frequencies, and relative frequencies, of course, do satisfy the probability calculus. We assume, what only a radical philosophical skeptic would deny, that we have adequately grounded (but nonetheless corrigible) knowledge of relative frequencies. It is this knowledge that serves as our ground for the application of probability to particular cases: the probability of heads on the next toss is approximately 1/2, the probability that the lady lacks the ability to discriminate is about 1/70.

Given knowledge of approximate frequencies in a body of knowledge K, what we need is a way of computing for each sentence S of the language an appropriate interval based on relative frequencies known within the knowledge base K.

There are three principles that may be called on to resolve issues concerning reference classes. They are *richness*, *specificity*, and *precision*. Specificity and richness deal with the case in which the import of two potential reference classes *differ*: the frequency interval characterizing one neither includes nor is included in the frequency interval characterizing the other.

The *principle of richness* provides that when K contains two differing items of statistical knowledge, one of which is a marginalization of the other, it is the richer knowledge that should determine the probability.

Example 1. [Richness] Suppose that our acceptance level (practical certainty) is 0.95, and that we either have an urn with 95% black balls (H_1), or an urn with 40% black balls (H_2). We have no prior probability: $Prob(H_1) = Prob(H_2) = [0,1]$.

We construct a test of hypothesis H_1: Draw a ball, and if it is white, reject H_1. The probability of false rejection — error of the first kind — is 0.05. We draw a ball. It is white. We reject H_1 and accept H_2. (Note that if the ball we draw is black, we can conclude nothing at the 0.95 level.)

Now suppose we know a little: that the probability of H_1 is [0.1,0.9]. We can calculate the conditional probability of H_1 given a white ball to be [0.009,0.429] and the conditional probability of its denial is [0.571,0.991]. The probability from the classical test is [0.05,0.05], which is included in the conditional probability: we ignore the conditional probability in favor of the testing probability.

And now suppose we know a little more: that the probability of H_1 is [0.4,0.8]. Then the probability of H_1 given a white ball is [0.053,0.250]. This *does* differ from the testing probability, and therefore, by the principle of richness, should rule.

The *principle of specificity* provides that when K contains two differing items of statistical knowledge, one of which concerns a subset of the reference class of the other, it is the more specific knowledge that should determine the probability.

Example 2. [**Specificity**] Suppose an experiment similar to that of the previous example, except that we know that we are presented with urns of each type equally often. We therefore know the overall frequency of black balls to be 0.675. But if we know in a particular instance that we have been presented with an urn of the second type, the probability of a black ball should be the proportion in that urn: [0.40,0.40].

The *principle of precision* provides that when the interval associated with a statistical statement in K includes the union of the intervals of all other statistical statements in K not ruled out by the principles of richness and specificity, this statement can be ignored.

Example 3. [**Precision**] Suppose we know that black balls are drawn at night with probability [0.3,0.8]; black balls in general are drawn with probability [0.4,0.6]; and dark colored balls are drawn at night with probability [0.35,0.5]. The first statement can be ignored as its interval is broader than and includes the intervals of the other two statements.

For every statement S and every body of knowledge K, these three principles, applied in the order: *richness, specificity, precision*, lead to a unique interval: the set-theoretic cover of the surviving intervals. We shall need to consider the cover of more than one interval only when we have reference classes characterized by *differing* intervals, and there is no resolution in terms of specificity or richness. In many ordinary cases, the intervals will lead to a single reference class.

6. Evidence and Error Frequency

It is all very well to say that we should take account of the evidence we have, and not worry about the evidence we don't have, but might have had. But that does not tell us *how* to take that evidence into account. We shall consider several stories in what follows.

6.1. *The Mixed Test*

One thing we should surely take account of is the known frequency of errors. In the case of the lady tasting tea, if we know that the test we applied was the first (reject the lady's claim unless she correctly identifies all the cups), then, if that is "all we know," and the lady does identify all the cups correctly, the probability that we are falsely rejecting the null hypothesis that she cannot tell the difference is about 0.014. In this significance testing example, if she *fails* to identify all the cups correctly, we cannot come to any conclusion at all, other than that we have "failed to reject" the null hypothesis that the lady cannot discriminate.

Suppose now we know that we employed the second test. If the lady is mistaken on no more than one cup, we reject the null hypothesis. In the long run, rejection under this test will be mistaken no more than a fraction 0.243 of the time.

Now let us consider the mixed test: the test in which we apply test A 5/8 of the time and test B 3/8 of the time. And let us apply it by testing the lady, observing her response, and *then* drawing a card from our 8-card deck.

Before conducting the test, we don't know which test, A or B, we will actually perform. We do know that in the long run this mixed test will lead to false rejection of the null hypothesis (that the lady cannot discriminate) about 10% of the time. It is safe to say, in advance of experimentation, that we will be led to a false rejection of the null hypothesis with a probability of about 0.10.

While this would be easy to automate, it seems clearly wrong. Our agent should know that the lady made one mistake, and that test B was applied, and that the probability in *this* case of false rejection is 0.243.

6.2. *Ancillary Statistics*

Kadane and Seidenfeld agree that *if* "...the (ancillary) statistic of which cups were treated 'milk first' is censored then ...there is consensus about a simple statistical distribution for the experimental outcomes." [3, p. 337] But they think censoring is a bad thing, and that "...once the researcher ...is made aware of the (ancillary) outcome of the randomization" the randomization frequencies are no longer "all we know": we also know the allocation of the treatments to the cups, and we should, of course, condition on it.

From a Bayesian point of view this is true, because from a traditional Bayesian point of view there is a precise, point-valued, probability for each outcome, conditioned on our knowledge of the allocation of the treatments.

Let us consider two cases. Suppose the experiment is performed with four red cups and four blue cups, and the result of randomization is that all the red cups get the same treatment. (God forbid! But it has to happen on average one time out of 70.) How does this affect the probability of false rejection of the null hypothesis H_0?

If the lady has no ability to discriminate, then it is at least credible that she might group cups of the same color together. Based on our vague knowledge of human psychology, we might suppose that the relative frequency with which people under similar circumstances do this lies between 0.10 and 0.90. Since the allocation is a result of randomization, we may suppose that the lady will select the right monocolored group of cups with a frequency between 0.05 and 0.45. If the lady lacks the ability, and the cups with a particular treatment are readily distinguishable, she will thus pass test A with a frequency between 0.05 and 0.45. This is different from the calculated frequency of 1/70, and it represents a subset of the trials for which we calculated that frequency.

Based on the principle of specificity of evidential probability, the probability of false rejection of the null hypothesis degenerates to the relatively broad interval [0.050,0.450] — a relatively uninformative result.

Here is the other case. Suppose we work conscientiously to render the cups indistinguishable, other than by the order in which milk and tea are poured in them. Of course we are imperfect, and there will no doubt be minor differences among the cups. Presumably there is a complex collection of properties that serves to distinguish those cups prepared with milk first from those cups prepared with tea first. It is possible that, consciously or unconsciously, the lady may be influenced by these properties.

If the lady has no ability to discriminate, then it is at least credible that her classification of the cups will be influenced, to some degree, by these properties. But since we can make no discriminations based on these properties, it is reasonable to suppose that they will not affect the discriminations made by the lady to any great degree. They might work against her, so that the frequency with which she would correctly pick the right cups is slightly *less* than 0.014; or they might work to help her mislead us by leading to a frequency of slightly *more* than 0.014.

If there are alternative frequency bounds for a subclass that are simply looser than the ones we started with, we should not attend to them, according to evidential probability: this is not *difference* but just vagueness or imprecision.

Note that the Bayesian analysis will treat these two cases just the same way. On the Bayesian view all the probabilities exist and are point-valued. Thus there is a real number that represents the (subjective) probability that the lady will correctly pick the four red cups, even though she does not possess any discriminatory ability, and *that* is the number we should take to be the probability that we will falsely reject the null hypothesis in that case. In the other case, even though we cannot perceive the differences in the cups, there will be another number that we will take to be the probability, possibly different from 1/70, that we will falsely reject the null hypothesis in this case.

In neither case, however, for the subjectivist Bayesian, will the probability be based on long run frequencies we have reason to believe.

6.3. Prior Probabilities

What is not discussed in [3] is that if we are really Bayesians trying to evaluate the probability that H_0 is being falsely rejected, even though the lady has got all four cups correctly, we should be evaluating $Prob(H_0|All)$. After all, if we are Bayesians, we will have a prior probability for H_0, we will have a probability for its denial, and conditional probabilities for the evidence All in either case. How does this fit in with what we have been saying?

To fix our ideas, suppose that there is only one alternative to H_0 (that the lady cannot taste the difference) and that is that if the lady can taste the difference at all, she can classify all the cups correctly 90% of the time. Let us also suppose that we know the relative frequency with which ladies can taste how their tea is made; let's suppose that the prior probability of H_0, based on this approximately known frequency, is pretty vague: say the interval $[0.1, 0.9]$. If we pump through the calculations, we discover bounds on the probability of falsely rejecting the null hypothesis given that the lady has got all four cups right: $Prob(H_0|All) = [0.0018, 0.1250]$. There is no *difference*, in our technical sense introduced in Section 5, here: $1/70 = 0.014$ falls within this interval, and if we suppose a small amount of fuzziness in the canonical probability on the grounds of imperfections in the cups, that will still fall in the interval we get for the conditional probability. The classical analysis goes through, since the richer Bayesian analysis yields only a broader interval, and the probability of falsely rejecting the null hypothesis is very close to the canonical 0.014.

Alternatively, suppose we enter the problem with fairly strong knowledge about how often ladies can tell how their tea is made. Suppose that frequency is known to fall in the interval $[0.1, 0.2]$; we take the prior probability of H_0 to be $[0.8, 0.9]$. Then we can calculate the probability of false rejection of H_0 to be: $Prob(H_0|All) = [0.0597, 0.1250]$. In this case, where we suppose our knowledge of the frequency with which ladies can tell how their tea is made to be fairly precise, it is clear that there *is* a difference from the canonical frequency of 0.014 (that is, the point 0.014 falls outside of the interval for $Prob(H_0|All)$), and that the interval $[0.0597, 0.1250]$ should be taken as the probability that the null hypothesis is falsely rejected in the face of a perfect score on the part of the lady.

What is reflected here is the relation of richness that is built into evidential probability: if the frequencies of two potential reference classes *differ* and one of them represents a conditional frequency not taken into account by the other, the conditional frequency should be governing.

Evidential probability does seem to steer a reasonable formal, knowledge based, course between the classical claim that only long run relative frequencies that can be established in general terms need be taken account of, and the Bayesian claim that the conditions required to translate these frequencies into probabilities can *never* be met.

7. Conclusion

Although the rationale for randomized tests does not seem to apply to science, the rationale for randomization of treatments does have some force. This force is particularly telling when the experiment concerns conscious agents who may undermine the frequency analysis of the experiment. The focus on objective long run frequencies embodied in the classical approach to testing statistical hypotheses seems perfectly correct.

Where it breaks down is in the demand that the long run frequencies be precisely known, and in the failure to provide a method for determining *which* frequencies to attend to. The Bayesian approach correctly focuses our attention on the particular instance we are confronting, and correctly insists on our using all the relevant information we have. In particular we may find one relative frequency of error appropriate *before* conducting the experiment, and a different relative frequency of error appropriate *after* conducting the experiment, when we have learned more about the specific conditions of the experiment.

The problem with the Bayesian approach is that it severs all connection to objective relative frequencies in the real world, replacing that connection with the subjective assessment of beliefs. The evidential approach retains both the focus on the individual case characteristic of the Bayesian view, and the connection to objective relative frequencies characteristic of the classical view.

References

1. D. Basu. An essay on the logical foundations of survey sampling. In V. Godambe and D. Sprott, editors, *Foundations of Statistical Inference*, pages 203–242. Rinehart and Winston, 1971.
2. Ronald A. Fisher. *The Design of Experiments*. Hafner, New York, 1971.
3. Joseph Kadane and Teddy Seidenfeld. Randomization in a Bayesian perspective. *Journal of Statistical Planning and Inference*, 25:329–345, 1990.
4. Henry E. Kyburg, Jr. and Choh Man Teng. *Uncertain Inference*. Cambridge University Press, New York, 2001.
5. E. L. Lehmann. *Testing Statistical Hypotheses*. Springer, New York, 1997.
6. Jerzy Neyman. Outline of a theory of statistical estimation based on the classical theory of probability. *Philosophical Transaction Of The Royal Society A*, pages 333–380, 1937.
7. Jerzy Neyman. Basic ideas and some recent results of the theory of testing statistical hypotheses. *Journal Of The Royal Statistical Society*, 105:292–327., 1942.
8. Jerzy Neyman and E.S. Pearson. On the problem of the most efficient tests of statistical hypotheses. *Philosophical Transactions Of The Royal Soc.*, A 2311:289–337, 1933.
9. D. B. Rubin. Bayesian inference for causal effects: The role of randomization. *Annals of Statistics*, 6:34–58, 1978.

An empirical complexity study for a 2CPA solver

M. Baioletti and A. Capotorti and S. Tulipani

Dipartimento di Matematica ed Informatica, Università degli Studi di Perugia
Perugia, Italy

Abstract

The computational decision problem CPA [1–4] is a variant of the probabilitistic satisfiability problem PSAT [5,11,15]. In this paper we investigate the behavior of an algorithm which decides CPA applied to the still NP-complete subproblem 2CPA, whose instances have at most two literals per clause. We locate, as it is done for some satisfiability problems [10,12–14,17], a critical value for the ratio $\alpha = m/n$, where m is the number of binary clauses present in the instance and n is the number of events. This point divides "almost all coherent" instances from "almost all not coherent"; moreover the most difficult instances lies near this point.

Keywords: *Probability assessments, Coherence decision, NP-complete problems, Simplification rules.*

We had the pleasure to work with our friend and colleague Sauro to this last job. He was always inspired by an interest of pure research and he has been our guide and promoter. This contribution is dedicated to him.

—Andrea & Marco

1. Introduction

Probabilistic models based on partial assessments play a central role in the treatment of partial knowledge and they have a wide relevance in both unconditional and conditional frameworks. For an exhaustive overview on this subject refer to [8] where there is a complete description of such methodology and where all the most recent developments have been summarized.

One of the major obstacles to the use of general probabilistic models in applications has been the high computational cost of the most common adopted methods. Anyway, in the last period several techniques have been developed to bypass such drawback, both in conditional assessments ([8], chapt. 14) and in unconditional assessments (see [16]).

We recently proposed a new approach [1-4] to the problem of the coherence of unconditional assessments by formulating an algorithm based on a variable elimination procedure in the style of Davis–Putnam procedure for satisfiability. This approach, in line with de Finetti thought [9], deals with probability assessments on events which are represented implicitly by their explicit logical relations. An instance of the problem, called CPA for "Coherent Probability Assessment", is an assessment on events, say $E_1, \ldots, E_n$, together with a set of dual clauses [1] on Boolean variables $X_1, \ldots, X_n$. Each dual clause determines a relation on $E_1, \ldots, E_n$ by substituting each variable X_i for the corresponding E_i and by letting the clause to be equate to 0, which represents "false".

Problem CPA is adequate to treat any partial probabilistic framework as well as the problem PSAT [5,11,15], to which it is naturally reducible [1]. Hence, CPA is a NP-complete problem. Actually, it is NP-complete also its restriction 2CPA to clauses with at most two literals.

In this paper we will investigate the behavior of our algorithm for CPA in the case of instances of 2CPA. We have already proved in [3] that a suitable elimination procedure, based on our rewriting rules introduced in [1,2], solves instances of 2CPA in polynomial average time. Here, we perform an experimental analysis, as announced in [4], on random instances.

In Section 2, we briefly present the more general problem CPA and the procedure based on simplification rules of instances.

In Section 3, we present our procedure to generate random 2CPA instances which has the peculiarity to avoid logically unsatisfiable or trivially incoherent instances. Finally, in Section 4, we report the experimental results of our procedure applied to such random instances.

We are able to observe that the behavior of our algorithm is related to the index $\alpha = m/n$, where m is the number of binary clauses present in the instance and n is the number of Boolean variables involved. Like most of the satisfiability problems [10,12-14,17], our procedure presents an "almost unimodal" path depending on the index α, with a "peak" in instances for which the α is quite concentrated around a critical value. This particular value of α is also a crossover where the instances of the problem pass from "almost all coherent" to "almost all not coherent".

---

[1] Dual means "in disjunctive normal form".

2. CPA and simplification rules

In this section we formalize the CPA problem in its general form and we describe the rules of simulations used in our decision procedure.

Let us give first the basic definitions.

Definition 1. An *instance of CPA* is given by a pair $(\mathcal{C}, p)$ where $p = (p_1, \ldots, p_n)$ is a vector of real numbers with $0 \leq p_i \leq 1$, $i = 1, \ldots, n$, and $\mathcal{C} = \{D_1, \ldots, D_m\}$ is a set of dual clauses in Boolean variables $X_1, \ldots, X_n$.
Each dual clause D_j is a conjunction of literals

$$D_j = X_{j_1}^{\varepsilon_1} \wedge X_{j_2}^{\varepsilon_2} \wedge \ldots \wedge X_{j_r}^{\varepsilon_r} \quad j_k \in \{1, \ldots, n\}, \varepsilon_k \in \{0, 1\}$$

where, as usual, $X_{j_k}^0 = X'_{j_k}$ (the negation of X_{j_k}) and $X_{j_k}^1 = X_{j_k}$.

It is understood that, under the substitution of each variable X_i for an event E_i, the instance $(\mathcal{C}, p)$ represents a probabilistic assessment $E_i \mapsto p_i$, $i = 1, \ldots, n$, and each clause D_j, for $j = 1, \ldots, m$, when equated to 0 (i.e. false) represents a Boolean relation among the events. Events E_i's generate a Boolean algebra $\mathcal{B}$ modulo the given relations, see [1], and it is not *trivial* if and only if the set of dual clauses $\mathcal{C}$ is zero–satisfiable.

Definition 2. An instance $(\mathcal{C}, p)$ is called *coherent*, or satisfiable, if there is a probability distribution $P : \mathcal{B} \to [0, 1]$ on the Boolean algebra described above such that $P(E_i) = p_i$ for $i = 1, \ldots, n$.

Actually, inside our procedure we will need to generalize the notion of CPA instance, first by considering an assessment that takes value into a generic interval $[0, p_0]$, instead of $[0, 1]$. This is required since, in the elimination process, the use of "Splitting Rule" [2] will divide an assessment of total mass q in two assessments of total masses q_1 and q_2, respectively, such that $q_1 + q_2 = q$.

Moreover, since the new assessments generated by the Splitting Rule are parametric, we need the elements of assessment p_i and the total mass p_0 to be linear polynomials of some real variables. Such variables could also be constrained by the a set of inequalities. Therefore an assessment can be generalized to a symbolic one as follows:

Definition 3. A *symbolic assessment* $\mathcal{S}$ is a pair $(\mathcal{C}, p)$ where $\mathcal{C}$ is a set of dual clauses, as in Definition 1, and $p = (p_0, p_1, \ldots, p_n)$ is an array of linear polynomials with real constant terms and integer coefficients for the real variables, say $\vec{z} = (z_1, \ldots, z_t)$. If $\mathcal{U}$ is a set of linear inequalities in the real variables $\vec{z}$, we say that $(\mathcal{S}; \mathcal{U})$ is a *symbolic assessment with constraints* $\mathcal{U}$ if, for every list $\vec{a}$ of real numbers

---

[2] This rule will be defined forward

which satisfy all the inequalities in $\mathcal{U}$ with the substitution of $\vec{z}$ for $\vec{a}$, the following condition holds
$$0 \leq p_i(\vec{a}) \leq p_0(\vec{a}) \qquad \text{for } i = 1, \ldots, n.$$

The notion of satisfiability can be easily extended to a symbolic assessment with constraints, see [1].

Now we present some rules for rewriting an instance of CPA into simpler instances. Each rule can produce, as a side effect, a set of constraints on the assessment values. So we work in general with a sequence
$$\mathcal{S}_1, \mathcal{S}_2, \ldots, \mathcal{S}_r; \mathcal{U} \tag{1}$$
of general assessments on the same set of constraints $\mathcal{U}$.

A sequence of symbolic constrained assessments on real variables $\vec{z}$ is satisfiable if there is a list of real numbers $\vec{a}$ which satisfies every constraint in $\mathcal{U}$ and such that each ground assessment $\mathcal{S}_i(\vec{a})$ is coherent.

The rules described below can be applied to any $\mathcal{S} = (\mathcal{C}, p)$ belonging to the list $\mathcal{S}_1, \mathcal{S}_2, \ldots, \mathcal{S}_r$. The new sequence is satisfiable if and only if the old sequence was such (for a proof see [1]).

To simplify the notation, if p_i is any polynomial in the list $(p_0, p_1, \ldots, p_n)$ and $\varepsilon \in \{0, 1\}$, we will denote by p_i^ε the polynomial p_i, if $\varepsilon = 1$, and the polynomial $p_0 - p_i$, if $\varepsilon = 0$.

For the sake of space limitation, we report here only the three most relevant rules. Anyway, each rule is numbered according to the list presented in [2] which we refer to for a complete description of all the rules.

R1: Unitary clause rule. If X_i^ε appears as a clause in $\mathcal{C}$ then
- Delete all clauses containing X_i^ε
- Delete the literal $X_i^{1-\varepsilon}$ in each clause where it appears
- Add the constraint $p_i^\varepsilon = 0$.

R5: Splitting Rule. Fix a variable that, without loss of generality, can be X_1. Then replace $\mathcal{S}$ by the two general assessments $\mathcal{S}^1 = (\mathcal{C}^1, p^1)$ and $\mathcal{S}^0 = (\mathcal{C}^0, p^0)$ in the Boolean variables $X_2, \ldots, X_n$ such that
- $p^1 = (p_1, z_2, \ldots, z_n)$ and $p^0 = (p_0 - p_1, p_2 - z_2, \ldots, p_n - z_n)$ where $z_2, \ldots, z_n$ are new real variables not already being used
- $\mathcal{C}^\varepsilon = \mathcal{C}[X_1 \leftarrow \varepsilon]$, for $\varepsilon = 0, 1$ where $[X_1 \leftarrow \varepsilon]$ means the substitution of variable X_1 for the Boolean value ε
- Add the constraints
$$0 \leq z_i \leq p_1, \quad 0 \leq p_i - z_i \leq p_0 - p_1$$
for $i = 2, \ldots, n$.

R8: Inclusion rule. If in $\mathcal{S} = (\mathcal{C}, p)$ all the clauses of $\mathcal{C}$ are binary clauses and the literal–literal graph $G(\mathcal{C})$ is bipartite, then
- Delete $\mathcal{S}$ from the sequence
- Add the constraints
$$p_i^\varepsilon + p_j^\eta \leq p_0 \quad \text{for all } X_i^\varepsilon \wedge X_j^\eta \text{ in } \mathcal{C}.$$

These rules are correct with respect to the notion of satisfiability. Hence they can be used in an algorithm which checks the coherence of a given probability assessment $(\mathcal{C}, p)$.

The algorithm starts with the symbolic assessment $\mathcal{S}; \emptyset$ as input, where $\mathcal{S} = (\mathcal{C}, (1, p_1, \ldots, p_n))$ and halts when a contradiction in $\mathcal{U}$ is found or when there are no more clauses. In this case the coherence of $(\mathcal{C}, p)$ is equivalent to the solvability of $\mathcal{U}$, the constraint system returned by the procedure, which can be checked by using one of several methods based on linear programming.

At each step the algorithm keeps the current sequence $\mathcal{S}_1, \mathcal{S}_2, \ldots, \mathcal{S}_r$ in a stack and applies one of the simplification rules to the topmost assessment, trying to use as late as possible the Splitting Rule.

3. Algorithm behavior for 2CPA: random instances generation

As already stated in the introduction, the main goal of this paper is to produce a qualitative analysis of the performance of the algorithm described in the previous section when it is applied to 2CPA instances, i.e. when the clauses D_j's, $j = 1, \ldots, m$, have at most two literals. Since, due to rule R1, unitary clauses would be immediately simplified, without loss of generality, we will focus on instances containing clauses with *exactly* two literals. The practical relevance of such instances and the good performance (polynomial average time complexity) of the algorithm on them were already discussed in [3], but the present empirical study will show interesting features hardly attainable by pure theoretical tools.

The first issue we had to face to perform good simulations was to find a sound random generator of 2CPA instances. In fact, a "fully" unconstrained generator is not suitable for our purposes because trivial not coherent instances can easily appear.

In this section we discuss three generators of random instances for the 2CPA problems; anyway, in the next section we will present only the empirical results obtained by the second and the third.

The first two generators share as a first common step the random generation of the probabilities p_i, associated to each event X_i, $i = 1, \ldots, n$, with a uniform distribution in $[0, 1]$.

The second step is the random generation of the clauses. The two generators differ in this step.

A first common principle used in both generators is that clauses must be zero–satisfiable, i.e. there must exists a truth assignment on the variables which falsifies all the clauses. In fact it is easy to show that a 2CPA instance whose clauses are not zero–satisfiable, is incoherent.

Fortunately, the problem of checking if a 2CPA has zero–satisfiable clauses is equivalent to 2SAT and then it is solvable in a time linear with respect the number of clauses.

A second principle is to avoid to generate instances whose clauses violate in an apparent way some rules of probability theory.

In particular, for each binary clause $X_i^\epsilon \wedge X_j^\eta$, where $\epsilon, \eta \in \{0, 1\}$, the constraint $p_i^\epsilon + p_j^\eta \leq 1$ must hold.

Otherwise the instance is not coherent and any procedure, based on our rules, would be able to detect the incoherence in a few steps. In fact applying the splitting rule (R5) on one of the two variables present in the clause, and then applying the unit clause rule (R1) on the other variable, two numerical contradictory constraints would be added to the system. This inconsistency would be immediately detected by the procedure.

When performing an empirical analysis on the percentage of coherent instances or on the difficulty of solution, the presence of instances with clauses violating $p_i^\epsilon + p_j^\eta \leq 1$ can cause a bias on the results of an empirical analysis because this kind of clauses are very easy to solve and always incoherent.

Moreover, a totally random generator of instances, i.e. which generates the p_i's independently of the clauses, has a very high probability (of order $1 - 2^{-n}$) to create at least one clause violating the former constraint.

Therefore a 2CPA instances generator must take into account the clauses D_j's when it generates the probabilities p_i's. On the other hand, it is computationally easier to reverse the process by taking into account the probabilities p_i's meanwhile the clauses D_j's are generated.

Now, we observe that the constraint reduces to $p_i + p_j \leq 1$ if $\epsilon = 1$ and $\eta = 1$, to $p_i + p_j \geq 1$ if $\epsilon = 0$ and $\eta = 0$, to $p_i \leq p_j$ if $\epsilon = 1$ and $\eta = 0$ and to $p_i \geq p_j$ if $\epsilon = 0$ and $\eta = 1$.

So, given p_i and p_j the polarities can be chosen according to the following table

$$
\begin{array}{|c|c|c|}
\hline
 & p_i + p_j \leq 1 & p_i + p_j \geq 1 \\
\hline
p_i \leq p_j & \begin{array}{c} \epsilon = 1, \eta = 0 \\ \text{or} \\ \epsilon = 1, \eta = 1 \end{array} & \begin{array}{c} \epsilon = 1, \eta = 0 \\ \text{or} \\ \epsilon = 0, \eta = 0 \end{array} \\
\hline
p_i \geq p_j & \begin{array}{c} \epsilon = 0, \eta = 1 \\ \text{or} \\ \epsilon = 1, \eta = 1 \end{array} & \begin{array}{c} \epsilon = 0, \eta = 1 \\ \text{or} \\ \epsilon = 0, \eta = 0 \end{array} \\
\hline
\end{array}
\quad (2)
$$

Except in cases where $p_i = p_j$ or $p_i + p_j = 1$, only two clauses, among the four possible, are admissible; moreover, one of them has equal polarities while the other has different polarities.

Hence a generator can first decide about equal or different polarities and later choose the right ones according to table (2), where, to be definite, in case $p_i = p_j$ it uses only the first line and in case $p_i + p_j = 1$ the first column.

Finally this way of selecting clauses also fulfills the first principle because the truth assignment

$$v(X_i) = \begin{cases} 0 & \text{if } p_i \leq 1/2 \\ 1 & \text{otherwise} \end{cases}$$

is able to zero–satisfy all the selected clauses.

The first generator [3] takes as input a positive integer n and a probability value p. Then, after randomly choosing the assessment vector $(p_1, \ldots, p_n)$, the generator decides, on the base of the fixed probability p, for every $1 \leq i \leq j \leq n$ if to generate a clause on the variables X_i, X_j or not. If yes, it chooses, with probability $1/2$, one of the two admissible clauses according to the above table (2).

This operational procedure generates a random instance of 2CPA where the expected value $\bar{\alpha}$ of M/n, where M is the random number of clauses, is

$$\bar{\alpha} = p\binom{n}{2}\frac{1}{n} = \frac{p(n-1)}{2}$$

The analysis of the experiments can be done by varying the probability p or, equivalently, by varying $\bar{\alpha}$ and taking $p = (2\bar{\alpha})/(n-1)$.

On the contrary, the analysis with the second generator of random clauses is done with respect to the fixed index $\alpha = m/n$. This generator, whose inputs are now m and n, after the first step draws randomly m couples of variables without replacement and it selects the polarities of the variables in each clause according to table (2).

An apparent advantage of the second generator is that the instances produced have a fixed number of clauses, while the first generator is only able to control the average number of clauses.

The third generator produces instances which are generally much harder than those produced by the first two. It exploits the linear–time reduction of the problem 3–COLORABILITY to 2CPA, which was already used in [1] to prove that CPA is NP–complete.

This generator has as input parameters v and p and generates a random graph G with v vertices and a random number E of edges, where each possible edge has probability p to be present in G.

Denoting by e the realization of E, G is then converted into a 2CPA instance with $n = 3v$ variables and $m = 3(v + e)$ clauses, and with all the event's probabilities set to $1/3$.

4. Algorithm behavior for 2CPA: empirical results

We have performed a series of experiments to determine the computational hardness to solve random instances of 2CPA and to estimate the percentage of those that are coherent.

---

[3] This generator was already used in a simplified form to prove that a procedure based on our rules is polynomial average-time on 2CPA [3]

Here, for the sake of synthesis, we report the results obtained by using only the second and the third random generator described in the previous section.

With the second generator, the parameter n varies among the integers from 20 to 45 by a step of length 5, while the parameter α varies in $[0,3]$ with a fineness of 0.05. For each joint combination of n and α, the algorithm solved 10000 random instances, storing the following data
- cp = percentage of coherent instances
- t = execution time
- nn = number of visited nodes in the search tree
- ps = percentage of instances solved by satisfiability of $\mathcal{U}$

In the following figure we report the graphs of cp against α. Note the path with a "threshold", typical of satisfiability problems. In fact, also in 2CPA we find that

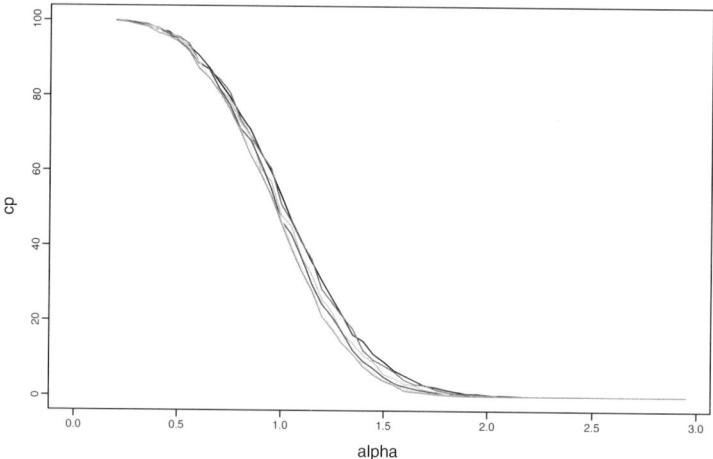

Fig. 1. Percentages of coherent instances, with n varying from 20 to 45 by a step of length 5

the percentage of coherent (the analogous of satisfiable for k–SAT) instances passes from values close to 100% to values almost null. This quick decrease happens in the neighborhood of a critical value of α, usually named "threshold" or "crossover" and denoted by α_c. Such behavior has been already observed in other combinatorial and physical problems and it has been named "phase transition" (see [10]).

In figure 2 the average hardness of the procedure measured by nn against α are plotted. Obviously, for any fixed value of α, nn increases according to the number n of variables.

All the paths share a common behavior. They are unimodal and strongly asymmetric, i.e. they are quite fast increasing till a value of α around 1.7, while they are slightly decreasing for higher values of α.

A similar behavior can be observed in figure 3, in which the average execution times in seconds are reported.

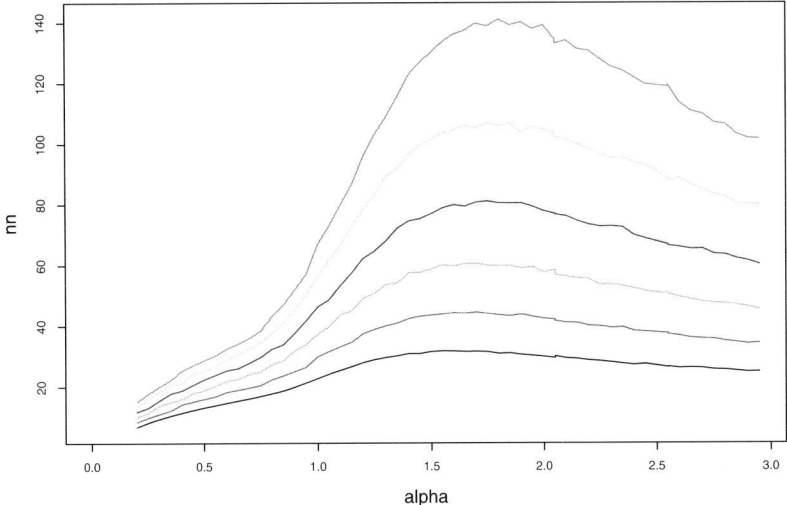

Fig. 2. Number of visited nodes in the search tree, with n varying from 20 to 45 by a step of length 5

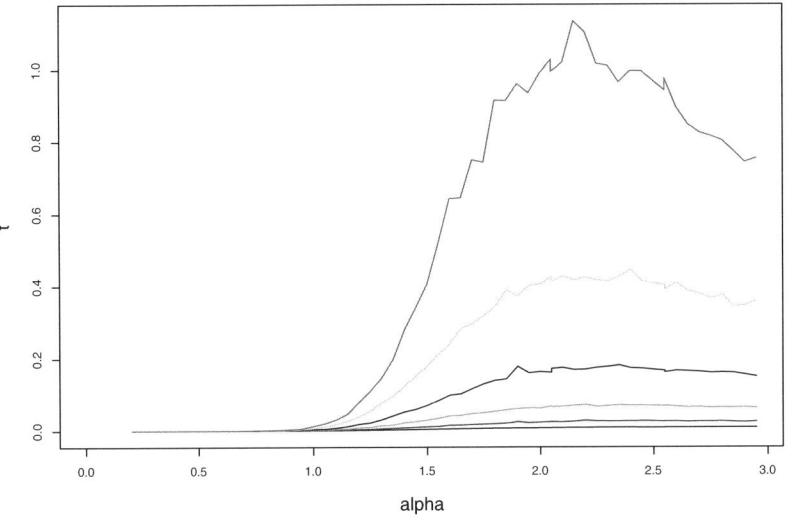

Fig. 3. Procedure execution times, with n varying from 20 to 45 by a step of length 5

On the contrary, in figure 4 the graphs of ps against α show more symmetrical paths. This is in accordance with the behavior of cp. In fact, varying the number of variables n, the maximum values accordingly locate close to the crossovers α_c. This phenomenon could suggest that far from the transition area 2CPA is essentially an almost purely combinatorial problem, while close to the crossover point it has also a numerical counterpart. Anyhow this aspect must be deepened in some future investigation.

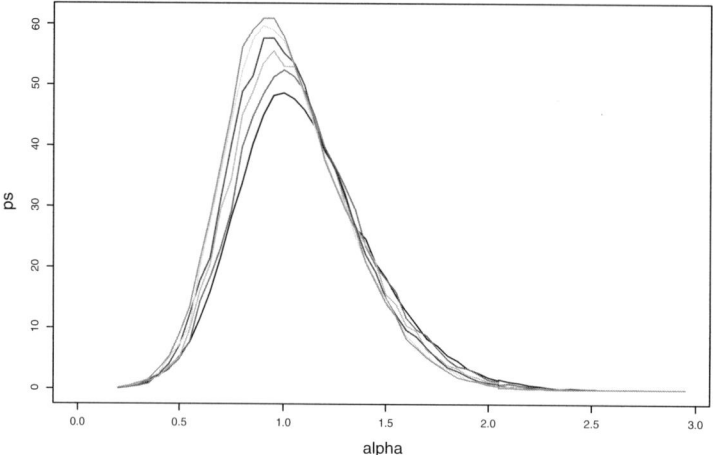

Fig. 4. Percentage of instances solved by satisfiability of $\mathcal{U}$, with n varying from 20 to 45 by a step of length 5

For the sake of comparison, we report also the results of runs performed with the third random generator. Due to hardness of instances generated in such a way, we restricted our attention only to instances generated by random graphs with the number or vertices in between 3 and 8. Note that in this case the potential value of

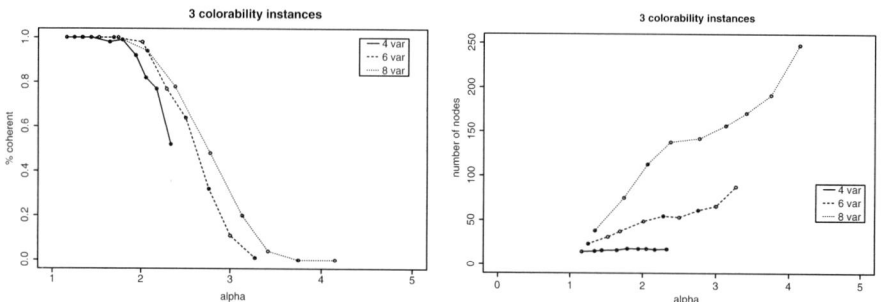

Fig. 5. Percentages of coherence and computational hardness for instances generated with random graphs with 4 (solid), 6 (dashed) and 8 (dotted) vertices

the crossover for cp should be between 2 and 3 and it is significantly influenced by the number of vertices of the graph (and hence by the number of variables of the instances). Moreover, we can underline that the hardness in solving such instances has an increasing path, which differs from that one "almost-unimodal" observed with the second generator. This was, in a way, an expected behavior since instances generated by the third generator are harder and of special type with respect to the other which are almost generic.

4.1. Crossover location

In figure 1, it appears that the crossover value should be close to 1. This, by the way, is the same results for the transition phase point for 2SAT [12,7,6]. Recall that the crossover is defined as the value α_c such that, in mean, the 50% of the instances are coherent. Hence, to better locate its value, we have used the following strategy.

First of all, for each run (of 10000 instances) with a fixed value of the parameter n, we have estimated the critical value $\alpha_c(n)$. Its computation has been done by a linear regression among the values of cp against α with the restriction to the central range, i.e. $cp \in [0.3, 0.7]$, where the paths are all almost linear.

The particular value $\alpha_c(n)$ has been computed as

$$\alpha_c(n) = \frac{0.5 - a_n}{b_n}$$

where a_n and b_n are the least squares estimates of the linear regression.

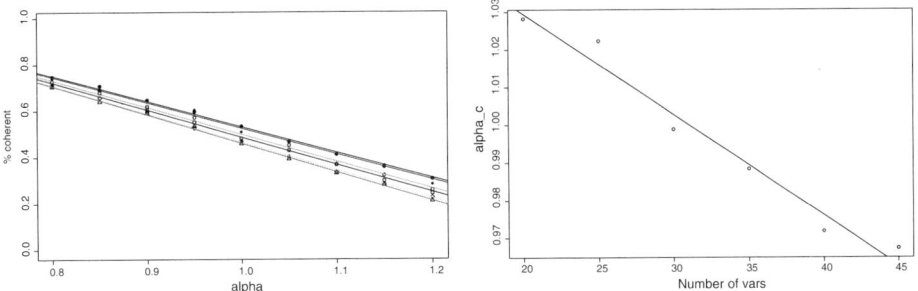

Fig. 6. Linear regressions of cp against α and of α_c against n

Varying n, we obtained a mean value of 0.9961396 with a standard deviation of 0.02530749. Anyway, the value of $\alpha_c(n)$ slightly decreases as n increases. Hence we have computed also the linear regression of $\alpha_c(n)$ against n, obtaining the following linear relation, with $R^2 = 0.9702$,

$$\alpha_c(n) = 1.082746 - 0.002665n.$$

These results are summarized in figure 4, where both linear regression and the locations of cp are plotted.

5. Conclusion

We can conclude saying that the empirical results confirm our theoretical believes about the behavior of the procedure. What we plan to do in the next future is, from the theoretical point of view, to try to prove that the real crossover point is 1, while from the operational side, to search for a more efficient algorithm which allows to solve instances with a higher number of variables.

References

1. M. Baioletti, A. Capotorti, S. Tulipani, B. Vantaggi (2000) Elimination of Boolean variables for probabilistic coherence. *Soft Computing* vol. 4 N. 2, 81–88
2. M. Baioletti, A. Capotorti, S. Tulipani, B. Vantaggi (2002) Simplification Rules for the Coherent Probability Assessment Problem. *Ann. of Math. and Artif. Intell.*, Vol. 35, 11–28.
3. M. Baioletti, A. Capotorti, S. Tulipani (2003) Polynomial average time complexity of an algorithm for 2CPA. submitted to *Information and Computation*.
4. M. Baioletti, A. Capotorti, S. Tulipani (2003) Procedures for the CPA problem based on the elimination of Boolean constraints, in *"Proceedings of Sixth International Conference on Theory and Applications of Satisfiability Testing SAT'03"*, S.Margherita Ligure - Portofino (Italy), May 5-8 2003.
5. G.Boole (1854) *An investigation of the laws of thought.* London: Walton and Maberley, (reprint New York: Dover 1958).
6. V. Chvatal, B. Read (1992) Mick gets some (the odds arc on his side), in *Proocedings of 33rd Ann. Symp. on Foundat. of Computer Science*, 620–627.
7. J.M. Crawford, L.D. Auton (1993) Experimental results on the crossover point in SAT problem, in *Proceedings of 8th AAAI*, 21–27.
8. G. Coletti, R. Scozzafava (2002) *Probabilistic Logic in a Coherent Setting*, Dordrecht: Kluwer, Series "Trends in Logic".
9. B. de Finetti (1970) *Teoria della probabilità vol.I,II*. Torino: Einaudi (Engl. Transl. (1974) Theory of probability vol.I,II, London: Wiley & Sons).
10. J. Franco and M. Paull (1983) Probabilistic analysis of the Davis Putnam procedure for solving the satisfiability problem. *Discrete Applied Math.* 5, 1983, 77-87.
11. G.Georgakopoulos, D.Kavvadias and C.H.Papadimitriou (1988) Probabilistic Satisfiability. *Journal of Complexity*, **4**, 1–11.
12. A. Goerdt (1992) A treshold for unsatisfiability, *Proceedings of 17th Int. Symp. Mathematical Foundations of Computer Science*, 264–274.
13. A. Goerdt (1999) A remark on random 2-SAT, *Discrete Applied Mathematics*,**96-97**, 107–110.
14. A. Goldberg, Jr. P.W. Purdom and C.A. Brown (1982) Average time analysis of simplified Davis-Putnam procedures. *Information Process. Lett.*, vol. 15, 72–75; see also "Errata", vol. 16, 1983, p.213.
15. T.Hailperin (1986) *Boole's logic and probability, studies in logic and the foundations of mathematics 85*. New York: North–Holland.
16. P.Hansen, B.Jaumard, M.Poggi de Aragão (1995) Boole's Conditions of Possible Experience and Reasoning Under Uncertainty. *Discrete Applied Mathematics*, **60**, 181–193.
17. D. Mitchell, B. Selman and H. Levesque (1992) Hard and easy distributions of SAT problems. In *Proceedings of the Tenth National Conference on Artificial Intelligence (AAAI-92), San Jose, CA, July 1992*, 459-465.

PREFERENCES

Consistency in preference modelling

José Luis García-Lapresta [a] and Javier Montero [b]

[a] Dep. de Economía Aplicada (Matemáticas), Universidad de Valladolid, Spain
[b] Dep. de Matemáticas, Universidad Complutense de Madrid, Spain

Abstract

Coherence in preference modelling has been introduced in standard decision making frameworks, taking many different formulations in each context, as a need in order to assure consistent decision making procedures. In the classical crisp context, preferences use to be assumed to be transitive *in order to assure consistent behavior. In the fuzzy framework, a standard assumption is the condition of* max-min transitivity; *alternatively, consistency has been understood by Cutello-Montero as a* rationality measure, *therefore allowing degrees of performance. In this paper we stress that, neither in the crisp nor in the fuzzy case, consistency should not be necessarily associated with underlying linear orders.*

Key words: Fuzzy preferences, Transitivity, Coherence measures
2000 MSC: 91B08, 90B50

1. Introduction

A wide class of possible conditions has been proposed in classical preference modelling in order to capture coherence, rationality or consistency in the pairwise comparison of a finite set of alternatives: linear orders and complete preorders (where both the preference and indifference relations are transitive); semiorders, interval orders, semitransitivity and quasitransitivity (where the strict preference relation is transitive but the indifference relation is not necessarily transitive); and acyclicity, where no cycles are allowed (see for instance [13,31]). All these structures come from transitivity and linear ordering, which is in some way conceived as the ideal structure for consistency, still acknowledging that natural observed decision making misbehavior should produce a relaxed definition for consistency (see, e.g., [22,32]).

In the fuzzy framework, transitivity plays again a crucial role in coherence modelling, since crisp behavior should appear as a particular case. Hence, crisp transitivity is generalized into fuzzy preference modelling, starting from Zadeh's max-min transitivity [36], where transitivity is imposed to every α-cut. However, there exists a great variety of fuzzy transitivity properties, each one offering a different consistency assumption (see for instance [11,12,16,18,34]). The problem of studying consistency of fuzzy preferences, and choosing the most appropriate one in a given decision making problem, may require much more effort than in the ordinary crisp case.

In fact, a key argument in [3] was that most standard fuzzy transitivity conditions in literature were crisp in nature, i.e., they either hold or not hold. But it is obvious that some situations are *extremely intransitive* while sometimes we only find small or unexpected transitivity violations that can be in some way bypassed in practice. Notice that these arguments are valid both in the crisp case and the fuzzy case, meanwhile a close enough transitive relation can be reached, by introducing some few modifications in decision maker preferences (see for instance [25]). Consistency in most cases allows different degrees, and it should be measured.

The axiomatic approach of [3,4] was a first proposal in this direction, proposing a particular family of conditions any *rationality measure* should verify within preference modelling. A rationality measure in [3] was defined as a mapping $\rho : \mathcal{P}(X) \to [0,1]$, where $\mathcal{P}(X)$ represents the universe of all possible fuzzy preference relations on a finite set X of alternatives. Given $R \in \mathcal{P}(X)$ with membership function $\mu_R : X \times X \longrightarrow [0,1]$, being $\mu_R(x,y)$ the degree to which alternative x is weakly preferred to alternative y. Then, $\rho(R)$ represents the degree of *consistency* of R, provided that such a mapping ρ verifies certain conditions (see [3] for details):

(i) *Foundation* (linear orders have the maximum degree of rationality).
(ii) *Invariance* (with respect to permutations of alternatives).
(iii) *Symmetry* (with respect to *dual* opinions).
(iv) *Principle of persistent degree of rationality* (behavior with respect to *new* alternatives).
(v) *Regularity* (with respect to preference modifications).

Of course, many different rationality measures can be in principle defined holding the above axiomatic, so a key problem is to find out a way of building up a particular one, being appropriated to the particular problem we are facing to. However, a positive test of mappings satisfying the proposed definition was missing in [3]. One possibility is to try a direct translation of models from the assumed crisp model, perhaps by imposing our crisp consistency definition for every α-cut of fuzzy preferences. Hence, consistency degrees may depend on the previous choice of a particular family of crisp preference structures (not necessarily the family of all linear orders), which is taken as a main argument for a rationality analysis for fuzzy preference relations (see also [33], where *coherency* is conceived in a more general setting).

2. Crisp consistency

In the crisp framework, the standard assumption is to assimilate *consistency* to linear ordering (if applied to *strict preferences*, so neither indifference or incomparability are allowed) or complete preordering (if applied to *weak preferences*: for every pair of alternatives x and y, either x is preferred to y or y is preferred to x, and indifference appears if both hold, in such a way that transitivity holds). But these are not the only available proposals. For example, quasitransitivity, interval orders and semiorders impose transitivity to strict preference, but not to indifference (the famous *sugar paradox* [19] is a nice argument against transitivity of indifference, see also [22]).

In fact, as pointed out in [15], there are many alternative definitions for *consistency*, each one still allowing a rich enough decision making model, fitting main restrictions of decision makers. But the family of consistent crisp preference relations may not be the family of all linear orders (see [15], where it is argued that decision makers may identify as consistent only *short* chains of alternatives: if decision makers can not deal with more than seven alternatives at once, for example, it is not clear at all why the mathematical model should force them to assume long chains of alternatives that decision makers will never be able to check if they define a linear order).

One possibility, considered in [15], is to assume that our decision maker has been able to define what consistency is, by listing a family $\mathcal{C}(X)$ of *consistent* crisp binary preference relations ($\mu_R(x, y) \in \{0, 1\}$ for all $x, y \in X$ and every $R \in \mathcal{C}(X)$), in such a way that $\rho(R) = 1$ if and only if $R \in \mathcal{C}(X)$. For example, invariance with respect permutations of the set of alternatives seems a natural condition that can be assumed for our family $\mathcal{C}(X)$ of *consistent* crisp preference relations. But we also need to assure that such a family is being built according to a *rule*, in such a way that elements in $\mathcal{C}(X)$ are connected by means of some unifying common criteria (perhaps a recursive construction can be tried, telling us how a new alternative can be *consistently* added to any given *consistent* crisp preference relation, as proposed in [5] in a different context). In other words, we expect a compact comprehensive definition associated with the standard extensive definition of consistent preference relations (sets can be defined in terms of the list of elements or in terms of the properties characterizing those elements as members of the set).

Moreover, we should keep in mind that consistency for strict preferences and consistency for indifference may require different models. Suppose for example individuals who have to show their crisp preferences among the alternatives of the set $X = \{x_1, \ldots, x_n\}$, where $n \geq 3$. A way of introducing crisp preference concepts is taking the strict preference as the primitive notion, through a binary relation P, where $x P y$ means "*x* is preferred to *y*" or "*x* is better than *y*". A basic assumption for P is asymmetry: $P \cap P^{-1} = \emptyset$. In this case the indifference relation I can be defined by the absence of preference: x is indifferent to y when neither x is preferred to y nor y is preferred to x in such a way that $I = (P \cup P^{-1})^c = P^c \cap (P^{-1})^c$. Then, I is reflexive and symmetric, and $P \cup I$ (the weak preference relation) is com-

plete. But once asymmetry is being assumed in order to assure the strict preference role, indifference is fixed but incomparability can not be represented.
(i) If P is transitive and I is antisymmetric we call it *linear order*.
(ii) If P and I are transitive, i.e., $P \cup I$ is transitive, we call it *complete preorder*. It is worth to emphasize that complete preorders satisfy the following properties (see for instance [13]):
- $(x_i \, P \, x_j$ and $x_j \, I \, x_k) \Rightarrow x_i \, P \, x_k$, for all $x_i, x_j, x_k \in X$.
- $(x_i \, I \, x_j$ and $x_j \, P \, x_k) \Rightarrow x_i \, P \, x_k$, for all $x_i, x_j, x_k \in X$.

(iii) If transitivity is imposed just to P, we call it *quasitransitive*.

According to [7,21], we can use an index d_{ij} in order to distinguish among the three possible cases of preference and indifference between x_i and x_j:

$$d_{ij} = \begin{cases} 1, & \text{if } x_i \, P \, x_j, \\ 0, & \text{if } x_i \, I \, x_j, \\ -1, & \text{if } x_j \, P \, x_i. \end{cases}$$

We can normalize this index by taking values into the unit interval if we define:

$$r_{ij} = \frac{d_{ij} + 1}{2} = \begin{cases} 1, & \text{if } x_i \, P \, x_j, \\ 0.5, & \text{if } x_i \, I \, x_j, \\ 0, & \text{if } x_j \, P \, x_i. \end{cases}$$

3. Fuzzy preferences

Main arguments above can be translated from the crisp into the fuzzy context, always taking into account the whole fuzzy preference structure that contains information about strict preference and indifference but also about incomparability (see [9,26]). Consistency should be developed allowing both indifference and incomparability, although it is quite often assumed in practice that they can not simultaneously appear.

We can therefore consider fuzzy binary relations as a generalization of the crisp ones, by considering the above indices r_{ij}, now belonging into the unit interval $[0, 1]$ instead of the set $\{0, 0.5, 1\}$. If R is a fuzzy binary relation on X with membership function $\mu_R : X \times X \longrightarrow [0, 1]$, we denote $r_{ij} = \mu_R(x_i, x_j)$. This value r_{ij} has been interpreted in the literature in mainly two ways (see [10]). For example, some authors (e.g., [29,30,1]) understand r_{ij} as the degree of certainty or confidence in the (strict or weak) preference of x_i over x_j. But for other authors r_{ij} denotes the intensity in which x_i is preferred to x_j (see for instance [2,10,27,28,35]).

Reciprocity is in this framework a common hypothesis: $r_{ij} + r_{ji} = 1$ for all pair of alternatives $x_i, x_j \in X$. The set of reciprocal fuzzy binary relations on X will be denoted by $\mathcal{R}(X)$. But notice that some authors (see, e.g., [2,28]) propose reciprocity with an exception: $r_{ii} = 0$. These authors assume that $r_{ij} = 0.5$ indicates indifference between x_i and x_j, and since the alternative x_i must be indifferent to itself, it should be $r_{ii} = 0.5$, just as happens under reciprocity. Thus, as the mentioned authors assert, $r_{ii} = 0$ is a convention.

Anyway, given $\alpha \in [0, 1]$, we can define the α-cut of $R \in \mathcal{R}(X)$:

$$P_\alpha = \{(x_i, x_j) \in X \times X \mid r_{ij} \geq \alpha\}.$$

And for any $\alpha \in [0, 1)$ we can define another ordinary binary relation, also associated with R:

$$P_{\overline{\alpha}} = \{(x_i, x_j) \in X \times X \mid r_{ij} > \alpha\}$$

Hence, $x_i P_\alpha x_j \Leftrightarrow r_{ij} \geq \alpha$ and, analogously, $x_i P_{\overline{\alpha}} x_j \Leftrightarrow r_{ij} > \alpha$.

We note that every reciprocal fuzzy binary relation defines, in a natural way, a set of preference ordinary relations. In this case, P_α and $P_{\overline{\alpha}}$ are ordinary preference relations, for each $\alpha \in (0.5, 1]$ and $\alpha \in [0.5, 1)$, respectively. The indifference relations associated with P_α (i.e., neither $x_i P_\alpha x_j$ nor $x_j P_\alpha x_i$ hold), and $P_{\overline{\alpha}}$ (i.e., neither $x_i P_{\overline{\alpha}} x_j$ nor $x_j P_{\overline{\alpha}} x_i$ hold), can be respectively defined by

$$x_i I_\alpha x_j \Leftrightarrow 1 - \alpha < r_{ij} < \alpha, \qquad x_i I_{\overline{\alpha}} x_j \Leftrightarrow 1 - \alpha \leq r_{ij} \leq \alpha.$$

In this way, fuzzy binary relations generalize ordinary binary relations. However, no reciprocal fuzzy binary relation is ordinary: from $r_{ii} = 0.5$ for all $x_i \in X$, we have $0.5 \in \mu_R(X \times X)$; hence, $\mu_R(X \times X) \subseteq \{0, 1\}$ is not being verified. Then, we say that $R \in \mathcal{R}(X)$ is *crisp* if $r_{ij} \in \{0, 0.5, 1\}$ for all $x_i, x_j \in X$ ($r_{ij} = 0.5$ implies $r_{ji} = 0.5$ and it is then being understood that x_i and x_j are indifferent).

In fact, many alternative transitivity conditions can be found in the fuzzy literature, in order to assure some kind of *consistency*. Among those transitivity definitions, the most frequent is *max-min* transitivity: $r_{ik} \geq \min\{r_{ij}, r_{jk}\}$ for all $x_i, x_j, x_k \in X$. Such a definition can be easily generalized by considering another t-norm instead of the *minimum* (see, e.g., [17]): a t-norm is a mapping

$$* : [0, 1] \times [0, 1] \to [0, 1]$$

being monotonic, commutative, associative, and verifying a particular boundary condition: $a * 1 = 1 * a = a$ for all $a \in [0, 1]$. Being a fuzzy preference relation *max-** transitive means that $r_{ik} \geq r_{ij} * r_{jk}$ for all $x_i, x_j, x_k \in X$. See for instance [18,25].

We characterize below max-min transitivity in the framework of the reciprocal fuzzy binary relations: the first item says us that this property is a natural extension of transitivity to the fuzzy case; the second item justifies why this property is called "*max-min*". The fourth item will shows us an undesirable side effect of this property.

Proposition 1. *For every $R \in \mathcal{R}(X)$ the following statements are equivalent:*
  (i) P_α *is transitive for all* $\alpha \in [0, 1]$.
  (ii) $r_{ik} \geq \max\{\min\{r_{ij}, r_{jk}\} \mid x_j \in X\}$ *for all* $x_i, x_k \in X$.
  (iii) $r_{ik} \geq \min\{r_{ij}, r_{jk}\}$ *for all* $x_i, x_j, x_k \in X$.
  (iv) $\min\{r_{ij}, r_{jk}\} \leq r_{ik} \leq \max\{r_{ij}, r_{jk}\}$ *for all* $x_i, x_j, x_k \in X$.

Remark 2. Suppose $R \in \mathcal{R}(X)$ is max-min transitive. We show some paradoxes:

(i) If $r_{ij} = r_{jk} = 0.9$, then necessarily $r_{ik} = 0.9$.
(ii) If $X = \{x_1, x_2, x_3, x_4\}$, $r_{12} = 0.7$, $r_{13} = 0.9$, $r_{23} = 0.5$, $r_{24} = 0.8$ and $r_{34} = 0.9$, then $\max\{0.7, 0.9\} = 0.9 \leq r_{14} \leq 0.8 = \min\{0.8, 0.9\}$, which is a contradiction.

These aspects could be considered as drawbacks of the max-min property under the reciprocity assumption. In this way, some restrictions have been considered in the literature. "Weak" (or "restricted") conditions are considered by [6,35], among others, when certain additional hypotheses are required. In this paper we consider preference intensities greater than 0.5 (or greater than or equal to 0.5) in order to avoid the mentioned drawbacks.

The next property, appearing in three equivalent ways, is a restricted version of the max-min transitivity. It has been considered under the reciprocity assumption by many authors (see [8,20], for example), in the framework of the probabilistic choice theory, with the name of *moderate stochastic transitivity*, and by [35], within the fuzzy decision theory, under the name of *fuzzy preference order*.

Proposition 3. *For every $R \in \mathcal{R}(X)$ the following statements are equivalent:*
(i) P_α is transitive for all $\alpha \in [0.5, 1]$.
(ii) $r_{ik} \geq \max\{\min\{r_{ij}, r_{jk}\} \mid x_j \in X, r_{ij} \geq 0.5, r_{jk} \geq 0.5\}$, for all $x_i, x_k \in X$.
(iii) $(r_{ij} \geq 0.5$ and $r_{jk} \geq 0.5) \Rightarrow r_{ik} \geq \min\{r_{ij}, r_{jk}\}$, for all $x_i, x_j, x_k \in X$.

In a similar way, 0.5 intensities can be excluded from the prerequisites, leading to the next generalization of quasitransitivity within the fuzzy framework.

Proposition 4. *For every $R \in \mathcal{R}(X)$ the following statements are equivalent:*
(i) P_α is transitive for all $\alpha \in (0.5, 1]$.
(ii) $P_{\overline{\alpha}}$ is transitive for all $\alpha \in [0.5, 1)$.
(iii) $r_{ik} \geq \max\{\min\{r_{ij}, r_{jk}\} \mid x_j \in X, r_{ij} > 0.5, r_{jk} > 0.5\}$, for all $x_i, x_k \in X$.
(iv) $(r_{ij} > 0.5$ and $r_{jk} > 0.5) \Rightarrow r_{ik} \geq \min\{r_{ij}, r_{jk}\}$, for all $x_i, x_j, x_k \in X$.

Now we introduce two classes of fuzzy transitivity properties, depending on binary operations which allow enforcement of preference intensities among preference-connected triplets of alternatives.

Definition 5. Let $R \in \mathcal{R}(X)$ and $*$ a binary operation on $[0.5, 1]$ (i.e., $a*b \in [0.5, 1]$ for all $a, b \in [0.5, 1]$) satisfying commutativity ($a * b = b * a$, for all $a, b \in [0.5, 1]$), monotonicity ($a' * b' \geq a * b$ whenever $a' \geq a$ and $b' \geq b$, for all $a, b \in [0.5, 1]$) and continuity.
  (i) R is *moderate max-$*$ transitive* if $(r_{ij} \geq 0.5$ and $r_{jk} \geq 0.5) \Rightarrow r_{ik} \geq r_{ij} * r_{jk}$ for all $x_i, x_j, x_k \in X$.
  (ii) R is *moderate max-$*$ quasitransitive* if $(r_{ij} > 0.5$ and $r_{jk} > 0.5) \Rightarrow r_{ik} \geq r_{ij} * r_{jk}$ for all $x_i, x_j, x_k \in X$.

Examples of binary operations verifying the required conditions are: $a *_1 b = 0.5$, $a *_2 b = \max\{a+b-1, 0.5\}$, $a *_3 b = \max\{ab, 0.5\}$, $a *_4 b = \min\{a,b\}$, $a *_5 b = \frac{a+b}{2}$ and $a *_6 b = \max\{a,b\}$. Some empirical studies of the fulfillment of moderate max-$*$ transitivity with respect to the above binary operations can be found in [11,12,34].

We note that if R is moderate max-max (max-$*_6$) transitive, $r_{ik} = 0.5$ whenever $r_{ij} = r_{jk} = 0.5$, for all $x_i, x_j, x_k \in X$; in other words, $I_{\overline{0.5}}$ is transitive.

4. Coherence measures

As already pointed out, there are many available models for rationality even in classical decision theory. Among the great variety of preference structures we can find in the literature (linear orders, complete preorders, semiorders, interval orders, semitransitivity, quasitransitivity and acyclicity, among others), at a first stage we propose to concentrate our attention in three of them (see, for instance, [13,31]).

Since each strong ordinary preference relation P on X can be considered as a crisp reciprocal fuzzy binary relation $R \in \mathcal{R}(X)$ by means of

$$r_{ij} = \begin{cases} 1, & \text{if } x_i P x_j, \\ 0.5, & \text{if } x_i I x_j, \\ 0, & \text{if } x_j P x_i \end{cases}$$

we can define some key ordinary preference structures through properties on R:
  (i) P is a linear order if and only if R is moderate max-min quasitransitive and $r_{ij} \in \{0,1\}$ for all $x_i, x_j \in X$.
  (ii) P is a complete preorder if and only if R is moderate max-max transitive.
  (iii) P is quasitransitive if and only if R is moderate max-min quasitransitive.

Now we introduce a way of defining a class of coherence measures in the framework of reciprocal fuzzy binary relations, taking into account the above crisp properties (compare with [3]). Let

$$\mathcal{R} = \bigcup_{X \text{ finite}} \mathcal{R}(X)$$

Definition 6. A *fuzzy coherence measure* is a mapping $\rho : \mathcal{R} \longrightarrow [0,1]$ satisfying at least the following properties:
  (i) $\rho(R) = 1$ for all $R \in \mathcal{C}$, being $\mathcal{C}$ a fixed family of binary relations which decision maker identifies as *consistent*.
  (ii) Neutrality: Let $\pi : \{1,\ldots,n\} \longrightarrow \{1,\ldots,n\}$ be a bijection and $R \in \mathcal{R}(X)$. If R^π is defined by $r_{ij}^\pi = r_{\pi(i)\pi(j)}$, then $\rho(R^\pi) = \rho(R)$.
  (iii) Reciprocity: Let $R \in \mathcal{R}(X)$. If R^{-1} is defined by $r_{ij}^{-1} = r_{ji}$, then $\rho(R^{-1}) = \rho(R)$.
  (iv) Monotonicity: Let $R, R' \in \mathcal{R}(X)$ such that R' and R coincide in $X \times X \setminus \{(x_i, x_k), (x_k, x_i)\}$. If $r'_{ik} \geq r_{ik}$ for each x_j such that $r'_{ij} = r_{ij} > 0.5$ and $r'_{jk} = r_{jk} \geq 0.5$, then $\rho(R') \geq \rho(R)$.

Let us suppose now an ordered list $\mathbf{T} = \{T_1, \ldots, T_s\}$ of moderate max-* transitivity (quasitransitivity) properties, where T_i is associated with the binary operation $*_i$ on $[0.5, 1]$ such that $a *_i b \le a *_j b$ for all $a, b \in [0.5, 1]$, whenever $i < j$. Consequently, T_j implies T_i if $i < j$.

Given $R \in \mathcal{R}(X)$, with $p_i(R)$ we denote the rate of triplets of X satisfying the property T_i; consequently, $p_i(R)$ is a relative measure of the accomplishment of T_i. The map $\mathbf{p} : \mathcal{R}(X) \longrightarrow [0,1]^s$ assigns the vector of fulfillment rates of properties T_i to each reciprocal fuzzy binary relation, $\mathbf{p}(R) = (p_1(R), \ldots, p_s(R))$. Since the binary operations $*_i$ provide greater results when i increases, the components of the vector $\mathbf{p}(R)$ are ordered in an increasing manner.

Definition 7. Let $\mathbf{T}$ be a list of fuzzy transitivity properties, $\mathbf{w} = (w_1, \ldots, w_s) \in [0,1]^s$ a vector of weights such that $w_1 + \cdots + w_s = 1$, and $\varphi : [0,1] \longrightarrow [0,1]$ an increasing function such that $\varphi(0) = 0$ and $\varphi(1) = 1$. The *fuzzy coherence measure* $\rho : \mathcal{R} \longrightarrow [0,1]$ *associated with* $\langle \mathbf{T}, \mathbf{w}, \varphi \rangle$ is defined by

$$\rho(R) = w_1 \cdot \varphi(p_1(R)) + \cdots + w_s \cdot \varphi(p_s(R)).$$

Now we show some simple examples of fuzzy coherence measures by considering concrete vectors of weights and functions φ.

(i) Absolute fulfillment of $T_i \in \mathbf{T}$:

$$w_j = \begin{cases} 1, & \text{if } j = i, \\ 0, & \text{if } j \neq i, \end{cases} \qquad \varphi(x) = \begin{cases} 1, & \text{if } x = 1, \\ 0, & \text{if } x < 1. \end{cases}$$

In this case, $\rho(R) = 1$ if and only if R satisfies T_i.

(ii) Relative fulfillment of $T_i \in \mathbf{T}$:

$$w_j = \begin{cases} 1, & \text{if } j = i, \\ 0, & \text{if } j \neq i, \end{cases} \qquad \varphi(x) = x.$$

Now $\rho(R)$ is the rate of fulfillment of T_i.

(iii) Detection of maximum fulfillment of properties in $\mathbf{T}$:

$$\mathbf{w} = \left(\frac{1}{s}, \ldots, \frac{1}{s}\right), \qquad \varphi(x) = \begin{cases} 1, & \text{if } x = 1, \\ 0, & \text{if } x < 1. \end{cases}$$

In this case $s \cdot \rho(R) = \max\{i \mid p_i(R) = 1\}$ indicates the maximum index i such that R satisfies T_i.

(iv) Average of relative fulfillment of the properties in $\mathbf{T}$:

$$\mathbf{w} = \left(\frac{1}{s}, \ldots, \frac{1}{s}\right), \qquad \varphi(x) = x.$$

Now $\rho(R)$ is the average of the rates of fulfillment of the properties in $\mathbf{T}$.

Of course, *consistency* can be addressed by defining a certain *distance* in some way telling us how close we are to a *consistent* set of (binary or non binary) relation. This is an underlying argument in [3], and indeed it allowed to get compositions and mixtures of rationality measures (see [4]). But apart from that rationality measure initially proposed in [22], defining non binary rationality measures seems to be a difficult task. Alternatively, we can consider all α-cuts, and evaluate whether each one belongs to $\mathcal{C}$. But this approach may imply big computation times, and still we may find extra difficulties in managing such a complex information (see [15]).

5. Final comments

We want to stress the amount of practical difficulties that will appear when the approach of [3] has to be developed. In particular, although in this paper we have pointed out that *consistency* should not be necessarily associated with linear orders, decision makers should declare in what they understand consistency is: on one hand, linear orders may not be the only fully consistent crisp preference relations; on the other hand, full consistency can be reached with fuzzy (non crisp) preference relations.

In addition, it should be noticed that consistency is conceived in most literature as a decision making requirement: if we must choose among several alternatives, better if the best alternative exists. In a more general decision making problem we may be forced to choose among some yet not defined subset of alternatives, so better if the best alternative exists for every subset of alternatives. Such a decision making oriented approach will obviously take us into some property closely related to transitivity. Such a decision making oriented approach can be seen as natural in the crisp case, where the sentence "alternative x is preferred" can be considered equivalent to "alternative x is chosen". But this is not the case in a fuzzy context: an alternative may be to some extent preferred, but still not chosen (the argument will be clearer when dealing with Goguen's L-fuzzy sets [14], which allow a multi-dimensional preference). If consistency is being seen as a basis for decision making, we need to impose a perhaps unnecessarily strong restriction (in order to choose among the elements of any possible subset of alternatives). The smallest chance of being non-transitive makes a decision rule unacceptable, as also shown in [23] in a group decision making context. But as pointed out in [24], our true objective should perhaps be just to help decision makers allowing a better understanding of the problem they are faced to. This is the proper objective of a decision making aid tool (showing conflict when there is a conflict). If *knowledge* becomes the problem instead of decision making, consistency may adopt weaker formulations. In this sense, a decision will be considered *rational* whenever it follows from a rational analysis. Rationality should refer to the decision process instead of the consistency of the set of solutions to all possible decision making problems, in the same way a *democratic* decision refers to a certain method to reach social consensus, no matter the final decision a group of people makes. Hence, information about criteria can be more relevant than information about alternatives (see, e.g., [15]). Decision making aid should focus on "why" rather than "what".

Acknowledgements: This research has been partially supported by the Government of Spain, grants BEC2001-2253 and BFM2002-0281.

References

1. Barrett, C.R., Pattanaik, P.K., Salles, M. (1986): "On the structure of fuzzy social welfare functions". *Fuzzy Sets and Systems* 19: 1–10.
2. Bezdek, J.C., Spillman, B., Spillman, R. (1978): "A fuzzy relation space for group decision theory: An application". *Fuzzy Sets and Systems* 1: 255–268.
3. Cutello, V., Montero, J. (1994): "Fuzzy rationality measures". *Fuzzy Sets and Systems* 62: 39–54.
4. Cutello, V., Montero, J. (1997): "Equivalence and compositions of fuzzy rationality measures". *Fuzzy Sets and Systems* 85: 31–43.
5. Cutello, V., Montero, J. (1999): "Recursive connective rules". *International Journal of Intelligent Systems* 14: 3–20.
6. Dasgupta, M., Deb, R. (1996): "Transitivity and fuzzy preferences". *Social Choice and Welfare* 13: 305–318.
7. Fishburn, P.C. (1973): *The Theory of Social Choice*. Princeton University Press, Princeton.
8. Fishburn, P.C. (1973): "Binary choice probabilities: on the varieties of stochastic transitivity". *Journal of Mathematical Psychology* 10: 327–352.
9. Fodor, J., Roubens, M. (1994): "Valued preference structures". *European Journal of Operational Research* 79: 277–286.
10. García-Lapresta, J.L., Llamazares, B. (2000): "Aggregation of fuzzy preferences: Some rules of the mean". *Social Choice and Welfare* 17: 673–690.
11. García-Lapresta, J.L., Meneses, L.C. (2003): "An empirical analysis of transitivity with four scaled preferential judgment modalities". *Review of Economic Design* 8: 335–346.
12. García-Lapresta, J.L., Meneses, L.C. (2005): "Individual valued preferences and their aggregation: Consistency analysis in a real case". *Fuzzy Sets and Systems* 151: 269–284.
13. García-Lapresta, J.L., Rodríguez-Palmero, C. (2004): "Some algebraic characterizations of preference structures". *Journal of Interdisciplinary Mathematics* 7: 233–254.
14. Goguen, J.A.: (1967): "L-fuzzy sets". *Journal of Mathematical Analysis and Applications* 18: 145–174.
15. Gómez, D., Montero, J., Yáñez, J., González-Pachón, J., Cutello, V. (2004): "Crisp dimension theory and valued preference relations". *International Journal of General Systems* 33: 115–131.
16. Herrera-Viedma, E., Herrera, F., Chiclana, F., Luque, M. (2004): "Some issues on consistency of fuzzy preference relations". *European Journal of Operational Research* 154: 98–109.

17. Klement, E.P., Mesiar, R., Pap, E. (2000): *Triangular Norms*. Kluwer, Dordrecht.
18. Klir, G.J., Folger, T.A. (1988): *Fuzzy Sets, Uncertainty and Information*. Prentice Hall, Englewood Cliffs, NJ.
19. Luce, R.D. (1956): "Semiorders and a theory of utility discrimination". *Econometrica* 24: 178–191.
20. Luce, R.D., Suppes, P. (1965): "Preferences, utility and subjective probability". In: *Handbook of Mathematical Psychology* III, R.D. Luce *et al.* (eds.), Wiley, New York; chap. 19.
21. May, K.O. (1952): "A set of independent necessary and sufficient conditions for simple majority decision". *Econometrica* 20: 680–684.
22. Montero, J. (1987): "Arrow's theorem under fuzzy rationality". *Behavioral Science* 32: 267–273.
23. Montero, J. (1987): "Social welfare functions in a fuzzy environment". *Kybernetes* 16: 241–245.
24. Montero, J. (2004): "Classifiers and decision makers". In: *Applied Computacional Intelligence*, D. Ruan *et al.* (eds.), World Scientific, Singapore; pp. 19–24.
25. Montero, J., Tejada, J. (1986): "Some problems on the definition of fuzzy preference relations". *Fuzzy Sets and Systems* 20: 45–53.
26. Montero, J., Tejada, J., Cutello, V. (1997): "A general model for deriving preference structures from data". *European Journal of Operational Research* 98: 98–110.
27. Nakamura, K. (1992): "On the nature of intransitivity in human preferential judgements". In: *Fuzzy Approach to Reasoning and Decision–Making*, Novák, V., Ramík, J. *et al.* (eds.), pp. 147–162. Kluwer Academic Publishers, Dordrecht.
28. Nurmi, H. (1981): "Approaches to collective decision making with fuzzy preference relations". *Fuzzy Sets and Systems* 6: 249–259.
29. Orlovsky, S.A. (1978): "Decision making with a fuzzy preference relation". *Fuzzy Sets and Systems* 1: 155–167.
30. Ovchinnikov, S.V. (1981): "Structure of fuzzy binary relations". *Fuzzy Sets and Systems* 6: 169–195.
31. Roubens, M., Vincke, P. (1985): *Preference Modelling*. Lecture Notes in Economics and Mathematical Systems, vol. 250. Springer–Verlag, Berlin.
32. Pattanaik, P.K. (1971): *Voting and collective choice*. Cambridge U.P., Cambridge.
33. Sancho, A., Verdegay, J.L. (2004): "On the definition of coherence measure for fuzzy sets". *International Journal of Uncertainty, Fuzziness and Knowledge-Based Systems* 12: 129–144.
34. Switalski, Z. (2003): "General transitivity conditions for fuzzy reciprocal preference matrices". *Fuzzy Sets and Systems* 137: 85–100.
35. Tanino, T. (1984): "Fuzzy preference orderings in group decision making". *Fuzzy Sets and Systems* 12: 117–131.
36. Zadeh, L.A. (1971): "Similarity relations and fuzzy orderings". *Information Sciences* 3: 177–200.

Transitive decomposition of min-transitive fuzzy relations

S. Díaz [a], B. De Baets [b] and S. Montes [c]

[a] Department of Statistics and O.R., University of Oviedo,
Calvo Sotelo s/n, 33071 Oviedo, Spain

[b] Department of Applied Mathematics, Biometrics and Process Control,
Ghent University, Coupure links 653, B-9000 Gent, Belgium

[c] Department of Statistics and O.R., University of Oviedo, Viesques Campus,
33271 Gijón, Spain

Abstract

Transitivity is a basic property in preference modelling and in particular in the study of preference structures. In this work, we consider min-transitive reflexive fuzzy relations and we identify the strongest types of transitivity of the corresponding indifference and strict preference relations generated by means of a Frank t-norm. We consider three different completeness conditions: the general case, the weakly complete case and the strongly complete case. We compare and discuss the results obtained.

Key words: completeness, Frank t-norm, min-transitivity, preference structure

1. INTRODUCTION

Transitivity is an important property in the study of preference structures. In the case of crisp relations, the transitivity of a complete relation R is characterized by the transitivity of the corresponding indifference relation I and strict preference relation P [10]. In this work, we study this decomposition in the framework of fuzzy

---

Email addresses: diazsusana@uniovi.es (S. Díaz), Bernard.DeBaets@UGent.be (B. De Baets), montes@uniovi.es (S. Montes).

preference structures. Our attention goes to the strongest type of T-transitivity for the fuzzy relation R, i.e. $T_\mathbf{M}$-transitivity. We identify the strongest types of transitivity that can be assured for the indifference relation I and strict preference relation P when they are generated by means of a member of a special family of operators: the Frank t-norm family. Different studies [4,5] have shown the importance of the completeness of the fuzzy relation R in the study of the propagation of the transitivity in fuzzy preference structures. This has motivated the study of three different situations: the general case in which we do not assume any completeness condition, the weakly complete case and the strongly complete case.

In recent years, other authors [1,2] have worked on the connection between the transitivity of R and the transitivity of I and P in the weakly complete case. They have studied whether I and P satisfy the same type of transitivity as R does. In this work, we not only investigate whether I and P are $T_\mathbf{M}$-transitive, but we also obtain the strongest type of transitivity they can exhibit. On the other hand, in this study we do not restrict ourselves to some particular generators as it is traditionally done in the literature, but we consider a whole family of t-norms to define the indifference and strict preference relations from R.

This work is organized in seven sections. After recalling some important concepts and results from the literature in 2, we center our attention on the indifference relation I in Section 3. We identify the greatest conjunctor expressing the transitivity of I when no completeness condition is imposed on R and discuss how the absence of completeness makes these results weaker than the ones obtained in the strongly complete case. In Section 4 we present the strongest implications for the strict preference relation and, as in the case of the indifference relation, we analyze how the implications become weaker in absence of completeness. We study the influence of the weak completeness of the fuzzy relation R in Section 5. We prove that restricting the study to this particular type of fuzzy relations allows to improve the implications obtained in the general case. We also compare these results to the implications known in the strongly complete case. Section 6 includes the strongest implications when considering the most restrictive situation: strong completeness of R. In the last section we summarize and briefly discuss the results obtained.

2. BASIC DEFINITIONS

Next we introduce some basic definitions and notations as well as some results established in previous works.

2.1. CRISP PREFERENCE STRUCTURES

A (large) preference relation R defined on a set of alternatives A is just a *reflexive* relation interpreted as follows: aRb *if and only if a is at least as good as b*. Such a relation R can be decomposed into disjoint parts: an irreflexive and asymmetric strict preference component P, a reflexive and symmetric indifference component

I and an irreflexive and symmetric incomparability component J such that those three relations and the transpose of P, denoted P^t, form a partition of A^2 ($P \cup P^t \cup I \cup J = A^2$). The triplet (P, I, J) is called a *preference structure*. Given those three components, the relation R can be rebuilt from P and I as their union, $R = P \cup I$.

If we denote the transitivity of a relation Q on A as $Q \circ Q \subseteq Q$, the characterization of the transitivity of a large preference relation R can be written as follows.

Theorem 2.1. [10] For any reflexive relation R with corresponding preference structure (P, I, J) it holds that

$$R \circ R \subseteq R \quad \Leftrightarrow \quad \begin{cases} P \circ P \subseteq P \wedge I \circ I \subseteq I \\ P \circ I \subseteq P \ \wedge I \circ P \subseteq P. \end{cases}$$

When R is complete (i.e. aRb or bRa for any $a, b \in A$) the previous characterization can be simplified. It is important to note that the completeness of R is equivalent to the emptiness of the incomparability relation ($J = \emptyset$). When this holds, the following characterization can be proven.

Theorem 2.2. [10] For any complete relation R with corresponding preference structure $(P, I, \emptyset)$ it holds that

$$R \circ R \subseteq R \quad \Leftrightarrow \quad (P \circ P \subseteq P \wedge I \circ I \subseteq I).$$

2.2. FUZZY PREFERENCE STRUCTURES

In fuzzy preference modelling, a reflexive fuzzy relation R on A can also be decomposed into what is called an (additive) fuzzy preference structure, by means of a generator i, which was defined in [3] as follows.

Definition 2.1. A *generator* i is a commutative $[0,1]^2 \to [0,1]$ mapping bounded by the Łukasiewicz t-norm $T_\mathbf{L}$ and the minimum operator $T_\mathbf{M}$, i.e. $T_\mathbf{L} \leq i \leq T_\mathbf{M}$.

Given a reflexive fuzzy relation R and a generator i, the three components of an additive fuzzy preference structure (AFPS) are defined as follows:

$$P(a,b) = p(R(a,b), R(b,a)) = R(a,b) - i(R(a,b), R(b,a)),$$
$$I(a,b) = i(R(a,b), R(b,a)),$$
$$J(a,b) = j(R(a,b), R(b,a)) = i(R(a,b), R(b,a)) - (R(a,b) + R(b,a) - 1).$$

The fuzzy relation R from which they are defined is then given by $R(a,b) = P(a,b) + I(a,b)$. When R is strongly complete (i.e. $\max(R(a,b), R(b,a)) = 1$ for any $a, b \in A$), the generator considered does not matter and the fuzzy preference structure obtained is always the same.

It is easy to realize that the definition of a generator does not imply that generators must satisfy the definition of a t-norm. However, most of the studies on the topic consider only t-norms as generators [8], i.e. they require that not only $i(x,y)$ is a t-norm, but also that $p(x, 1-y)$ and $j(1-x, 1-y)$ are t-norms. In [3] it was proven that this requirement is equivalent to saying that i, the generator of the indifference relation, belongs to the Frank family.

The Frank family is a parametric family of continuous t-norms. They are usually denoted as $T_\lambda^\mathbf{F}$ where the parameter λ can take any value in $[0, \infty]$. For $\lambda \in \,]0,1[\cup\,]1,\infty[$, these t-norms are defined by

$$T_\lambda^\mathbf{F}(x,y) = \log_\lambda\left(1 + \frac{(\lambda^x - 1)(\lambda^y - 1)}{(\lambda - 1)}\right).$$

For the three remaining values it holds $T_0^\mathbf{F} = T_\mathbf{M}$, $T_1^\mathbf{F} = T_\mathbf{P}$ and $T_\infty^\mathbf{F} = T_\mathbf{L}$. For any $\lambda \in \,]0,\infty[$, the corresponding Frank t-norm $T_\lambda^\mathbf{F}$ is a strict t-norm, meaning that it can be expressed as a transform of the algebraic product $T_\mathbf{P}$ by means of a multiplicative generator denoted ϕ_λ. This function is defined on $[0,1]$ as the identity function for $\lambda = 1$, $\phi_1(x) = x$, and it can be written as follows

$$\phi_\lambda(x) = \frac{\lambda^x - 1}{\lambda - 1}, \text{ for } \lambda \in \,]0,1[\cup\,]1,\infty[.$$

Given these expressions, it holds that $T_\lambda^\mathbf{F}(x,y) = \phi_\lambda^{-1}(\phi_\lambda(x) \cdot \phi_\lambda(y))$, for $\lambda \in \,]0,\infty[$. An important property the Frank family satisfies and that has been very useful in this work is the following equality [8]:

$$T_{1/\lambda}^\mathbf{F}(x,y) = x - T_\lambda^\mathbf{F}(x, 1-y),$$

for any $x, y \in [0,1]$ and any $\lambda \in [0, \infty]$.

A fuzzy relation Q is called T-transitive if $T(Q(a,b), Q(b,c)) \leq Q(a,c)$, for any $a, b, c \in A$, and it can be denoted as $Q \circ_T Q \subseteq Q$. With this notation a generalization of Theorems 2.1 and 2.2 has been obtained in the particular case of a strongly complete preference relation R. In more general situations, no results have been reported so far.

Theorem 2.3. [4] Consider a strongly complete fuzzy relation R with corresponding fuzzy preference structure $(P, I, \emptyset)$. For any t-norm $T \geq T_\mathbf{L}$ it holds that:

$$R \circ_T R \subseteq R \quad \Leftrightarrow \quad \begin{cases} P \circ_{T_\mathbf{M}} P \subseteq P \wedge I \circ_T I \subseteq I \\ P \circ_{T_\mathbf{L}} I \subseteq P \ \wedge I \circ_{T_\mathbf{L}} P \subseteq P. \end{cases}$$

2.3. CONJUNCTORS

The concept of transitivity in fuzzy set theory is traditionally related to t-norms, but this property can be defined for more general operators: conjunctors.

Definition 2.2. A conjunctor f is an increasing binary operation on $[0,1]$ which coincides on $\{0,1\}^2$ with the Boolean conjunction.

Often, additional properties will be imposed, such as having neutral element 1.

Definition 2.3. Consider a conjunctor f. A fuzzy relation Q on a set of alternatives A is called f-transitive if it holds that

$$(\forall (a,b,c) \in A^3)(f(Q(a,b), Q(b,c)) \leq Q(a,c)).$$

In this work we will consider the latter definition. We will present the strongest types of f-transitivity that I and P satisfy where f stands for a conjunctor.

3. FROM PREFERENCE TO INDIFFERENCE RELATIONS

In the context of fuzzy preference structures it is necessary to consider a generator if we want to construct an AFPS from a given reflexive fuzzy relation R. However, indifference relations, also called symmetric kernels, are studied outside the theory of fuzzy preference structures too, and in this case indifference relations can be built not only by means of a generator but in general by any commutative conjunctor. In this more general context, we obtained the results concerning the transitivity of the indifference relation mentioned below.

Theorem 3.1. [6] Consider a conjunctor f and a bisymmetric generator i such that $f \geq i$. For any reflexive fuzzy relation R with corresponding indifference relation I generated by means of i, it holds that

$$R \text{ is } f\text{-transitive} \Rightarrow I \text{ is } i\text{-transitive}.$$

Proposition 3.2. [6] Consider a conjunctor g. If for any reflexive fuzzy relation R with corresponding indifference relation I generated by means of a generator i it holds that

$$R \text{ is } T_{\mathbf{M}}\text{-transitive} \Rightarrow I \text{ is } g\text{-transitive},$$

then $g \leq i$.

As a direct consequence of these results we obtain the following corollary for the Frank t-norm family.

Corollary 3.3. For any reflexive fuzzy relation R with corresponding indifference relation I generated by means of $T_\lambda^{\mathbf{F}}$, $\lambda \in [0, \infty]$, it holds that

$$R \text{ is } T_{\mathbf{M}}\text{-transitive} \Rightarrow I \text{ is } T_\lambda^{\mathbf{F}}\text{-transitive}.$$

Moreover, this is the strongest result possible.

In the particular case that R is $T_\mathbf{M}$-transitive, we can extend this result to any bisymmetric generator.

Theorem 3.4. For any reflexive fuzzy relation with corresponding indifference relation I generated by means of a bisymmetric generator i, it holds that

$$R \text{ is } T_\mathbf{M}\text{-transitive} \Rightarrow I \text{ is } i\text{-transitive}.$$

Moreover, this is the strongest result possible.

This is a first difference with the strongly complete case. When a strongly complete fuzzy relation R is considered, the indifference relation I inherits at least the same type of transitivity that R satisfies, in our case this is $T_\mathbf{M}$-transitivity. Thus, not only in the classical case, when the relations are crisp, the completeness of the (large) preference relation is an important factor, but also in the fuzzy case. In Sections 5 and 6 we will see how the different types of completeness of the fuzzy relation R allow to improve the foregoing results.

4. FROM PREFERENCE TO STRICT PREFERENCE RELATIONS

In the same way as the transitivity of I is much weaker in absence of completeness, the transitivity of the strict preference relation P is also influenced by the completeness of R and we prove below how the implication presented in the literature for the strongly complete case can only be guaranteed in absence of completeness when the generator is the minimum operator.

An important t-norm in the implications shown in this section is the nilpotent minimum [7]. This left-continuous t-norm, usually denoted as $T_{\mathbf{nM}}$, is defined by

$$T_{\mathbf{nM}}(x,y) = \begin{cases} 0 & \text{, if } x+y \leq 1, \\ \min(x,y) & \text{, otherwise.} \end{cases}$$

Given a $[0,1]$-automorphism φ, the φ-transform of $T_{\mathbf{nM}}$ is the t-norm $T_{\mathbf{nM}}^\varphi$ given by

$$T_{\mathbf{nM}}^\varphi(x,y) = \begin{cases} 0 & \text{, if } \varphi(x)+\varphi(y) \leq 1, \\ \min(x,y) & \text{, otherwise.} \end{cases}$$

Proposition 4.1. For any reflexive fuzzy relation R with corresponding strict preference relation P generated by means of $T_\mathbf{L}$, it holds that

$$R \text{ is } T_\mathbf{M}\text{-transitive} \Rightarrow P \text{ is } T_{\mathbf{nM}}\text{-transitive}.$$

Moreover, this is the strongest result possible.

Theorem 4.2. For any reflexive fuzzy relation R with corresponding strict preference relation P generated by means of $T_\lambda^{\mathbf{F}}$, $\lambda \in \,]0,\infty[$, it holds that

$$R \text{ is } T_{\mathbf{M}}\text{-transitive} \Rightarrow P \text{ is } T_{\mathbf{nM}}^{\varphi_{1/\lambda}}\text{-transitive},$$

where φ_λ is the $[0,1]$-automorphism defined by $\varphi_\lambda(x) = \phi_\lambda^{-1}\left(\sqrt{\phi_\lambda(x)}\right)$.
Moreover, this is the strongest result possible.

Observe how in both cases the transitivity obtained for the strict preference relation is defined by transforms of the nilpotent minimum. These t-norms are strictly smaller than the minimum which defines the transitivity that P satisfies in the strongly complete case. Therefore, the implications in the general case are weaker than the results known in the strongly complete case. Proposition 4.1 and Theorem 4.2 confirm what we have already explained, the completeness of the reflexive relation R from which we build the fuzzy preference structure plays an important role in the propagation of the transitivity from R to the components of the fuzzy preference structure.

The following proposition shows the strongest result when the generator is also the strongest one possible, the minimum.

Proposition 4.3. For any reflexive fuzzy relation R with corresponding strict preference relation P generated by means of $T_{\mathbf{M}}$ it holds that

$$R \text{ is } T_{\mathbf{M}}\text{-transitive} \Rightarrow P \text{ is } T_{\mathbf{M}}\text{-transitive}.$$

Moreover, this is the strongest result possible.

We have proven that the following limits hold

$$\lim_{\lambda \to 0} T_{\mathbf{nM}}^{\varphi_{1/\lambda}} = T_{\mathbf{nM}}, \quad \lim_{\lambda \to \infty} T_{\mathbf{nM}}^{\varphi_{1/\lambda}} = T_{\mathbf{M}}.$$

Hence, we could talk about the family of t-norms $T_{\mathbf{nM}}^{\varphi_{1/\lambda}}$ with $\lambda \in [0,\infty]$ and summarize the above results as follows.

Corollary 4.4. For any reflexive fuzzy relation R with corresponding strict preference relation P generated by means of $T_\lambda^{\mathbf{F}}$, $\lambda \in [0,\infty]$, it holds that

$$R \text{ is } T_{\mathbf{M}}\text{-transitive} \Rightarrow P \text{ is } T_{\mathbf{nM}}^{\varphi_{1/\lambda}}\text{-transitive}.$$

Moreover, this is the strongest result possible.

5. THE WEAKLY COMPLETE CASE

Once the relevance of the concept of completeness is demonstrated, the study of the previous implications when considering the weak completeness condition arises as a natural question. A fuzzy relation R is called weakly complete if $R(a,b) +$

$R(b,a) \geq 1$ for any $a, b \in A$. Weak completeness is an intermediate situation between the general case, no completeness condition, and the particular case of strong completeness. The following results prove that this restriction on the reflexive fuzzy relation R from which the AFPS is obtained allows to improve the transitivity of P and I compared to the general case.

The following theorem about the transitivity of the indifference relation I not only concerns the Frank t-norm family but a general commutative conjunctor c with neutral element 1.

Theorem 5.1. For any weakly complete reflexive relation R with corresponding indifference relation I generated by means of a commutative conjunctor c with neutral element 1 it holds that

$$R \text{ is } T_\mathbf{M}\text{-transitive} \Rightarrow I \text{ is } \bar{f}_\mathbf{M}^c\text{-transitive},$$

where $\bar{f}_\mathbf{M}^c$ is the commutative operator defined by

$$\bar{f}_\mathbf{M}^c(x,y) = \begin{cases} \inf_{z \in [x, 1-y]} c(z, 1-z) & \text{, if } x + y \leq 1, \\ c(x,y) & \text{, otherwise.} \end{cases}$$

Moreover, when c is continuous this is the strongest result possible.

Note that the implication is true in general, not only for continuous operators. The continuity is only required to prove that no stronger result is possible. If we center our attention on the Frank t-norm family, we can write $\bar{f}_\mathbf{M}^c$ explicitly.

Corollary 5.2. For any weakly complete reflexive fuzzy relation R with corresponding indifference relation I generated by means of $T_\lambda^\mathbf{F}$, $\lambda \in [0, \infty]$, it holds that

$$R \text{ is } T_\mathbf{M}\text{-transitive} \Rightarrow I \text{ is } \bar{f}_\mathbf{M}^\lambda\text{-transitive},$$

where $\bar{f}_\mathbf{M}^\lambda$ is the commutative operator defined by $\bar{f}_\mathbf{M}^\lambda(x,y) = T_\lambda^\mathbf{F}(x, \max(1-x, y))$ for $x \leq y$.

Obviously, it holds that $\bar{f}_\mathbf{M}^\lambda \geq T_\lambda^\mathbf{F}$. In particular, for the three important cases $\lambda \in \{0, 1, \infty\}$ we have $\bar{f}_\mathbf{M}^0 = T_\mathbf{M}$, $\bar{f}_\mathbf{M}^\infty = T_\mathbf{L}$ and

$$\bar{f}_\mathbf{M}^1(x,y) = \min(x,y) \cdot \max(1 - \min(x,y), \max(x,y)).$$

Note that $\bar{f}_\mathbf{M}^\lambda$ is not a t-norm for any $\lambda \in]0, \infty[$ since it is not associative.

Remark that although for the extreme cases $\lambda = 0$ and $\lambda = \infty$, the results obtained coincide with the strongest implications in the general case, for any $\lambda \in]0, \infty[$, the conjunctor obtained in the weakly complete case is greater than the one obtained in the general case. It is clear that $\bar{f}_\mathbf{M}^\lambda(x,y) > T_\lambda^\mathbf{F}(x,y)$ for $x + y \leq 1$.

Next we study the transitivity of the strict preference relation.

Proposition 5.3. For any weakly complete reflexive fuzzy relation R with corresponding strict preference relation P generated by means of $T_{\mathbf{L}}$, it holds that

$$R \text{ is } T_{\mathbf{M}}\text{-transitive} \Rightarrow P \text{ is } \bar{g}_{\mathbf{M}}^{\infty}\text{-transitive,}$$

where

$$\bar{g}_{\mathbf{M}}^{\infty}(x,y) = \begin{cases} 0 & \text{, if } x+y \leq 1, \\ \max(x,y) & \text{, otherwise.} \end{cases}$$

Moreover, this is the strongest result possible.

Theorem 5.4. For any weakly complete reflexive fuzzy relation R with corresponding strict preference relation P generated by means of $T_\lambda^{\mathbf{F}}$, $\lambda \in \,]0,\infty[$, it holds that

$$R \text{ is } T_{\mathbf{M}}\text{-transitive} \Rightarrow P \text{ is } \bar{g}_{\mathbf{M}}^{\lambda}\text{-transitive,}$$

where $\bar{g}_{\mathbf{M}}^{\lambda}$ is the commutative operator defined by

$$\bar{g}_{\mathbf{M}}^{\lambda}(x,y) = \begin{cases} 0 & \text{, if } \varphi_{1/\lambda}(x) + \varphi_{1/\lambda}(y) \leq 1, \\ x & \text{, if } \varphi_{1/\lambda}(x) + \varphi_{1/\lambda}(y) > 1 \\ & \quad \text{and } y \leq \max(\varphi_{1/\lambda}(x), 1 - \varphi_{1/\lambda}(x)), \\ \varphi_{1/\lambda}^{-1}(y) & \text{, otherwise,} \end{cases}$$

for $x \leq y$.

Note that the conjunctor $\bar{g}_{\mathbf{M}}^{\lambda}$ does not have neutral element 1. It is therefore not surprising that $\bar{g}_{\mathbf{M}}^{\lambda} \leq T_{\mathbf{M}}$ does not hold.

Proposition 5.5. For any weakly complete reflexive fuzzy relation R with corresponding strict preference relation P generated by means of $T_{\mathbf{M}}$, it holds that

$$R \text{ is } T_{\mathbf{M}}\text{-transitive} \Rightarrow P \text{ is } \bar{g}_{\mathbf{M}}^{0}\text{-transitive,}$$

where

$$\bar{g}_{\mathbf{M}}^{0}(x,y) = \begin{cases} \min(x,y) & \text{, if } 1 + \min(x,y) \geq 2\max(x,y) \text{ or } \min(x,y) = 0, \\ 2\max(x,y) - 1 & \text{, otherwise.} \end{cases}$$

Moreover, this is the strongest result possible.

Again the conjunctor $\bar{g}_{\mathbf{M}}^{0}$ does not have neutral element 1. Surprisingly, in this case it holds that $T_{\mathbf{M}} < \bar{g}_{\mathbf{M}}^{0}$. As for the family $T_{n\mathbf{M}}^{\varphi_\lambda}$, we have proven that the following limits hold

$$\lim_{\lambda \to \infty} \bar{g}_{\mathbf{M}}^{\lambda} = \bar{g}_{\mathbf{M}}^{\infty}, \quad \lim_{\lambda \to 0} \bar{g}_{\mathbf{M}}^{\lambda} = \bar{g}_{\mathbf{M}}^{0}.$$

Therefore, we can also talk about the family of conjunctors $\bar{g}_{\mathbf{M}}^{\lambda}$, with $\lambda \in [0,\infty]$. Obviously, it holds that $\bar{g}_{\mathbf{M}}^{\lambda} \geq T_{n\mathbf{M}}^{\varphi_{1/\lambda}}$.

Corollary 5.6. For any weakly complete reflexive fuzzy relation R with corresponding strict preference relation P generated by means of $T_\lambda^{\mathbf{F}}$, $\lambda \in [0, \infty]$, it holds that

$$R \text{ is } T_{\mathbf{M}}\text{-transitive} \Rightarrow P \text{ is } \bar{g}_{\mathbf{M}}^\lambda\text{-transitive}.$$

6. THE STRONGLY COMPLETE CASE REVISITED

In this section we return to the strongly complete case and, in particular, to Theorem 2.3. We want to stress that that result does not show the strongest possible implication as we have done in Sections 3–5,.

Theorem 6.1. For any strongly complete reflexive fuzzy relation R with corresponding indifference and strict preference relations I and P, it holds that

$$R \text{ is } T_{\mathbf{M}}\text{-transitive} \Rightarrow \begin{cases} P \text{ is } \bar{\bar{g}}_{\mathbf{M}}\text{-transitive,} \\ I \text{ is } T_{\mathbf{M}}\text{-transitive,} \end{cases}$$

where

$$\bar{\bar{g}}_{\mathbf{M}}(x, y) = \begin{cases} 0 & \text{, if } \min(x, y) = 0, \\ \max(x, y) & \text{, otherwise.} \end{cases}$$

Once again, we can see how completeness conditions are relevant in the propagation of the transitivity. The strong completeness of the large preference relation allows to improve the results obtained under the weak completeness assumption. Indeed, it holds that $\bar{\bar{g}}_{\mathbf{M}} \geq \bar{g}_{\mathbf{M}}^0$.

7. CONCLUSION

In this work we have completed the study of the propagation of the $T_{\mathbf{M}}$-transitivity in AFPS in three different situations, the general case, the weakly complete case and the strongly complete case, when the generator of the AFPS is any t-norm in the Frank family. We have proven that in the general case, only when the generator is the minimum operator we can assure for I the same type of transitivity that is obtained in the strongly complete case, the one defined by $T_{\mathbf{M}}$. We have also seen that the results obtained are much weaker when other generators are considered. The transitivity obtained for P in absence of completeness is weaker than the one proven in the strongly complete case for all the generators studied. Concerning the weakly complete case, we have proven that this condition allows to improve the results that hold in general, although obviously the strongest implications obtained considering weak completeness are not as strong as the ones known when working under the strong completeness assumption. The main results are summarized in the following table.

	General Case	Weak Compl.	Strong Compl.
I	$T_\lambda^{\mathbf{F}}$	$\bar{f}_{\mathbf{M}}^\lambda$	$T_{\mathbf{M}}$
P	$T_{\mathrm{nM}}^{\varphi_{1/\lambda}}$	$\bar{g}_{\mathbf{M}}^\lambda$	$\bar{g}_{\mathbf{M}}$

Table 1
Transitivity of I and P generated from a $T_{\mathbf{M}}$-transitive R by means of $i = T_\lambda^{\mathbf{F}}$.

Acknowledgements

The research reported on in this paper has been partially supported by project MTM2004-01269.

References

1. M. Dasgupta and R. Deb, *Transitivity and fuzzy preferences*, Social Choice and Welfare **13** (1996), 305–318.
2. M. Dasgupta and R. Deb, *Factorizing fuzzy transitivity*, Fuzzy Sets and Systems **118** (2001), 489–502.
3. B. De Baets and J. Fodor, *Generator triplets of additive fuzzy preference structures*, Proc. Sixth Internat. Workshop on Relational Methods in Computer Science (Tilburg, The Netherlands), 2001, pp. 306–315.
4. B. De Baets, B. Van De Walle and E. Kerre, *Fuzzy preference structures without incomparability*, Fuzzy Sets and Systems **76** (1995), 333–348.
5. S. Díaz, B. De Baets and S. Montes, *Study of the transitivity of fuzzy indifference relations involving the nilpotent minimum*, Proc. Second Internat. Summer School on Aggregation Operators and their Applications (Alcalá de Henares, Spain), 2003, pp. 61–66.
6. S. Díaz, S. Montes and B. De Baets, *Transitivity bounds in additive fuzzy preference structures*, IEEE Transactions on Fuzzy Systems, submitted.
7. J. Fodor, *Contrapositive symmetry of fuzzy implications*, Fuzzy Sets and Systems **69** (1995), 141–156.
8. J. Fodor and M. Roubens, *Fuzzy Preference Modelling and Multicriteria Decision Support*, Kluwer Academic Publishers, 1994.
9. E.P. Klement, R. Mesiar and E. Pap, *Triangular Norms*, Kluwer Academic Publishers, 2000.
10. M. Roubens and Ph. Vincke, *Preference modelling*, Lecture Notes in Economics and Mathematical Systems, Vol. **76**, Springer-Verlag, 1985.

Decision Making with Fuzzy Ternary Relations

S. Ovchinnikov [a]

[a]Mathematics Department
San Francisco State University
San Francisco, CA 94232
E–mail: sergei@sfsu.edu

Abstract

In this paper we study three models of choice in a fuzzy environment. The first model is based on maximizing sets defined for interval scales. The second model defines a fuzzy choice set by means of a fuzzy ternary relation. Finally, we introduce an abstract model of fuzzy choice functions which extends some classical ideas of rational choice behavior. We prove that these three models generate equivalent choice mechanisms.

Key words: Maximizing set, Fuzzy ternary relation, Fuzzy choice function

1. Introduction

In the paper we consider the optimization problem in a general framework of best alternative choice [1]. Many problems in decision theory, especially in economical, psychological, and social applications, can be reduced to making the best choice from a set of alternatives with respect a given optimality criterion. Very often this criterion is a real–valued function on the set of all alternatives. The main objectives of the theory in question are a study of the sets of best alternatives and establishing relations between different mechanisms of choice, rather then calculating the optimum.

The classical theory of choice considers the following framework (see, for instance, [1]). Let A be a finite set of alternatives (the 'universe' of alternatives). A function $f : A \to \mathbb{R}$ is said to be a *criterion* (scale, goal function, utility function, etc.). Values of this function are assumed to be measurements in an ordinal scale [6,7]. It means that two such functions f and g are equivalent ordinal scales if there is a strictly increasing bijection $\varphi : \mathbb{R} \to \mathbb{R}$ such that $g = \varphi \circ f$. The criterion f generates the following mechanism of choice:

$$C_X^f = \{y \in X : f(y) \geq f(x), \forall x \in X, \tag{1.1}$$

where $X \subseteq A$ is the set of submitted alternatives. This choice mechanism is equivalent to

$$C_X^f = \{y \in X : \text{there is no } x \in X \text{ such that } f(x) > f(y)\}. \tag{1.2}$$

For a given criterion f on A, the function $C^f : \mathbf{2}^A \to \mathbf{2}^A$ defined by (1.1) is an example of a 'choice function'. Elements of C_X^f are the 'best alternatives' in the submitted set X. According to (1.1) an alternative $x \in X$ is a best one in X if the function f assumes its maximum value on the set X at x. Thus the alternatives in C_X^f 'optimize' the criterion f. The two choice mechanisms (1.1) and (1.2) have different meanings despite their mathematical equivalence: mechanism (1.1) defines C_X^f as the set of 'dominating alternatives' as opposed to (1.2) which defines this set as the set of 'non–dominated' alternatives.

The choice mechanism defined by (1.1) can be called an 'ordinal scale' mechanism, since $C_X^f = C_X^g$, for all $X \subset A$ if and only if f and g are equivalent ordinal scales.

One standard result in the choice theory is that a criterion (assumed to be an ordinal scale) defines a mechanism of choice which is equivalent to the pair–dominant mechanism of choice, i.e., a mechanism based on a binary relation on A. In fact, the criterion mechanism is the same as the one generated by weak ordering relations. Moreover, it is possible to describe the class of 'choice functions' in the form C^f by some characteristic properties of abstract choice functions. Here, an abstract choice function is a function in the form $C : X \mapsto Y$ where Y is a nonempty subset of X (i.e., $C_X \subseteq X$). The following is one of standard 'characteristic' properties of abstract choice functions.

Strict Heritage or Constancy condition (K):

$$X' \subseteq X, \ X' \cap C_X \neq \emptyset \ \Rightarrow \ C_{X'} = C_X \cap X'.$$

Remark. This property was introduced by Chernoff (postulate 6 in [3]. It is also known as the "weak axiom of revealed preferences" (axiom C4 in [2]). "Condition(K) requires that the options chosen from the initial set X and left in the narrowed one X' and only such options be chosen from X'..." [1].

The purpose of this paper is to suggest an extension of the classical choice theory to the case when criteria are interval scales. Let, for example, f_1 and f_2 be two criteria which are equivalent ordinal scales but there are no constants $\alpha > 0$ and β such that $f_1 = \alpha f_2 + \beta$. Then f_1 and f_2 are not equivalent interval scales, although they yield the same choice mechanisms by (1.1). Thus the classical theory is not able to distinguish optimizations in scales that are stronger than ordinal ones and we 'loose information' passing from criteria to choice functions. It turns out that there is a model of choice based on fuzzy set theory which provides the classical correspondences between the 'criterion language', the 'relation language', and the 'choice function language' for the interval scales. This model utilizes a notion of a maximizing set introduced by Zadeh in 1972 [10], (see also [4]).

We define a maximizing set for a function f on a finite set X as a fuzzy set M by its membership function $M(x)$ as follows (see [4, p.101]):

$$M(x) = \frac{f(x) - \min f}{\max f - \min f}, \qquad (1.3)$$

(we set $M = X$ if f is a constant function). Then two functions f_1 and f_2 are equivalent interval scales if and only if they define the same maximizing set by (1.3).

Intuitively, the grade of membership of $x \in X$ in M represents the degree to which f approximates to $\max f$ relative to the range of f.

Clearly, the membership function M and the function f are equivalent interval scales.

The notion of a maximizing set permits to give a proper generalization of choice mechanisms (1.1) and (1.2) that turned out to be equivalent to triple–dominant mechanisms of choice based on fuzzy ternary relations.

2. Fuzzy Choice Functions

We denote $\tilde{P}(A)$ the set of fuzzy sets with a finite universe A and $carX$ the *carrier* of a fuzzy set X, i.e., the crisp set

$$\{x \in A : X(x) > 0\}$$

where $X(x)$ is the membership function of X. We write $x \in X$ if $x \in carX$.

Definition 2.1. A *choice function* C is a mapping $C : \tilde{P}(A) \to \tilde{P}(A)$ assigning a nonempty fuzzy set $C_X \subseteq X$ to every nonempty fuzzy set X with the universe A.

The subset C_X of X is considered to be the subset of 'best' elements in X. The number $C_X(x)$ may be regarded as a 'degree of goodness' of the element $x \in X$ with respect to the choice function C.

Examples of choice functions can be found in Section 3 where a particular class of choice functions is defined by means of criteria and triple–dominant choice mechanisms. This class can be also described in an external way by some properties of abstract choice functions. One of these properties has no analog in the classical theory. This is the Separation property:

Separation (S):

$$C_X = C_{carX} \cap X, \quad \forall X \in \tilde{P}(A).$$

Intuitively, the number $C_X(x)$ is the degree to which the alternative x is 'chosen' as the 'best' one from the fuzzy set X. The Separation property asserts that this degree is determined by the choice from the crisp set $carX$ and the value $X(x)$ of the membership function of the fuzzy set X.

Another property is similar to the Strict Heritage property (K) of non fuzzy choice functions.

For a nonempty fuzzy set X, a *normalizer* of X is a fuzzy set $N(X)$ with a membership function (cf. (1.3))

$$N(X)(x) = \frac{X(x) - \min X(x)}{\max X(x) - \min X(x)},$$

if $X(x)$ is not a constant function, and $N(X) = carX$ if $X(x)$ is a constant function.

Strict Heritage (K):
If $X' \subseteq X$ are nonempty crisp sets, then

$$C_{X'} = N(C_X \cap X').$$

Clearly, this property is of the same nature as the classical one described in Section 1.

3. Choice Theory for Interval Scales

In this section we present a model of optimal choice for interval scales.

Definition 3.1. Let f be a function (criterion) on the universe of alternatives A. A *dominating subset* of a fuzzy subset $X \subseteq A$ with respect to f is a fuzzy subset D_X^f of X defined by

$$D_X^f(x) = \frac{f(x) - m^f(X)}{M^f(X) - m^f(X)} \wedge X(x), \tag{3.1}$$

where $m^f(X) = \min_{x \in X} f$, $M^f(X) = \max_{x \in X} f$. For a constant function f, $D_X^f = X$.

Clearly, dominating subsets defined by (3.1) are invariant under positive affine transformations that define the class of interval scales [6,7]. It is easy to prove that two criteria f_1 and f_2 are equivalent interval scales if and only if $D_X^{f_1} = D_X^{f_2}$ for all $X \in \tilde{P}(A)$. We consider D_X^f's as values of a fuzzy choice function C.

Theorem 3.1. Let C be a fuzzy choice function. The following statements are equivalent:
(i) $C_X = D_X^f$ for some criterion f;
(ii) C satisfies properties (S) and (K).

Proof. (i) $\Rightarrow$ (ii).

Clearly, (S) holds for C defined by (3.1). Let $X' \subseteq X$ be two crisp subsets of A. Then

$$N(D_X^f \cap X')(x) = \frac{D_X^f(x) - m^{D_X^f}(X')}{M^{D_X^f}(X') - m^{D_X^f}(X')}$$

$$= \frac{\frac{f(x)-m^f(X)}{M^f(X')-m^f(X')} - \min_{x \in X'} \frac{f(x)-m^f(X)}{M^f(X')-m^f(X')}}{\max_{x \in X'} \frac{f(x)-m^f(X)}{M^f(X')-m^f(X')} - \min_{x \in X'} \frac{f(x)-m^f(X)}{M^f(X')-m^f(X')}}$$

$$= \frac{f(x) - \min_{X'} f}{\max_{X'} f - \min_{X'} f} = D_{X'}^f(x),$$

for $x \in X'$.

Thus condition (K) holds for C.

(ii) $\Rightarrow$ (i).

Let us define $f(x) = C_A(x)$. Then

$$D_X^f(x) = \frac{f(x) - m^f(X)}{M^f(X) - m^f(X)} \wedge X(x) = \frac{C_A(x) - \min_{x \in X}\{C_A(x)\}}{\max_{x \in X}\{C_A(x)\} - \min_{x \in X}\{C_A(x)\}} \wedge (X(x))$$

$$= (N(C_A \cap carX))(x) \wedge X(x) = C_{carX}(x) \wedge X(x) = C_X(x),$$

by properties (K) and (S). □

Thus the Separation and Strict Heritage properties completely characterize fuzzy choice functions defined by criteria which are interval scales.

It turns out that there is a mechanism of choice based on hyper dominant relations [1] which yields an equivalent description of choice in the case of interval scales. Informally, this mechanism can be described as follows. Let R be a relation between elements of A and 2–element subsets of A. Then a *weakly dominant* crisp choice function is defined by

$$C_X = \{x \in X : \text{for every } y \in X \text{ and, for at least one pair } \{y, z\} \subseteq X, \quad (3.2)$$
$$\text{holds } xR\{y, z\}\}.$$

For our purposes it is more convenient to represent R as a fuzzy ternary relation on A. Then we have the following extension of (3.2):

Definition 3.2. Let R be a fuzzy ternary relation on A. A fuzzy choice function C_X^R based on R is defined by its membership function as follows:

$$C_X^R(x) = \left[\bigwedge_{y \subset X} \bigvee_{z \in X} R(x, y, z) \right] \wedge X(x) \quad (3.3)$$

In this paper we consider only those choice mechanisms (3.3) that are based on triple–dominant relations defined as follows:

Definition 3.3. A fuzzy ternary relation R is said to be a *triple–dominant relation* if it satisfies the following conditions:

(i) $R(x, y, z) = R(x, z, y)$, $\forall x, y, z \in A$;

(ii) $R(x, y, y) \wedge R(x, z, z) \leq R(x, y, z) \leq$

$$\leq R(x, y, y) \vee R(x, z, z);$$

(iii) There is a weak ordering $\preceq$ on A such that
$$R(x, y, y) = R(x, x, y) = \begin{cases} 1, & \text{if } y \preceq x, \\ 0, & \text{if } x \prec y; \end{cases}$$

(iv) $R(x, u, v) = \dfrac{R(x, y, z) - R(u, y, z)}{R(v, y, z) - R(u, y, z)},$

if $y \preceq u \preceq x \leq v \preceq z$ and $u \prec v$.

We define $x \prec y$ if $x \preceq y$ but $y \not\preceq x$, and $x \sim y$ if $x \preceq y$ and $y \preceq x$.

Our last theorem establishes equivalence of choice mechanisms based on interval scales and on fuzzy triple–dominant relations.

Theorem 3.2. *For a criterion f there is a fuzzy triple–dominant relation R such that $D^f = C^R$. Conversely, for any fuzzy triple–dominant relation R there is a criterion f such that $C^R = D^f$.*

Proof. (i) Let f be an interval scale on A. We define

$$R(x, y, z) = \tfrac{f(x) - m^f(\{x,y,z\})}{M^f(\{x,y,z\}) - m^f(\{x,y,z\})}, \tag{3.4}$$

if f is not a constant function on $\{x, y, z\}$, and

$$R(x, y, z) = 1, \tag{3.5}$$

if f is a constant function on $\{x, y, z\}$.

Thus defined R is a triple–dominant relation. Indeed, property (i) in Definition 3.3 clearly holds. We have

$$R(x, y, y) = \begin{cases} 1, & \text{if } f(x) \geq f(y), \\ 0, & \text{if } f(x) < f(y), \end{cases} \tag{3.6}$$

and the same equation holds for $R(x, x, y)$. It is easy to see now that property (ii) in Definition 3.3 holds.

Let us define a relation $\preceq$ on A by

$$x \preceq y \iff f(x) \leq f(y).$$

Thus defined $\preceq$ is a weak ordering on A. Clearly, property (iii) in Definition 3.3 holds.

Finally, let us verify property (iv) in Definition 3.3. Suppose that $y \preceq u \preceq x \preceq v \preceq z$ and $u \prec v$. Then

$$f(y) \leq f(u) \leq f(x) \leq f(v) \leq f(z)$$

and $f(u) < f(v)$ and we have
$$R(v,y,z) = \frac{f(v)-f(y)}{f(z)-f(y)}$$
$$R(u,y,z) = \frac{f(u)-f(y)}{f(z)-f(y)}$$
$$R(x,y,z) = \frac{f(x)-f(y)}{f(z)-f(y)}$$
$$R(x,u,v) = \frac{f(x)-f(u)}{f(v)-f(u)}$$

Hence,
$$\frac{R(x,y,z)-R(u,y,z)}{R(v,y,z)-R(u,y,z)} = \frac{\frac{f(x)-f(y)}{f(z)-f(y)} - \frac{f(u)-f(y)}{f(z)-f(y)}}{\frac{f(v)-f(y)}{f(z)-f(y)} - \frac{f(u)-f(y)}{f(z)-f(y)}} = \frac{f(x)-f(u)}{f(v)-f(u)} = R(x,u,v).$$

It remains to show that $C^R = D^f$.

For given $x, y \in X$ we have
$$\bigvee_{z \in X} R(x,y,z) = 1,$$
if $f(y) \le f(x)$. Indeed, for $z = y$ we have, by (3.6), $R(x,y,z) = 1$.

Suppose now that $f(y) > f(x)$. If $f(z) \ge f(x)$, then $R(x,y,z) = 0$. If $f(z) < f(x)$, then
$$R(x,y,z) = \frac{f(x)-f(z)}{f(y)-f(z)}.$$

Therefore,
$$\bigvee_{z \in X} R(x,y,z) = \bigvee_{z \in X} \frac{f(x)-f(z)}{f(y)-f(z)} = \frac{f(x)-f(z_0)}{f(y)-f(z_0)},$$
where $f(z_0) = m^f(X)$.

Now, for $f(y_0) = M^f(X)$, we have
$$C_X^R(x) = \left[\bigwedge_{y \in X} \bigvee_{z \in X} R(x,y,z)\right] \wedge X(x) = \frac{f(x)-f(z_0)}{f(y_0)-f(z_0)} \wedge X(x) = D_X^f(x).$$

(ii) Suppose now that R is a triple–dominant relation on A. We define a function f on A by
$$f(x) = R(x, y_0, z_0), \qquad (3.7)$$
where y_0 and z_0 are maximal and minimal elements in A with respect to the relation $\preceq$. By part (i) of the proof, it suffices to prove (3.4) and (3.5) for the function f defined by (3.7).

First we prove that (3.7) defines an increasing function with respect to $\preceq$. More precisely, we prove that
$$x \prec y \quad \Leftrightarrow \quad f(x) < f(y)$$
and
$$x \sim y \quad \Leftrightarrow \quad f(x) = f(y).$$

Suppose $x \preceq y$. Then $z_0 \preceq x \preceq y \preceq y_0$. If $z_0 \prec y$, then, by conditions (iv), (iii), and (i) of Definition 3.3,

$$R(x, z_0, y) = \frac{R(x, z_0, y_0) - R(z_0, z_0, y_0)}{R(y, z_0, y_0) - R(z_0, z_0, y_0)} = \frac{R(x, z_0, y_0)}{R(y, z_0, y_0)} = \frac{f(x)}{f(y)} \leq 1.$$

Hence, $f(x) \leq f(y)$.

If $x \prec y_0$, then, by conditions (iv), (i) and (iii) of Definition 3.3,

$$R(y, x, y_0) = \frac{R(y, z_0, y_0) - R(x, z_0, y_0)}{R(y_0, z_0, y_0) - R(x, z_0, y_0)} = \frac{f(y) - f(x)}{1 - f(x)} \geq 0. \quad (3.8)$$

Thus $f(x) \leq f(y)$, since condition (iv) of Definition 3.3 implies

$$R(x, z_0, y_0) \neq R(y_0, z_0, y_0).$$

Suppose now that $y \preceq z_0$ and $y_0 \preceq x$. Then $z_0 \sim x \sim y \sim y_0$ and by conditions (ii) and (iii) of Definition 3.3,

$$R(x, y_0, z_0) \geq R(x, y_0, y_0) \wedge R(x, z_0, z_0) = 1$$

and

$$R(y, y_0, z_0) \geq R(y, y_0, y_0) \wedge R(y, z_0, z_0) = 1,$$

i.e., $f(x) = f(y) = 1$.

We proved that f is an increasing function on A with respect to the relation $\preceq$.

Finally, let $x \prec y$. Then, by condition (iv) of Definition 3.3 applied to $z_0 \preceq x \preceq x \prec y \preceq y_0$,

$$R(x, y_0, z_0) \neq R(y, y_0, z_0).$$

Hence, $f(x) < f(y)$.

Suppose f is a constant function on $\{x, y, z\}$. Then $x \sim y \sim z$ and, by conditions (ii) and (iii) of Definition 3.3, $R(x, y, z) = 1$, i.e., (3.5) holds.

Now we prove that (3.4) holds for f defined by (3.7) and R. Both sides of (3.4) are symmetric with respect to y and z. Hence it suffices to consider the case when $y \preceq z$. We consider the following possible cases.

$y \sim z$. Then the right side of (3.4) is 1 if $y \sim z \prec x$, and is 0 if $x \prec y \sim z$. By conditions (iii) and (iv) of Definition 3.3, the left side of (3.4) takes the same values.

$x \prec y \prec z$. Then $R(x, y, z) = 0$, by conditions (iii) and (iv) of Definition 3.3; the right side of (3.4) equals zero because $f(x)$ is the minimal value of f on $\{x, y, z\}$.

$y \preceq x \preceq z$ and $y \prec z$. Then, by condition (iv) of Definition 3.3,

$$R(x, y, z) = \frac{R(x, z_0, y_0) - R(y, z_0, y_0)}{R(z, z_0, y_0) - R(y, z_0, y_0)} = \frac{f(x) - f(y)}{f(z) - f(y)}$$
$$= \frac{f(x) - m^f(\{x, y, z\})}{M^f(\{x, y, z\}) - m^f(\{x, y, z\})}$$

$y \prec z \preceq x$. By conditions (iii) and (iv) of Definition 3.3, $R(x, y, z) = 1$; the right side of (3.4) equals 1, since $f(x)$ is the maximal value of f on $\{x, y, z\}$.

□

4. Conclusion

We have shown (Theorem 3.2) that choice mechanisms based on criteria which are measurements in interval scales can be equivalently described as choice mechanisms based on fuzzy triple–dominant relations.

References

1. M. Aizerman and F. Alekserov, *Theory of Choice* (North–Holland, Amsterdam, 1995).
2. K.J. Arrow, Rational choice functions and orderings, *Economica* **26** (1959) 121–127.
3. H. Chernoff, Rational selection of decision functions, *Econometrica* **22** (1954) 422–443.
4. D. Dubois and H. Prade, *Fuzzy Sets and Systems* (Academic Press, New York, 1980).
5. S. Ovchinnikov and T. Riera, On fuzzy classifications. In *R.R. Yager, ed., Recent Developments in Fuzzy Set and Possibility Theory* (Pergamon Press, New York, 1981).
6. J. Pfanzagl, *Theory of Measurement* (John Wiley and Sons, New York, 1968).
7. F.S. Roberts, *Measurement Theory* (Addison–Wesley Publ. Co., Reading, MA, 1979)
8. E. Szpilrajn, Sur l'extension de l'ordre partiel, *Fundamenta Mathematicae* **16** (1980) 386–389.
9. L.A. Zadeh, Similarity relations and fuzzy orderings, *Inf. Sci.* **3** (1971) 177–200.
10. L.A. Zadeh, On fuzzy algorithms, Memorandum No. UCB/ERL M325, College of Engineering, UC Berkeley, 1972.

New Consistency Properties for Preference Relations

F. Chiclana [a], E. Herrera-Viedma [b] and F. Herrera [b]

[a]Centre for Computational Intelligence, School of Computing
De Montfort University, Leicester LE1 9BH - U.K.
chiclana@dmu.ac.uk

[b]Dept. of Computer Science and Artificial Intelligence
University of Granada, 18071 - Granada, Spain
viedma,herrera@decsai.ugr.es

Abstract

Consistency of preference relations is associated with the study of the transitivity property. In this paper, we analyze the properties to be verified by a function, T, in order to obtain the value of preference of the alternative x_i over the alternative x_k when we already have the values of the preference of x_i over x_j, and of x_j over x_k. As a consequence, we define T-additive transitivity property as a new consistency property for fuzzy preference relations and T-multiplicative transitivity property for the case of multiplicative preference relations.

Keywords: *Decision making; Consistency; Transitivity; Fuzzy preference relations; Multiplicative preference relations.*

1. Introduction

It is widely acknowledged that fuzzy sets play an important role in modelling decision processes because human judgements, including preferences, are often vague. We should consider, for instance, the situation when a set of feasible options have to be pairwise compared. In this case, the opinions of the experts are usually described using preference relations. Many important decision models have been developed using mainly two kinds of preference relations: *fuzzy preference relations* [1–3,7,16] and *multiplicative preference relations* [2,5,6,11–13].

In order to make consistent choices when dealing with preference relations a set of properties or restrictions to be satisfied by such preference relations have been suggested. In the multiplicative model, a multiplicative preference relation is consistent when it verifies the so called multiplicative consistency property [11]. The results obtained in [2] imply that a fuzzy preference relation is consistent if and only if the corresponding multiplicative preference relation is consistent. Therefore, a fuzzy preference relation is considered consistent when it verifies the so-called additive consistency property.

However, there exists a conflict between the multiplicative and additive consistency properties and the scales used to assign preference values to judgements. There exist many arguments to support that a change in the scales used in the multiplicative and fuzzy models seems unpractical and unrealistic. Therefore, a possible solution to overcome the existing conflict seems to be a change in the definition of those consistency properties. In this paper we address this problem and study the properties for a fuzzy reciprocal preference relation to be considered a consistent one. We will study the general conditions of a function $T : [0,1] \times [0,1] \longrightarrow [0,1]$ to obtain p_{ik} from the pair of values (p_{ij}, p_{jk}). Using this function, we introduce the concepts of the T-additive consistency property in the case of fuzzy preference relations, which consist of a relaxation of the additive consistency property. Using the results obtained in [2], the concept of T-multiplicative consistency property is defined for multiplicative preference relations.

The paper is laid out as follows. In section 2, we present an overview of the consistency properties defined for preference relations. In section 3, we show the existence of a conflict between the additive and multiplicative consistency properties and the scales used to provide preference relations. In section 4, we study properties to be verified by a function, T, in order to obtain the preference value p_{ik} when the pair of preference values (p_{ij}, p_{jk}) is known. As a result of this, in section 5 the concepts of T-additive and T-multiplicative transitivity properties are introduced. Finally, in section 6 we draw our conclusions.

2. Consistency Properties and Preference Relations

In a preference relation an expert associates to each pair of alternatives a real number that reflects the preference degree, or the ratio of preference intensity, of the first alternative over, or to that of, the second one. Two questions immediately arise when doing this:
- Which scale should be used to associate preference values to judgements?
- Which conditions have to be satisfied in order to obtain consistent results?

The answer to the first question depends on the selection model we are working with. Two of the most well-known selection models are:
   (i) *Fuzzy model*, in which preferences are represented by a *fuzzy preference relation* P on a set of alternatives X, i.e. a fuzzy set on the product set $X \times X$, which is characterized by its membership function $\mu_P : X \times X \longrightarrow [0,1]$ [17].

This implies that the scale to use in the fuzzy model is the closed interval $[0,1]$.

(ii) *Multiplicative model*, in which preferences are represented using a *multiplicative preference relation*, $A = (a_{ij})$, on a set of alternatives X, being a_{ij} interpreted as the ratio of the preference intensity of alternative x_i to that of x_j. According to Miller's study [10], Saaty suggests measuring a_{ij} using as ratio scale, and precisely the $1-9$ scale [11], or more generally the closed interval $[1/9, 9]$.

With respect to the second question, we agree with Saaty [11] in the sense that lack of consistency in decision making can lead to inconsistent conclusions. In a crisp context, where an expert provides his/her opinion on the set of alternatives, $X = \{x_1, x_2, \ldots, x_n; n \geq 2\}$, by means of a binary preference relation, R, the concept of consistency has traditionally been defined in terms of acyclicity [14], that is the absence of sequences such as $x_1, x_2, \ldots, x_k (x_{k+1} = x_1)$ with $x_j R x_{j+1} \forall j = 1, \ldots, k$. In a fuzzy context, a traditional requirement to characterize consistency is using transitivity, in the sense that if an alternative x_i is preferred to alternative x_j and this one to x_k then alternative x_i should be preferred to x_k, although stronger conditions have been given to define consistency [9,15–17]. In the multiplicative model, what Saaty means by *consistency* is what he calls *cardinal transitivity* in the strength of preferences, which is a stronger condition than the traditional requirement of the transitivity of preferences. Thereby, the definition of consistency proposed by Saaty is the following [11]

Definition 1. *A reciprocal multiplicative preference relation* $A = (a_{ij})$ *is consistent if*

$$a_{ij} \cdot a_{jk} = a_{ik} \quad \forall i, j, k = 1, \ldots, n.$$

Inconsistency for Saaty is a violation of proportionality which may nor entail violation of transitivity [11]. We will use the term *multiplicative consistency property* to refer to this consistency property for multiplicative reciprocal preference relations.

Some of the suggested properties in the case of fuzzy preference relations are:

(i) *Triangle condition [9]*: $p_{ij} + p_{jk} \geq p_{ik} \quad \forall i, j, k$
(ii) *Weak transitivity [16]*: $\forall i, j, k: \min\{p_{ij}, p_{jk}\} \geq 0.5 \Rightarrow p_{ik} \geq 0.5$
(iii) *Max-min transitivity [4,17]*: $p_{ik} \geq \min\{p_{ij}, p_{jk}\} \quad \forall i, j, k$
(iv) *Max-max transitivity [4,17]*: $p_{ik} \geq \max\{p_{ij}, p_{jk}\} \quad \forall i, j, k$
(v) *Restricted Max-min transitivity [16]*: $\forall i, j, k: \min\{p_{ij}, p_{jk}\} \geq 0.5 \Rightarrow p_{ik} \geq \min\{p_{ij}, p_{jk}\}$
(vi) *Restricted Max-max transitivity [16]*: $\forall i, j, k: \min\{p_{ij}, p_{jk}\} \geq 0.5 \Rightarrow p_{ik} \geq \max\{p_{ij}, p_{jk}\}$
(vii) *Multiplicative transitivity [16]*: $\frac{p_{ji}}{p_{ij}} \cdot \frac{p_{kj}}{p_{jk}} = \frac{p_{ki}}{p_{ik}} \quad \forall i, j, k$
(viii) *Additive transitivity [15,16]*: $(p_{ij} - 0.5) + (p_{jk} - 0.5) = (p_{ik} - 0.5) \quad \forall i, j, k$ or equivalently $p_{ij} + p_{jk} + p_{ki} = \frac{3}{2} \quad \forall i, j, k$

In [2] we obtained the transformation function between multiplicative and fuzzy preference relations, which is given in the following result:

Proposition 1. *Suppose that we have a set of alternatives, $X = \{x_1, \ldots, x_n\}$, and associated with it a multiplicative reciprocal preference relation $A = (a_{ij})$, with $a_{ij} \in [1/9, 9]$ and $a_{ij} \cdot a_{ji} = 1, \forall i, j$. Then the corresponding fuzzy reciprocal preference relation, $P = (p_{ij})$, associated to A, with $p_{ij} \in [0, 1]$ and $p_{ij} + p_{ji} = 1, \forall i, j$, is given as follows:*

$$p_{ij} = f(a_{ij}) = \frac{1}{2}(1 + \log_9 a_{ij}).$$

The above transformation function is bijective and, therefore, allows us to transpose concepts that have been defined for fuzzy preference relations to multiplicative preference relations. Indeed, applying the above function we show that additive transitivity property for fuzzy preference relation can be seen as the parallel concept of Saaty's multiplicative consistency property:

Proposition 2. *Suppose that $A = (a_{ij})$ is a multiplicative consistent preference relation. Then, the corresponding reciprocal fuzzy preference relation, $P = f(A)$, associated with A, being $p_{ij} = f(a_{ij}) = \frac{1}{2} \cdot (1 + \log_9 a_{ij})$ verifies additive transitivity property.*

This result suggests the following definition of a consistent fuzzy reciprocal preference relation [8]:

Definition 2. *A fuzzy reciprocal preference relation $P = (p_{ij})$ is consistent if*

$$p_{ij} + p_{jk} + p_{ki} = \frac{3}{2} \quad \forall i, j, k = 1, \ldots, n.$$

We will use the term *additive consistency property* to refer to this consistency property for fuzzy reciprocal preference relations.

3. Consistency Properties and Scales Conflict

The following simple example will show that there exists a conflict between the scales used to associate multiplicative preference values to judgements and the multiplicative consistency property.

Let us suppose a set of three alternatives $\{x_1, x_2, x_3\}$ on which an expert provides the following judgements: alternative x_1 is *considerably more important than* alternative x_2 and this one *demonstrably or overwhelming more important than* alternative x_3. In such a case, using Saaty's 1-9 scale, we would have the values $a_{12} = 5$ and $a_{23} = 7$.

Firstly, if we want to maintain the multiplicative consistency property then, according to Saaty [11], we would have to assign the value $a_{13} = a_{12} \cdot a_{23} = 35$, and the only solution would be using the following consistent reciprocal multiplicative preference relation

$$A = \begin{pmatrix} 1 & 5 & 35 \\ 1/3 & 1 & 7 \\ 1/35 & 1/5 & 1 \end{pmatrix}$$

We observe that the application of the multiplicative consistency property results in obtaining values outside the scale $[1/9, 9]$. This means that a different scale to $[1/9, 9]$ would be needed for providing judgements. The use of any other scale of the form $[1/a, a]$, $a \in \mathbb{R}^+$, no matter how large the value of a, would not make this conflict disappear which means that to overcome this conflict the scale of pairwise comparison from 0 to $+\infty$ would have to be used. However, as Saaty points out in [11], this "may not be useful at all because it assumes that the human judgement is capable of comparing the relative dominance of any two objects, which is not the case."

Secondly, if we restrict the possible values of a_{13} to be in $[1/9, 9]$, then applying transitivity alternative x_1 should be considered as overwhelming more important than alternative x_3, and therefore the value of a_{13} should be greater or equal to 7. In [11] Saaty shows that a reciprocal multiplicative preference relation is multiplicative consistent if and only if its maximum or principal eigenvalue λ_{max} is equal to the number of alternatives n. However, because perfect consistency is difficult to obtain in practice, especially when measuring preferences on a set with a large number of alternatives, Saaty defined a *consistency index (CI = $\lambda_{max} - n$)* that reflects the deviation from consistency of all the a_{ij} of a particular reciprocal multiplicative preference relation from the estimated ratio of priorities w_i/w_j. A measure of inconsistency independent of the order of the reciprocal multiplicative preference relation is defined as the *consistency ratio (CR)*. This is obtained by taking the ratio of CI to the *random index (RI)*, which is an average consistency index of a sample set of randomly generated reciprocal matrices from the scale 1 to 9 (size 500 up to 11 by 11 matrices, and size 100 for squares matrices of orders 12, 13 14 and 15). For this consistency measure, he proposed a threshold of 0.10 to accept a reciprocal multiplicative preference relation as consistent. When the CR is greater than 0.10 then, in order to improve consistency, those judgements with a greater difference a_{ij} and w_i/w_j, are usually modified and a new priority vector is derived. In our example, if $a_{13} = 7$ we get a C.R. value of 0.25412; with $a_{13} = 8$ a C.R. value of 0.212892; and with $a_{13} = 9$ a C.R. value of 0.179714. In any case, the application of the scale results in the impossibility of obtaining a consistent reciprocal multiplicative preference relation for this particular situation, which should not be the case.

Obviously, a similar analysis in the case of working with the fuzzy model can be carried out concluding that the same conflict also exists.

In conclusion, if we do not change the scale used to associate preference values to judgement or we want to have a homogeneous scale when working in a group decision context, then the above definition 1 and definition 2 of consistency of preference relations should be modified. In the next section, we will study the general conditions to be satisfied by a function $T: [0,1] \times [0,1] \longrightarrow [0,1]$ so that it can be used to obtain the preference value of the alternative x_i over the alternative x_k, p_{ik}, from the preference values of x_i over x_j and of x_j over x_k, $\{p_{ij}, p_{jk}\}$.

4. The value of p_{ik} with known (p_{ij}, p_{jk})

If we want to compare the alternatives x_i and x_k, but cannot do it directly, and have an alternative x_j of which we know the exact values of p_{ij} and p_{jk}, then we can establish a broad comparison between alternatives x_i and x_k on the basis of the values p_{ij} and p_{jk}. Indeed, we can distinguish the following cases:

Case 1. $p_{ij} = 0.5$ $(p_{jk} = 0.5)$ which means that $x_i \sim x_j$ $(x_j \sim x_k)$ and as a consequence the strength of preference between x_i and x_k should be the same as the one between x_j and x_k. We then have: $p_{ik} = p_{jk}$ $(p_{ik} = p_{jk})$.

Case 2. $p_{ij} > 0.5$ and $p_{jk} > 0.5$. In this case, alternative x_i is preferred to alternative x_j $(x_i \succ x_j)$ and alternative x_j is preferred to alternative x_k $(x_j \succ x_k)$. We then have that $x_i \succ x_j \succ x_k$ which implies $x_i \succ x_k$ and therefore $p_{ik} > 0.5$. Furthermore, in these cases restricted max-max transitivity should be imposed, which means that x_i should be preferred to x_k with a degree of intensity at least equal to the maximum of p_{ij} and p_{jk}: $p_{ik} \geq max\{p_{ij}, p_{jk}\}$, where the equality holds only when there exists indifference between at least one of the alternatives x_i or x_k and x_j, i.e., $p_{ij} = 0.5$ or $p_{jk} = 0.5$, as we have said in case 1. As a result, in this case $p_{ik} > max\{p_{ij}, p_{jk}\}$ should be verified.

Case 3. $p_{ij} > 0.5$ and $p_{jk} < 0.5$ which is equivalent to $p_{ij} > 0.5$ and $p_{kj} = 1 - p_{jk} > 0.5$, that is: $x_i \succ x_j$ and $x_k \succ x_j$. The comparison of alternatives x_i and x_j is done by comparing the intensities of preferences of them over the alternative x_j. An indifference situation between x_i and x_k would exist only when both alternatives are preferred over x_j with the same intensity, while the alternative with greater intensity of preference over x_j should be preferred to the other one. This is summarized in the following way:

$$\left\{ \begin{array}{l} x_i \sim x_k \text{ if } p_{ij} = p_{kj} \Leftrightarrow p_{ij} + p_{jk} = 1 \\ x_i \succ x_k \text{ if } p_{ij} > p_{kj} \Leftrightarrow p_{ij} + p_{jk} > 1 \\ x_i \prec x_k \text{ if } p_{ij} < p_{kj} \Leftrightarrow p_{ij} + p_{jk} < 1 \end{array} \right\} \Leftrightarrow \left\{ \begin{array}{l} p_{ik} = 0.5 \text{ if } p_{ij} + p_{jk} = 1 \\ p_{ik} > 0.5 \text{ if } p_{ij} + p_{jk} > 1 \\ p_{ik} < 0.5 \text{ if } p_{ij} + p_{jk} < 1 \end{array} \right\}$$

It is obvious that the greater the value $|p_{ij} + p_{jk} - 1|$ the greater $|p_{ik} - 0.5|$.

Case 4. $p_{ij} < 0.5$ and $p_{jk} > 0.5$. This case is analogous to case 3 and the same conclusion is obtained.

Case 5. $p_{ij} < 0.5$ and $p_{jk} < 0.5$. This case is analogous to case 2 and we obtain that $p_{ik} < \min\{p_{ij}, p_{jk}\}$.

Cases 1 to 5 suggest that the value of $p_{ik} - 0.5$ is related to the value $p_{ij} + p_{jk} - 1 = (p_{ij} - 0.5) + (p_{jk} - 0.5)$, and therefore there exists a function
$$T : [0,1]^2 \longrightarrow [0,1],$$
such that
$$p_{ik} = T(p_{ij}, p_{jk}).$$
The above cases mean that function T verifies:
(i) $T(0.5, y) = y \ \forall y$
(ii) T is increasing in the interval $[0.5, 1] \times [0.5, 1]$ with respect to the value $\max\{x, y\}$ and $T(x, y) \geq \max\{x, y\}$ being equal only in the case $\min\{x, y\} = 0.5$.
(iii) T is increasing in the interval $[0, 0.5] \times [0, 0.5]$ with respect to the value $\min\{x, y\}$ and $T(x, y) \leq \min\{x, y\}$ being equal only in the case $\max\{x, y\} = 0.5$.
(iv) T is increasing in the sets $[0, 0.5) \times (0.5, 1]$ and $(0.5, 1] \times [0, 0.5)$ with respect to the value $x + y - 1$ and takes the value 0.5 when $x + y - 1 = 0$.
(v) T is a symmetric function, i.e $T(x, y) = T(y, x) \ \forall x, y$
Applying this property and reciprocity of fuzzy preference relations we have
$$T(1 - p_{ij}, 1 - p_{jk}) = T(p_{ji}, p_{kj}) = T(p_{kj}, p_{ji}) = p_{ki} = 1 - p_{ik} = 1 - T(p_{ij}, p_{jk})$$
and therefore function T should also verify the following additional condition:
$$T(1 - x, 1 - y) = 1 - T(y, x) \ \forall x, y$$
Another desirable property to be verified by function T should be that of continuity as it is expected that a slight change of the values in (p_{ij}, p_{jk}) should produce a slight change in the value p_{ik}.

In order to know more about possible function T satisfying the above conditions, we may start assuming that $T(x, y) = f(x + y)$, with $f : [0, 2] \to [0, 1]$ a continuous and increasing such that $f(1) = 0.5$. The linear solutions are $f_1(z) = z/2$ and $f_2(z) = z - 0.5$.

The first linear solution gives $p_{ik} = T(p_{ij}, p_{jk}) = (p_{ij} + p_{jk})/2$, which fails to satisfy property restricted max-max transitivity, because $\min\{p_{ij}, p_{jk}\} \leq (p_{ij} + p_{jk})/2 \leq \max\{p_{ij}, p_{jk}\}$ and in the case of $p_{ij} \to 0.5 \ \wedge \ p_{jk} \to 1 \ (p_{ij} \to 1 \ \wedge \ p_{jk} \to 0.5)$ we get that $p_{ik} \to 0.75$ instead of $p_{ik} \to p_{jk} = 1 \ (p_{ik} \to p_{ij} = 1)$.

With the second linear solution we get $p_{ik} = T(p_{ij}, p_{jk}) = p_{ij} + p_{jk} - 0.5$, which coincides with additive transitivity. In this case T verifies restricted max-max transitivity but fails to satisfy $p_{ij} \to 0 \ \wedge \ p_{jk} \to 0 \ (p_{ij} \to 1 \ \wedge \ p_{jk} \to 1) \Rightarrow p_{ik} \to 0 \ (p_{ik} \to 1)$.

In fact, if $x, y \leq 0.5$ and $x + y \leq 0.5$ then the above function gives negative values of p_{ik}, while in the case of $x, y \geq 0.5$ and $x + y \geq 1.5$ we obtain values of p_{ik} greater than 1. We can overcome this problem by defining T as a piecewise function. A possible modification of function T would be the following:

$$T(x,y) = \begin{cases} \min\{x,y\} & x+y \leq 0.5 \\ \max\{x,y\} & x+y \geq 1.5 \\ x+y-0.5 & \text{otherwise} \end{cases}$$

This function has a drawback in that it treats an infinite number of different cases as equal. For example when $p_{ij} = 0.9$ and $p_{jk} \in [0.6, 0.9]$ this function returns the value $p_{ij} = 0.9$ and it is obvious that x_i should be preferred to x_k with a degree of intensity in the case of $p_{jk} = 0.9$ greater than when $p_{jk} = 0.6$. Furthermore, this function it is not continuous because

$$\lim_{x+y \to 1.5^-} T(x,y) = 1$$

and

$$\lim_{x+y \to 1.5^+} T(x,y) = \max\{x,y\},$$

being these limits the same only when $x \to 1$ or $y \to 1$. The same can be said when $x+y \to 0.5$.

5. T-additive transitivity and T-multiplicative transitivity

If we want function T to be continuous, then we have to narrow the application of additive transitivity to the case of $(p_{ij}, p_{jk}) \in [0, 0.5) \times (0.5, 1] \cup (0.5, 1] \times [0, 0.5)$ where it shows good behaviour, that is:

$$T(x,y) = \begin{cases} \min\{x,y\} & x,y \in [0, 0.5] \\ \max\{x,y\} & x,y \in [0.5, 1] \\ x+y-0.5 & \text{otherwise} \end{cases}$$

This last expression of function T, although continuous, presents the same behaviour as the previous one in the sense of treating an infinite number of different cases as equal. Again, the same value is obtained for the two different pairs of values $(0.6, 0.9)$ and $(0.9, 0.9)$. So, some kind of strength with respect to the maximum (minimum) has to be incorporated in function T to differentiate those tuples of values with the same minimum (maximum) value.

As a consequence, a better expression of such a function T would be the following one:

$$T(x,y) = \begin{cases} \min\{x,y\} - h_1(x,y) & x,y \in [0, 0.5] \\ \max\{x,y\} + h_2(x,y) & x,y \in [0.5, 1] \\ x+y-0.5 & \text{otherwise} \end{cases}$$

where

$$h_1 : [0, 0.5]^2 \longrightarrow [0, \min\{x, y\}] \subseteq [0, 0.5]$$

and

$$h_2 : [0.5, 1]^2 \longrightarrow [0, 1 - \max\{x, y\}] \subseteq [0, 0.5]$$

are continuous and increasing functions satisfying

$$\min\{x, y\} \to 0.5 \Rightarrow h_1(x, y) \to 0$$

and

$$\max\{x, y\} \to 0.5 \Rightarrow h_2(x, y) \to 0$$

respectively.

All these considerations allow us to define a new transitivity condition, that we name T-additive transitivity:

Definition 3. *A fuzzy preference relation P is T-additive transitive if $p_{ik} = T(p_{ij}, p_{jk})$ being $T : [0,1] \times [0,1] \longrightarrow [0,1]$ a function verifying:*
  (i) $T(x, y) \geq \max\{x, y\}$ $\forall x, y \in [0.5, 1]$
  (ii) $T(x, y) \leq \min\{x, y\}$ $\forall x, y \in [0, 0.5]$
  (iii) $T(x, y) = x + y - 0.5$ otherwise

It is obvious that T-additive transitivity implies restricted max-max transitivity:

Proposition 3. *T-additive transitivity implies restricted max-max transitivity, restricted max-min transitivity and weak transitivity.*

In the case of working with multiplicative preference relations, T-multiplicative transitivity can be defined by using the definition of T-additive transitivity for fuzzy preference relations and the bijective transformation function that relates both preference structures. By doing that, we have:

Definition 4. *A multiplicative preference relation A is T-multiplicative transitive if $a_{ik} = T(a_{ij}, a_{jk})$ being $T : [1/9, 9] \times [1/9, 9] \longrightarrow [1/9, 9]$ a function verifying:*
  (i) $T(x, y) \geq \max\{x, y\}$ $\forall x, y \in [1, 9]$
  (ii) $T(x, y) \leq \min\{x, y\}$ $\forall x, y \in [1/9, 1]$
  (iii) $T(x, y) = xy$ otherwise

6. Conclusions

In order to make consistent choices when dealing with preference relations a set of properties or restrictions to be satisfied by such preference relations have been suggested. In the multiplicative model, a multiplicative preference relation is consistent when it verifies the so called multiplicative consistency property. In the additive model, a fuzzy preference relation is considered consistent when it verifies the so called additive consistency property.

However, there exists a conflict between the multiplicative and additive consistency properties and the scales used to assign preference values to judgements. There exist many arguments to support that a change in the scales used in the multiplicative and fuzzy models seems unpractical and unrealistic. Therefore, the only possible solution to overcome the existing conflict seems to be a change of the definition of the consistency properties.

In this paper we have addressed this problem and have studied the properties to be verified for a preference relation to be considered a consistent one. We have introduced the concepts of T-additive consistency property in the case of fuzzy preference relations and T-multiplicative consistency property for multiplicative preference relations which consist of a relaxation of the additive and multiplicative consistency properties.

References

1. F. Chiclana, F. Herrera, E. Herrera-Viedma, Integrating three representation models in fuzzy multipurpose decision making based on fuzzy preference relations, Fuzzy Sets and Systems 97 (1998) 33–48.
2. F. Chiclana, F. Herrera, E. Herrera-Viedma, Integrating multiplicative preference relations in a multipurpose decision making model based on fuzzy preference relations, Fuzzy Sets and Systems 112 (2001) 277–291.
3. B. De Baets, M. Delgado, F. Herrera, E. Herrera-Viedma, J. Fodor, L. Martínez (Guest Editors), Preference Modelling and Applications (Special Issue), Fuzzy Sets and Systems 137 (1) (2003) 1–190.
4. D. Dubois, H. Prade, Fuzzy Sets and Systems: Theory and Application, (Academic Press, New York, 1980).
5. E. Forman, S. Gass, The analytic hierarchy process-An exposition, Operations Research 49 (2001) 469–86.
6. F. Herrera, E. Herrera-Viedma, F. Chiclana, Multiperson decision making based on multiplicative preference relations, European Journal of Operational Research 129 (2001) 372–385.
7. E. Herrera-Viedma, F. Herrera, F. Chiclana, A consensus model for multiperson decision making with different preference structures, IEEE Transaction on Systems, Man and Cybernetics - Part A: Systems and Humans 32 (2002) 394–402.
8. E. Herrera-Viedma, F. Herrera, F. Chiclana, M. Luque, Some issues on consistency of fuzzy preference relations, European Journal of Operational Research 154 (1) pp. 98–109.
9. R.D. Luce, P. Suppes, Preferences, Utility and subject probability. In: R.D. Luce et al., Eds., Handbook of Mathematical Psychology, Vol. III, (Wiley, New York, 1965) 249–410.

10. G. A. Miller, The magical number seven plus or minus two: some limits on our capacity of processing information, Psychological Review 63 (1956) 81–97.
11. Th. L. Saaty, The Analytic Hierarchy Process (McGraw-Hill, New York, 1980).
12. Th. L. Saaty, Fundamentals of Decision Making and Priority Theory with the AHP (RWS Publications, Pittsburg, 1994).
13. Th. L. Saaty ,L. Vargas, Models, Methods, Concepts and Applications of the Analytic Hierarchy Process (Kluwer, Boston, 2000).
14. A. K. Sen, Social Choice Theory : A Re-Examination, Econometrica, 45 (1977) 53–89. 45-53.
15. T. Tanino, Fuzzy preference orderings in group decision making, Fuzzy Sets and Systems 12 (1984) 117–131.
16. T. Tanino, Fuzzy preference relations in group decision making. In: J. Kacprzyk, M. Roubens (Eds.), Non-conventional Preference Relations in Decision Making (Springer-Verlag, Berlin, 1988) 54–71.
17. H.-J. Zimmermann, Fuzzy Set Theory and Its Applications (Kluwer, Dordrecht, 1991).

Management of uncertainty orderings through ASP

Andrea Capotorti [a] and Andrea Formisano [b]

[a] Dipartimento di Matematica e Informatica, Università di Perugia, Italy
[b] Dipartimento di Informatica, Università dell'Aquila, Italy

Abstract

Traditionally, most of the proposed probabilistic models of decision under uncertainty rely on numerical measures and representations. Alternative proposals call for qualitative (non-numerical) treatment of uncertainty, based on preference relations and belief orders. The automation of both numerical and non-numerical frameworks surely represents a preliminary step in the development of inference engines of intelligent agents, expert systems, and decision-support tools.

In this paper we exploit Answer Set Programming to formalize and reason about uncertainty expressed as belief orders. The availability of ASP-solvers supports the design of automated tools to handle such formalizations. Our proposal reveals particularly suitable whenever the domain of discernment is partial. *We first illustrate how to automatically "classify", according to the most well-known uncertainty frameworks, any given qualitative uncertainty assessment. Then, we show how to compute an enlargement of the assessment, to any other new inference target.*

Key words: Uncertainty orderings, ASP, partial assessments, general inference

Introduction

Uncertainty orderings are receiving wider and wider attention in AI literature, either as theoretical tools to deal directly with belief management [1,6,8], or inside the more articulated framework of decision-making theory [9–11,13]. This burst of interest translates into a wider application of uncertainty orderings, as qualitative assessments better fit the nature of human judgments, while do not suffer intrinsic difficulties typical of numerical elicitations. As happened for numerical methods, there have been proposed various uncertainty orderings different from traditional probabilistic ones. The main purpose of all of these proposals is to generalize the "additive" character of (unconditional) probabilities. Clearly, different generalizations are possible and several families of qualitative judgments appeared in literature. All of them share common basic properties, but differentiate on the way of combining pieces of information. By following [5,8,16,17], in [2–4] various preference orderings have been fully classified according to their agreement with the most well-known numerical models; both for "complete" (i.e. defined on well structured and closed supports) and "partial" assessments (i.e. defined only among some of the quantities involved). Such axiomatic classifications revealed a coarser grained differentiation with respect to numerical models: different uncertainty measures share the same qualitative properties in combining pieces of information.

The detected classes have been characterized by identifying specific axioms that the orderings must satisfy. Apart from qualitative probabilities, such axioms are of direct declarative reading, as they involve only logical and preference relations. As we will see, such a declarative character supports a straightforward translation of the axioms within the logical framework of ASP. Consequently, we immediately obtain an executable ASP-specification able to discriminate between the different uncertainty orderings. More specifically, this is done by exploiting an ASP-solver (in our case SModels, cf. [18]) that determines which axioms are violated by the given preference relation expressing user's believes comparisons.

Notice that, by proceeding in this way, we actually invert the usual attitude towards qualitative management of uncertainty. In fact, specific axioms are usually set in advance, so that only relations satisfying them are admitted. Here, on the contrary, given a fixed preference relation, our goal consists in ascertain which are the reasonable rules to work with.

In this paper, we mainly focus on the treatment of partial orderings, even if also total relations can be dealt with by the very same machinery. The rational behind this choice is that incomplete assessments appear more realistic models of phenomena which are open to include new (and maybe unexpected) evidences or considerations. In this frame of mind, an interesting problem is that of finding an extension of a preference relation so as to take into account any further event extraneous to the initial assessment. This should be achieved in a way that the initial ordering and its extension satisfy the same axioms. Hence, first, the initial (partial) preference relation is classified by identifying its characterizing rules Then, by exploiting the same approach the extension sought for is determined.

1. Axioms characterizing partial uncertainty orderings

In [2–4] axioms have been introduced to distinguish alternative possible approaches to qualitative uncertainty. In particular, according to the major uncertainty frameworks, a full classification of partial orderings has been proposed in [4]. In what follows we face a problem left open in [4]. Namely, we propose an inferential system to classify a given partial ordinal relation into one of the classes.

Let us start by briefly recalling the basic notions on uncertainty orderings and on their axiomatic classification. We will not enter into the details of the motivations for such classification, the reader is referred to [2–4]. The domain of discernment will be represented by a finite set of events $\mathcal{E} = \{E_1, \ldots, E_n\}$. Among them, ϕ and Ω will denote the impossible and the sure event, respectively. The events in $\mathcal{E}$ are seen as the relevant propositions on which the subject of the analysis can, or wants, to express his/her opinion. Hence, usually $\mathcal{E}$ does not represent a full model, i.e. it does not comprehend all elementary situations and all of their combinations. For this reason, a crucial component of partial assessments is the knowledge of the logical relationships holding among the events E_i's. Usual relationships are those of incompatibility, implication, combination and equivalence. Anyhow, any logical constraint can be potentially expressed. Such constraints are usually represented as a set $\mathcal{C}$ of clauses among the E_i's and such clauses are intended to be always verified. Taking into account $\mathcal{C}$, the family $\mathcal{E}$ spans a minimal Boolean algebra $\mathcal{A_E}$ containing $\mathcal{E}$ itself. Note that $\mathcal{A_E}$ is only implicitly defined via $\mathcal{E}$ and $\mathcal{C}$ and it is not a part of the assessment. Anyway, $\mathcal{A_E}$ will be referenced as a supporting structure. More formally, we have:

Definition 1. Let $\mathcal{E}$ be a set of events and $\mathcal{C}$ a collection of constraints on $\mathcal{E}$. $\mathcal{A_E}$ is the minimal algebra $(\mathcal{A}, \vee, \wedge, ^-, \phi, \Omega)$ satisfying $\mathcal{C}$ and such that $\mathcal{E} \subseteq \mathcal{A}$.

Clearly, such an algebra induces a lattice structure on $\mathcal{A}$. The ATOMS of $\mathcal{A_E}$ are the minimal elements of the (sub-)lattice $\mathcal{A_E} \setminus \{\phi\}$. Consequently, each event corresponds to a set of atoms, and $\mathcal{A_E}$ is (partially) ordered by set inclusion.

An useful piece of notation: in what follows, given any binary relation R, the writing $\neg(ARB)$ will mean that the pair $\langle A, B \rangle$ does not belong to R.

Definition 2. Let $\mathcal{A_E}$ be an algebra of events. A binary relation $\preccurlyeq^*$ over $\mathcal{A}$ is a (TOTAL) PREFERENCE ORDER if it satisfies the following conditions:
(A1) $\preccurlyeq^*$ is a pre-order, i.e. it is reflexive, transitive, and total;
(A2) $\phi \preccurlyeq^* \Omega$ and $\neg(\Omega \preccurlyeq^* \phi)$;
(A3) for all events A, B, $A \subseteq B \rightarrow (A \preccurlyeq^* B)$.
Let $\preccurlyeq^*$ be a total preference order. Then, $\sim^*$ is its SYMMETRICAL PART, i.e. $\forall E_1, E_2 \ (E_1 \sim^* E_2 \leftrightarrow E_1 \preccurlyeq^* E_2 \wedge E_2 \preccurlyeq^* E_1)$. Moreover, $\prec^*$ is the ASYMMETRICAL PART of $\preccurlyeq^*$, i.e. $\forall E_1, E_2 \ (E_1 \prec^* E_2 \leftrightarrow E_1 \preccurlyeq^* E_2 \wedge \neg(E_2 \sim^* E_1))$.

Definition 3. Let $\preccurlyeq$ and $\prec$ be two binary relations over a set of events $\mathcal{E}$, such that $E_1 \prec E_2 \rightarrow E_1 \preccurlyeq E_2$. The pair $\langle \preccurlyeq, \prec \rangle$ is a WEAK PREFERENCE STRUCTURE for $\mathcal{E}$ (w.p.s., for short) if exists a total preference order $\preccurlyeq^*$ over $\mathcal{A_E}$ such that:
$$\forall E_1, E_2 \in \mathcal{E} \ \big((E_1 \preccurlyeq E_2 \rightarrow E_1 \preccurlyeq^* E_2) \wedge (E_1 \prec E_2 \rightarrow E_1 \prec^* E_2)\big).$$

Notice that Definition 3 does not require neither $\preccurlyeq$ or $\prec$ to be total orders, nor $\prec$

to be the asymmetrical part of $\preccurlyeq$. On the other hand, it is required that $\preccurlyeq^*$ extends $\preccurlyeq$, and that $\prec^*$ (the asymmetrical part of $\preccurlyeq^*$) extends $\prec$.

For any weak preference structure $\langle \preccurlyeq, \prec \rangle$ for $\mathcal{E}$, the following properties hold:
(A1') if there exist $E_1, \ldots, E_n \in \mathcal{E}$ such that $E_1 \preccurlyeq E_2 \preccurlyeq \ldots \preccurlyeq E_n \preccurlyeq E_1$, then $\neg(E_i \prec E_j)$ for all $i, j \in \{1, \ldots, n\}$;
(A2') $\neg(\Omega \preccurlyeq \phi)$;
(A3') for all $E_1, E_2 \in \mathcal{E}$, $E_1 \prec E_2 \to E_2 \not\sqsubseteq E_1$.
Conditions **(A1')**–**(A3')** ensure the existence of a total preference order $\preccurlyeq^*$ which enlarges $\langle \preccurlyeq, \prec \rangle$. As a matter of fact, Capacities constitute the most general numerical tool to manage uncertainty, as they express "common sense" behaviors. In our context, any reasonable relation $\preccurlyeq$ must be representable by a partial Capacity (i.e., a restriction of a Capacity measure to the set of events at hand). This corresponds exactly to the satisfaction of the conditions **(A1')**–**(A3')**. Mathematical properties of orders satisfying such *basic axioms* are deeply investigated in [6].

Definition 4. Let $\mathcal{E}$ be a set of events. A total preference order $\preccurlyeq^*$ over $\mathcal{A}_\mathcal{E}$ is said to be REPRESENTABLE by a numerical measure $f : \mathcal{A}_\mathcal{E} \to [0, 1]$ iff for all $E_1, E_2 \in \mathcal{A}_\mathcal{E}$ it holds that $E_1 \preccurlyeq^* E_2 \leftrightarrow f(E_1) \leqslant f(E_2)$.

A w.p.s. $\langle \preccurlyeq, \prec \rangle$ for $\mathcal{E}$ is said to be REPRESENTABLE by a partial uncertainty measure $g : \mathcal{E} \to [0, 1]$ iff it admits an enlargement $\preccurlyeq^*$ over $\mathcal{A}_\mathcal{E}$ which is representable by an uncertainty measure $g^* : \mathcal{A}_\mathcal{E} \to [0, 1]$ extension of g to $\mathcal{A}_\mathcal{E}$.

Differentiation among ordinal relations can be done on the basis of more specific way of combining different pieces of information. Below, we list the axioms characterizing each class. [1]

Comparative probabilities. A w.p.s. $\langle \preccurlyeq, \prec \rangle$ for $\mathcal{E}$ can be extended to a total preference order $\preccurlyeq^*$ over $\mathcal{A}_\mathcal{E}$ *representable by a probability function* iff **(CP)** for any $A_1, \ldots, A_n, B_1, \ldots, B_n \in \mathcal{E}$, with $B_i \preccurlyeq A_i, \forall i = 1, \ldots, n$, such that for some $r_1, \ldots, r_n > 0$ $\sup \sum_{i=1}^n r_i(a_i - b_i) \leq 0$ implies that $A_i \sim B_i$, for all $i = 1, \ldots, n$ (a_i, b_i denote the indicator functions of A_i, B_i, resp.).

Comparative believes. A w.p.s. $\langle \preccurlyeq, \prec \rangle$ for $\mathcal{E}$ can be extended to a total preference order $\preccurlyeq^*$ over $\mathcal{A}_\mathcal{E}$ *representable by a belief function or by a n-monotone function* (with $n \geq 2$) iff for all $A, B, C, D \in \mathcal{E}$ s.t. $A \subset B, C \subset D \subset B, D \setminus C \subseteq B \setminus A$ it holds
(B') $A \sim B \to \neg(C \prec D)$.

Comparative lower-probabilities. A w.p.s. $\langle \preccurlyeq, \prec \rangle$ for $\mathcal{E}$ can be extended to a total preference order $\preccurlyeq^*$ over $\mathcal{A}_\mathcal{E}$ *representable by a lower-probability function or by a 0-monotone function* [2] iff for all $A, B, C \in \mathcal{E}$ s.t. $A \subset B, C \subseteq B \setminus A$ it holds

---

[1] We introduce a single axiom for each class, while [4] uses two axioms, since in our characterization we close $\preccurlyeq$ by monotonicity (i.e. $A \subseteq B \to A \preccurlyeq B$).
The name of the classes comes from the representability of $\preccurlyeq^*$ by corresponding numerical measures (recall that qualitative classes are coarser than numerical measures). Axiom **(CP)** was introduced in [5], while **(B')** derives from the analogous axiom introduced for total orders in [17].
[2] "0-monotone" functions are "super-additive" i.e. $H \wedge K = \phi \to f(H \vee K) \geq f(H) + f(K)$.

(**L'**) $A \sim B \to \neg(\emptyset \prec C)$.

Comparative plausibilities. A w.p.s. $\langle \preccurlyeq, \prec \rangle$ for $\mathcal{E}$ can be extended to a total preference order $\preccurlyeq^*$ over $\mathcal{A}_\mathcal{E}$ representable by a plausibility function or by a n-alternating function (with $n \geq 2$) iff for all $A, B, C, D \in \mathcal{E}$ s.t. $A \subset B$, $C \subset D \subset B$, $D \setminus C = B \setminus A$ it holds
(**PL'**) $A \prec B \to \neg(C \sim D)$.

Comparative upper-probabilities. A w.p.s. $\langle \preccurlyeq, \prec \rangle$ for $\mathcal{E}$ can be extended to a total preference order $\preccurlyeq^*$ over $\mathcal{A}_\mathcal{E}$ representable by an upper-probability function or by a 0-alternating function [3] iff for all $A, B \in \mathcal{E}$ s.t. $A \subset B$, it holds
(**U'**) $A \prec B \to \neg(\emptyset \sim B \setminus A)$.

Comparative lower/upper-probabilities. A w.p.s. $\langle \preccurlyeq, \prec \rangle$ for $\mathcal{E}$ can be extended to a total preference order $\preccurlyeq^*$ over $\mathcal{A}_\mathcal{E}$ representable by both a lower-probability function and by an upper-probability function iff it satisfies both (**L'**) and (**U'**).
Note that only (**CP**) does not have a pure qualitative nature since it involves also indicator functions and summations. It is the only one that should require an external numerical elaboration (e.g. involving some linear programming tool like the simplex or the interior point methods). We also considered the following *necessary* axiom (i.e. it alone does not guarantee the representability of $\preccurlyeq^*$ by a probability function, but its failure ensure the not representability):

Weak comparative probabilities. If $\langle \preccurlyeq, \prec \rangle$ can be extended to a total preference order $\preccurlyeq^*$ over $\mathcal{A}_\mathcal{E}$ representable by a probability function then
(**WC**) $A \preccurlyeq B \to \neg(B \vee C \prec A \vee C)$ for all $A, B, C \in \mathcal{E}$ s.t. $A \wedge C = B \wedge C = \phi$

2. Answer set programming

In the following sections we show how to obtain executable specifications from the axiomatic classification of preference orders described so far. To this end, we employ Answer Set Programming (ASP, for short).

Let us first briefly recall the basics of such alternative style of logic programming [15]. A problem can be encoded—by using a function-free logic language—as a set of properties and constraints which describe the (candidate) solutions. More specifically, an *ASP-program* is a collection of *rules* of the form

$L_1; \ldots ; L_k; \text{not } L_{k+1}; \ldots ; \text{not } L_\ell \leftarrow L_{\ell+1}, \ldots, L_m, \text{not } L_{m+1}, \ldots, \text{not } L_n$

where $n \geqslant m \geqslant \ell \geqslant k \geqslant 0$ and each L_i is a literal, i.e., an atom A or a negation of an atom $\neg A$. The symbol $\neg$ denotes classical negation, while *not* stands for negation-as-failure (Notice that ',' and ';' stand for logical conjunction and disjunction, respectively.) The left-hand side and the right-hand side of the clause are said *head* and *body*, respectively. A rule with empty head is a *constraint*. The literals in the body of a constraint cannot be all true, otherwise they would imply falsity.

Semantics of ASP is expressed in terms of *answer sets* (or equivalently *stable models*, cf. [12]). Consider first the case of an ASP-program P which does not

---
[3] "0-alternating" functions are "sub-additive" i.e. $H \wedge K = \phi \to f(H \vee K) \leq f(H) + f(K)$.

involve negation-as-failure (i.e., $\ell = k$ and $n = m$). In this case, a set X of literals is said to be closed under P if for each rule in P, whenever $\{L_{\ell+1}, \ldots, L_m\} \subseteq X$, it holds that $\{L_1, \ldots, L_k\} \cap X \neq \emptyset$. If X is inclusion-minimal among the sets closed under P, then it is said to be an answer set for P. Such a definition is extended to any program P containing negation-as-failure by considering the *reduct* P^X (of P). P^X is defined as the set of rules of the form $L_1; \ldots; L_k \leftarrow L_{\ell+1}, \ldots, L_m$ for all rules of P such that X contains all the literals $L_{k+1}, \ldots, L_\ell$, but does not contain any of the literals $L_{m+1}, \ldots, L_n$. Clearly, P^X does not involve negation-as-failure. The set X is an answer set for P if it is an answer set for P^X.

Once a problem is described as an ASP-program P, its solutions (if any) are represented by the answer sets of P. Notice that an ASP-program may have none, one, or several answer sets.

Let us consider the program P consisting of the two rules $p; q \leftarrow$ and $\neg r \leftarrow p$. Such a program has two answer sets: $\{p, \neg r\}$ and $\{q\}$. If we add the rule (actually, a constraint) $\leftarrow q$ to P, then we rule-out the second of these answer sets, because it violates the new constraint. This simple example reveals the core of the usual approach followed in formalizing/solving a problem with ASP. Intuitively speaking, the programmer adopts a "generate-and-test" strategy: first (s)he provides a set of rules describing the collection of (all) potential solutions. Then, the addition of a group of constraints rules-out all those answer sets that are not desired real solutions.

To find the solutions of an ASP-program, an ASP-solver is used. Several solvers have became available (cf. [18], for instance), each of them being characterized by its own prominent valuable features. In this work we choose smodels as solver, together with its natural front-end lparse [14].

Expressive power of ASP, as well as, its computational complexity have been deeply investigated. The interested reader can refer to the survey [7], among others.

Let us give a simple example of ASP-program. In doing this, we will recall the syntax and the main features of lparse/smodels which will be exploited in the rest of the paper (see [14], for a more details). The problem we want to formalize in ASP is the well-known *n-queens* problem: "Given a $n \times n$ chess board, place n queens in such a way that no two of them attack each other". The two clauses below state that a candidate solution is any disposition of the queens, provided that each column of the board contains one and only one queen. (The fact that a queen is placed on the nth column and on the mth row is encoded by the atom queen(n,m).) [4]

    pos(1..n).   1{queen(Col,Row) : pos(Col)}1 :- pos(Row).

The second rule is a particular form of constraint available in smodels' language. The general form of such a kind of clauses is

$$k\{\langle property\_def \rangle : \langle range\_def \rangle\}m :-\langle search\_space \rangle$$

where: the conditions $\langle search\_space \rangle$ in the body define the set of objects of the domain to be checked; the atom $\langle property\_def \rangle$ in the head defines the property to be

---

[4] In the syntax of smodels ':-' denotes implication $\leftarrow$. The value of the constant n occurring in the first clause is a parameter of the program supplied to lparse at run-time.

checked; the conjunction ⟨range_def⟩ defines the possible values that the property may take on the objects defined in the body, namely by providing a conjunction of unary predicates each of them defining a range for one of the variables that occur in ⟨property_def⟩ but not in ⟨search_space⟩; k and m are the minimum and maximum number of values that the specified property may take on the specified objects.

We now introduce two constraints, in order to rule out those placements where two queens control either the same row or the same diagonal of the board:[5]

:- queen(C,R1), queen(C,R2), pos(C;R1;R2), R1<R2.
:- queen(C1,R1), queen(C2,R2), pos(C1;C2;R1;R2), R1<R2, abs(C1-C2)==abs(R1-R2).

Here is one of the answer sets produced by smodels, when fed with our program (in this case we put n= 8): Answer: 1. queen(4,1) queen(6,2) queen(1,3) queen(5,4) queen(2,5) queen(8,6) queen(3,7) queen(7,8)

Notice that lparse offers some elementary built-in arithmetic functions (such as abs(), in the above clause) that can be used to perform simple arithmetics. More in general, lparse allows the user to employ user-defined C or C++ functions within an ASP-program. The object code of these functions is linked with lparse at run time (cf. [14]). We exploited this feature (not available in some other solvers) to implement a basic library of functions aimed at handling sets and operation on sets.

The pair lparse/smodels constitutes an essential and neat tool for fast prototypical development. Notable facilities come from the simple albeit useful integration capabilities with the C programming language, the prompt availability of the source-code and documentation, and the ease of use.

3. Preference classification

Our first task consists in writing an ASP-program able to classify any given w. p. s. ⟨≼, ≺⟩ w.r.t. the axioms seen in Sec. 1 (Except for (CP), that, up to our knowledge, does not admit a purely declarative formulation). We start by defining in ASP the predicates prec(·,·), precneq(·,·), and equiv(·,·), to render the relators ≼, ≺, and ∼, resp. Moreover, the fact of "being an event" (i.e. a member of $\mathcal{E}$) is stated through the monadic predicate event(·).[6] Auxiliary predicates/functions are used to render set-theoretical construcs, such as ∩, ∪, and ⊆, whose implementations rely on user-defined C-libraries. The characterization of potential legal answer sets is done by asserting properties of prec(·,·), precneq(·,·), and equiv(·,·), as follows:

prec(A,B) :- event(A;B), equiv(A,B).

prec(B,A) :- event(A;B), equiv(A,B).

:- precneq(A,B), event(A;B), equiv(A,B).

---

[5] Here pos(C;R1;R2) is a shorthand notation for the three facts pos(C), pos(R1), pos(R2).
[6] Actually, in our program, events are denoted by integer numbers. Here, for the sake of readability, we systematically denote events by capital letters.

prec(A,B) :- event(A;B), precneq(A,B).

equiv(A,B) :- event(A;B), prec(B,A), prec(A,B).

Also axioms **(A1')**–**(A3')** must be imposed. For instance **(A3')** is rendered by weeding out all answer sets where $A \subseteq B \land B \prec A$ holds for some events A and B:

:- event(A;B), subset(A,B), precneq(B,A).

Consider now one of the axioms of Sec. 1, say **(B')**, for simplicity. Since, in this phase, we do not want to impose such axiom, but we just want to test whether or not it is satisfied by the preference relation at hand, we use a rule of the form:

failsB1 :- event(A;B;C), subset(A,B), A!=B, empty(B∩C), precneq(A,B), prec(B∪C,A∪C).

Having in mind **(B')** of Sec. 1, this clause is of immediate reading: the fact failsB1 is true (i.e. belongs to the answer set) whenever there exist events falsifying **(B')**. All other axioms have been treated similarly. When smodels is fed with such program and a description of an input preference relation (i.e., a collection of facts of the forms prec(·,·), precneq(·,·), and equiv(·,·)), different outcomes may be obtained:

a) If no answer set is produced, then the input weak preference structure violates some basic requirement, such as axioms **(A1')**–**(A3')**.

b) Otherwise, if an answer set is generated, there exists a numerical (partial) model representing the input weak preference structure. Moreover, the presence in the answer set of a fact of the form fails$\mathcal{C}$ (say failsL1, for example), witnesses that the corresponding axiom (**(L')** in the case) is violated by the given preference order. Consequently, the given order (as well as its extensions) is not compatible with the uncertainty framework ruled by $\mathcal{C}$ (in the case of failsL1, the given order cannot be represented by a partial Lower probability).

Example 1. Suppose a physician wants to perform a preliminary evaluation about the reliability of a test for SARS (Severe Acute Respiratory Syndrome). Up to his/her knowledge, the SARS diagnosis is based on moderate or severe respiratory symptoms and on the positivity or indeterminacy of an adopted clinical test about the presence of the SARS-associated antibody coronavirus SARS-CoV). The elements appearing in his/her analysis can be schematized as:

A ≡ *Normal respiratory symptoms*, B ≡ *Moderate respiratory symptoms*,
C ≡ *Severe respiratory symptoms*, D ≡ *Moderate or severe respiratory symptoms*,
E ≡ *Death from pulmonary diseases*, F ≡ *Positive or indeterminate clinical test*,

subject to these (logical) restrictions: A∩B=∅, B∩C=∅, A∩C=∅, A∪B∪C=Ω, D=B∪C, E⊂C, F∩A=∅. Consider the w.p.s. $\langle \preccurlyeq, \prec \rangle$ so described: precneq(∅,C). precneq(C,B). prec(B,A). precneq(C,D). precneq(E,C). precneq(E,D). precneq(F,A). equiv(A∪E,A∪C). Due to events' meaning, such order seems reasonable. If it is given as input to smodels, the answer set found includes the facts failsB1 and failsWC. This means that the given preference relation agrees with the basic axioms, however it cannot be managed by using neither a Probability nor a Belief function. Nevertheless, one can use comparative Lower probabilities or comparative Plausibilities. □

4. Partial-order extension

An interesting problem is that of finding an extension of a preference relation so as to take into account any further event extraneous to the initial assessment. This should be achieved in a way that the extension retains the same character of the initial order (e.g., both satisfy the same axioms). More precisely, let be given an initial (partial) assessment expressed as a (partial) order $\preccurlyeq$ over set of known events $\mathcal{E}$. Assume that $\preccurlyeq$ satisfies the axioms characterizing a specific class, say $\mathcal{C}$, of orders (cf. Sec. 3). Consider a new event S (not in $\mathcal{E}$), implicitly described by a collection $\mathcal{C}'$ of set-theoretical constraints involving the events of $\mathcal{E}$. In the spirit of [5, Thm. 3], the problem we are going to tackle is: Determine which is the "minimal" extension $\preccurlyeq^+$ (over $\mathcal{E} \cup \{S\}$) of $\preccurlyeq$, induced by the new event, which still belongs to the class $\mathcal{C}$. In other words, we are interested in ascertaining how the new event S must relate to the members of $\mathcal{E}$ in order that $\preccurlyeq^+$ still is in $\mathcal{C}$. To this aim we want to determine the sub-collections $\mathcal{L}_S$, $\mathcal{WL}_S$, $\mathcal{U}_S$, and $\mathcal{WU}_S$, of $\mathcal{E}$ so defined:

$E \in \mathcal{L}_S$ iff no extension $\preccurlyeq^*$ of $\preccurlyeq$ can infer that $S \preccurlyeq^* E$
$E \in \mathcal{WL}_S$ iff no extension $\preccurlyeq^*$ of $\preccurlyeq$ can infer that $S \prec^* E$
$E \in \mathcal{U}_S$ iff no extension $\preccurlyeq^*$ of $\preccurlyeq$ can infer that $E \preccurlyeq^* S$
$E \in \mathcal{WU}_S$ iff no extension $\preccurlyeq^*$ of $\preccurlyeq$ can infer that $E \prec^* S$

Consequently, in order to satisfy the axioms characterizing $\mathcal{C}$, any weak preference structure $\langle \preccurlyeq^+, \prec^+ \rangle$ extending $\langle \preccurlyeq, \prec \rangle$ must, at least, impose that:

$E \prec^+ S \, \forall E \in \mathcal{L}_S, \quad E \preccurlyeq^+ S \, \forall E \in \mathcal{WL}_S, \quad S \prec^+ E \, \forall E \in \mathcal{U}_S, \quad S \preccurlyeq^+ E \, \forall E \in \mathcal{WU}_S.$

We describe now an ASP-program that solves this problem by taking advantage from the computation done during the classification phase: It gets as input the knowledge regarding the satisfied axiom(s), the preference and logical relations on the original set of events, and the description of the new event (see Example 2).

The handling of the axioms is done by ASP-rules of the form (we give here the rule for (**L'**). Other axioms are treated similarly):

:- holdsL1, event(A;B), empty(N), empty(A∩B), precneq(N,A), prec(A∪B,B).

Rules of this kind (actually, constraints, in the sense described in Sec. 2), declare "undesirable" any extension for which the axiom is violated. For instance, consider a ground instance of the above rule; whenever the fact holdsL1 is present (i.e. is true in an answer set), then to make the (ground) clause satisfied, at least one of the other literals must not belong to the answer set. (Notice that, these literals are all true exactly when (**L'**) is violated.) Consequently, in order to activate this constraint (i.e. to impose axiom (**L'**), for the case at hand) it suffices to add the fact holdsL1 to the input of the solver.

A further rule describes the potential answer set we are interested in:

1{ precneq(A,B), equiv(A,B), precneq(B,A) }1 :- event(A;B).

This rule simply asserts that any computed answer-set must predicate on each pair A,B of events by stating exactly one, and only one, of the three facts precneq(A,B), equiv(A,B), and precneq(B,A). Then, smodels calculates the answer sets fulfilling the desired requirements and encoding "legal" total orders.

The collections $\mathcal{L}_S$, $\mathcal{WL}_S$, $\mathcal{U}_S$, and $\mathcal{WU}_S$ can be obtained by computing the intersection Cn of all these answer sets. (Or, equivalently, by computing the set of logical consequences of the ASP-program. Notice that, in general, Cn needs not to be an answer set by itself.) Unfortunately, not all the available ASP-solvers offer the direct computation of Cn as a built-in feature (DLV, for instance does, while smodels does not, cf. [18]). In general, a simple inspection of the answer sets generated by smodels allows one to detect the minimal extension of the preference relation which is mandatory for each total order. We designed a simple post-processor which filters smodels' output and produces the imposed extension of $\preccurlyeq$.

Example 2. Consider the weak preference structure of Example 1 and the new event
$$S \equiv \text{The real state of having SARS}$$
subject to these restrictions: $S \subset F$ and $F \cap E \subset S$. Since in Example 1 we discovered that the initial preference relation satisfies axiom **(PL')**, we want to impose such axiom and compute the extension of the initial order. Once filtered smodels' output, we obtained the following result:[7] precneq(S,A∪C) precneq(S,A∪E) precneq(S,D) precneq(S,A) precneq(S,Ω) prec(∅,S) prec(S,F) ... showing that, apart from obvious relations induced by monotonicity, no significant constraint involving S can be inferred. Since S and E can be freely compared, this result suggests that either further investigation about relevance of the clinical test or a revision of the initial preference relation, should be performed. □

The availability of automated tools able to extend preference orders, whenever new knowledge (new events) is acquired, directly suggests applications in expert systems and decision-support tools. In automated diagnosis, planning, or problem solving, to mention some examples, one could easily imagine scenarios where knowledge is not entirely available from the beginning. We could outline how a rudimental inference process could develop, by identifying the basic steps an automated agent should perform:
0) Acquisition of an initial collection of observations (events) about the object of the analysis, together with a (qualitative) partial preference assessment;
1) Detection of which is the most adequate (i.e., the most discriminant) uncertainty framework, through a "preference classification phase" (cf. Sec. 3);
2) Whenever new knowledge becomes available, refine agent's description of the real world by performing order extension (which substantially corresponds to knowledge inference. Cf. Sec. 4).
The results of step 2) could be then exploited to guide further investigations on the real world, in order to obtain new information. Then, step 2) will be repeated and the process will continue until further pieces of knowledge are obtainable or an enough accurate degree of believe is achieved.

---

[7] We list here only the portion of the extension involving the new event S.

Conclusions

In this paper we started an exploration of the potentialities offered by ASP for building decision support systems based on qualitative judgments. The implementation of what could be thought as a kernel of an inference engine sprouted almost naturally. Certainly, our research is at an initial stage and the implementation we reported on is just a prototype. Next step in this research would consist in validating the proposed approach by means of a number of benchmarks aimed at testing our prototype on the ground of real applications. Results of this activity will help in consolidating the prototype. In this context, a further goal consists in completing our approach so as to handle comparative Probabilities too. Since no axiomatic characterization of comparative Probabilities is known (up to our knowledge), this aim should be achieved through integration with efficient linear optimization tools (such as the column generation techniques). More in general, we envisage the design of a full-blown automated system which integrates different (in someway complementary) techniques and methods for uncertainty management; comprehending mixed numerical/qualitative assessments and conditional frameworks.

References

1. T. Bilgiç (2001) Fusing interval preferences, in *Proc. of EUROFUSE Workshop on Preference Modelling and Applications*, pp. 253–258.
2. A. Capotorti, G. Coletti, and B. Vantaggi (1998) Non additive ordinal relations representable by lower or upper probabilities. *Kybernetika*, **34**(1):79–90.
3. A. Capotorti and B. Vantaggi (1998) Relationships among ordinal relations on a finite set of events. In *Information, Uncertainty, Fusion*, Eds. B. Bouchon-Meunier, R. R. Yager and L. A. Zadeh, pp. 447–458.
4. A. Capotorti and B. Vantaggi (2000) Axiomatic characterization of partial ordinal relations. *Int. J. of Approximate Reasoning*, **24**:207–219.
5. G. Coletti (1990) Coherent qualitative probability. *J. Math. Psych.*, **34**:297–310.
6. G. de Cooman (1997) Confidence Relations and Ordinal Information. *Inform. Sci.*, **104**.
7. E. Dantsin, T. Eiter, G. Gottlob, and A. Voronkov (2001) Complexity and expressive power of logic programming. *ACM Comput. Surveys*, **33**(3):374–425.
8. D. Dubois (1986) Belief Structure, Possibility Theory and Decomposable Confidence Measures on Finite Sets. *Comput. Artif. Intell.*, **5**(5):403–416.
9. D. Dubois, H. Fargier, and H. Prade (1997) Decision-making under ordinal preferences and uncertainty, *AAAI Spring Symposium on Qualitative Preferences in Deliberation and Practical Reasoning*, pp. 41–46.
10. D. Dubois, H. Prade, and R. Sabbadin (1997) A possibilistic logic machinery for qualitative decision, *AAAI Spring Symposium on Qualitative Preferences in Deliberation and Practical Reasoning*, pp. 47–54.

11. P. H. Giang, P. P. Shenoy (2001) A comparison of axiomatic approaches to qualitative decision making under possibility theory, *Proc. of the 17th Conf. on Uncertainty in Artificial Intelligence UAI01*, pp. 162–170.
12. M. Gelfond and V. Lifschitz (1988) *The stable model semantics for logic programming*, Proc. ILPS-5, pp. 1070–1080.
13. D. Lehmann (1996) Generalized qualitative probability: Savage revisited, *Proc. of 12th Conf. on Uncertainty in Artificial Intelligence UAI96*, pp. 381–388.
14. T. Syrjänen (2001) *Lparse 1.0 User's Manual*.
15. W. Marek and M. Truszczyński (1999) *Stable models and an alternative logic programming paradigm*. The Logic Programming Paradigm: a 25-Year Perspective, Springer, pp. 375–398.
16. P. Walley and T. Fine (1979) Varieties of modal (classificatory) and comparative probability. *Synthese*, **41**:321–374.
17. S. K. M. Wong, Y. Y. Yao, P. Bollmann, and H. C. Bürger (1991) Axiomatization of Qualitative Belief Structure. *IEEE Trans. on System, Man, and Cybernetics*, **21**:726–734.
18. Web resources for ASP solvers. CModels: `www.cs.utexas.edu/users/tag/cmodels.html`; DLV: `www.dbai.tuwien.ac.at/proj/dlv`; SModels: `www.tcs.hut.fi/Software/smodels`;

CLASSIFICATION AND DATA MINING

Automating the quality assurance of an on-line knowledge-based classifier by fusing multiple off-line classifiers

Piero P. Bonissone

General Electric Global Research, Schenectady, NY 12309, USA

Abstract

We address two problems in the lifecycle of a production classifier: the monitoring of its decisions quality and the updating of the classifier over time. The proposed architecture consists of four off-line classifiers and an associative fusion module. The fusion is a T-norm based outer-product of the classifiers' normalized outputs. By attaching a confidence measure to each output of the fusion, we generate a distribution of the production classifier's quality. The lower tail of this distribution identifies the least reliable cases, which become candidates for auditing and manual QA. The upper tail identifies the most reliable cases, which become candidates for updating the standard reference data set used to design and tune the production classifier. We illustrate this approach with an insurance underwriting problem.

Key words: Classification, Fusion, T-norms, Fuzzy Constraints

1. Introduction

The automation of real-world decision-making processes requires addressing the lifecycle of its underlying decision engines. The development and deployment of such engines represent the first stage of their lifecycle. Once an engine has been placed in production, it is important to monitor its performance and probe the quality of its decisions. In previous papers we have described the design and optimization of two decision engines for underwriting insurance applications. Both engines, based on fuzzy constraints and fuzzy case-based reasoning [1,3], used an evolutionary algorithm to optimize their underlying parameters and minimize the cost of misclassification [4]. The core of this optimization was the generation of a set of Standard Reference Decisions (SRD). In ref. [5] we discussed the lifecycle of a classifier with an emphasis on its validation, verification, and knowledge-base maintenance. In this paper we focus on the monitoring and quality assurance of the production classifier.

2. The Classification Problem

As presented in ref. [5], we use the process of underwriting insurance applications as our representative classification problem. Insurance underwriting (UW) is a complex decision-making task traditionally performed by trained individuals. An underwriter must evaluate each insurance application in terms of its potential risk for generating a claim, e.g. mortality in the case of term life insurance. The application is then classified into one of the risk categories available for the type of insurance requested by the applicant. The estimated risk, in conjunction with factors such as gender, age, and policy face value, will determine the appropriate premium for the insurance policy. We define an insurance application as an input vector $\overline{X}$ containing discrete, continuous, and attribute variables. These variables represent the applicant's medical information that has been identified by actuarial studies to be pertinent to the estimation of the applicant's claim risk. Similarly, we define the output space $\overline{Y}$, e.g. the underwriting decision space, as an ordered list of rate-classes. The underwriting process can be summarized as a discrete classifier that maps an input vector $\overline{X}$ into a decision space $\overline{Y}$, where: $|\overline{X}| = n$ and $|\overline{Y}| = T$.

The UW problem is further complicated by these factors: (i) the mapping from $\overline{X}$ to $\overline{Y}$ is a *highly nonlinear;* (ii) the UW guidelines require *interpretations* to find the correct balance between *risk-tolerance*, necessary to maintain price competitiveness, and *risk-avoidance*, necessary to prevent overexposure to risk; (iii) legal and compliance regulations require that the models used to make the underwriting decisions be *transparent* and *interpretable*.

We extended traditional AI reasoning methodologies, such as rule-based and case-based reasoning, with soft computing techniques, such as fuzzy logic and evolutionary algorithms. With these hybrids systems, we provide flexibility and consistency, while maintaining interpretability and accuracy.

3. The Production Classifier

For this application we used a Fuzzy Logic Engine (FLE) based on rule-encoded underwriting standards. Each rule set is an intersection of fuzzy constraints defining the boundaries between rate classes. First, these constraints were determined from underwriting guidelines. Then, they were refined using knowledge engineering sessions with expert underwriters to identify factors such as blood pressure levels and cholesterol levels, which were critical in defining the applicant's risk and corresponding premium. The goal of the classifier is to assign an applicant to the most competitive rate class, providing that the applicant's vital data meet all of the constraints of that particular rate class to a minimum degree of satisfaction. The constraints for each rate class r are represented by n fuzzy sets: $A_i^r(x_i)$ $i=1,...,n$. Each value $A_i^r(x_i)$ is interpreted as the *degree of preference* induced by value x_i for satisfying constraint A_i^r. After evaluating all constraints, we compute two measures for each rate class r. The first one is the *degree of intersection* of all constraints and measures the *weakest* constraint satisfaction:

$$I(r) = \bigcap_{i=1}^{n} A_i^r(x_i) = Min_{i=1}^{n} A_i^r(x_i) \quad ^1 \tag{1}$$

The second one is a *cumulative* measure of missing points (the complement of the average satisfaction of all constraints), and measures the *overall tolerance* allowed to each applicant i.e.:

$$MP(r) = \sum_{i=1}^{n} (1 - A_i^r(x_i)) = n\left(1 - \frac{1}{n}\sum_{i=1}^{n} A_i^r(x_i)\right) = n(1 - \overline{A}^r) \tag{2}$$

The final classification is obtained by comparing the two measures, *I(r)* and *MP(r)* against two lower bounds defined by thresholds τ_1 and τ_2. The parametric definition of each fuzzy constraint $A_i^r(x_i)$ and the values of τ_1 and τ_2 are design parameters that were initialized with knowledge engineering sessions. After a parametric optimization and a five-fold cross-validation, described in [4,5,8] the classifier was placed in production.

4. Lifecycle Stages after Deployment: Monitoring and Maintenance

A serious challenge to the successful deployment of intelligent systems is their ability to remain valid and accurate over time, while compensating for drifts and accounting for contextual changes that might otherwise render their knowledge-base stale or obsolete. This issue has been an ongoing concern in deploying AI expert systems and continues to be a critical issue in deploying knowledge-based classifiers. The maintenance of a classifier is essential to its long-term usefulness since, over time, the configuration of a FLE may become sub-optimal. It is necessary to modify the SRD over time to reflect these contextual changes. We developed specialized editors to achieve this objective. By modifying the SRD to incorporate the desired changes (by altering previous standard reference decisions), we create a new *target* for the classifier. Then, we use the same evolutionary optimization tools to find a new configuration for the classifier to *approximate the new target*.

It is equally important to monitor the classifier performance over time to identify those new, highly reliable cases that could be used to update the SRD. To address this objective, we have implemented an off-line quality assurance (QA) process, based on a fusion module, to test and monitor the production FLE that performs on-line rate classification. At periodic intervals, e.g., every week, the fusion module and its components will review the decisions made by the FLE during the previous week. The purpose of this fusion is to assess the quality of the FLE performance over that week. This fusion will identify the *best* cases, which could be used to tune the production engine, and *controversial* or *unusual* cases, which could be audited or reviewed by human underwriters.

In our approach we designed the classifiers around a set of *Standard Reference Decisions* (SRD), which embodies the results of the ideal behavior that we want to *reach* during development and that we want to *track* during production use. The SRD are the training and validation set for the classifier, and in general are a benchmark set that must be maintained over time. To this end we propose to use a fusion module for updating the SRD with new cases, without requiring expensive manual screenings [5].

---

[1] This expression implies that each criterion has equal weight. If we want to attach a weight w_i to each criterion A_i we could use the weighted minimum operator:

$$I'(r) = \bigcap_{i=1}^{n} W_i A_i^r(x_i) = Min_{i=1}^{n}\left(Max\left((1-w_i), A_i^r(x_i)\right)\right), \text{ where } w_i \in [0,1].$$

5. Architecture for the Quality Assurance

To ensure the integrity of the cases used to update the SRD, we decided to develop a collection of independent classifiers specially tuned for accuracy. These classifiers, which do not need to meet the same interpretability requirements as the FLE, are part of the fusion process described in Figure 1.

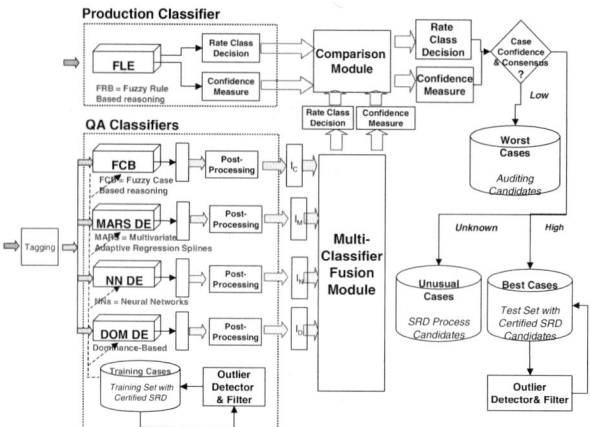

Figure 1: Top-level Fusion Architecture

This process is decomposed into four steps that will be discussed in Section 7: (i) tag inputs, and post-process classifiers' outputs; (ii) combine decisions via the associative fusion of the classifiers' outputs; (iii) determine a confidence measure; (iv) identify candidate cases for auditing and SRD updating.

6. Classifiers Used in the Fusion Module

6.1 Fuzzy Case-Based Engine

Rule-based engines are *generative* approaches to develop knowledge-based solutions, while Case-based (CB) engines are *analogical* approaches to solve the same problems. Knowledge engineering is used to determine the most efficient indices for representing cases, to define the fuzzy similarity metric that induces the best ranking upon the retrieved cases, and to adapt the solution of the closest cases to the application on hand. The parameters used by case-based systems to search for similar cases and to rank them are design choices that need to be determined and maintained over time for optimal performance. The CB engine executes four basic steps [1,3]: (i) compares a probe against the CB of past cases and retrieves cases that are similar to the probe; (ii) calculates a distance between each retrieved case and the probe to quantify the similarity between the two cases; (iii) generates a weighted histogram of the rate-class distribution for the retrieved neighboring cases; (iv) determines a solution for the probe case using the median of the resulting histogram.

6.2. Feed-forward Neural Network (NN) Classifier

A NN with multiple output nodes is the typical design for multiple-class classifiers. However, these NN's have large number of weights and biases. As such, they require large training sets and long training time. Since in the UW problem the size of the training set is relatively small (in comparison with the number of features and classes) we used multiple binary NN's to perform the multi-class classification. This approach not only reduces the complexity of the network and its training time, but also improves the classification performance. Each binary network has the structure of 12-5-1, i.e., 12 input nodes, 5 hidden neurons, and 1 output node. Activation functions for both hidden and output neurons are logistic sigmoidal functions. The range of target values is scaled to [0.1 0.9] to prevent saturation during training process. The Levenberg-Marquardt numerical optimization technique is used as the back-propagation learning algorithm to achieve second-order training speed. Each binary network represents an individual rate class and is trained with the targets of one-vs-other. During classification for an unknown case, each network generates a partial membership value of the unknown case to the class represented by the network. The *max* rule determines the final rate-class assignment of the unknown case.

6.3. MARS-Based Classifier

MARS (multivariate regression splines) [7] is an adaptive nonparametric regression technique, able to capture main and interaction effects in a hierarchical manner. Being a piecewise-linear adaptive regression procedure, MARS can approximates very well any non-linear structure, if present. However, global models cannot easily incorporate jumps in decision boundaries of a large number of variables in an extremely small bounded range. To address this problem we used a *Tag* encoding (section 7.1), which leverages domain knowledge to help MARS search algorithm in initializing the "knots" in the right place. Then we created a collection of MARS models, each of which solves a two-class problem, and we collated their outputs in a manner similar to the one used for the NN classifiers.

6.4. Dominance-Based Classifier

All input variables in a vector $\overline{X}$ describing an application can be constructed such as smaller values represent more desirable values. We use the partial order induced by the "≤" operator over the input vectors to indicate this preference. When vector $\overline{X}_1$ *dominates* $\overline{X}_2$, then we know that its associated rate-class cannot be worse than the one associated with $\overline{X}_2$. Using this dominance concept, we generated two subsets for each rate-class: the *Pareto-best* subset and the *Pareto-worst* subset, representing the *least risky* and the *most risky* candidates within the same rate-class. These subsets are samples of two risk surfaces in the feature space that bound the rate-class from above and below. The classifier will assign a rate-class to a new candidate by verifying if it lies within these two bounding risk surfaces. When this occurs, the decision is always correct. Since, this situation is not very frequent (~20% coverage in the UW problem), this classifier produces very low coverage at maximum accuracy.

7. Fusion module

7.1 Input Tagging, Output Generation, Discounting, and Outputs Post-processing

Tagging. Data-driven algorithms can improve their performance if they can leverage domain-knowledge. In our case, we wanted to use existing knowledge about risk classification to influence the classifiers. Using data-mining experiments, we identified four input variables, among the ones defined by actuarial studies, which had the highest impact on the rate-class decision. Since the same studies indicate the critical thresholds that govern such risk, there was no reason to re-learn the thresholds and guidelines. We defined a set of inequality constraints on these four variables and represented them as crisp rules. With these rules, we created a *tag*, which was an ordinal variable developed from a collection of indicators for the various decision boundaries defined by human experts. The use of available domain knowledge boosted the classifiers' performance, leading to an average accuracy improvement of ~1-2%.

Output Generation. The output of each classifier is a distribution representing the degree to which a rate class is selected. The set of all possible rate classes represents the universe of answers that can be considered by the classifiers. An assignment to the universe represents the classifier's *ignorance*. Specifically, each module generates an output vector $I = [I(1), I(2), \ldots I(N+1)]$ where $I(i) \in [0, M]$ where M is a large real value and N is the number of rate-classes. Each entry $I(i)$, for $i=1, \ldots, N$, is the un-normalized degree to which the case could be classified in rate class i. The last element, $I(N+1)$ indicates the degree to which the case cannot be decided and the entire universe is selected.

Discounting. The reliability of each classifier can be represented by a static or dynamic discounting factor, which reflects the expected accuracy of the classifier. In a manner similar to Shafer's belief theory [10], a static discounting factor represents a *prior* expectation about the classifier's reliability, e.g., the average past accuracy of the classifier.

Post-processing. A dynamic discounting represents a *conditional* assessment of the classifier's reliability. The post-process computes a set of features: *cardinality, entropy, the difference between the distribution's mode and the second highest value.* These features are compared with experimentally determined thresholds to assess the validity of the model's output. If the output does not meet these constraints, the model's decision is replaced by ignorance.

7.2. Combining Decisions via Associative Fusion of Models' Outputs

The different semantics of the classifiers pose a challenge to the fusion operation. While the outputs of some classifiers could be interpreted as probability densities (e.g., the histograms of cases retrieved by the CB engine), other models, such as the NN or MARS, generate possibilistic distributions or scores. We can only interpret these distributions as membership functions with a normalized cardinality, without necessarily assigning any probabilistic semantics to them. Furthermore, all classifiers share a common preprocessing annotation (Tagging) that could potentially introduce a common bias. To combine the outputs of the classifiers we propose an aggregation method that does not require orthogonality among the classifiers. The proposed method is also associative. Let us define m classifiers $S_1, \ldots S_m$, such that the output of classifier S_j is the vector I^j showing the normalized decision of such classifier to the N classes. In this case, the last $(N+1)^{th}$ element represents the universe of all classes, U, and is used to indicate the classifier's lack of commitment:

$$I^j = [\, I^j(1),\, I^j(2),\, ...,\, I^j(N+1)], \text{ where } I^j(i) \in [0,1] \text{ subject to: } \sum_{i=1}^{N+1} I^j(i) = 1$$

The un-normalized fusion of the outputs of two classifiers S_1 and S_2 is:

$$F(I^1, I^2) = Extraction\left[Outerproduct(I^1, I^2, T)\right] = Extraction[A] \qquad (3)$$

where the outer-product is a well-defined mathematical operation, which takes as arguments two N-dimensional vectors I^1 and I^2 and generates as output the NxN dimensional array A. Each element $A(i,j)$ is the result of applying the operator T to the corresponding vector elements, namely $I^1(i)$ and $I^2(j)$, i.e.:

$$A(i,j) = T[I^1(i), I^2(j)]. \qquad (4)$$

The *Extraction* operator recovers the un-normalized output in vector form:

$$Extraction[A] = [I'(1), I'(2), ..., I'(N+1)] \qquad (5)$$

$$\text{where: } I'(i) = A(i,i) + A(i, N+1) + A(N+1, i) \text{ for } i = 1, N \qquad (6)$$

$$\text{and } I'(N+1) = A(N+1, N+1) \qquad (7)$$

Equations (6) and (7) are justified by the case analysis shown in equation (10). We can derive the associativity of the fusion from that of the T-norms:

$$F(I^1, F(I^2, I^3)) = F(F(I^1, I^2), I^3), \qquad (8)$$

providing that equation (4) only contains one term. This occurs when: a) there is *no lack of commitment* in the classifiers [$A(i,N+1)=A(N+1,i)=0$ for $i=1,..., N$]; b) the *lack of commitment is complete* in one classifiers [$A(i,i)=0$ for $i=1,..., N$ and either $A(i,N+1)=I^1(i)$ & $A(N+1,i)=0$ or $A(N+1,i)= I^2(i)$ & $A(i,N+1)=0$]; c) the *lack of commitment is complete* in both classifiers [$eq(6) = 0$ & $eq(7) = 1$]. In any other case, we need the distributivity of the T-norm over the addition operator of equation (6) to preserve associativity. This distributivity is satisfied only by the scalar product. For any other T-norm the lack of associativity means that the outer-product A defined by equation (4) must be computed on all dimensions at once, using a dimensionally extended Schweizer & Sklar T-norm:

$$T_p(x_1,...,x_k) = \left[\sum_{i=1}^{k} x_i^{-p} - k + 1\right]^{-1/p} \text{ if } (p>0) \text{ or } (p<0) \text{ and } \left[\sum_{i=1}^{k} x_i^{-p}\right] \geq (k-1) \qquad (9)$$

Each element $A(i,j)$ represents the fused assignment of the two classifiers to the intersection of rate classes r_i and r_j. Given our premise that the classes are disjoint, we have four possible situations:

$$i=j \text{ and } i < (N+1) \text{ then } r_i \cap r_j = r_j \cap r_i = r_i \qquad (10a)$$
$$i=j \text{ and } i = (N+1) \text{ then } r_i \cap r_j = U \text{ (the universe of classes)} \qquad (10b)$$
$$i \neq j \text{ and } i < (N+1) \text{ and } j < (N+1) \text{ then } r_i \cap r_j = \phi \text{ (the empty set)} \qquad (10c)$$
$$i \neq j \text{ and either } i = (N+1) \text{ then } U \cap r_j = r_j \text{ or } j = (N+1) \text{ then } r_i \cap U = r_i \qquad (10d)$$

The decisions for each rate-class can be gathered by adding up *all* the weights assigned to them. According to the four possible situations described above, weights can be assigned to a specific rate class only in situations 10a) and 10d):

$$Weight(r_i) = A(i,i) + A(i,N+1) + A(N+1,i) \qquad (11)$$

$$Weight(U) = A(N+1, N+1) \qquad (12)$$

The final output is a rate-class distribution and a measure of conflict among all the classifiers. We normalize the final output (showing the degree of rate-class selection as a percentage) and identify the strongest selection of the fusion.

7.3. Determination of a Confidence Measure

We propose to use a measure of the scattering of the weights around the main diagonal as a confidence metric for the fusion. The more weights are assigned to elements outside the main diagonal, the larger is the amount of conflict among the classifiers. We can represent this concept by defining a penalty matrix $P = [P(i, j)]$ of the form:

$$P(i, j) = \begin{cases} \max(0, (1 - W * |i - j|))^d & \text{for } 1 \leq i \leq N \text{ and } 1 \leq j \leq N \\ 1 & \text{for } i = (N+1) \text{ or } j = (N+1) \end{cases} \quad (13)$$

This function rewards the presence of weights on the main diagonal, indicating agreement between the two classifiers, and penalizes the presence of weights off the main diagonal, indicating conflict. The conflict increases in magnitude as the distance from the main diagonal increases. We could use other functions to penalize elements off the main diagonal. This type of penalty function indicates that *conflict is gradual*, since the rate-classes are ordered. We want to represent the notion that the difference between r_1 and r_2 is smaller than then the one between r_1 and r_3. The shape of the penalty matrix P captures this concept, as P shows a confidence that decreases non-linearly with the distance from the main diagonal. A measure of the normalized confidence $\hat{C}$ is the sum of element-wise products between $\hat{A}$ and P, e.g.:

$$\hat{C} = \text{Normalized Confidence } (\hat{A}, P) = \sum_{i=1}^{N+1} \sum_{j=1}^{N+1} \hat{A}(i, j) * P(i, j) \quad (14)$$

and $\hat{A}$ is the normalized matrix A: $\hat{A} = A / |A|$

7.4. Identification of Candidate Cases for Auditing and Updating the SRD

Finally, we use the confidence measure and the agreement between the fusion's and the production engine's decisions to assess the quality of the latter. When the fusion produces a *low* degree of confidence, the case is flagged for *auditing*. When the fusion produces a *high* degree of confidence and agrees with the decision of the production engine, the case is selected for *augmenting the SRD*. When the fusion is non-committal, the case is selected for *review by senior underwriters* who will generate a standard reference decision. These cases will be later used to retrain the offline classifiers.

8. Experimental Results

8.1. Selecting the Lowest Quality Cases for QA.

The fusion module was tested with 1,875 applications of non-nicotine users. For a given confidence threshold ($T1=0.2$), we had an agreement between the fused decision and the engine in 92.75% of the cases, while in 2.35% the fusion did not make any decision. In 4.9% of the cases, the fusion disagreed with the production engine, identifying possible candidates for an audit. Table 1 shows the effect of changing the confidence threshold $T1$. Each column shows the number of cases whose confidence measure $\hat{C}$ is greater or equal to $T1$. As this threshold increases, so does the number of *No Fused Decision*.

Table 1: Output of Fusion for *Low* Confidence Threshold $T1$ (for non- nicotine users)

T=Product, W=0.2, d=7	Confidence Threshold T1										
	1	0.9	0.8	0.7	0.6	0.5	0.4	0.3	0.2	0.1	0
No Fused Decisions	1875	381	270	193	127	78	61	52	44	40	39
Complete asagreement	0	1462	1558	1625	1666	1686	1688	1688	1690	1692	1692
False Positive	0	14	17	18	29	41	50	54	59	59	59
False Negatives	0	13	19	24	28	43	46	48	49	49	49
Corrections	0	4	10	14	22	24	27	28	28	28	28
Complete diasagreement	0	1	1	1	3	3	3	5	5	7	8
Total	1875	1875	1875	1875	1875	1875	1875	1875	1875	1875	1875

Table 2: Summary of Fusion of Non-nicotine users (for threshold $T1 = 0.2$)

	Non-Nicotine Users (Threshold = 0.2)	
	No Fused Decisions	44
	Agreements	1690
	False Positive	59
	False Negatives	49
	Corrections	28
	Complete diasagreement	5
	Total	1875

Table 2 shows the results of our experiments on the set of 1,875 applications of non-nicotine users. Note that in a production environment we only have FLE and Fusion available. We can only use the SRD during the training phase of the models and the fusion module. For a given confidence threshold of 0.20, we eliminated 44 cases for which the result of the fusion was deemed *too weak to be used*. Of the remaining 1,831 cases in which the fusion module delivered a decision, it disagreed with the FLE production engine in (28+59+5=92) cases. These are the least reliable cases that we would like to select for manual auditing. This subset represents a **4.9%** of the entire case population. In 28 of the 92 cases, the FLE decision was incorrect (i.e. it disagreed with the SRD). An auditing based on this information would have been productive, finding ~30% of the sample to be incorrect decisions. There are still 49 cases of false negatives, where the fusion agrees with the FLE and they are both wrong.

8.2. Selecting the Best Cases to Augment the SRD

By pushing the threshold T1 to the other extreme, we can select cases with the least amount of conflict among the classifiers. These cases are the best candidates to augment and update the SRD. Their final selection would be based on a rate-class stratification, to insure a balanced updating. For instance, in our test data set, 169 cases had a confidence measure C greater or equal to 0.987. Except for one case, the remaining 168 cases are correct decisions. This set represents the most reliable **9%** of all cases.

8.3. Experiments Results using different T-Norms

The results in Tables 2 are computed using the *scalar product* as the outer-product operator. When this choice is combined with a strict determination of the conflict (e.g. for d=infinite in the computation of penalty matrix P), we have an aggregation analogous to Dempster-Shafer's rule of combination. This aggregation relies on the sources being evidentially uncorrelated. However, in reality this is not an easy constraint to satisfy. In our case, we have used a pre-processing stage (*Tagging*) to annotate the input data with domain knowledge. Since this pre-processing stage is applied to a common set of inputs for *all* models, it is possible to inject a common bias; hence the models could exhibit partial positive correlation. To account for this positive correlation we use a t-norm operator different from the scalar product to generate the outer product. We used Schweizer and Sklar's parameterized family of T-norms [9], which has been studied by many researchers [2,6], and performed some experiments for positive values of parameter p.

Table 3: Fusion as a function of T-norms (for non- nicotine users)

	T-Norm [p]			
$W=0.2, d=7. T1=0.2$	$T[p\to 0]$	$T[p=0.5]$	$T[p=1]$	$T[p\to\infty]$
No Fused Decisions	44	39	42	42
Agreements	1690	1702	1690	1690
False Positive	59	50	60	60
False Negatives	49	43	48	48
Corrections	28	36	28	29
Complete disagreement	5	5	7	6
Total	1875	1875	1875	1875

Table 3 was constructed using the same penalty matrix derived from $W=0.2$ and $d=7$ and using the same threshold confidence $T1=0.2$. From this table we observe that a minor adjustment for positive correlation ($p=0.5$) produces the Pareto-best results for the fusion operator. The 39 cases for which the fusion makes no decisions provide relevant information. In 35 cases, the FLE also avoids making any decision by sending the application to a human underwriter, while the SRD assigns it to the least-desirable rate class. In the remaining 4 cases, the FLE fully disagrees with the SRD, by selecting different classes. Hence these four cases can be easily identified for auditing.

9. Conclusions and Future Work

We have focused our efforts on two problems: *monitoring* the quality of a knowledge-based classifier used in daily production, and *supporting* the classifier's lifecycle, by updating its Standard Reference Decisions. To address these problems, we have developed four off-line classifiers built on different technologies: case-based, neural networks, multiple adaptive splines, and Pareto dominance. We needed to fuse the classifiers' outputs and compare them with that of the production classifier. Given the heterogeneous semantics of the off-line classifiers, we could not use traditional probabilistic approaches to fusion.

We considered the output of each classifier as a weight assignment, representing the un-normalized degree to which a given rate-class was selected by the classifier. As in DS theory, the assignment of weights to the universe all rate-classes represented the lack of commitment to a specific decision. After a post-processing stage, in which weak outputs were removed and replaced with non-committing statements, the weight distributions were normalized to have unit-valued cardinality. We combined the normalized outputs by using an associative fusion operator. The fusion mechanism was based on an outer-product of the outputs, using a Triangular norm as the operator. The output of the fusion was a rate-class distribution and a measure of conflict among all the classifiers. We normalized the final output, identified the strongest selection of the fusion, and qualified the decision with an associated confidence measure. Finally, we used the confidence measure to assess the quality of the production engine. When the degree of confidence of a fused decision was below a lower confidence bound, that case became a candidate for *auditing*. When the degree of confidence of a fused decision was above an upper confidence bound, that case became a candidate for *augmenting the SRD*. We tested the fusion module with data sets for nicotine and non-nicotine users. In an analysis of 1,875 non-nicotine applications, we generated a distribution of the quality of the production engine. By focusing on the two tails of such distribution, we identified **~9%** of the most reliable decisions and **4.9%** of the least reliable ones.

The proposed fusion module plays a key role in supporting the quality assurance of the knowledge-based classifier, by selecting the most questionable cases for auditing. At the same time, the fusion module supports the SRD lifecycle by identifying the most reliable cases used for updating it.

References

[1] K. Aggour, M. Pavese, P. Bonissone and W. Cheetham. SOFT-CBR: A Self-Optimizing Fuzzy Tool for Case-Based Reasoning, *5th Int. Conf. on Case-Based Reasoning (ICCBR)*, pp. 5-19, Springer-Verlag, Trondheim, Norway, 2003.

[2] P. Bonissone and K.S. Decker. Selecting Uncertainty Calculi and Granularity: An Experiment in Trading-off Precision and Complexity, in Kanal and Lemmer (eds.) *Uncertainty in Artificial Intelligence*, pp. 217-247, North-Holland, 1986.

[3] P. Bonissone, W. Cheetham. Fuzzy Case-based Reasoning for Decision Making, *IEEE Int. Conf. on Fuzzy Systems,* Melbourne, Australia, 2001.

[4] P. Bonissone, R. Subbu, K. Aggour. Evolutionary Optimization of Fuzzy Decision Systems for Automated Insurance Underwriting, *IEEE Int. Conf. on Fuzzy Systems (FUZZ-IEEE '02)*, pp 1003-1008, Honolulu, Hawaii, USA, 2002.

[5] P. Bonissone. The life cycle of a Fuzzy Knowledge-based Classifier, *NAFIPS 2003*, pp. 488-494, Chicago, IL, Aug. 2003.

[6] D.Dubois and H. Prade. Criteria aggregation and ranking of alternatives in the framework of fuzzy set theory, *TIMS/Studies in the Management Science*, Zimmerman, Zadeh, Gaines (eds.), Vol. 20, pp. 209-240, Elsevier, 1984.

[7] J.H. Friedman. Multivariate Adaptive Regression Splines. *Annals of Statistics*, 19: 1-141, 1991.

[8] A. Patterson, P. Bonissone, and M. Pavese. Six Sigma Quality Applied Throughout the Lifecycle of and Automated Decision System, *Journal of Quality and Reliability International* 21:275-292, 2005.

[9] B. Schweizer and A. Sklar. *Probabilistic Metric Spaces*, North Holland, New York, NY, USA, 1986.

[10] G. Shafer. *A mathematical theory of evidence*, Princeton University Press, Princeton, NJ, USA, 1976.

Qualitative Classification with Possibilistic Decision Trees

Nahla Ben Amor[a] and Salem Benferhat[b] and Zied Elouedi[a]

[a]Institut Supérieur de Gestion de Tunis,
41 Avenue de la liberté, 2000 Le Bardo, Tunis, Tunisia
nahla.benamor@gmx.fr, zied.elouedi@gmx.fr
[b]CRIL - CNRS, Université d'Artois,
Rue Jean Souvraz, SP 18 62307 Lens, Cedex France
benferhat@cril.univ-artois.fr

Abstract

This paper presents a classification method, in an uncertain context, using decision trees. Our method will use qualitative possibility theory in order to represent uncertainty on the attributes' values of each object to classify. Examples related to intrusion detection field illustrating the ability of our approach to classify objects with uncertain attributes are presented.

Key words: Decision trees, Possibility theory, Classification.

1. Introduction

Various learning methods have been developed to ensure classification [16]. One of the most commonly used methods in supervised learning is the decision tree [4,13,15]. Decision trees are characterized by their capability to break down a complex decision problem into several simpler ones. They represent a sequential procedure for deciding the class membership of a given instance. Their major advantage resides in providing a powerful formalism for presenting comprehensible classifiers often easy to interpret by experts and even by ordinary users.

Standard decision trees are appropriate when attribute's values of objects to classify are precisely defined. However, in practical applications like in intrusion detection systems, attributes are partially defined and some of them can be even missing.

This paper investigates different ways to classify objects with uncertain/missing attributes using qualitative possibility theory. We show that a direct application of min/max operators, as it is used in some developments related to fuzzy decision trees [10], is not completely satisfactory. Solutions based on leximin/leximax operators taking into account the gain ratio of attributes are proposed. We illustrate our approach with a same running example from an intrusion detection systems area. Intrusion detection in the context of information systems is regarded as a set of attempts to compromise a computer network resource security[2].

Section 2 provides a brief description of the basics of decision trees. The necessary background on possibility theory is recalled in Section 3. Then in Section 4, our method named qualitative decision tree is detailed. Finally, Section 5 concludes the paper and presents some future extensions.

2. Decision trees

Decision trees in the machine learning community are considered as a solution to classification applications. Their popularity is due to their ability to handle complex problems by providing an understandable representation easier to interpret and also their adaptability to the inference task by producing logical rules of classification.

A decision tree consists of nodes for testing attributes, edges for branching by values of the selected attribute and leaves labeling classes where for each leaf a unique class is attached.

A decision tree is made up of two major procedures: One to build the tree, the other for the knowledge inference i.e. classification.

- *Building the tree.* Constructing a decision tree is a top-down building procedure. It starts at the root with the whole training set. The objective is to find in each decision node of the tree, the best test attribute allowing to diminish as much as possible the mixture of classes between each subset created by the test. This process will continue for each sub decision tree until reaching leaves and fixing their corresponding classes.

- *Classification.* Classifying new objects is based on the induced tree. So, to classify an object, we start from the root, we evaluate the relative test attribute and we take the branch corresponding to the test's outcome. This process is repeated until a leaf is encountered. The new object is then classified to the class labeling the leaf.

In a decision tree, each path from the root to a leaf corresponds to a conjunction of test attributes and the tree is considered as a disjunction of these conjunctions.

There are several algorithms for building decision trees such as *ID3* and *C4.5* algorithms developed by Quinlan [13,15] considered as the most popular ones. We can also mention the *CART* algorithm of Breiman and al. [4]. A generic decision tree algorithm is characterized by the next properties:

- *The attribute selection measure* allowing to choose an attribute that generates partitions where objects are distributed less randomly. In other words, this measure should consider the ability of each attribute A_k to determine training objects' classes.

The measure used in this paper is the gain ratio of Quinlan [15], based on the Shannon entropy, where for an attribute A_k and a set of objects T, it is defined as follows:

$$Gain(T, A_k) = Info(T) - Info_{A_k}(T) \qquad (1)$$

where

$$Info(T) = -\sum_{i=1}^{n} \frac{freq(c_i, T)}{|T|} log_2 \frac{freq(c_i, T)}{|T|} \qquad (2)$$

$$Info_{A_k}(T) = \sum_{a_k \in D(A_k)} \frac{|T_{a_k}^{A_k}|}{|T|} Info(T_{a_k}^{A_k}) \qquad (3)$$

and $freq(c_i, T)$ denotes the number of objects in the set T belonging to the class c_i and $T_{a_k}^{A_k}$ is the subset of objects for which the attribute A_k has the value a_k (belonging to the domain of A_k denoted $D(A_k)$).

Then, $Split\_Info(A_k)$ is defined as the information content of the attribute A_k itself [15]:

$$Split\_Info(T, A_k) = -\sum_{a_k \in D(A_k)} \frac{|T_{a_k}^{A_k}|}{|T|} log_2 \frac{|T_{a_k}^{A_k}|}{|T|} \qquad (4)$$

So, the gain ratio is the information gain calibrated by Split_Info:

$$Gain\_ratio(T, A_k) = \frac{Gain(T, A_k)}{Split\_Info(A_k)} \qquad (5)$$

- *The partitioning strategy* dividing the current training set into several subsets by taking into account the values of the selected test attribute.
- *The stopping criteria* stopping the growth of a part of the decision tree and consequently declaring the training subset as a leaf.

3. Possibility theory

This subsection gives a brief recalling on possibility theory (for more details see [6]).

Uncertainty is here assumed to be represented qualitatively by a finite and totally ordered scale denoted by $L = \{\alpha_0 = 1, \alpha_1, ..., \alpha_n, \alpha_{n+1} = 0\}$ such that $\alpha_0 = 1 > \alpha_1 > ... > \alpha_n > \alpha_{n+1} = 0$.

If A is a set of uncertainty degrees, we define $Min(A) = \alpha_j$ (resp. $Max(A) = \alpha_j$) such that $\alpha_j \in A$ and $\nexists \alpha_k \in A$ such that $\alpha_k < \alpha_j$ (resp. $\alpha_k > \alpha_j$).

The basic concept of possibility theory, when uncertainty is represented qualitatively, is the notion of *Qualitative Possibility Distribution* (QPD), simply denoted by π.

A QPD π is a function which associates to each element ω of the universe of discourse Ω an element from L, (π encodes our beliefs on a real world). By convention, $\pi(\omega) = 1$ means that it is completely possible ω is the real world, $\pi(\omega) = 0$ means that ω cannot be the real world, and $\pi(\omega) \geq \pi(\omega')$ means that ω is at least as possible as ω' to be the real world. A QPD π is said to be normalized if there exists at least one state ω which is totally possible (i.e. $\pi(\omega) = 1$).

We define the *possibility measure* of any event $\omega \subseteq \Omega$ by:

$$\Pi(\phi) = max\{\pi(\omega); \omega \models \phi\}. \tag{6}$$

This measure evaluates at which level ϕ is consistent with our knowledge represented by π.

4. Qualitative classification with possibilistic decision trees

Our approach begins by using the C4.5 algorithm [15] to construct a decision tree form a given training set, i.e. where its attribute values or in its classes are defined precisely. Once the tree is constructed, the major objective of our paper is to develop a method, based on decision trees, able to classify objects characterized by uncertain attributes' values where the uncertainty is presented by qualitative possibility distributions.

We assign for each attribute a possibility distribution expressing the uncertainty in a qualitative way by encoding it in a totally ordered scale L.

Let $A_1, ..., A_n$ be different attributes of the problem. The instance to classify is described by a vector of possibility distributions $\vec{v} = (\pi_{A_1}, ..., \pi_{A_n})$. An attribute A_i is precisely defined if there exists exactly one value $a \in D_{A_i}$ such that $\pi_{A_i}(a) = 1$, and for all other values $a' \in D_{A_i} \neq a, \pi_{A_i}(a') = 0$. A missing data regarding an attribute A_i, is represented by a uniform possibility distribution π_A (i.e., $\forall a \in D_A, \pi_A(a) = 1$).

Example 1. : In order to illustrate different notions presented in this paper, we will consider an example in the intrusion detection field (the small example is extracted from KDD'99 data sets [11]).

The training set given in Table 1 is composed of an extract of different connections corresponding to a TCP/IP dump rows.

Note that, for the sake of simplicity, each connection is described by only three discrete attributes which are: *proctocle_type*, *service* and *flag*.

Domains of these attributes are:
- $D_{proctocle\_type} = \{tcp, udp\}$,
- $D_{service} = \{http, domain\_u, private\}$,
- $D_{flag} = \{SF, REJ, RSTO\}$.

We also handle three classes:
$C = \{Normal\ (N), DOS\ (D), Probing\ (P)\}$; where *Normal* corresponds to a normal connection while *DOS* and *Probing* are relative to two categories of attacks.

Table 1
Training set

protocol_type	service	flag	C
tcp	http	SF	N
tcp	private	SF	N
tcp	http	RSTO	N
tcp	http	REJ	D
tcp	private	SF	N
tcp	private	REJ	D
tcp	private	RSTO	D
tcp	private	RSTO	D
tcp	http	RSTO	N
tcp	http	SF	N
udp	private	SF	P
udp	domain_u	SF	N
udp	private	SF	P
udp	domain_u	SF	N
udp	domain_u	RSTO	P
udp	http	REJ	D
udp	http	SF	P

Following the algorithm C4.5, the corresponding tree is given by Figure 1.

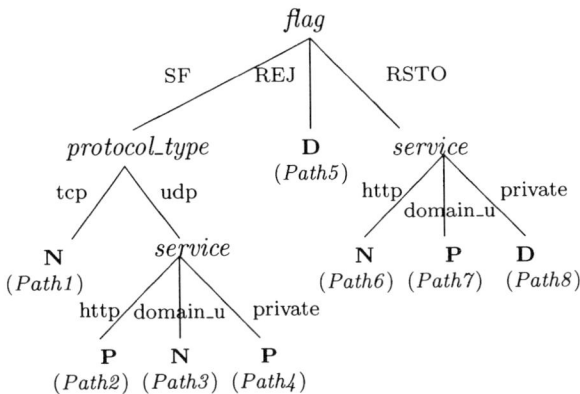

Fig. 1. Example of decision tree in intrusion detection field

Assume that the connection to classify is
$\vec{i_1} = (\pi_{protocol\_type}, \pi_{service}, \pi_{flag})$ with the possibility distributions given in Table 2.

Table 2
Possibility distributions on $\vec{i_1}$

$\pi_{protocol\_type}$		$\pi_{service}$		π_{flag}	
tcp	α_2	http	α_1	SF	1
udp	1	domain_u	α_4	REJ	α_3
		private	1	RSTO	1

In standard decision trees, only one path will be selected to find the membership leaf of the object to classify. Within qualitative decision trees, we need to explore all the tree's paths in order choose the most plausible one(s). The following subsections present different strategies to select plausible classes.

4.1. Using min/max operators

In standard possibility theory, the basic operators min/max are used in order to choose the more plausible path in the tree. At first, we should compute the possibility degree of each path (from a root to a leaf class) by applying the minimum operator on its attributes values. Then, the most plausible path is the one presenting the highest possibility degree. In other words, we should apply the maximum operator on these paths' degrees. Hence the class of the object to classify is the one labeling the leaf corresponding to this path.

Example 2. : Let us continue Example 1, then according to the induced decision tree 1 we have height paths, then applying the minimum operator on the different degrees relative to each path, we get:
Path1 : $min(1, \alpha_2) \Rightarrow (N, \alpha_2)$
Path2 : $min(1, 1, \alpha_1) \Rightarrow (P, \alpha_1)$
Path3 : $min(1, 1, \alpha_4) \Rightarrow (N, \alpha_4)$
Path4 : $min(1,1, 1) \Rightarrow (P, 1)$
Path5 : $min(\alpha_3) \Rightarrow (D, \alpha_3)$
Path6 : $min(1, \alpha_1) \Rightarrow (N, \alpha_1)$
Path7 : $min(1, \alpha_4) \Rightarrow (P, \alpha_4)$
Path8 : $min(1, 1) \Rightarrow (D,1)$

According to the maximum operator, the most plausible paths are 4 and 8, thus the connection $\vec{i_1}$ will be classified as Probing or DOS attack with a possibility degree 1.

This approach in not satisfactory since it is somewhat cautions, and the number of candidate classes can be very important.

The situation is even worst when the number of missing attributes is important.

Another reason why minimim/maximum combination operators is not satisfactory is the fact that it is not discriminatory. Indeed, we can check that, for any attribute A, and for any value a of D_A such that $\pi_A(a) = \alpha_i \neq 1$, replacing $\pi_A(a)$ by 0 does not change the selected candidate classes. This is explained by the fact that if π_A's are normalized, then there exists at least one path from the root to a leaf class such that the possibility degree of each node's value in this path is equal to 1. Hence, with min/max combination mode, only paths where possibility degrees of attributes values are equal to 1 are considered.

4.2. Using min/leximax operators

As it is said above, the use of the maximum operator makes difficult to choose between the equally plausible paths leading to different classes. For instance in the example 2, we cannot decide whether the connection pertains to Probing or DOS attacks. In such a case we propose to extend the *maximum* operator by using the *leximax* criterion which is a natural extension of the *maximum* operator used in the qualitative setting [12] defined by:

Definition 1. Let $\vec{u} = \{u_1, ..., u_n\}$ and $\vec{v} = \{v_1, ..., v_n\}$ be two vectors of possibility degrees, and let σ and τ be two permutations of indices such that $\forall i \in \{1,...,n\}, u_{\sigma(i)} >_\Pi u_{\sigma(i+1)}$ and $v_{\tau(i)} >_\Pi v_{\tau(i+1)}$. Then, $\vec{u}$ is said to be leximax-preferred to $\vec{v}$, denoted by $\vec{u} >_{leximax} \vec{v}$, if and only if there exists i such that $u_{\sigma(i)} >_\Pi v_{\tau(i)}$ and $\forall j < i, u_{\sigma(j)} =_\Pi v_{\tau(j)}$.

Let $(P_1, ...P_n)$ be the set of all different paths from the root to leaves. We denote by $deg(P_i)$ as simply the minimum of possibility degrees of attribute's values in the path P_i.

For each class C, we associate a vector $\vec{C} = (C_1, ..., C_n)$ such that:

$$C_i = \begin{cases} deg(P_i) & if C \text{ is the leaf of the path } P_i \\ 0 & otherwise. \end{cases} \quad (7)$$

Definition 2. The class C is min/leximax preferred if there is no class C', such that $C' >_{leximax} C$, where $>_{leximax}$ is given in Definition 1.

In the following, and for the sake of simplicity and clarity only values different from 0 are explicitly precised in $\vec{C}$'s.

Example 3. : Let us continue the previous example. According to the induced tree, we get three vectors of possibility degrees relative to different classes: $\vec{N} = (\alpha_2, \alpha_4, \alpha_1)$, $\vec{D} = (\alpha_3, 1)$, $\vec{P} = (\alpha_1, 1, \alpha_4)$.

At the first step, DOS and Probing are leximax-preferred to Normal since their maximum is superior than the one relative to Normal class. Refining this result between DOS and Probig, we get that Probing is leximax-preferred to DOS, thus the new connection will be classified to as a Probing attack.

4.3. Using leximin/leximax operators

The selection modes based on *min/max* and *min/leximax* combination operators proceed in two steps: first, they use the minimum operator to select a first set of candidate classes, then they refine this set with the maximum or *leximax* combination operator. However, the minimum operator is not selective, and one way to overcome this limitation is to replace, in the first step, the minimum operator with *leximin* and to maintain the *leximax* in the second step.

The above subsections only use possibility degrees to select best classes. This subsection goes one step further and proposes to take into account the gain ratio criterion in the selection process.

One idea to overcome drawbacks of the min/max combination is to extend these two operators by using *leximin* and *leximax* criteria which are natural extensions of the minimum and maximum operators used in the qualitative setting [12] and in different areas like in handling conflicts in knowledge bases [3]. We first define the leximin ordering (which is the dual of leximax ordering given in Definition 1):

Definition 3. Let $\vec{u} = \{u_1, ..., u_n\}$ and $\vec{v} = \{v_1, ..., v_n\}$ be two vectors, and let σ and τ be two permutations of indices such that $\forall i \in \{1, .., n\}, u_{\sigma(i)} >_\Pi u_{\sigma(i+1)}$ and $v_{\tau(i)} >_\Pi v_{\tau(i+1)}$. Then,
- $\vec{u}$ is said to be leximin-preferred to $\vec{v}$, denoted by $\vec{u} >_{leximin} \vec{v}$, if and only if there exists i such that $u_{\sigma(i)} >_\Pi v_{\tau(i)}$ and $\forall j > i, u_{\sigma(j)} =_\Pi v_{\tau(j)}$ (resp. $\forall j < i, u_{\sigma(j)} =_\Pi v_{\tau(j)}$).
- $\vec{u}$ is said to be leximin-equal (resp. leximax-equal) to $\vec{v}$, denoted by $\vec{u} =_{leximin} \vec{v}$ (resp. $\vec{u} =_{leximax} \vec{v}$), if and only if $\forall i, u_{\sigma(i)} =_\Pi v_{\tau(i)}$.

The selection mode based on the leximin/leximax operators proceeds in two steps:
(i) Establish a total pre-order of all paths using leximin operator based on the gain ratio.
(ii) Select a first set of candidate classes corresponding to classes labeling best paths in the total pre-order of paths. If this set contains more than one class, refine it by selecting its leximax-preferred class(es) using the leximin-leximax order.

4.3.1. *Establishing a total leximin pre-order of all paths*

The application of the leximin criterion requires that all paths should be described by the same attributes already defined in the training set. However, since paths are pruned, the idea will be to assign a degree 1 to the missing values. In fact, if in a given path labeled with a class C, an attribute A is missing, this means that this attribute does not affect the class C. In other terms it can be obtained even with the most plausible instances of A namely those having the degree 1 since only normalized distributions are considered.

Furthermore, the application of the *leximin* requires pre-order between different attributes. For this purpose, we propose to use the same criterion used for building the tree, namely the *gain ratio* (see Equation (5)). This criterion is appropriate since it gives for each training subset the attribute having the highest discriminative power.

Assume we have a training set T with three attributes A, B, and C. Suppose that $Gain\_ratio(T,A) > Gain\_ratio(T,B) > Gain\_ratio(T,C)$. So, A is the most discriminative attribute and will be considered as the first criterion within the leximin method. However, even it is true that in the first level $Gain\_ratio(T,B) > Gain\_ratio(T,C)$, this does not mean that this inequality is true once A is fixed.

The discriminative power of different attributes can be found directly from the tree since we use the same principle, which is the gain ratio, to build it.

The procedure allowing to establish the total pre-oder based on leximin and gain ratio is described as follows:

1. *Sort in a decreasing order the different path sets relative to each of the children of the root taking into account the possibility degree relative to branches leading to these children.*

2. *For each path set containing more than one path repeat the same process, recursively. The process will be ended when each induced set path contains only one path.*

Once this first step ended, we cannot usually have a total pre-order on all paths since in some levels of the previous process some set of paths may have the same ranking (i.e. they have the same possibility degree).

In order to obtain the total pre-order we will proceed in an incremental manner by refining these equalities (in each level) as follows:

3. *For equally ranked set of paths, we will group first (resp. second, third, etc.) elements of each of them. Elements belonging to the same group are equally preferred. Then, we re-order paths by considering that the group of first elements is preferred to the one containing second elements and so on.*

4.3.2. Selecting best class(es)

From the total pre-order established in the previous step, we will select a first set of candidate classes corresponding to classes labeling best paths. Let C be this set of classes. If C contains more than one class we will refine it by selecting its leximax-preferred class(es) using the leximin-leximax order given by the following definitions:

Definition 4. Let $\vec{C_k} = \{P_{C_k,1}, ..., P_{C_k,m}\}$ and $\vec{C_l} = \{P_{C_l,1}, ..., P_{C_l,n}\}$ be two vectors relative to paths leading to C_k and C_l.

Let σ and τ be two permutations of indices such that $\forall i \in \{1,..,n\}$, $P_{C_k,\sigma(i)} >_{leximin} P_{C_k,\sigma(i+1)}$ and $P_{C_l,\tau(i)} >_{leximin} P_{C_l,\tau(i+1)}$.

- $\vec{C_k}$ is said to be leximin-leximax preferred to $\vec{C_l}$, denoted by $\vec{C_k} >_{leximin-leximax} \vec{C_l}$,
  - if there exists $i \in \{1,..min(n,m)\}$ such that $P_{C_k,\sigma(i)} >_{leximin} P_{C_l,\sigma(i)}$ and $\forall j < i, P_{C_k,\sigma(j)} =_{leximin} P_{C_l,\sigma(j)}$.
  - or if $\forall i \in \{1,..min(n,m)\}$, $P_{C_k,\sigma(i)} =_{leximin} P_{C_l,\tau(i)}$ and $m > n$ (i.e. C_k is supported by a greater number of paths than C_l) .
- $\vec{C_k}$ is said to be leximin-leximax equal to $\vec{C_l}$, denoted by $\vec{C_k} =_{leximin-leximax} \vec{C_l}$, if and only if $n = m$ and $\forall i, P_{C_k,\sigma(i)} =_{leximin} P_{C_l,\tau(i)}$.

Definition 5. Let $C = \{C_1, ...C_m\}$ be a set of classes, the class C_i is leximin-leximax preferred iff there is no class C_j, such that $\vec{C_j} >_{leximin-leximax} \vec{C_i}$.

Example 4. : Let us classify the connection given in Example 1.

From the tree, the first attribute to be used in the leximin order is flag which is the root of the induced tree. This attribute shows that the path P_5 is the worst one in the total leximin order since it has the lowest possibility degree.

Next, the set of paths from P_1 to P_4 can be partitioned using the protocol_type, then the service attribute. This leads to this pre-order $P_4 >_{leximin} P_2 >_{leximin} P_3 >_{leximin} P_1$. As the same manner, the remaining set of paths from P_6 to P_8 will be partitioned using the service attribute, then the protocol_type which gives $P_8 >_{leximin} P_6 >_{leximin} P_7$.

Thus, we will group P_4 and P_8 (resp. P_2 and P_6, P_3 and P_7) together which leads to this total pre-order $P_8 =_{leximin} P_4 >_{leximin} P_2 =_{leximin} P_6 >_{leximin} P_3 =_{leximin} P_7 >_{leximin} P_1 >_{leximin} P_5$.

Therefore, $C = \{P, D\}$ which are the classes labeling P_8 and P_4, respectively. In other terms the connection will be classified as a Probing or a DOS attack.

Then, $\vec{P} = (P_4, P_2, P_7) >_{leximin-leximax} \vec{D} = (P_8, P_5)$ since $P_4 =_{leximin} P_8$ and $P_2 >_{leximin} P_5$. Thus, it is possible to have a more precise result and the connection will be classified as a Probing attack.

5. Conclusion

In this paper, we have proposed different ways to classify objects with uncertain/missing attributes in decision trees. The uncertainty on the attributes' values is represented qualitatively in the possibilistic framework.

First, we have shown that using basic min/max operators of possibility theory, as it is used in fuzzy decision trees [10], is not suitable since it is not enough discriminatory. Then, solutions based on $leximin/leximax$ operators taking into account the gain ratio of attributes are proposed. The developed approaches are illustrated by an example on intrusion detection systems area.

In [1] a syntactic machinery based on possibilistic knowledge bases has been proposed. This is important, for instance, for explanation purpose. A future work is to provide syntactic counterparts for $min/leximax$ and $leximin$ selection combination modes.

6. Acknowledgments

This work is supported by a french national project ACI (Action Concerte Incitative) Sécurité Informatique entitled DADDi (Dependable Anomaly Detection with Diagnosis)).

References

1. Ben Amor N., Benferhat S., Elouedi Z., Mellouli K.: Decision Trees and Qualitative Possibilistic Inference: Application to the Intrusion Detection Problem. Proceedings of European Conference of Symbolic and Quantitative Approaches to Reasoning and Uncertainty (ECSQARU'2003), 419-431, 2003.
2. Axelsson, S.: Intrusion detection systems: a survey and taxonomy. Technical report 99-15, March 2000.
3. Benferhat S., Cayrol C., Dubois D, Lang J., Prade H.: Inconsistency management and prioritized syntax-based entailment. Proceedings of Intlernational Joint Conference on Artificial Intelligence (IJCAI'93), 640-645, 1993.
4. Breiman, L., Friedman, J. H., Olshen, R. A., Stone, C. J.: Classification and regression trees. Monterey, CA, Wadsworth & Brooks, 1984.
5. Denoeux T., Skarstein-Bjanger M.: Induction of decision trees for partially classified data. Proceedings of the IEEE International Conference on Systems, Man, and Cybernetics, Nashville, USA, 2923-2928, 2000.
6. D Dubois and H. Prade: Possibility theory: An approach to computerized. Processing of uncertainty. Plenium Press, New York, 1988.
7. Dubois, D, Lang, J., Prade, H.: Possibilistic logic. In Handbook on Logic in Artificial Intelligence and Logic Programming, 3, 439-513, 1994.
8. Elouedi Z., Mellouli K., Smets P.: Belief decision trees: Theoretical foundations. International Journal of Approximate Reasoning 28, 91-124, 2001.
9. Hullermeier E., Possibilistic induction in decision-tree learning,. Proceedings of European Conference on Machine Learning (ECML'02), 2002.
10. Maher P. E., St. Clair, D., Uncertain reasoning in an ID3 machine learning framework, Proceedings of the Second IEEE International Conference on Fuzzy Systems, FUZZ-IEEE'93, Vol 1, 7-12, 1993.
11. http://kdd.ccs.uci.edu/databases/kddcup99/task.html.
12. Moulin H.: Axioms for cooperative decision-making. Cambridge University Press, 1988.
13. Quinlan, J. R.: Induction of decision trees. Machine Learning 1, 1-106, 1986.
14. Quinlan, J. R.: Probabilistic decision trees. Machine Learning, Vol. 3, Chap. 5, Morgan Kaufmann, 267-301, 1990.
15. Quinlan, J. R.: C4.5: Programs for machine learning. Morgan Kaufmann San Mateo Ca, 1993.
16. Weiss, S. M., Kulikowski, C. A., Computer systems that learn, San Mateo, California, Morgan Kofmann Publishers, 1991.

Discovery of Abstract Knowledge from Non-Atomic Attribute Values in Fuzzy Relational Databases

Rafal A. Angryk[a] and Frederick E. Petry[b,c]

[a]Department of Computer Science, Montana State University
Bozeman, MT 59717-3880, USA
angryk@cs.montana.edu
[b]Naval Research Laboratory, Mapping, Charting and Geodesy,
Stennis Space Center, MS 39529, USA
fpetry@nrlssc.navy.mil
[c]Electrical Engineering and Computer Science Department, Tulane University
New Orleans, LA 70118, USA

Abstract

In this paper we introduce attribute-oriented induction with partial vote propagation – a new approach allowing acquisition of generalized knowledge from uncertain data. We utilize a proximity-based fuzzy relational database as the medium carrying the original information, where the lack of precise information about an entity is reflected via insertion of multiple attribute values, and the fuzzy relation of α-proximity replaces the classical equivalence relation. Following a well-known approach for generalization of exact data in ordinary databases [9], we introduce a new method for induction of tuples with non-atomic attribute values. In our approach we take advantage of the implicit information about the generalized attributes in the fuzzy database model and apply it to generalize imprecise information.

Keywords: Data Mining, Fuzzy Databases, Attribute-Oriented Induction, Uncertain Data.

1. Introduction

Attribute-Oriented Induction (AOI) is a descriptive database mining technique, which compresses the original set of data into a generalized relation, providing concise and summarative information about the massive set of the original data. This technique enables a transformation of similar data collections, expressed originally in a database at a low (primitive) level, into more abstract conceptual representations.

The generalization of database records is performed on an attribute-by-attribute basis, utilizing a separate concept hierarchy for the each of the generalized attributes included in the relation of task-relevant data. Each concept hierarchy reflects background knowledge about the domain, which is going to be generalized. The concept hierarchies progressively increase the abstraction of the generalization concepts at each new level, allowing the gradual aggregation of attribute values stored in the original tuples.

In contrast to simplified, non-hierarchical data summarization, a gradual attribute-oriented induction through concept hierarchies allows detailed tracking of all records, and can lead to the discovery of interesting patterns among data at the lowest abstraction level of their occurrence. In effect we are able to avoid unnecessary loss of information due to the overgeneralization. Moreover, thorough attribute-oriented induction allows extraction of generalized knowledge, without omitting even rare attribute values. It might occur that such atypical values, despite being initially (at a low level of the generalization hierarchy) infrequent, can sum up to meaningful numbers when generalized to a sufficiently high abstraction level.

In this work we focus on the extraction of generalized knowledge from the imprecise data stored in the fuzzy relational database. In real life, imperfect information occurs very frequently (e.g. caused by the lack of suitable precision during measurements; inconsistency of the data coming from multiple sources; uncertainty in judgments performed by human beings caused by the lack of their objective assessment), and in the miscellaneous areas (e.g. weather maps, genotype characteristics, census data, etc.). An ability to mine knowledge from such data, in spite of the occurring imperfections, has significance for real-world applications. A choice of a suitable approach for generalization of original data can have a fundamental influence on retrieved results, regardless of further data mining techniques.

In the next section we provide a brief review of research conducted on AOI. We also give an overview of a proximity based fuzzy database model, which we utilized as the basis for our generalization approach. Then we present how the fuzzy proximity relation can be applied to build generalization hierarchies, and finally introduce our method allowing attribute-oriented induction of imperfect data.

2. Background

2.1 Attribute-Oriented Induction (AOI)

The idea of applying concept hierarchies to generalize database records for data mining purposes was initially developed by Han et al. [8-10] and extended further by Hamilton et al. [5, 11]. The majority of this work focuses on attribute-oriented induction with utilization of crisp concept hierarchies, where each attribute value (concept) can have only one direct abstract to which it fully belongs.

Several groups of researchers have investigated applications of fuzzy concept hierarchies for AOI. Fuzzy hierarchies of concepts seem to better model real life dependencies, since they are able to reflect the degree with which one concept belongs to its direct abstract and more than one direct abstract of a single concept is also allowed. Lee and Kim [13] used ISA hierarchies, from area of data modeling, to generalize database records to more abstract concepts. Lee [14] applied fuzzy generalization hierarchies to mine generalized fuzzy quantitative association rules. Cubero et al. [6] presented fuzzy gradual rules for data summarization. Raschia and Mouaddib [17] implemented the SaintEtiq system for data summarization through extended concept hierarchies. Consistent fuzzy concept hierarchies, where each degree of membership is normalized to preserve an exact vote propagation of each tuple when generalized, were recently investigated by the authors [1-2].

2.2 Proximity-based Fuzzy Relational Database

The similarity-based fuzzy model of a relational database, proposed originally by Buckles and Petry [4, 16], is actually a formal generalization of the ordinary relational database model introduced by Codd [7]. The fuzzy model, based on the max-min composition of a fuzzy similarity relation, which replaces the classical equivalence relation coming was further extended by Shenoi and Melton [12, 18-19] with the concept of the proximity relation and because of its more general character, we utilized an extension for this approach.

The most distinctive qualities of the fuzzy relational database are: (1) allowing non-atomic domain values, when characterizing attributes of an entity and (2) generation of equivalence classes with the support of a proximity relation applied in the place of traditional identity relation.

As mentioned above, each attribute value of the fuzzy database record is allowed to be a subset of the whole base set of attribute values describing a particular domain. Formally, if we denote a set of acceptable attribute values as D_j, and we let d_{ij} to symbolize a particular (j^{th}) attribute value, characterizing the ith entity; the original Codd's principle $d_{ij} \in D_j$ is replaced in the fuzzy database schema with the set $d_{ij} \subseteq D_j$. Any member of the power set of accepted domain values can be inserted as an attribute descriptor except the null set. Therefore a fuzzy database relation is actually a subset of the cross product of all power sets of its constituent attributes $2^{D_1} \times 2^{D_2} \times ... \times 2^{D_m}$. This property permits fuzzy database to store imprecision coming from the original source of information. In cases when the particular entity cannot be clearly characterized by a single descriptor, the uncertainty can be reflected by multiple attribute values.

A proximity-based fuzzy database uses an explicitly declared proximity relation of which both the identity and similarity relations are special cases. Since a fuzzy proximity relation (also called tolerance relation) is only reflexive and symmetric, which is not sufficient to obtain equivalence classes, transitivity of proximity relation was an extension. This is achieved by modifying the original definition of fuzzy proximity relations with transitivity via similarity paths (sequences of similarities), using Tamura chains [20]. The definition of α-proximity relation employed in this approach is:

If P is a proximity relation on D_j, then given an $\alpha \in [0, 1]$, two elements $x, z \in D_j$ are α-similar (denoted by $xP_\alpha z$) if and only if $P(x,z) \geq \alpha$, and are said to be α-proximate (denoted by $x P_\alpha^+ z$) if and only if they are (1) either α-similar or (2) there exists a sequence $y_1, y_2, \ldots, y_m \in D_j$, such that $xP_\alpha y_1 P_\alpha y_2 P_\alpha .. P_\alpha y_m P_\alpha z$.

Table 1: Proximity table for a domain HAIR COLOR.

	black	d. brown	auburn	red	Blond	bleached
black	1.0	0.8	0.6	0.5	0.3	0.1
d. brown	0.8	1.0	0.7	0.6	0.5	0.2
auburn	0.6	0.7	1.0	0.8	0.4	0.3
red	0.5	0.6	0.8	1.0	0.5	0.4
blond	0.3	0.5	0.4	0.5	1.0	0.8
bleached	0.1	0.2	0.3	0.4	0.8	1.0

Each of the attributes in the fuzzy database has its own *proximity table*, which includes the *degrees of proximity* (called above α-*similarity*) between all values occurring for the particular attribute. A proximity table for the domain of HAIR COLOR, which we will use as an example for our further analysis, is presented in the Table 1. Since it is not necessary to preserve max-min transitivity when defining the proximity values the relation becomes much easier to specify.

As proposed by Tamura [20], the proximity table can be transformed to reflect the α-*proximity relation*. The results of such a transformation are seen in Table 2.

Table 2: α-proximity table for a domain HAIR COLOR.

	black	d. brown	auburn	red	blond	bleached
black	1.0	0.8	0.7	0.7	0.5	0.5
d. brown	0.8	1.0	0.7	0.7	0.5	0.5
auburn	0.7	0.7	1.0	0.8	0.5	0.5
red	0.7	0.7	0.8	1.0	0.5	0.5
blond	0.5	0.5	0.5	0.5	1.0	0.8
bleached	0.5	0.5	0.5	0.5	0.8	1.0

Now the disjoint classes of attribute values, considered to be equivalent at the specific α-level, can be extracted from the table. They are marked by shadings in Table 2. Such a separation of the equivalence classes arises due to the sequential similarity proposed by Tamura. For instance, despite the fact that the proximity degree, presented in Table 1, between the concepts *red* and *black* is *0.5*, the α-proximity is 0.7. Via the sequence of the original proximity degrees: *black P_α d.brown=0.8* ∧ *d.brown P_α auburn=0.7* ∧ *auburn P_α red=0.8*, we get *black P_α^+ red=0.7*, which is shown in Table 2.

3. Attribute-Oriented Induction from fuzzy tuples

3.1 Building concept hierarchy from α-proximity table

The creation of an *α-proximity* relation for a particular domain D_j can lead to the extraction of a crisp concept hierarchy, allowing attribute-oriented induction on such a domain. From the propagation of shadings in the Table 2, we can easily observe that the equivalence classes marked in the table have a nested character.

As in the case of a fuzzy similarity relation [21], each *α-cut* (where $\alpha \in [0, 1]$) of a fuzzy binary relation in Table 2 creates disjoint equivalence classes in the domain D_j. If we let Π_α denote a single equivalence class partition induced on domain D_j by a single *α-level-set*, then by an increase of the value of α to α' we are able to extract the subclass of Π_α, denoted $\Pi_{\alpha'}$ (a refinement of the previous equivalence class partition). A nested sequence of partitions $\Pi\alpha^1$, $\Pi\alpha^2$,..., $\Pi\alpha^k$, where $\alpha^1 < \alpha^2 < ... < \alpha^k$, may be represented in the form of a *partition tree*, as in Figure 1.

This nested sequence of partitions in the form of a tree has a structure identical with the crisp concept hierarchy used for AOI. The increase of conceptual abstraction in the partition tree is denoted by decreasing values of α; lack of abstraction during generalization (0-abstraction level at the bottom of generalization hierarchy) complies with the 1-cut of the similarity relation ($\alpha=1.0$), and is denoted as $S_{1.0}$.

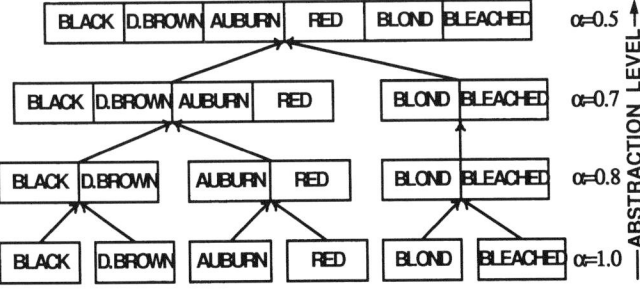

Figure 1: Partition tree of domain HAIR COLOR, built on the basis of Table 2.

An advantage of the utilization of the proximity-based fuzzy model is that such a hierarchy, by definition implemented in every such fuzzy database, can be extracted automatically for a user who has no background knowledge about the specific domain.

The only thing differentiating the hierarchy in the Figure 1 from the crisp concept hierarchies applicable for AOI is the lack of abstract concepts, which are used as the labels characterizing the sets of generalized (grouped) concepts. To create a complete set of the abstract labels it is sufficient to choose only one value of the attribute per the equivalence class at the each level of hierarchy (α), and assign a unique abstract descriptor to it. Sets of such definitions (value of attribute and value of α linked with an abstract name) can be stored as a relational database table (Table 3), where the first two columns create a natural key for this relation.

Table 3: Table of abstract descriptors (for Figure 1).

ATTRIBUTE VALUE	ABSTRACTION LEVEL (α)	ABSTRACT DESCRIPTOR
black	0.8	DARKISH
red	0.8	REDDISH
blond	0.8	BLONDISH
black	0.7	DARK
blond	0.7	BLONDISH
black	0.5	ANY

The combination of partition tree in Figure 1 and the table of abstract descriptors allow us to build the generalization hierarchy in the form shown in Figure 2.

The disjoint character of equivalence classes generated from the α-proximity table does not allow any concept in the hierarchy to have more than one direct abstract at every level of generalization hierarchy. Therefore this approach can be utilized only to form a crisp generalization hierarchy. Such a hierarchy, however, can be then successfully applied as a foundation to the development of a fuzzy concept hierarchy – by extending it with additional edges to represent partial membership of the lower level concepts in their direct abstract descriptors. Depending on the assigned memberships, reflecting preferences of the user, this can create consistent or inconsistent fuzzy concept hierarchies.

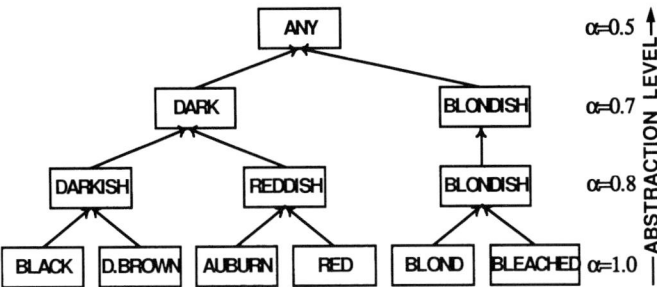

Figure 2: Crisp generalization hierarchy formed using Tables 2 and 3.

3.2 Character of imprecision reflected in fuzzy records

Before introducing our approach to AOI from imprecise data, let us analyze briefly the nature of the uncertainty representation allowed in the fuzzy database model. There are two actual representations of imprecision in the fuzzy database schema. First, as already mentioned, is the occurrence of multiple attribute values. Obviously, the more descriptors we use to characterize a particular record in the database, the more imprecise is its depiction. Uncertainty about the description is also implicitly reflected in the similarity of values characterizing a particular entity. e.g. when we describe someone's hair as *{black, dark brown, red, auburn}* we have more doubt about the person's hair colour than in the case when we characterize it as *{blond, dark blond, light brown, brown}*, since this description would be rather immediately interpreted as "blondish". There are the same number of attribute values in each case, however the higher similarity of values utilized in the second set results in the higher informativeness carried by the second example.

The imprecision of the original information is actually reflected both in the number of inserted descriptors for a particular attribute and in the similarity of these values. In Table 4 we summarize observations concerning their relationship. The domain called *Quantity of attribute values* is a discrete set of integer numbers (> 0, since the fuzzy model does not allow empty attributes); the *Similarity of attribute values* is characterized in fuzzy databases with a continuous set of real numbers in a range [0, 1] – the values of α.

Table 4: Character of information stored in the Fuzzy Databases.

Quantity of attr. values \ Similarity of attr. values	LOW	HIGH
SMALL	Imprecise	Precise
LARGE	Imprecise (Error suspected)	Precise (Confirmed)

The simplified characterization of data imprecision presented in Table 4 can be enhanced with a brief analysis of the boundary values. The measure of imprecision can be thought of ranging between 0 (i.e. the lack of uncertainty about results) and infinity (maximum imprecision). The common opinion that even flawed information is better than lack of the information, leads us to say that imprecision reaches its maximum limits when there is no data inserted at all. Since the fuzzy database model does not allow empty attributes we will not consider this further. The minimum imprecision (0-level) is achieved by a single attribute value. If there are no other descriptors or auxiliary information, we must assume the inserted value is a perfect characterization of the particular entity's feature. The same minimum can be also accomplished with multiple values if they all have identical meaning (synonyms). Despite the fact that multiple, identical descriptors additionally confirm an initially inserted value, they cannot lead to further reduction of imprecision, since it already has the minimal value. Therefore the descriptors, which are so similar that they are considered to be identical, can be reduced to a single descriptor. Obviously, some attribute values, initially considered as different, may be treated as identical at a higher abstraction level. Therefore we can conclude that the practically achievable minimum of imprecision depends on the abstraction level of employed descriptors, and can reach its original 0-level only at the lowest level of abstraction (for $\alpha=1.0$ in our fuzzy database model).

3.3 Partial Vote Propagation to generalize imprecise data

Since the fuzzy database model permits the reflection of uncertainty about the value characterizing each feature via insertion of multiple attribute descriptors, it is necessary to provide a mechanism allowing AOI from such data. In this section we propose a method enabling generalization of multiple attribute values, based on the dependencies presented in the previous section.

In the case of attribute generalization with utilization of a concept hierarchy (Figure 2), we have single attribute values at the bottom level of the hierarchy. Therefore the generalization of tuples with single descriptors is straightforward. A problem arises with the case of multiple attribute values describing a single entity. Where should we assign a person whose hair was described as *{d.brown, auburn, red}*? Our solution is based on partial vote propagation, where a single vote, corresponding to one database record, is partitioned to represent each of the originally inserted attribute values. During AOI all fractions of this vote propagate gradually through multiple levels of generalization hierarchy, the same way as the regular (precise) records do. The only difference is that the record with uncertainty has multiple generalization paths (different paths for different vote's fractions), whereas each of the precise records has only one generalization path.

The most trivial solution would be to split the vote equally among all inserted descriptors: *{d.brown|0.(3), auburn|0.(3), red|0.(3)}*. This approach however does not take into consideration real life dependencies, which are reflected not only in the number of inserted descriptors, but also in their similarity. We propose replacement of the even distribution of vote with a nonlinear spread, dependent on the similarity and the number of inserted values. Using the partition tree (Figure 1), we can extract from the set of the originally inserted values the concepts which are more similar to each other than to the remaining descriptors; we call these subsets of resemblances (e.g. *{red, auburn}* from the above-mentioned example). Then we use the subset as a base for calculating new vote's fractions. An important aspect of this approach is extraction of the subsets of similarities at the lowest possible level of their occurrence, since the nested character of α-proximity relation guarantees that above this α-level they will always occur together. Repetitive extraction of such subsets could unbalance the original dependencies among inserted values.

The proposed approach is rather straightforward given (1) a set of attribute values inserted as a description of particular entity (i.e. *Set of Descriptors*), and (2) a hierarchical structure (tree) reflecting Zadeh's partition tree for the particular attribute (Figure 1). We want to extract the list of all subsets of similarities from the given *Set of Descriptors*, with the highest *Level of α-proximity* of their common occurrence. This is achieved by preorder recursive traversal of the partition tree.. Searching from the root of the tree, if any subset of the given *Set of Descriptors* occurs at a particular node of the concept hierarchy, we store the values that were recognized as similar, and the value of α. In Figure 3 we present an example of such a search for subsets of similarities for a record with values *{black, d.brown, blond, red}*. Numbers on the links in the tree represent the order in which the particular subsets of similarities were extracted.

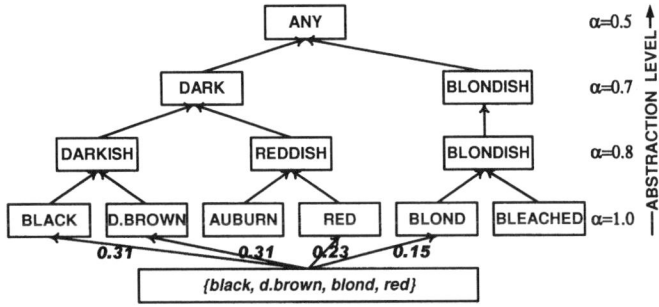

Figure 3: Subsets of similar values extracted from the original set of descriptors.

After extracting the subsets of similarities (Figure 3), we summarize α values as a measure reflecting both the frequency of occurrence of the particular attribute values in the subsets of similarities, as well as the abstraction level of these occurrences. Since value *blond* appeared only at the top and the bottom level, we assign it a grade *1.5 (1.0+0.5)*. The remaining attribute values were graded as follows:

black|(1.0 + 0.8 + 0.7 + 0.5) = black|3.0
d.brown|(1. 0 + 0.8 + 0.7 + 0.5) = d.brown|3.0
red|(1.0 + 0.7 + 0.5)= red|2.2

In the next step, we use the sum of all generated grades *(1.5+3.0 + 3.0 + 2.2 = 9.7)* in order to normalize the grades finally assigned to each of the participating attribute values:

black|(3.0/9.7) = black|0.31
d.brown|(3.0/9.7) = d.brown|0.31
red|(2.2/9.7) = red|0.23
blond|(1.5/9.7) = blond|0.15

This new distribution of the vote's fractions more accurately reflects real life dependencies than a linear approach. The final results are shown in Figure 4.

Normalization of the initial grades has a crucial meaning for preservation of the generalization model's completeness. It guarantees that each of the records is represented as a unity, despite being variously distributed at each of the generalization levels.

During the AOI process all fractions of the vote may gradually merge to finally become unity at the level of abstraction high enough to erase the originally occurring imprecision. In such a case, we observe that there is a removal of imprecision from data due to its generalization. Such a connection between the precision and certainty seems to be natural and was already noted by other researchers [3, 15]. In general, very abstract statements have a greater probability to be "correct" than more detailed ones.

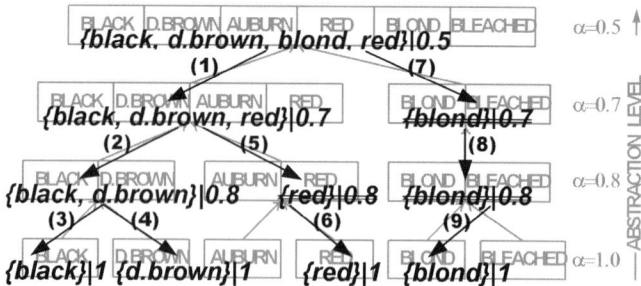

Figure 4: Partial Vote Propagation for records with uncertainty.

4 Conclusions

An acceptance of non-atomic values for an attribute may lead to the occurrence of imprecision, when a single attribute is described by multiple values which are not considered to be equal at the given level of detail. In this paper we presented a new approach allowing Attribute-Oriented Induction in such cases.

In our approach, multiple descriptors with high similarity are allowed to dominate distribution of the vote's fractions, which seems to more accurately reflect the actually occurring dependencies. Such a nonlinear distribution of the record's vote, based on the similarities among attribute values, implicitly supports a reduction of the original data's inconsistency.

In this paper we utilized a proximity-based fuzzy relational database model, however the proposed mechanism of generalization via partial vote distribution based on the shape of concept hierarchy seems to be applicable to AOI on any data with non-atomic attribute values. Applying this approach to mine abstract knowledge from imprecise data stored in other types of databases remains an interesting challenge for our future work.

Acknowledgements

We would like to thank the Naval Research Laboratory's Base Program, Program Element No. 0602435N for sponsoring this research.

References

1. R.A. Angryk and F.E. Petry, "Consistent fuzzy concept hierarchies for attribute generalization," *Proceeding of the IASTED International Conference on Information and Knowledge Sharing (IKS '03)*, Scottsdale, AZ, USA, November 2003, pp. 158-163.
2. R.A. Angryk and F.E. Petry, "Data Mining Fuzzy Databases Using Attribute-Oriented Generalization," *Proceeding of The Third IEEE International Conference on Data Mining (ICDM '03), Workshop on Foundations and New Direction in DM*, Melbourne, FL, USA, November 2003, pp. 8-15.
3. P. Bosc and H. Prade, "An introduction to fuzzy set and possibility theory based approaches to the treatment of uncertainty and imprecision in database management systems", *Proceedings of the 2nd Workshop on Uncertainty Management in Information Systems (UMIS'94): From Needs to Solutions*, Catalina, CA, USA, 1994.
4. B.P. Buckles and F.E. Petry, "A fuzzy representation of data for relational databases", *Fuzzy Sets and Systems*, 7(3), 1982, pp. 213-226.
5. C.L. Carter and H.J. Hamilton, "Efficient Attribute-Oriented Generalization for Knowledge Discovery from Large Databases", *IEEE Transactions on Knowledge and Data Engineering*, 10(2), 1998, pp. 193-208.
6. J. C. Cubero, J.M. Medina, O. Pons, M.A. Vila, "Data Summarization in Relational Databases through Fuzzy Dependencies", *Inf. Sciences*, 121(3-4), 1999, pp. 233-270.

7. F.E. Codd, "A relational model of data for large share data banks", *Communications of the ACM, 13*(6), 1970, pp. 377-387.
8. J. Han, Y. Cai, and N. Cercone, "Knowledge discovery in databases: An attribute-oriented approach", *Proc. 18th Int. Conf. VLDB*, Vancouver, Canada, 1992, pp. 547-559.
9. J. Han and Y. Fu, "Exploration of the Power of Attribute-Oriented Induction in Data Mining", in U.M. Fayyad, G. Piatetsky-Shapiro, P. Smyth, and R. Uthurusamy (Eds.), *Advances in Knowledge Discovery and Data Mining*, AAAI/MIT Press, Menlo Park, CA, 1996, pp. 399-421.
10. J. Han and M. Kamber, *Data Mining: Concepts and Techniques*, Morgan Kaufmann, New York, NY, 2000.
11. R.J. Hilderman, H.J. Hamilton, and N. Cercone, "Data mining in large databases using domain generalization graphs", *Journal of Intelligent Information Systems, 13*(3), 1999, pp. 195-234.
12. S. Kumar De, R. Biswas, and A. R. Roy, "On extended fuzzy relational database model with proximity relations", *Fuzzy Sets and Systems, 117*(2), 2001, pp.195-201.
13. D.H. Lee and M.H. Kim, "Database summarization using fuzzy ISA hierarchies", *IEEE Transactions on Systems, Man, and Cybernetics - part B, 27*(1), 1997, pp. 68-78.
14. K.-M. Lee, "Mining generalized fuzzy quantitative association rules with fuzzy generalization hierarchies", *Proc. Joint 9th IFSA World Congress and 20th NAFIPS Int'l Conf.*, Vancouver, Canada, 2001, pp. 2977-2982.
15. S. Parsons, Current approaches to handling imperfect information in data and knowledge bases, *IEEE Trans. on Knowledge and Data Eng., 8*(3), 1996, pp. 353-372.
16. F.E. Petry, *Fuzzy Databases: Principles and Applications*, Kluwer Academic Publishers, Boston, MA, 1996.
17. G. Raschia and N. Mouaddib, "SAINTETIQ: a fuzzy set-based approach to database summarization", *Fuzzy Sets and Systems, 129*(2), 2002, pp. 137–162.
18. S. Shenoi and A. Melton, "Proximity Relations in the Fuzzy Relational Database Model", *International Journal of Fuzzy Sets and Systems, 31*(3), 1989, pp. 285-296.
19. S. Shenoi, A. Melton, and L. T. Fan, "Functional Dependencies and Normal Forms in the Fuzzy Relational Database Model", *Information Sciences, 60*(1-2), 1992, pp. 1-28.
20. S. Tamura, S. Higuchi, and K. Tanaka, "Pattern Classification Based on Fuzzy Relations", *IEEE Trans. on Systems, Man, and Cybernetics, SMC-1*(1), 1971, pp. 61-66.
21. L.A. Zadeh, "Similarity relations and fuzzy orderings", *Information Sciences, 3*(2), 1970, pp. 177-200.

Kernel-based outlier preserving clustering with representativity coefficients

M.-J. Lesot

LIP6, 8 rue du capitaine Scott, 75015 Paris, France

Abstract

Kernel learning methods provide a framework to implicitly enrich data representation and to handle non-vectorial data without requiring to adapt to each data representation or nature. In this paper, we consider the kernel extension of the Outlier Preserving Clustering Algorithm in order to identify both major trends and atypical behaviours in datasets and to define exceptionality coefficients to measure the subgroups' representativeness, independently of the data nature. We illustrate its principles on an artificial two-dimensional dataset and on XML data representing student results to several exams.

Key words: clustering, outlier handling, kernel methods

1. Introduction

Unsupervised learning aims at extracting regularities from datasets, in order to simplify their description by reducing them to their most characteristic elements. In particular, clustering decomposes datasets into subgroups which then constitute a summary of the initial data. Now a simplified and still accurate description should contain information about the major trends present in the dataset but also about the atypical behaviours, together with exceptionality coefficients to measure the extent to which the subgroups are representative of the whole dataset. This is illustrated by the example of a device having three modes, linguistically described as "high", "low" and "abnormally low": this natural description mentions the two major cases together with the exceptional one, which is indeed necessary: it is important to know that the device may be in such a state, which should not be overlooked. Moreover, the adverb "abnormally" underlines the fact that the three modes do not have the same representativeness, and distinguishes the device from a process having three normal modes, described as "high", "low" and "very low" for instance.

The outlier preserving clustering algorithm (OPCA) [1] provides the previous information in the case of vectorial data, by means of a partition and exceptionality coefficients [2] that indicate the extent to which the subgroups are characteristic of the whole dataset, modelling the role of the adverbs in the previous linguistic description. In this paper, we consider the extension of this algorithm in the kernel learning framework so as to make it independent of the data representation: kernel methods [3,4] do not involve data points as such but only rely on their pairwise scalar products; they make it possible to implicitly enrich the data representation and to consider more appropriate feature spaces than the input space; the latter should facilitate the identification of the underlying structure of the data, without increasing the computational costs. They also make it possible to handle non-vectorial data, such as trees or graphs, or more generally structured data without requiring to modify the algorithms to adapt to these specific data.

The paper is organised as follows: section 2 recalls the principles of OPCA and some elements about kernel learning methods. Section 3 describes the kernel extension of OPCA and section 4 the associated definition of exceptionality coefficients. Lastly section 5 illustrates some experimental results on an artificial dataset and an XML dataset representing student results to several exams.

2. Background

2.1. Outlier Preserving Clustering Algorithm

The Outlier Preserving Clustering Algorithm (OPCA) [1] aims at identifying both major trends and atypical behaviours in datasets, so as to provide complete and accurate descriptions: it identifies subgroups as any clustering algorithm, but also one-point clusters, corresponding to outliers, and lastly intermediate clusters, corresponding to small sets of similar outliers, which can be overlooked by both clustering techniques and outlier detection methods. Indeed, it considers that outliers or outlying groups should not be regarded as aberrations or noisy points as is usually the case, but as specific cases which are to be preserved.

OPCA is based on the combination, in an iterative process, of two clustering algorithms, so as to exploit their respective properties: it couples the agglomerative hierarchical clustering algorithm with single linkage (denoted AHC_{min} in the following) and the fuzzy c-means (denoted fcm in the following): AHC_{min} is sensitive to the minimum distance between data points assigned to different subgroups, thus it particularly identifies separable clusters. The fuzzy c-means algorithm optimises the homogeneity of the clusters, and thus provides compact groups. Their combination makes it possible to get both compact and separable clusters, which corresponds to the clustering double objective. Moreover, it allows to get over their respective difficulties: *fcm* are disrupted by the presence of outliers, whereas AHC_{min} identifies them easily; conversely AHC_{min} suffers from the chaining effect case, which can be handled by *fcm*: when natural subgroups are connected through a "bridge" of close points, the single linkage hierarchical algorithm can not split them whereas it is no difficulty for *fcm*.

Lastly the OPCA iterative process makes it possible to take into account several distance scales, and thus to handle datasets with varying densities. OPCA can be seen as a divisive clustering algorithm that, at each step, selects between AHC_{min} and *fcm* the most appropriate algorithm to split the considered subgroup and determines the most appropriate parameter values, as a function of the considered group properties.

2.2. Kernel learning methods

Kernel methods [3,4] are algorithms which exclusively depend on the data scalar products and not on the data themselves. The *kernel trick* then consists in replacing the classic euclidian scalar product by a so-called *kernel function* which is defined as a function $k : \mathcal{X} \times \mathcal{X} \to \mathbb{R}$ that corresponds to a scalar product in some implicit *feature space* ($\mathcal{X}$ denotes the input space): k is such that there exists a Hilbert space $\mathcal{F}$ and a transformation function $\phi : \mathcal{X} \to \mathcal{F}$ such that $\forall x, y \in \mathcal{X}$, $k(x,y) = \langle \phi(x), \phi(y) \rangle$.

This implies that through the kernel the algorithm is implicitly applied in the feature space $\mathcal{F}$ that can be of high or infinite dimension, which corresponds to an implicit data representation enrichment. Besides, these principles make it possible to handle non-vectorial data, such as sequences, trees or graphs: the algorithm only needs the kernel matrix, i.e. the pairwise values of the scalar products for all data points, but does not depend on the exact data nature.

In order to define a kernel extension of OPCA it is necessary to have a kernel variant of the hierarchical algorithm and of the fuzzy *c*-means.

2.2.1. Hierarchical clustering with kernels

Extending hierarchical clustering methods to the kernel framework is straightforward as they do not involve data points as such, but only their pairwise distances: replacing the euclidian distance with a kernel-based one

$$d_K(x,y) = \sqrt{k(x,x) - 2k(x,y) + k(y,y)} = \|\phi(x) - \phi(y)\| \tag{1}$$

one can apply the same process as in the non-kernel case. The algorithm is then implicitly applied in the feature space.

2.2.2. Fuzzy c-means with kernels

The kernel extension of the fuzzy *c*-means is less direct as this algorithm explicitely uses the data points themselves. It consists in transposing the cost function to the feature space, i.e. applying it to $\phi(x_i)$ instead of x_i. Provided the cluster centres are looked for as linear combinations of the data, which is consistent with the centre expression obtained in the non-kernel case, it can be shown [5] that the update equations for the linear combination coefficients and the membership degrees only depend on the scalar products and thus on the kernel.

It is to be noticed that there exist other approaches to replace the euclidian distance by more appropriate ones in the fuzzy c-means algorithm, as the fuzzy shell approach for instance [6]. Yet the aim of the latter differs from that of kernel methods: they look for clusters whose prototypes have a different nature than the data point, as for instance lines or quadric curves; therefore they require a modification of the distance between data points and cluster centres. In the kernel case, the point of view is different: there is no explicit representation of the cluster prototypes, and the comparison function involves pairs of data points, and not cluster centres. Kernels indicate more directly which points should be kept together, without considering the reference of a cluster centre.

3. Kernel-based outlier preserving clustering algorithm

The kernel extension of OPCA, denoted kOPCA in the following, is therefore based on the combination, in an iterative process, of the kernel agglomerative hierarchical clustering algorithm with single linkage (denoted $kAHC_{min}$) and the kernel fuzzy c-means (denoted kfcm) [5], as indicated in table 1: it considers a data subgroup G and tests its separability in the feature space. If G contains well separated clusters, $kAHC_{min}$ is applied as being the most appropriate algorithm; otherwise, the group's compactness in $\mathcal{F}$ is measured to determine whether it requires a subdivision (e.g. in chaining effect cases). If its homogeneity is low, G is split by kfcm. The process is then iterated on the obtained subgroups: as its non-kernel equivalent, kOPCA follows a divisive approach, determining at each step the most appropriate algorithm according to the considered group properties. The following sections detail the criteria used to determine which algorithm is to be applied at each step, and how its parameters are defined; some of them are simple transpositions to $\mathcal{F}$ of the criteria used in the non-kernel case.

3.1. Kernel hierarchical algorithm

The selection criterion for $kAHC_{min}$ must indicate whether it is justified to apply $kAHC_{min}$, i.e. whether the considered group (denoted G in the following) is separable in the feature space $\mathcal{F}$. Thus one must evaluate if the data distribution presents gaps in $\mathcal{F}$. This is measured by the quotient between the maximal merging distance and a minimal significant distance

$$C_{kAHC} = \frac{\max D}{\min D} \qquad (2)$$

where D is the vector containing the cost of the successive merges proposed by $kAHC_{min}$ when clustering G. Its maximal value, $\max D$, corresponds to the costs

Table 1
KOPCA procedure. $X = \{x_i, i = 1..n\}$ denotes the dataset.

Initialisation

Fix the parameter α (involved in eq. (3))

Compute the kernel matrix $K = (k(x_i, x_j)), 1 \leq i, j \leq n$

Set G = X

Algorithm

If G is separable according to C_{kAHC} (eq. (2))

    Compute threshold s^* according to eq. (3)

    Split G using $kAHC_{min}$ and s^*

Else, if G is not compact according to C_{diam} (eq. (4))

    Compute c^* according to eq. (6)

    If kfcm is justified according to KTA (eq. (5))

        Split G using kfcm with $c = c^*$

Iterate on each obtained subgroup, extracting the corresponding kernel submatrix.

of not splitting the group and considering it as a cluster as such: it takes high values if G contains well separated subgroups and should be divided by $kAHC_{min}$. The minimal value of D equals the minimal distance between distinct points in the group: $\min D = \min_{x,y \in G} d_K(x,y)$; this denominator involves local information in the definition of the separability criterion: for instance in low density groups, it has a high value, and an especially high maximal merging distance is required to imply that the group should be split by $kAHC_{min}$. It makes it possible to handle data with variable densities, without considering a single distance scale.

If $kAHC_{min}$ is selected, it is necessary to choose its parameter: hierarchical algorithms provide sequences of nested partitions, one of which must be selected as the clustering result. The criterion we use consists in carrying out the less expensive among the proposed merges, more precisely the merges whose cost is lower than the threshold

$$s^* = \bar{D} + \alpha\sigma(D) \qquad (3)$$

where $\bar{D}$ and $\sigma(D)$ are the average and standard deviation of the previous D vector and α is a user-defined parameter. Indeed, the more expensive merges correspond to fusing outliers to other clusters, they should not be carried out, thus their costs should be higher than s^* so that they can be left as single-point clusters. This criterion is equivalent to performing a fixed proportion of the proposed merges at each step, the proportion being ruled by parameter α that should depend on the expected proportion of outliers. Again, this definition is local, which means that the algorithm can identify outliers or outlying groups at several distance scales, at each step of its iterative application.

All quantities considered above are distances and thus can be computed in the feature space, using the kernel-based distance as indicated in eq. (1) instead of the euclidian one, to apply to the kernel framework.

3.2. Kernel fuzzy c-means

The selection criterion for *kfcm* must indicate whether a non-separable group G (i.e. a group which cannot be split by $kAHC_{min}$) should be split using *kfcm*, i.e. whether it is not sufficiently compact in the feature space. To that aim we use two criteria: the first one is defined as the group diameter

$$C_{diam} = \max_{x,y \in G} d_K(x,y) \qquad (4)$$

which is a measure of the group homogeneity: if the diameter is small, an additional split by *fcm* is rejected as unnecessary.

Beside, we use a second criterion to measure if the split proposed by *kfcm* is relevant: there exist criteria (cf. following paragraph) to compare the partitions obtained for various c values, but it is also necessary to measure the quality of the optimal one. To that aim, we use the Kernel Target Alignment KTA quantity [7] which was originally proposed as a measure of the quality of a kernel for a learning task and has many theoretical advantages: it measures the correlation between kernel values, interpreted as similarity measures (as scalar products), and data classes. Indeed data assignments and kernel values are consistent if high kernel values are associated to points belonging to the same class and small values to points assigned to different classes. Its computation is based on a reference matrix, defined as $R_{ij} = 1$ if x_i and x_j belong to the same group, and -1 otherwise: it corresponds to an assignment-based similarity. KTA is then defined as

$$KTA = \frac{\langle K, R \rangle}{\sqrt{\langle K, K \rangle \langle R, R \rangle}} \qquad (5)$$

where for any two matrices $\langle A, B \rangle = \sum_{ij} A_{ij} B_{ij}$. It measures the correlation between the assignment-based similarity and the kernel similarity itself. This quantity in particular verifies the separability of the obtained subgroups as it requires that points assigned to different groups have small kernel values. Likewise, it verifies the compactness as points belonging to the same group should have high kernel values, but this should not be a problem according to the kernel fuzzy c-means principles.

If *kfcm* is applied, the optimal c value should be selected, there exist many criteria, cf. [8-11] for instance; we apply a stability-based approach: it relies on the empirical observation that the kernel fuzzy c-means provide a highly stable result with respect to the random initialisation of the centres, provided the c value is lower than the actual number of subgroups present in the data. If c is higher, the algorithm exploits the available degrees of freedom and does not converge to the same solution each time. Therefore, we propose to test several c values and select the last one before destabilisation, the stability being measured by

$$C_{kfcm}(c) = \frac{\sigma(J_{kfcm})}{\bar{J}_{kfcm}} \qquad (6)$$

where J_{kfcm} denotes the kernel fuzzy c-means cost function, $\bar{J}_{kfcm}$ and $\sigma(J_{kfcm})$ its average and standard deviation with respect to random initialisation of the centres.

3.3. *kOPCA parameters*

As a consequence of the previous definitions, kOPCA depends on two parameters: the first one is the α value, involved in equation (3) to select the threshold for the hierarchical algorithm. It rules the proportion of proposed merges which are performed at each step and should be determined depending on the expected proportion of outliers: the latter corresponds to merges whose cost should be higher than the threshold.

The second parameter is the kernel itself, which greatly influences the clustering results. This influence is identical to the influence of attributes in the non-kernel case: the choice of the optimal kernel is equivalent to the problem of feature selection and data representation for vectorial data.

It is to be noticed that the non-kernel algorithm OPCA [1] contains more parameters that enable the user to incorporate *a priori* semantic information, as for instance the maximal diameter value or a minimal significant distance. In the kernel case, these quantities are defined in the feature space and thus are difficult to interpret, therefore they are not considered as parameters.

4. Exceptionality coefficients

In the previous section, we described the clustering algorithm, as a means to determine a partition of the data into subgroups identifying simultaneously major trends and atypical behaviours. In fact, due to its iterative process, kOPCA provides additional information which lead to a valuable clustering enrichment, in the form of exceptionality coefficients.

4.1. *Principles*

Natural linguistic descriptions provide information about major trends and atypical behaviours present in datasets, but they also preserve information about their representativity, by means of adverbs indicating the extent to which the trends are characteristic of the whole datasets: in the example mentioned in the introduction we considered a device having three modes described as "high", "low" and "abnormally low"; the additional information is provided by the adverb "abnormally" which underlines the specificity of the third mode. Now kOPCA, as well as OPCA [2], makes it possible to retrieve such information in the form of exceptionality coefficients, due to its iterative process: as we underlined in the previous section, parameters are defined locally, taking into account the local data distribution, and the algorithm considers progressively refined distance scales. This property can be used to define exceptionality coefficients.

Indeed, it means that an outlier defined at the end of the process is only a local outlier, whereas a point isolated at the first step is a global outlier whose representativity of the whole dataset is very low: the isolation date of a cluster provides information about the distance to its nearest neighbour; it can be considered that the earlier a cluster is identified, the more exceptional it is.

This consideration must be balanced by the cluster size: a large and well-separated group may represent the whole dataset better than smaller groups identified later. More generally, it seems natural that a big cluster be more characteristic of the whole dataset than a small one.

4.2. Definition

Based on the two previous intuitive properties, one can define an exceptionality coefficient for any cluster C to be inversely proportional to its size, denoted $|C|$, and to its isolation date, denoted $h(C)$:

$$cExc(C) = \frac{1}{Z} \frac{Z_{h(C)}}{|C|} \frac{\max_\Gamma h(\Gamma)}{h(C)} \qquad (7)$$

In this equation, $Z_{h(C)}$ denotes the average size of clusters identified at step $h(C)$ in order to measure a local lack of balance of C size; the cluster isolation date $h(C)$ is compared to the maximal isolation date, $\max_\Gamma h(\Gamma)$, i.e. the total number of steps of the iterative process. Lastly Z is a normalising factor which ensures that the minimal exceptionality coefficient equals 1, so as to have a reference value.

With this definition, the exceptionality is maximal for early identified clusters of small size, which are indeed the least representative groups. Due to the normalisation, the exceptionality coefficient is to be compared to the reference value 1 that is associated to clusters which are totally characteristic of the dataset.

It is to be underlined that this definition is similar to the definition used in the non-kernel case [2]: indeed it does not use any data point relative information, thus it can be transposed to the feature space directly. This is due to the fact that exceptionality coefficients take into account a high abstraction level, and do not depend on data points themselves.

5. Numerical experiments

In this section we illustrate the results obtained with KOPCA and the exceptionality coefficients on an artificial two-dimensional dataset and real XML data corresponding to tree data.

5.1. Artificial data

Figure 1a represents a ring type dataset, made of a central uniform distribution surrounded by a noisy ring and linked to it through a bridge of regularly spaced

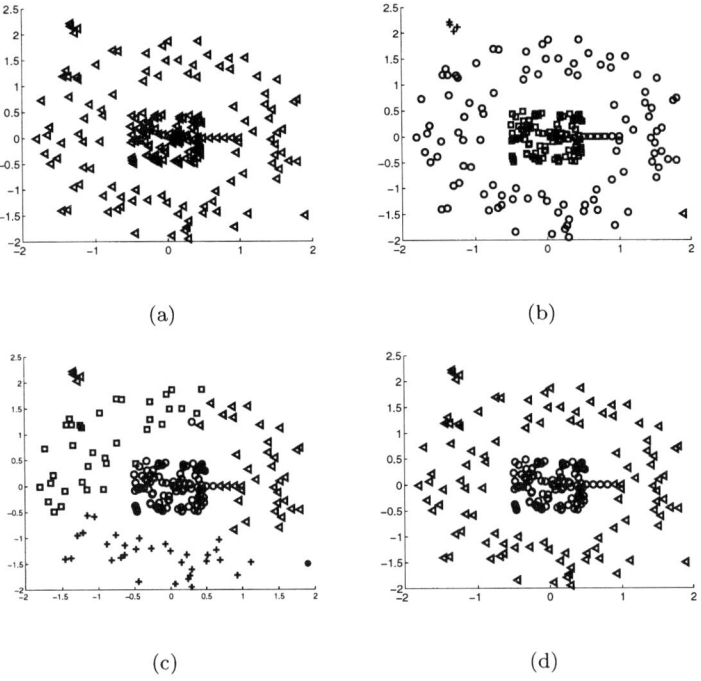

Fig. 1. Clustering results using several clustering algorithms: (a) Considered dataset; (b) KOPCA (4 clusters); (c) OPCA (6 clusters); (d) kernel fcm (2 clusters).

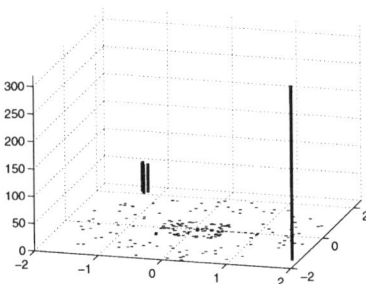

Fig. 2. Exceptionality coefficients for the artificial dataset represented on fig. 1.

data leading to a chaining effect; it also contains a small outlying group located around (-1.4, 2.1) and an outlier located in (1.9, -1.5).

Figure 1b shows that KOPCA, applied with a gaussian kernel of variance 0.32 and $\alpha = 4$, identifies the expected clusters: the ring and the internal distribution are associated to exceptionality coefficients of 1 (see fig. 2) which indicate they are totally representative of the whole dataset. The small outlying group is less representative, with $cExc = 53$; the outlier itself has a very high exceptionality of

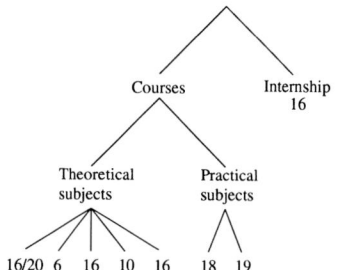

Examples of depths of deepest common node (tree leaves, corresponding to fields, are numbered from left to right) :

p(1, 8) = 0
p(1, 2) = 2

Fig. 3. Left: example of a considered data point: XML structure and field values; right: examples of depths of deepest common node for two field couples.

319.

Figure 1c illustrates the OPCA results and thus the kernel advantage: using the euclidian distance, the ring cluster is not compact enough and must be split into four subgroups; still, outliers are identified. Figure 1d shows the results using *kfcm*: as it is also based on the gaussian kernel, it identifies the ring cluster, but it fails to isolate the outliers, be it the small outlying group or the outlier point. It assigns them to the ring cluster, loosing information about the specificity of these data points.

5.2. XML *data*

We consider an application to real data corresponding to XML data representing student results to several exams, as illustrated on figure 3: the XML structure represents the relationships between the exams, for instance opposing theoretical subjects to practical ones. This structure provides information which should be taken into account to enrich the classic euclidian distance: it suggests that attributes are not independent one from another and that their correlation should be involved.

Therefore we propose to measure the similarity between students as

$$k(x,y) = \sum_{i=1}^{d}\sum_{j=1}^{d} \lambda_{ij} x_i y_j \quad \text{with} \quad \lambda_{ij} = \delta_{ij} + \frac{l}{P - p(i,j)}(1 - \delta_{ij})$$

where d denotes the number of fields in the XML structure, $l < 1$ is a user-defined parameter, P the depth of the XML tree and $p(i,j)$ the depth of the deepest common node for fields i and j (see fig. 3 right); this corresponds to a weighted euclidian scalar product, where the weights are derived from the structure. If $i = j$, one still has $\lambda_{ij} = 1$, but if $i \neq j$, $\lambda_{ij} \neq 0$, it takes a value which depends on the XML structure: if two distinct fields i and j have nothing in common, their deepest common node is the root, which leads to $\lambda_{ij} = l/P$; if they belong to the same branch of the tree, $\lambda_{ij} = l$ because $p(i,j) = P - 1$; thus they have a higher influence in the comparison of the corresponding values in the kernel definition.

Figure 4 represents an example of obtained clusters, in the case $l = 0.9$ and $\alpha = 2$, represented as sequences of the field values, table 2 indicates the associated

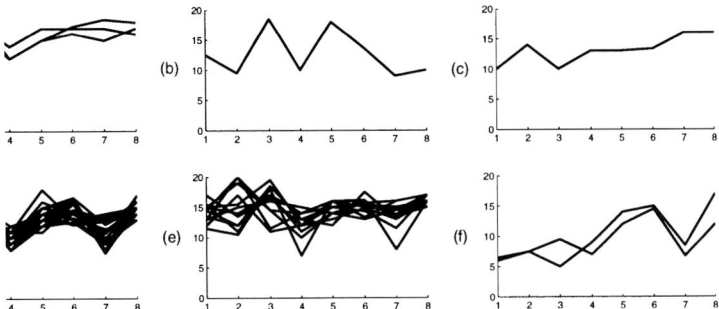

Fig. 4. Clustering result for XML data, represented as sequences of their field values.

Table 2
Exceptionality coefficients for the clusters obtained with the XML data (see fig. 4).

Cluster	a	b	c	d	e	f
$cExc$	16.47	42.23	21.00	1.00	1.75	24.71

exceptionality coefficients. It can be seen that the cluster constitution indeed takes into account some correlation about the fields, in particular for cluster (e): it can be interpreted as students having almost perfect results for the theoretical exams 2 and 3, one compensating for the other. Together with the exceptionality coefficients, the obtained partition indicates that the class is made of two main groups (cluster (d) and (e)), associated to exceptionality coefficients lower than 2, cluster (d) corresponding to students having slightly lower results than those of cluster (e). The other groups have much lower representativity measures and correspond to specific profiles: the most atypical one is cluster (b), associated to $cExc = 42.23$, which corresponds to the student having the worst note for the internship although his results were acceptable or high for all exams. Cluster (f) corresponds to the students who failed at the theoretical exams; cluster (c) is close to cluster (d) but is isolated because the corresponding student got especially good results on exams 4 and 7 when compared to cluster (d); with $cExc = 24.7$ and 21.0 respectively, these two clusters are not to be considered as very representative of the whole class. Lastly, cluster (a), which is slightly more representative ($cExc = 16.5$), can be interpreted as students having especially good results to all exams.

6. Conclusion

We proposed a technique to provide a simplified and accurate description of a dataset, containing information about the major trends present in the dataset as well as the atypical behaviours, together with exceptionality coefficients to measure the extent to which the subgroups are representative of the whole dataset. The proposed method belongs to the kernel framework and thus can be applied to any kind of data, be it vectorial data with several scalar products or structured data as XML trees for instance.

In the considered application, the quality of the obtained clusters was visually assessed. Perspectives include the definition of numerical quality measures, leading to objective evaluation. Such a criterion could induce a method to optimise the parameters of the algorithm which are here empirically set.

Another perspective concerns the application of the algorithm to other structured data, in particular in the bio-informatics context where sequences are to be handled, e.g. sequences representing temporal evolution of gene expression. In such contexts, the application of the kernel outlier preserving clustering algorithm may be particularly useful.

References

1. M.-J. Lesot, B. Bouchon-Meunier, Descriptive concept extraction with exceptions by hybrid clustering, in: Proc. of the IEEE Int. Conf. on Fuzzy Systems, FUZZ-IEEE'04, 2004, pp. 389–394.
2. M.-J. Lesot, B. Bouchon-Meunier, Cluster characterization through a representativity measure, in: Proc. of Flexible Query Answering Systems, FQAS'04, 2004, pp. 446–458.
3. V. Vapnik, The nature of statistical learning theory, Springer, New York, 1995.
4. B. Schölkopf, A. Smola, Learning with kernels, MIT Press, 2002.
5. Z. Wu, W. Xie, J. Yu, Fuzzy c-means clustering algorithm based on kernel method, in: Proc. of the 5th Int. Conf. on Computational Intelligence and Multimedia Applications, ICCIMA'03, 2003, pp. 1–6.
6. F. Klawonn, R. Kruse, H. Timm, Fuzzy shell cluster analysis, in: G. della Riccia, H. Lenz, R. Kruse (Eds.), Learning, networks and statistics, Springer, 1997, pp. 105–120.
7. N. Cristianini, J. Shawe-Taylor, A. Elisseeff, J. Kandola, On kernel-target alignment, in: Advances in Neural Information Processing Systems NIPS 14, 2002, pp. 367–373.
8. J. Bezdek, Cluster validity with fuzzy sets, Journal of Cybernetics 3 (3) (1974) 58–73.
9. J. Bezdek, Mathematical models for systematics and taxonomy, in: Proc. of the 8th Int. Conf. on Numerical Taxonomy, Freeman, 1975, pp. 143–166.
10. X. Xie, G. Beni, A validity measure for fuzzy clustering, IEEE Transactions on pattern analysis and machine intelligence 13 (4) (1991) 841–846.
11. M. Rezaee, B. Lelieveldt, J. Reiber, A new cluster validity index for the fuzzy c-means, Pattern Recognition Letters 19 (1998) 237–246.

Fuzzy C-medoids clustering models for time-varying data

R. Coppi [a] and P. D'Urso [b] and P. Giordani [a]

[a] Dipartimento di Statistica, Probabilità e Statistiche Applicate,
Università di Roma "La Sapienza",
Rome, Italy.
[b] Dipartimento di Scienze Economiche, Gestionali e Sociali,
Università del Molise,
Campobasso, Italy.

Abstract

In this paper, by considering suitable dissimilarity measures for multivariate time trajectories (time series) [1–3], we suggest different fuzzy C-medoids clustering models, which are particular relational versions of the dynamic clustering models proposed in [2,3]. In particular, our models classify time trajectories and select, in the set of the observed trajectories, typical trajectories that synthetically represent the structural characteristics of the identified clusters (medoid time trajectories). A simulation study and an application are also discussed.

Key words: Time data array, Medoid time trajectory, Instantaneous and/or velocity fuzzy C-medoids clustering
2000 MSC: 62H30, 62B10

1. Introduction

In the literature, there are various works adopting classification methods for time-varying data both in an exploratory framework (see, e.g., [1–6]) and in an inferential framework (see, e.g., [7–9]). In this paper, we suggest different dynamic partitioning models by adopting an exploratory formalization of the time array. We analyze the classification problem based on an algebraic-geometric representation of the time array. In particular, we propose three fuzzy C-medoids clustering models for time-varying data. In the following section, we briefly show the algebraic and geometric formulation of the time data array, the instantaneous and longitudinal features of the so-called time trajectories (geometric representation of the time data array), the dissimilarity measures for comparing time trajectories and illustrate the dynamic clustering problem. In Section 3, we propose dynamic fuzzy C-medoids clustering models for classifying time trajectories and selecting, in the set of the observed trajectories, typical trajectories that synthetically represent the structural characteristics of the identified clusters (medoid time trajectories). A simulation study and an application are discussed, respectively, in Sections 4 and 5.

2. Fuzzy Clustering for Time Data Arrays

2.1. *Algebraic and Geometric Representation of Time Data Arrays*

A time data array can be represented in the following way: $\mathbf{X} \equiv \{x_{ijt} : i = 1, \ldots, I; j = 1, \ldots, J; t = 1, \ldots, T\}$, where i $(i = 1, \ldots, I)$ indicates the generic observation unit, j $(j = 1, \ldots, J)$ the generic variable, and t $(t = 1, \ldots, T)$ the generic time point. Therefore, x_{ijt} represents the j-th variable observed on the i-th observation unit at time occasion t. Furthermore, $\mathbf{X}$ can be represented as a bi-dimensional matrix (stacked matrix) by combining two of the three indices i, j, t on the rows and assigning the remaining index to the columns. The various types of matrices are respectively: $\mathbf{X}_i \equiv \{x_{ijt} : j = 1, \ldots, J; t = 1, \ldots, T\}$, $\mathbf{X}_j \equiv \{x_{ijt} : i = 1, \ldots, I; t = 1, \ldots, T\}$ and $\mathbf{X}_t \equiv \{x_{ijt} : i = 1, \ldots, I; j = 1, \ldots, J\}$. Geometrically, $\mathbf{X}$ can be represented on a suitable vectorial space. By treating the elements of one of the three possible classification modes as vectors of a vectorial space, defined with respect to the other ones, we have: 1) the space of the observation units $\Re^{J+1}$; 2) the space of the variables $\Re^{I+1}$; 3) the space of the time occasions $\Re^{IJ}$. In particular, in the space $\Re^{J+1}$ (the first J dimensions correspond to the J variables and the last dimension refers to the time occasion), each observation unit i is represented, for each time point t, by the vector $\mathbf{y}_{it} = (x_{i1t}, \ldots, x_{ijt}, \ldots, x_{iJt}, t)'$, $i = 1, \ldots, I; t = 1, \ldots, T$. For fixed t, the matrix $\mathbf{X}_t$ is represented by the scatter $S_I(t) \equiv \{\mathbf{y}_{it} : i = 1, \ldots, I\}$. Then $\{S_I(t) \equiv \{\mathbf{y}_{it} : i = 1, \ldots, I\} : t = 1, \ldots, T\}$ represents the set of scatters located on T hyperplanes parallel to the co-ordinate subspace $\Re^J$. Conversely, for fixed i, the matrix $\mathbf{X}_i$ is represented by the scatter $S_T(i) \equiv \{\mathbf{y}_{it} : t = 1, \ldots, T\}$ that describes the *time trajectory* of the i-th observation unit. Then, the set of scatters $\{S_T(i) \equiv \{\mathbf{y}_{it} : t = 1, \ldots, T\} : i = 1, \ldots, I\}$ represents the set of the time trajectories of the I observation units. Each time trajectory crosses the T hyperplanes. Here, we consider only the case in which the time array $\mathbf{X}$ is represented in the space of the observation units $\Re^{J+1}$ and then we analyze the aggregative behavior of the time trajectories of observation units $S_T(i) \equiv \{\mathbf{y}_{it} : t = 1, \ldots, T\}$ in this data space. Notice that, in the following, in the formalization of the definition of time trajectory, we do not consider the co-ordinate t, because this does not affect the clustering procedure. Thus, $\mathbf{X}_i \equiv \{\mathbf{x}_{it} : t = 1, \ldots, T\}$ uniquely represents the

i-th time trajectory, where $\mathbf{x}_{it} \equiv (x_{i1t}, ..., x_{ijt}, ..., x_{iJt})$, $i = 1, ..., I$, $t = 1, ..., T$.

2.2. Instantaneous and Longitudinal Features of Time Trajectories and Dissimilarity Measures

In order to identify time trajectories with similar instantaneous and longitudinal characteristics we can define suitable dissimilarities that we subsequently incorporate in the objective function of the suggested clustering models. An *instantaneous dissimilarity* between a pair of trajectories is:

$$_1d_{il}^2 = \sum_{t=1}^{T} (_1w_{t1}d_{ilt})^2 = \sum_{t=1}^{T} (_1w_t \|\mathbf{x}_{it} - \mathbf{x}_{lt}\|)^2, \tag{1}$$

where $\mathbf{x}_{it}$ and $\mathbf{x}_{lt}$ are the vectors of the i-th and l-th time trajectories at time t, $_1w_t$ is the t-th instantaneous weight associated to the instantaneous Euclidean distance $_1d_{ilt}$. In the previous dissimilarity measure, we do not take into account the evolutive (longitudinal) features of the trajectories. If we want to capture the differences concerning the *variational* pattern of the trajectories, then we can consider a dissimilarity measure that compares the so-called velocity vectors associated with the trajectories. Thus, to take into account the longitudinal (variational) information of each observed time trajectory, we consider a (squared) distance to compare the dynamic features in each time interval of the time trajectories. In particular in the interval $[t-1, t]$ we compare the velocities of the trajectories, by considering the following *velocity dissimilarity* between a pair of trajectories:

$$_2d_{il}^2 = \sum_{t=2}^{T} (_2w_{t2}d_{ilt})^2 = \sum_{t=2}^{T} (_2w_t \|\mathbf{v}_{it} - \mathbf{v}_{lt}\|)^2, \tag{2}$$

where $_2w_t$ is a weight in $[t-1, t]$ ("velocity" weight); $_2d_{ilt} = \|\mathbf{v}_{it} - \mathbf{v}_{lt}\|$ is the Euclidean distance between the velocities of the trajectories of the i-th and l-th observation units. Notice that, we have defined, for the i-th time trajectory, the concept of velocity in the time interval $[t-1, t]$, as $\mathbf{v}_{it} = \frac{(\mathbf{x}_{it} - \mathbf{x}_{it-1})}{t - (t-1)} = (\mathbf{x}_{it} - \mathbf{x}_{it-1})$. Then, for each variable j, v_{ijt} can be greater (less) than zero according to whether the i-th observation unit presents an increasing (decreasing) rate of change of its position in $[t-1, t]$; $v_{ijt} = 0$ if the observation unit does not change position from t-1 to t. Moreover, we observe that, for any time trajectory, the velocity pertaining to each pair of successive time points represents the slope of the straight line passing through them: if the velocity is negative (positive) the slope will be negative (positive) and the angle made by each segment of the trajectory with the positive direction of the t-axis will be obtuse (acute) [1]. Then, the squared Euclidean distance $_2d_{ilt}^2$ compares the slopes (velocities) in each time interval $[t-1, t]$ of the segments of the time trajectory concerning the i-th observation unit with the corresponding slopes of the l-th time trajectory. Summing up, this distance is able to capture and thus to measure similarities of shapes of the time trajectories by taking into account the trajectories as piecewise linear functions and measuring the

difference of slopes (velocities) between them.
The instantaneous and longitudinal (velocity) dissimilarities emphasize two different pieces of information embodied in the data set (cross sectional and longitudinal information). When both are considered important the simultaneous dissimilarity $\sum_{s=1}^{2} \sum_{t} ({}_s w_{ts} d_{ilt})^2$ can be chosen for the clustering task.

2.3. Dynamic Fuzzy Clustering Models

By taking into account the previous instantaneous, velocity and mixed dissimilarity measures between the time trajectories and the centroid time trajectories defining the various clusters [2–4], dynamic versions of the well-known fuzzy C-means algorithm suggested in [10–12] have been proposed: the so-called Instantaneous, Velocity and Simultaneous fuzzy C-means clustering models. Notice that dynamic fuzzy C-means clustering models for fuzzy (imprecise) time trajectories have been proposed in [13–16].

3. Dynamic Fuzzy C-Medoids Clustering Models

By means of the previously mentioned clustering models, we determine fuzzy partitions of the set of the time trajectories and, then, we estimate (unobserved) typical trajectories (the *centroid trajectories*) that synthetically represent the features of the trajectories belonging to the corresponding clusters. However, there are several situations in which it is more realistic, in the clustering process, to identify typical trajectories belonging to the set of observed trajectories that synthesize the cluster information (the *medoid trajectories*) (see Figure 1; in particular, on the left side, we show six observed trajectories and two clusters (with two medoid trajectories); on the right side, we display four observed trajectories and two clusters (with two centroid trajectories)). In a two-way framework ($T = 1$), the idea to cluster objects around representative objects (centrotype, median or medoid) was introduced in [17] and later discussed in [18–20]. Successively, different clustering techniques by means of medoids have been suggested: Partitioning Around Medoids (PAM) [21]; Clustering Large Applications (CLARA) [22]; Clustering Large Applications based on Randomized Search (CLARANS) [23,24]; Clustering Large Applications based on Simulated Annealing (CLASA) [25–27]; Fuzzy C-Medoids Algorithm (FCMdd) [28,29]; Multi-centroid, Multi-Run Sampling Scheme [30]; Incremental Multi-centroid, Multi-Run Sampling Scheme [31]; Genetic C-Medoids Algorithm (GFCM) [32]; Fuzzy C Trimmed Medoids Algorithm (FCTMdd) [28,29]. In this paper, for clustering time trajectories, we propose a dynamic version of the two-way fuzzy C-medoids model suggested in [28,29]. The adoption of a *fuzzy* clustering model for multivariate time trajectories is justified on the grounds of at least two considerations. First of all the "complexity" of the trajectories (various observational times, several variables) suggests thinking in terms of "degrees" of

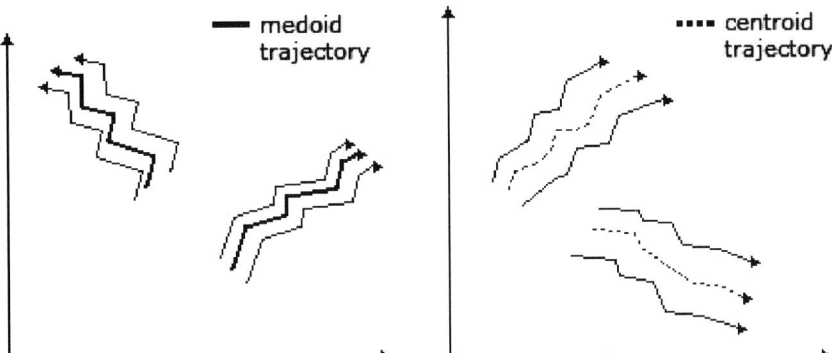

Fig. 1. Clusters, Centroid and medoid trajectories

membership to given clusters rather than in terms of total membership vs. non-membership. In fact, a crisp definition of clusters contrasts for example with the ambiguities presented in the following instances. 1) "Switching time trajectories" may occur, namely, trajectories showing a pattern typical of a given cluster during a certain time period and a completely different pattern (characteristic of another cluster) in another time period. 2) The time evolution of the variables defining an observation may follow a given pattern (belonging to a specific cluster) for a subgroup of variables, and a remarkably different pattern (another cluster) for a different subgroup of variables. Moreover, the following considerations support the adoption of the fuzzy approach. 1) Greater *adaptivity* in defining the "prototypes" (i.e. the "typical" trajectories). This can be better appreciated when the observed time patterns do not differ too much from each other. In this case, the fuzzy definition of the clusters allows us to single out underlying prototypes, if these are likely to exist in the given array of data. 2) Greater *sensitivity*, in capturing the details characterizing the time pattern of the observations. The dynamics are often drifting or switching and the standard clustering approaches are likely to miss this underlying structure. On the contrary, the switches from one time state to another, which are usually vague and not focused on any particular time point, can be naturally treated by means of fuzzy clustering.

By considering the instantaneous characteristics of the trajectories, the so-called *Instantaneous fuzzy C-medoids clustering model* can be formalized as follows:

$$\begin{cases} \min : {}_mJ({}_1\mathbf{U}, {}_1\mathbf{w}, \tilde{\mathbf{X}}; \mathbf{X}) = \sum_{i=1}^{I}\sum_{c=1}^{C} {}_1u_{ic}^m \sum_{t=1}^{T} \left({}_1w_t {}_1d_{ict}\right)^2 \\ \qquad\qquad\qquad\qquad\quad = \sum_{i=1}^{I}\sum_{c=1}^{C} {}_1u_{ic}^m \sum_{t=1}^{T} \left({}_1w_t \|\mathbf{x}_{it} - \tilde{\mathbf{x}}_{ct}\|\right)^2; \\ \sum_{c=1}^{C} {}_1u_{ic} = 1, {}_1u_{ic} \geq 0; \quad \sum_{t=1}^{T} {}_1w_t = 1, {}_1w_t \geq 0. \end{cases} \qquad (3)$$

where $_1\mathbf{U} = \{_1u_{ic} : i = 1,...,I; c = 1,...C\}$ is the fuzzy membership degrees matrix, in which $_1u_{ic}$ represents the extent to which the i-th observation unit belongs to the c-th cluster; $_1\mathbf{w}$ represents the vector of the instantaneous weights; $\tilde{\mathbf{X}}$ is a sub-set of $\mathbf{X}$ with cardinality C; $_1d_{ict} = \|\mathbf{x}_{it} - \tilde{\mathbf{x}}_{ct}\|$ denotes the Euclidean distance between the i-th observed time trajectory and the c-th medoid time trajectory at time t, $t = 1,\ldots,T$; $m \in [1,\infty)$ is the "fuzzifier". We observe that the aims of the previous model are: 1) to suitably select specific observed time trajectories as representative trajectories of the corresponding clusters (medoid time trajectories); 2) to determine the degrees of membership of each observed time trajectory in the various clusters identified by their representative trajectories; 3) to weigh objectively the observational times.

The membership degrees and the instantaneous weights can be defined heuristically in many different ways. For instance, we can adopt the membership degrees and the instantaneous weights obtained by means of the Instantaneous fuzzy C-means clustering model [2,3]:

$$_1u_{ic} = \frac{1}{\sum_{c'=1}^{C}\left[\frac{\sum_{t=1}^{T}(_1w_{t\,1}d_{ict})^2}{\sum_{t=1}^{T}(_1w_{t\,1}d_{ic't})^2}\right]^{\frac{1}{m-1}}}, \quad _1w_t = \frac{1}{\sum_{t'=1}^{T}\left[\frac{\sum_{i=1}^{I}\sum_{c=1}^{C}{}_1u_{ic}^m{}_1d_{ict}^2}{\sum_{i=1}^{I}\sum_{c=1}^{C}{}_1u_{ic}^m{}_1d_{ict'}^2}\right]}. \quad (4)$$

When $_mJ\left(_1\mathbf{U},_1\mathbf{w},\tilde{\mathbf{X}};\mathbf{X}\right)$ is minimized, the $\tilde{\mathbf{X}}$ corresponding to the solution provides an instantaneous fuzzy partition and a velocity weighting system via (4). However, similarly to the two-way case, $_mJ\left(_1\mathbf{U},_1\mathbf{w},\tilde{\mathbf{X}};\mathbf{X}\right)$ cannot be minimized by means of the alternating optimization algorithm, because the necessary conditions cannot be derived by differentiating it with respect to the medoids. Nonetheless, following Fu's heuristic algorithm for a crisp version of $_mJ\left(_1\mathbf{U},_1\mathbf{w},\tilde{\mathbf{X}};\mathbf{X}\right)$, a fuzzy clustering algorithm that minimizes $_mJ\left(_1\mathbf{U},_1\mathbf{w},\tilde{\mathbf{X}};\mathbf{X}\right)$ can be built up as follows [29].

Instantaneous Fuzzy C-Medoids Algorithm

Fix C and max_iter; set $iter = 0$; pick up initial medoids $\tilde{\mathbf{X}} = \left\{\tilde{\mathbf{X}}_1,\ldots,\tilde{\mathbf{X}}_C\right\}$;
Repeat
Compute $_1\mathbf{U}$ and $_1\mathbf{w}$ by using (4);
Store the current medoids: $\tilde{\mathbf{X}}_{OLD} = \tilde{\mathbf{X}}$;
Compute the new medoids $\tilde{\mathbf{X}}_c$, $c = 1,\ldots,C$:
$q = \underset{1 \leq i' \leq I}{\arg\min} \sum_{i''=1}^{I} {}_1u_{i''c}^m \sum_{t=1}^{T}(_1w_{t\,1}d_{i'i''t})^2$, $\tilde{\mathbf{X}}_c = \mathbf{X}_q$;
$iter = iter + 1$;
Until ($\tilde{\mathbf{X}}_{OLD} = \tilde{\mathbf{X}}$ or $iter = max\_iter$).

We remark that, similarly to the two-way version, this algorithm falls in the category of Alternating Cluster Estimation paradigm [33]; furthermore, it is not guaranteed to find the global minimum. Thus, more than one random start is suggested. Kamdar and Joshi [34] observe that "since the medoid always has a membership of 1 in the cluster, raising its membership to the power m has no effect. Thus, when m is high, the mobility of the medoids may be lost. [...] For this reason, a value between 1 and 1.5 for m is recommended".

In order to take into account the evolutive (velocity) features of the time trajectories in the clustering process, we propose the following *Velocity fuzzy C-medoids clustering model*:

$$\begin{cases} \min :_m J(_2\mathbf{U}, _2\mathbf{w}, \tilde{\mathbf{X}}; \mathbf{X}) = \sum_{i=1}^{I} \sum_{c=1}^{C} {}_2u_{ic}^m \sum_{t=2}^{T} (_2w_t \, _2d_{ict})^2 \\ \qquad\qquad\qquad\quad = \sum_{i=1}^{I} \sum_{c=1}^{C} {}_2u_{ic}^m \sum_{t=2}^{T} (_2w_t \, \|\mathbf{v}_{it} - \tilde{\mathbf{v}}_{ct}\|)^2; \\ \sum_{c=1}^{C} {}_2u_{ic} = 1, {}_2u_{ic} \geq 0; \quad \sum_{t=2}^{T} {}_2w_t = 1, {}_2w_t \geq 0. \end{cases} \quad (5)$$

Analogously to the instantaneous model, the membership degrees and the velocity weights are:

$$_2u_{ic} = \frac{1}{\sum_{c'=1}^{C}\left[\frac{\sum_{t=2}^{T}(_2w_t \, _2d_{ict})^2}{\sum_{t=2}^{T}(_2w_t \, _2d_{ic't})^2}\right]^{\frac{1}{m-1}}}, \quad _2w_t = \frac{1}{\sum_{t'=2}^{T}\left[\frac{\sum_{i=1}^{I}\sum_{c=1}^{C} {}_2u_{ic}^m \, _2d_{ict}^2}{\sum_{i=1}^{I}\sum_{c=1}^{C} {}_2u_{ic}^m \, _2d_{ict'}^2}\right]}, \quad (6)$$

where the notation is similar to the instantaneous model (in particular $\tilde{\mathbf{v}}_{ct}$ denotes the vector of the velocity of the c-th medoid trajectory). Notice that, also in this case, following Fu's heuristic algorithm a fuzzy clustering algorithm that minimizes $_mJ(_2\mathbf{U}, _2\mathbf{w}, \tilde{\mathbf{X}}; \mathbf{X})$ can be considered.

Similarly to the mixed (instantaneous-velocity) fuzzy C-Means clustering model, a *Mixed fuzzy C-medoids clustering model* can be considered for taking into account in the clustering process simultaneously the instantaneous and longitudinal (velocity) features of the time trajectories. We observe that, analogously to the two-way case, a robust version of our previous dynamic fuzzy clustering models can be considered, by extending, in a dynamic framework, the Fuzzy C Trimmed Medoids Algorithm (FCTMdd) [28,29].

4. Simulation study

In this section we provide the results of a simulation study carried out in order to assess how our clustering models work. In particular we study whether our models recover the known medoid which characterizes each cluster and how well they are able to reconstruct the cluster memberships of the trajectories that belong to one of the $C = 2$ clusters. We consider $I = 10$ or $I = 18$ trajectories characterized by $J = 2$ variables at $T = 6$ or $T = 12$ times. The experiment consists of two parts. in the first part the instantaneous clustering model is tested, whereas the second part is devoted to assessing the longitudinal model. Concerning the former study, the trajectories belonging to each cluster are constructed as follows. We assume that the first $I/2$ trajectories belong to Cluster 1 and the remaining $I/2$ ones to Cluster 2. For each cluster, we construct the medoid trajectory, which is, thus, known in advance. The remaining trajectories belonging to the involved cluster are obtained by modifying the medoid trajectory by means of added constant values. More specifically, let $\mathbf{X}_1 \equiv \{x_{1jt} : j = 1, 2; t = 1, \ldots, T\}$ be the medoid trajectory for Cluster 1 (without loss of generality we assume that the first trajectory belonging to each cluster is the medoid). The remaining trajectories belonging to Cluster 1 are $\mathbf{x}_{i1} \equiv \{x_{11t} : t = 1, \ldots, T\}, i = 2, \ldots, I/2$; and $\mathbf{x}_{i2} \equiv \{x_{12t} + k : t = 1, \ldots, T\}, i = 2, \ldots, I/2$; where $k = \pm 0.2, \pm 0.5$, when $I = 10$ and $k = \pm 0.2, \pm 0.5, \pm 1.0, \pm 1.5$, when $I = 18$. Similarly, the medoid trajectory for Cluster 2 is $\mathbf{X}_{I/2+1} \equiv \{x_{I/2+1jt} : j = 1, 2; t = 1, \ldots, T\}$ and the remaining trajectories belonging to Cluster 2 are $\mathbf{x}_{i1} \equiv \{x_{I/2+11t} : t = 1, \ldots, T\}, i = I/2 + 2, \ldots, I$; and $\mathbf{x}_{i2} \equiv \{x_{I/2+12t} + k : t = 1, \ldots, T\}, i = I/2 + 2, \ldots, I$. This leads to the structure of clusters given in Figure 2 (*instantaneous* case). The membership of the trajectories to the clusters depends on their instantaneous features. In this case, the instantaneous fuzzy C-medoids clustering model is performed in order to classify the trajectories.

With reference to the second part of the study, we use the following set-up to

Fig. 2. Instantaneous case: Cluster 1 (continuous line) and Cluster 2 (dotted line)

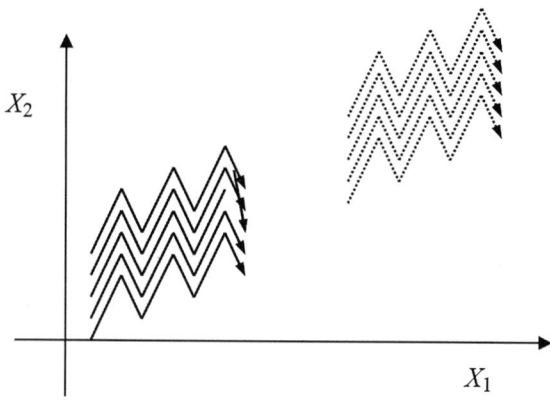

construct trajectories, which are then analyzed by means of the longitudinal fuzzy C-medoids clustering model. In this case, the classification of the trajectories is obtained taking into account the evolutive (longitudinal) features (*longitudinal* case) as one can see in Figure 3. With respect to Cluster 1 (and similarly for Cluster 2), the

Fig. 3. Longitudinal case: Cluster 1 (continuous line) and Cluster 2 (dotted line)

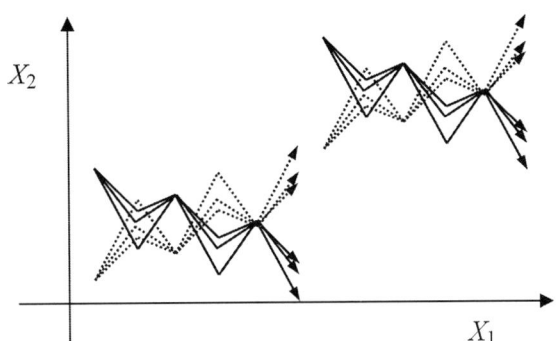

medoid trajectory is $\mathbf{X}_1 \equiv \{x_{1jt} : j = 1, 2; t = 1, \ldots, T\}$ and the remaining trajectories belonging to Cluster 1 are $\mathbf{x}_{i1} \equiv \{x_{11t} : t = 1, \ldots, T\}, i = 2, \ldots, I/2$; and $\mathbf{x}_{i2} \equiv \{x_{12t} : t = 1, 3, \ldots, T-3, T-1\}, i = 2, \ldots, I/2$; $\mathbf{x}_{i2} \equiv \{x_{12t} + k : t = 2, 4, \ldots T-2, T\}$, $i = 2, \ldots, I/2$; where $k = \pm 0.2, \pm 0.5$, when $I = 10$ and $k = \pm 0.2, \pm 0.5, \pm 1.0, \pm 1.5$, when $I = 18$. Moreover, for each cluster, the last $I/4$ trajectories of each cluster are shifted by means of $K = 1.7$ so that they have the same evolutive features as for the first $I/4$ trajectories (and different instantaneous profiles). We then have (for Cluster 1) $\mathbf{x}_{i2} \equiv \{x_{12t} + K : t = 1, 3, \ldots, T-3, T-1\}, i = I/4+1, \ldots, I/2$; $\mathbf{x}_{i2} \equiv \{x_{12t} + k + K : t = 2, 4, \ldots, T-2, T\}, i = I/4+1, \ldots, I/2$. The results are summarized in Table 1. Notice that, we set $m = 1.25$ and, for each case, we consider 50 random starts. The results are summarized in Table 1. The first column refers

Table 1
Performance of the models

Condition	Recovering Medoid (%)	Membership	Condition	Recovering Medoid (%)	Membership
$I = 10, T = 6$ (C)	100.0	100.0	$I = 10, T = 12$ (C)	100.0	100.0
$I = 10, T = 6$ (L)	100.0	100.0	$I = 10, T = 12$ (L)	100.0	99.8
$I = 18, T = 6$ (C)	65.0	94.3	$I = 18, T = 12$ (C)	68.0	94.3
$I = 18, T = 6$ (L)	69.0	100.0	$I = 18, T = 12$ (L)	56.0	88.9

to the involved condition. The second column contains the relative frequency of times in which the model at hand (instantaneous or longitudinal according to the structure of the clusters) recovers the known medoids of the clusters considering the 50 random starts. The third column displays the relative frequency of times in which the model at hand (instantaneous or longitudinal according to the structure of the clusters) exactly classifies the trajectories. Notice that we assign a trajectory to the class with the highest membership degree (hard clustering). On the whole, we can state that the results strongly depend on the number of trajectories. The number of occasions slightly affects the results. Finally, the results do not depend on the type of performed model (instantaneous or longitudinal). From Table 1, we can observe that the models classify the trajectories well. On average the trajectories are exactly assigned to the clusters in 97.7% of cases. In practice, when $I = 10$, the misclassifications rate is null (the rate is 5.6% when $I = 18$). Moreover, we can observe that the models very often detect the known medoids that characterize the clusters. In fact, this occurs in 82.3% of cases. Specifically, when $I = 10$, all of the 50 random starts lead to the same solution. On the contrary, when the number of trajectories increases, the algorithm does not always end up to the known medoids. In these cases, as one may expect, the trajectories setting $k = \pm 0.2$ are very often considered to be the medoid trajectories. We can conclude that several random starts should be used especially when the number of trajectories increases.

5. Application

The data examined in this application refer to the Web traffic concerning $I = 19$ Web sites (see Table 2). More specifically, the data refer to the percentage of Internet users that surf each Web site and the average time per person spent in each site ($J = 2$) during $T = 6$ time occasions. Before performing the fuzzy clustering models, we preprocess the data by standardizing them using the mean and the standard deviation obtained considering, for each variable, the scores pertaining to all the Web sites at all the times. This helps us to get rid of unwanted differences among the variables. In order to classify the Web sites, we apply the mixed fuzzy C-medoids clustering model. After running several analyses, we set $m = 1.25$ and $C = 3$. In this respect, we obtain the membership degrees matrix given in Table 2. Moreover, we obtain the following system of weights: $_1w_1 = 0.14$, $_1w_2 = 0.14$, $_1w_3 = 0.14$, $_1w_4 = 0.17$, $_1w_5 = 0.21$, $_1w_6 = 0.20$; $_2w_2 = 0.24$, $_2w_3 = 0.08$, $_2w_4 = 0.18$, $_2w_5 = 0.18$, $_2w_6 = 0.32$. Thus, we can observe that the instantaneous weights slightly differ, even if the weights pertaining to the last three time occasions are slightly higher than the remaining ones. On the contrary, the third and fifth velocity weights are, respectively, sensibly smaller and higher than those pertaining to the remaining time intervals. The medoids are MSN (Cluster 1), Time Warner (Cluster 2) and Altavista (Cluster 3). The clusters contain, respectively, three, eight and six trajectories with high membership degrees. Only two Web sites present consistently fuzzy membership degrees (Geocities and Lycos Network). In fact, they appear to belong to both Clusters 2 and 3. They can be considered as switching time trajectories between the involved clusters. The analysis of the medoid trajectories allows us to interpret the obtained clusters. Web sites reached by a very high percentage of Internet users form the first cluster. Clusters 2 and 3 are characterized by Web sites reached by a smaller percentage of Internet users. The average time spent surfing on the Web sites plays a relevant role in assigning the remaining Web Sites to Clusters 2 and 3. Specifically, Web sites with a high average time per person are assigned to Cluster 2. On the contrary, when the average time spent on the Web sites is low, the involved Web sites belong to Cluster 3.

Table 2
Membership degrees matrix

WEB SITES	C1	C2	C3	WEB SITES	C1	C2	C3	WEB SITES	C1	C2	C3
Altavista	0	0	1	Excite Network	0.06	0.90	0.04	MSN	1	0	0
Amazon	0.00	0.88	0.12	Geocities	0.00	0.55	0.45	Snap	0.00	0.02	0.98
AOL Websites	0.92	0.05	0.03	GO Network	0.01	0.95	0.04	Time Warner	0	1	0
AT&T	0.00	0.98	0.02	InfoSpace	0.00	0.01	0.99	Xoom	0.00	0.01	0.99
Blue Mountain Arts	0.00	0.94	0.06	Lycos Network	0.00	0.54	0.46	Yahoo!	0.99	0.01	0.00
Broadcast.com	0.00	0.01	0.99	Microsoft	0.00	0.97	0.03	ZDNet	0.00	0.97	0.03
CNET	0.00	0.24	0.76								

References

1. D'Urso, P., JISS, 1-3, 2000, 533.
2. D'Urso, P., IJUFKBS, 12, 2004, 287.
3. D'Urso, P., IEEE Trans. Fuzzy Syst., 2005, in press.
4. Carlier, A, COMPSTAT'86, 1986, p. 140, Physica-Verlag.
5. Košmelj, K., Batagelj, V., J. Class., 7, 1990, 99.
6. Sato, M., Sato, Y., IJUFKBS, 2, 1994, 127.
7. Kakizawa, Y., Shumway, H., Taniguchi, M., JASA, 93, 1998, 328.
8. Maharaj, E.A., Patt. Recogn., 32, 1999, 1129.
9. Maharaj, E.A., J. Class., 17, 2000, 297.
10. Bezdek, J.C., J. Math. Biol., 1, 1974, 57.
11. Bezdek, J.C., Pattern Recognition with Fuzzy Objective Function Algorithms, Plenum Press.
12. Dunn, J.C., J. Cybern., 3, 1974, 32.
13. Coppi, R., D'Urso, P., SMA, 11, 2002, 21.
14. Coppi, R., D'Urso, P., CSDA, 43, 2003, 149.
15. Coppi, R., D'Urso, P., CSDA, 2005, in press.
16. Coppi, R., D'Urso, P., Giordani, P., in: Lopez-Diaz, M., Gil, M.A., Grzegorzewski, P., Hryniewicz, O., Lawry, T., (Eds.), Springer-Verlag, p. 463.
17. Vinod, H., JASA, 64, 1969, 506.
18. Rao, M.R., JASA, 66, 1971, 622.
19. Church, R., in: ORSA/TIMS Joint National Meeting.
20. Mulvey, J., Cowder, H., Manag. Sci., 25, 1979, 329.
21. L. Kaufman, P.J. Rousseeuw, in: Dodge, Y., (Ed.) North-Holland, 405.
22. Kaufman, L., Rousseeuw, P.J., Finding Groups in Data: An Introduction to Cluster Analysis, J. Wiley and Sons.
23. Ng, R., Han, J. (1994) in, Twentieth International Conference on Very Large DataBases, Santiago, Morgan Kaufmann, 1994, 144.
24. Ng, R., Han, J., IEEE Trans. Knowl. Data Engin., 14, 2002, 1003.
25. Kirkpatrick, S., Gelatt Jr., C., Vecchi, M.P., Science, 220, 1983, 671.
26. Chu, S.-C., Roddick, J.F., Pan, J.S., Fifth International Conference on Optimization: Techniques and Applications, Hong Kong, 2001, 1708.

27. Huang, H.C., Pan, J.S., Lu, Z.M., Sun, S.H., Hang, H.M., Sig. Process., 81, 2001, 1513.
28. Krishnapuram, R., Joshi, A., Yi, L., FUZZIEEE99, 1999, 1281.
29. Krishnapuram, R., Joshi, A., Nasraoui, O., Yi, L., IEEE Trans. Fuzzy Syst., 9, 2001, 595.
30. Chu, S.-C., Roddick, J.F., Pan, J.S., Workshop on Mining Data for CRM, 2002, Taipei.
31. Chu, S.-C., Roddick, J.F., Pan, J.S., Tech. Rep. KDM-02-2002, Knowledge Discovery and Management Laboratory, Flinders University of South Australia.
32. Lucasius, C.B., Dane, A.D., Kateman, G., An. Chim. Acta, 1993, 647.
33. Runkler, T.A., Bezdek, J.C., IEEE Trans. Fuzzy Syst., 5, 1999, 270-293.
34. Kamdar, T., Joshi, A., Tech. Rep. TR-CS-2000-05, Department of Computer Science and Electrical Engineering, University of Maryland, Baltimore County.

Improving the K2 Algorithm Using Association Rule Parameters

Evelina Lamma, Fabrizio Riguzzi and Sergio Storari [*]

Dipartimento di Ingegneria, Università di Ferrara, Via Saragat 1, 41100 Ferrara, Italy

Abstract

A Bayesian network is an appropriate tool to work with the uncertainty that is typical of real-life applications. Bayesian network arcs represent statistical dependence between different variables and can be automatically elicited from database by Bayesian network learning algorithms such as K2. In the data mining field, association rules can also be interpreted as expressing statistical dependence relations. In this paper we present an extension of K2 called K2-rules that exploits a parameter normally defined in relation to association rules for learning Bayesian networks. We compare K2-rules with K2 and TPDA on the problems of learning four Bayesian networks. The experiments show that K2-rules improves both K2 and TPDA with respect to the quality of the learned network and K2 with respect to the execution time.

Key words: Bayesian Networks. Machine Learning. Association Rules.

1. Introduction

A Bayesian network [1,2] is an appropriate tool to work with the uncertainty that is typical of real-life applications. A Bayesian network is a directed, acyclic graph (DAG) whose nodes represent random variables. In a Bayesian network each node

---

[*] Corresponding author.
 Email addresses: elamma@ing.unife.it (Evelina Lamma), friguzzi@ing.unife.it (Fabrizio Riguzzi), sstorari@ing.unife.it (Sergio Storari).

is conditionally independent from any subset of nodes that are not its descendants, given its parents.

By means of Bayesian networks, we can use information about the values of some variables to obtain probabilities for other variables. A probabilistic inference takes place once the probabilities functions of each node conditioned to just its parents are given. These are usually represented in a tabular form, called Conditional Probability Table (CPT).

Given a training set of examples, learning a Bayesian network is the problem of finding the structure of the direct acyclic graph and the CPT associated with each node that best match (according to some scoring metric) the dataset. Optimality is evaluated with respect to a given scoring metric (e.g., description length or posterior probability [3–10]). A procedure for searching among possible structures is needed. However, the search space is so vast that any kind of exhaustive search cannot be considered, and often a greedy approach is followed.

The K2 algorithm [4] is a typical search and score method. It starts by assuming that a node has no parents, after which, in every step it adds incrementally the parent whose addition mostly increases the probability of the resulting structure. K2 stops adding parents to the nodes when the addition of a single parent cannot increase the probability of the network given the data. Other search and score methods include the MDL algorithm [10] and the CB algorithm [11].

In this work, we propose the algorithm K2-rules that improves the quality of learned networks and reduces the computational resources needed. This algorithm uses data mining techniques, and in particular the computation of parameters normally defined in relation to association rules [12], to obtain new knowledge to be used for improving some of the steps of K2. Association rules describe correlation of events, and can be viewed as probabilistic rules. Two events are "correlated" when they are frequently observed together. Both Bayesian network arcs and association rules represent dependence relations among variables so it is natural to integrate these methodologies in order to improve Bayesian network learning. Each association rule is characterized by several parameters which can be used to identify the absence of dependence among the nodes. In this work, we exploit in particular the leverage parameter.

The paper presents the results of a comparison between K2, K2-rules and TPDA [13], another well-known learning algorithm. TPDA computes the mutual information of each pair of nodes as a measure of dependence and creates the network using this information.

The paper is structured as follows. Section 2 describes the K2 algorithm. In Section 3, we briefly present association rules. Section 4 illustrates the algorithm K2-rules. In Section 5, we show an experimental comparison between K2, K2-rules and TPDA considering four of the most known Bayesian networks. Section 6 discusses related works. Finally, in Section 7, we conclude and present future work.

2. The K2 algorithm

In the literature, there are different approaches for Bayesian network learning. Some of them are based on the search and score methodology [3–10], and the others follow an information theory based approach [11,13].

A procedure frequently used for learning the structure of a Bayesian network from data is the K2 algorithm [4]. Given a database D, this algorithm searches for the Bayesian network structure G^* with maximal $\Pr(G^*|D)$, where $\Pr(G|D)$ is the probability of network structure G given the database D. Since $\Pr(G_1|D)/\Pr(G_2|D) = \Pr(G_1,D)/\Pr(G_2,D)$ (where G_1 and G_2 are two Bayesian network structures), the authors look for a method to compute $\Pr(G,D)$. Let $V(G)$ be a set of n discrete variables, where a variable $V_i \in V(G)$ has r_i possible value assignments v_{ik} $k = 1,\ldots,r_i$. Let D be a database of m cases, where each case contains a value assignment for each variable in $V(G)$. Let G denote a directed acyclic graph representing the structure of a Bayesian network containing just the variables in $V(G)$, and let GPr be the associated set of conditional probability distributions. Each node $V_i \in V(G)$ has a set of parents $\pi(V_i)$. Let w_{ij} denote the j-th unique instantiation of $\pi(V_i)$ relative to D. Suppose there are q_i unique instantiations of $\pi(V_i)$, so $j = 1,\ldots,q_i$. Define N_{ijk} to be the number of cases in D in which variable V_i has the value v_{ik} and $\pi(V_i)$ is instantiated as w_{ij}. Let

$$N_{ij} = \sum_{k=1}^{r_i} N_{ijk}$$

Given a Bayesian network structure G, assuming that the cases occur independently and the conditional probability density function $f(GPr|G)$ is uniform, then it follows that

$$\Pr(G,D) = \Pr(G) \prod_{i=1}^{n} \prod_{j=1}^{q_i} \frac{(r_i-1)!}{(N_{ij}+r_i-1)!} \prod_{k=1}^{r_i} N_{ijk}!$$

The K2 algorithm looks for a network structure G that maximizes $\Pr(G,D)$. In particular, assuming that an ordering on the variables is available and that all structures are equally similar, it adopts a greedy method for maximizing $\Pr(G,D)$. This method consists in searching, for each node V_i, for the set of parent nodes that maximizes the function:

$$g(i,\pi(V_i)) = \prod_{j=1}^{q_i} \frac{(r_i-1)!}{(N_{ij}+r_i-1)!} \prod_{k=1}^{r_i} N_{ijk}! \tag{1}$$

K2 starts by assuming that a node lacks parents, after which in every step it adds incrementally the parent whose addition mostly increases $g(i,\pi(V_i))$. K2 stops adding parents to a node when the addition of a single parent cannot increase $g(i,\pi(V_i))$.

A pseudo code representation of K2 algorithm is shown in Figure 1.

```
1 For i = 1 to n
{
    1.1 π(V_i) = ∅
    1.2 Repeat
    {
        1.2.1 Select V_j ∈ {V_1,...,V_{i-1}} − π(V_i) that
              maximizes g(i, π(V_i) ∪ {V_j})
        1.2.2 Δ = g(i, π(V_i) ∪ {V_j}) − g(i, π(V_i))
        1.2.3 If Δ > 0 then π(V_i) = π(V_i) ∪ {V_j}
    } until Δ < 0 or π(V_i) = {V_1,...,V_{i-1}}
}
```

Fig. 1. Pseudo code representation of the K2 algorithm

3. Association Rules

Association rules [12] describe co-occurrence of events, and can be regarded as probabilistic rules. A good example of association rules is taken from the domain of sale transactions: an association rule in this domain expresses what items are usually bought together, information that is used for developing successful marketing strategies.

Consider a database D consisting of a single table. An association rule [12] is a rule of the form

$$A_1 = v_{A_1}, A_2 = v_{A_2}, \ldots, A_j = v_{A_j} \Rightarrow B_1 = v_{B_1}, B_2 = v_{B_2}, \ldots, B_k = v_{B_k}$$

where $A_1, A_2, \ldots, A_j, B_1, B_2, \ldots, B_k$ are attribute names and $v_{A_1}, v_{A_2}, \ldots, v_{A_j}, v_{B_1}, v_{B_2}, \ldots, v_{B_k}$ are values such that v_{A_i} (v_{B_h}) belongs to the domain of the attribute $A_i(B_h)$ for $i = 1, \ldots, j$ ($h = 1, \ldots, k$).

More formally, an association rule can be defined as follows.

An *item* is a literal of the form $Attribute_i = v_{Attribute_i}$ where $v_{Attribute_i}$ belongs to the domain of $Attribute_i$. Let M be the set of all the possible items. A *transaction* T is a record of the database.

An *itemset* X is a set of items that is consistent, that is a set X such that $X \subseteq M$ and an attribute $Attribute_i$ does not appear twice in X. We say that a transaction T *contains* an itemset X if $X \subseteq T$ or, alternatively, if T satisfies all the literals in X.

The *support* of an itemset X (indicated by $support(X)$) is the fraction of transactions in D that contain X.

An *association rule* is an implication of the form $X \Rightarrow Y$, where X and Y are itemsets and $X \cap Y = \emptyset$. For each association rule $X \Rightarrow Y$ we define the following parameters:

- The *support* of $X \Rightarrow Y$ (represented by $support(X \Rightarrow Y)$) is defined as $support(X \cup Y)$;
- The *leverage* [14] of $X \Rightarrow Y$ (represented by $leverage(X \Rightarrow Y)$) is defined as

$leverage(X \Rightarrow Y) = support(X \cup Y) - support(X) \times support(Y)$. (this parameter is similar to the Absolute Confidence Difference to Prior defined in [15]). It can assume positive and negative values. Since $support(X)$ can be interpreted as $\Pr(X)$, the leverage can be interpreted as $\Pr(X,Y) - \Pr(X) \times \Pr(Y)$. Therefore the more the leverage is close to 0 the more X and Y are statistically independent from each other.

In this paper we consider association rules where both X and Y contain a single item. In this way the leverage of the rule can be interpreted as a measure of the dependence between the two items contained respectively in X and Y.

4. K2-rules algorithm

In this section we describe the K2-rules algorithm which improves the K2 algorithm described in Section 2 by exploiting the leverage parameter of association rules. In order to work, the K2 algorithm requires the total ordering of the nodes. K2 has a high computational cost and produces a significant number of extra arcs in the learned network.

The high computational cost is due to Formula 1 (see Section 2) which requires many computational resources especially for nodes characterized by a great number of parents.

The extra arc problem arises especially when the network is characterized by a lot of root nodes (nodes without parents). During network learning, the algorithm tries to add parents to each of these nodes until it maximizes $g(i, \pi(V_i))$. The algorithm will add at least one arc to a root node because the value of the heuristic for this new structure is always better than the value of the previous structure.

The new proposed approach considers all the association rules containing a single item in the body and a single item in the head. In order to obtain the leverage of these rules, we do not employ an algorithm that learns association rules (such as APRIORI [16]), but we consider all the possible two items rules and for each we compute the leverage. The K2-rules algorithm first computes, for each stochastic variable V_i, the maximum and the minimum of the leverage of the association rules that have an item that refers to V_i. Let $MaxLev(V_i)$ and $MinLev(V_i)$ be these figures.

Then K2-rules finds the minimum of all the $MaxLev(V_i)$ and the maximum of all the $MinLev(V_i)$. Let $MaxLeverage$ and $MinLeverage$ be these figures. Using these parameters, K2-rules deletes nodes from the list of possible parents of a node Q (those that precede it in the order). These parameters are used as thresholds for considering a couple of nodes statistically independent: if the leverage of a rule involving the two nodes is between $MinLeverage$ and $MaxLeverage$, then the two variables are considered independent. Therefore the node that precedes the other in the given order can be removed from the list of parents of the other node.

This method is implemented by the function $FindAllowableParents$ that, given a node, returns the set of allowable parents. We have also considered a more con-

> Given the set of network nodes V and the set of learned association rules AR:
> 1 For $i = 1$ to n
> {
>   1.1 Select the subset $AR(V_i)$ of association rules from AR
>   which involve V_i;
>   1.2 Find the minimum and maximum value of leverage of rules in $AR(V_i)$
>   and call them $MinLev(V_i)$ and $MaxLev(V_i)$;
> }
> 2 Find the global minimum and maximum for all the network nodes:
> $MinLeverage = max_{V_i \in V}\{MinLev(V_i)\}$ and
> $MaxLeverage = min_{V_i \in V}\{MaxLev(V_i)\}$
> 3 For $i = 1$ to n
> {
>   3.1 $\pi(V_i) = \emptyset$
>   3.2 Compute $FindAllowableParents(V_i)$ or $FindAllowableParents\_All(V_i)$
>   which return a list $AllowableParents$ of allowable nodes
>   3.3 Repeat
>   {
>   3.3.1 Select $V_j \in AllowableParents - \pi(V_i)$ that
>   maximizes $g(i, \pi(V_i) \cup \{V_j\})$
>   3.3.2 $\Delta = g(i, \pi(V_i) \cup \{V_j\}) - g(i, \pi(V_i))$
>   3.3.3 If $\Delta > 0$ then $\pi(V_i) = \pi(V_i) \cup \{V_j\}$
>   } until $\Delta < 0$ or $\pi(V_i) = \{V_1, \ldots, V_{i-1}\}$
> }

Fig. 2. Pseudo code representation of the K2-rules algorithm

> Given the ordered list of network nodes L, a node Q and the set of learned
> association rules AR, the $FindAllowableParents$ function:
> 1 Associates a list $AllowableParents$ of possible parents to Q
>   composed by the nodes that precede Q in the list L
> 2 Selects the subset $AR(Q)$ of association rules from AR which involve Q
> 3 For each node P in $AllowableParents$
>   3.1 if at least a rule R in $AR(Q)$
>   exists that involves P and Q, and that has
> $MinLeverage < leverage(R) < MaxLeverage$ then
>   3.1.1 Removes P from $AllowableParents$
> 4 Return $AllowableParents$

Fig. 3. $FindAllowableParents$ function

servative method to remove nodes from the set of allowable parents.

This method is implemented by the function $FindAllowableParents\_All$. This

Given the ordered list of network nodes L, a node Q and the set of learned association rules AR, the $FindAllowableParents\_All$ function:
 1 Associates a list $AllowableParents$ of possible parents to Q
   composed by the nodes that precede Q in the list L
 2 Selects the subset $AR(Q)$ of association rules from AR which involve Q
 3 For each node P in $AllowableParents$
   3.1 if all the rules R in $AR(Q)$
     which involve P and Q have
     $MinLeverage < leverage(R) < MaxLeverage$ then
   3.1.1 Removes P from $AllowableParents$
 4 Return $AllowableParents$

Fig. 4. $FindAllowableParents\_All$ function

function deletes a node P from the list of parents of a node Q only if all the rules involving Q and P are such that their leverage is between $MinLeverage$ and $MaxLeverage$. The K2-rules algorithm is described in pseudo code in Figure 2. The functions $FindAllowableParents$ and $FindAllowableParents\_All$ are presented in Figures 3 and 4 respectively.

5. Experimental comparisons

We compared K2 and K2-rules on four different Bayesian networks:
- "Visit to Asia": a network for a fictitious medical example about whether a patient has tuberculosis, lung cancer or bronchitis, depending on their X-ray, dyspnea, visit-to-Asia and smoking status. It has 8 nodes and 8 arcs, and is described in [17].
- "Car_diagnosis": a network to diagnose the reason why a car does not start, based on spark plugs, headlights, main fuse, etc. It has 18 nodes and 20 arcs, and is described in [18];
- "ALARM": ALARM stands for "A Logical Alarm Reduction Mechanism". This is a medical diagnostic network to monitor patients. It is a nontrivial network with 8 diagnoses, 16 findings and 13 intermediate variables (37 nodes and 46 arcs), and is described in [19].
- "Boelarge92": A subjective belief network for a particular scenario of neighborhood events, that shows how even distant concepts have some connection. It has 24 nodes and 35 arcs. It is described in [20];

The dataset of examples used for rule learning has been obtained with the NETICA tool [18]. This tool, given the structure and the CPTs of a Bayesian network is able to generate automatically a dataset of N examples. Each experiment was conducted by first generating a dataset from one of the networks above and then trying to learn back the network using K2, K2-rules using $FindAllowableParents$ (K2-r-

	K2				K2-r-FAP				K2-r-FAPA				TPDA	
Data Set	MA	EA	LS	NN	MA	EA	LS	NN	MA	EA	LS	NN	MA	EA
1,000	0	4	66	2280	1	2	52	1980	1	2	52	1980	1	0
5,000	0	2	61	1608	0	1	50	1416	0	1	50	1416	1	0
10,000	0	1	57	1224	1	0	40	900	1	2	44	960	1	0
20,000	0	1	57	1224	1	0	39	852	1	1	47	1020	1	0

Table 1
Comparison of K2, K2-r-FAP and K2-r-FAPA on the Visit-to-Asia network.

	K2				K2-r-FAP				K2-r-FAPA				TPDA	
Data Set	MA	EA	LS	NN	MA	EA	LS	NN	MA	EA	LS	NN	MA	EA
1,000	3	9	396	21705	4	6	270	16710	4	9	331	20679	8	0
5,000	1	7	395	26817	2	2	214	17631	1	7	325	24375	6	0
10,000	1	7	395	26817	2	1	201	16716	1	5	334	24837	7	0
20,000	1	7	395	26817	1	0	206	17490	1	4	311	23745	6	0

Table 2
Comparison of K2, K2-r-FAP and K2-r-FAPA on the Car_diagnosis network.

	K2				K2-r-FAP				K2-r-FAPA				TPDA	
Data Set	MA	EA	LS	NN	MA	EA	LS	NN	MA	EA	LS	NN	MA	EA
1,000	3	13	1793	252120	23	3	143	11919	2	1	937	155178	37	37
5,000	1	11	1771	204462	27	4	119	20163	1	0	685	91572	37	36
10,000	1	11	1771	204462	22	3	148	23782	1	0	771	95235	37	35

Table 3
Comparison of K2, K2-r-FAP and K2-r-FAPA on the ALARM network.

FAP), K2-rules using *FindAllowableParents_All* (K2-r-FAPA) and TPDA. The learned networks are compared to the original network in tables 1, 2, 3 and 4. For each algorithm we indicate: the numbers of missing and extra arcs (MA and EA, respectively); the Log Score (LS) indicating the number of computations of the function $g(i, \pi(V_i))$; the number of computation of N_{ijk} (NN). The last two parameters represent the computational resources needed by the K2, K2-r-FAP and K2-r-FAPA algorithms.

Analyzing these experimental results we can observe that K2-r-FAP and K2-r-FAPA have a number of missing arcs comparable with that of K2 (apart from K2-r-FAP applied to ALARM) but have lower numbers of extra arcs. Moreover, the computational costs of both K2-rules algorithms are significantly lower than those required for K2. In particular, K2-r-FAP is more selective than K2-r-FAPA so it requires the least amount of resources.

Comparing K2-r-FAP and K2-r-FAPA with TPDA we can observe the following: TPDA underestimates the probabilistic relations so it produces a high number of missing arcs while K2-r-FAP and K2-r-FAPA overestimate the probabilistic rela-

	K2				K2-r-FAP				K2-r-FAPA				TPDA	
Data Set	MA	EA	LS	NN	MA	EA	LS	NN	MA	EA	LS	NN	MA	EA
1000	10	3	554	1194	10	1	196	4056	10	1	196	4056	13	1
5,000	7	2	585	14244	7	0	172	4068	7	0	176	4140	12	0
10,000	7	4	601	15732	8	2	199	5136	7	2	202	5284	13	0
20,000	7	4	615	17172	8	3	161	4320	7	3	268	4500	12	0

Table 4
Comparison of K2, K2-r-FAP and K2-r-FAPA on the Boelarge network.

tions so they produce a low number of missing arcs but introduce some extra arcs. The total number of erroneous (missing and extra) arcs of TPDA is higher than the one of the new K2-rules algorithms (especially K2-r-FAPA) except for Visit to Asia and the first two datasets of Car_diagnosis.

6. Related Works

In this paper we present an approach for exploiting parameters related to association rules in order to improve the performance of an algorithm for learning Bayesian networks. Such an approach is not limited to the K2 algorithm only. In fact, in [21], we have applied the same methodology to the TPDA algorithm [13] that is based on an information theory approach rather than on a search and score methodology. In particular, we have exploited association rules parameters for improving the drafting phase of TPDA. This phase is devoted to learn an initial sketch of the network structure.

In [21] we have used the parameters leverage, conviction, lift, Pearson X^2 and Cramer index. We have tested our algorithm (called BNL-rules) with each parameter on four networks together with TPDA. In each test three dimensions of the database were considered: 5,000, 20,000 and 100,000. Of all the algorithm tested, BNL-rules with Pearson X^2 gave the best results outperforming TPDA in five cases in terms of number of missing and extra arcs, equating it in six cases and having a lower performance in only one case.

7. Conclusions

In this work we describe a method for improving K2, one of the most known algorithm for learning Bayesian network, by exploiting association rules parameters.

The K2 algorithm starts by assuming that a node has no parents, after which in every step it incrementally adds the parent whose addition mostly increases the probability of the resulting structure. K2 stops adding parents to the nodes when the addition of a single parent cannot increase the probability of the resulting network structure given the data.

In this work, we propose a method for improving the K2 algorithm, reducing the set of allowable parents from which the algorithm selects actual parents and avoiding extra arc insertions. This new methodology uses data mining techniques, and in particular the computation of association rules parameters from a database of examples, in order to learn the structure of a Bayesian network. Association rules describe correlation of events, and are characterized by several parameters that can be used in structure learning. We have presented the K2-rules algorithm (K2 with association rules) that exploits the leverage parameter of association rules in order to improve the performance of the K2 algorithm.

Experiments discussed in the paper have shown that the proposed approach solves the problem of extra arcs and also notably reduces the computational cost. They also showed the validity of the new algorithms with respect to TPDA.

In future, we plan to compare K2-rules with MDL [10] and other Bayesian network learning algorithms.

Acknowledgments

We would like to thank Andrea Stambazzi and Rossella Bozzini for their help with the experiments. This work is partially funded by the Information Society Technologies programme of the European Commission under the IST-2001-32530 SOCS project.

References

1. J. Pearl, Probabilistic reasoning in intelligent systems: networks of plausible inference, Morgan Kaufmann, San Francisco, 1988.
2. J. H. Kim, J. Pearl, A computational model for combined causal and diagnostic reasoning in inference systems, in: Proceedings of the Eight International Joint Conference on Artificial Intelligence (IJCAI83), Los Angeles, 1983, pp. 190–193.
3. H. Akaike, A new look at statistical model identification, IEEE Trans. Automatic Control 19 (1974) 716–723.
4. G. Cooper, E. Herskovits, A bayesian method for the induction of probabilistic networks from data, Machine Learning 9 (1992) 309–347.
5. D. Heckerman, D. Geiger, D. Chickering, Learning bayesian networks: the combination of knowlegde and statistical data, Machine Learning 20 (1995) 197–243.
6. D. Heckerman, Tutorial on learning in bayesian networks, in: M. Jordan (Ed.), Learning in Graphical Models, MIT Press, Cambridge, MA, 1999, pp. 301–354.
7. E. H. Herskovits, Computer-based probabilistic-network construction, Ph.D. thesis, Medical Informatics, Stanford University (1991).
8. D. Madigan, A. Raftery, Model selection and accounting for model uncertainty in graphical models using occam's window, J. Am. Statist. Association 89 (1994) 1535–1546.

9. J. Rissanen, Stochastic complexity (with discussion), J. Roy. Statist. Soc. B 49 (1987) 223–239.
10. J. Suzuki, Learning bayesian belief networks based on the mdl principle: An efficient algorithm using the branch and bound technique, IEICE Transactions on Communications Electronics Information and Systems.
11. M. Singh, M. Valtorta, Construction of bayesian network structures from data: a brief survey and an efficient algorithm, International Journal of Approximate Reasoning 12 (1995) 111–131.
12. R. Agrawal, T. Imielinski, A. Swami, Mining association rules between sets of items in large databases, in: P. Buneman, S. Jajodia (Eds.), Proceedings of the 1993 ACM SIGMOD International Conference on Management of Data, Washington, D.C., May 26-28, 1993, ACM Press, 1993, pp. 207–216.
13. J. Cheng, R. Greiner, J. Kelly, D. Bell, W. Liu, Learning bayesian networks from data: An information-theory based approach, Artificial Intelligence 137 (1–2) (2002) 43–90.
14. I. Witten, E. Frank, Weka (2003).
URL http://www.cs.waikato.ac.nz/~ml/weka/doc_gui/weka.associations.ItemSet.html#leverageForRule
15. C. Borgelt, Absolute confidence difference to prior (2004).
URL http://fuzzy.cs.uni-magdeburg.de/~borgelt/doc/apriori/apriori.html#diff
16. R. Agrawal, R. Srikant, Fast algorithms for mining association rules, in: J. Bocca, M. Jarke, C. Zaniolo (Eds.), Proceedings of the 20th International Conference on Very Large Data Bases (VLDB'94), Morgan Kaufmann, 1994, pp. 487–499.
17. S. L. Lauritzen, D. J. Spiegelhalter, Local computations with probabilities on graphical structures and their application to expert systems, J. Royal Statistics Society B 50 (2) (1988) 157–194.
18. Norsys, Netica, http://www.norsys.com (2004).
19. I. Beinlich, H. Suermondt, R. Chavez, G. Cooper, The alarm monitoring system: A case study with two probabilistic inference techniques for belief networks, in: J. Bocca, M. Jarke, C. Zaniolo (Eds.), Proceedings of the Second European Conference on Artificial Intelligence in Medicine (AIME 89), Springer, 1989, pp. 247–256.
20. B. Boerlage, Link strength in bayesian networks, Master's thesis, Dept. Computer Science, Univ. of British Columbia (1992).
21. E. Lamma, F. Riguzzi, A. Stambazzi, S. Storari, Improving the SLA algorithm using association rules, in: A. Cappelli, F. Turini (Eds.), Ottavo Congresso Nazionale dell'Associazione Italiana per l'Intelligenza Artificiale (AI*IA2003), Pisa, 23-26 September 2003, no. 2829 in LNAI, Springer Verlag, Heidelberg, Germany, 2003, pp. 165–175.

AGGREGATION AND MULTI-CRITERIA DECISION MAKING

OWA Aggregation on an Interval Argument

Ronald R. Yager

Machine Intelligence Institute, Iona College
New Rochelle, NY 10801
yager@panix.com

Abstract

We briefly describe the OWA operator. We provide an extension of the OWA operator to the case in which our argument is a continuous interval rather then a finite set of values. We look at some examples of this type of aggregation. We consider the extension of the continuous interval argument OWA operator to the more general case in which the argument values have importance weights. We use this to introduce the idea of an operative value associated with a random variable.

Keywords: Aggregation, Ordered weighted averaging, probability

1. Introduction

The OWA operator [2] provides a parameterized family of averaging operators. It has as its argument a finite collection of values. Here we extend the applicability of the OWA operator to the situation in which the argument is a continuous interval. We point out the role of the attitudinal character of the OWA weighting vector in this aggregation process. We also consider the extension of the continuous interval argument OWA operator to the more general case in which the argument values have importance weights. This allows us to introduce the idea of an operative value associated with a continuous random variable. We shown how this operative value can provide an attitudinal based scalar representative value for a random variable. We discuss how this operative value can provide an alternative to expected value for tasks in which a representative scalar value of a random variable is needed.

2. Basic Concepts of the OWA Operator

In the following we discuss some basic properties of the OWA operator more details can be found in [2-4]. An OWA operator of dimensions n is a mapping F: $R^n \to R$ such that $F(a_1, ..., a_n) = \sum_{j=1}^{n} w_j b_j$ where b_j is the jth largest of the a_i and the w_j are weights satisfying $w_j \in [0, 1]$ and $\sum_{j=1}^{n} w_j = 1$. If index(j) is the index of the jth largest of the a_i then $b_j = a_{index(j)}$.

The OWA operator provides a class of averaging operators parameterized by the weighting vector W. The type of average is determined by the weighting vector W. Some notable examples are: $\mathbf{W_*}$ where $w_n = 1$ and $w_j = 0$ for $j \neq n$ here $F(a_1, ..., a_n) = Min_i[a_i]$., $\mathbf{W^*}$ where $w_1 = 1$ and $w_j = 0$ for $j \neq 1$ here $F(a_1, ..., a_n) = Max_i[a_i]$ and $W = \mathbf{W_N}$ where $w_j = 1/n$ here $F(a_1, ..., a_n) = \frac{1}{n}\sum_{i=1}^{n} a_i$. Various other well known averages can be obtained by appropriate selection of the weights [2].

An important measure associated with an OWA aggregation with weighting vector W is its **Attitudinal–Character** [2] defined as $A\text{-}C(W) = \sum_{j=1}^{n} w_j \frac{n-j}{n-1}$. It is known that $A\text{-}C(W) \in [0, 1]$ and $A\text{-}C(W^*) = 1$, $A\text{-}C(W_N) = 0.5$ and $A\text{-}C(W_*) = 0$. If W is symmetrical $w_j = w_{n-j+1}$ then $A\text{-}C(W) = 0.5$. This measure provides a characterization of the type of aggregation being performed. An A-C value near one indicates a bias toward the larger values in the argument while an A-C value near zero indicates preference is being given to the smaller values in the argument. An A-C value near 0.5 is an indication of a neutral type aggregation.

In [3] it was suggested that the OWA weights can be parameterized by a function Q: $[0, 1] \to [0, 1]$ having the properties: **1.** $Q(0) = 0$, **2.** $Q(1) = 1$ and **3.** $Q(x) \geq Q(y)$ if $x > y$. These function where denoted as BUM functions. Using a BUM function we can obtain the OWA weights as $w_j = Q(\frac{j}{n}) - Q(\frac{j-1}{n})$. Among the benefits of using these BUM functions to parameterize the OWA operator is that it provides a dimension independent description of the desired aggregation, we can use the same function Q to define the weights for any dimension n. Another benefit of this approach is that we can, with the add of Zadeh's paradigm of computing with words [7, 8], relate the aggregation to some linguistically expressed imperative. Here starting with some linguistic concept we represent this with the add of fuzzy logic as a BUM function Q.

Some notable examples of these BUM functions are the following. Q^* where $Q^*(0) = 0$ and $Q^*(y) = 1$ for all $y > 0$. Q_* where $Q_*(y) = 0$ for $y < 1$ and $Q_*(1) = 0$. Q_N where $Q_N(y) = y$ for all y. A further example of these BUM functions is $Q(y) = y^r$ where $r > 0$. We note that $Q(y) = \text{Sin}(\frac{\pi}{2}y)$ and more generally $Q(y) = (\text{Sin}(\frac{\pi}{2}y))^r$ for $r > 0$ are BUM functions Another example of a BUM function is $Q(y) = \frac{1 - e^{-ay}}{1 - e^{-a}}$ and more generally $Q(y) = (\frac{1 - e^{-ay}}{1 - e^{-a}})^r$ for $r > 0$

The concept of attitudinal character can be associated directly with a function Q. In this case

$$A\text{-}C(Q) = \int_0^1 Q(y)\, dy.$$

It is the area under Q, $A\text{-}C(Q) \in [0, 1]$. We will find it useful to denote $A\text{-}C(Q)$ as λ
There exists a useful alternative expression for $A\text{-}C(Q)$ [6]

Theorem: $A\text{-}C(Q) = \int_0^1 Q(y)\, dy = 1 - \int_0^1 y\, \frac{dQ}{dy}\, dy$

3 Continuous Interval Argument OWA Aggregation

In the preceding we have defined the OWA aggregation of a finite argument collection where the aggregation is guided by a BUM function Q. We denote this $F_Q(a_1, ..., a_n)$. Here we extend this operation to case when the arguments are all the values in the interval a to b. Thus here we want to find the Q OWA average of [a, b] we shall denote this as $F_Q([a, b])$. We note that since [a, b] is an interval the arguments are pre-ordered we need not do a re-ordering. In the discrete case $F_Q(d_1, ..., d_n) = \sum_{i=1}^{n} (Q(\frac{i}{n}) - Q(\frac{i-1}{n}))d_{\text{index}(i)}$. We shall obtain $F_Q([a, b])$ by generalizing this. First we take a finite approximation of $F_Q([a, b])$. We let $\delta = \frac{b-a}{n}$. Using this $d_{\text{index}(i)} = b - i\delta$, when $i = 0$ we get $d_{\text{index}(0)} = b$ and when $i = n$ we get $d_{\text{index}(n)} = a$. It is clear that $d_{\text{index}(i)} \geq d_{\text{index}(k)}$ if $i < k$. Using this we have as an approximation

$$F_Q([a, b]] \approx F_Q(d_1, ..., d_n) \approx \sum_{i=1}^{n} (Q(\tfrac{i}{n}) - Q(\tfrac{i-1}{n}))(b - i\delta).$$

Letting $\Delta y = 1/n$ we get

$$F_Q([a, b]) \approx \sum_{i=1}^{n} (Q(i\, \Delta y) - Q(i\, \Delta y - \Delta y))(b - \tfrac{i(b-a)}{n})$$

$$F_Q([a, b]) \approx \sum_{i=1}^{n} (Q(i\, \Delta y) - Q(i\, \Delta y - \Delta y))(b - i\, \Delta y(b - a)).$$

Multiplying by $\frac{\Delta y}{\Delta y}$ gives us

$$F_Q([a,b]) \approx \prod_{i=1}^{n} \frac{(Q(i\,\Delta y) - Q(i\,\Delta y - \Delta y))}{\Delta y}(b - i\,\Delta y(b-a))\,\Delta y.$$

Finally letting $n \to \infty$, denoting $y = i\,\Delta y$ and noting that as i goes from 0 to n we have $y \in [0, 1]$ we get

$$F_Q([a,b]) = \int_0^1 \frac{dQ(y)}{dy}(b - y(b-a))\,dy$$

We now observe some properties of this aggregation operator. Proofs of these can be found in [6].

Observation: If the interval shrinks to a point $b = a$ then $F_Q([a,b]) = b(Q(1) - Q(0)) = b$

This operator is monotonic with respect to the argument values

Theorem: Assume $a_1 \geq a_2$ and $b_1 \geq b_2$ then for all Q we have $F_Q([a_1, b_1]) \geq F_Q([a_2, b_2])$.

This operator exhibits a monotonicity with respect to Q.

Definition: If Q_1 and Q_2 are such that $Q_1(y) \geq Q_2(y)$ for all $y \in [0, 1]$ we denote this as $Q_1 \geq Q_2$.

Theorem: If $Q_1 \geq Q_2$ then $F_{Q_1}([a,b]) \geq F_{Q_2}[(a,b)]$.

This interval type OWA operator is also bounded.

Theorem: For all Q we have $a \leq F_Q([a,b]) \leq b$

From the results of the preceding theorems we see that $F_Q([a,b])$ is a mean operator.

We look at $F_Q([(a,b])$ for some special case of Q. First we consider the linear function, $Q(y) = y$. For this we get $F_Q([a,b]) = 0.5(b+a)$. This is the usual average of an interval. Consider now the function Q where $Q(y) = 0$ for $y < q$ and $Q(y) = 1$ for $y \geq q$. In this case $\frac{dQ(y)}{dy} = \delta(y - q)$, the Dirac delta function focused at q. Using this we get $F_Q([a,b]) = aq + (1-q)b$. If $q = 0$, we get $F_Q((a,b) = b = \text{Max}[a, b]$, if $q = 1$ then we get $F_Q([a,b]) = a = \text{Min}[a, b]$ and if $q = \frac{1}{2}$, then we get $F_Q((a,b) = \frac{1}{2}(a+b)$ the median, the average.

For $Q(y) = y^r$ we get $F_Q([a,b]) = b - \frac{(b-a)}{r+1} = \frac{b+ra}{r+1}$. More generally we can show [6] that if $r = \frac{K}{N}$ then $F_Q([a,b)] = \frac{Nb + Ka}{K+N}$

A general closed form representation of $F_Q([a,b])$ can be obtained [6].

Theorem: If λ is the attitudinal character of Q then $F_Q([a,b]) = \lambda b + (1-\lambda)a$.

$F_Q([a,b])$ is always the weighted average of end points based on the attitudinal character.

In [5] we introduced a class of OWA weights called the E-Z OWA weights based on the Q function where $Q(y) = 0$ for $y \leq \alpha$, $Q(y) = 1/(\beta-\alpha)$ for $\alpha \leq y \leq \beta$ and $Q(y) = 1$ for $y \geq \beta$. For this function $\lambda = A-C(Q) = 1 - 0.5 (\alpha + \beta)$. We point out if $\beta = 1$ then $\lambda \leq 0.5$ and if $\alpha = 0$ then $\lambda \geq 0.5$. For this function $F_Q([a, b]) = b\lambda + a(1 - \lambda) = b - 0.5 (b-a)(\beta + \alpha)$.

4. Importance Weighted Aggregations

In [4] we described a methodology for performing the OWA aggregation when the arguments had associated importance weights. We briefly describe the procedure in anticipation of extending it to the case of continuous arguments. Let Q be a BUM function. Let $[(a_1, u_1), ..., (a_n, u_n)]$ be a collection of tuples where a_j is called the argument value and u_j is its associated importance weight, the importance weights are non-negative. Without loss of generality we shall assume that the a_j are ordered so that $a_1 \geq a_2 ... \geq a_n$. In [4] it was suggested that the OWA aggregation of the a_j with these importance's is $F_Q((a_1, u_1), ..., (a_n, u_n)) = \sum_{j=1}^{n} w_j a_j$

where $w_j = Q(\frac{S_j}{T}) - Q(\frac{S_{j-1}}{T})$. Here $S_j = \sum_{i=1}^{j} u_i$, $S_0 = 0$ and $T = S_n$.

We now extend this importance weighted aggregation to the continuous case. Assume we have an interval [a, b] and a non-negative function f(z) defined on [a, b] where f(z) corresponds to the "importance weight" associated with the value $z \in [a, b]$. We let Q be a BUM function. Then the OWA aggregation of ([a, b], f) guided by the aggregation imperative Q, denoted $F_Q([a, b], f)$, is obtained as follows:

1. Normalize f on [a, b]: $g(z) = \dfrac{f(z)}{\int_a^b f(x)dx}$.

2. Obtain for $x \in [a, b]$ $y = H(x) = \int_x^b g(z)dz$.

3. Obtain for $y \in [0, 1]$ the inverse of H: $x = x(y) = H^{-[1]}(y)$.
4. The OWA aggregation is

$$F_Q([a, b], f) = \int_0^1 \frac{dQ(y)}{dy} H^{-[1]}(y)dy$$

We look at some examples to assure ourselves that this is working correctly. Consider the case $f(z) = K$ for $z \in [a, b]$. In this case 1. $g(z) = 1/(b-a)$ 2. Using this $y = (b-x)/(b-a)$. 3. The inverse of this is $x = b - (b - a)y$. Using this we get

$$F_Q[[a, b], K] = \int_0^1 \frac{dQ(y)}{dy}(b - (b-a)y)\, dy$$ which is the formula we originally introduced.

For the special case where assume $Q(y) = y$ and we have an arbitrary $f(z)$ [6] we get $F_Q([a, b], f] = \int_a^b x\, g(x)\, dx$, the usual weighted average over the interval.

We consider some examples of our approach to importance weighted continuous OWA aggregation. As a first illustration we consider the case where $f(z) = (b-z)/(b-a)$ for $a \le z \le b$ and $Q(y) = y^p$ ($p \ge 0$). In [6] we shown that for this case $F_Q([a, b], f] = \frac{1}{2p+1}(b + 2pa)$. We see that when $p \to 0$, we get b the Max, when $p \to \infty$ we get a, the Min and with $p \to 1$ we get $\frac{b+2a}{3}$.

We now consider the weighted formulation for the case where Q is the E-Z OWA aggregation operator: $Q(y) = 0$ for $y \le \alpha$, $Q(y) = 1/(\beta-\alpha)$ for $\alpha \le y \le \beta$ and $Q(y) = 1$ for $y \ge \beta$. We shall assume we have g, obtained by normalization of some general f, and calculate $F_Q([a, b], g)$. Here from the definition of Q we get

$$F_Q([a, b], f) = \int_0^1 \frac{dQ(y)}{dy} H^{[1]}(y)\, dy = \frac{1}{\beta - \alpha}\int_\alpha^\beta H^{[1]}(y)\, dy$$

However we recall that $H^{-[1]}(y) = x$ so we can express $F_Q([a, b], f) = \frac{1}{\beta - \alpha}\int_\alpha^\beta x\, dy$.

We further recall that $y = \int_x^b g(z)\, dz$ and hence $dy = -g(x)dx$. Using this we get $F_Q([a, b], g) = -\frac{1}{\beta - \alpha}\int_{x_\alpha}^{x_\beta} x\, g(x)\, dx$ where x_β is the value on the interval $[a, b]$ such that $\beta = \int_{x_\beta}^b g(z)\, dz$ and x_α is the value on the interval $[a, b]$ where $\alpha = \int_{x_\alpha}^b g(z)\, dz$. Since $\alpha < \beta$ then $x_\beta < x_\alpha$ and hence we get

$$F_Q([a, b], g) = \frac{1}{\beta - \alpha}\int_{x_\beta}^{x_\alpha} x\, g(x)dx$$

Let us now summarize for this case of using E-Z OWA aggregation imperative

1. Calculate x_α and x_β such that $\alpha = \int_{x_\alpha}^{b} g(z)dz$ and $\beta = \int_{x_\beta}^{b} g(z)dz$

2. Calculate $F_Q([a, b], g) = \dfrac{1}{\beta - \alpha} \int_{x_\beta}^{x_\alpha} x\, g(x)\, dx$

What is interesting to note is the similarly of this formulation to the ordinary expected value, $\int_a^b x\, g(x)\, dx$. Here we are getting some variation of the ordinary expected value.

In [5] we discussed two important special cases of this E-Z OWA Q. In the first case we assume $\alpha = 0$. Here we have that $\lambda = 1 - 0.5\, \beta$. Thus when $\beta = 0$ we get $\lambda = 1$ and when $\beta = 1$ we get $\lambda = 0.5$. Thus assuming $\alpha = 0$ we have $0.5 \leq \lambda \leq 1$. Thus we can model any attitudinal character greater or equal 0.5 by making $\alpha = 0$ and selecting some $\beta \in [0, 1]$. In this case $F_Q([a, b], g) = \dfrac{1}{\beta} \int_{x_\beta}^{b} x\, g(x)\, dx$. If we specify a value for λ that is greater then 0.5 then solving $\lambda = 1 - 0.5\, \beta$ we get the associated value for β. Using this we obtain x_β.

In the second special case $\beta = 1$. Here we have that $\lambda = \dfrac{1}{2}(1 - \alpha)$. Thus for $\alpha = 0$ we get $\lambda = \dfrac{1}{2}$ and for $\alpha = 1$ we get $\lambda = 0$. Thus here $0 \leq \lambda \leq 0.5$. This allows us to model attitudinal character less than or equal 0.5 by selecting $\alpha \in [0, 1]$. In this case where we have assumed $\beta = 1$ we get $x_\beta = a$ and therefore $F_Q[a, b], g) = \dfrac{1}{1 - \alpha} \int_a^{x_\alpha} x\, g(x)\, dx$. This allows us to specify $\lambda \leq 0.5$ and since $\alpha = 2\lambda - 1$ we can use this to get x_α.

5. Operative Values of Random Variables

In many applications involving random variables we make use of a unique scalar value as a replacement for the more complex probability distribution.. This simplification allows us to perform many tasks, such as comparisons, which may be very difficult if not impossible using probability distributions. The expected value is most often used to provide this representative scalar value. What must be emphasized is the choice of using the expected value is based on some subjective preference of the analyst using it. This use of the expected is a reflection, although implicit, of the analyst's attitude with regard to the ultimate resolution of the uncertainty modeled by the random variable. Although in many cases the choice of the expected value to provide the scalarization is a good one it is by no means the only one. One can easily envision situations in which the use of the smallest or largest values in the range the random variable may the one chosen by the analyst. The methodology we have developed in the preceding allows us to introduce a general attitudinal based approach to obtaining a representative scalar value for a random variable. We shall refer to the scalar value obtained in this manner as an operative value. As we shall see the expected value is a very important special case of this general class of operative values.

Let R be a random variable taking values in the interval [a, b] and let f be the associated probability density function. We define the operative value of R with respected to attitude Q as $F_Q([a, b], f)$. If $Q(y) = y$ then this reduces to the usual expected value. The approach here allows us to consider other types operative values.

In order to get some understanding of this idea of operative values we shall consider as an example the special situation of the exponential probability distribution [1]. We recall a continuous random variable R whose probability density function is given by $f(x) = \rho e^{-\rho x}$ for $x \geq 0$ and $f(x) = 0$ for $x < 0$ for some $p > 0$, is said to be an exponential random variable. The exponential distribution is often used to model uncertainties associated with the amount of time before some special event occurs. The usual expected value of an exponential random variable is $1/\rho$. In this case the expected value provides a scalar value representative of how long before some event will happen, for example the next major terrorist attack.

We now consider using the operative value of this exponential distribution to provide the representative value. Here shall parameterize this operative value by using as Q the one from the E–Z OWA aggregation with parameters α and β. In this case $F_Q([0, \infty], f) = \frac{\rho}{\beta - \alpha} \frac{1}{\rho^2} [(\rho x_\beta + 1)e^{-\rho x_\beta} - (\rho x_\alpha + 1)e^{-\rho x_\alpha}]$ where $\beta = \int_{x_\beta}^{\infty} \rho e^{-\rho z} dz$ and $\alpha = \int_{x_\alpha}^{\infty} \rho e^{-\rho z} dz$. From the form of α and β we can show that $x_\alpha = -\frac{\ln(\alpha)}{\rho}$ and $x_\beta = -\frac{\ln(\beta)}{\rho}$. Using this we get

$$F_Q([0, \infty], f) = \frac{1}{\beta - \alpha} \frac{1}{\rho} [\beta(1 - \ln(\beta)) - \alpha(1 - \ln(\alpha))]$$

Let us consider two special cases. The first is where $\beta = 1$. Here $F_Q([0, \infty], f) = \frac{1}{\rho}[1 + \frac{\alpha \ln(\alpha)}{(1 - \alpha)}]$. When $0 < \alpha \leq 1$, since $\ln(\alpha) < 0$ we get $F_Q([0, \infty], f] \leq \frac{1}{\rho}$ and $\alpha = 0$ we get $F_Q([0, \infty], f] = \frac{1}{\rho}$ the usual expected value. Thus here we tend to reduce the operative value with respect to the expected time.. As α increases $F_Q([0, \infty], f]$ decreases culminating in the extreme case $F_Q([0, \infty], f] \to 0$ as $\alpha \to 1$. For $\beta = 1$ we have $0 \leq \lambda \leq 0.5$, thus we see that selecting $\lambda < 0.5$ results in reduction in the time to the special event.

In this case with $\alpha = 0$ we have $F_Q([0, \infty], f] = \frac{1}{\rho}(1 - \ln(\beta))$. If $\beta = 1$

then we get $F_Q([0, \infty], f] = \frac{1}{\rho}$, the expected value. More generally for $\beta < 1$ t as β decreases $F_Q([0, \infty], f]$ increases. This culminates in the extreme case $F_Q([0, \infty], f] \to \infty$ as $\beta \to 0$. We recall for $\alpha = 0$ we have that $0.5 \le \lambda \le 1$, thus we see that selecting $\lambda > 0.5$ essentially results in an increase in the operative

We can relate α and β to attitudinal character λ. We can attain any attitudinal character $\lambda \in [0, 0.5]$ by selecting $\beta = 1$ and letting $\alpha = 1 - 2\lambda$ and we can attain any attitudinal character $\lambda \in [0.5, 1]$ by selecting $\alpha = 0$ and letting $\beta = 2(1 - \lambda)$. Using this we can express get $F_Q([0, \infty], f] = \frac{1}{\rho} M(\lambda)$ where

$$M(\lambda) = \left[1 + \frac{(1 - 2\lambda)\ln(1 - 2\lambda)}{2\lambda}\right] \quad \text{for } \lambda \in [0, 0.5]$$

$$M(\lambda) = 1 - \ln(2(1 - \lambda)) \quad \text{for } \lambda \in [0.5, 1]$$

When $\lambda = 0.5$ we get that $M(\lambda) = 1$.

6. References

1. T. Bedford and R. Cooke, Probabilistic Risk Analysis: Foundations and Methods. Cambridge University Press: New York, 2001.
2. R. R. Yager, On ordered weighted averaging aggregation operators in multi-criteria decision making. In IEEE Transactions on Systems, Man and Cybernetics 18, 1988, pp 183-190.
3. R. R. Yager, Quantifier guided aggregation using OWA operators. In the International Journal of Intelligent Systems 11, 1996, pp 49-73.
4. R. R. Yager, On the inclusion of importances in OWA aggregations. In The Ordered Weighted Averaging Operators: Theory and Applications, edited by Yager, R. R. and Kacprzyk, J., Kluwer Academic Publishers: Norwell, MA, 1997, pp 41-59.
5. R. R. Yager, E-Z OWA weights. In the Proceedings of the 10th International Fuzzy Systems Association World Congress-IFSA, Istanbul, 2003, pp 39-42.
6. R. R. Yager, OWA aggregation over a continuous interval argument with applications to decision making. In IEEE Transactions on Systems, Man and Cybernetics Part B 35, 2004, pp 1952-1963.
7. L. A. Zadeh, Fuzzy logic = computing with words. In the IEEE Transactions on Fuzzy Systems 4, 1996, pp 103-111.
8. L. A. Zadeh and J. Kacprzyk, Computing with Words in Information/Intelligent Systems 1. Physica-Verlag: Heidelberg, 1999.

On Bi-Capacity-based Concordance Rules in Multicriteria Decision Making

A. Rolland

LIP6 – Université Paris VI
Paris – FRANCE

Abstract

Several models have been proposed in multi-criteria decision making relying on ordinal information to aggregate the performances on different criteria in order to rank the alternatives, but some situations can still not be well described by these models. We propose here to investigate the interest of new fuzzy measures (bi-capacities) in ordinal aggregation procedures.

Key words: multicriteria decision making, aggregation methods, fuzzy measure

1. Introduction

In the field of multicriteria decision making (MCDM), many models have been proposed to describe preference relations. A first school (see e.g. Keeney and Raiffa [9]) is based on a numerical representation of preferences and put forwards the aggregation of marginal scaled utility functions into a global preference function, using for example the weighted sum or other additive utilities. Some generalizations, using non-additive functions, have been proposed based on the Choquet integral (see e.g. Schmeidler [15], Grabisch [6], Marichal [11]). But in many cases in MCDM, the information available about the alternatives is not sufficient to measure precisely the utility of each alternative on each criterion, or to guaranty the commensurability of the criteria. In such cases, non-numerical approaches based on the use of preferences graphs are useful. In the relational approach of preference models, preferences along each criteria (whether numerical or not) are represented by a binary preference relation, and aggregation methods like votes, majority rules or concordance rules are used to perform criteria aggregation (see e.g. Roy [13], Fodor and Roubens [5],

Perny and Roubens [12]). All these methods are based on evaluating the importance of the coalitions of criteria which favor an alternative over another. In this idea, the importance of each criterion, or coalition should be evaluated by a weight, or a fuzzy measure (see Sugeno [16]), or capacity (see Choquet [3]). This has been much studied in the numerical approach, but it has been less studied in preference aggregation (see e.g. the concordance rules proposed by Dubois and Al. [4]). But the use of a capacity to describe the importance of criteria coalitions is sometimes not sufficient. Grabisch and Labreuche [7] recently proposed bi-capacities as a useful generalization of capacities.

The aim of this paper is to investigate the description potential of bi-capacities in graphs-based aggregation methods like concordance rules and to provide representation theorems for bi-capacity-based concordance relations

Section (2) presents the general framework and points out the descriptive limits of some ordinal MCDM models. Section (3) introduces preference models using ordinal bi-capacities and reference points. Section (4) presents the main results : a characterization of preference models using bi-capacities with and without a reference point. All the proofs are relegated in the appendix in order to facilitate the reading.

2. Motivations

2.1. *Notations and definitions*

Notations

A multicriteria decision problem is characterized by a set X of alternatives and a set $N = \{1, \ldots, n\}$ of attributes used to describe the alternatives. We note $\mathcal{P}(N)$ the set of subsets of N. Let $(X_i, \succsim_i)$ denote a finite ordered scale where X_i is the set of attribute values for component $i \in N$, and $\succsim_i$ is a complete weak-order on X_i. $X = X_1 \times \ldots \times X_n$ is said to be the multicriteria space. We suppose that each attribute set X_i is composed by at least 3 different levels.

We note $C_\succ(x,y)$ the set $\{j \in N, \ x_j \succ_j y_j\}$.

An aggregation procedure consists in deriving a global preference relation $\succsim$ on X from partial preferences relations $\succsim_j$ on each criterion $X_1, \ldots, X_n$. $\succsim$ is supposed to be a weak-order, i.e. a transitive and reflexive binary relation.

Many models have been proposed to describe aggregation procedures in the frame of ordinal multicriteria decision making, see for example Roy [14] for a review.

Generalized Concordance Rules

Dubois and al. [4] have introduced the Generalized Concordance Rules in a purely ordinal frame as follow:

Definition 1. A generalized concordance rule defines a preference relation $\succsim$ on X from the relations $\succsim_j$ on X_j, $\forall j = 1,..,n$ as follows :

$$x \succsim y \iff C_\succ(x,y) \succsim_N C_\succ(y,x)$$

where $\succsim_N$ is a relative importance relation on $\mathcal{P}(N)$

Capacity-based Concordance Rules
Let us recall the definition of fuzzy measures, or capacities for finite sets. For more details, see e.g. Sugeno and Murofushi [17], Grabisch and Roubens [8] and Grabisch and Labreuche [7].

Definition 2. A capacity $\mu : 2^N \rightarrow \mathbb{R}^+$ is a set function such that $\mu(\emptyset) = 0$, and $A \subseteq B \subseteq N$ implies $\mu(A) \leq \mu(B)$. The capacity is normalized if in addition $\mu(N) = 1$.

An instance of the general model introduced in definition 1 is:

Definition 3. A capacity-based concordance rule defines a preference relation $\succsim$ on X from the relations $\succsim_j$ on X_j, $\forall j = 1,..,n$ and a capacity μ on $\mathcal{P}(N)$ as follows :

$$x \succsim y \iff \mu(C_\succ(x,y)) \geq \mu(C_\succ(y,x))$$

2.2. *Some limits of existing models*

Even if the Capacity-Based Concordance Rules and the Generalized Concordance Rules can describe many preference relations, the following examples show different situations where Capacity-Based Concordance Rules, or even Generalized Concordance Rules are unable to explain the proposed preferences.

Example 1. Let us consider the following example, giving evaluations obtained by several cars following three criteria : Comfort (1), Price (2) and Consumption (3). The performances on each criteria are evaluated on three different scales : three levels "+", "=" and "-" for the comfort, five categories from A (the cheapest) to E (the more expensive) for he price, and the consummation in liter for hundred kilometers.

	1	2	3
x^1	+	B	8
x^2	+	E	6.5
x^3	-	B	6.5

Assume that the decision maker has the following preferences : she prefers x^1 to x^3 (so $x^1 \succ x^3$), but she has no preferences between x^1 and x^2, and x^2 and x^3 (so $x^1 \sim x^2$ and $x^2 \sim x^3$).

The question is : can we represent these preferences with a Capacity-Based Concordance Rule? In this model, we have $x \succsim y$ if and only if $\mu(C_\succ(x,y)) \geq$

$\mu(C_{\succ}(y,x))$. We can easily see that in the present situation, $x^1 \sim x^2$ implies that $\mu(\{2\}) = \mu(\{3\})$, $x^2 \sim x^3$ implies that $\mu(\{1\}) = \mu(\{2\})$ while $x^1 \succ x^3$ implies that $\mu(\{1\}) > \mu(\{3\})$: there is an impossibility.

Remark : We have shown in this example that some preference relations cannot be represented by a Capacity-Based Concordance Rule. But these preferences can be represented by a Generalized Concordance Rule with a non transitive importance set relation $\succsim_N$ specifying $\{M\} \sim_N \{P\}$, $\{P\} \sim_N \{C\}$ and $\{M\} \succ_N \{C\}$. These relations can also be represented by a Bi-Capacity-Based Concordance relation, as seen below.

Example 2. Let us consider now the following example in the same frame than example (1), including a fourth criterion representing the available options (airbags, high fidelity radio...) evaluating by 1 (few options), 2 or 3 (many options).

	1	2	3	4
x^1	+	C	8	2
x^2	+	C	6	1
x^3	=	A	8	2
x^4	=	A	6	1

Assume that the decision maker has the following preferences : he prefers x^1 to x^2 (so $x^1 \succ x^2$), and x^4 to x^3 (so $x^4 \succ x^3$).

The question is : can we represent preferences $x^1 \succ x^2$ and $x^4 \succ x^3$ using a Capacity-Based Concordance rule or even a Generalized Concordance Rule defined in definition 1 ? We can easily see that in the present situation, $x^1 \succ x^2$ implies that $\{3\}$ is more important than $\{4\}$, while $x^4 \succ x^3$ implies the contrary : there is an impossibility. The Concordance rules introduced above are not sufficient to be able to describe some existing preferences.

3. Bi-capacity-based concordance models

We propose in this section preference models using a bi-capacity to represent the issue of conflicting coalitions in concordance rules.

We will first recall the definition of bi-capacities. Let us denote $\mathcal{Q}(N) = \{(A,B) \in \mathcal{P}(N) \times \mathcal{P}(N) \mid A \cap B = \emptyset\}$, where $\mathcal{P}(N)$ stands for 2^N as introduced in Grabisch and Labreuche [7].

Definition 4. A function $\nu : \mathcal{Q}(N) \to \mathbb{R}$ is a bi-capacity if it satisfies :
 (i) $\nu(\emptyset, \emptyset) = 0$
 (ii) $A \subseteq B$ implies $\nu(A,.) \leq \nu(B,.)$ and $\nu(.,A) \geq \nu(.,B)$
In addition, ν is normalized if $\nu(N, \emptyset) = 1 = -\nu(\emptyset, N)$.

We can then define bi-capacity-based concordance rules as follows :

Definition 5. A bi-capacity-based concordance rule defines a preference relation $\succsim$ on X from the relations $\succsim_j$ on X_j, $\forall j = 1, .., n$ and a bi-capacity ν on $\mathcal{P}(N) \times \mathcal{P}(N)$ as follows :

$$x \succsim y \iff \nu(C_\succ(x,y), C_\succ(y,x)) \geq 0$$

Return to Example 1 : *The preference relations described in Example 1 can easily be built using a Bi-Capacity-Based Concordance rule as follows :*

$$\nu(\{2\},\{3\}) = 0$$
$$\nu(\{1\},\{2\}) = 0$$
$$\nu(\{1\},\{3\}) = 1$$

Note that the use of the bi-capacity-based concordance relations is interesting only if $C_\succ(x,y) \neq N \backslash C_\succ(y,x)$. If not, the bi-capacity reduces to a capacity μ by setting $\mu(A) = (\nu(A, \overline{A}) + 1)/2$.

Return to Example 2 : *The preference relations described in Example 2 can not be built using a Bi-Capacity-Based Concordance rule, as seen below :* $C_\succ(x^1, x^2) = C_\succ(x^3, x^4) = \{4\}$, $C_\succ(x^2, x^1) = C_\succ(x^4, x^3) = \{3\}$, *so* $x^1 \succ x^2$ *implies that* $\nu(\{4\},\{3\}) > 0$ *and* $x^4 \succ x^3$ *implies that* $\nu(\{3\},\{4\}) > 0$, *which is not coherent.*

Introducing a reference point in a bi-capacity-based concordance rule means that the preference relation between two elements x and y will no longer depend on the position of x relatively to y. Only the respective position of each alternative compared to a reference point p are taken into account to compare x and y. We will note $p = (p_1, \ldots, p_n) \in X$ the *reference point*, and assume that
- $\forall j \in N$, $\exists x, y \in X$ such that $x_j \succ_j p_j \succ_j y_j$ (p is neither majoring nor minoring any criteria).
- $\forall j \in N$, $\forall x \in X$, $x_j \succsim_j p_j$ or $p_j \succsim_j x_j$ (each element of X_j is comparable to p_j for $j = 1, \ldots, n$).

We can define a bi-capacity-based concordance rule with a reference point as follow :

Definition 6. A bi-capacity-based concordance rule with a reference point defines a preference relation $\succsim$ on X from the relations $\succsim_j$ on X_j, $\forall j = 1, .., n$, a bi-capacity ν on $\mathcal{P}(N) \times \mathcal{P}(N)$ and a reference point p as follows : $x \succsim y \iff \nu(C_\succ(x,p), C_\succ(p,x)) \geq \nu(C_\succ(y,p), C_\succ(p,y))$

Return to example 2 : *Let us take* $p=(=,C,6,2)$ *as a reference profile for a car. Then* $C_\succ(x^1, p) = \{1\}$, $C_\succ(p, x^1) = \{3\}$, $C_\succ(x^2, p) = \{1\}$, $C_\succ(p, x^2) = \{4\}$, $C_\succ(x^3, p) = \{2\}$, $C_\succ(p, x^3) = \{3\}$, $C_\succ(x^4, p) = \{2\}$, $C_\succ(p, x^4) = \{4\}$. *Hence, preferences* $x^1 \succ x^2$ *and* $x^4 \succ x^3$ *are easily represented by a Bi-Capacity-Based Concordance rule with* $\nu(\{1\},\{3\}) > \nu(\{1\},\{4\})$ *and* $\nu(\{2\},\{4\}) > \nu(\{2\},\{3\})$.

We have seen above that the introduction of a reference point allows the decision maker to sort the value of each alternative on each criterion in two categories : good (better than p) or bad (worse than p). In order to be a little bit more discriminating, we can introduce a second reference point, with for example $p_i^1 \succ_i p_i^2 \; \forall \, i \in N$, which consists, for each criteria, in partitioning the different criterion values in three categories : good (better than p_i^1), medium (between p_i^1 and p_i^2) and bad (worse than p_i^2). Several approaches can then be considered to compare the alternatives to p^1 and p^2. We choose here an up to down filtering, where the alternatives are first compared to p^1 and then to p^2, in order to select first the best alternatives, but other choices are also possible. We will so define a bi-capacity-based concordance rule with two reference points as follow :

Definition 7. A bi-capacity-based concordance rule with two reference points defines a preference relation $\succsim$ on X from the relations $\succsim_j$ on X_j, $\forall j = 1, .., n$, a bi-capacity ν on $\mathcal{P}(N) \times \mathcal{P}(N)$ and two reference points p^1 and p^2 as follows :
$$x \succsim y \iff \nu(C_\succ(x, p^1), C_\succ(p^2, x)) \geq \nu(C_\succ(y, p^1), C_\succ(p^2, y))$$

Example 3. In this example, we show the interest of the introduction of a second reference point. The context is the same as in example 2.

	1	2	3	4
x^1	+	A	6	2
x^2	+	C	6	2
x^3	+	E	6	2
x^4	-	C	9	3

Assume that the decision maker has the following preferences : she prefers $x^1 \succ x^2$ and $x^2 \succ x^3$. Assume also that she prefers $x^2 \succ x^4$, which shows that preference $\succsim$ does not depend only on criterion (2).

The question is : can we represent these preferences with a bi-capacity-based concordance rule with only one reference point p? Suppose that it is possible, and let us note $p = (p_1, p_2, p_3, p_4)$ the reference point. We show that in these conditions, there is not acceptable value for one of the p_i, value of p on criterion i. First, the fact that $x^1 \succ x^2$ gives, on criterion 2, that $A \succ_2 p_2 \succsim_2 C$, because it is the only mean to distinguish x^1 and x^2. Then, the fact that $x^2 \succ x^3$ gives, on the same criterion, that $C \succ_2 p_2 \succsim_2 E$. so we have $p_2 \succsim_2 C \succ p_2$ which is not possible. We cannot represent these preferences with this model.

But these preferences can easily be build with a bi-capacity-based concordance rule with two reference points p^1 and p^2 as follow : let us take $p^1 = (=, B, 7, 2)$ and $p^2 = (=, D, 9, 2)$. Then, following the definition (7), we have

$$x^1 \succ x^2 \Rightarrow \nu(\{1, 2, 3\}, \emptyset) > \nu(\{1, 3\}, \emptyset)$$
$$x^2 \succ x^3 \Rightarrow \nu(\{1, 3\}, \emptyset) > \nu(\{1, 3\}, \{2\}).$$

4. Axiomatization

Establishing a representation theorem for a specific decision model consists in giving a set of conditions on the preference relation $\succsim$, through some testable axioms, and proving that they are necessary and sufficient for $\succsim$ to be represented by the proposed model. A representation theorem of a model allows to justify theoretically the use of this model in a specific context. Several general representation theorems on product sets have been proposed in conjoint measurement theory (see e.g. Luce *et al.* [10], Bouyssou and Pirlot [2]). Specific representation theorems for concordance rules have been proposed by Bouyssou and Pirlot [1] and Dubois *et al.* [4]. In this section, we establish three representation theorems to characterize preference structures which are compatible with a bi-capacity-based concordance rule as expressed by the relations defined in definition 5, 6 and 7.

4.1. *Bi-capacity-based concordance model*

First of all, we need to specify that the preference structure is ordinal-based. This is what the following axiom, introduced in Dubois *et al.* [4], says.

Axiom 1. Neutrality and Independence (NI)
$\forall x, y, z \in X$, $[C_{\succ}(x,y) = C_{\succ}(z,w)$ and $C_{\succ}(y,x) = C_{\succ}(w,z)] \Rightarrow [x \succsim y \iff z \succsim w]$

Then, it seems reasonable for the preference structure to have also a unanimity property on the criteria.

Axiom 2. Unanimity (UNA)
$$\forall i = 1, \ldots, n, \quad x_i \succsim_i y_i \Rightarrow x \succsim y$$

These two axioms are enough to specify which kind of preference structures can be characterized by a bi-capacity-based concordance rule, as shown in the following theorem:

Theorem 1. *If the preference relation $\succsim$ and the weak-orders $\succsim_j$ satisfy axioms (NI) and (UNA), then a bi-capacity ν exists such that :*
$$x \succsim y \iff \nu(C_{\succ}(x,y), C_{\succ}(y,x)) \geq 0$$

4.2. *Bi-capacity-based concordance model with a reference point*

Introducing a reference point in a bi-capacity-based concordance rule means that the NI axiom is no longer respected. It is now important to notice that only the respective position of each alternative compared to the reference point p are taken into account to compare two different alternatives. This is the meaning the following axiom:

Axiom 3. Neutrality and Independence with respect to a Reference Point (NIp)

$$\forall x, y \in X, \begin{cases} C_\succ(x,p) = C_\succ(y,p) \\ C_\succ(p,x) = C_\succ(p,y) \end{cases} \Rightarrow x \sim y$$

Associated with the unanimity axiom, (NIp) is sufficient to characterize the preference relations which can be represented by a bi-capacity-based concordance relation, as shown in the following theorem:

Theorem 2. If $\succsim$ and $\succsim_j$ satisfies axioms (NIp) and (UNA), then a bi-capacity ν exists such that : $x \succsim y \iff \nu(C_\succ(x,p), C_\succ(p,x)) \geq \nu(C_\succ(y,p), C_\succ(p,y))$

Remark : as we have seen before in Example 2, bi-capacity-based concordance rule using a reference point allows us to capture by ordinal concordance rules preference relations which were not modelled before.

4.3. Bi-capacity-based concordance model with two reference points

The neutrality and independence axiom should take into account the existence of two different reference points as follow :

Axiom 4. Neutrality and Independence with respect to two Reference Points (NI2p)
$\forall x, y \in X,$
$$\begin{cases} C_\succ(x,p^1) = C_\succ(y,p^1) \\ C_\succ(p^2,x) = C_\succ(p^2,y) \end{cases} \Rightarrow x \sim y$$

As above, this axiom is sufficient, associated with an unanimity axiom, to characterize the bi-capacity-based concordance rules with two reference points, as shown in the following theorem:

Theorem 3. If $\succsim$ and $\succsim_j$ satisfies axioms (NI2p) and (UNA), then a bi-capacity ν exists such that: $x \succsim y \iff \nu(C_\succ(x,p^1), C_\succ(p^2,x)) \geq \nu(C_\succ(y,p^1), C_\succ(p^2,y))$

5. Conclusion

New models using bi-capacity based concordance rules have been proposed to enlarge the description capacity of Concordance rules in ordinal MCDM. For examples, in the situations where the preference relations are semi-transitives, bi-capacity based concordance relations cannot be reduced to capacity based concordance relations.

On another hand, the introduction of reference points in such models, allows us to get out the frame of the so-called Arrow's impossibility theorem, and so to obtain transitive and non dictatorial preference rules based on the aggregation of ordinal preferences.

Appendix

We define $z = (x_j, y_{-j})$ as the element of X such as $z_j = x_j$ and $z_i = y_i$ $i \neq j$, with $j \in N$ and $x, y \in X$. More generally, $z = (x_A, y_{-A})$ is defined as the element of X such as $z_j = x_j$ if $j \in A$ and $z_j = y_j$ if $j \notin A$, with $A \subset N$ and $x, y \in X$.

Proof of theorem 1

Let us define a function f from $\mathcal{P}(N) \times \mathcal{P}(N)$ to $\{-1, 0, 1\}$ by :
$f(A, B) = 1 \iff \exists x, y \in X | C_\succ(x, y) = A, \ C_\succ(y, x) = B$ and $x \succ y$
$f(A, B) = 0 \iff \exists x, y \in X | C_\succ(x, y) = A, \ C_\succ(y, x) = B$ and $x \sim y$
$f(A, B) = -1 \iff \exists x, y \in X | C_\succ(x, y) = A, \ C_\succ(y, x) = B$ and $y \succ x$

Let us show that the function f is well defined : suppose that $\exists \ (x, y)$ and $(z, w) \in X \times X$ such as $C_\succ(x, y) = C_\succ(z, w) = A$ and $C_\succ(y, x) = C_\succ(w, z) = B$. As $\succsim$ respects the axiom (NI), we are sure that $x \succsim y \iff z \succsim w$, and so there is no ambiguity on the value of $f(A, B)$. We now show that f is a bi-capacity.

- $f((\emptyset, \emptyset)) = 0$: if $C_\succ(x, y) = C_\succ(y, x) = \emptyset$, it means that $\forall i \in N$, $x_i = y_i$, and so $x = y$ an $dx \sim y$, which means that $f((\emptyset, \emptyset)) = 0$.
- Monotonicity : suppose that $\exists x, y, z \in X$ such as $C_\succ(x, y) = A$, $C_\succ(z, y) = A'$, $C_\succ(y, x) = C_\succ(y, z) = B$ and $A \subseteq A'$. Do we have $f(A', B) \geq f(A, B)$? Let us take $w \in X$ such as $\forall i \in N$, $w_i = max_{\succsim_i}\{x_i, z_i\}$. We have $\forall i \in N$, $w_i \succsim_i x_i$, so as $\succsim$ respects (UNA), $w \succsim x$. Moreover, as $A \subseteq A'$, $C_\succ(w, y) = A'$ and $C_\succ(y, w) = B$. So $w \succsim y \iff z \succsim y$.
  · if $f(A, B) = -1$, then $f(A', B) \geq -1$ and so $f(A', B) \geq f(A, B)$
  · if $f(A, B) = 0$, we have $x \sim y$, and, by transitivity, $w \succsim y$. By (NI), we have $z \succsim y$ and so $f(A', B) \geq 0 = f(A, B)$.
  · if $f(A, B) = 1$, we have $x \succ y$, and, by transitivity, $w \succ y$. By (NI), we have $z \succ y$ and so $f(A', B) = 1 \geq f(A, B)$.

So if $A \subseteq A'$, we always have $f(A, .) \leq f(A', .)$. We can show on the same idea that if $A \subseteq A'$, we always have $f(., A) \geq f(., A')$.

This proves that f is a bi-capacity. □

5.1. *Proof of theorem 2*

Let us define a relation $\succsim'$ on $\mathcal{Q} \times \mathcal{Q}$ by $(A,B) \succsim' (C,D) \iff \exists x, y \in X \mid \begin{cases} A = C_\succ(x,p) \\ B = C_\succ(p,x) \\ C = C_\succ(y,p) \\ D = C_\succ(p,y) \end{cases}$ and $x \succsim y$.

We show that this relation is a complete weak order on $\mathcal{Q}$.

Let us demonstrate first that the relation $\succsim'$ defined above exists. The relation $\succsim'$ defined above should not depend on the elements x and y chosen during the construction. For this, we should show that if two couples of $X \times X$, (x,y) and (z,w), exist such that $\begin{cases} A = C_\succ(x,p) = C_\succ(z,p) \\ B = C_\succ(p,x) = C_\succ(p,z) \end{cases}$ and $\begin{cases} C = C_\succ(y,p) = C_\succ(w,p) \\ D = C_\succ(p,y) = C_\succ(p,w) \end{cases}$, then

$x \succsim y \iff z \succsim w$. This is obvious, following (NIp), because $\begin{cases} C_\succ(x,p) = C_\succ(z,p) \\ C_\succ(p,x) = C_\succ(p,z) \end{cases}$

and $\begin{cases} C_\succ(y,p) = C_\succ(w,p) \\ C_\succ(p,y) = C_\succ(p,w) \end{cases}$ give $x \sim z$ and $y \sim w$.

Let us now demonstrate that $\succsim'$ is a weak-order on $\mathcal{Q}$.
- **asymmetry of $\succ'$**: if $(A,B) \succ' (C,D)$, this means that exist $x, y \in X$ such that $\begin{cases} A = C_\succ(x,p) \\ B = C_\succ(p,x) \end{cases}$, $\begin{cases} C = C_\succ(y,p) \\ D = C_\succ(p,y) \end{cases}$ and $x \succ y$. If $(A,B) \prec' (C,D)$, this means that exist $z, w \in X$ such that $\begin{cases} A = C_\succ(z,p) \\ B = C_\succ(p,z) \end{cases}$, $\begin{cases} C = C_\succ(w,p) \\ D = C_\succ(p,w) \end{cases}$ and $w \succ z$. Following (NIp), we have $x \sim z$ and $y \sim w$, which is in contradiction with $x \succ y$ and $w \succ z$. So we can't have on the same time $(A,B) \succ' (C,D)$ and $(A,B) \prec' (C,D)$, which proves the asymmetry of $\succ'$.
- **symmetry of $\sim'$**: on the same idea, symmetry $\sim'$ is easily shown based on the symmetry of $\sim$ and (NIp).
- **transitivity of $\succsim'$**: if $(A,B) \succsim' (C,D)$ and $(C,D) \succsim' (E,F)$, then exist $x, y, y', z \in X$ such that $\begin{cases} A = C_\succ(x,p) \\ B = C_\succ(p,x)) \end{cases}$, $\begin{cases} C = C_\succ(y,p) \\ D = C_\succ(p,y) \end{cases}$ and $x \succsim y$, and $\begin{cases} C = C_\succ(y',p) \\ D = C_\succ(p,y') \end{cases}$, $\begin{cases} E = C_\succ(z,p) \\ F = C_\succ(p,z) \end{cases}$ and $y' \succsim z$. Axiom (NIp) implies that $y \sim y'$, and transitivity of $\succsim$ implies $x \succsim z$, which shows the transitivity of $\succsim'$.

We now show the completeness of $\succsim'$. As we have $\forall i \in N, \exists\ x_i, y_i$ such that $x_i \succ_i$

$p_i \succ_i y_i$, we can build for all $(A, B) \in \mathcal{Q}$ a element $z \in X$ such that $C_\succ(z,p) = A$
and $C_\succ(p, z) = B$: we just have to take
$$\begin{cases} z_i = a_i \text{ if } i \in A \\ z_i = b_i \text{ if } i \in B \\ z_i = p_i \text{ if not} \end{cases}, \text{ with } a_i \succ_i p_i \forall i \in N$$
and $b_i \prec_i p_i \forall i \in N$. Completeness of $\succsim$ gives the completeness of $\succsim'$.

As $\succsim'$ is complete and $\mathcal{Q}$ is finite, there is a function $\nu : \mathcal{Q} \to \mathbb{R}$ such that $(A,B) \succsim' (C,D) \iff \nu(A,B) \geq \nu(C,D)$. We now show that this set-function ν is a bi-capacity. Suppose that $A \subseteq B$. Let compare $\nu(A,C)$ and $\nu(B,C)$, with $A \cap C = B \cap C = \emptyset$. Suppose $x \in X$ such that $C_\succ(x,p) = A$ and $C_\succ(p,x) = C$. Suppose $y \in X$ such that $C_\succ(y,p) = B$ and $C_\succ(p,y) = C$. Let denote $z = (x_{A \cup N \setminus B}, y_{B \setminus A})$. Following axiom (UNA), $z \succsim x$, because $\forall j \in N$, $z_j \succsim_j x_j$. Actually, if $j \in B \setminus A$, we have $z_j = y_j \succ_j p_j$ and $x_j = p_j$. So $z \succsim x$ gives $(B,C) \succsim' (A,C)$, which implies $\nu(B,C) \geq \nu(A,C)$. We have shown that $A \subseteq B \Rightarrow \nu(A,\cdot) \leq \nu(B,\cdot)$. On the same way, we can show that $A \subseteq B \Rightarrow \nu(\cdot,A) \geq \nu(B,\cdot)$. Then, ν is a bi-capacity if $\nu(\emptyset, \emptyset) = 0$. If not, we just have to take $\nu' = \nu - \nu(\emptyset, \emptyset)$ to have a bi-capacity. □

Proof of theorem 3

let us define a relation $\succsim'$ on $\mathcal{Q} \times \mathcal{Q}$ by $(A,B) \succsim' (C,D) \iff \exists x,y \in$
$$X| \begin{cases} A = C_\succ(x, p^1) \\ B = C_\succ(p^2, x) \\ C = C_\succ(y, p^1) \\ D = C_\succ(p^2, y) \end{cases} \text{ and } x \succsim y.$$

We show that this relation is a complete weak order on $\mathcal{Q}$.

Let us demonstrate first that the relation $\succsim'$ defined above exists. The relation $\succsim'$ defined above should not depend on the elements x and y chosen during the construction. For this, we should show that if two couples of $X \times X$ (x,y) et (z,w) such that $\begin{cases} A = C_\succ(x, p^1) = C_\succ(z, p^1) \\ B = C_\succ(p^2, x) = C_\succ(p^2, z) \end{cases}$ and $\begin{cases} C = C_\succ(y, p^1) = C_\succ(w, p^1) \\ D = C_\succ(p^2, y) = C_\succ(p^2, w) \end{cases}$, then

$x \succsim y \iff z \succsim w$. It is obvious following (NI2p) : $\begin{cases} C_\succ(x, p^1) = C_\succ(z, p^1) \\ C_\succ(p^2, x) = C_\succ(p^2, z) \end{cases}$ and
$\begin{cases} C_\succ(y, p^1) = C_\succ(w, p^1) \\ C_\succ(p^2, y) = C_\succ(p^2, w) \end{cases}$ gives $x \sim z$ and $y \sim w$.

We now demonstrate that $\succsim'$ is a weak order on $\mathcal{Q}$.
- **asymmetry of $\succ'$** : if $(A,B) \succ' (C,D)$, this means that exist $x,y \in X$ such that $\begin{cases} A = C_\succ(x, p^1) \\ B = C_\succ(p^2, x)) \end{cases}$, $\begin{cases} C = C_\succ(y, p^1) \\ D = C_\succ(p^2, y) \end{cases}$ and $x \succ y$. If $(A,B) \prec' (C,D)$, this means

that exist $z, w \in X$ such that $\begin{cases} A = C_\succ(z, p^1) \\ B = C_\succ(p^2, z) \end{cases}$, $\begin{cases} C = C_\succ(w, p^1) \\ D = C_\succ(p^2, w) \end{cases}$ and $w \succ z$.

Following the axiom (NI2p), we have $x \sim z$ and $y \sim w$ which is in contradiction with $x \succ y$ and $w \succ z$. So we can't have on the same time $(A, B) \succ' (C, D)$ and $(A, B) \prec' (C, D)$, which proves the asymmetry of $\succ'$.

- **symmetry of $\sim'$** : on the same idea, symmetry $\sim'$ is easily shown based on the symmetry of $\sim$ and (NIp).
- **transitivity of $\succsim'$** : If $(A, B) \succsim' (C, D)$ and $(C, D) \succsim' (E, F)$, then exist $x, y, y', z \in X$ such that $\begin{cases} A = C_\succ(x, p^1) \\ B = C_\succ(p^2, x)) \end{cases}$, $\begin{cases} C = C_\succ(y, p^1) \\ D = C_\succ(p^2, y) \end{cases}$ and $x \succsim y$, and $\begin{cases} C = C_\succ(y', p^1) \\ D = C_\succ(p^2, y') \end{cases}$, $\begin{cases} E = C_\succ(z, p^1) \\ F = C_\succ(p^2, z) \end{cases}$ and $y' \succsim z$. Axiom (NI2p) implies that $y \sim y'$, and transitivity of $\succsim$ implies $x \succsim z$, which proves the transitivity of $\succsim'$.

We now demonstrate the completeness of $\succsim'$. As we supposed that $\forall i \in N, \exists\ x_i, y_i$ such that $x_i \succ_i p_i^1$ and $p_i^2 \succ_i y_i$, we can build for all $(A, B) \in \mathcal{Q}$ an element $z \in X$ such that $C_\succ(z, p^1) = A$ and $C_\succ(p^2, z) = B$: we just have to take

$\begin{cases} z_i = a_i \text{ if } i \in A \\ z_i = b_i \text{ if } i \in B \\ z_i = c_i \text{ if not} \end{cases}$, with $a_i \succ_i p_i^1\ \forall i \in N$, $b_i \prec_i p_i^2\ \forall i \in N$ and $p_i^1 \succsim_i c_i \succsim_i p_i^2$

$\forall i \in N$. Completeness of $\succsim$ implies the completeness of $\succsim'$. As $\succsim'$ is complete and $\mathcal{Q}$ is finite, there is a function $\nu : \mathcal{Q} \to \mathbb{R}$ such that $(A, B) \succsim' (C, D) \iff \nu(A, B) \geq \nu(C, D)$. We now show that this function ν is a bi-capacity. Suppose that $A \subseteq B$. Let compare $\nu(A, C)$ and $\nu(B, C)$, with $A \cap C = B \cap C = \emptyset$. Let take $x \in X$ such that $C_\succ(x, p^1) = A$ and $C_\succ(p^2, x) = C$. Let take $y \in X$ such that $C_\succ(y, p^1) = B$ and $C_\succ(p^2, y) = C$. We note $z = (x_{A \cup N \setminus B}, y_{B \setminus A})$. Following axiom (UNA), $z \succsim x$, because $\forall j \in N$, $z_j \succsim_j x_j$. Actually, if $j \in B \setminus A$, we have $z_j = y_j \succ_j p_j^1$ and $p_j^1 \succsim_j x_j \succsim_j p_j^2$. $z \succsim x$ gives $(B, C) \succsim' (A, C)$, which gives $\nu(B, C) \geq \nu(A, C)$. we have shown that $A \subseteq B \Rightarrow \nu(A, \cdot) \leq \nu(B, \cdot)$. On the same way, we can show that $A \subseteq B \Rightarrow \nu(\cdot, A) \geq \nu(\cdot, B)$. Then, ν is a bi-capacity if $\nu(\emptyset, \emptyset) = 0$. If not, we just have to take $\nu' = \nu - \nu(\emptyset, \emptyset)$ to have a bi-capacity. $\square$

References

1. D. Bouyssou and J.C. Pirlot. A characterization of strict concordance relations. In *Aiding decisions with multicriteria*, pages 121–146. Kluwer's academic publishers, 2002.
2. D. Bouyssou and M. Pirlot. Non transitive decomposable conjoint measurement. *Journal of Mathematical Psychology*, 46:677–703, 2002.
3. G. Choquet. Theory of capacities. *Annales de l'Institut Fourier*, (5):131–295, 1953.

4. D. Dubois, H. Fargier, P. Perny, and H. Prade. A characterization of generalized concordance rules in multicriteria decision making. *International Journal of Intelligent Systems, special issue on preference modeling application*, (18):751–774, 2003.
5. J. Fodor and M. Roubens. *Fuzzy preference modelling and multicriteria decision support*. Kluwer Academic Publishers, 1994.
6. M. Grabisch. The application of fuzzy integrals in multicriteria decision making. *European Journal of Operational Research*, 89:445–456, 1996.
7. M. Grabisch and C. Labreuche. Bi-capacities. In *1st Joint International Conference on Soft Computing and Intelligent Systems and 3rd International Symposium on Advanced Intelligent Systems*, 2002.
8. M. Grabisch and M. Roubens. Application of the Choquet integral in multicriteria decision making. In M. Grabisch, T. Murofushi, and M. Sugeno, editors, *Fuzzy Measures and Integrals - Theory and Applications*, pages 348–374. Physica Verlag, 2000.
9. R.L. Keeney and H. Raiffa. *Decisions with multiple objectives: Preferences and value tradeoffs*. J. Wiley, New York, 1976.
10. R.D. Luce, D.H. Krantz, P. Suppes, and A. Tversky. *Foundations of measurement*, volume 3: Representation, axiomatisation and invariance. Academic Press, New York, 1990.
11. J.L. Marichal. An axiomatic approach of the discrete Choquet integral as a tool to aggregate interacting criteria. *IEEE Transactions on Fuzzy Systems*, 8(6):800–807, December 2000.
12. P. Perny and M. Roubens. *Preference Modelling*, pages 69–101. Kluwer Academic Publishers, 1998.
13. B. Roy. How outranking relations helps multiple criteria decision making. In J. Cochrane and M. Zeleny, editors, *Multicriteria Decision Making*, pages 179–201. University of Carolina, 1973.
14. B. Roy. *Multicriteria Methodology for Decision Aiding*. Kluwer Academic, Dordrecht, 1996.
15. D. Schmeidler. Integral representation without additivity. *Proc. Amer. Math. Soc.*, (97):255–261, 1986.
16. M. Sugeno. *Theory of fuzzy integrals and its applications*. PhD thesis, Tokyo Institute of Technology, 1974.
17. M. Sugeno and T. Murofushi. Choquet integral as an integral form for a general class of fuzzy measures. In *2nd IFSA Congress*, pages 408–411, 1987.

Information Evaluation in fusion: Formalization of informal recommendations

Laurence Cholvy [a]

[a] ONERA Centre de Toulouse, BP 4025, 2 av Ed Belin, 31055 Toulouse, France

Abstract

This paper examines a case study of information fusion[1]. It focuses on some recommendations defined by NATO relatively to information evaluation in intelligence. These recommendations, written in natural language, are ambiguous and imprecise and we discuss the fact that they define a scale for evaluating information. We then propose a model of information evaluation, which takes into account the main notions which underline the recommendations and we show its use in the fusion process.

Key words:
Information evaluation, information fusion, logic.

1. Introduction

An important step in the intelligence gathering process is the fusion of information provided by several sources. The objective of this process is to build an up-to-date and correct view of the current situation with the overall available information in order to make adequate decisions.

Moreover, to succeed in this process, it is important to associate with each available information, some attributes like the number of the sources that support it, their reliability, the degree of truth of the information etc. For the moment, these attributes are managed by the human operator when he fuses information provided

---
[1] This work was supported by ONERA under grant ONERA/DSG/RGF/PR 08180

by the different sources. But there is no real methodology to do this in a formal manner. And, when relaying this fusion process to a machine, we need to develop formal definitions and algorithms to manage these attributes in addition to fusing information. Furthermore, in a context of interoperability where different systems exchange information, common definitions of these attributes have to be shared. The Standardization Agreements (STANAG) 2022 of North Atlantic Treaty Organization (NATO) defines a framework for such common definitions.

The aim of this paper is to analyse the STANAG 2022 recommendations about information evaluation and to define a formal and non ambiguous system for evaluating information. Indeed, as it will be shown, the present recommendations, written in natural language are rather ambiguous and imprecise and are subject to discussion.

Consequently, the main contribution of this paper is not a new theory for information fusion, but is to show how to adapt some existing theory to the case of information evaluation in intelligence agreeing with recommendations of NATO.

This paper is organized as follows. Section 2 presents STANAG 2022 recommendations. It also lists some criticisms that can be done and points out the main notions that underline these recommendations. Section 3 presents a formal model for evaluating information which tends to agree with these notions. Section 4 shows the application of this model in information fusion process. An example is described in section 5. Finally, section 6 is devoted to a discussion.

2. Discussion on STANAG 2022 recommendations

The Annex to STANAG 2022 (Edition 8) [1] explicitly mentions that *the aim of information evaluation is to indicate the degree of confidence that may be placed in any item of information which has been obtained for intelligence. (...) This is achieved by adopting an alphanumeric system of rating which combines a measurement of the reliability of the source of information with a measurement of the credibility of that information when examined in the light of existing knowledge.*

Examining the whole text leads us to point out that the two main notions of this evaluation system are *the reliability* of the sources and *the credibility* of the information. These notions are defined in the STANAG 2022 recommendations, as follows:

Reliability of the source is designated by a letter between A and F signifying various degrees of confidence as indicated below.
– a source is evaluated A if it is completely reliable. It refers to a tried and trusted source which can be depended upon with confidence
– a source is evaluated B if it is usually reliable. It refers to a source which has been successfully used in the past but for which there is still some element of doubt in particular cases.
– a source is evaluated C if it is fairly reliable. It refers to a source which has occasionally been used in the past and upon which some degree of confidence can

be based.
- a source is evaluated D if it is not usually reliable. It refers to a source which has been used in the past but has proved more often than not unreliable.
- a source is evaluated E if it is unreliable. It refers to a source which has been used in the past and has proved unworthy of any confidence.
- a source is evaluated F if its reliability cannot be judged. It refers to a source which has not been used in the past.

Credibility of information is designated by a number between 1 and 6 signifying varying degrees of confidence as indicated below.
- If it can be stated with certainty that the reported information originates from another source than the already existing information on the same subject, then it is classified as "confirmed by other sources" and rated 1.
- If the independence of the source of any item of information cannot be guaranteed, but if, from the quantity and quality of previous reports, its likelihood is nevertheless regarded as sufficiently established, then the information should be classified as "probably true" and given a rating of 2.
- If, despite there being insufficient confimation to establish any higher degree of likelihood, a freshyly reported item of information does not conflict with the previously reported behaviour pattern of the target, the item may be classified as "possibly true" and given a rating of 3.
- An item of information which tends to conflict with the previously reported or established behaviour pattern of an intelligence target should be classified as "doubtful" and given a rating of 4
- An item of information which positively contradicts previously reported information or conflicts with the established behaviour pattern of an intelligence target in a marked degree should be classified as "improbable" and given a rating of 5
- An item of information is given a rating of 6 if its truth cannot be judged.

The previous definitions of information evaluation can be discussed. Indeed, since they are given in natural language, they are quite imprecise and ambiguous. Let us discuss three points.

According to the previous recommendations, the reliability of a source is defined in reference to its use in the past. It can be measured for example, as the ratio of the number of times it gave a true information to the number of times it gave information. However, this definition does not take into account the actual environment of use of the information source. For instance, even if it is known to be reliable, an infra-red sensor loose reliability when it rains.

Concerning the credibility of information, it seems that the rating defined according to the recommendations does not qualify an unique property. For instance, how should we note an item of information supported by several sources of information which is also conflictual with some already registered information ? According to these definitions, this item should be given a rating of 1 and should also be given a rating of 5.

Furthermore, according to the recommendations, a rating of 6 should be given to an item whose truth cannot be judged. This suppposes that the other ratings (1...5) concern the evaluation of the truth of information. If so, rating of 1 should be given to a true information. But, as it is defined, rating of 1 should be given to an item supported by at least two sources. This is questionable since, the different sources (even if they agree) may emit false information.

However, even if the previous recommendations can be discussed, one can see that the three main notions which underline the evaluation system are :
- the number of independent sources that support an information
- their reliability
- the fact that the information tends to conflict or conflicts with some available information

These three characteristics are independent. For instance, two sources, one being fully reliable and the other not usually reliable may have emitted the same piece of information. Furthermore, this piece of information may be contradictory with another piece of information.

In the following, we present a model of evaluation which takes into account the number of the sources and their reliability but which does not make a distinction between "tending to conflict" and "conflicting". In this model, that unique notion of conflict is represented by the property of inconsistency.

3. Proposal for a formal model of evaluation

In order to define an evaluation as close as possible to the one recommended by the STANAG, an information evaluation will still be a pair. But the meaning of the two members of that pair will be different. This meaning is given below.

We consider a propositional language L, used to express information. Information will then be formulas of L. $Mod(F)$ will demote the set of models of the formula F.

We consider several sources of information which deliver information about an observed situation.

Each source of information is associated with its degree of reliability, which is a letter belonging to $\{A, ..., E\}$ depending on the fact that this source is judged more or less reliable. Notice that this definition could be refined by defining the degree of reliability of a source according to the probability that this source gives true information in the current context of use. Refining this definition is not necessary for the following.

Each information emitted by a source is stored in a database DB with its evaluation as defined by the following definition.

Definition. The evaluation of a formula F, denoted $eval(F)$, is a pair $< V, m >$, such that :
- V is a vector of letters belonging to $\{A, B, C, D, E\}$. The length of this vector indicates the number of sources which support the information and the contents of the vector reflects their reliability degrees.
- m is an integer which is equal to 1 iff the information is consistent with the other avalaible information stored in DB or equal to 2 else.

Examples. The evaluation $< (A), 1 >$ is associated with an information which has been emitted by a completely reliable source and which is consistent with the current state of DB.

The evaluation $< (A, C), 2 >$ is associated with an information which is supported by two sources, one being completely reliable, the other one being fairly reliable, and which is inconsistent with the current state of DB.

One can notice that in a given state of DB, the evaluation of an information is unique. However, an information evaluation may change during time as it will be shown in the following.

4. Application of this model in fusion

In this section, we show how to apply this previous model is the process of information fusion. That process is the following: as soon as an item of information is emitted by a source (sensor, human), it is stored in DB with its appropriate evaluation. From time to time, queries are asked to DB in order to make decisions. Besides DB, we also have a set of constraints, IC, stating what is true for certain in the real world. For instance IC may contain the following rules *if the observed object is a plane, then it is not an helicopter, if a vehicule moves north, then it does not move south, etc..*

4.1. Registering an information into DB

Let us consider an information F emitted by a source whose reliability is r. The following algorithm describes the registration, in DB, of F associated with its evaluation.
- If F is not yet stored in DB.
  · F is consistent with $DB \cup IC$.
    Then F is stored in DB with the evaluation $<< r >, 1 >$.
  · F is inconsistent with $DB \cup IC$.
    Then F is stored in DB with the evaluation $<< r >, 2 >$.
    Let $S_i = \{F_i^1, ... F_i^{n_i}\}$ (i = 1...n) the minimal subsets of DB inconsistent with $F \cup IC$.
    Then $\forall i = 1...n$ $\forall j = 1...n_i$, if the evaluation of F_i^j was $< V_i^j, m >$ then it is updated and becomes $< V_i^j, 2 >$.
- If F is already stored in DB.
    Assume that F is stored in DB with the evaluation $<< V >, m >$. Then this evaluation becomes $< V', m >$ where V' is the vector obtained by agregating V with r.
    Notice that the length of the vector has been incremented by 1 (indeed, one more source supports F), but m is not changed : even if one more source emitted F, this does not change the fact that F is (or not) consistent with $DB \cup IC$.

Remark. In this last case, we should also check the independance of the different sources of information which have emitted F. But, in order to simplify the presentation of the model, we assume independence of these sources.

So, finally DB is a finite set of formulas associated with their evaluation. We can then write $DB = \{< F_1, eval(F_1) > .... < F_n, eval(F_n) >\}$.

4.2. Querying DB

The problem is now to answer a query addressed to DB. Let Q be a formula expressing this query. We denote $||Q||_{DB,IC}$ the answer to Q addressed to DB under the constraints IC.

In the following, we show that given IC, DB can be associated with an unique consistent set of formulas of L, denoted $merge(DB, IC)$ and we will define $||Q||_{DB,IC}$ according to the satisfaction of Q in this set. $merge(DB, IC)$ is here defined by extending a majority merging operator by taking into account weigthed sum instead of sum. The weigths here will be numbers (5, 4, 3, 2, 1) which intend to represent, on a numerical scale, the different degrees of reliability of the sources (A, B, C, D, E).

4.2.1. Definition of $\Delta_{W\Sigma}$

We recall here some definitions introduced by Konieczny and Pino-Pérez [2] [3] and adapt them for our purpose.

Let $db_1...db_n$ be n sets of formulas of L and IC a set of integrity constraints. Konieczny and Pino-Pérez defined a majority merging operator, denoted $\Delta_{\Sigma,IC}$, such that the set of models of the information source which is obtained from merging $db_1 ... db_n$ with this operator, is semantically characterized by:

$$Mod(\Delta_{\Sigma,IC}([db_1, ..., db_n])) = \min_{\leq^\Sigma_{[db_1...db_n]}} (Mod(IC))$$

$\leq^\Sigma_{[db_1...db_n]}$ is a total pre-order on $Mod(IC)$ defined by:

$$w \leq^\Sigma_{[db_1...db_n]} w' \text{ iff } d_\Sigma(w, [db_1...db_n]) \leq d_\Sigma(w', [db_1...db_n])$$

with

$$d_\Sigma(w, [db_1...db_n]) = \sum_{i=1}^{n} \min_{w' \in Mod(db_i)} d(w, w')$$

where $d(w, w')$ is the Hamming distance (i.e, the number of propositional letters whose valuation differs from w to w').

In other words, when merging $db_1...db_n$ with the operator $\Delta_{\Sigma,IC}$, the result is semantically characterized by the models of IC which are minimal according to the pre-order $\leq^\Sigma_{[db_1,...,db_n]}$.

As Konieczny and Pino-Pérez explicitely mentionned it in conclusion of [2], this merging operator $\Delta_{\Sigma,IC}$ can be extended by taking into account a weigthed sum instead a simple sum However, the properties of this operator remain to be studied. In the following, we suggest such an extension, which fully agrees with the weighted model-fitting approach of Revesz [4] to the revision of a (possibly inconsistent) weighted knowldege-base by a formula.

We assume now that any db_i is associated with an integer denoted $r(db_i)$. We define $\Delta_{W\Sigma,IC}$ by :

$$Mod(\Delta_{W\Sigma,IC}([db_1,...,db_n])) = \min_{\leq^{W\Sigma}_{[db_1...db_n]}} (Mod(IC))$$

$\leq^{W\Sigma}_{[db_1...db_n]}$ is a total pre-order on $Mod(IC)$ defined by:

$$w \leq^{W\Sigma}_{[db_1...db_n]} w' \text{ iff } d_{W\Sigma}(w,[db_1...db_n]) \leq d_{W\Sigma}(w',[db_1...db_n])$$

with

$$d_{W\Sigma}(w,[db_1...db_n]) = \sum_{i=1}^{n} \min_{w' \in Mod(db_i)} d(w,w').r(db_i)$$

i.e,

$$d_{W\Sigma}(w,[db_1...db_n]) = \sum_{i=1}^{n} r(db_i). \min_{w' \in Mod(db_i)} d(w,w')$$

4.2.2. Definition of $merge(DB, IC)$.
Consider $DB = \{< F_1, eval(F_1) > .... < F_n, eval(F_n) >\}$.
For $i = 1...n$, let us denote $eval(F_i) =< (d_i^1...d_i^{p_i}), m_i >$,
Then we associate DB with $db_1^1...db_1^{p_1}...db_n^1...db_n^{p_n}$ where :
- $\forall i = 1...n$, $db_i^1 = db_i^2 = ... = db_i^{p_i} = \{F_i\}$
- $\forall j = 1...p_i$, $r(db_i^j) = 5$ $(resp, 4, 3, 2, 1)$ iff $d_i^j = A$ $(resp, B, C, D, E)$

$merge(DB, IC)$ is the consistent set of formulas of L so that

$$Mod(merge(DB, IC)) = \Delta_{W\Sigma,IC}([db_1^1...db_n^{p_n}])$$

4.2.3. Definition of the answer to Q
When addressed to DB, the answer to query Q is defined by:
$||Q||_{DB,IC} = YES$ iff $\models merge(DB, IC) \rightarrow Q$
$||Q||_{DB,IC} = NO$ iff $\models merge(DB, IC) \rightarrow \neg Q$
$||Q||_{DB,IC} =?$ $else$

4.2.4. An alternative to answers definition.
According to the approach adopted here, one can check that, in order to remain as close as possible to the recommendations, we have considered a second attribute in the evaluation of a piece of information, intending to represent its degree of inconsistency, but this attribute is not useful: the conflictual aspect of an information is taken into account in the fusion process when querying the database.

However, since the conflictual aspect of an information seems to be important for intelligence, we suggest to modify the definition of answers as it is done in [5].

There, we suggest to associate answers with explanations as follows. Let Q be a query, the possible answers that the evaluator can generate are:

- *Yes, and there is no proof against it* (resp, *No, and there is no proof against it*) when some source prove Q and no other source provide $\neg Q$.

- *Yes, by majority* (resp, *No, by majority*) when the number of the sources which prove Q (resp, $\neg Q$) is strictly greater than the number of the sources which provide $\neg Q$ (resp, Q)

- *Don't know, due to a balanced inconsistency* when the number of the sources which provides Q is equal to the number of the sources which provide $\neg Q$.

- *Dont't know, due to a lack of information* when no source provide Q nor $\neg Q$.

In the first case, the explanation means that the information Q is supposed to be true and this is not conflictual. In the second case, the explanation means that even if, by the majority merging process, Q is supposed to be true, this is somewhat conflictual. In the third case, the explanation means that Q is highly conflictual and the majority vote cannot help to decide.

We do not give more detail about this alternative definition.

5. An exemple

We assume a propositional language with letters a, b and c. And we assume a set of constraints $IC = \{\neg a \vee \neg b, \neg a \vee \neg c\}$.

For instance, a could mean *the observed object is a plane*, b could mean *the observed object is an helicopter* and c could mean *the altitude of the observed object is less than 3 km*

We consider four information sources called $One, Two, Three$ and $Four$, whose reliability are respectively A, B, C and D. We consider the following flow of emissions:

$$One \text{ emits } b, \text{ then}$$
$$Two \text{ emits } a, \text{ then}$$
$$Three \text{ emits } a, \text{ then}$$
$$Four \text{ emits } c, \text{ then}$$
$$One \text{ emits } c.$$

At this step, we have

$$DB = \{< a, < (B,C), 2 >>, < b, < (A), 2 >>, < c, < (D,A), 2 >>\}$$

The questions that raise are: is a true ? is b true ? is c true ?...

By the previous definitions, we can define:
$$db_1^1 = \{a\} \text{ and } r(db_1^1) = 4$$

$$db_1^2 = \{a\} \text{ and } r(db_1^2) = 3$$
$$db_2^1 = \{b\} \text{ and } r(db_2^1) = 5$$
$$db_3^1 = \{c\} \text{ and } r(db_3^1) = 2$$
$$db_3^2 = \{c\} \text{ and } r(db_3^2) = 5$$

The five models of IC are: $w_1 = \{a, \neg b, \neg c\}$, $w_2 = \{\neg a, b, c\}$, $w_3 = \{\neg a, b, \neg c\}$, $w_4 = \{\neg a, \neg b, c\}$ and $w_5 = \{\neg a, \neg b, \neg c\}$. Then we can compute the following distances:

$$d_{W\Sigma}(w_1, [db_1^1...db_3^2]) = 12$$
$$d_{W\Sigma}(w_2, [db_1^1...db_3^2]) = 7$$
$$d_{W\Sigma}(w_3, [db_1^1...db_3^2]) = 14$$
$$d_{W\Sigma}(w_4, [db_1^1...db_3^2]) = 12$$
$$d_{W\Sigma}(w_5, [db_1^1...db_3^2]) = 19$$

Thus, $Merge(DB, IC) = w_2 = \{\neg a, b, c\}$.

Then finally, $||a||_{DB,IC} = NO$, $||b||_{DB,IC} = YES$, $||c||_{DB,IC} = YES$.

Coming back to the intuitive meaning we gave to letters, it would mean that, given what has been registered in DB until now by the different sources and given their reliability, the most plausible answer is that *the observed object is not a plane, it is an helicopeter which flies at less than 3km high.*

6. Discussion

This works intended to formalize some informal recommendations about information evaluation in information fusion.

Most of the informal notions underlying the recommendations have been given a formal interpretation. However, some of them have not yet been taken into account.

For instance, in this present work, we made no difference between "being conflictual" and "tending to be conflictual". This last notion assumes that there is a scale for defining conflicts. In the present work, this scale is binary and the formal notion which represents the conflict is the logical inconsistency. Extension to graded conflict is foreseen in future work.

Another point which has been left aside is the total ignorance about the reliability of a given source, which was a case forseen in the recommendations. In the present formalization, it seems difficult to represent that. Indeed, which number can be attached to a source whose reliability is not known ? That is an open question.

However, this formalization proved that the second attribute in the evaluation of an information is not necessary. Thus, the evaluation of an information could be simplified and memorizing only the number of the sources that emitted it and their reliability is enough.

As for the method of fusion, we have chosen a weighted majority because it takes into account the number of the sources and their reliability. If the number of the sources had not been so important, we could have chosen a method taking into account the reliability of the sources only (see [6], [7], [8] for instance). As for arbitration merging operator as characterized in [2] or [3], it does not consider as essential the number of sources which support an information.

As for implementation issues, in order to automatically compute the answers to queries, we suggest to slightly modify the query-evaluator defined in [9] by taking into account the reliability of the sources. That extension is obvious. However, it must be recalled that this evaluator is valid only in some particular case. More specifically, when $\forall i = 1...n \ \forall j = 1...p_i \quad db_i \cup IC$ is equivalent to a set of atomic formulas, which is the case of the example given in section 5.

References

1. Annex to STANAG 2022 (Edition 8) North Atlantic Treaty Organization (NATO) Information Handling Services, DODSID, Issue DW9705
2. S. Konieczny and R. Pino-Pérez. On the logic of merging. In *Principles of Knowledge Representation and Reasoning (KR'98)*, pages 488–498, 1998.
3. S. Konieczny and R. Pino-Pérez. Merging with Integrity Constraints In *Proceedings of ESCQARU'99*
4. P. Z. Revesz. On the semantics of arbitration. In *International Journal of Algebra and Computation*, vol 7, no 2, pp 130–160, 1997.
5. L. Cholvy and C. Garion. Querying several conflicting databases Journal of Applied Non-Classical Logics, 14(3), 2004.
6. C. Baral and S. Kraus and J. Minker and V.S. Subrahmanian. Combining multiple knowledge bases. *IEEE Trans. on Knowledge and Data Engineering, 3(2), 1991*
7. L. Cholvy. Proving theorems in a multi-sources environment. *Proceedings of IJCAI, 1993*
8. C. Liau. A conservative Approach to Distributed Belief Fusion *Proceedings of FUSION, 2000*
9. L. Cholvy and C. Garion. Answering queries addressed to merged databases: a query evaluator which implements a majority approach. In M-S Hacid, Z.W. Raś, D.A. Zighed, and Y. Kodratoff, editors, *Proc. of ISMIS-2002, LNAI n° 2366*, p 131–139. Springer, june 2002.

Application of uncertainty-based methods to fuse language identification expert decisions

J. Gutiérrez and J.-L. Rouas and R. André-Obrecht

Institut de Recherche en Informatique de Toulouse
Université Paul Sabatier
31062 Toulouse Cedex 9, France

Abstract

Relying on uncertainty theories, a formal methodology to fuse automatic language identification expert decisions is presented. Special attention is focused on representing and making use of a priori knowledge about the performance of experts: the Discriminant Factor Analysis method is applied to compute performance confidence indices at the class level. Experimentation results support the hypothesis that implementing some uncertainty-based inference techniques issued from recent research advances in Evidential or Possibility theories appears not only as a feasible fusion alternative to empirical weighted techniques but also as the one which best exploits the knowledge provided by such indices while delivering better language identification rates.

Key words: Multicriteria Decision Making, Information Fusion, Performance Confidence Indices, Discriminant Factor Analysis, Automatic Language Identification.

1. Introduction

In the field of Automatic Language Identification (ALI), experts are primary systems, also known as sources of decision information, whose aim is to identify as soon as possible the language in which an utterance has been pronounced. An ALI system can be composed of several experts whose architecture allows them to take advantage of language-discriminant specific features and characterises them as:

- Acoustic Expert: vocalic and consonant phones and their frequency of occurrence differ from language to language [12]; the acoustic information of each language is modelled by Gaussian Mixture Models (GMM) or Hidden Markov Models (HMM) [16];
- Phonotactic Expert: specific sequences of phonetic units appear at different occurrence rate in each language [16]; bi-gram or tri-gram models translate the language phonotactic rules;
- Prosodic Expert: sound duration, fundamental frequency, intensity variation and rhythm are language discriminant lineaments [14]; this expert is mostly based on statistical moments computed on the rhythm and the fundamental frequency.

In taking into account the identification decisions issued from experts, an ALI system faces the problem of merging (fusing) them in a suitable way. Till now several merging techniques have been implemented and have evolved from the application of empirical operators (average, addition, multiplication, consensus, and so forth) still used not long ago, to nowadays estimations of confidence indicators [13] regarding the performance of experts; this is applied as heuristics-like a priori knowledge by weighting the expert decisions.

Both generation and application of confidence indices are carried out in an empirical iterative way by testing and adjusting values with no clear formal background: good performance is often obtained though [9]. So, great efforts have started to be deployed to try to formally justify such techniques [4] [10]. We propose an original method to fuse language identification expert decisions. It consists of developing a formal methodology to:

- represent and compute confidence indices by extracting language-discriminant information while processing a development corpus and using the Discriminant Factor Analysis (DFA) method in the decision score field. The DFA projection is used to obtain the confusion matrix and to provide expert and class performance confidence indices.
- model the language identification process by means of the concept of a Linguistic Variable, so that we can work on the scores in the domains of Possibility and Evidence Theories, where respectively:
  · we implement a hierarchical searching inference mechanism based on the class confidence indices and apply an Adaptive Fusion [8] technique to compute the possibility degree of each language;
  · we assign basic belief mass values to the language occurrence events [5], weight such event mass values [1] with the class confidence indices, apply Dempster's orthogonal rule to fuse them and derive the pignistic probability [15] of each language.

Thus, in section 2 we present the methodology used to represent expert information such as the collected expert decisions and the computed performance confidence indices. In section 3 we describe the empirical weighted fusing techniques while the uncertainty-based fusion models and methodologies are elaborated and depicted in section 4. Experiments are explained in section 5.

2. Information Representation

2.1. Expert Decisions are Scores

ALI experts accept a speech utterance called the observation, as input, and provide the class (or language) decision as output, after computing language-score values; mostly a statistical model is used and the language score is the language likelihood; so that the experts handle a vector of language-likelihood values. Given M languages to identify, L_i, $1 \leq i \leq M$, and N experts, s_j, $1 \leq j \leq N$, we obtain for each observation, N vectors of M values, each one ranging from 0 to 1; the higher the value, the more confident the expert is that the corresponding language is the right one. This global observation is represented as a score matrix: $\delta = [d_{ij}]_{1 \leq i \leq M, 1 \leq j \leq N}$ (Table 1), where $L = \{L_1, L_2, \ldots, L_i, \ldots L_M\}$ is the set of languages and $S = \{s_1, s_2, \ldots s_j, \ldots, s_N\}$ is the set of experts.

Table 1
The matrix $\delta = [d_{ij}]_{1 \leq i \leq M, 1 \leq j \leq N}$, is composed of the scores corresponding to each observation.

L \ S	s_1	s_2	...	s_j	...	s_N
L_1	d_{11}	d_{12}	...	d_{1j}	...	d_{1N}
L_2	d_{21}	d_{22}	...	d_{2j}	...	d_{2N}
...	...	...	...	...	...	...
L_i	d_{i1}	d_{i2}	...	d_{ij}	...	d_{iN}
...	...	...	...	...	...	...
L_M	d_{M1}	d_{M2}	...	d_{Mj}	...	d_{MN}

2.2. Computation of Confidence Indices

Estimation of expert performance, with a view to provide the language identification process with heuristic-like information, can be achieved beforehand by means of an evaluation phase where the expert is tested on a set of segments whose language is known. We split a global speech corpus into three partitions: a learning corpus $X = \{x_{learn}\}$, a test corpus $Y = \{y_{test}\}$ and a development corpus $Z = \{z_{dev}\}$. We use the last one to compute the two families of indices: the performance expert and class indices. In order to explain our future fusion techniques, it is necessary to define not only such indices, but also the observation performance confidence indices which represent for each expert the confidence of the decision made for the observation. The two first families of indices are independent of the current observation.

We collect the score matrices corresponding to the acoustic segments of the development corpus; each expert s_j, $1 \leq j \leq N$, contributes with a score vector corresponding to an acoustic segment and is represented by column j, in the score matrix (Table 1). Then a matrix M_j (set of score vectors from expert s_j) will correspond to several

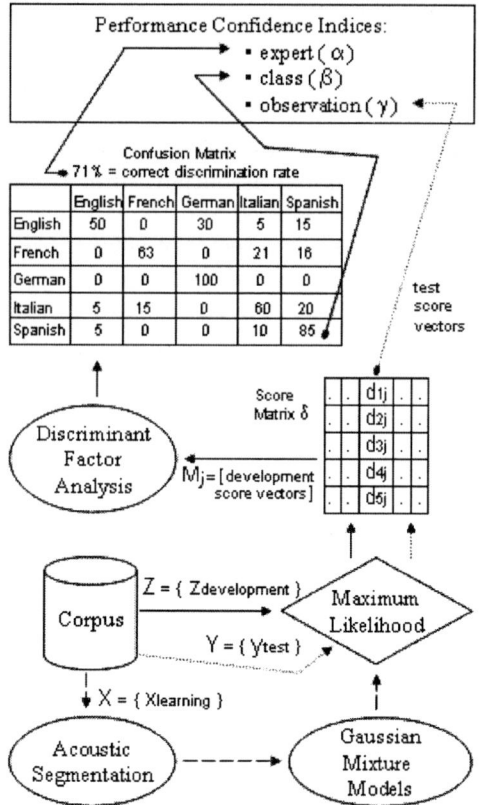

Fig. 1. Computing expert (α), class (β) and observation (γ) confidence indices.

acoustic segments. For each expert s_j, we apply the DFA statistical method to its matrix M_j in order to search for an appropriate representation space for them and a way of obtaining performance confidence indices on a correct discrimination rate basis: we use the $M-1$ factorial axis corresponding to the $M-1$ eigen-values and project the set M_j of score vectors into this subspace. In building the corresponding confusion matrix (Figure 1), the class confidence indices ($\beta_{ij}, 1 \leq i \leq M$) are directly mapped from the diagonal values of it while the expert confidence index must be computed as an averaged value:

$$\alpha_j = \frac{1}{M} \sum_{i \in [1,M]} \beta_{ij} \qquad (1)$$

Many solutions may be proposed to define the observation confidence indices. We retain two formulas to be applied to test-corpus matrices: given an identification expert s_j and $\hat{i}$ the decision class, $d_{\hat{i}j} = \max_k(d_{kj}), k \in [1,M]$,

$$\gamma_j = d_{\hat{i}j} - \max_{k \neq \hat{i}} d_{kj} \qquad (2)$$

$$\gamma_j = d_{\hat{i}j} - \frac{1}{M-1} \sum_{k \neq \hat{i}} d_{kj} \qquad (3)$$

3. Empirical Fusion

The most current operations to empirically fuse decision scores are the so called linear and logarithmic ones that are respectively implemented by summing and multiplying score values. In addition, the estimated performance of each expert can be taken into account to weight its own scores in a heuristic-like way. The concept of weighting by expert estimated performance [4] matches the one of weighting by the expert confidence index α described above. Thus, a language is considered as the identified one if it corresponds to the greatest value computed with the following weighted rules:

$$\text{Sum } L^* = \arg \max_{i \in [1,M]} [\sum_{j \in [1,N]} \alpha_j d_{ij}] \qquad (4)$$

$$\text{Product } L^* = \arg \max_{i \in [1,M]} [\prod_{j \in [1,N]} d_{ij}^{\alpha_j}] \qquad (5)$$

4. Modelling under Uncertainty

Let Ψ be a linguistic variable that is represented by a triplet (Figure 2) [2]:

$$\Psi = (\delta, \mathbb{R}^{M \times N}, L) \qquad (6)$$

- δ is a simple variable representing the score matrix, corresponding to an acoustic segment y, that is defined in the reference space $\mathbb{R}^{M \times N}$;
- $\mathbb{R}^{M \times N} = \{x | x = [d_{ij}], 1 \leq i \leq M, 1 \leq j \leq N\}$ is the set of all score matrix values that δ can take;
- $L = \{L_1, L_2, \ldots, L_m, \ldots, L_M\}$ is a finite set composed of fuzzy sets L_m, that is to say the set of different languages to be identified that characterise the variable δ and define its value constraints in $\mathbb{R}^{M \times N}$.

L_m is an infinite fuzzy set that is defined a priori by a membership function that associates to each element $x \in \mathbb{R}^{M \times N}$ the degree $\mu_{L_m}(x)$, within the range [0,1], with which x belongs to L_m:

$$\mu_{L_m} : \mathbb{R}^{M \times N} \to [0,1]; \qquad (7)$$

and can be denoted either in ordered-pair notation:

$$L_m = \{(\mu_{L_m}(x), x); x \in \mathbb{R}^{M \times N}\} \qquad (8)$$
$$= \{(\mu_{L_m}([d_{ij}]), [d_{ij}]); [d_{ij}] \in \mathbb{R}^{M \times N}, 1 \leq i \leq M, 1 \leq j \leq N\}, \qquad (9)$$

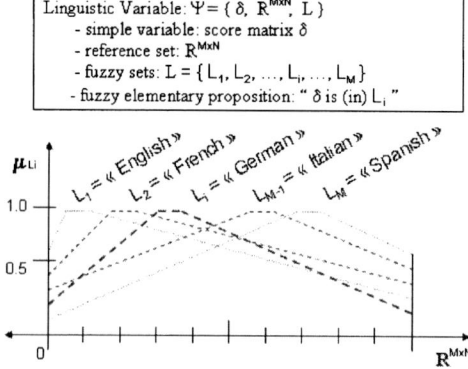

Fig. 2. Automatic language identification is modelled as a linguistic variable concept.

or in additive continuous notation [2]:

$$L_m = \int_x \mu_{L_m}(x)/x = \int_{[d_{ij}]} \mu_{L_m}([d_{ij}])/[d_{ij}]. \qquad (10)$$

Making an identification decision is figured out by means of fuzzy elementary propositions such as "(score matrix) δ is (in language) L_m". Such proposition is an a posteriori description that vaguely describes the language employed to pronounce an acoustic segment y, and it indicates the membership degree of the variable δ to language L_m.

If for each language L_m we associate a possibility distribution to a fuzzy elementary proposition [2]:

$$\forall x \in \mathbb{R}^{M \times N}, \pi_{\delta, L_m}(x) = \mu_{L_m}(x); \qquad (11)$$

then we will be able to make an identification decision after computing the possibility degree $\pi_{\delta, L_m}(x)$ to which δ belongs to each language L_m. This can be accomplished by means of directly applying uncertainty-based fusion techniques [8] on the matrix score values of the variable δ.

Taking into account each score value d_{ij} in matrix δ is a language-likelihood value, we can consider them as possibility values x_{ij} [5] [8] after normalising them:

$$x_{ij} = d_{ij} / \max_{k \in [1, M]} d_{kj}; \qquad (12)$$

so that we can compute $\pi_{\delta, L_m}(x)$ for each language L_m by means of fusing all possibility values in δ.

4.1. Possibility Theory

Before the fusion operation takes place, we exploit the *a priori* expert performance information provided by the class confidence indices ($\beta_{ij}, 1 \le i \le M, 1 \le j \le N$) to

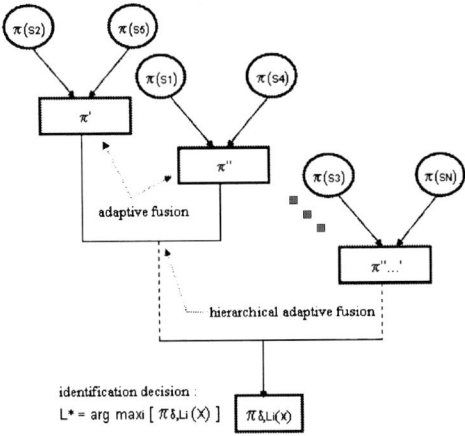

Fig. 3. Hierarchical adaptive fusion of expert decisions

implement a hierarchical tree (Figure 3) of experts with a view to fuse their scores on a priority basis. The higher the performance of the experts at the class (language) level, the first they appear in the hierarchical tree. Each node of the tree comprises similarly-performing experts.

We apply the Adaptive Fusion [8] technique to fuse the score values issued from the experts that are inside each node of the tree. This technique implies computing the consistency index γ (a sort of observation confidence index) of the experts on a score matrix basis:

$$\gamma_{rk} = \text{supremum}_{L_m \in L}[\min(\pi_{\delta, L_m}(s_r), \pi_{\delta, L_m}(s_k))], \tag{13}$$

so that conjunctive or disjunctive fusion can be done adaptively at the class level for each node:

$$\pi_{\delta, L_m}(x) = \max[\pi\text{conj}_{\delta, L_m}(s_r, s_k)/\gamma_{rk}, \min(1 - \gamma_{rk}, \pi\text{disj}_{\delta, L_m}(s_r, s_k))]. \tag{14}$$

The rules employed for conjunctive and disjunctive fusion are:

$$\pi\text{conj}_{\delta, L_m}(s_r, s_k) = \min(\pi_{\delta, L_m}(s_r), \pi_{\delta, L_m}(s_k)); \tag{15}$$

$$\pi\text{disj}_{\delta, L_m}(s_r, s_k) = \max(\pi_{\delta, L_m}(s_r), \pi_{\delta, L_m}(s_k)). \tag{16}$$

Results from pairs of adjacent nodes are fused in an adaptive way as well. We start the fusion process from the upper node and end up with the lower node so that a global possibility value $\pi_{\delta, L_m}(x)$ is obtained as result. We compute the consistency index γ and apply the adaptive rule the same way we explained above, but the conjunctive and disjunctive rules [8] between nodes are respectively the following:

$$\pi\text{conj}_{\delta, L_m}(x)^{',''} = \min[\pi_{\delta, L_m}(x)', \max(\pi_{\delta, L_m}(x)'', 1 - \gamma^{',''})]; \tag{17}$$

$$\pi\text{disj}_{\delta, L_m}(x)^{',''} = \max[\pi_{\delta, L_m}(x)', \min(\pi_{\delta, L_m}(x)'', 1 - \gamma^{',''})]; \tag{18}$$

Having M languages L_m, we compute M global possibility distribution functions $\pi_{\delta,L_m}(x)$ to make an identification decision by considering as the identified language the one that has been assigned to the score-matrix variable δ with the maximum possibility degree:

$$L^* = \arg \max_m [\pi_{\delta,L_m}(x)]. \tag{19}$$

4.2. Theory of Evidence

Let $L = \{L_1, L_2, \ldots, L_i, \ldots, L_M\}$ denote the finite set of possible languages to be identified; this set L is composed of M exhaustive and exclusive hypotheses of the decision process and we assume every union of hypotheses may be a response of the decision process. The set 2^L of all possible events A based on L is the set of all subsets of L, $2^L = \{A | A \subseteq L\}$, $|2^L| = 2^M$, that is to say:

$$2^L = \{\emptyset, \{L_1\}, \ldots, \{L_m\}, \ldots, \{L_M\}, \{L_1, L_2\}, \ldots, \{L_{M-1}, L_M\}, \ldots, L\}. \tag{20}$$

For each unknown utterance, and for each expert s_j, we define a basic belief mass function $m_L^{s_j}$, which explains how the decision L^* belongs to the subset A of L: $m_L^{s_j} : 2L \to [0,1]$ with the constraints: $\sum_{A \subseteq L} m_L^{s_j}(A) = 1$ and $m_L^{s_j}(\emptyset) = 0$. The basic belief mass function $m_L^{s_j}$ is built from the score matrix values of the utterance; we assign basic belief mass values from the distances between their corresponding possibility values [1] [5] [7]. Let A_k represent an event A in position k when all the singleton events have been arranged in decreasing order taking into account its corresponding possibility value π_k. In the case of events that are different than singletons, the corresponding possibility value is the minimum value found among the several possibility values that correspond to the participating singletons [5]. If $\pi_1 = 1 > \pi_2 > \ldots \pi_k > \ldots \pi_M > \pi_{M+1} = 0$; then $m_L^{s_j}(A_k) = 0$ if A_k represents $\emptyset$; but for any non-empty set A, at least two mass-value assignment ways can be considered:
- Case 1. Straightforward assignment [1] [5] [7]: $m_L^{s_j}(A_k) = \pi_k - \pi_{k+1}$;
- Case 2. Level-cut assignment [7]: $m_L^{s_j}(A_{ij}) = \sum_{k=1,M} (\pi_k - \pi_{k+1}) |\Phi_k|^{-1} \mathcal{K}_{\Phi_k}(x_{ij})$; where Φ_k represents the level cuts (corresponding to the same values x_{ij} that come out of the distribution functions π_k) and $\mathcal{K}_{\Phi_k}(x_{ij}) = 1$ if $x_{ij} \geq$ level-cut threshold value, otherwise $\mathcal{K}_{\Phi_k}(x_{ij}) = 0$.

In order to verify the constraints above, we normalise all the belief values after computing a normalisation factor:

$$R_j = 1/ \sum_{A_k \subseteq L} m_L^{s_j}(A_k); \tag{21}$$

and we apply it as a multiplying factor:

$$m_L^{s_j}(A_r) = R_j m_L^{s_j}(A_k); \forall A_r \subseteq L. \tag{22}$$

Thus the set of focal elements includes all the subsets A such as its corresponding $m_L^{s_j}(A_r) > 0$.

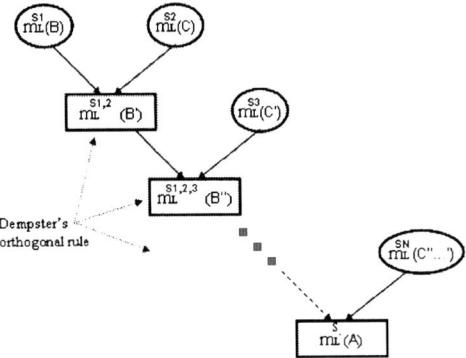

Fig. 4. Cascade-like application of Dempster's orthogonal rule.

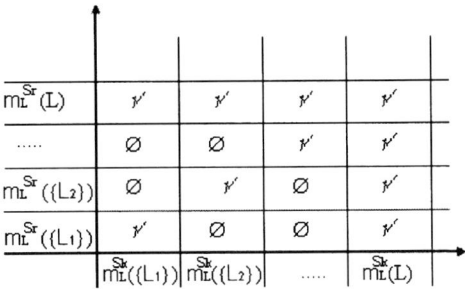

Fig. 5. Orthogonal combination of basic belief mass values of expert focal elements.

Let (s_k, s_r) represent any pair of the N experts, we may combine the belief mass values of the focal elements (B, C, etc.) of these experts on a cascade-like pair basis (Figure 4) by applying Dempster's orthogonal combination rule:

$$m_L^{s_{r,k}}(A) = K_L . \sum_{B \cap C = A} m_L^{s_k}(B).m_L^{s_r}(C); \qquad (23)$$

where $K_L = 1/[1 - \sum_{B \cap C = \emptyset} m_L^{s_k}(B).m_L^{s_r}(C)]$ is a normalisation factor taking into account the case where the empty set results from conjoining focal elements (Figure 5). We obtain thus a global belief mass function, noted $m_L^S(A)$, for each event A.

We weight basic belief mass functions [1] of the events (B, C, etc.) by discounting the expert and class confidence indices (respectively α and β before normalising to do the orthogonal operation:

$$m_L^{s_j, \beta_{ij}}(C) = \beta_{ij}.m_L^{s_j}(C), \forall C \neq L, |C| = 1; \qquad (24)$$
$$m_L^{s_j, \alpha_j}(C) = \alpha_j.m_L^{s_j}(C), \forall C \neq L, |C| > 1; \qquad (25)$$
$$m_L^{s_j, \alpha_j}(L) = (1 - \alpha_j) + \alpha_j.m_L^{s_j}(L). \qquad (26)$$

In order to make a language identification decision, we use the pignistic transformation [15] to derive a probability on L, from the belief mass values:

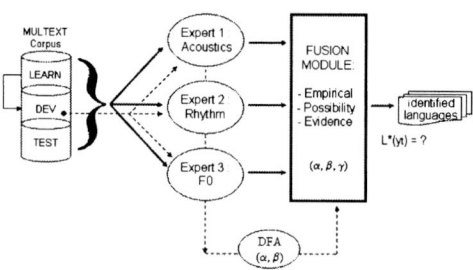

Fig. 6. Architecture of the Fusion System.

$$BetP(L_m) = \sum_{L_m \in A} m_L^S(A)/|A|. \qquad (27)$$

Thus, the decision process can be carried out by maximum pignistic probability [6]:

$$L^* = \arg\max_m [BetP(L_m)]. \qquad (28)$$

5. Experimentation

5.1. Preliminaries

Acoustic data is provided by the MULTEXT corpus [3] which comprises a set of 20 kHz 16-bit sampled records in 5 languages: English, French, German, Italian and Spanish. Data consists of read passages from the EUROM1 corpus pronounced by 50 different speakers (5 males and 5 females per language). The mean duration of each passage is 20.8 seconds. The global corpus is split into three partitions for each language: the learning corpus, the development corpus and the test corpus (2 speakers: 1 male and 1 female who do not belong to the other corpora).

The ALI system is based on three ALI experts and a fusion module (see Figure 6):
- Acoustics Expert [12]: After an automatic vowel detection, each vocalic segment is represented with a set of 8 Mel-Frequency Cepstral Coefficients and 8 δ-MFCC, augmented with the Energy and delta Energy of the segment. This parameter vector is extended with the duration of the underlying segment providing a 19-coefficient vector. A cepstral subtraction performs both blind removal of the channel effect and speaker normalisation. For each recording sentence, the average MFCC vector is computed and subtracted from each coefficient.
- Rhythm Expert [14]: Syllable may be a first-rate candidate for rhythm modelling. Nevertheless, segmenting speech in syllables is typically a language-specific mechanism and thus no language independent algorithm can be derived. For this reason, we have introduced the notion of pseudo-syllables derived from the most frequent syllable structure in the world, namely the CV structure. Using the vowel-non vowel segmentation, speech signal is parsed in patterns matching

the structure: $.C^nV$. Each pseudo-syllable is then characterised by its consonant global duration, its vocalic duration, its complexity (the number of consonant segments), and its energy.
- Fundamental Frequency Expert [14]: The fundamental frequency outlines are used to compute statistics within the same pseudo-syllable frontiers (previously defined) in order to model intonation on each pseudo-syllable. The parameters used to characterise each pseudo syllable intonation are a measurement of the accent location (maximum f0 location in regard to vocalic onset) and the normalised fundamental frequency bandwidth on each syllable.

For each expert, we applied the same learning-testing procedure: for each language, a Gaussian Mixture Model (GMM) is trained using EM algorithm with LBG initialisation [11]. The optimal number of components of the mixture is obtained from experiments on the learning part of the corpus. During the test, the decision relies on a Maximum Likelihood procedure.

The performance of these three experts is given in Table 2, and is considered as a reference to be compared with. We may observe the relatively bad performance of: the fundamental frequency-based expert in general and the three experts on the test set number two (see next section) in particular.

5.2. Tests

Three sets of the test corpus (2 speakers out of 10: 1 male and 1 female) are selected and tested on a round-robin basis with a view to analyse the fusion system behaviour over representative expert performance data of good (set 1) and rather-bad examples (sets 2 and 3).

The three techniques of fusion (empirical, possibility-based and evidential ones) are experimented to merge the decision scores (outputs of the three experts) as explained in the previous sections.

The development corpus is used to compute the class and expert performance confidence indices while the test corpus is used to compute the observation index. The information provided by these indices drive in a heuristic-like way the uncertainty-based inference.

The empirical fusion techniques are tested in their non-weighted and weighted versions. The expert confidence index is used for the weighted versions.

Minimum and maximum operations are selected and tested as conjunctive and disjunctive possibility-based aggregation techniques; we use them while applying the adaptive fusion technique explained above.

Regarding the evidential fusion techniques, the straightforward and level-cut cases of mass-value assignment are tested. Two versions of focal element sets are tested depending on what events can participate to compose them: I) any event $A \subseteq L$ is eligible; and II) any event $A \subseteq L$ such that $|A|=1$ and the event $A=L$ are eligible.

Furthermore, 2-expert fusion is also tested to observe which combinations could provide better results and how efficient the fusion techniques are in obtaining the best identification rates when combining 3 experts at a time.

5.3. Results

Most important results in fusing the three experts are the following (see Table 2):
- The empirical fusion delivers better identification rates than those of any expert for sets 1 and 3 (up to 84%), but for set 2. Weighted versions work out better than non-weighted versions for set 1 (good-example data) only.
- The possibility fusion generally attains a good identification-rate delivery level: up to 85%. But it fails in set 2 (bad-example data).
- Excepting the evidential fusion (version II), all the others fail in set 2 (bad-example data). The performance of evidential fusion version II is better than version I for bad-example data (where the incoherence degree between experts is too high: from 0.5 to 0.9).
- The best identification rates are reached by the fusion system using the evidential method with data from either the good-example set or the bad-example set (version II only where the two cases of assignment provide similar performance): up to 90%.
- Regarding the 2-expert fusion, we observe that two combinations barely deliver better identification rates than the 3-expert combination for the empirical (experts 2 and 3, set 1: 85%) and possibility (experts 1 and 2, set 2: 65%) fusion approaches. This scenario does not take place for the evidential fusion.

Table 2
Results of Fusion Strategies - Total Success Rate (%).

		1st set	2nd set	3rd set
Reference Experts	Expert 1: acoustics	79	41	62
	Expert 2: rhythm	71	63	60
	Expert 3: fundamental frequency	35	37	48
Empirical Fusion Techniques	Addition	83	60	69
	Product	67	49	68
	Weighted Addition	84	58	67
	Weighted Product	68	51	67
Uncertainty-Based Fusion Methods	Possibility Theory	85	52	69
	Theory of Evidence version I			
	- case 1	85	56	69
	- case 2	90	56	69
	version II	90	64	75

6. Conclusion

Uncertainty-based fusion methods can be applied properly to model the language identification expert process of interaction in the presence of robust confidence indices that reflect a priori knowledge on expert performance, like those computed by the Discriminant Factor Analysis method. This fusion methodology comes out as a formal strong alternative to empirical techniques.

Both Possibility and Evidence Theories provide us with inference techniques that can take advantage of weighting values in a more refined way: not only at the expert level but also at the class and observation levels, so that they will generally deliver better identification rates compared to empirical techniques.

The evidence approach has been explored to a rather acceptable extent, so that better results have been obtained if we compare it to the possibility approach. Nevertheless, keeping in mind that an in-depth exploration goal of uncertainty-based fusion methods is pursued, the latter cannot be discarded yet since there are several unexplored aggregation techniques that could allow us to obtain a performance analogous to that of Dempster's orthogonal combination rule [8].

Thus, future works could include experimenting with: a) other conjunctive and disjunctive operations in the possibility/fuzzy domain where there is a pool of t-norm and t-conorm operators: probabilistic ones, Lukasiewicz, Hamacher, Weber, etc.; and b) possibility-to-probability transformations [7] in search of a common risk-based function to make fused decisions in the probabilistic domain (note that the pignistic probability has already been computed from the evidential domain).

References

1. Appriou A. Multisensor signal processing in the framework of the theory of evidence. In NATO/RTO - Lecture Series 216 on Application of Mathematical Signal Processing Techniques to Mission systems, 1999.
2. Bouchon-Meunier B. Théorie des possibilités et variables linguistiques. In La Logique Floue et ses Applications. Addison-Wesley, Paris, 1995.
3. Campione E. and Véronis J. A multilingual prosodic database. In Proceedings of the conference ICSLP'1998, Sidney, Australia, 1998.
4. Cooke R.M. Experts in uncertainty. Oxford University Press, Oxford, United Kingdom, 1991.
5. Denoeux T. and Zouhal L.M. Handling possibilistic labels in pattern classification using evidential reasoning. In Fuzzy Sets and Systems, volume 122(3), pages 409-424, 2001.
6. Denoeux T. Pattern recognition using belief function. In Proceedings of the conference SFC'2002, Toulouse, France, 2002.
7. Dubois D., Prade H. and Sandri S. On possibility-probability transformations. In Fuzzy Logic, Lowen R. and Roubens M., Kluwer Academic, pages 103-112, Dordrecht, Holland, 1993.

8. Dubois D. and Prade H. Possibility theory and data fusion in poorly informed environments. In Control Engineering Practice, volume 2(5), pages 811-823, 1994.
9. Hazen T.J., and Zue V.W. Segmented-based automatic language identification. Journal of the Acoustical Society of America, 4(101), 1997.
10. Kittler J., Hojjatoleslami A.J. and Windeatt T. Weighting factors in multiple expert fusion. In Proceedings of the conference BMVCŠ97, pages 41-50, Essex University, United Kingdom, 1997.
11. Linde Y., Buzo A. and Gray R.M. An algorithm for vector quantizer design. IEEE Transaction on Communications, volume 28, no. 1, pages 84-95, 1980.
12. Pellegrino F., André-Obrecht R. Automatic language identification: an alternative approach to phonetic modelling. In Signal Processing, Elsevier Science North Holland, volume 80, pages 1231-1244, 2000.
13. Rahman A. and Fairhurst M. A novel confidence-based framework for multiple expert decision fusion. In Proceedings of the conference BMVC'98, University of Southampton, United Kingdom, 1998.
14. Rouas J.L., Farinas J. and Pellegrino F. Automatic modelling of rhythm and intonation for language identification. In 15th International Congress of Phonetic Sciences (15th ICPhS), 2003, pages 567-570, Barcelona, Spain, 2003.
15. Smets P. Constructing the pignistic probability function in a context of uncertainty. In Uncertainty in Artificial Intelligence 5, Elsevier Science North-Holland, pages 29-39, 1990.
16. Zissman M. and Berkling K.M. Automatic language identification. In Speech Communication, volume 35, pages 115-124, 2001.

Intelligent Multiattribute Decision Support Model for Medical Triage

F. Burstein[a], Jocelyn San Pedro[b], Leonid Churilov[a], Jeff Wassertheil[a]

[a]*Monash University, Melbourne, PO Box 197, Caulfield East, Victoria, 3145, Australia*

[b]*Institutional Markets and Services, National Australia Bank Limited, 32/500 Bourke St, Melbourne, VIC, 3000*

Abstract

The paper describes a model for intelligent multiattribute decision support for medical triage. Triage is a preliminary clinical assessment of a patient aimed at categorising the treatment category according to priority level or urgency. The model uses a combination of rule-based reasoning and multiattribute decision-making to assist a nurse in selecting the best treatment category for a patient. The model uses a combination of rule-based reasoning and multiattribute decision-making to assist a nurse in selecting the best treatment category for a patient in emergency care. The proposed model can potentially address the issues of accuracy, consistency and timeliness in medical triage decisions.

Keywords: intelligent decision support, multiattribute decision-making, triage
2000 MSC: 68T37, 68T20, 62C12, 90B50

1. Introduction

Triage refers to a preliminary clinical assessment of a patient aimed at categorising the treatment category according to priority level or urgency. The word triage is derived from the French word "trier", which means, "to sort, pick out, classify or choose" [1]. In medical emergency situations, most nurse.s rely on their expert judgment to identify the treatment category for a patient who is critically injured or ill. Accurate, triage decisions must be produced within short time frame (e.g. 2- 5 minutes) and should be consistent with operational strategies and existing triage guidelines. Triage can be considered decision-making process under uncertainty for several reasons. For one, a nurse's expert judgment is usually subjective in nature and depends on experience and expertise of the nurse on duty, availability of medical supplies, beds, or doctors and the severity of illness or injury of patient. Another reason is that the treatment category depends on the level of urgency of medical attention, and decisions based on nurse's primary observations must be produced in the shortest time possible Further, in practice triage decisions are not consistent with existing triage guidelines because of the ad hoc nature with which triage decisions are made especially in rare and severe medical emergencies.

In this paper we describe a model for intelligent multiattribute decision support (IMDS) to address the issues of accuracy, consistency and timeliness of triage decisions [2]. The model combines rule-based reasoning and multiattribute decision-making methodology to support a triage nurse in selecting the best treatment category for a triage patient. Rule-based reasoning reasons in the form of "if X then Y" rules. Multiattribute decision-making methods solve a decision problem by evaluating and comparing a number of alternatives based on multiple attributes and selecting the best alternatives based on some aggregation of these evaluations and comparisons. By combining reasoning and decision-making techniques, we can provide intelligent decision support for triage and potentially address the three main issues in triage.

2. Background

The purpose of triage is to determine a patient's need for time-critical intervention, and identify any immediate care needs. The patients who are most likely to suffer severe consequences if treatment is delayed should be treated in a higher acuity than those who are not facing severe outcomes. One of the difficulties in triage is to determine which criteria should be used to categorize the patients. In Australia, the Australian College of Emergency Medicine (ACEM) adopts the Australian Triage Scale (ATS) as part of its triage policy [3]. The ATS comprises five categories (see Table 1).

A patient with symptoms assessed as immediately life-threatening is allocated to category 1, in which he will receive immediate aggressive intervention. A patient who is deteriorating rapidly or experiencing very severe pain may be allocated to category 2, in which he will be treated within 10 minutes.

The quality of a triage decision may be reflected by its accuracy, consistency, and timeliness. Because the accuracy of triage decisions has a major influence on whether or not a patient may receive medical intervention in an appropriate time frame, it is critical for the health outcomes of the patient. The three possible outcomes of a triage are: expected/correct triage, over triage, or under triage [4].

Correct triage relates to the appropriate allocation of a triage category in which a doctor treats the patient within a suitable time frame. Over triage refers to the allocation of a triage category with higher acuity in which the medical intervention is shorter than demanded. Over triage is not desired as it may potentially result in the waste of resources and the adverse effect on other patients. Under triage refers to the allocation of a triage category with lower acuity, in which the medical intervention is longer than anticipated. It should be avoided because under triage may have potential for patients to deteriorate or develop life or limb threatening complications and to prolong their pain and suffering.

Consistency refers to a patient should be allocated correctly to the same triage category when presenting the same symptoms regardless of hospitals, nurses who are examining them, or activities at emergency departments.

Timeliness is important as any triage decision-making process intends to minimize the delays of medical intervention. Triage decision-making is a tradeoff between the thoroughness of examination and timeliness. A correct triage decision should be made within an appropriate time frame, which ensures the intervention of medical treatment takes place in time. Timeliness is also defined in ATS as an indicator to measure the performance of emergency departments.

In reality, the accuracy, consistency and timeliness of triage may not be simultaneously achieved. It is anticipated that some factors such as triage nurse experience and ED environment may more or less influence the quality of triage. Research has shown that accuracy and consistency of application of ATS very with respect to a number of specific characteristics identified by triage nurses [5]. It may, however, be necessary to find out some ways to enhance the quality of triage by improving its accuracy, consistency, or timeliness, or all of them.

Table 1: Australian Triage Scale Categories (adapted from [3])

ATS Category	Description of Category	Response
1	Immediately life-threatening	Immediately
2	Imminently life-threatening; important time-critical treatment; very severe pain	Assessment and treatment within 10 minutes
3	Potentially life-threatening; situational urgency; human practice mandates the relief of severe discomfort; distress within 30 minutes	Assessment and treatment start within 30 minutes
4	Potentially life-serious; situational urgency; significant complexity or severity; human practice mandates the relief of severe discomfort; distress within 60 minutes	Assessment and treatment start within 60 minutes
5	Less urgent; clinico-administrative problems	Assessment and treatment start within 120 minutes

In the following section, we propose a model for intelligent decision support (IDS) for triage. Our hypothesis is that by providing IDS, we can address the issues of accuracy, consistency and timeliness in triage. By IDS, we mean any type of support that enhances a human decision-maker to perform the cognitive tasks of "learning", "reasoning" or "remembering" to support decision-making [6]. The proposed IDS model combines rule-based reasoning and multiattribute decision-making to support a triage nurse to select the best treatment category for a triage patient [2].

3. Intelligent Multiattribute Decision Support Model for Triage

In this section, we formulate triage as a multiattribute decision-making problem.

We then propose a heuristic-based strategy for selecting the best treatment category of a triage patient. We also discuss strategies that allow a triage nurse to express his/her subjective judgment and store the judgment in a knowledge base for future use.

Let $A = \{a_1, a_2, ..., a_n\}$ be a set of attributes arranged from most important to least important, and $C = \{c_1, c_2, ..., c_m\}$ be a set of treatment categories arranged from highest to lowest priority. That is, $c_1 \succ c_2 \succ ... \succ c_m$ where $c_i \succ c_j$ implies c_i has higher priority than c_j. In this paper, we consider as attributes some physiological discriminators that are important in differentiating the priority levels of treatment of a triage patient.

For example, as seen in Table 2, $a_1 = $ "*Air way*" is the most important attribute in classifying treatment for an adult patient. Thus, if air way is obstructed, the patient's treatment category is c_1, if other attributes are not considered.

Table 2. Physiological Discriminator List (adapted from [3]. DCS - Disability Conscious State, GCS – Glascow Coma Scale)

Category	Air Way	Breathing	Circulation	Disability Conscious State
1	Obstructed Partially obstructed airway	Absent respiration or hypoventilation Severe respiratory distress, e.g. Severe use accessory muscles Unable to speak Central cyanosis Altered conscious state	Absent circulation Severe haemodynamic compromise, e.g. Absent peripheral pulses Skin pale, cold, moist Significant alteration in HR Altered conscious state Uncontrolled hemorrhage	GCS<8
2	Patent airway	Moderate respiratory distress, e.g. Moderate use accessory muscles Speaking in words Skin pale/peripheral cyanosis	Moderate haemodynamic compromise, e.g. Absent radial pulse but palpable brachial pulse Skin pale, cool, moist Moderate alteration in HR	GCS 9-12
3	Patent airway	Mild respiratory distress, e.g. Mild use accessory muscles Speaking in sentences Skin pink	Mild haemodynamic compromise, e.g. Palpable peripheral pulses Skin pale, cool, dry Mild alteration in HR	GCS>=13
4	Patent airway	No respiratory distress, e.g. No use accessory muscles Speaking in full sentences	No haemodynamic compromise, e.g. Palpable peripheral pulses Skin pink, warm, dry	Normal GCS Or no acute change to usual GCS
5	Patent airway	No respiratory distress, e.g. No use accessory muscles Speaking in full sentences	No haemodynamic compromise, e.g. Palpable peripheral pulses Skin pink, warm, dry	Normal GCS Or no acute change to usual GCS

We will also consider Table 2 as a set of rules for classifying treatment category for an adult triage patient according to attribute values. In practice, triage starts from the most important attribute to the least important. Once c_1 category is established using one or more attributes, or when the nurse is confident with his/her categorical decision, the triage process ends.

Let us denote by x_{ij} the ith attribute value corresponding to category c_j. We may represent Table 2 as a relation $R = \{r(x_{ij}) = c_j \mid c_j \in C \text{ for } i = 1, 2, \ldots, n; j = 1, 2, \ldots, m\}$.

Note that R is a one-to-many relation. To illustrate, consider x_{ij} = "*no respiratory distress*". Based on Table 2, the treatment category based on breathing attribute is either c_4 or c_5. We can regard R as a set of standard rules that map an attribute assessment x_{ij} to at least one treatment category in C according to attribute a_i. Thus, if we use rule-based reasoning, we can say that "if patient has *no respiratory distress*, then treatment category is either c_1 or c_2" if all other attributes are not considered.

When there is a unique category matching a given attribute value, we are simply supporting the nurse to follow the rules to achieve consistency in triage. When a unique category is not found for a particular clinical characteristic, we may consider the following three strategies to support the triage nurse's decision-making task:

Strategy 1.

Allow the nurse to select a category based on his/her expert judgment.

This corresponds to the cognitive process of "knowing" based on undifferentiated familiarity and retrieval of specific contextual and conceptual information [7, 8]. For an expert triage nurse faced with a difficult and stressful situation when immediate reaction is necessary, this strategy will yield a robust decision, because the decision can be established quickly. In this context, by allowing the nurse to choose between c_4 and c_5 on the spot, based on his/her experience and domain knowledge, a categorical decision will be achieved in a timely manner.

To facilitate learning from past judgments, a scale from 1 to 10, for example, may be used to convert the nurse's expert judgment into an ordinal ranking. Thus, in implementing Strategy 1, we can provide a slide bar on the screen of a mobile device to allow the triage nurse to position the bar in the scale according to her best judgment. The system then assigns a score correspondingly.

For example, a score of $s(x_{ij}) = 2$ may be assigned to the clinical characteristic x_{ij} = "skin pink, warm and dry" corresponding to c_5, while a score of $s(x_{ij}) = 4$ may be assigned to the same clinical characteristic corresponding to c_4. Thus, the higher the score in the scale from 1 to 10, the higher is the treatment category.

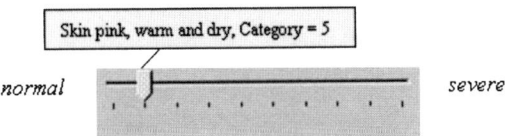

Figure 1: Slide bar indicating the severity of circulation

Strategy 2.

Allow the triage nurse to consider the succeeding attributes until a unique or higher category is established.

This corresponds to the boundedly rational "Take-The-Best" (TTB) heuristic proposed in probabilistic mental models [9]. In TTB method, given a set of cues (object attributes) ordered according to their decreasing validity, "if the best (i.e., the most valid) cue discriminates, then the object favored by this cue is chosen, and further search is terminated" [10].

Referring to our example patient who has no respiratory distress, if the same patient has no haemodynamic compromise, the corresponding categories are still c_4 and c_5. This implies that circulation attribute is not discriminating enough to identify a unique category. Considering the next important attribute, if the patient has Glasgow Coma Scale, GCS = 14, then a higher treatment category, c_3 will be selected based on Table 2. In this case, GCS is a discriminating cue, so that the category corresponding to GCS = 14 is selected. If nurse is satisfied with this category, triage ends.

A multiattribute value tree may be used to represent the hierarchy of attributes according to their degree of importance. If the categorical decision at each level of hierarchy is recorded as shown in Figure 2, we can facilitate learning from past decisions by recording such value tree in a knowledge base, and applying data-mining or knowledge discovery techniques later when there is sufficient information in the knowledge base to derive new rules.

Strategy 3.

Allow the nurse to differentiate two categories based on the same attributes by modifying attribute values to reflect which category is better.

For our example if the patient has no respiratory distress under "Breathing" attribute, the nurse might identify that the patient has *pale*, *warm* and *dry* skin instead of *pink*, *warm* and *dry* skin. By simple use of linguistic terms *pale* or *pink*, two or more categories can be differentiated. We can support this type of reasoning by converting the linguistic terms into an ordinal ranking (i.e., *pink* "*is better than*" *pale*).

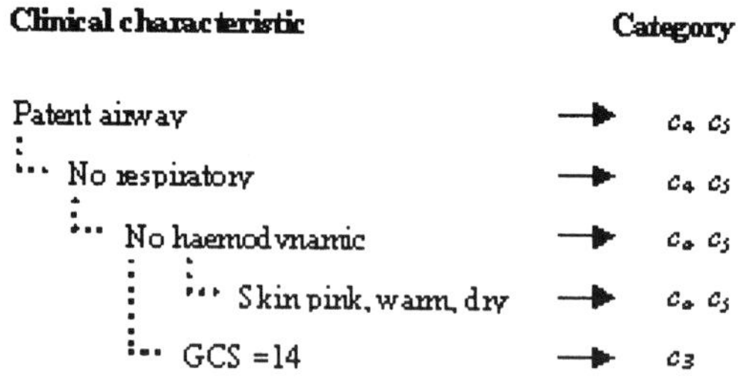

Clinical characteristic	Category
Patent airway	→ c_4 c_5
⋯ No respiratory	→ c_4 c_5
⋯ No haemodynamic	→ c_4 c_5
⋯ Skin pink, warm, dry	→ c_4 c_5
⋯ GCS =14	→ c_3

Figure 2: Multiattribute value tree and corresponding categorical decision

We can allow a nurse to modify the value of an attribute by providing an edit box as shown in Figure 3. Note that if the mobile device has a transcriber facility that recognises words, phrases and numbers written in cursive or print styles, overwriting or completing the edit box is as natural as writing the description on a pad. An ordinal ranking can be achieved by positioning the bar in a scale (e.g., from 1 to 10 as shown in Figure 3) to reflect why such description should be classified under a higher or lower category.

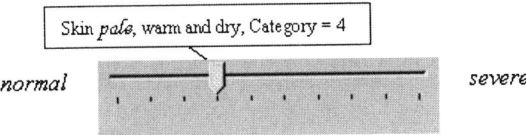

Figure 3: Edit box and slide bar indicating the severity of circulation

We can also use fuzzy sets to indicate the imprecision or uncertainty in identifying the treatment category.

For example, as shown in Figure 4, we can describe the state of consciousness (disability) as a fuzzy membership function that converts a GCS value to linguistic term severe, moderate or normal and assigns a score between 0 and 1. In this function, 1 will indicate normal condition while 0 will indicate severe conscious state.

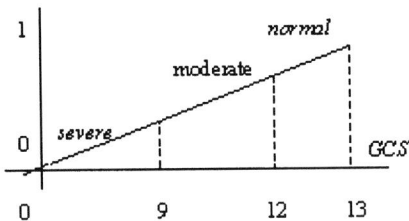

Figure 4: Fuzzy membership function indicating disability- conscious state

To formalise the above triage process, we define a, multiattribute choice model that identifies the most suitable treatment category for a triage patient based on some physiological discriminators provided by medical authorities [7].

Let us first denote by p_i the nurse's assessment of a patient's health condition based on the ith attribute. Let $D = \{d(p_i) = c_j \mid c_j \in C$ for $i \in \{1, 2, \ldots, n\}; j \in \{1, 2, \ldots, m\}\}$ be the set of nurse's categorical decisions c_j's where c_j is the treatment category associated with p_i for some attribute a_i regardless of other attributes. We assume that c_j will be derived by applying the rule set R, and any one of the three strategies when a unique category is not found using R. The best category d^* from the set of candidate categories D is selected using the following steps:

Step 1. Set $i = 1$. Assess the patient according to the most important attribute, a_i. Denote by p_i the assessment of patient according to attribute a_i.

Step 2. Match p_i against an existing rule R. If there does not exist a x_{ij} that exactly matches p_i for $j \in \{1, 2, ..., m\}$, go to Step 6. Otherwise, there exist a $x_{ij} = p_i$ and a rule $r(x_{ij}) = c_j$ so that $r(p_i) = c_j$. If there is only one c_j corresponding to x_{ij} in R, then we can set $d(p_i) = \overline{c}_j = c_j$. If there are two or more c_j's, then go to Step 7.

Step 3. If $\overline{c}_j \neq c_l$, go to Step 4. Otherwise, $\overline{c}_j = c_l$. The best treatment category $d^* = \overline{c}_j$ is achieved because c_l has the highest level of priority. STOP.

Step 4. If there are no more attributes to consider, STOP. Else, assess the patient according to the next most important attribute. Set $i = i + 1$.

Step 5. If $d(p_i) \succ d^*$, set $d^* = d(p_i)$. If d^* is a satisfactory treatment category, then STOP. Otherwise, go back to Step 4.

Step 6. Assign the patient a category $\overline{c}_j$ according to the attribute a_i using expert judgment. Because there is no such rule to verify such assignment, store this decision as in a knowledge base future use. Data-mining techniques can be used at a later stage to derive new rules. Go back to Step 3.

Step 7. Assign the patient a treatment category $\overline{c}_j$ according to the attribute a_i using either Strategy 1, 2 or 3. If Strategy 1 is selected, go to Step 6. If Strategy 2 is selected, go to Step 4. If Strategy 3 is selected, modify p_i to differentiate the matching categories based on current attribute, then go to Step 6.

4. Discussions and Ongoing Research

A summary of the proposed IMDS model is illustrated in Figure 5. As shown in the flowchart in Figure 5, we support the nurse's decision-making tasks by providing three alternative strategies to select the best treatment category based on nurse's expert judgment. It is also assumed that a rule base is available, and that a knowledge base will be created for future use. When the knowledge base has sufficient information to be used as training set deriving new rules, we recommend that the rule base be updated.

The proposed model can be regarded as providing intelligent decision support because it implements "reasoning" based on existing rules; it supports "learning" of new rules based on historical decisions that are stored in knowledge base; and allows the triage nurse to exercise his/her expert judgment when making categorical decisions.

The proposed IMDS model may lead to a timely categorical decision. There is no need to consider less important attributes as soon a c_l category is established, or as soon as the nurse is satisfied with the selection made. Thus the proposed model is following a non-compensatory strategy as there is no need to aggregate all attribute values, and robust decision can be made based on discriminating subset of the attributes. Also, by embedding the rules in the system, real-time expert advice is available. Thus, the time needed to come up with a decision may be reduced because there is no need for nurse to recall the rules from his/her mind, or to consult a supervisor to give expert advice.

The proposed model may also reduce inconsistency in triage as the decisions are guided by rules that are based on standard ATS. When a nurse's decision is highly inconsistent with the system's rules, alert tools may be provided in the system to advise the nurse about possible error in the decision. If such alert is not ignored, then the model potentially can also produce better or more accurate results. The accuracy however, will only be based on existing rules or on historical expert judgment of the nurse, if such data is available. If rules are regularly updated to include "best practice" and past correct decisions of expert nurses, then eventually, we can expect the triage process to be consistent and accurate according to the ATS. However, without actual field-testing, we cannot support our claims.

So far, we have developed a multiattribute choice model to provide an algorithm for selecting best treatment category for a triage patient. In our ongoing research we will also be introducing intelligent technologies and soft computing methodologies to build IDS system for triage. We will be exploring the use of fuzzy sets to allow flexibility in rule-based reasoning; fuzzy logic to derive new rules based on historical decisions; different knowledge discovery techniques until we find the most appropriate one for triage; other multiattribute decision models to reflect nurse's preferences and other techniques to address the issues on timeliness, accuracy and accuracy in triage. We have taken advantage of mobile technologies for developing a system that can support triage anywhere, anytime. A prototype using strategy 2 has been implemented and tested in the laboratory settings involving a specialist doctor and twenty nine senior nursing students [11] The preliminary findings of each triage test case based on paper-based scenarios has highlighted the potential benefits of the use of the prototype for decision-making and training for triage in emergency healthcare [12]. This system can be particularly beneficial to Australia as there is increased need for timely, accurate and consistent triage especially in remote areas where residents have longer waiting time to access healthcare services and products. Adding intelligence features to the decision support system architecture would further enhance the possibility to improve the process and outcomes in medical triage.

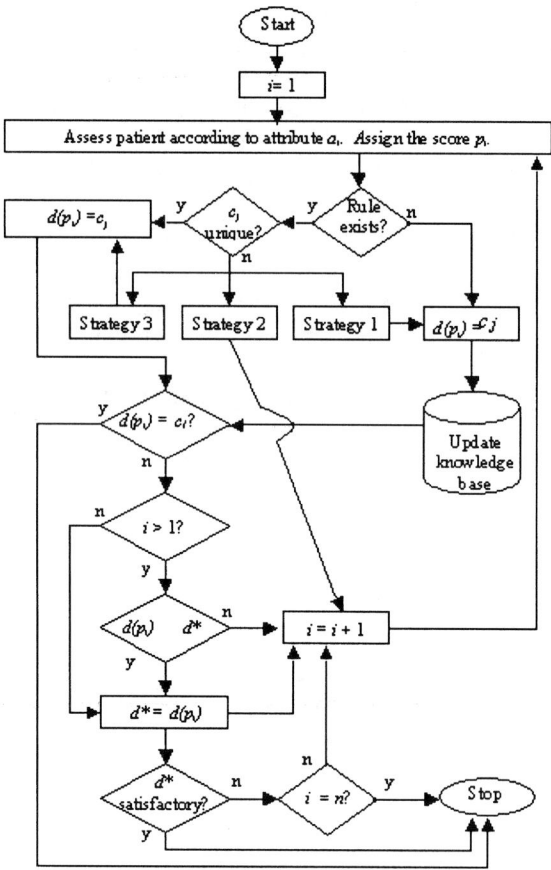

Figure 5: Intelligent multiattribute decision support model for triage

5. Conclusions

In this paper, we described triage as a multiattribute decision making problem and developed a heuristic-based choice model that selects the best treatment category for a triage patient based on some physiological discriminators. We introduced three strategies to support the triage nurse in his/her selection when standard rules fail to produce a unique category. The first strategy is based on the cognitive process of "knowing" and allows the nurse to exercise his/her expert judgment. The second strategy is based on the "Take-The-Best" heuristic that selects the best treatment corresponding to the most discriminating attributes. The third strategy allows the nurse to modify description of the observed attributes to discriminate the best category from the others. We combined these three strategies with a rule-based reasoning to provide intelligent decision support to the triage nurse. If implemented, the proposed model for IDS may address the issues of consistency, accuracy and timeliness in triage. First, by embedding the standard rules in the system and making them available anywhere, anytime, expert advice can be made available whenever inconsistencies occur. Second, if alerts for inconsistencies are not ignored by the triage nurse, then the quality of the nurse's decision may be improved, and the triage process may produce more accurate results. Third, because of the simplicity and robustness of the proposed multiattribute treatment selection process, and availability of real-time expert advice, the proposed IDS model may produce timely triage decisions.

Acknowledgement

This project is funded by Monash University research grant "Towards Mobile Real -Time Multicriteria Decision Support for Open-Field Triage in Contingency Management" and "Empirical Testing of the Mobile Triage Decision Support System". The authors would like to acknowledge help and support of Ms Nyree Parker, Mr Bernard Hornblower, Mr Patrick Cao, Mr Nitin Arora and Associate Professor Arkady Zaslavsky in developing *iTriage* system and organising its empirical evaluation.

References

1. Victorian Department of Human Services. Consistency of Triage in Victoria's Emergency Departments: Summary Report. Melbourne, Australia, 2001a.
2. San Pedro, J., Burstein, F., Churilov, L., Wassertheil, J. , Cao P. Intelligent Multi-Attribute Decision Support Model For Triage, Proceedings of the Tenth International Information Processing and Management of Uncertainty in Knowledge-based Systems IPMU2004, July 4-9, 2004, Perugia, Italy, 2004, 1559-1566.
3. Victorian Department of Human Services. Consistency of Triage in Victoria's Emergency Departments: Gidelines for Triage Education and Practice. Melbourne, Australia, 2001b.
4. Victorian Department of Human Services. Consistency of Triage in Victoria's Emergency Departments: Education and Quality Report. Melbourne, Australia. 2001c.
5. Victorian Department of Human Services. Consistency of Triage in Victoria's Emergency Departments: Triage Consistency Report. Melbourne, Australia. 2001d
6. San Pedro, J. Burstein, F. , Sharp, A. Toward case-based fuzzy multicriteria decision support model for tropical cyclone forecasting, European Journal of Operational Research, Special Issue on Tools for Decision Support Systems, Vol 160/2,2005, 308-324.
7. Mandler, G. Recognizing: The judgment of previous occurrence. Psychological Review, 87, 1980, 252-271.
8. Mandler, G. Your face looks familiar but I can't remember your name: A review of dual process theory. In W.E. Hockley & S. Lewandowsky (Eds.), Relating theory and data: Essays on human memory in honor of Bennet B. Murdock, 1991, 207-225. Hillside, NJ: Erlbaum.

9. Gigerenzer, G., Hoffrage, U., Kleinbolting, H. Probabilistic mental models: A Brunswikian theory of confidence. Psychological Review, 98, 1991, 506-528.
10. Broder, A. Assessing the empirical validity of the "Take-The-Best" heuristic as a model of human probabilistic inference. Journal of Experimental Psychology: learning, memory, and Cognition, 26(5), 2000, 1332-1346.
11. San Pedro, J., Burstein, F., Wassertheil, J., Arora, N., Churilov L., Zaslavsky, A. On Development and Initial Evaluation of Prototype Mobile Decision Support for Hospital Triage", Proceedings of the 38th Annual Hawaii International Conference on System Sciences (HICSS'05), IEEE Publication, 2005.
12. Padmanabhan, N., Burstein, F., Churilov, L., Wassertheil, J., Hornblower, B. Experimental evaluation of mobile decision support prototype for emergency triage, Proceedings of the 8th International Conference of the SIG Decision Support Systems, Brazil, 2005.

Interval-Based Multicriteria Decision Making

Martine Ceberio and François Modave

University of Texas at El Paso
Computer Science Department
500 West University Avenue
El Paso, Texas 79968-0518
{mceberio,fmodave}@cs.utep.edu

Abstract

The aim of this paper is to show how non-additive measures and intervals can be combined in order to provide a simple and accurate approach to multi-criteria decision making problems. We construct an interval-based Choquet integral in order to derive preferences over a set of multidimensional alternatives. Preferences are no longer real number comparisons, but interval comparisons, which is not straightforward to interpret. In this paper, we propose strategies of choice, and explain how we can integrate additional information – such as probabilities – to intervals, so as to ease the choice.

Key words: AI, multi-criteria decision making, interval computations, Choquet integral, preferences.

1. Introduction

In multicriteria decision making, we aim at ordering multidimensional alternatives and giving a semantic interpretation of the results. A traditional approach for the ordering problem is to use a weighted sum that ensures low complexity ($O(n)$) and ease of use and where each weight represents the (subjective) importance given by a decision maker to a particular attribute or criterion.

Despite its simplicity, it is difficult to deal with dependencies between criteria using additive approaches. To prevent this problem, non-additive measures and integrals can be used to represent preferences. An axiomatization of multi-criteria decision making using the Choquet integral (a particular case of non-additive integral) was provided in [9].

We are interested in providing a practical solution for such problems using the Choquet integral. An inherent problem of non-additive measures is their exponential cost. However, the notion of 2-additive measures (see [5]) allows us to limit this cost to a $O(n^2)$. Besides, a convenient representation of the 2-additive Choquet integral allows us to express the Choquet integral in terms of complementary, redundant and independent criteria which is a natural extension of the weighted sum.

In practical problems, we only require the decision maker to provide importance and interaction indices which are sufficient to define preferences over the alternatives as long as we assume the measure to be 2-additive. However, it is unlikely that the decision maker can give precise values for these indices. Nevertheless, this is not a major problem as we can reasonably expect the decision maker to be able to give intervals of values.

Therefore, the aim of this paper is to present a Choquet integral based on intervals that allows us to express intervals of preferences for multidimensional alternatives. This will allow us to have a simple, yet accurate model of preferences.

First, we recall the essentials of MCDM and non-additive integration. Then, we present intervals and their operations, and describe how to combine these two theories to obtain interval of preferences in a MCDM setting. Finally, we present strategies of choice between intervals of preferences, and describe how to integrate probabilistic information in the intervals to free the choice from strategies.

2. Non-additive measures in MCDM

2.1. Multicriteria decision making

Let us define a multicriteria decision making problem as a triple $(X, I, (\succeq_i)_{i \in I})$ where $X \subset X_1 \times \cdots \times X_n$ is the set of alternatives of our problem and each set X_i is the set of values of attribute i. I is the (finite) set of criteria or attributes. And for all $i \in I$, $\succeq_i$ is a preference relation (a weak order) over X_i.

The problem is to "combine" the preference relations (or partial preferences) $\succeq_i$ in a rational way, in agreement with the decision maker's partial preferences.

2.2. Utility functions

A first step to achieve the construction of a global preference relation is to put all values of attributes over a common scale.

In this paper, we assume all the sets X_i to be order-separable. Then, we are guaranteed the existence of n monodimensional utility functions $u_i : X_i \to \mathbb{R}$ such that for all $x_i, y_i \in X_i$, $x_i \succeq y_i$ if and only if $u_i(x_i) \geqslant u_i(y_i)$ (see [7]).

In order to define a global preference $\succeq$ over X that is "consistent" with the partial orders, we now need to define a global utility function $u : X \to \mathbb{R}$ that aggregates the monodimensional utility functions u_i, that is, we need to build an aggregation operator $\mathcal{H} : \mathbb{R}n \to \mathbb{R}$ such that:

$$\forall x, y \in X , x \succeq y \Leftrightarrow \mathcal{H}(u_1(x_1), \cdots , u_n(x_n)) \geqslant \mathcal{H}(u_1(y_1), \cdots , u_n(y_n)) \quad (1)$$

with $x = (x_1, \cdots , x_n)$ and $u(x) = \mathcal{H}(u_1(x_1), \cdots , u_n(x_n))$.

In the sequel, we denote the global utility function by $u(x) = \mathcal{H}(u_1(x_1), \cdots u_n(x_n))$ for $x \in X$. By consistent, we mean that the choice of the aggregation operator should reflect the preferences of the decision maker.

A very natural and simple approach for such a problem is to use a simple weighted sum. The decision maker is asked to provide weights $\alpha_i \in [0, 1]$ that reflect the importance of each criterion and such that $\sum_{i=1}^{n} \alpha_i = 1$. The utility function is then defined by:

$$\forall x \in X , u(x) = \sum_{i=1}^{n} \alpha_i u_i(x_i) \quad (2)$$

However, we can show that using an additive aggregation operator such as a weighted sum is equivalent to assuming some kind of independence property (namely that all the attributes mutually preferentially independent ([8]).

This is not always desirable so, we need to turn to non-additive approaches.

The notion of mutual preferential independence is formally equivalent to the notion of the sure-thing principle in Decision under Uncertainty ([4]). The sure-thing principle also leads to paradoxes in Decision under Uncertainty and Schmeidler ([11], [12]) had proposed the use of non-additive measures and the Choquet integral as representation tools. We follow the same approach, and see how non-additive measures and the Choquet integral leads to more adequate representation of preferences in an MCDM context.

2.3. *Non-additive measures and integrals*

For the sake of our applications, we restrict ourselves to the finite case. However, these definitions can be extended to infinite sets (see [6] for a detailed presentation of fuzzy integration).

In the following definition, $\mathcal{P}(I)$ represents the power set of I.

Definition 1. Let I be the set of attributes (or any set in a general setting). A set function $\mu : \mathcal{P}(I) \to [0, 1]$ is called a non-additive measure (or fuzzy measure) if it satisfies the three following axioms:
(1) $\mu(\varnothing) = 0$: the empty set has no importance
(2) $\mu(I) = 1$: the maximal set has maximal importance
(3) $\mu(B) \leqslant \mu(C)$ if $B, C \subset I$ and $B \subset C$: a new criterion added cannot make the importance of a coalition (a set of criteria) diminish.

As the values of the empty set and of the maximal set are fixed, we need $2^n - 2$ values or coefficients to define a non-additive measure. So, there is a trade-off between complexity and accuracy. We will see later (Subsection 2.4) that we can reduce the complexity in order to guarantee that non-additive measures are used in practical applications.

Definition 2. Let μ be a non-additive measure on $(I, \mathcal{P}(I))$ and an application $f : I \to \mathbb{R}+$. The Choquet integral of f w.r.t μ is defined by:

$$(C) \int_I f d\mu = \sum_{i=1}^{n} (f(\sigma(i)) - f(\sigma(i-1))) \mu(A_{(i)}).$$

where σ is a permutation of the indices in order to have $f(\sigma(1)) \leqslant \cdots \leqslant f(\sigma(n))$, $A_{(i)} = \{\sigma(i), \ldots, \sigma(n)\}$ and $f(\sigma(0)) = 0$, by convention.

When there is no risk of confusion, we will write (i) for $\sigma(i)$. A Choquet integral ([3]) is a sort of weighted mean taking into account the importance of every coalition of criteria and is an extension of the Lebesgue integral.

2.4. *Representation of preferences*

We are now able to present how non-additive measures can be used in lieu of the weighted sum and other more traditional aggregation operators in a multicriteria decision making framework.

It was shown in [9] that under rather general assumptions over the set of alternatives X, and over the weak orders $\succeq_i$, there exists a unique non-additive measure μ over I such that:

$$\forall x, y \in X \ , \ x \succeq y \Leftrightarrow u(x) \geqslant u(y) \tag{3}$$

where:

$$u(x) = \sum_{i=1}^{n} [u_{(i)}(x_{(i)}) - u_{(i-1)}(x_{(i-1)})] \mu(A_{(i)}) \tag{4}$$

which is simply the aggregation of the monodimensional utility functions using the Choquet integral w.r.t. μ.

We are still facing two crucial problems. First, the proof of the above result is not constructive. Second, as we have said before, evaluating a non-additive measure requires $O(2^n)$ values. We are going to see that we can overcome these difficulties and that using non-additive measures (coupled with intervals) offers a nice solution to multi-criteria decision making problems.

Let us start with a couple of definitions that will allow us to show how to limit the complexity to a $O(n^2)$.

The global importance of a criterion is given by evaluating what this criterion brings to every coalition it does not belong to, and averaging this input. This is given by the Shapley value or index of importance (see [5]).

Definition 3. Let μ be a non-additive measure over I. The Shapley value of index j is defined by:
$$v(j) = \sum_{B \subset I \setminus \{j\}} \gamma_I(B)[\mu(B \cup \{j\}) - \mu(B)]$$
with $\gamma_I(B) = \frac{(|I|-|B|-1)! \cdot |B|!}{|I|!}$, $|B|$ denotes the cardinal of B.

The Shapley value can be extended to degree two, to define the indices of interactions (between attributes). Indeed, as we will see below, the Shapley value defines the importance of an attributes, whereas the interaction indices define the level of interaction between attributes, which is interesting to give a semantic interpretation of the Choquet integral.

Definition 4. Let μ be a non-additive measure over I. The interaction index between i and j is defined by:
$$I(i,j) = \sum_{B \subset I - \{i,j\}} \xi_I(B) \cdot (\mu(B \cup \{i,j\}) - \mu(B \cup \{i\}) - \mu(B \cup \{j\}) + \mu(B))$$
with $\xi_I(B) = \frac{(|I|-|B|-2)! \cdot |B|!}{(|I|-1)!}$.

The interaction indices belong to the interval $[-1, +1]$ and
- $I(i,j) > 0$ if the attributes i and j are complementary;
- $I(i,j) < 0$ if the attributes i and j are redundant;
- $I(i,j) = 0$ if the attributes i and j are independent.

Interactions of higher orders can also be defined, however we will restrict ourselves to second order interactions which offer a good trade-off between accuracy and complexity. Indeed, we are interested in defining an approach that is both accurate and tractable. Defining the importance of attributes and the interaction between attributes is generally enough in MCDM problems, and restricting ourselves to interaction between two attributes guarantees us to be at most quadratic with respect to the number of attributes. To do so, we define the notion of 2-additive measure.

Definition 5. A non-additive measure μ is called 2-additive if all its interaction indices of order equal or larger than 3 are null and at least one interaction index of degree two is not null.

In this particular case of 2-additive measures, we can show ([5]) that the Shapley value and the interaction indices (of order two and higher) offer us an other way to represent a Choquet integral, as follows:

Theorem 1. Let μ be a 2-additive measure. Then the Choquet integral can be computed by:

$$(C) \int_I f d\mu = \sum_{I_{ij}>0} (f(i) \wedge f(j)) I_{ij} + \sum_{I_{ij}<0} (f(i) \vee f(j)) |I_{ij}| + \sum_{i=1}^{n} f(i)(I_i - \frac{1}{2} \sum_{j \neq i} |I_{ij}|). \tag{5}$$

Note that this expression justifies the above interpretation of interaction indices, as a positive interaction index corresponds to a conjunction (complementary) and a negative interaction index corresponds to a disjunction (redundant).

In the weighted sum case, we assume that the decision maker can provide us with the weights she/he puts on each criterion. However, we know that this model is inaccurate when trying to deal with dependencies. We could use a Choquet integral instead, as we have seen that they are a convenient and precise tool to model preferences. However, the complexity is very high. Therefore, in order to combine the best of the two worlds, we can ask the decision maker to give the Shapley values, as well as the interaction indices, and then use the reconstruction theorem 1 to obtain the aggregation operator, which is a Choquet integral w.r.t. to a 2-additive measure. Of course, we have to assume the measure to be 2-additive to use theorem 1. However, this is not a serious limitation as the importance and the 2-order interaction are enough to give a thorough semantic interpretation of the results.

Nevertheless, such an approach raises an other problem. How can we expect the decision maker to give a precise value for the importance and interaction indices? In order to overcome this hurdle, we introduce the concept of interval and see how it can be used efficiently to derive "interval of preferences".

3. Intervals

3.1. Interval Arithmetic

Interval Arithmetic is an arithmetic over sets of real numbers called *intervals*. Interval arithmetic has been proposed by Ramon E. Moore [10] in the late sixties in order to model uncertainty, and to tackle rounding errors of numerical computations. For a complete presentation of interval arithmetic, we refer the reader to [1].

Definition 6 (Interval). An *interval* is a closed and connected set of real numbers. The set of intervals[1] is denoted by $\mathbb{IR}$. Every $x \in \mathbb{IR}$ is denoted by $[\underline{x}, \overline{x}]$, where its bounds are defined by $\underline{x} = \inf x$ and $\overline{x} = \sup x$.

---

[1] Note that, in order to represent the real line with closed sets, $\mathbb{R}$ is compactified in the obvious way with the infinities $\{-\infty, +\infty\}$. The usual conventions apply: $(+\infty) + (+\infty) = +\infty$, *etc.*

For every $a \in \mathbb{R}$, the interval point $[a, a]$ is also denoted by a.

Given a subset ρ of $\mathbb{R}$, the *convex hull* of ρ is the interval $\text{Hull}(\rho) = [\inf \rho, \sup \rho]$. The *width* of an interval $\boldsymbol{x}$ is the real number $w(\boldsymbol{x}) = \overline{x} - \underline{x}$. Given two real intervals $\boldsymbol{x}$ and $\boldsymbol{y}$, $\boldsymbol{x}$ is said to be *tighter than* $\boldsymbol{y}$ if $w(\boldsymbol{x}) \leqslant w(\boldsymbol{y})$.

Interval Arithmetic operations are set theoretic extensions of the corresponding real operations. Given $\boldsymbol{x}, \boldsymbol{y} \in \mathbb{IR}$ and an operation $\diamond \in \{+, -, \times, \div\}$, we have: $\boldsymbol{x} \diamond \boldsymbol{y} = \text{Hull}\{x \diamond y \mid (x, y) \in \boldsymbol{x} \times \boldsymbol{y}\}$.

Due to properties of monotonicity, these operations can be implemented by real computations over the bounds of intervals. Given two intervals $\boldsymbol{x} = [a, b]$ and $\boldsymbol{y} = [c, d]$, we have for instance: $\boldsymbol{x} + \boldsymbol{y} = [a + c, b + d]$. The associative law and the commutative law are preserved over $\mathbb{IR}$. However, the distributive law does not hold. In general, only a weaker law is verified, called semi-distributivity. We observe in particular that equivalent expressions over the real numbers are no longer equivalent when handling intervals: different symbolic expressions may lead to different interval evaluations.

For instance, consider the following three expressions equivalent over the real numbers: $x^2 - x$, $x(x-1)$ and $(x - \frac{1}{2})^2 - \frac{1}{4}$. When evaluated over the intervals, with $\boldsymbol{x} = [0, 1]$, we obtain the following results: $\boldsymbol{x}^2 - \boldsymbol{x} = [-1, 1]$, $\boldsymbol{x}(\boldsymbol{x} - 1) = [-1, 0]$, $(\boldsymbol{x} - \frac{1}{2})^2 - \frac{1}{4} = [-\frac{1}{4}, 0]$. Expressions formerly equivalent over the real numbers are not necessarily equivalent when extended to the intervals. This problem is known as the dependency problem of interval arithmetic, and a fundamental problem in interval arithmetic consists in finding expressions that lead to tight interval computations.

3.2. Interval Extensions

Interval arithmetic is particularly appropriate to represent outer approximations of real quantities. The range of a real function f over a domain D, denoted by $\boldsymbol{f}^u(D)$, can be computed by interval extensions.

Definition 7 (Interval extension). An *interval extension* of a real function $f : D_f \subset \mathbb{R}^n \to \mathbb{R}$ is a function $\varphi : \mathbb{IR}^n \to \mathbb{IR}$ such that

$$\forall \mathbf{X} \in \mathbb{IR}^n, (\mathbf{X} \in D_f \Rightarrow \boldsymbol{f}^u(\mathbf{X}) = \{f(\boldsymbol{x}) \mid \boldsymbol{x} \in \mathbf{X}\} \subseteq \varphi(\mathbf{X})).$$

This inclusion formula is called *Fundamental Theorem of Interval Arithmetic*. Interval extensions are also called *interval forms* or *inclusion functions*.

This definition implies the existence of infinitely many interval extensions of a given real function. In particular, the weakest and tightest extensions are respectively defined by: $\mathbf{X} \mapsto [-\infty, +\infty]$ and $\mathbf{X} \mapsto \text{Hull} \boldsymbol{f}^u(\mathbf{X})$.

The most common extension is known as the *natural extension*. Natural extensions are obtained from the expressions of real functions, and are *inclusion mono-*

tonic[2], which means that given a real function f, its natural extension, denoted $\boldsymbol{f}$, and two intervals $\boldsymbol{x}$ and $\boldsymbol{y}$ such that $\boldsymbol{x} \subset \boldsymbol{y}$, then $\boldsymbol{f}(\boldsymbol{x}) \subset \boldsymbol{f}(\boldsymbol{y})$. Since natural extensions are defined by the syntax of real expressions, two equivalent expressions of a given real function f generally lead to different natural interval extensions. In Figure 1, we see that both interval functions define interval extensions of f. However, one function is clearly better.

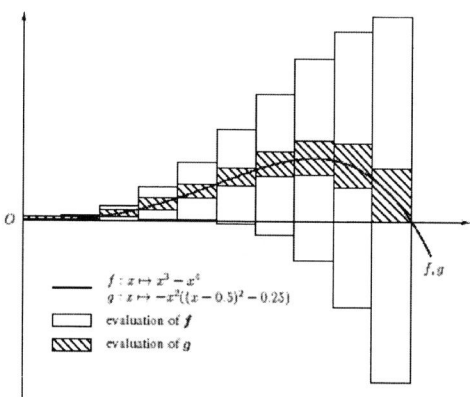

Fig. 1. Natural interval evaluations of two expressions of a real function f.

The overestimation problem, known as *dependency problem of IA*, is due to the decorrelation of the occurrences of a variable during interval evaluation. For instance, given $\boldsymbol{x} = [a, b]$ with $a \neq b$, we have: $\boldsymbol{x} - \boldsymbol{x} = [a - b, b - a] \not\supseteq 0$. An important result is Moore's theorem known as the *theorem of single occurrences*.

Theorem 2 (Moore [10]). Let t be a Σ-term and let the real function $f : D_f \subset \mathbb{R}^n \to \mathbb{R}$, $(x_1, \ldots, x_n) \mapsto t(x_1, \ldots, x_n)$ be the interpretation of t. If each x_i occurs only once in t, $1 \leqslant i \leqslant n$, then $\forall \mathbf{X} \in \mathbb{IR}^n, (\mathbf{X} \subseteq D_f \Rightarrow \boldsymbol{f}^u(\mathbf{X}) = \boldsymbol{f}(\mathbf{X}))$.

In other words, there is no overestimation if all variables occur only once in the given expression.

---

[2] This property follows from the monotonicity of interval operations

4. Intervals of preferences

As we have seen before, to define preferences over alternatives, the user is required to provide importance and interaction indices, but is more likely to establish intervals of values than precise values. In this section, we explain how such interval information can be integrated in the scheme of computation of the Choquet integral, by extending its definition to Interval Arithmetic.

Since the user is not longer asked for precise values of indices I_{ij} and I_i, but for intervals [3], we consider intervals of values of these indices, and we respectively denote them $\boldsymbol{I_{ij}}$ and $\boldsymbol{I_i}$, $i, j \in \{1, \ldots, n\}$. As a consequence, the formula for the computation of the Choquet integral is now given by:

$$(C_\mathbb{I}) \int_I f d\mu = \sum_{\boldsymbol{I_{ij}} > 0} (f(i) \wedge f(j)) \boldsymbol{I_{ij}} \\ + \sum_{\boldsymbol{I_{ij}} < 0} (f(i) \vee f(j)) |\boldsymbol{I_{ij}}| + \sum_{i=1}^{n} f(i)(\boldsymbol{I_i} - \frac{1}{2}\sum_{j \neq i} |\boldsymbol{I_{ij}}|). \quad (6)$$

$(C_\mathbb{I})$ means that the interpretation of this formula is performed using IA. As a consequence, the value of the integral is an interval, which we hope is the tightest one regarding the interval information provided by the user.

However, using IA means that overestimation of the range of real functions may occur, due to the above-mentioned dependency problem of IA. In particular, in the case of Equation 6, every interval variable $\boldsymbol{I_{ij}}$ occurs twice, with different monotonicities (once positively, once negatively), which inevitably leads to overestimating the expected range of values. Therefore, the right part of the formula is rewritten so as to obtain single occurrences only:

$$(C_\mathbb{I}) \int_I f d\mu = \sum_{\boldsymbol{I_{ij}} > 0} \left((f(i) \wedge f(j)) - \frac{1}{2}(f(i) + f(j)) \right) \boldsymbol{I_{ij}} \\ + \sum_{\boldsymbol{I_{ij}} < 0} \left((f(i) \vee f(j)) - \frac{1}{2}(f(i) + f(j)) \right) |\boldsymbol{I_{ij}}| + \sum_{i=1}^{n} f(i)\boldsymbol{I_i}$$

This formula contains only single occurrences of interval variables, which is a guarantee to obtain the exact range of possible values, given the intervals of preferences of the user.

4.1. Traditional against interval Choquet integral

It is worth noting that if the decision maker gives precise values for the importance and interaction indices (*i.e.*, real values), then the interval-based Choquet integral restricts theoretically to a standard Choquet integral and the intervals of preferences

---

[3] We will make the assumption (not restrictive) that the decision maker cannot give an interval whose interior contains 0, which would be a contradictory information.

are real valued numbers. In practice however (i.e., when using a computer), when evaluating the *interval* Choquet integral on "real numbers", the evaluation turns out to be still an interval. Yet, this is an interesting feature since:
- if all intermediate values of the computation of the Choquet integral are floating-point numbers, the interval result will be an interval $[a, a]$, where a is the floating-point value of the Choquet integral;
- and otherwise, the computation of the interval Choquet integral results in an interval $[a, b]$, where a and b are floating-points, $a \leqslant c \leqslant b$, and c is the actual (expected) value of the Choquet integral.

In both cases, we retrieve the actual value of the Choquet integral (exactly or included).

4.2. Making decisions: an issue when using intervals

Two alternatives are compared w.r.t. the corresponding interval values of their interval integral of Choquet. Unfortunately, intervals may not be as easy to compare as real numbers.

The ideal case is the following:

$$(C_\mathbb{I}) \int_I f d\mu \succeq (C_\mathbb{I}) \int_I g d\mu \overset{def}{\Leftrightarrow} \overline{(C_\mathbb{I}) \int_I f d\mu} \geqslant \overline{(C_\mathbb{I}) \int_I g d\mu}$$

when the intervals of preferences do not intersect. In this case, alternative f is evaluated with values that are all better than those of alternative g. Here the preference is clear, and is interpreted as the alternative f is preferred to the alternative g.

However, the above case is very specific and may unfortunately not always happen. Indeed it may rather happen that:

$$(C_\mathbb{I}) \int_I f d\mu \cap (C_\mathbb{I}) \int_I g d\mu \neq \varnothing$$

In such a case, we need to define a degree of preference corresponding to the intersection of the intervals. Next section describes strategies to make decisions in such cases.

5. Strategies of preference

5.1. Naive strategy

A trivial solution could consist in having a look :
- either at the upper bounds and give preference to the highest upper bound, which corresponds to an optimistic behavior: the preference is given to the alternative more likely to have a high Choquet integral value;
- at the lower bounds and give preference the the highest lowest bound which then corresponds to a pessimistic behavior: the preference is given to the alternative less likely to have a low Choquet integral value.

However, many alternatives between the very optimistic case and the very pessimistic case are possible. It is our feeling that we need to look simultaneously at the upper and lower bounds as well as the width of the intervals. Indeed, in many situations, the decision maker will exhibit some sort of aversion of risk and will want to have intervals as tight as possible, that is restrict the degree of uncertainty. In particular, we can already draw some strategies of choice as follows.

5.2. Intermediate strategies

Suppose that we consider two intervals I and J, corresponding respectively to:

$$(C_\mathbb{I}) \int_I f d\mu \quad \text{and} \quad (C_\mathbb{I}) \int_I g d\mu.$$

If the configuration is such that $\overline{I} > \overline{J}$ and $\underline{I} > \underline{J}$, then an optimistic strategy could consist in preferring to interval I, since I offers the possibility of having higher Choquet integral values. It is not as simple when J is included in I.
• Indeed, when the configuration is such that $\underline{J} - \underline{I} = \overline{I} - \overline{J}$, without more information, we can guess that there is the same probability for values in I to be smaller than values in J, as to be greater. As a consequence, a reasonable strategy could consist in giving preference to J since J is tighter and therefore more accurate.

One the other hand, a risky but defensible strategy would consist in preferring I, in the hope of getting better values, $i.e.$, those greater than J's.
• When interval I is not as well-balanced around J as it was in the previous configuration, two configurations are to be considered. In such cases, our feeling is that we may have to give preference to the interval that minimizes the risk of having small Choquet integral values.
⋆ The first case is defined by: $\underline{J} - \underline{I} > \overline{I} - \overline{J}$. A safe strategy may consist in preferring J for which the probability of obtaining small Choquet integral values is less than for I.
⋆ On the contrary, the second case is defined by: $\underline{J} - \underline{I} < \overline{I} - \overline{J}$, and a safe strategy would then consist in preferring I for the same reason as just mentioned.

5.3. Degree of preference and corresponding strategies

It is our feeling that we need to look simultaneously at the upper and lower bounds as well as the width of the intervals. Indeed, in many situations, the decision maker will exhibit some sort of aversion of risk and will want to have intervals as tight as possible, that is restrict the degree of uncertainty.

In this respect, we define hereafter a degree of preference $d(I, J)$, which is intended to express the extent to which a better value of the Choquet integral is likely to lie in interval I, instead of in interval J. It is defined as follows: $d : \mathbb{I}^2 \to [0, 1]$, where:

$$d(I,J) = \begin{cases} \dfrac{\overline{I}-\overline{J}}{|(\overline{I}-\overline{J})+(\underline{J}-\underline{I})|} & \text{if } \overline{I} > \overline{J} \text{ and } \underline{J} \geqslant \underline{I} \\ 1 & \text{if } \overline{I} = \overline{J} \text{ and } \underline{I} > \underline{J} \\ & \text{or: if } \overline{I} > \overline{J} \text{ and } \underline{I} \geqslant \underline{J} \\ & \text{or: if } \overline{I} = \overline{J} \text{ and } \underline{I} = \underline{J} \\ 1-d(J,I) & \text{otherwise} \end{cases} \quad (7)$$

Using this definition, we evaluate the chances to get a better value in interval I by comparing the "positive"[4] width of interval $[\overline{J}, \overline{I}]$, i.e., the interval where a better value of I could lie, to that of interval $[\underline{I}, \underline{J}]$, i.e., the interval where a worse value of I could lie.

5.3.1. Strategies associated to degrees of preference.

Any strategy can then be defined by a degree, above which the interval with the largest upper bound is preferred to the other. In particular, we can categorize strategies as follows:
- a risky strategy will be associated with a low degree d: this is an optimistic scenario in which, even if it is more likely[5] to get a worse value in interval I than in J, the strategy focuses on the slight, yet existing, possibility of getting a better value in I;
- a safe strategy will be associated with a high degree d: this is a pessimistic scenario where below degree d, even if there are chances to get better values in I, the focus is made on the remaining possibilities that this case does not happen, i.e., that we get worse values in I.

As a result, we will always be able to compare two strategies, in term of safeness or riskiness, regarding their associated degree.

5.3.2. Comparison of intervals.

The above-described degree of preference allows us to compare intervals resulting from the computation of interval Choquet integrals. In particular, given two intervals I and J, with $\overline{I} \geqslant \overline{J}$, and a strategy s associated with a degree $d \in [0,1]$, interval I is preferred to interval J if and only if $d(I,J) \geqslant d$:

$$I \succeq J \stackrel{def.}{\Leftrightarrow} \begin{cases} d(I,J) \geqslant d \\ \overline{I} \geqslant \overline{J} \end{cases} \stackrel{def.}{\Leftrightarrow} J \not\succeq I$$

(otherwise we note $J \succeq I$)

---
[4] By positive, we mean that if $\overline{J} > \overline{I}$, then interval $[\overline{J}, \overline{I}]$ is not an interval (bounds inverted) and its width is going to be $-w([\overline{I}, \overline{J}])$
[5] The likeliness is based upon the width of intervals only.

The comparison relies indeed on the capacity of the interval of largest upper bound to provide a better value.

Proposition 1. Relation $\succeq$ implies a partial order on the set $\mathbb{I}$ of intervals.

Proof. A complete proof can be found in [2]. □

5.3.3. *Need for generalization.*
We must point out that this evaluation of the degree relies on the fact that any values are equally possible in the compared intervals. However, this does not necessarily hold: situations may arise in which the user has more knowledge about the indices than only intervals of values, *i.e.*, bounds. Indeed, the user may have a stronger intuition about the part of the interval where the actual value may lie. This knowledge may be of different kinds. In particular, we address, in [2], the case in which the user is able to provide probabilistic distributions in addition to intervals of values.

6. Conclusion

In this paper, we have presented a simple computation scheme, combining the Choquet integral (in the 2-additive case) with interval arithmetic that allows us to give intervals of preferences over multidimensional alternatives. The approach is very attractive as it reflects more accurately what we can really expect from a decision maker, yet remains simple and still allows us to represent dependencies between attributes which is not possible with more traditional approaches such as the weighted sum.

In the case where the intervals of preferences are disjoint, the order of alternatives is clearly established. However, it is not as trivial in the (more probable) case where the intervals have an intersection. In this case, strategies have been presented, as well as a general degree of preference.

Future work will consist in extending our interval-decision framework to other kinds of knowledge provided by the user, such as general distributions.

References

1. G. Alefeld and J. Herzberger. *Introduction to Interval Computations*. Academic Press Inc., New York, USA, 1983. Traduit par Jon Rokne de l'original Allemand 'Einführung In Die Intervallrechnung'.
2. M. Ceberio and F. Modave. Interva-based multi-criteria decision making. Technical report, University of Texas at El Paso, 2004.
3. G. Choquet. Theory of capacities. *Annales de l'Institut Fourier*, 5, 1953.

4. F. Modave D. Dubois, M. Grabisch and H. Prade. Relating decision under uncertainty and multicriteria decision making models. *International Journal of Intelligent Systems*, 15:967–979, 2000.
5. M. Grabisch. *Fuzzy measures and integrals. Theory and applications*, chapter The interaction and Mobius representations of fuzzy measures on finite spaces, k-additive measures: a survey. Physica Verlag, to appear.
6. M. Grabisch, H. T. Nguyen, and E. A. Walker. *Fundamentals of Uncertainty Calculi with Applications to Fuzzy Inference*. Kluwer Academic Publisher, Dordrecht, 1995.
7. D. Krantz, R. Luce, P. Suppes, and A. Tverski. *Foundations of Measurement*. Academic Press, 1971.
8. F. Modave and M. Grabisch. Preferential independence and the Choquet integral. In *8th Int. Conf. on the Foundations and Applicatons of Decision under Risk and Uncertainty (FUR)*, Mons, Belgium, 1997.
9. F. Modave and M. Grabisch. Preference representation by the Choquet integral: the commensurability hypothesis. In *Proc. 7th Int. Conf. on Information Processing and Management of Uncertainty in Knowledge- Based Systems (IPMU)*, Paris, France, July 1998.
10. R. E. Moore. *Interval Analysis*. Prentice-Hall, Englewood Cliffs, N.J., 1966.
11. D. Schmeidler. Integral representation without additivity. *Proc. of the Amer. Math. Soc.*, 97(2):255–261, 1986.
12. D. Schmeidler. Subjective probability and expected utility without additivity. *Econometrica*, 57(3):571–587, 1989.

A Linguistic Hierarchical Evaluation Model for Engineering Systems

L. Martínez [a] and L. G. Pérez [a] and J. Liu [b]
J.B. Yang [c] and F. Herrera [d]

[a] Dpt. of Computer Sciences, University of Jaén, Jaén, Spain
[b] School of Computing and Mathematics, University of Ulster, Jordanstown, UK
[c] Manchester Business School, University of Manchester, Manchester, UK
[d] Dpt. Computer Sciences and A.I., University of Granada, Granada, Spain

Abstract

Before implementing a design of a large engineering system different design proposals are evaluated and ranked based on subjective assessments of different criteria. The knowledge about these criteria might be vague and incomplete. So, to deal with this kind of information we shall use linguistic approaches and Dempster-Shafer theory of evidence. In this chapter we propose an evaluation model based on the criteria of Safety and Cost. The safety assessments will be obtained using the fuzzy rule-based evidential reasoning (FURBER) approach and the cost assessments are supplied by the experts. Both subjective criteria are usually assessed in different utility spaces. The aim of this contribution is to evaluate the different design options by means of a decision model applying a linguistic hierarchical process to avoid loss of information.

Key words: Engineering systems, cost, safety, evaluation, linguistic information

1. Introduction

In the design of large engineering products such as offshore topsides, and offshore cranes, an efficient design may be evaluated and selected by means of Multi-Criteria Decision Making (MCDM) techniques. The decision of implementing a design will depend on that satisfies technical and economical constraints. In this chapter is proposed a linguistic evaluation model that takes into account the criteria of *Safety* and *Cost*. Hence, subjective safety and cost assessments can be studied together to determine the best risk reduction action and to choose the best design/operation option. So, multiple safety analysts can provide their subjective judgments for each design option on both cost and safety aspects.

Different safety assessment approaches may be difficult to use in situations where there is a lack of information, past experience, or ill-defined situation in risk analysis [11]. Therefore, linguistic descriptors, such as, "*Likely*", "*Impossible*", are used to describe an event due to the fact they are used commonly by engineers and safety analysts. Hence, the use of the fuzzy linguistic approach [14] is a good model to analyze the safety of engineering systems with incomplete information. Also the estimation of the cost is a ill-defined situation, therefore the use the linguistic approach is adequate too.

In engineering safety analysis, intrinsically vague information may coexist with conditions of "lack of specificity" originating from evidence not strong enough to completely support a hypothesis but only with degrees of belief or credibility. Dempster-Shafer (D-S) theory of evidence [7,9] based on the concept of belief function. D-S theory enlarges the scope of traditional probability theory, describes and handles uncertainties using the concept of the degrees of belief, which can model incompleteness and ignorance explicitly. Besides, the D-S theory also shows great potentials in multiple attribute decision analysis under uncertainty [13].

The aim of this paper is to develop a linguistic decision model that evaluates different design options for a large engineering system according to safety and cost criteria. To do so, we propose:

(i) An evaluation framework to assess the safety and cost criteria.
   - Safety will be assessed based on fuzzy logic and the evidential reasoning approach, referred to as a FURBER approach [5], which is based on the RIMER approach proposed recently in [12].
   - The synthesis of the safety assessments for each option is expressed and implemented using a linguistic 2-tuple scheme [3].
   - The cost assessments of each design option will be synthesized based on the assessments of each cost factor that are supplied directly by the experts in terms of linguistic labels. The assessments of each criterion are conducted in different utility spaces from each other.

(ii) An evaluation model based on a Multi-Expert MCDM process.
   - These assessments are the input values for a Multi-Expert Multi-Criteria Decision Making (MEMC-DM) problem defined in a multi-granular linguistic domain.
   - In the evaluation process the cost and safety assessments will be unified in a common utility space by means of linguistic hierarchies [4] and the linguistic 2-tuple representation model and after combined to obtain a degree of suitability for each design option to choose the best one.

In order to do so, this chapter is structured as follows: in Section 2 we make a brief review of linguistic tools. In Section 3 we describe the evaluation framework for safety and cost modelling of large engineering systems. In Section 4 it will be presented the application of the Hierarchical linguistic decision model to evaluate the design options. And finally, some conclusions are pointed out.

2. Linguistic Background

In this section we shall review some core concepts about linguistic information. We review briefly the *2-tuple Linguistic model* and the *Linguistic Hierarchies*.

2.1. *The 2-tuple Linguistic Model*

This model was presented in [3], for overcoming the drawback of the loss of information presented by the classical linguistic computational models: (i) The semantic model [1], (ii) and the symbolic one [2]. The 2-tuple fuzzy linguistic representation model is based on the symbolic method and takes as the base of its representation the concept of Symbolic Translation.

Definition 1. The Symbolic Translation of a linguistic term $s_i \in S = \{s_0, \cdots, s_g\}$ is a numerical value assessed in $[-0.5, 0.5)$ that supports the "difference of information" between an amount of information $[0, g]$ and the closest value in $\{0, \cdots, g\}$ that indicates the index of the closest linguistic term in $S(s_i)$, being $[0, g]$ the interval of granularity of S.

From this concept a linguistic representation model is developed, which represents the linguistic information by means of 2-tuples (s_i, α_i), $s_i \in S$ and $\alpha_i \in [-0.5, 0.5)$. This model defines a set of functions between linguistic 2-tuples and numerical values.

Definition 2. Let $S = \{s_0, \cdots, s_g\}$ be a linguistic term set and $\beta \in [0,]$ a value supporting the result of a symbolic aggregation operation, then the 2-tuple that expresses the equivalent information to β is obtained with the following function:

$$\Delta : [0, g] \to S \times (-0.5, 0.5)$$

$$\Delta(\beta) = (s_i, \alpha), with \begin{cases} s_i & i = round(\beta) \\ \alpha = \beta - i \; \alpha \in [-0.5, 0.5) \end{cases} \quad (1)$$

where s_i has the closest index label to "β" and "α" is the value of the symbolic translation.

Proposition 1. Let $S = \{s_0, \cdots, s_g\}$ be a linguistic term set and $(s_i, \alpha_i$ be a linguistic 2-tuple. There is always a Δ^{-1} function, such that, from a 2-tuple it returns its equivalent numerical value $\beta \in [0, g]$.

Proof. It is trivial, we consider the following function:

$$\Delta^{-1} : S \times [-0.5, 0.5) \to [0, g]$$

$$\Delta^{-1}(s_i, \alpha) = i + \alpha = \beta \quad (2)$$

Remark 1. *From Definitions 1 and 2 and Proposition 1, the conversion of a linguistic term into a linguistic 2-tuple consist of:* $s_i \in S \to (s_i, 0)$

In addition this model has a computational technique based on the 2-tuples were presented in [3].

2.2. Linguistic Hierarchies

The hierarchical linguistic contexts were introduced in [4] to improve the precision of the processes of Computing with Words in multi-granular linguistic contexts, that it is the aim of this contribution.

A Linguistic Hierarchy is a set of levels, where each level represents a linguistic term set with different granularity to the remaining levels. Each level is denoted as $l(t, n(t))$ being,
- t a number that indicates the level of the hierarchy.
- $n(t)$ the granularity of the term set of the level t.

The levels belonging to a linguistic hierarchy are ordered according to their granularity, i.e., for two consecutive levels t and $t+1$, $n(t+1) > n(t)$. Therefore, the level $t+1$ is a refinement of the previous level t.

From the above concepts, we define a linguistic hierarchy, LH, as the union of all levels t:

$$LH = \cup_t l(t, n(t))$$

Given a LH, we denote as $S^{n(t)}$ the linguistic term set of LH corresponding to the level t of LH characterized by a granularity of uncertainty $n(t)$:

$$S^{n(t)} = \{s_0^{n(t)}, \ldots, s_{n(t)-1}^{n(t)}\}$$

Generically, we can say that the linguistic term set of level $t+1$ is obtained from its predecessor as:

$$l(t, n(t)) \longrightarrow l(t+1, 2 \bullet n(t) - 1)$$

A graphical example of a linguistic hierarchy can be seen in Figure 1:

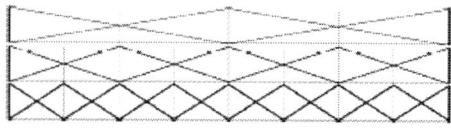

Fig. 1. Linguistic Hierarchy

In [4] were developed different transformation functions between labels of different levels without loss of information.

Definition 3. Let $LH = \cup_t l(t, n(t))$ be a linguistic hierarchy whose linguistic term sets are denoted as $S^{n(t)} = \{s_0^{n(t)}, \ldots, s_{n(t)-1}^{n(t)}\}$, and let us consider the 2-tuple linguistic representation. The transformation function from a linguistic label in level t to a label in level t' is defined as:

$$TF_{t'}^{t} : l(t, n(t)) \longrightarrow l(t', n(t'))$$

$$TF_{t'}^{t}(s_i^{n(t)}, \alpha^{n(t)}) = \Delta_{n(t')} \left(\frac{\Delta_{n(t)}^{-1}\left(s_i^{n(t)}\right) \bullet (n(t') - 1)}{n(t) - 1} \right) \qquad (3)$$

Proposition 2. The transformation function between linguistic terms in different levels of the linguistic hierarchy is bijective:

$$TF_t^{t'}(TF_{t'}^{t}(s_i^{n(t)}, \alpha^{n(t)})) = (s_i^{n(t)}, \alpha^{n(t)})$$

3. Evaluation Framework for Engineering Systems

In this section we show briefly how are the assessments for safety using the FURBER approach [5,12] and how are the cost assessments provided by the experts.

3.1. Safety Evaluation Framework

A generic framework for modelling system safety estimate using FURBER approach and for safety synthesis is outlined, more details see [5,12].

Step #1: Identification of causes/factors: it can be done by a panel of experts during a brainstorming session at the early concept design stages.

Step #2: Identify and definite fuzzy input and fuzzy output variables (i.e., safety estimates)

The three fundamental parameters used to assess the safety level of an engineering system on a subjective basis are the failure rate (**FR**), consequence severity (**CS**) and failure consequence probability (**FCP**). Subjective assessments are more appropriate for analysis using these three parameters as they are always associated with great uncertainty.

Safety estimates is the only output fuzzy variable used to produce safety evaluation for a particular cause to technical failure. This variable is described linguistically, which is described and determined by the above parameters. In safety is common to express a safety assessment in the following linguistic term set [10], that we note as, S_S:

$$S_S = \{Poor, Low, Average, High, Good\}$$

which are referred to as safety expressions.

Step #3: Construct a fuzzy rule-base

Fuzzy logic systems are knowledge-based or rule-based ones constructed from human knowledge in the form of fuzzy IF-THEN rules. We shall use to build our fuzzy rule base a linguistic term set with seven labels for **failure rate** (i.e., $J_1 = 7$); five labels for **consequence severity** (i.e., $J_2 = 7$), seven labels for **failure consequence probability** (i.e., $J_3 = 7$). Therefore, being L the total number of rules, in this case we use a sample of $L = 245$ rules [5].

Step #4: Fuzzy rule-base inference mechanism.

Suppose a fuzzy rule-base with the belief structure is given by $R = \{R_1, \cdots, R_L\}$. The kth rule can be represented as follows:

R_k : IF U is A^k THEN **safety estimate** is D with belief degree Y_k

where U represents the antecedent attribute vector (**FR, CS, FCP**), A^k the packet antecedents $\{A_1^k, A_2^k, A_3^k\}$, D the consequent vector $(D_1, \cdots, D_N)$, Y_K the vector of the belief degrees $(Y_{ik}, \cdots, Y_{nk})$ and $k \in 1, \cdots, L$.

Once a rule-base is built up its knowledge can be used to perform the inference procedure. In order to reach a safety assessment the fuzzy reasoning system expresses the safety estimates $S(e_i(a_l))$ as follows for the assessment done by the ith expert on the lth potential cause to a technical failure:

$$S(e_i(a_l)) = \left\{ (Poor; \Theta_{1i}^l); (Low; \Theta_{2i}^l); (Average; \Theta_{3i}^l); (High; \Theta_{4i}^l); (Good; \Theta_{5i}^l) \right\}$$

where e_i represents the ith expert ($i = 1, \cdots, p$) and a_l represents the lth ($l = 1, \cdots, q$) potential cause to a technical failure. Θ_{ti}^l represents the belief degree to which the safety of a_l is believed to be assessed to D_t by the expert e_i. The inference procedure is based on fuzzy rule-base and evidential reasoning approach, referred to as a fuzzy rule-based evidential reasoning approach - FURBER approach [5]. The final result is still a belief distribution on safety expression, which gives a view about the safety level for a given input.

In this phase for the synthesis purpose, we transform the safety estimate into a linguistic 2-tuple, i.e., transform the distribution assessment $S(e_i(a_l))$ on the S_S into linguistic 2-tuples over the S_S. A function X_i^l is introduced that transforms a distribution assessment in a linguistic term set S_S into a linguistic 2-tuple in S_S:

$$\chi_i^l : S(e_i(a_l)) \to S_S \times [-0.5, 0.5)$$

$$\chi_i^l \left(\{ (s_t; \Theta_{ti}^l), t = 0, \ldots, g-1 \} \right) = \Delta \left(\frac{\sum_{t=0}^{g} t\Theta_{ti}^l}{\sum_{t=0}^{g} \Theta_{ti}^l} = \beta_i^l \right) \quad (4)$$

3.2. Cost Modelling

Cost and safety are two of the most important features for the engineering systems, but usually they are conflicting because higher safety leading to higher costs. The cost incurred for safety improvement associated with a design/operation option is usually affected by many factors that often have large uncertainties of estimation. Therefore, it may be more appropriate to model the cost incurred in safety improvement associated with the design option on a subjective basis.

In the literature [10,11] these assessments are described by means of linguistic values. In our proposal we are interested in develop a model without loss of information using the linguistic hierarchies. To do so and due to the safety is assessed in a linguistic term set with five labels, the experts will express the cost assessments in a linguistic term set with nine labels, S_C. We propose the following term set (triangular shaped and symmetrically distributed):

$S_C = \{None, VeryLow, Low, ModeratelyLow, Average, ModeratelyHigh, High, VeryHigh, Unacceptable\}$

In our proposal the experts provide directly the cost assessments by means of labels in S_C.

Remark 2. *Cost assessments have a different interpretation that safety assessments, i.e., high cost indicates low suitability of the design option.*

4. Evaluation Model: Ranking Engineering Design Options

The aim we pursue solving this problem is to choose the most suitable design option for an engineering system taking into account features from safety and cost. So far, the assessments of safety are assessed in S_S while the assessments of the cost are assessed in S_C. Then to evaluate and rank the options we shall apply the multi-granular linguistic decision model presented in [4] in order to solve our problem. This model uses linguistic hierarchies to manage decision making problems defined in multi-granular linguistic domains without loss of information, that it is a very important feature in the development of engineering systems. After choosing a LH for the evaluation framework the evaluation model will consist of two phases:

– Aggregation phase: it combines safety and cost assessments to obtain an overall suitability assessment for each option. This phase has two steps:
 (i) Normalization process: it unifies the multi-granular linguistic information.
 (ii) Aggregation process: it obtains an overall value of suitability for each design option.
– Exploitation phase: it ranks the different design options according to assessments obtained in the aggregation phase by means of a choice degree.

4.1. Safety and Cost Problem Modelled by means of Linguistic Hierarchies

So far, we have the Safety and Cost assessments of each design option expressed by means of linguistic values assessed in different linguistic utility spaces with five and nine labels respectively. Therefore, we have to choose a linguistic hierarchy, LH, for modelling our problem. We shall choose a LH that contains levels with five and nine labels respectively (see Fig. 2):

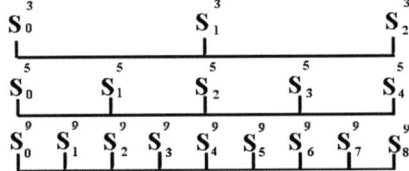

Fig. 2. Linguistic Hierarchy 3,5 and 9 labels

4.2. Evaluation based on a Decision Process

Here, we describe in detail the steps of the evaluation model used to solve our problem that is modelled as a Multi-Expert Multi-Criteria Decision Making problem where each expert i, provides assessments for the cost and from his/her opinions are synthesized assessments for the safety (See Table 1):

Table 1
Expert's assessments

Design Options		
Expert i	Safety	Cost
O_1	(s_{i1}, α)	(c_{i1}, α)
...	...	...
O_n	(s_{in}, α)	(c_{in}, α)

Where (s_{ij}, α) are the safety assessments synthesized from the opinions of the expert e_i for the design option o_j, i.e., estimated based on the fuzzy rule-based system, and then synthesized to obtain the safety assessment of the system by means of linguistic 2-tuples in the linguistic term set, S_S. While (c_{ij}, α) are the overall cost assessment obtained aggregating the cost of the different cost factors, provided by the expert e_i for the design option O_j, assessed in the linguistic term set S_C (These values are transformed into 2-tuples according to Remark 1).

4.2.1. Aggregation Phase

In this phase the information is combined to obtain collective preference values for each design option according to the assessments of the different experts and criteria. This model combines the multi-granular linguistic information in two steps.

(i) Normalization Process:

We are dealing with multi-granular linguistic information, to manage it the model unifies it in a common utility space called, Basic Linguistic Term Set (BLTS). We propose as the common utility space for expressing the overall utility of each design option the following linguistic term set, with five labels:

$S_T = \{SlightlyPreferred, ModeratelyPreferred, Average, Preferred, GreatlyPreferred\}$

Remark 3: during the aggregation process is used the notation, s_i^5, to refer to the aggregated values to avoid misunderstandings with cost meaning.

In this case our model chooses the BLTS as the second level of the linguistic hierarchy shown in the (Fig. 2) which granularity is five labels.

Once we have chosen the common utility space to express the preferred design options we have to transform the safety and cost assessments to the BLTS. Let's suppose the following assessments (See Table 2):

The multi-granular information is unified by means of the transformation function between the levels of the hierarchy (Def. 3). The safety assessments of safety are already expressed in the BLTS, while the cost assessments are

Table 2
Linguistic Safety and cost assessments in S_S

	Safety			Cost		
Opts	Experts					
	E#1	...	E#M	E#1	...	E#M
O_1	(poor,0.2756)	...	(poor,0)	(ModerateHigh,0)	...	(Average,0)
⋮		...			...	
O_n	(Low,-0.459)	...	(poor,0.445)	(High,0)	...	High,0)

unified by means of $TF_5^9(c,\alpha)$. This process is applied to all the experts opinions. So, the safety and cost assessments of the expert i are expressed by means of linguistic 2-tuples in the common utility space, BLTS (See table 3):

Table 3
Linguistic Safety and Cost assessments expressed in the BLTS

	Safety			Cost		
Opts	Experts					
	E#1	...	E#M	E#1	...	E#M
O_1	$(s_0^5, 0.2745)$	...	$(s_0^5, 0)$	$(s_3^5, -0.5)$	...	$(s_2^5, 0)$
⋮		...			...	
O_n	$(s_1^5, -0.4594)$	...	$(s_0^5, 0.4453)$	$(s_3^5, 0)$	...	$(s_3^5, 0)$

(ii) Aggregation Process: it combines the cost and safety assessments to obtain a global value for each design option in a two-step process:

(a) Obtain a global value for cost and safety of each design option expressed in a linguistic value in the BLTS. To do so, we can use different aggregation operators for linguistic 2-tuples defined in [3]. In this paper we use the weighted average operator to obtain a global value for cost and safety, (See Table 4):

Table 4
Global assessments for Safety and Cost

	Safety	Cost
O_1	$(s_1^5, -0.3)$	$(s_3^5, -0.12)$
...	...	...
O_n	$(s_0^5, 0.34)$	$(s_3^5, 0.23)$

(b) Obtain an evaluation value for each design option in the BLTS. To do so, we have a set of pairs of assessments $\{(s_i,\alpha),(c_i,\alpha)\}$ for each design option, the applying a weighted aggregation operator taking into account the remark 2 the aggregated value for each design option is obtained with the following expression:

$$W_{AM}\left((s_i,\alpha),(c_i,\alpha)\right) = \Delta\left(\Delta^{-1}(s,\alpha) \cdot w + \Delta^{-1}\left(Neg(c,\alpha)\right) \cdot (1-w)\right)$$

Where $Neg(c_i,\alpha)$ is the assessment for the cost of the design option i taking into account its decreasing interpretation and (s_i,α) is the assessment for the safety of the option i. And w is the weight for the safety assessment and $1-w$ the weight for the cost assessment. Let suppose a value of $w=0.5$ then from Table 4:

Table 5
Design Options Utility Assessments

Design Options	
O_1	(Moderated Preferred, 0.44)
$\vdots$	$\vdots$
O_n	(Moderated Preferred, 0.05)

Now we have got an overall value of each design option expressed by means of a linguistic 2-tuple in S_T for each expert. To obtain a global assessment for each option we shall apply another aggregation operator to the global assessments of all experts. We could consider that all the experts are equally important or we could assign different weights to each experts.

4.2.2. Exploitation Phase

Finally the decision process applies a choice degree to obtain a selection set of alternatives. Different choice functions has been proposed in the choice theory literature [6,8]. The choice functions rank the alternatives according to different possibilities and from the ranking obtained the best one/s.

In our problem the information is expressed by linguistic 2-tuples that have defined a total order over itself. In our problem we shall rank the results using this order. Let's suppose an only expert then from Table 7 we shall choose as the best design option: O_1

5. Conclusions

The evaluation of different designs before implementing a large engineering system is a common task. In this paper we have proposed an evaluation model based on an MEMCDM problem that evaluates the engineering systems according to its Safety and Cost. The main advantage of this evaluation model is that it manages multi-granular linguistic information without loss of information.

Acknowledgments

This work has been supported by the Research Project TIC 2002-03348.

References

1. R. Degani and G. Bortolan. The problem of linguistic approximation in clinical decision making. *Int. Journal of Approximate Reasoning*, 2:143–162, 1988.
2. M. Delgado, J.L. Verdegay, and M.A Vila. Linguistic decision making models. *International Journal of Intelligent Systems*, 7:479–492, 1992.
3. F. Herrera and L. Martínez. A 2-tuple fuzzy linguistic representation model for computing with words. *IEEE Trans. on Fuzzy Systems*, 8(6):746–752, 2000.
4. F. Herrera and L. Martínez. A model based on linguistic 2-tuples for dealing with multigranularity hierarchical linguistic contexts in multiexpert decision-making. *IEEE Transactions on Systems, Man and Cybernetics. Part B: Cybernetics*, 31(2):227–234, 2001.
5. J. Liu, J.B. Yang, J. Wang, H.S. Sii, and Y.W. Wang. Fuzzy rule-based evidential reasoning approach for safety analysis. *International Journal of General Systems*, page In press, 2004.
6. S.A. Orlovsky. Decision-making with a fuzzy preference relation. *Fuzzy Sets Systems*, 1:155–167, 1978.
7. Dempster A. P. A generalization of bayesian inference. *Journal of the Royal Statistical Society, Series B*, 30:205–247, 1968.
8. M. Roubens. Some properties of choice functions based on valued binary relations. *European Journal of Operational Research*, 40:309–321, 1989.
9. G. Shafer. , *A Mathematical Theory of Evidence*. Princeton, N.J.: Princeton University Press, 1976.
10. J. Wang, J.B. Yang, and P. Sen. Safety analysis and synthesis using fuzzy sets and evidential reasoning. *Reliability Eng. System Safety*, 41:103–118, 1995.
11. J. Wang, J.B. Yang, and P. Sen. Multi-person and multi-attribute design evaluations using evidential reasoning based on subjective safety and cost analyses. *Reliability Engineering and System Safety*, 52(2):113–129, 1996.
12. J. B. Yang, J. Liu, J. Wang, and H. S. Sii. A generic knowledge-base inference methodology using the evidential reasoning approach - RIMER. *IEEE Transactions on Systems, Man, and Cybernetics*, page To appear, 2004.
13. J.B. Yang. Rule and utility based evidential reasoning approach for multi-attribute decision analysis under uncertainties. *European Journal of Operational Research*, 131:31–61, 2001.
14. L.A. Zadeh. The concept of a linguistic variable and its applications to approximate reasoning. *Information Sciences, Part I, II, III*, 8,8,9:199 249,301 357,43–80, 1975.

KNOWLEDGE REPRESENTATION

Non Monotonic Aggregates Applying to Fuzzy Sets in Flexible Querying

Patrick Bosc[a] and Ludovic Liétard[b]

[a]IRISA/ENSSAT, Technopole anticipa BP 447,
22305 Lannion Cedex, France

[b]IRISA/IUT, Rue Edouard Branly BP 30219
22302 Lannion Cedex, France

Abstract

This paper considers flexible queries against relational databases using fuzzy set theory. More precisely, it is concerned with fuzzy conditions involving an aggregate operator (such as the maximum or the sum). In the general case, the interpretation of such conditions is not trivial since the aggregate applies to a fuzzy referential as in the condition "the average of high salaries is over $2000" where the aggregate average applies to the fuzzy set of high salaries. Our objective is to give an interpretation for conditions where the aggregate not only applies to a fuzzy set of items but is also confronted to a fuzzy condition. The contribution of this paper is to propose an interpretation which deals with any kind of aggregates (monotonic or non monotonic).

Key words: relational databases, flexible querying, fuzzy sets, aggregate functions.

1. Introduction

This paper deals with flexible queries addressed to relational databases. In this context, atomic conditions define preferences instead of strict requirements and the set of answers returned to the user is discriminated. Several approaches to define flexible querying have been proposed and it has been shown [1] that fuzzy set theory is a unifying framework to define flexible queries. Atomic conditions are defined by fuzzy sets and are then called "vague" or "fuzzy" predicates. Such vague conditions can be aggregated using various operators (e.g., generalized conjunctions and disjunctions, linguistic quantifiers) and an extension of the SQL query language (called SQLf) has been proposed [2].

In SQLf, as well as in SQL, it is possible to consider aggregates which are functions applying to a set of items (such as the cardinality, the sum, the maximum or the average). Aggregates can be integrated into flexible queries such as "retrieve the firm where the average salary is *around $2000*". Its expression in SQLf is:

    select #cmp **from** EMP **group by** #firm
    having avg(salary) = *around(2000)*,

assuming that relation EMP(#emp, #cmp, salary) describes employees working into different companies. The average salary of each company is computed and confronted to the fuzzy condition *around(2000)* to get a degree of satisfaction of them with respect to the condition: "the *average* salary of its employees is *around $2000*". The higher this degree, the more the company belongs to the answer to the query.

In the previous example, we are in a simple situation where the aggregate can be easily computed since it applies to a crisp set. However, when the items to aggregate are issued from a fuzzy condition, the interpretation is no longer trivial as in the query aiming at the retrieval of companies where "the average of *high* salary is *around $2000*" which could be expressed in SQLf as:

    select #cmp **from** EMP **where** salary = *high*
    group by #firm
    having avg(salary) = *around(2000)*.

Here for a given company, the value of the aggregate "average" has to be computed on the fuzzy set made of its *high* salaries and is confronted to the vague condition *around(2000)*. In this general case, the difficulty is mainly to compute the value of the aggregate (average) since it applies to a fuzzy set (of *high* salaries).

The objective of this paper is to propose an interpretation for conditions where the aggregate applies to a fuzzy set of items and is confronted to a fuzzy predicate. The desired interpretation must deliver a degree of satisfaction in order to be coherent with other predicates in the framework of SQLf.

In the following, an aggregate is denoted by agg, a (fuzzy) set of elements to be aggregated is denoted by A and the statement "agg(A) is C" is considered. In addition, the truth value of any expression *expr* (Boolean or fuzzy) is denoted by truth[*expr*]. With these notations, the condition appearing in the previous example is rewritten: "avg(*high* salaries) is *around(2000)*" and truth[avg(*high* salaries) is *around(2000)*] expresses the extent to which this flexible condition (predicate) is satisfied.

Previous propositions suggested for determining the truth value for "agg(A) is C" either are limited to monotonic aggregates and monotonic predicates [3], or lead to an imprecise degree of truth [4] (made of two indices : the degrees of possibility and certainty that the condition is satisfied). Such approaches are not convenient for SQLf where a unique degree of truth is required and where any kind of aggregates or predicates must be acceptable. The contribution of this paper is to propose (in section 2) an approach to determine a unique degree of truth in the general case (i.e., applicable in particular in the presence of non monotonic aggregates and predicates). Section 3 is devoted to the position of this proposition with respect to the algebraic property stating that "agg(A) is C" and "agg(A) is not C" are the negation one of the other. A conclusion is given in section 4.

2. The proposed approach

According to our proposition, the fuzzy set A is viewed as a collection of its α-cuts which represent different interpretations (at different levels) of A. The value of the aggregate for A_α is denoted by $agg(A_\alpha)$ and the extent to which it satisfies the fuzzy condition C is given by $\mu_c[agg(A_\alpha)]$.

Example 1. The statement "avg(A) is *high*" is considered with the following fuzzy set A :

$$0.1/0 + 0.1/1 + 0.1/2 + 0.1/3 + 0.1/4 + 0.1/10 + 0.2/200 + 0.5/700 + 0.8/500 + 1/600.$$

The different interpretations A_α of A are obtained for α in $\{0.1, 0.2, 0.5, 0.8, 1\}$. If we assume that: $\mu_{high}(202) = 0.2$, $\mu_{high}(500) = 0.8$, $\mu_{high}(550) = 0.9$ and $\mu_{high}(600) = 1$, we get :

α	0.1	0.2	0.5	0.8	1
$avg(A_\alpha)$	202	500	600	550	600
$\mu_{high}[avg(A_\alpha)]$	0.2	0.8	1	0.9	1

Table 1. The truth values of $\mu_{high}[avg(A_\alpha)]$

For instance, in the previous table, when $\alpha = 0.5$, $\mu_{high}[avg(A_{0.5})] = 1$ since $A_{0.5} = \{700, 500, 600\}$, $avg(A_{0.5}) = 600$ and $\mu_{high}(600) = 1$. ♦

The question now is about the integration of the various results obtained for the interpretations of A. Intuitively, it seems reasonable to think that the more often the aggregate satisfies C, the more "agg(A) is C" is true.

A way is to look for the highest degree of satisfaction β such that, for each interpretation A_α, "agg(A_α) is C" is at least equal to β. In other words :

$$\text{truth}[agg(A) \text{ is } C] = \max_{\beta \text{ in } [0,1]} \min(\beta, \text{each}(\beta)), \quad (1)$$

where each(β) means "for each interpretation A_α, $\mu_c[agg(A_\alpha)] \geq \beta$". Obviously, this definition depends on that of each(β). The simplest case is when each(β) is Boolean and equals 1 as soon as each interpretation reaches the threshold β :

each(β) = 1 if $\forall \alpha$, $\mu_c[agg(A_\alpha)] \geq \beta$
0 otherwise.

It is easy to show that this expression defines the truth value of "agg(A) is C" as the minimum among all the values $\mu_C[agg(A_\alpha)]$ and expression (1) becomes :

$$\text{truth}[agg(A) \text{ is } C] = \min_\alpha \mu_C[agg(A_\alpha)].$$

Example 2. If we come back to example 1, the truth value for the statement "avg(A) is *high*" is given by: $\min_\alpha \mu_{high}[avg(A_\alpha)] = 0.2$. This low value may seem to be a bit strange since the average strongly satisfies *high* for each α-cut except the lowest one (see table 1), i.e., when elements which belong weakly to A are taken into account. ♦

The previous example shows that a Boolean interpretation for each(β) (1 when β is reached for each $\mu_C[agg(A_\alpha)]$, 0 otherwise) is not appropriate. A definition delivering a degree is more convenient and we propose to sum the lengths of intervals (of levels) where the threshold β is reached :

$$\text{each}(\beta) \;=\; \sum_{\substack{]\alpha_i,\alpha_j] \text{ such that } \forall \alpha \in]\alpha_i,\alpha_j],\\ \mu_C[agg(A_\alpha)] \text{ is defined and } \mu_C[agg(A_\alpha)] \geq \beta}} (\alpha_j - \alpha_i). \qquad (2)$$

= 0 when $\forall\, \alpha \in [0, 1]$, $\mu_C[agg(A_\alpha)]$ is not defined or $\mu_C[agg(A_\alpha)] < \beta$.

The higher each(β), the more numerous the levels α for which $\mu_C[agg(A_\alpha)] \geq \beta$. In particular, each(β) equals 1 means that for each level α, $\mu_C[agg(A_\alpha)]$ is larger than (or equal to) β.

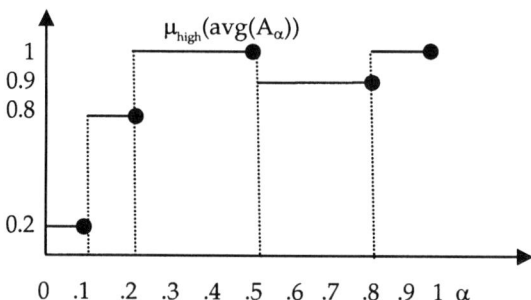

Figure 1. α–cuts of the predicate "avg(A) is *high*"

Example 3. Let us consider figure 1 which summarizes the results of table 1. In particular, for β = 0.95, we get:

$$\text{each}(0.95) \;=\; \sum_{\substack{]\alpha_i,\alpha_j] \text{ such that } \forall \alpha \in]\alpha_i,\alpha_j],\\ \mu_{high}[avg(A_\alpha)] \text{ is defined and } \mu_{high}[avg(A_\alpha)] \geq 0.95}} (\alpha_j - \alpha_i).$$

$= (0.5 - 0.2) + (1 - 0.8) = 0.5$.

Similarly, each(0.6) = 0.9. ♦

This second definition for each(β) (i.e., expression (2)) is used in the rest of the paper. At first glance,, from a computational point of view, the definition of truth[agg(A) is C] (expression (1)) needs to handle an infinity of values β. However, it is possible to restrict the computations to β values belonging to the set of "effective" $\mu_c[agg(A_\alpha)]$ values, according to the following formula:

(3) $\quad$ truth[agg(A) is C] = $\max_{\beta \in D} \min(\beta, each(\beta))$,

where $D = \{\beta \mid \exists \alpha \text{ such that } \beta = \mu_c[agg(A_\alpha)]\}$.

Proof. We consider expression (1) and we show that a value λ out of D can be omitted in the computations. When λ is out of V, two cases can be considered.

Case 1. When λ is larger than the maximum value of $D = \{\beta \mid \exists \alpha \text{ such that } \beta = \mu_c[agg(A_\alpha)]\}$, we get :

$$each(\lambda) = \sum_{\substack{]\alpha_i,\alpha_j] \text{ such that } \forall \alpha \in]\alpha_i,\alpha_j], \\ \mu_C[agg(A_\alpha)] \text{ is defined and } \mu_C[agg(A_\alpha)] \geq \beta}} (\alpha_j - \alpha_i) = 0$$

and consequently min(λ,each(λ)) = 0. Since the maximum value is retained in formula (1), value λ can be discarded since its contribution is 0.

Case 2. When λ is not larger than the maximum value of $D = \{\beta \mid \exists \alpha \text{ such that } \beta = \mu_c[agg(A_\alpha)]\}$, there are values of $\mu_c[agg(A_\alpha)]$ such that $\lambda \leq \mu_c[agg(A_\alpha)]$. We denote by $\mu_c[agg(A_{\alpha'})]$ (associated to level α') the smallest one. We have:

$each(\lambda) = each(\mu_c[agg(A_{\alpha'})])$ and $\lambda \leq \mu_c[agg(A_{\alpha'})]$,

and we get :

$\min(\lambda,each(\lambda)) \leq \min(\mu_c[agg(A_{\alpha'})], each(\mu_c[agg(A_{\alpha'})]))$.

Here again, as the maximum value is retained to define truth[agg(A) is C], such a value λ can be omitted.●

Example 4. Let us consider the context of example 1 devoted to the statement "avg(A) is *high*". From table 1 we get :

$D = \{\beta \mid \exists \alpha \text{ such that } \beta = \mu_c[agg(A_\alpha)]\} = \{0.2, 0.8, 0.9, 1\}$,

and from figure 1:

each(0.2) = 1, each(0.8) = 0.9, each(0.9) = 0.8 and each(1) = 0.5.

According to (3), the final result is:

truth[avg(A) is *high*] = max(min(0.2, 1) min(0.8, 0.9) min(0.9, 0.8) min(1, 0.5))
= 0.8.

The statement "avg(A) is *high*" is rather true (at degree 0.8) since every interpretation of the fuzzy set A (except the lowest one) strongly satisfies the flexible condition "the average is *high*" (at least at degree 0.8). ♦

One may remark that the result only depends on the sum of the lengths of the intervals where β is reached and not on the quality of the cuts. For example, 0.8 is also obtained in the situation depicted in figure 2.

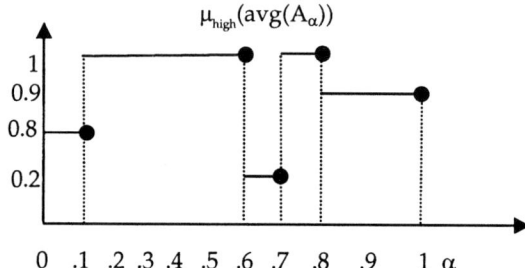

Figure 2. α–cuts of the predicate "avg(A) is *high*"

3. Condition with an aggregate and its negation

This section investigates the situation of the given approach with respect to the algebraic property expressing that "agg(A) is C" and "agg(A) is not C" are the negation of each other. It turns out that the normalization (or not) of the fuzzy set A onto which the aggregate applies, may have a crucial importance. In fact, this is related to the applicability of an aggregate in the presence of a regular empty set. More precisely, two cases are now dealt with: a) the aggregate is meaningless for the empty set and A is not normalized, and b) either the aggregate makes sense when it applies to the empty set or A is normalized.

3.1 First case

We consider the situation where the fuzzy set A is not normalized and the aggregate is not defined for the empty set (such as the maximum). The next example illustrates this situation.

Example 5. The statement "max(A) is *high*" is considered with the following fuzzy set A:

0.1/500 + 0.1/700 + 0.2/550 + 0.5/500.

Here, A is not normalized and the aggregate is not defined for the empty set. The different values for β (with $\mu_{high}(500) = 0.8$, $\mu_{high}(550) = 0.9$ and $\mu_{high}(700) = 1$) are :

α	0.1	0.2	0.5
max(A_α)	700	550	500
β = μ_{high}(max(A_α))	1	0.9	0.8

We get β ∈ D = {0.8, 0.9, 1} and from expression (2) :

$$\text{each}(\beta) = \sum_{\substack{]\alpha_i,\alpha_j] \text{ such that } \forall \alpha \in]\alpha_i,\alpha_j], \\ \mu_{high}[\max(A_\alpha)] \text{ is defined and } \mu_{high}[\max(A_\alpha)] \geq \beta}} (\alpha_j - \alpha_i).$$

However, we cannot take into consideration α-cuts having a level over 0.5 (which are empty) in the computation of a value each(β). This is due to the fact that $\mu_{high}(\max(A_\alpha))$ is not defined for them since the aggregate maximum cannot apply. As we get :

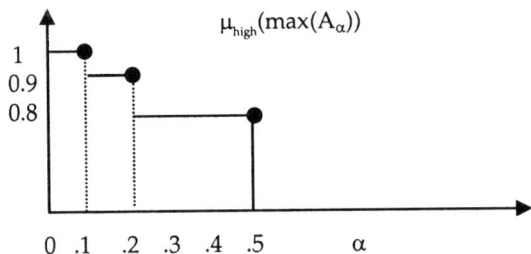

we can compute : each(0.8) = 0.5, each(0.9) = 0.2 and each(1) = 0.1. Finally :

truth[max(A) is *high*] = max(min(0.8, 0.5) min(0.9, 0.2) min(1, 0.1)) = 0.5.

Despite of the fact that each α-cut has a very high satisfaction for "the maximum is *high*", we do not obtain a high truth value for "max(A) is *high*". This is due to the fact that A is not normalized and consequently A is more or less equal to the empty set (depending on $\sup_x \mu_A(x)$). As the aggregate maximum does not apply to the empty set, the truth value of "max(A) is *high*" more or less reflects this impossibility to compute the aggregate. ♦

This example illustrates a behaviour of our proposition which can be formalized by the following property stating that truth[agg(A) is C] is bounded by the maximum membership in A.

Property 1. When the aggregate agg is not defined for the empty set and the fuzzy set A is not normalized:

$$\text{truth}[\text{agg}(A) \text{ is } C] \leq \sup_x \mu_A(x).$$

Proof. The value $\sup_x \mu_A(x)$ is denoted λ. In this context, some α-cuts are empty (since A is not normalized), namely the ones having a level over λ. Since the aggregate cannot apply to these α-cuts we get λ for the largest each(β) and :

$$\forall \beta \in D: \text{each}(\beta) \leq \lambda, \text{ and then :}$$

$$\forall \beta \in D: \min(\beta, \text{each}(\beta)) \leq \min(\beta, \lambda) \leq \lambda.$$

Consequently :

$$\text{truth}[\text{agg}(A) \text{ is } C] = \max_{\beta \in D} \min(\beta, \text{each}(\beta)) \leq \lambda. \bullet$$

Example 6. Let us consider the fuzzy set A:

0.1/100 + 0.1/10 + 0.1/20000 + 0.2/300,

and the statement "max(A) is *high*". The fuzzy set A is close to the empty set and the maximum does not apply to the empty set, truth[max(A) is *high*] cannot be expected to be over 0.2. This result complies with the intuition. ♦

As a consequence, when the aggregate agg is not defined for the empty set and the fuzzy set A is not normalized, "agg(A) is C" and "agg(A) is not C" cannot be the negation of each other. This property is illustrated by the data of example 6 where truth[max(A) is *high*] ≤ 0.2 and truth[max(A) is not *high*] ≤ 0.2 (due to property 1).

3.2 Second case

The situation considered here is the opposite of the previous one. The fuzzy set A is assumed to be normalized or the aggregate (e.g., the cardinality) is defined for the empty set. In this case, the property related to the value of a statement and its opposite holds.

Property 2. When the aggregate agg is defined for the empty set or when the fuzzy set A is normalized:

$$\text{truth}[\text{agg}(A) \text{ is } C] = 1 - \text{truth}[\text{agg}(A) \text{ is not } C]$$

Proof. This demonstration is based on the properties of the weighted maximum operator.

The definition of truth[agg(A) is C] can be rewritten :

$$\text{truth}[\text{agg}(A) \text{ is } C] = \max_{1 \leq i \leq n} \min(\beta_i, \text{each}(\beta_i))$$

where values from $D = \{\beta \mid \exists \alpha \text{ such that } \beta = \mu_c[\text{agg}(A_\alpha)]\}$ are increasingly ranked :

$$\beta_1 < \beta_2 < \ldots < \beta_n.$$

The value $\text{truth}[\text{agg}(A) \text{ is } C]$ is a weighted maximum of β_i's where the weights are the values $\text{each}(\beta_i)$. Since β values are increasingly ranked:

$$\text{each}(\beta_1) > \text{each}(\beta_2) > \ldots > \text{each}(\beta_n),$$

where $\text{each}(\beta_1) = 1$. With these conditions on β_i's and $\text{each}(\beta_i)$'s, we get [5]:

$$\text{truth}[\text{agg}(A) \text{ is } C] = \min_{1 \leq i \leq n} \max(\beta_i, \text{each}(\beta_{i+1}))$$

with $\text{each}(\beta_{n+1}) = 0$. Then:

$$1 - \text{truth}[\text{agg}(A) \text{ is } C] = 1 - \min_{1 \leq i \leq n} \max(\beta_i, \text{each}(\beta_{i+1}))$$
$$= \max_{1 \leq i \leq n} \min(1 - \beta_i, 1 - \text{each}(\beta_{i+1}))$$
(4).

Here, the expression of $\text{truth}[\text{agg}(A) \text{ is not } C]$ is obtained since :

a) expression (4) is a weighted maximum of the $(1 - \beta_i)$ values which are coming from the set :

$$\{\beta' \mid \exists \alpha \text{ such that } \beta' = 1 - \mu_c[\text{agg}(A_\alpha)]\}$$

as it is the case for $\text{truth}[\text{agg}(A) \text{ is not } C]$

b) $1 - \text{each}(\beta_{i+1}) = \text{each}(1 - \beta_i)$ (result established hereafter), and expression (4) becomes:

$$\max_{1 \leq i \leq n} \min(1 - \beta_i, \text{each}(1 - \beta_i))$$

which is nothing but the expression of $\text{truth}[\text{agg}(A) \text{ is not } C]$.

The value $(1 - \text{each}(\beta_{i+1}))$ equals $\text{each}(1 - \beta_i)$ since:

$$1 - \text{each}(\beta_{i+1}) = 1 - \sum_{]\alpha_i, \alpha_j] \text{ such that } \forall \alpha \in]\alpha_i, \alpha_j], \mu_C[\text{agg}(A_\alpha)] \geq \beta_{i+1}} (\alpha_j - \alpha_i)$$

$$= 1 - \sum_{]\alpha_i, \alpha_j] \text{ such that } \forall \alpha \in]\alpha_i, \alpha_j], \mu_C[\text{agg}(A_\alpha)] > \beta_i} (\alpha_j - \alpha_i)$$

$$= \sum_{\substack{]\alpha_i,\alpha_j] \text{ such that } \forall \alpha \in]\alpha_i,\alpha_j], \mu_C[agg(A_\alpha)] \leq \beta_i}} (\alpha_j - \alpha_i)$$

$$= \sum_{\substack{]\alpha_i,\alpha_j] \text{ such that } \forall \alpha \in]\alpha_i,\alpha_j], 1-\mu_C[agg(A_\alpha)] \geq 1-\beta_i}} (\alpha_j - \alpha_i) \quad = each(1 - \beta_i). \bullet$$

4. Conclusion

This paper is situated in the area of flexible queries against usual relational databases using fuzzy set theory. It addresses the issue of interpreting conditions involving aggregates applying to fuzzy sets. More precisely, conditions of the type "agg(A) is C" are taken into consideration where agg is any aggregate function, A is a fuzzy set of items and C is a vague predicate. The interpretation of such conditions is not trivial since the aggregate applies to a fuzzy set.

As a unique degree of truth is required in the context we are interested in (SQLf query language), the interpretation leading to an imprecise degree of truth [4] cannot be considered. A proposition (based on the Sugeno integral) which delivers a unique degree of truth has been previously proposed [3], but it is limited to monotonic aggregates and predicates.

The contribution of this paper is to propose an approach to compute a degree to evaluate conditions of type "agg(A) is C" in the general case (where no assumption is made about monotonicity). In the approach suggested here, the fuzzy set onto which the aggregate applies is viewed as a collection of crisp sets, namely its α-level cuts. The truth value of the statement "agg(A) is C" is a degree δ such that the higher δ, the more α-cuts satisfy "the value of the aggregate is C" with a high level of satisfaction. In other words, the higher the truth value of "agg(A) is C", the more α-cuts of A have a high value for $\mu_C[agg(A_\alpha)]$. It is worth noticing that the quality of α-cuts is not taken into account in this approach. Such a concern will be a matter for future research.

We have shown that the truth value obtained for "agg(A) is C" is the negation of that of "agg(A) is not C" only when A is a normalized fuzzy set or the aggregrate is defined for the empty set. Otherwise, this property does not hold. Instead, the truth value of these two statements is bounded by the heigth of the fuzzy set A which indeed reflects the inapplicability of the aggregate.

In the near future, we aim at designing algorithms for an efficient evaluation of conditions calling on aggregates. Moreover, we would like to assess the extra cost to pay for such queries with respect to "similar" regular (Boolean) queries.

References

1. P. Bosc, O. Pivert (1992), Some Approaches for Relational Databases Flexible Querying. *Journal of Intelligent Information Systems*, vol. 1, pages 323-354.
2. P. Bosc, O. Pivert (1995), SQLf: A relational database language for fuzzy querying. *IEEE Transactions on Fuzzy Systems*, vol. 3, pages 1-17.
3. P. Bosc, L Liétard, O. Pivert (2003), Sugeno Fuzzy integral as a basis for the interpretation of flexible queries involving monotonic aggregates. *Information Processing and Management*, vol. 39, pages 287-306.

4. D. Dubois, H. Prade (1990), Measuring Properties of Fuzzy Sets: a General Technique and its Use in Fuzzy Query Evaluation, *Fuzzy Sets and Systems*, vol. 38, pages. 137-152.
5. D. Dubois, H. Prade, C. Testemale (1988), Weighted fuzzy pattern matching. *Fuzzy Sets and Systems*, vol. 28, pages 315-331.

Fuzzy spatial data modeling: an extended bitmap approach

Jörg Verstraete and Guy De Tré and Axel Hallez

Dept. Telecommunications and Information processing, Ghent University
Sint-Pietersnieuwstraat 41, 9000 GENT, Belgium

Abstract

In this chapter, a technique for the modeling of a geographic region containing fuzzy information is presented. This technique is a raster technique, based on the existing concept of bitmaps in Geographic Information Systems. The fuzzy information modelled can consist of membership grades (to represent geographic fuzziness) and fuzzy numbers (to represent fuzzy values), and also type-2 fuzzy sets (to provide a richer model) and possibilistic truth values (i.e. to represent query-results). In each of the cases, the model is presented along with appropriate operators.

Key words: fuzzy spatial data, fuzzy bitmap

1. Introduction

One of the latest developments in Geographic Information Systems (or GIS for short), is adopting them to handle *uncertain* and *imprecise* information [13],[16],[21]. The core of a GIS is a database in which geospatial data (information on locations, i.e. the exact position of a house in a navigation system) and related attribute data (information that is related to a location, e.g. the temperature at the location or the house number itself) are stored. To model and manipulate the required data and to query the database in an adequate way, special data structures and operations are used. Commonly, the geographic information and the related attribute data are often obtained through measurements in the field, by extracting data from images (satellite or aerial) or by applying various sensing techniques [15]. As it is physically impossible to measure values or to record data on every square millimeter, the information is very prone to imprecision or uncertainty. Basically imprecision and uncertainty can occur (separately or combined) in two different contexts: either imprecision and/or uncertainty in the spatial domain, or imprecision and/or uncertainty concerning the attribute data themselves. The former occurs when the position of a known object (e.g. a house) is imprecise or uncertain; the latter occurs when attribute data of an object (e.g. a house number, it is between 60 and 70) is imprecise or uncertain. Hence, handling these cases of fuzziness and uncertainty more adequately logically leads to more general database models and has to provide for more flexible querying methods [5].

Generally, data in a GIS are stored in *layers*. Each layer contains one kind of information: i.e. the GIS could have a layer containing information about altitudes, another layer containing measured temperatures, etc. In order to answer a query, different kinds of information (thus stemming from different layers) may have to be combined; this operation is called *overlay*. Within a layer, there basically are two main approaches for modeling information [15], [17]: an *entity-based* approach and a *field based* approach. In an entity-based approach, objects and their locations are modeled (e.g. locations of houses, roads, ...) using basic geometric structures such as points, lines and regions (delimited by polygons). A lot of work has already been done in extending entity based approaches, often by using some form of contourlines to model vague regions [1],[2],[9],[10],[18]. These basically are regions with *undetermined boundaries*, or regions located at uncertain or imprecise positions. In a field based approach, *global* data — i.e. data that are present over the entire area under consideration — are modeled (e.g. temperatures, population densities, ...). For the modeling of this type of data, bitmaps, tesselations (both regular and irregular) and even halfplanes are commonly used. In [19], we presented a technique based on triangulated irregular networks to model fuzzy information in a field based approach.

In this chapter, the focus will be on field-based models; more specifically the bitmap technique that exists in GIS is adopted for the modeling of imprecision and/or uncertainty about the attribute data associated with points in the entire area of interest. The technique has however been adopted to model fuzzy entities as well.

2. Definition, notation and spatial representation

Representing field based data is possible with a bitmap approach, which retains information that is associated with a number of points, grouped in a *cell* of a *mesh* that covers the region of interest. Hence, the bitmap model is a kind of a discrete model, sometimes also called a *spatial resolution model*, where the considered tiles stem from the used partitioning.

Only bitmaps with rectangular cells are considered in this chapter but unlike in [20] the cells can differ in size (changes which are reflected in formulas as well). The presented extensions are also possible for regular bitmaps with e.g. hexagonal cells. The two dimensional space (limited by the map) is thus partitioned in a finite

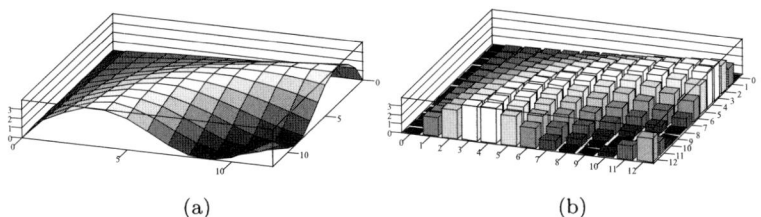

(a)   (b)

Fig. 1. geographically dependent values in continuous and bitmap representation.

number of cells. The size of the cells determines the *resolution* at which the data is to be modelled. Basically, a *cell* is a convex polygon, which can be defined by stating that all of the points of a line-segment connecting two points within the polygon are located inside the polygon.

A *grid* — in this context — is a collection of non-overlapping cells (i.e. their interiors are disjoint) that together cover the considered region U in the universe X. A cell thus has a dimension, but the attribute data values of all the points in the cell are represented by one single value associated with the cell. A grid is defined by

$$G = \{(c \subseteq X) | \forall c_1, c_2 \in G : c_1 \cap c_2 = \emptyset \wedge \bigcup_i c_i \in G = U, i = 1..T\} \quad (1)$$

where T is the total number of cells in the grid. The following explanation will be made by means of a regular two-dimensional $N \times M$ grid of rectangular cells or *pixels*. A cell has a location in the plane, consisting of the two coordinates n and m where $0 \leq n \leq N$ and $0 \leq m \leq M$, and will be denoted $c(n, m)$. A *bitmap* is defined as a set of cells, each representing an associated data value $B = (G, f)$

Using the Z-axis to represent the associated data value, a continuous three dimensional function can be visualized as shown in Fig. 1a. The bitmap structure B can be used to model a property dependent on a geographic location by approximating the property values in the associated data value of each cell, as shown on Fig. 1b. Examples of applications are the modeling of population densities, temperatures, recorded noise-levels, ... The bitmap structure as defined above is traditionally used to model crisp data. It does however allow for a number of extensions to accommodate fuzzy information.

3. Extended bitmap models: EBs

3.1. *EBs with membership grades*

In a first extension, the bitmap structure is adapted using membership grades. With every location (thus every cell in the bitmap model), a membership grade is associated. As the model requires values associated with every cell, it necessary to

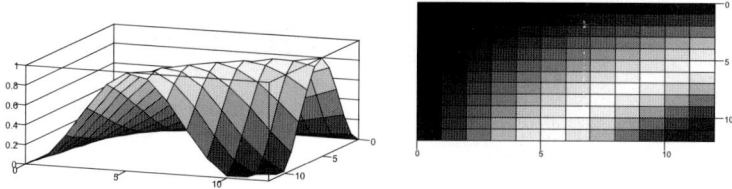

Fig. 2. sample function f_1.

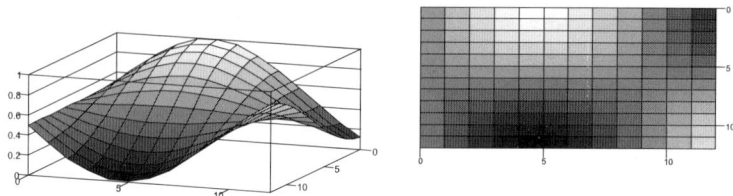

Fig. 3. sample function f_2.

include 0 as a possible value, hence the membership grades in the model are in the range $[0, 1]$. An extended bitmap with membership grades $\tilde{EB}$ is defined as

$$\tilde{EB} = \{(G, \mu_F\} \text{ where } \mu_F : G \to [0, 1], c \mapsto \mu_F(c), \forall c \in G \tag{2}$$

and represents the extent to which the property F is satisfied in cell c. This structure can be used to model properties regarding a geographic location, e.g. the property "near Ghent". A value 0 implies the cell is not considered to be "near Ghent", whereas e.g. a value 0.6 is considered to be more or less near Ghent (all values in $[0, 1]$ can occur). In a sense, this bitmap structure is a fuzzy set over a two-dimensional domain.

Suppose we have two different properties F_1 (e.g. "near Ghent") and F_2 (e.g. "alongside the river Schelde"), obtained by sample functions f_1 and f_2 as represented in Figs. 2 and 3; two extended bitmaps $\tilde{EB}_{F_1}$ resp. $\tilde{EB}_{F_2}$ are used to represent the grades μ_{F_1} and μ_{F_2} to which extent the properties are satisfied with respect to the considered area. Sometimes, data from the two EBs may need to be combined, for which any of the common aggregation operations (t-norms, t-conorms, ...) are applicable. An example of such a combination is "near Ghent and alongside the river Schelde".

Ideally, the extended bitmaps $\tilde{EB}_{F_1}$ and $\tilde{EB}_{F_2}$ should be based on the same grid and thus both should have the same resolution and size; otherwise one bitmap has to be approximated using the other bitmaps grid. For the sake of argumentation, the extended bitmaps $\tilde{EB}_{F_1}$ and $\tilde{EB}_{F_2}$ are considered to be based on the same grid and therefore both have the same resolution and size; they are defined as shown respectively in Fig. 2 and Fig. 3).

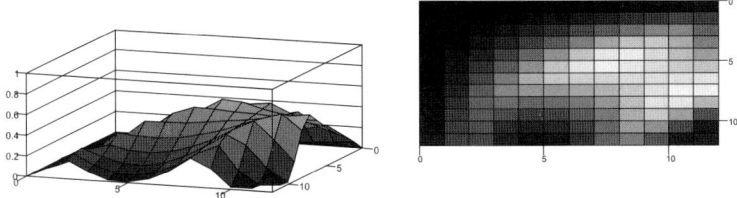

Fig. 4. minimum: min(f_1, f_2)

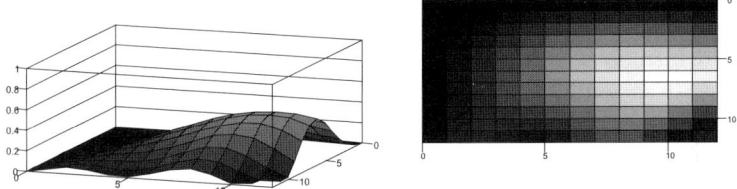

Fig. 5. product: $f_1 \times f_2$

The aggregation methods described here can be categorized as local [17] operations: the value of a cell in the result is only dependent on the value of the cells on the same position in the input. The operations and functions work cell by cell thus for an operator o and the cells $c_i \in \tilde{EB}_i$ this yields:

$$\mu_{F_3}(c_3(n,m)) = o(\mu_{F_1}(c_1(n,m)), \mu_{F_2}(c_2(n,m))) \qquad (3)$$

Considering the example of "near Ghent and alongside the river Schelde", a t-norm can be used to model the "and". In Fig. 4, the minimum operations on the two bitmap structures represented in Figs. 2 and 3 is illustrated. Likewise, in Fig. 5 the product of two bitmap structures is shown. Both the three dimensional ideal (continuous) solution and the related bitmap approximation are printed. The above definition allows for other t-norms as well as t-conorms or other operations to be used.

3.2. EBs with fuzzy numbers

Due to the simplicity of the bitmap-structure, the bitmap can easily be extended to represent more complex data. A very useful extension is the use of fuzzy numbers to represent the attribute data value per cell: e.g. this would also allow the modeling of approximate numerical data, which is beneficial for instance in the modeling of predictions or in the analysis of evolutions.

To achieve this, the modelled data — contained within the data field for every cell — are now extended from single values to fuzzy sets. It is important to notice that the co-domain $co(f)$ is the domain of the modelled values: in the definition of a bitmap, f maps a cell c onto an associated value $f(c)$. As a result, extending the associated value from a single value to a fuzzy set requires the fuzzy set to be defined on $co(f)$. The extended bitmap then is

$$\overline{EB} = (G, g) \text{ where } g : G \to \tilde{\wp}(co(f)), c \mapsto g(c), \forall c \in G \tag{4}$$

with $\tilde{\wp}(co(f))$ the powerset over $co(f)$, i.e. the set containing all fuzzy sets over the set $co(f)$. This association indicates that a fuzzy set is associated with the data field of each cell. For fuzzy numbers, the set $co(f)$ will be $\mathbb{R}$

There is a major conceptual difference between this extended bitmap model and the extended bitmap with membership grades as defined previously. Initially, geographic data was modeled using an extended bitmap with membership grades, which indicated e.g. a degree of similarity (or satisfaction) with regard to a given property F. In the extended bitmap with fuzzy numbers, there is a fuzzy set for every cell of the bitmap, which corresponds to the fuzzy number representing the attribute data value taken associated with the cell. This allows to express that the data value is cursed with imprecision, contained within the defined fuzzy set. This means that if a traditional operator op is used to combine that data from two bitmaps (with mapping functions g_1 and g_2), the resulting bitmap then is defined as:

$$\overline{EB} = \{(G, \tilde{op}(g_1, g_2))\} \tag{5}$$

where the operator op is extended using Zadeh's extension principle:

$$\mu_{\tilde{op}(g_1(c), g_2(c))}(x) = \begin{cases} \sup_{(x_1, x_2) \in op^{-1}(x)} \min\{\mu_{g_1(c)}(x_1), \mu_{g_2(c)}(x_2)\} \\ 0 \quad \text{if } op^{-1}(x) = \emptyset \end{cases} \tag{6}$$

where $x \in co(f)$.

Zadeh's extension principle is a point wise definition, which implies that it is directly applicable on the extended bitmap model (in essence a discrete model): calculations are performed cell by cell.

Every traditional mathematical operation that is extended, will work on a per cell basis. The model puts no constraints or limits on the membership functions that can be associated in a data field. One might opt for a triangular fuzzy set representation of the fuzzy numbers, or more generally a piece wise linear function representation, or perhaps even for other types of functions, but it doesn't impact the interpretation, nor the functionality of the bitmap.

This structure now permits the modeling of data such as e.g. temperature, but with imprecise or uncertain values. This also allows for a modeling of the uncertainty and/or imprecission associated with making predictions (e.g. about population densities).

3.3. EBs with type-2 fuzzy sets

In the previous section, the associated value in each cell has been represented by a fuzzy number. This approach can be used to generalize the EB-model with membershipgrades as presented in 3.1.

Intuitively, a type-2 fuzzy set can be defined as [11]: $\tilde{A} = (x, \mu_{\tilde{A}}(x)) \mid \forall x \in X$ in which $\mu_{\tilde{A}}(x)$ is a secondary membership function, defined as

$$\mu_{\tilde{A}}(x') = \int_{u \in J_{x'}} f_{x'}(u)/u \qquad (7)$$

where $J_{x'} \subseteq [0,1]$. This in turn means that $\tilde{A}$ can be expressed as

$$\tilde{A} = \int_{x \in X} \mu_{\tilde{A}}(x)/x = \int_{x \in X} [\int_{u \in J_x} f_x(u)/u]/x \qquad (8)$$

where $J_x \subseteq [0,1]$

Incorporating type-2 fuzzy sets in the bitmap-model appears very similar to the extension towards fuzzy numbers, yet there is a huge difference in meaning and interpretation. Type-2 fuzzy sets are a generalization of regular fuzzy sets [11],[12], in that they permit imprecision as well as uncertainty regarding the membership grades to be modeled. The example for EBs with membership grades in section 3.1 concerned the proposition "near Ghent". However, when describing the whereabouts of a person, there might be doubt on where he/she is located. The person could be located near Ghent, but also near Brussels. A type-2 fuzzy set allows this doubt to be modeled. As a result, in this approach, the membership grade associated with a cell is extended to a fuzzy set over the domain $[0,1]$. The extended bitmap with type-2 fuzzy sets is then defined as

$$\overline{\tilde{B}} = (G, g) \text{ where } g : G \to \tilde{\wp}([0,1]) \mapsto g(c), \forall c \in G \qquad (9)$$

A similar notation as before is used, with $\tilde{\wp}([0,1])$ being the set of all fuzzy sets over the interval $[0,1]$.

The various set-theoretic operators are defined by Mendel in [12], the maximum operation is used for the union and a general t-norm ($\star$) is used for the intersection (instead of the minimum). Consider two type-2 fuzzy sets $\tilde{A}$ and $\tilde{B}$:

$$\tilde{A} = \int_X \mu_{\tilde{A}}(x)/x = \int_X \int_{u \in J_x^u} f_x(u)/u \qquad (10)$$

where $J_x^u \subseteq [0,1]$ and

$$\tilde{B} = \int_X \mu_{\tilde{B}(x)}/x = \int_X \int_{w \in J_x^w} g_x(w)/w \qquad (11)$$

where $J_x^w \subseteq [0,1]$. The union of these two type-2 fuzzy sets can be defined as:

$$\tilde{A} \cup \tilde{B} = \int_X \mu_{\tilde{A} \cup \tilde{B}}/x = \int_{u \in J_x^u} \int_{w \in J_x^w} f_x(u) \star g_x(w)/v \qquad (12)$$

where $v = u \cup w$. In a completely analog matter, the intersection can be defined as:

$$\tilde{A} \cap \tilde{B} = \int_X \mu_{\tilde{A} \cap \tilde{B}}/x = \int_{u \in J_x^u} \int_{w \in J_x^w} f_x(u) \star g_x(w)/v \qquad (13)$$

where $v = u \cap w$. Following the same approach, the complement operator is then defined as:

$$\overline{\tilde{A}} = \int_X \mu_{\overline{\tilde{A}}}/x = \int_{u \in J_x^u} f_x(u)/(1-u) \qquad (14)$$

Apart from these set-theoretic operations on type-2 fuzzy sets, algebraic operations on type-1 fuzzy numbers have also been defined. As it extends beyond the scope of this paper, we refer to [12] for these definitions.

The above definitions for the operators on type-2 fuzzy sets are easily applicable in the bitmap model: the discrete domain of the bitmaps facilitates both the adaptation of the theoretical calculations as well as the implementations.

3.4. *EBs based on possibilistic truth values*

In the previous section, the extended bitmap structure was presented for the representation of goegraphical data (membership grades, fuzzy numbers or fuzzy membership grades).

These sections concerned the modeling of data (e.g. for storage in the database). Introducing fuzziness in the database also impacts the evaluation of queries. In traditional crisp systems, a query condition (e.g. "temperature is more than 30 °C" evaluates to either true or false for any given crips data. However, when the model is enriched to contain fuzzy numbers, the standard boolean turns out to be insufficiant. If the temperature is expressed by a fuzzy number (e.g. to model between 26 °C and 32 °C, the truth of the condition when this value is used is no longer true or false. Furthermore, there is an interest toward using natural language queries (using propositions like "warm", "high temperature", ... where this linguistic term is defined by means of a fuzzy set). As a result, there must be a mechanism present to determine the extent to which a value (e.g. "between 26 °C and 32 °C") is considered to mach a given fuzzy set (e.g. a set describing the linguistic term "warm", or the crisp value "30 °C").

There are a various approaches to indicate degrees of truth [14] [6]: membership grades, possibility measures and possibilistic truth values [3],[4],[8] can be used. The latter case will be explained in further detail. Possibilistic truth values indicate the truth by means of two values: a degree to indicate the extent to which a proposition is true, and a degree to indicate the extent to which the same proposition is false. In order to define possibilistic truth values, the set $\tilde{\wp}(I)$ of all fuzzy sets over the universe $I = \{T, F\}$ is considered (where T represents true and F represents false). A possibilistic truth value is associated with every location. The traditional truth value t of a proposition p, element of a set of propositions P is defined as $t : P \rightarrow I, p \mapsto t(p)$ The possibilistic truth value (or PTV) $\tilde{t}(p)$ of a proposition $p \in P$ is defined by means of the mapping function $\tilde{t}$

$$\tilde{t} : P \rightarrow \tilde{\wp}(I), p \mapsto \tilde{t}(p) \tag{15}$$

With each $p \in P$ a fuzzy set $\tilde{t}(p)$ is associated; the semantics of this associated fuzzy set are defined in terms of a possibility distribution Π:

$$\forall x \in I : \Pi_{t(p)}(x) = \mu_{\tilde{t}(p)}(x) \tag{16}$$

i.e.

$$\forall p \in P : \Pi_{t(p)} = \tilde{t}(p) \tag{17}$$

Using possibilistic truth values, the bitmap can hence be extended to

$$\overline{EB} = (G, g) \text{ where } g : G \rightarrow \tilde{\wp}(\{T, F\}), c \mapsto g(c), \forall c \in G \tag{18}$$

with $\tilde{\wp}(\{T, F\})$ the powerset of $\{T, F\}$, i.e. the set containing all fuzzy sets over $\{T, F\}$.

Hence cell-wise, a possibilistic truth value is associated with the attribute data value to express the degree of truth regarding the value associated with a cell in an query-expression.

The operator to compare a possibility distribution with a fuzzy set is the IS operator; it is of the form A IS L and returns a possibilistic truth value, indicating the extent to which the value of a property A (e.g. temperature), represented by a possibility distribution, matches a linguistic term L (e.g. "warm"), represented by a fuzzy set. A can therefor be either a crisp a fuzzy number, as presented in the previous sections. A IS L will yield a possibilistic truth value for which

$$\mu_{\tilde{t}(A \text{ IS } L)}(T) = \sup_{x \in dom(A)} \min(\pi_A(x), \mu_L(x)) \tag{19}$$

$$\mu_{\tilde{t}(A \text{ IS } L)}(F) = \sup_{x \in dom(A)} \min(\pi_A(x), 1 - \mu_L(x)) \tag{20}$$

Apart from the IS operator, common logical operators are needed. For PTVs, the rule for conjunction is $\forall p, q \in P : \tilde{t}(pANDq) = \tilde{t}(p) \tilde{\wedge} \tilde{t}(q)$ where

$$\tilde{\wedge} : \tilde{\wp}(I) \times \tilde{\wp}(I) \rightarrow \tilde{\wp}(I), (\tilde{U}, \tilde{V}) \mapsto \tilde{U} \tilde{\wedge} \tilde{V} \tag{21}$$

is defined by applying Zadeh's extension principle to the operator $\wedge$:

$$\mu_{\tilde{U} \tilde{\wedge} \tilde{V}}(T) = min(\mu_{\tilde{U}}(T), \mu_{\tilde{V}}(T))$$

and

$$\mu_{\tilde{U} \tilde{\wedge} \tilde{V}}(F) = max \begin{pmatrix} min(\mu_{\tilde{U}}(T), \mu_{\tilde{V}}(F)) \\ min(\mu_{\tilde{U}}(F), \mu_{\tilde{V}}(T)) \\ min(\mu_{\tilde{U}}(F), \mu_{\tilde{V}}(F)) \end{pmatrix}$$

Similarly, the disjunction, negation and other operators can be defined [6]. Sometimes it is more useful to use alterative definitions for these operators, as presented in [7].

Every cell will now have a possibilistic truth value associated with it, as defined above. The other operations (conjunction, disjunction, ...) on possibilistic truth values can also be defined on a per cell basis to suit the bitmap model. Again, the PTVs can be extended to extended possibilistic truth values [6], by using the domain $\{T, F, \perp\}$ instead of $\{T, F\}$, where $\perp$ means undefined and is used if the proposition is inapplicable. The EBs with PTVs are not intended for storage within the database; this structure is mainly intended for representing (intermediate or final) query results.

4. Conclusion

The bitmap structure adopted as described above is suitable for many purposes, both in modeling fuzzy data as in representing results from a fuzzy query (be it on crisp or fuzzy data). Various operations can easily be defined; the translation from the theoretical definitions to implementations proves also to be straightforward. A downside from a practical point of view is that bitmap models require large amounts of data to be accurate. Bitmaps can be used to approximate a continuous model (e.g. based on triangulated irregular networks [19]) for implementation purposes: new operations can be tried faster as the bitmap model allows easier definitions. Visualizing an extended bitmap with membership grades is relatively easily accomplished (e.g. using colours or a third dimension); visualizing an extended bitmap with fuzzy numbers, type-2 fuzzy sets or PTVs is far more challenging, as there basically are four dimensions to be dealt with: two coordinates, a modeled value and its membership grades (i.e. a membership function) per cell.

References

1. Clementini E., Di Felice P.; An algebraic model for spatial objects with undetermined boundaries; 1994; GISDATA Specialist Meeting - revised version.
2. Cohn A. G., Gotts N. M.; Spatial regions with undetermined boundaries; 1994; Proc. of the Second ACM Workshop on Advances in Geographic Information Systems; pages 52–59.
3. de Cooman, G.; Towards a possiblistic logic; 1995; Fuzzy set theory and advanced mathematical applications, Ruan D. Kluwer Academic publishers, pages 89–133.

4. de Cooman, G.; From possibilistic information to Kleene's strong multi-valued logics; 1999; Fuzzy sets, logics and reasoning about knowledge
5. De Tré G., De Caluwe R., Hallez A., Verstraete J.; Fuzzy and Uncertain Spatio-Temporal Database Models: A Constraint-Based Approach; 2002; Proc. of the Conference IPMU 2002, July 1-5, Annecy, France; pp. 1713-1720.
6. De Tré G.; 2002 Extended Possibilistic Truth Values; International Journal of Intelligent Systems, volume 17, no. 4, April 2002, Wiley Publishers, pages 427–446.
7. De Tré G., Hallez A., Verstraete J., Verkeyn A.; 2002; Beyond Conjucative Aggregation of Possibilistic Truth Values in Database Systems; The Seventh Meeting of the EURO Working Group on Fuzzy Sets; pages 137–142.
8. Dubois D., Prade H.; 2001; Possibility theory, probability theory and multiple-valued logics: A clarification. *Annals of Mathematics and Artificial Intelligence*, volume 32, pages 35–66.
9. Gotts N. M., Cohn A. G.; 1995; A mereological approach to representing spatial vagueness; Working Papers, Ninth International Workshop on Qualitative Reasoning; pages 246–255.
10. Hallez A., Verstraete J., De Tré G., De Caluwe R.; 2002; Contourline Based Modelling of Vague Regions; Proc. of the Conference IPMU 2002, July 1-5, Annecy, France.
11. Klir G. J., Yuan B.; 1995; Fuzzy sets and fuzzy logic: Theory and applications; New Jersey: Prentice Hall.
12. Mendel J. M.; 2001; Uncertain Rule-Based Fuzzy Logic Systems, Introduction and New Directions. Prenctice Hall PTR.
13. Morris A.; Why Spatial Databases Need Fuzziness; 2001; Proc. of Nafips 2001; pages 2446–2451.
14. Prade H.; Possibility sets, fuzzy sets and their relation to Lukasiewicz logic; In: Proc 12th Int Symp on Multiple-Valued Logic,; 1982; pages 223–227.
15. Rigaux P., Scholl M., Voisard A.; 2002; Spatial Databases with Applications to GIS. Morgan Kaufman Publishers.
16. Schneider M.; 1999; Uncertainty management for spatial data in databases : fuzzy spatial data types; 6th Int. Symp. on Advances in Spatial Databases (SSD), LNCS 1651, Springer Verlag; pages 330–351.
17. Shekhar S., Chawla S.; 2003; Spatial Databases: A tour; Pearson Education Inc.
18. Vertraete J., Van Der Cruyssen B., De Caluwe R.; 2000; Assigning Membership Degrees to Points of Fuzzy Boundaries: In *Proc. of the Conference NAFIPS 2000*, pages 444–447.
19. Verstraete J., De Tré G., Hallez A.; 2002; Adapting TIN-layers to Represent Fuzzy Geographic Information; The Seventh Meeting of the EURO Working Group on Fuzzy Sets; pages 57–62.
20. Verstraete J., De Caluse R., De Tré G., Hallez A.; Bitmap techniques for the modeling of fuzzy spatial data; In *Proc. of the 10th International Conference IPMU 2004*; pages 19–26
21. Zimmerman H-J.; 1999; Practical Applications of Fuzzy Technologies; Kluwer Academic Publishers.

Introducing λ-Specialization into the Fuzzy EER Model

Guoqing Chen, Ling Lin and Xunhua Guo

School of Economics and Management, Tsinghua University,
Beijing, China

Abstract

The entity-relationship (ER) model and its extensions (EER) have been widely used as conceptual models in database design and business modeling. In recent years fuzzy EER models have attracted attention of researchers, aimed at enriching semantics and dealing with uncertainty. This paper further extends the notions of total and partial specializations by introducing λ-specialization so as to reflect degrees of participation constraints in a gradual manner. In doing so, a general form of λ-specialization is proposed, along with a few specific forms with various fuzzy operators. Moreover, related semantics and properties are discussed.

Keywords: Fuzzy EER Model, λ-Specialization, Participation Constraint.

1. Introduction

The entity-relationship (ER) model, initially proposed in 1976 [3], is a powerful means for business and data modeling that helps identify essential elements of the domains of interest in a conceptual and integrated manner. The ER model describes the real world in terms of entities, relationships and attributes. This methodology had itself evolved considerably and rapidly became widely accepted as a standard design tool for relational databases. During the past decades, both practitioners and academics had been working with the application and development of the ER model and a number of new concepts have been introduced [4, 6, 9-10]. Some of the efforts gave rise to the so-called enhanced (or extended) entity-relationship (EER) models, which incorporates such notions as subclass/superclass, specialization/generalization, inheritance, aggregation, etc. [9-10]. These extensions are deemed important in enriching ER/EER models' expressiveness and usefulness for describing the real world conceptually.

To model uncertainty and imprecision inherent in reality, Zvieli and Chen [13] applied fuzzy logic [12] to some of the basic ER concepts, followed by several attempts on fuzzy ER/EER model (e.g., [1-2, 5, 7-8, 11]). A series of efforts have been made by Chen and Kerre since 1998 [1-2], resulting in fuzzy extensions of the important EER concepts including superclass/subclass, inheritance, generalization/specialization, shared subclass, category and constraints.

Specialization is the focal point of this paper. As an example, Figure 1 shows a superclass Employee with two specializations; both are attribute-based with one being conventional and the other being fuzzy. Notably, subclasses EmployeeWithBachelor(EB), EmployeeWithMaster (EM) and EmployeeWith Doctor (ED) are the result of specialization of Employee based on crisp values (Bachelor, Master, and Doctor) of attribute Degree-earned, while subclasses YoungEmployee (YE), MiddleAgedEmployee (ME), and OldEmployee (OE) are the result of specialization of Employee based on fuzzy values (Young, Middle-Aged, and Old) of attribute Age.

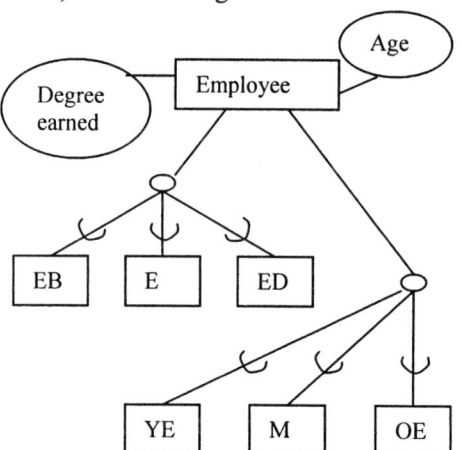

Figure 1. Specializations in a fuzzy EER model.

In the fuzzy EER model [1-2], the degrees to which an entity instance e belongs to a superclass (e.g., E) and to a subclass (e.g., E_i) are denoted as μ_E and μ_{Ei}. Generally, both μ_E and μ_{Ei} fall in [0, 1], and $\forall e, \mu_{Ei}(e) \leq \mu_E(e)$. Detailed treatments of how an entity type is generalized have been discussed by Chen and Kerre [2]. It has been proved that conventional specialization is a special case of fuzzy specialization.

Moreover, in terms of participation constraints, a specialization is called total if all the entities with nonzero membership in the superclass also have nonzero membership in at least one of its subclasses. Otherwise, the specialization is called partial. Such constraints are a kind of business rules and usually need to be modeled and enforced [2].

The target of this paper is set to extend such two-valued constraints to a more general setting so as to reflect the degrees of membership in related super/subclasses. Accordingly, λ- specialization will be introduced, where λ can be regarded as the strength of participation of entities in the specialization concerned, $\lambda \in [0, 1]$.

2. λ-specialization

The traditional ER model consists of three basic concepts, namely entity, relationship and attribute. An ER model M can be denoted as $M=(E, R, A)$, in which E, R, A are sets of entity types, relationship types, and attributes, respectively. An entity type E in an ER model is an element of E, namely $E \in E$. At the same time, E is a set of entity instances [3]. In an EER model, E_i is a subclass of E, if and only if $\forall e \in E_i$, $e \in E$. The process of classifying the entities in E into several subclasses $E_1, E_2 ... E_n$ is called specialization. A specialization is total if $\forall e \in E, \exists i$, s.t. $e \in E_i$, and partial otherwise [9, 10].

In the fuzzy ER/EER model, the degree to which an entity instance e belongs to an entity type E is represented as $\mu_E(e)$, $\mu_E(e) \in [0, 1]$. E is the superclass of E_i and E_i is the subclass of E if and only if $\forall e$, $\mu_{Ei}(e) \leq \mu_E(e)$. A specialization is total if $\forall e$ with $\mu_E(e) > 0$, $\exists E_i$ such that $\mu_{Ei}(e) > 0$; partial otherwise.

With this setting, we do not distinguish the magnitude of the degrees as long as they are nonzero. Concretely, for example, suppose there are three specializations, each of which comprises two subclasses. The membership of the entities is shown in Table 1, where it can be inspected that both specializations I and II are total, though the membership degrees differ significantly. Meanwhile, specialization III is partial, but it is more similar to specialization II than to specialization I.

Table 1. Examples of specializations

Specialization I				Specialization II			
Entities	$\mu_E(e)$	$\mu_{E1}(e)$	$\mu_{E2}(e)$	Entities	$\mu_E(e)$	$\mu_{E1}(e)$	$\mu_{E2}(e)$
e_1	1	1	1	e_1	1	0.1	0.1
e_2	1	1	1	e_2	1	0.1	0.1
...	...	...	...	...	...	...	...
e_n	1	1	1	e_n	1	0.1	0.1

Specialization III			
Entities	$\mu_E(e)$	$\mu_{E1}(e)$	$\mu_{E2}(e)$
e_1	1	0.1	0.1
e_2	1	0.1	0.1
...	...	...	...
e_{k-1}	1	0.1	0.1
e_k	*1*	*0*	*0*
e_{k+1}	1	0.1	0.1
...	...	...	...
e_n	1	0.1	0.1

Note that the traditional total specialization can be represented as the truth value of the proposition: if $\forall e$, $e \in E$ then $\exists i$, s.t. $e \in E_i$. From a logic point of view, in the fuzzy context, $e \in E$ and $e \in E_i$ can both be modeled with degrees such as $\mu_E(e)$ and $\mu_{Ei}(e)$ in [0, 1]. Thus, fuzzy implication operators may play an important role in the setting for λ-specialization.

Definition 1: The degree of strength that an entity e participates in a specialization is defined as $\lambda(e) = \mu_E(e) \rightarrow (\mu_{E1}(e) \vee \mu_{E2}(e) \vee ... \vee \mu_{En}(e))$, where $\mu_E(e)$ is the membership degree of e in superclass E, $\mu_{Ei}(e)$ is the membership degree of e in subclass E_i ($i = 1, 2, ..., n$), $\rightarrow$ is a fuzzy implication operator, and $\vee$ is a disjunction operator. The degree of specialization is then $\wedge_e(\lambda(e))$, where $\wedge$ is a conjunction operator. A specialization is called a λ-specialization if the degree of the specialization equals λ, i.e., $\lambda = \wedge_e(\lambda(e))$.

Apparently, total specialization is 1-specialization, and partial specialization is 0-specialization.

Definition 1 provides a general form of λ-specialization. Specific forms can be obtained when specific operators are used. As an example, with $x \wedge y = \min(x, y)$, $x \vee y = \max(x, y)$ and $x \rightarrow y = \max(1-x, y)$, in Table 1, the degree of specialization II is $\min_e (1 \rightarrow \max (0.1, 0.1, ... 0.1)) = \min_e(\max(1-1, 0.1)) = 0.1$.

In database modeling, a threshold for the specialization degree λ_0 can be set by experts or users as a participation constraint so that database updates can only be allowed when the constraint is satisfied.

Definition 2: A specialization satisfies λ_0-constraint iff $\lambda \geq \lambda_0$.

Note that here the threshold λ_0 is an extensional parameter whose value is set specifically with domain knowledge when modeling, while the degree of specialization λ is intentional and can be calculated from the entity membership values.

Graphically, λ_0-constraint can be represented by marking λ_0 alongside of the line of specialization. For example, a 0.8-constraint is represented as shown in Figure 2.

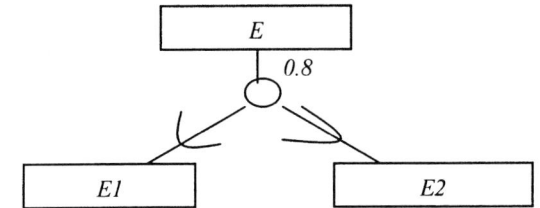

Figure 2. Graphic representation of 0.8-specialization.

If a specialization satisfies λ_1-constraint, and $\lambda_1 > \lambda_2$, then such a specialization also satisfies λ_2-constraint.

3. Specific forms of λ-specialization

Different fuzzy implication operators (FIOs) used in $\lambda(e)$ will result in different forms of λ-specialization. In choosing FIOs, the following properties are required to be held:

1) $I(1, 0) = 0$ (The degree to which an entity participates in a specialization is the lowest when its membership degree in the superclass is the highest and that in the subclasses is the lowest);

2) $I(a, 1) = 1$ (The degree to which an entity participates in a specialization is the highest when its membership degree in the subclasses is the highest);

3) $I(a, \bullet)$ is decreasing (with respect to a) and $I(\bullet, b)$ is increasing (with respect to b).

Hereby we examine three FIOs that are commonly used with the above properties. Concretely, minimum for conjunction, three FIOs namely Gödel, Kleene-Dienes, and Lukasiewicz, and maximum and Lukasiewicz for disjunction are discussed for calculating $\lambda(e)$. As a result, the combinations of these operators lead to six specific forms, as shown in Tables 2 and 3.

Table 2. Different operators' combinations.

	Implication	Disjunction
1	$I_1(a,b) = \begin{cases} 1, a \leq b \\ b, a > b \end{cases}$	$D_1(a, b) = \max(a, b)$
2	$I_1(a,b) = \begin{cases} 1, a \leq b \\ b, a > b \end{cases}$	$D_2(a, b) = \min(1, a+b)$

3	$I_2(a, b) = \max(1-a, b)$	$D_1(a, b) = \max(a, b)$
4	$I_2(a, b) = \max(1-a, b)$	$D_2(a, b) = \min(1, a+b)$
5	$I_3(a, b) = \min(1, 1-a+b)$	$D_1(a, b) = \max(a, b)$
6	$I_3(a, b) = \min(1, 1-a+b)$	$D_2(a, b) = \min(1, a+b)$

Table 3 Combinations and degrees of strength.

	$\lambda(e)$
1	$\lambda(e) = \begin{cases} 1, \max_i \mu_{Ei}(e) = \mu_E(e) \\ \max_i \mu_{Ei}(e), \max_i \mu_{Ei}(e) < \mu_E(e) \end{cases}$
2	$\lambda(e) = \begin{cases} 1, \sum_i \mu_{Ei}(e) \geq \mu_E(e) \\ \sum_i \mu_{Ei}(e), \sum_i \mu_{Ei}(e) < \mu_E(e) \end{cases}$
3	$\lambda(e) = \max(1 - \mu_E(e), \max_i \mu_{Ei}(e))$
4	$\lambda(e) = \max(1 - \mu_E(e), \min(1, \sum_i \mu_{Ei}(e)))$
5	$\lambda(e) = 1 - \mu_E(e) + \max_i \mu_{Ei}(e))$
6	$\lambda(e) = \min(1, 1 - \mu_E(e) + \sum_i \mu_{Ei}(e))$

It can be seen that total and partial specializations can be represented as special cases of the proposed extensions. For example, for specific form 1, we have

$$\forall e \in E, \max_i \mu_{Ei}(e) = \mu_E(e) = 1, \text{ so } \lambda = 1 \qquad (1)$$

It can be proved that $\lambda = 1$ also holds for other specific forms. For traditional partial specialization, we have $\exists e_0$, $\mu_E(e_0) = 1$ and $\mu_{E1}(e) = \mu_{E2}(e) = ... = \mu_{En}(e) = 0$. In specific form 1, we have $\forall e \in E, \max_i \mu_{Ei}(e_0) = 0 < \mu_E(e_0) = 1$, so $\lambda \leq \lambda(e_0) = 0$. It can also be proved that $\lambda = 0$ in other forms.

3.1. Semantics

Different forms of λ-specialization reflect different semantics and constraints. Let us discuss them with an example. In a market research on the IT services industry, IT services vendors are classified into hardware services vendors, software services vendors and IT consulting companies. The membership degree of a vendor belonging to a particular subclass may be determined in various ways, say, by domain experts, or for instance, it may be determined partly with information about revenues gained in proportion in the industry concerned. The fuzzy EER model for the IT services industry is shown in Figure 3.

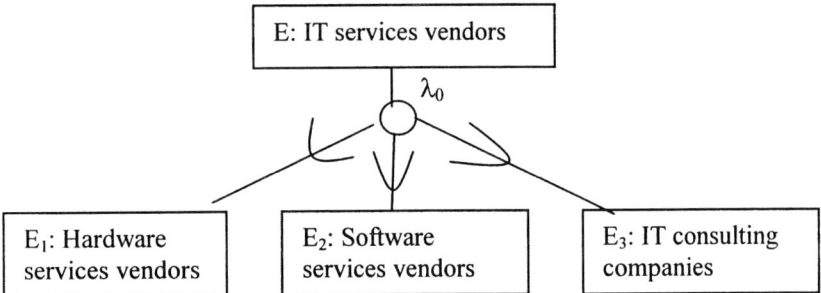

Figure 3. IT services vendors.

Given a threshold λ_0, when Lukasiewicz disjunction and implication and the conjunction minimum are chosen, we have

$$\forall e, \; \lambda(e) = \min(1, \; 1-\mu_E(e)+\Sigma_i\mu_{Ei}(e)) \geq \lambda_0 \qquad (2)$$

which means that, for instance, for each vendor, the sum of the revenue from each submarket must be close to the total revenue of IT services. If for each vendor the sum of the revenue from all the submarkets is equal to the total IT services revenue, it can be inferred that the subclasses considered in the specialization have covered all the IT services completely, so $\lambda(e)=1$. Otherwise the degree of specialization has to be decided according to the difference between the two:

$$\lambda = \min_e(\min(1,1-(\mu_E(e)-\Sigma_i\mu_{Ei}(e)))) \qquad (3)$$

Generally speaking, for the disjunction operators, maximum focuses on the maximal membership in all the subclasses, expressing the semantics such as "the *best* performance of the vendors in the submarkets must achieve a certain level (higher than the threshold)". While Lukasiewicz disjunction considers the sum of the membership, expressing the semantics such as "the *total* revenue must achieve a certain level".

For FIOs, Gödel implication requires that for each entity the membership in the subclasses should be above either λ_0 or the membership in the superclass. Kleene-Dienes implication represents the semantics that only the entities with membership higher than $1-\lambda_0$ in the superclass are needed to have their membership higher than λ_0 in the subclasses. In the IT services example, it can express that a *leading* IT services vendor must have a *good* performance in the three submarkets. The Lukasiewicz implication requires the difference between the membership in the superclass and that in the subclasses to be as little as possible.

Therefore, in real world applications, different specific forms may be chosen depending on the problems at hand in consideration of semantics to express and constraints to enforce.

3.2. Properties

Definition 3: Let F_1 and F_2 be two specific forms of λ-specialization with the degrees λ_1 and λ_2 respectively. Then F_1 is called stricter than F_2 if $\lambda_1 \leq \lambda_2$.

Apparently, if F_1 is stricter than F_2, then for a given threshold λ_0, if F_1 satisfies λ_0-constraint then so is F_2.

Suppose specific forms in Table 2 and 3 are $F_1, F_2, \ldots, F_6$ respectively, and the degree of F_i is λ_i, $i = 1, 2, \ldots 6$. We have

$$\forall e, \max(1-\mu_E(e), \max_i \mu_{Ei}(e)) \leq \min(1, 1-\mu_E(e)+\Sigma_i \mu_{Ei}(e)) \quad (4)$$

That is, $\lambda_3 \leq \lambda_6$, which means that F_3 is stricter than F_6. Similarly, it can be proved that $\lambda_3 \leq \lambda_4 \leq \lambda_6$, $\lambda_3 \leq \lambda_5 \leq \lambda_6$ and $\lambda_1 \leq \lambda_2 \leq \lambda_6$.

Since λ-specialization is a fuzzy extension to the traditional definition of total/partial specialization, it must preserve the semantics and properties in the traditional model. Such preservation of semantics and properties will be discussed as follows.

Similar to that in the traditional model, it is desirable that if for each entity e, there exists a subclass in which the membership of e is the same as in the superclass, the specialization degree must be at the highest level, i.e. $\lambda=1$. Specific forms 1, 2, 5 and 6 in Table 2 and 3 preserve this property, i.e. $\lambda=1$ if $\forall e$, $\max_i \mu_{Ei}(e)=\mu_E(e)$.

On the other hand, the specialization is partial in the traditional cases if there exists an entity in the superclass whose membership in all of the subclass is zero. In the fuzzy context of λ-specialization, only specific forms 1 and 2 in Table 2 and 3 possess this property, i.e. $\lambda=0$ if $\exists e$, $\max_i \mu_{Ei}(e_0)=0$. In the other forms, $\lambda = \min_e(1-\mu_E(e))$, if $\exists e$, $\max_i \mu_{Ei}(e_0) = 0$. The semantics in the latter case can be interpreted as "the total specialization constraint can be relaxed for the entities which partially belong to the superclass".

Particularly, in F_3, since $\max(1-\mu_E(e), \max_i \mu_{Ei}(e)) \geq \lambda_0$, we have $\mu_E(e) \leq 1-\lambda_0$ or $\mu_E(e) \geq \max_i \mu_{Ei}(e) \geq \lambda_0$, so when $\lambda_0 > 0.5$, for those entities whose membership in the superclass is in the interval $[1-\lambda_0, \lambda_0]$, the constraint will never be satisfied no matter what the membership in the subclasses is.

Suppose $S_1=\{E, (E_1, E_2, \ldots, E_m, F_1, F_2, \ldots, F_n)\}$ and $S_2=\{E, (F_1, F_2, \ldots, F_n, G_1, G_2, \ldots, G_k)\}$ are two specializations with the same superclass E, and $E_1, E_2, \ldots, E_m$, $F_1, F_2, \ldots, F_n, G_1, G_2, \ldots, G_k$ are subclasses, where $F_1, F_2, \ldots, F_n$ are the common subclasses of S_1 and S_2. Let $S_1 \cup S_2 = \{E, (E_1, E_2, \ldots, E_m, F_1, F_2, \ldots, F_n, G_1, G_2, \ldots, G_k)\}$. In the traditional model, if one of S_1 and S_2 is total, then for each entity e in the superclass E, e belongs to one of $E_1, E_2, \ldots, E_m, F_1, F_2, \ldots, F_n, G_1, G_2, \ldots, G_k$, hence $S_1 \cup S_2$ must be total too. If $S_1 \cup S_2$ is partial, then there exists such an entity e_0 that none of $E_1, E_2, \ldots, E_m, F_1, F_2, \ldots, F_n, G_1, G_2, \ldots, G_k$ contains e_0, therefore S_1 and S_2 are both partial. So it can be concluded that $\lambda[S_1 \cup S_2] \geq \lambda[S_1] \vee \lambda[S_2]$, where $\lambda[S_1 \cup S_2], \lambda[S_1], \lambda[S_2]$ are specialization degrees of $S_1 \cup S_2, S_1$ and S_2 respectively.

In the fuzzy model, such a property is held by specific forms 1, 3 and 5. Taking specific form 1 for example, we will provide a brief proof as follows.

Proof:

For specialization $S = \{E, (E_1, E_2, ..., E_n)\}$, let $S^i = \{E, (E_i)\}$, $i = 1, 2, ..., n$.

For each $e \in E$, if there exists such an i that $\mu_{Ei}(e) = \mu_E(e)$, then $\lambda[S^i](e) = 1$ and $\max_i \mu_{Ei}(e) = \mu_E(e)$, therefore $\lambda[S](e) = 1$, so $\lambda[S](e) = \max_i \lambda[S^i](e)$;

Otherwise, if for each i, $\mu_{Ei}(e) < \mu_E(e)$, then $\lambda[S^i](e) = \mu_{Ei}(e)$ and $\max_i \mu_{Ei}(e) < \mu_E(e)$, therefore $\lambda[S](e) = \max_i \mu_{Ei}(e) = \max_i \lambda[S^i](e)$.

So it can be concluded that $\forall e \in E$, $\lambda[S](e) = \max_i \lambda[S^i](e)$.

For $S_1 = \{E, (E_1, E_2, ..., E_m, F_1, F_2, ..., F_n)\}$, we have:
$\lambda[S_1](e) = \max (\lambda[\{E, E_1)\}](e), \lambda[\{E, (E_2)\}](e), ..., \lambda[\{E, (E_n)\}](e),$
$\lambda[\{E, (F_1)\}](e), \lambda[\{E, (F_2)\}](e), ..., \lambda[\{E, (F_m)\}](e))$.

Similarly,
$\lambda[S_2](e) = \max (\lambda[\{E, (F_1)\}](e), \lambda[\{E, (F_2)\}](e), ..., \lambda[\{E, (F_m)\}](e),$
$\lambda[\{E, (G_1)\}](e), \lambda[\{E, (G_2)\}](e), ..., \lambda[\{E, (G_k)\}](e))$.

$\lambda[S_1 \cup S_2](e) = \max (\lambda[\{E, (E_1)\}](e), \lambda[\{E, (E_2)\}](e), ..., \lambda[\{E, (E_n)\}](e),$
$\lambda[\{E, (F_1)\}](e), \lambda[\{E, (F_2)\}](e), ..., \lambda[\{E, (F_m)\}](e),$
$\lambda[\{E, (G_1)\}](e), \lambda[\{E, (G_2)\}](e), ..., \lambda[\{E, (G_k)\}](e))$

So $\lambda[S_1 \cup S_2](e) = \max (\lambda[S_1](e), \lambda[S_2](e))$, and
$\lambda[S_1 \cup S_2] = \min_e \lambda[S_1 \cup S_2](e) = \min_e \max(\lambda[S_1](e), \lambda[S_2](e))$
$\geq \max (\min_e \lambda[S_1](e), \min_e \lambda[S_2](e)) = \max (\lambda[S_1], \lambda[S_1])$,

the "=" holds if and only if $\forall e$, $\lambda[S_1](e) = \lambda[S_2](e)$.

Note that all the three specific forms 1, 3 and 5 take "max" as the conjunction.

4. The impact of λ-specialization on database updates

In the traditional EER model, the constraints will affect database maintenance when updating data. With total specialization, an entity must be inserted into at least one subclass if it is inserted into the superclass; an entity must be deleted from the superclass or inserted into another subclass if it is deleted from a subclass and does not belong to any other subclass. In the setting of λ-specialization, a change in the entity membership between nonzero values will cause a change in the degree of specialization; hence the updating strategy will be different. It is important to note that in each specific form, the specialization degree λ is a non-increasing function of the membership in the superclass $\mu_E(e)$, and a non-decreasing function of the membership in the subclasses $\mu_{Ei}(e)$. So the strategy for update is:

1. When the membership of an entity in the superclass increases, making the degree of specialization lower than the threshold λ_0, the membership in one or more of the subclasses must be increased accordingly.

2. When the membership of an entity in one of the subclasses decreases, making the degree of specialization lower than the threshold λ_0, either the membership in the superclass must be decreased, or the membership in other subclasses must be increased accordingly.

For example, consider the IT services industry again with $\lambda_0=0.8$ and specific form 6 in Table 2 and 3, using minimum for conjunction. Suppose the IT services revenue of company A, all of which comes from hardware services, is only 20% of the total revenue. Suppose e_1 represents A in the model, and E, E_1, E_2, E_3 represent the superclass "IT services vendors" and the subclasses "hardware services vendors", "software services vendors" and "IT consulting companies" respectively, then $\mu_E(e_1)=0.2$, $\mu_{E1}(e_1)=0.2$, $\lambda(e_1)=\min(1, 1-0.2+0.2)=1$. Now the business of company A has developed and the IT services revenue has reached 90% of the total, so $\mu_E(e_1)=0.9$, $\lambda(e_1)=\min(1, 1-0.9+0.2)=0.3<\lambda_0$. The increase of the IT services revenue must come from one or more of the submarkets. Suppose the increase all comes from hardware services. Only when a correct update is conducted, for example, $\mu_{E1}(e_1)=0.9$, will the constraint be satisfied, that is $\lambda(e_1)=\min(1, 1-0.9+0.9)=1$. Otherwise, company A will not be allowed in the database.

5. Concluding remarks

In this paper, a general form and several specific forms of λ-specialization have been presented, along with discussions of respective semantics and properties. The settings of λ-specialization extend the notions of total/partial specialization and enable us to reflect the degrees of strength for entities participating in the specialization. In real applications, different specific forms may be chosen depending on the problems at hand in consideration of semantics to express and constraints to enforce.

Ongoing studies center on further explorations of the properties and impact on databases maintenance. Another possible form is also being investigated, such as $$\frac{\sum_e (\lambda(e))}{\|\sup p(E)\|} = \lambda,$$ in which λ represents the proportion of the entities satisfying the constraint to all the entities in the entity set, so as to express the constraint from a different perspective of semantics.

Acknowledgements

The work was partly supported by the National Natural Science Foundation of China (79925001/70231010), the MOE Funds for Doctoral Programs (20020003095), and the Bilateral Scientific & Technological Cooperation between China and Flanders/Czech.

The authors wish to thank Peng Yan for the discussions related to the work.

References

1. G. Chen and E. E. Kerre, Extending ER/EER Concepts towards Fuzzy Conceptual Data Modeling. In Proceedings of IEEE World Congress WCCI'98, Alaska, 1998
2. G. Chen, Fuzzy logic in data modeling, Boston, Mass: Kluwer Academic, 1998
3. P. P. Chen, The Entity-Relationship Model-Toward a Unified View of Data. In ACM Transactions on Database Systems, Vol. 1, No. 1. March 1976, Pages 9-36.
4. C. Dos Santos, E. Neuhold and A. Furtado, A Data Type Approach to the Entity-Relationship Model. In Proceedings of ER Conference'79, 1979
5. D. Dubois, H.Prade and J. P. Rossazza. Vagueness, Typicality and Uncertainty in Class Hierarchies. In International Journal of Intelligent Systems 6, 1991, pp167-183
6. R. Elmasri, J. Weeldreyer, A. Hevner, The Category Concpet: an Extension to the Entity-Relationship Model. In International Journal on Data and Knowledge Engineering 1985; 1:1
7. E. E. Kerre, G. Chen, An Overview of Fuzzy Data Models, In Studies in Fuzziness: Fuzziness in Database Management Systems. P. Bosc and J. Kacprzyk, eds. Physica-Verlag, 1995.
8. E. Ruspini, Imprecision and Uncertainty in the Entity-relationship Model. In Fuzzy Logic in Knowledge Engineering, H. Prade and C. V. Negoita (eds.), Verlag TUV Rheinland, 18-22, 1986.
9. P. Scheuermann, G. Scheffner and H. Weber, Abstraction Capabilities And Invariant Properties Modelling Within The Entity-Relationship Approach. In Entity-Relationship Approach to Systems Analysis and Design, P. Chen, Ed. North-Holland, Amsterdam, 1980, pp. 121-140.
10. John. M. Smith and D. C.P. Smith, Database Abstractions: Aggregation and Generalization. In ACM Transactions on Database Systems, Vol. 2, No. 2, June 1977, Pages 105-133.
11. R. Vandenberghe, R. De Caluwe, An Entity-Relationship Approach to the Modeling of Vagueness in Databases. Symbolic and Quantitative Approaches to Uncertainty. In Proceedings of the European Conference ECSQAU, Marseille, France, October 1991 (eds. R. Kruse & P. Siegel), Springer-Verlag, Berlin, 1991, pp. 338-343.
12. L. A. Zadeh. Fuzzy sets. In Inform. and Control 8 (1965) 338-353
13. Zvieli and P.P. Chen, Entity-Relationship Modeling and Fuzzy Database. In Proceedings of the 2nd Conference on Data Engineering L.A. 1985

A logical reasoning framework for modelling and merging uncertain semi-structured information

Anthony Hunter [a] and Weiru Liu [b]

[a] Department of Computer Science, University College London,
Gower Street, London WC1E 6BT, UK
[b] School of Computer Science, Queen's University Belfast,
Belfast, Co Antrim BT7 1NN, UK

Abstract

Semi-structured information in XML can be merged in a logic-based framework [7,9]. This framework has been extended to deal with uncertainty, in the form of probability values, degrees of beliefs, or necessity measures, in the XML documents [8]. In this paper, we discuss how this logical framework can be used to model and reason with structured scientific knowledge on the Web in medical and bioscience domains. We will demonstrate how multiple summaritive and evaluative knowledge under uncertainty can be merged to obtain less conflicting and better confirmed results in response to users queries. We will also show how reliability of a source can be integrated into this structure. A number of examples are deployed to illustrate potential applications of the framework.

Key words: Semi-structured information fusion, uncertain information in XML

1. Introduction

XML has been used extensively on the Web for representing and exchanging a variety of static and dynamic information, such as database query results. Along with its increasing use in a wider range of activities, the need to represent uncertain information has rapidly emerged recently, since in real life, information is often uncertain and incomplete.

Two typical examples of integrating uncertainty into the XML structure are [6] and [10], both methods assign probabilistic values to elements in an XML document. A probability value can either be assigned to a leaf node (a textentry) or a tagname, but these two approaches offer different methods to calculate a final probability for a query of XML information. Another attempt to model uncertainty in XML is reported in [1] where numerical values representing the importance of tags are attached to tagnames. These values are interpreted in fuzzy theory and used to calculate the importance of a set of tagnames in comparison to other sets of tagnames, so that more important information can be used first to make decisions. Its primary application domain is service related information gathering in which customers have choices over a set of options. With a decision tailored to options that are more important, a customer is more likely to be satisfied by the service provided. Also, under the umbrella of making Web information more meaningful, a proposal was reported in [11] which integrates probabilities into DAML+OIL, a commonly used ontology language in the Semantic Web. Uncertain statements are marked with probability values instead of assuming that every statement is either true or false as in the current language format.

In contrast to the approaches above, our logic-based framework aims at establishing a formal structure that can facilitate uncertainty reasoning in formal logics that in turn make use of knowledge in the background knowledgebase to assist querying and merging. The framework has proved to be capable of modelling a variety of forms of uncertainty and has advantages over both approaches [6,10].

In this paper, we discuss how this extended logical framework can be used for modelling and reasoning with structured scientific knowledge on the Web in medical and bioscience domains. We will demonstrate how multiple summaritive and evaluative knowledge under uncertainty can be easily merged to obtain less conflicting and better confirmed results in response to users queries. A number of examples are deployed to illustrate potential applications of the framework. We will proceed as follows. Section 2 discusses what constitutes structured scientific knowledge and the need for modelling uncertainty in XML. Section 3 reviews the basic definitions in the logical fusion framework with examples. Section 4 investigates how the reliability of a source can be explicitly represented in the framework and how it is integrated with other types of uncertainty in the process of answering a user's query. Section 5 looks at the issue of merging multiple XML documents for both probability values and mass functions. Section 6 summarizes the paper.

2. Structured scientific knowledge

Structured scientific knowledge We use XML documents to represent semi-structured information such as structured scientific knowledge (SSK). Each SSK report describes information in one or more scientific datasources (such as journals, databases of empirical results, etc). The format of an SSK report is an XML document. Each SSK report contains **summaritive information** about the datasource (e.g. information from an abstract, summary of techniques used, etc) plus **evaluative information** about the datasource (eg. delineation of uncertainties and errors in the information source, qualifications of the key findings, etc). Each SSK report can be constructed by hand, by information extraction systems (e.g. [3]), or as the result of querying and analysing scientific databases in [10,12].

For instance, in the medical community, the number of journals and conferences having articles that are relevant to a single specific topic is extremely large and fast growing. This makes it very difficult for physicians to keep pace of all new results reported in their fields and makes it even harder for patients to find relevant information. There is an increasing need to better summarize this raw information so that different types of user can get more satisfactory summaritive and evaluative information.

In [5], a system called *Persival* was developed which aims at providing tailored presentation of relevant medical literature for both physicians and lay consumers. Based on a user's query, the system takes documents (including images and video) as input, and generates one or more paragraphs of summary from the input documents, highlighting the common points and the differences among these input documents. The summaries can also be provided at different levels of granularity depending on who the user is. Each summary follows a fixed structure including *introduction, methods, results, and discussion*. For documents with patient medical records, the output is in a more structured format which can be easily represented with XML documents. Already in [12], the query results of medical journals are directly expressed as XML documents and these results are merged to reduce incompleteness and error messages.

Another source of SSK reports can be obtained as a by-product of querying databases. There are many online information resources for bioinformatics. Most of the information in these sites is in a semi-structured format. For example, when searching for information related to a specific protein, a bioscientist may invoke specialised database search tools, such as BLAST. The results of such searches are in semi-structured format and may need to be saved by the user and then searched. It is desirable to collect these results and extract summary information from them. Such information may then be integrated with searches of abstracts such as those stored in PubMed.

As more and more individual SSK reports accumulate, there is an urgent need to integrate them. An example of integrating query results in XML format is reported in [13] where the main focus is on semantic integration of life science databases. As it was argued that publically available biological knowledge is scattered over many hundred internet accessible data sources, data integration is a fundamental prerequisite for answering complexity queries. Another example of this kind is from [2] which focuses on merging temporal aspects of multimedia semi-structured data in clinical information. Temporal clinical semi-structured information is first modelled in a graphical model and then translated into XML documents.

In summary, with XML being increasingly used as a standard data exchange format, integrating information in XML documents is a pressing task in making the best use of available data sources. Furthermore, in real-world applications, many summaritive and evaluative information and query results are often subject to uncertainty and inconsistency. Therefore, an automated XML integration tool should be able to deal with inconsistencies and uncertainties in information when they arise.

In repsonse to this need, we have been developing a logic-based fusion framework that supports context-dependent representation and reasoning involving uncertainty in information. In our approach, each SSK report is regarded as a tree and this can isomorphically be represented as a logical term. Therefore, logical reasoning technologies can be applied. A query of merging some SSK reports can be handled by recursive calls to a logical reasoning tool to merge the subtrees in the SSK reports. This gives a context-dependent logic-based approach to merging that is sensitive to the uncertain information in the SSK reports and to the background knowledge in the knowledgebase. The apparent structural difference of multiple XML documents can be resolved by using XSLT which is able to transform one XML document into the format of another XML document. Therefore, in this paper, we don't consider structural heterogeneity in XML documents.

Uncertainty in XML An important feature of SSK reports is the ability to represent **uncertainty**. Much leading-edge scientific information is subject to uncertainty, and of diverse types, including empirical methods (such as the nature of populations and samples, estimates of experimental errors, etc), statistical analysis (such as mean, standard deviation, probability statements, correlation, significance tests, etc), and subjective assessments drawn on the basis of the evidence. For example, a probability distribution over a set of possible outcomes as textentries $\tau_1,..,\tau_n$ for a tagname ϕ, where x_i is the probability of τ_i, can be represented by the following piece of XML that would be nested in an SSK report.

$$\langle\phi\rangle\langle\text{prob value} = \text{``}x_1\text{''}\rangle\tau_1\langle/\text{prob}\rangle...\langle\text{prob value} = \text{``}x_n\text{''}\rangle\tau_n\langle/\text{prob}\rangle\langle/\phi\rangle$$

Encoding probabilities (or uncertainty values) involves refining the DTD for SSK reports to enforce the use of specific tags for uncertain information. We represent uncertainty in the XML for SSK reports as developed in [8] where uncertainty can be modelled in either probability theory, belief function theory [14], or possibility theory [4].

The primary objective of **merging** SSK reports is to decrease redundancy between SSK reports, to address incompleteness in individual SSK reports, and most importantly to minimize the inconsistencies and uncertainties arising in SSK reports. So that merging would provide a better and more complete summary and evaluation of the datasources involved. For example, if two SSK reports are on the same subject and they are mutually conflicting, i.e the union of them is highly inconsistent, then they reveal that either one or both sources are not correct. This can then be a qualification assigned to the evaluative information in the SSK reports that indicates there is a problem with one or both datasources. This can be very useful especially for empirical data in datasources.

3. A logical fusion framework

We review some of the basic definitions in the framework [8].

Definition 1. Structured Scientific Knowledge Report (SSK report): If φ is a tagname (i.e an element name), and ϕ is textentry, then $\langle\varphi\rangle\phi\langle/\varphi\rangle$ is an SSK report. If φ is a tagname, ϕ is a textentry, θ is an attribute name, and κ is an attribute value, then $\langle\varphi\ \theta = \kappa\rangle\phi\langle/\varphi\rangle$ is an SSK report. If φ is a tagname and $\sigma_1, ..., \sigma_n$ are SSK reports, then $\langle\varphi\rangle\sigma_1...\sigma_n\langle/\varphi\rangle$ is an SSK report.

Definition 2. Abstract term: Each SSK report is isomorphic with a ground term (of classical logic) called an abstract term. This isomorphism is defined inductively as follows: (1) If $\langle\varphi\rangle\phi\langle/\varphi\rangle$ is an SSK report, where ϕ is a textentry, then $\varphi(\phi)$ is an abstract term that is isomorphic with $\langle\varphi\rangle\phi\langle/\varphi\rangle$; (2) If $\langle\varphi\ \theta = \kappa\rangle\phi\langle/\varphi\rangle$ is an SSK report, where ϕ is a textentry, then $\varphi(\phi, \kappa)$ is an abstract term that is isomorphic with $\langle\varphi\ \theta = \kappa\rangle\phi\langle/\varphi\rangle$; and (3) If $\langle\varphi\rangle\phi_1..\phi_n\langle/\varphi\rangle$ is an SSK report, and ϕ'_1 is an abstract term that is isomorphic with ϕ_1, ..., and ϕ'_n is an abstract term that is isomorphic with ϕ_n, then $\varphi(\phi'_1, .., \phi'_n)$ is an abstract term that is isomorphic with $\langle\varphi\rangle\phi_1..\phi_n\langle/\varphi\rangle$.

Clearly each SSK report is isomorphic to a tree with the non-leaf nodes being the tagnames and the leaf nodes being the textentries. This isomorphism allows us to give a definition for an *abstract term* of an SSK report. Via this isomorphic relationship, we can refer to a branch of an abstract term by using the branch of the isomorphic SSK, and we can refer to a subtree of an abstract term by using the subtree of the isomorphic SSK.

Definition 1 describes how an XML document can be defined recursively starting from the simplest one which has only one tagname and one value associated with the tagname. Definition 2 defines how a tree structure like XML document can be equally described as a logical term which also reflects the relationship between tagnames and their values. For instance, XML information $\langle\text{date}\rangle 03/03/99\langle/\text{date}\rangle$ is denoted as $\text{date}(03/03/99)$ in logics where $03/03/99$ can be understood as the value of attribute date.

We consider two types of uncertainty in this paper, probability values and mass functions in DS theory [14]. A mass function, m, is defined on a set of mutually exclusive and exhaustive set of values Ω called a *frame of discernment* (or simply *frame*), as $m(\emptyset) = 0$ and $\Sigma_{A \subseteq \Omega}\ m(A) = 1$. The formal modelling approach to representing these two types of uncertainty is given in the following two definitions.

Definition 3. The SSK report $\langle\text{probability}\rangle\sigma_1, .., \sigma_n\langle/\text{probability}\rangle$ is a **probability-valid component (ProVC)** iff each $\sigma_i \in \{\sigma_1, .., \sigma_n\}$ is of the form $\langle\text{prob value} = \kappa\rangle\ \phi\langle/\text{prob}\rangle$ where $\kappa \in [0, 1]$ and ϕ is a textentry.

```
⟨report⟩
  ⟨prostate cancer prediction⟩
  ⟨reliability = "0.7"⟩
    ⟨author⟩unknown ⟨/author⟩
    ⟨title⟩Prostatic Specific Antigen Screening Test⟨/title⟩
    ⟨url⟩http : //medic.med.uth.tmc.edu/ptnt/00000390.htm⟨/url⟩
      ⟨PSA range = "0.0 − 3.9"⟩
        ⟨conclusion⟩NoCancer⟨/conclusion⟩
      ⟨/PSA⟩
      ⟨PSA range = "4.0 − 9.9"⟩
        ⟨conclusion⟩
          ⟨probability⟩
            ⟨prob value = "0.22"⟩Cancer⟨/prob⟩
            ⟨prob value = "0.78"⟩NoCancer⟨/prob⟩
          ⟨/probability⟩
        ⟨/conclusion⟩
      ⟨/PSA⟩
      ⟨PSA range > "10.0"⟩
        ⟨conclusion⟩
          ⟨probability⟩
            ⟨prob value = "0.65"⟩Cancer⟨/prob⟩
            ⟨prob value = "0.35"⟩NoCancer⟨/prob⟩
          ⟨/probability⟩
        ⟨/conclusion⟩
      ⟨/PSA⟩
  ⟨/reliability⟩
  ⟨/prostate cancer prediction⟩
⟨/report⟩
```

Fig. 1. An XML document with uncertain information

Definition 4. The SSK report ⟨belfunction⟩ $\sigma_1,..,\sigma_n$⟨/belfunction⟩ is a **belfunction-valid component (BelVC)** iff for each $\sigma_i \in \{\sigma_1,..,\sigma_n\}$ σ_i is of the form ⟨mass value = κ⟩$\sigma_1^i,...,\sigma_m^i$⟨/mass⟩ and for each $\sigma_j^i \in \{\sigma_1^i,..,\sigma_m^i\}$, σ_j^i is of the form ⟨massitem⟩ϕ⟨/massitem⟩ where $\kappa \in [0,1]$ and ϕ is a textentry.

All textentries in the above two definitions are elements of a pre-defined set Ω in the background knowledgebase. We also require that $\Sigma_i \kappa_i = 1$ for both cases to preserve the constrains in both theories.

Let us take prostate cancer prediction and diagnosis as an example. There are two types of methods available for users to get some initial information. One method is based on the Prostate Specific Antigen (PSA) value through a blood test. Higher PSA values can flag the possibility of cancer. However, this method is subject to inaccuracy, due to the fact that a higher PSA value can be influenced by many other factors, such as prostate inflammation and horse riding, before taking the blood sample. In general, this method is about 70% accurate in cancer diagnosis (http://medic.med.uth.tmc.edu/ptnt/00000390.htm). This high level summary can be represented in an XML document as shown in Figure 1.

In this example, we use two ProVCs to represent the conclusions drawn form certain PSA values. Furthermore, since this diagnosis is not absolutely accurate, we insert a reliability factor into the XML to indicate how much credence we should give to this piece of information. Obviously, there is a need to formalize the reliability factor into the diagnostic result. We look at this issue next.

4. Integrating reliability of SSK into XML

The reliability value in the above example is different from probability distributions on text entries such as Cancer or NoCancer. The former identifies how reliable a conclusion, or a source, or an experiment, is. In this section, we investigate the method to integrate this factor with other uncertainty components (ProVCs, BelVCs) in XML documents when answering a query For this purpose, we look at the discounting operator in DS theory.

Discounting is useful and essential when a belief function (or a mass function) fails to take into account some particular uncertainty affecting the evidence as a whole [14]. Assume that the evidence is accurate to α degree, then the information provided by the evidence should be discounted by degree $1 - \alpha$. Let m be a mass function on Ω provided by a piece of evidence which is in turn has the degree of reliability (or trust) α, then a new mass function m' defined by

$$m'(A) = \begin{cases} \alpha m(A) & \text{when } m(A) > 0, A \subset \Omega \\ (1 - \alpha) + \alpha m(A) & \text{when } A = \Omega \end{cases}$$

has taken into account the impact of imprecision of the evidence.

Definition 5. A SSK report $\langle\sigma_1\rangle\langle\text{reliability} = \kappa^1\rangle\sigma_1^1,..,\sigma_n^1\langle/\text{reliability}\rangle\langle/\sigma_1\rangle$ $,..,\langle\sigma_t\rangle\langle\text{reliability} = \kappa^t\rangle\sigma_1^t,..,\sigma_m^t\langle/\text{reliability}\rangle\langle/\sigma_t\rangle$ is a **reliability-valid component (RelVC)** where $\kappa^i > 0$ and each $\sigma_i^l \in \{\sigma_1^1,\ldots,\sigma_n^1\} \cup \ldots \cup \{\sigma_1^t,\ldots,\sigma_m^t\}$ is a valid SSK report.

Definition 6. Let a section of a RelVC for tag σ be $\langle\sigma\rangle\langle\text{reliability} = \kappa_t\rangle\sigma_1,..,\sigma_n$ $\langle/\text{reliability}\rangle\langle/\sigma\rangle$ and any σ_i does not contain any further RelVC components. Let σ_i be a BelVC with structure in Figure 1 left, then the transformed σ_i' defined in Figure 2 right is a BelVC incorporating the value of the reliability. The original section of the RelVC for tag σ is thus revised as $\langle\sigma\rangle\sigma_1',..,\sigma_n'\langle\sigma\rangle$, where each σ_i' has the reliability factor being integrated.

The last section with $\langle\text{mass value} = 1 - \kappa_t\rangle$ is the value assigned to the frame Ω, if there is no mass value assigned to it in the initial XML document. Otherwise, this section has appeared as a σ_j above and should not be added again here.

Starting with an XML document that contains both reliability factors and uncertainty components, the above definition generates a new XML document from it consisting of only uncertainty components.

Example Since a PSA value only provides an approximate prediction and suffers from drawbacks of inaccuracy, more comprehensive methods have been proposed to analyze patient's tests results thoroughly. Here, we look at one of such methods. Assume that for each patient, there is a blood serum mass spectrum. The features of a spectrum are defined as the x-axis locations within the spectrum that are able to distinguish healthy and cancerous status based on y-axis values. The full resolution of a spectrum can contain 15000 features and may be subject to noise. Usually, it is possible to smooth the spectrum to produce less features and to reduce noise. Commonly, feature numbers are reduced by half in each smoothing stage.

$\langle\varphi_1\rangle$
  $\langle\varphi_l\rangle$
    $\langle$belfunction$\rangle$
      $\langle$mass value $= \kappa_1^i\rangle$
        $\langle$massitem$\rangle\phi_1^1\langle$/massitem$\rangle$...
        $\langle$massitem$\rangle\phi_m^1\langle$/massitem$\rangle$
      $\langle$/mass$\rangle$
                    :
      $\langle$mass value $= \kappa_j^i\rangle$
        $\langle$massitem$\rangle\phi_1^j\langle$/massitem$\rangle$...
        $\langle$massitem$\rangle\phi_n^j\langle$/massitem$\rangle$
      $\langle$/mass$\rangle$
    $\langle$/belfunction$\rangle$
  $\langle/\varphi_l\rangle$
    :
$\langle/\varphi_1\rangle$

$\langle\varphi_1\rangle$
  $\langle\varphi_l\rangle$
    $\langle$belfunction$\rangle$
      $\langle$mass value $= \kappa_1^i \times \kappa_t\rangle$
        $\langle$massitem$\rangle\phi_1^1\langle$/massitem$\rangle$...
        $\langle$massitem$\rangle\phi_m^1\langle$/massitem$\rangle$
      $\langle$/mass$\rangle$
                    :
      $\langle$mass value $= \kappa_j^i \times \kappa_t\rangle$
        $\langle$massitem$\rangle\phi_1^j\langle$/massitem$\rangle$...
        $\langle$massitem$\rangle\phi_n^j\langle$/massitem$\rangle$
      $\langle$/mass$\rangle$
      $\langle$mass value $= 1 - \kappa_t\rangle$
        $\langle$massitem$\rangle\forall\psi \in \Omega\langle$massitem$\rangle$...
      $\langle$/mass$\rangle$
    $\langle$/belfunction$\rangle$
  $\langle/\varphi_l\rangle$
    :
$\langle/\varphi_1\rangle$

Fig. 2. Transformation of a reliability factor

For the sample data at http://clinicalproteomics.steem.com/download-prost.php, a Bayesian Classifier program (by Dr. Cheng) runs these data first with a full resolution giving 15000 features, then with lower resolutions having 15000/2 (giving 7500 features), $15000/2^2$, $15000/2^3$, and $15000/2^4$ features respectively. The relative accuracies of cancer diagnosis under these five resolutions are 90%, 92.68%, 91.75%, 92.33%, and 85.81% respectively. The experimental result of this analysis is then summarized in the following XML document.

$\langle$report$\rangle$
  $\langle$prostate cancer prediction$\rangle$
    $\langle$author$\rangle$Jie Cheng$\langle$/author$\rangle$
    $\langle$title$\rangle$Bayesian Classifier of prostate cancer$\langle$/title$\rangle$
    $\langle$url$\rangle$http : //clinicalproteomics.steem.com/download $-$ prost.php$\langle$/url$\rangle$
    $\langle$dataName$\rangle$accuracy of blood serum mass spectrum$\langle$dataName$\rangle$
    $\langle$features $= 15000\rangle$
    $\langle$conclusionAccuracy$\rangle$"0.9"$\langle$/conclusionAccuracy$\rangle$
    $\langle$/features$\rangle$
    $\langle$features $= 7500\rangle$
    $\langle$conclusionAccuracy$\rangle$"0.9268"$\langle$/conclusionAccuracy$\rangle$
    $\langle$/features$\rangle$
    $\langle$features $= 3750\rangle$
    $\langle$conclusionAccuracy$\rangle$"0.9175"$\langle$/conclusionAccuracy$\rangle$
    $\langle$/features$\rangle$
    $\langle$features $= 1875\rangle$
    $\langle$conclusionAccuracy$\rangle$"0.9233"$\langle$/conclusionAccuracy$\rangle$
    $\langle$/features$\rangle$
    $\langle$features $= 937\rangle$
    $\langle$conclusionAccuracy$\rangle$"0.8581"$\langle$/conclusionAccuracy$\rangle$
    $\langle$/features$\rangle$
  $\langle$/prostate cancer prediction$\rangle$
$\langle$/report$\rangle$

When a patient's spectrum is analysed using this classifier under a specific resolution, for instance, the full resolution, a conclusion will be drawn as to whether the patient has cancer. Assume that the conclusion is Cancer, then the degree of accuracy of this analysis under *this* resolution shall be taken into account, so the conclusion is revised as *the patient is having cancer with chance* 90%. This statement also implies that with 10% chance we do not know what the conclusion would be, e.g., either Cancer or NoCancer.

This XML document can be used to derive diagnosis for individual patients. For example, assume that patient J Sky's spectrum is known and features have been selected under the full resolution. Feeding these values into the Bayesian Classifier, a diagnosis will be conducted with a probability attached to each of the two possible outcomes, Cancer or NoCancer. The corresponding XML document is as follows.

```
⟨report⟩
  ⟨prostate cancer prediction⟩
    ⟨author⟩Jie Cheng⟨/author⟩
    ⟨title⟩Bayesian Classifier ⟨/title⟩
    ⟨patient⟩J. Sky⟨/patient⟩
    ⟨date⟩06/11/2003⟨/date⟩
    ⟨dataName⟩blood serum mass spectrum⟨dataName⟩
    ⟨features = 15000⟩
       ⟨reliability = "0.9"⟩
          ⟨conclusion⟩
             ⟨probability⟩
                ⟨prob value = "0.4985569"⟩Cancer⟨/prob⟩
                ⟨prob value = "0.5014431"⟩NoCancer⟨/prob⟩
             ⟨/probability⟩
          ⟨/conclusion⟩
       ⟨/reliability⟩
    ⟨/features⟩
  ⟨/prostate cancer prediction⟩
⟨/report⟩
```

Since a ProVC can be seen as a special case of BelVC and we have a predicate to convert a ProVC into a BelVC [8], it is possible to first convert the ProVC for J Sky into a BelVC and then apply Definition 6 to generate an XML document with the reliability degree being integrated into the BelVC . The newly derived BelVC gives $m(\text{Cancer}) = 0.44870121, m(\text{NoCancer}) = 0.45129879, m(\text{Cancer}, \text{NoCancer}) = 0.1$ and the BelVC segment is

```
⟨belfunction⟩
  ⟨mass value = "0.44870121"⟩
     ⟨massitem⟩Cancer⟨/massitem⟩
  ⟨/mass⟩
  ⟨mass value = "0.45129879"⟩
     ⟨massitem⟩NoCancer⟨/massitem⟩
  ⟨/mass⟩
  ⟨mass value = "0.1"⟩
     ⟨massitem⟩Cancer⟨/massitem⟩
     ⟨massitem⟩NoCancer⟨/massitem⟩
  ⟨/mass⟩
⟨/belfunction⟩
```

5. Merging multiple uncertainty information

Merging occurs when multiple sources of information available concerning the same issue. We first review the predicate for merging two BelVCs.

Definition 7. ([8]) Let $\langle\text{belfunction}\rangle\sigma_1^1,..,\sigma_p^1\langle/\text{belfunction}\rangle$ and $\langle\text{belfunction}\rangle$ $\sigma_1^2,..,\sigma_q^2\langle/\text{belfunction}\rangle$ be two BelVCs, where
  (i) $\sigma_i^1 \in \{\sigma_1^1,..,\sigma_p^1\}$ is of the form $\langle\text{mass value} = \kappa_i^1\rangle\psi_i^1\langle/\text{mass}\rangle$
  (ii) the (subset, mass) pair collection is $S_1 = \{(\psi_1^1, \kappa_1^1), \ldots, (\psi_p^1, \kappa_p^1)\}$,
  (iii) $\sigma_j^2 \in \{\sigma_1^2,..,\sigma_q^2\}$ is of the form $\langle\text{mass value} = \kappa_j^2\rangle\psi_j^2\langle/\text{mass}\rangle$
  (iv) the (subset, mass) pair collection is $S_2 = \{(\psi_1^2, \kappa_1^2), \ldots, (\psi_q^2, \kappa_q^2)\}$.
Let the **combined BelVC** be $\langle\text{belfunction}\rangle\sigma_1,..,\sigma_s\langle/\text{belfunction}\rangle$ where each $\sigma_k \in \{\sigma_1,..,\sigma_s\}$ is of the form $\langle\text{mass value} = \kappa_k\rangle\psi_k\langle/\text{mass}\rangle$ and $\kappa_k = \frac{\Sigma \kappa_i^1 \times \kappa_j^2}{1 - \Sigma \kappa_n^1 \times \kappa_m^2}$ such that $\psi_k = \psi_i^1 \cap \psi_j^2$ for the (ψ_i^1, κ_i^1) and (ψ_j^2, κ_j^2) pairs, and $\psi_n^1 \cap \psi_m^2 = \emptyset$ for the (ψ_n^1, κ_n^1) and (ψ_m^2, κ_m^2) pairs, and ψ_k is of the form $\langle\text{massitem}\rangle\phi_{k_1}\langle/\text{massitem}\rangle,\ldots,$ $\langle\text{massitem}\rangle\phi_{k_z}\langle/\text{massitem}\rangle$.

The value $\kappa_\perp = \Sigma \kappa_n^1 \times \kappa_m^2$ (that is, $\Sigma_{A \cap B = \emptyset}(m_1(A) \times m_2(B))$) indicates how much of the total belief has been committed to the empty set while combining two pieces of uncertain information. A higher $\kappa_\perp$ value reflects either an inconsistency among the two sources or lower confidence in any of the possible outcomes from both sources.

Following the above example, if J Sky's PSA gives $PSA > 10$, then based on the XML document in Section 3, a new XML is generated for J Sky using his PSA value after integrating the method's reliability. This segment of the XML is

```
⟨belfunction⟩
   ⟨mass value = "0.455"⟩
      ⟨massitem⟩Cancer⟨/massitem⟩
   ⟨/mass⟩
   ⟨mass value = "0.245"⟩
      ⟨massitem⟩NoCancer⟨/massitem⟩
   ⟨/mass⟩
   ⟨mass value = "0.3"⟩
      ⟨massitem⟩Cancer⟨/massitem⟩
      ⟨massitem⟩NoCancer⟨/massitem⟩
   ⟨/mass⟩
⟨/belfunction⟩
```

Merging this BelVC with the one at the end of Section 4 using the procedure in Definition 7, we obtain a final diagnostic result with $m(\text{Cancer}) = 0.5609$, $m(\text{NoCancer}) = 0.3952$ and $m(\text{Cancer}, \text{NoCancer}) = 0.0438$ which strongly suggest that J Sky may have cancer.

6. Conclusion

A logical fusion framework that enables an easy modelling and merging of multiple summaritive and evaluative knowledge with uncertainty in XML, especially in medical or bioscience domains, is reported in this paper. As XML is being increasingly used on the Web as a standard for data storage and exchange, modelling uncertain and incomplete information as well as merging these pieces of information have become an important and urgent issue. We believe our framework provides a formal platform for addressing these issues and has the potential to standardize the various proposals of modelling uncertain information in XML available so far.

Acknowledgement We would like to thank Dr Jie Cheng for providing the experimental results used in this paper.

References

1. P Ceravolo, E Damiani and B Oliboni. Fuzzy technique for medadata construction. *Proc. of IPMU'04*:1019-1026. 2004.
2. C Combi, B Oliboni, and R Rossato. Merging multimedia presentations and semi-structured temporal data: a graph-based model and its application to clinical information. *Artificial Intelligence in Medicine*, 2005.
3. J Cowie and W Lehnert. Information extraction. *Comm. of the ACM*, 39:81–91, 1996.
4. D Dubois and H Prade. *Possibility theory: An approach to the computerized processing of uncertainty*. Plenum Press, 1988.
5. N Elhadad, M Kan, J Klavans, and K McKeown. Customization in a unified framework for summarizing medical literature. *Artificial Intelligence in Medicine* 33,179-198, 2005.
6. M van Keulen, A de Keijzer and W Alink. A probabilistic XML approach to data integration. *Proceedings of ICDE'05*, 459-470, 2005.
7. A Hunter. Logical fusion rules for merging structured news reports. *Data and Knowledge Engineering*, 42:23–56, 2002.
8. A Hunter and W Liu. Fusion rules for merging uncertain information. *Information Fusion* (in press), 2005.
9. A Hunter and R Summerton. Fusion rules for context-dependent aggregation of structured news reports. *Journal of Applied Non-classical Logic* 14(3):329-366, 2004.
10. A Nierman and H Jagadish. ProTDB: Probabilistic data in XML. In *Proc. of VLDB'02*, LNCS2590: 646–657. Springer, 2002.
11. H Nottelmann and N Fuhr. pDAML+OIL: A probabilistic extension to DAML+OIL based on probability datalog. *Proc. of IPMU'04*:227-234, 2004.
12. T Pankowski and E Hunt. Data merging in life science data integration systems. *Intelligent Information Systems, Advances in Soft Computing*, Springer, 2005.

13. S Philippe and J Köhler. Using XML technology for ontology-based semantic integration of life science databases. *IEEE Trans. on Information Technology in Bioinformatics* 8(2):154-160, 2004.
14. G Shafer. *A Mathematical Theory of Evidence*. Princeton University Press, 1976.

APPLIED DOMAINS

Machine learning and the prediction of protein structure: the state of the art

Rita Casadio[a] and Remo Calabrese[a] and Emidio Capriotti[a] and Mario Compiani[a] and Piero Fariselli[a] and Paola Marani[a] and Ludovica Montanucci[a] and Pier Luigi Martelli[a] and Ivan Rossi[a] and Gianluca Tasco[a]

[a]Biocomputing Group, Department of Biology/Interdepartmental Center for Biotechnological Research, University of Bologna, Via Irnerio, 42-40126 Bologna

Abstract

In the genomic era machine learning algorithms that improve automatically through experience have proven to be among the most successful methods for addressing relevant problems of Computational Molecular Biology, including protein structure prediction. The increasing amount of information stored in publicly available biological data bases is retrieved to find approximate solutions relating sequence to protein structure. This may be useful in different fields of Bioinformatics, from structural, functional and comparative genomics, to protein engineering and molecular medicine. How far can we go if we have a protein sequence and we do not know the corresponding structure? Also, why is it so important to know the protein structure? This and related issues will be discussed in the following.

Key words: Machine learning, neural networks, hidden Markov models, protein structure prediction, homology building, threading, fold recognition

1. Introduction

Presently, the amount of biological sequences in the publicly available data bases is increasing with a hyperbolic rate due to the continuous flux of results produced by the different genome sequencing projects. Billions of nucleotide sequences, coding for millions of proteins in different organisms, from bacteria to man, are already stored in electronic archives and contain all the relevant information on molecular evolution, gene differentiation, pathogenic mutations and molecular genetics (Figure 1). It is therefore urgent to retrieve all the general rules that data mining can extract from the archives, in order to understand the molecular bases of living processes at large. Also, based on a molecular approach, it is possible to understand and eventually find remedies to genetic diseases [1].

The number of sequences, including that of protein sequences is however several order of magnitudes higher than the number of structures known at atomic resolution (Figure 1). The question then poses as to whether it is feasible to compute the three-dimensional (3D) structure from protein sequences, considering that in spite of several efforts high-throughput crystallography is still not able to cope with the enormous amount of known genes. In the sixties, Christian Anfinsen first proposed that the information determining the tertiary structure of a protein resides in the chemistry of its amino acid sequence. The so called "protein folding problem" however has been never solved by means of computational analytical approaches trying to simulate and optimize all the ion-pair interactions of the protein embedded in the polar solvent environment (*http://www.nobel.se/chemistry/laureates/*).

However with the increase of the amount of protein structures known at atomic resolution, heuristic methods have been developed that take advantage of the information stored in the different protein structures and for which the solution to protein folding problem is available. These methods are approximate and their state of the art is routinely assessed during international experiments (CASPs, (Critical Assessment of protein Structure Prediction techniques). The results of the different CASPs editions tell us that it is presently conceivable to model 3D structure of a protein starting from its covalent structure under specific constraints (*http://predictioncenter.llnl.gov/*).

2. Methods for protein structure predictions

2.1. *Building by homology*

Protocols for protein structure predictions generally start with sequence alignment of the *target* (the sequence of unknown structure) with sequences of known structure. This procedure allows to retrieve sequences of known structures (if present) with some level of identity with the target. If this is so, provided that sequence identity is above 30%, the scaffold of the protein of known structure (the *template*) can be used to compute the 3D structure of the target protein. The method is called building by homology and the different CASP editions have demonstrated that the higher the sequence identity, the higher the probability of computing a structure very similar to the expected one, if available. The results confirm that proteins belonging to the same family, may adopt the same structure and that this is often related to the same function (*http://predictioncenter.llnl.gov/*).

By following this procedure, it has been possible to compute structures for fractions of whole genomes ranging from 20 up to 50 % of the proteome, depending on the level of identity of the different sequences with the different templates in the data bank of protein structures (PDB). Presently we can therefore count on repositories of structural models that may be publicly available and can be browsed to find the "pet" protein structure (http://salilab.org/; http://www.bioinformatics.buffalo.edu/current_buffalo/skolnick/services.html).

However quite often, even in the case of well annotate genomes, it is difficult to find homologues in the data bases of sequences and/or structures for all of the putative proteins predicted/found in the proteome. Under these circumstances alternative methods that make it possible to give approximate solutions to the protein folding problem are to be taken into considerations.

2.2. *Threading and ab initio methods*

Methods that can solve the problem of computing the 3D structure of proteins when sequence identity id below 30% can essentially be grouped into two main categories: fold recognition or threading methods and "ab initio" methods. With approaches complimentary to sequence comparison, including alignment of secondary structures and weighted comparison of sequence profiles, it is possible to search for distantly related proteins that may have the same fold (fold recognition). Threading methods are based on the notion that the sequence at hand may be folded according to different typical folds present in the data base and that each fold may or may not optimize the structure of the target sequence. Ab initio methods are an alternative when new folds or old folds need to be spatially arranged without taking into consideration all the structural information in the available data base (for recent reviews, see [2,3]). Among these, one particularly successful is a fragment based methods that recently allowed to engineering a small protein with a new fold [4].

3. General characteristics of machine learning-based predictors

Since a decade it has been debated that most of the successful methods sequence analysis and protein structure prediction are based on machine learning algorithms that automatically extracts if existing rules of associations between two related sets of variables. The most widely used are neural networks (NN) and hidden Markov models (HMM) that are at the basis of several predictors publicly available at different websites and trying to address several problems of sequence analysis and protein structure predictions (for a recent comprehensive review see [5]).

Our group in Bologna through the years has been focusing on the prediction of structural features of protein structure starting from sequences (www.biocomp.unibo.it). Our strategy consists in posing a problem and carefully deriving a non redundant subsets of structures from the data base of protein structures (PDB) with different constraints, depending on the problem at hand. In the following we will briefly outline some of the characteristics of our predictors, basically consisting of neural networks, hidden Markov models or a combination of both (Hidden Neural Networks).

3.1. Neural network-based predictors

A neural network is a massively parallel-distributed processor designed to extract and store experimental knowledge and to make it available for use. Each processing unit is called neuron in analogy with the biological neurons in the human brain. Similarly an artificial neural network is a highly complex, connected, non-linear and parallel computing system. In artificial neural networks (NNs) knowledge is acquired through a learning/training process and is stored in the inter-neuron connections referred to as synaptic weights. The learning process is performed with a learning algorithm.

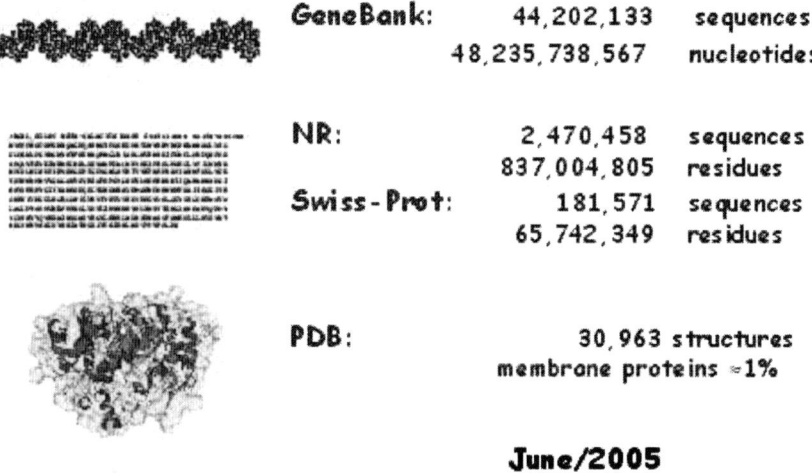

Fig. 1. The number of bio-sequences and structures in the currently available primary data bases

Neural networks are candidates to solve problems with the following characteristics: i) there is a large set of data for the training phase; ii) no simple first-principles or model-based solution is available. Given the billions of biosequences that are stored in the data bases (Figure 1), specific patterns relating sequences to given structural motifs or functions or folds can be found. A general strategy to address the folding problem is therefore to recognise the most likely fold that a given sequence may adopt. In this respect, neural networks are tools suited to bridge the gap between sequence and protein 3D structure.

Specific tasks of computational biology have been addressed with feedforward neural networks trained with the backpropagation algorithm, particularly multilayered perceptrons with hidden layers of neurons. Supervised networks are endowed with a feed-back mechanism (learning algorithm) that adjusts the connections so as to minimise an error function which measures the discrepancy between the actual response of the network to the current input and the desired output as specified by the supervisor. The stage in the course of which the weights are changed is termed learning phase and comes to an end when the error falls below a given (small) value. The main adjustable features of a multilayer feedforward perceptron are:
− the input coding;
− the amplitude of the sliding window;
− the number of hidden layers and neurons;
− the learning rate.

By performing a search in the parameter space of the network, different problems of Computational Biology have been satisfactorily investigated. Sequence homology is routinely kept as low as possible (<= 25%) in order to achieve optimal generalisation. Once weights are fixed, the network can act as a predictor for the specific task at hand (Figure 2). The predictive performance is computed by evaluating different statistical indexes that highlight different aspects of the predictive power. For brevity, the accuracy (the number of correct predictions over the total ones) is routinely evaluated. For large training sets, as for the tasks reviewed in this paper, a cross validation procedure is necessary in order to score the prediction. The training set is divided into subsets and each subset at a time is removed from the training set and used as testing set. In this case, the values of the statistical coefficients are computed as average values over the subsets.

A local coding scheme is normally used to avoid undesired coding-induced correlation among patterns. For protein sequences, each residue in each site within the input window is coded by 20 input neurons; 19 of them have activation values set to zero except for the activated neuron (with unit activation value) whose position within the 20-tuple corresponds to the actual residue. On the whole 20 x W neurons are needed for representing all the W residues of the input window.

Most of the predictors based on neural networks take as input from the amino acid sequence. Alternative inputs are based on the evaluation of an array for each residue in the protein sequence, which contains the frequency of each aminoacid, aligned in that position in the protein family (sequence profile) [5,6].

3.2. Hidden Markov Model based predictors

A Hidden Markov Model (HMM) is a probabilistic system designed to model a sequence as a result of a markovian process that cannot be observed. In a generative point of view, a sequence is an outcome of a path among the states of a Markov model: each state can emit a character in the alphabet of the 20 amino acids with

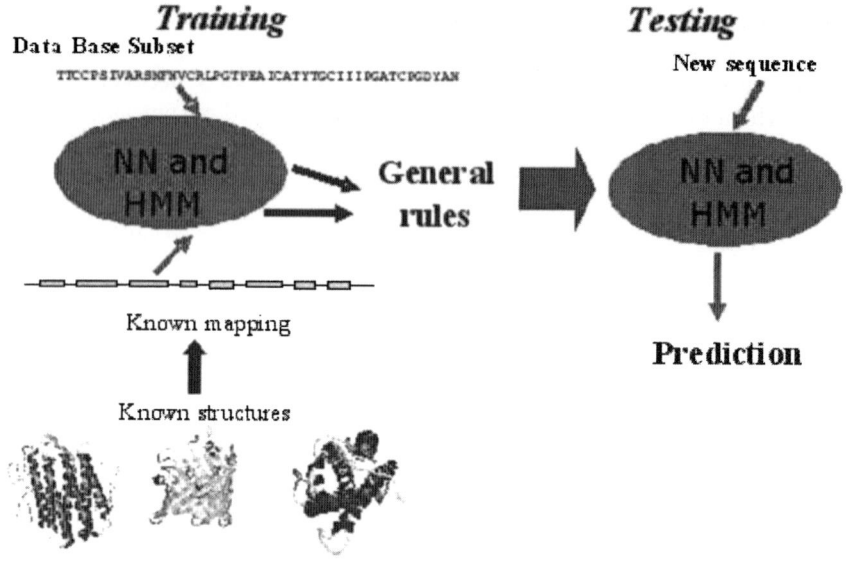

Fig. 2. A general scheme of a predictor based on machine learning approaches

an emission probability solely depending on the state. The sequence is generated by two concomitant stochastic processes: the transition between states and the emission of a letter from each state.

For modelling the protein structure, a Markov model casting all the known constraints on the feature we want to study has to be hypothesized. The training procedure, based on the Expectation-Maximisation algorithm, set all the transition and the emission probabilities in order to maximise the probability of generating the sequences of the training set. In this point of view, a HMM is a machine learning method for modelling a class of protein sequences. A trained HMM is able to compute the probability of generating any new sequence: this probability value can be used for discriminating if the new sequence belongs to the family modelled HMM. Moreover, the HMM computes for each residue in the sequence the state that most probably has emitted it: this procedure allows mapping the residue sequence into a sequence of states and is the basis of the HMM based predictor. For example, membrane proteins can be modelled by means of a set of transmembrane states and a set of loop states connected with transition probabilities. Each state is, generally speaking, characterised by his peculiar set of emission probabilities over the alphabet of the 20 amino acids. After the training, the reconstruction of the most probable mapping between the sequence and the sequence of states can be used to predict the membrane spanning segments along the protein sequence [7].

The HMM are extremely useful in the prediction of protein structure, when the

feature we want to map on the protein sequence is constrained by a grammar, that can be easily cast into a HMM.
Recently HMMs able to analyse the evolutionary information contained in sequence profiles have been proposed and it was possible to enrich input also with sequence profiles, increasing the performance of the predictors [8].

3.3. *Hidden Neural Network-based predictors*

With neural networks input presentation through a sliding window allows to include all the local information conducive to a given output; with HMM, a global model of the sequence at hand for a given feature is computed. The success of either method depends on the problem: for secondary structure prediction NNs are scoring higher, for fold recognition HMMs are more suited. Recently methods have been developed for predicting whether a cysteine residue is involved or not in a disulfide bridge that take advantage of both local and global information, by considering the neural network output as the emission probability of a HMM (Hidden Neural Networks) [9].

4. Machine learning-based predictors in Bologna

At our web site, predictors are available for different problems of Computational Biology (Figure 3). Basically with a given sequence at hand one can predict: the secondary structure, the solvent accessibility of each residue, the coordination number of each residue, the bonding state of cysteines, the contact map of proteins and surface patches of interacting proteins. Furthermore if a sequence is that of a membrane protein, we have predictors suited to predict both the topography and topology of the protein with respect to the membrane. All our predictors have been described at length in the literature, and are top scoring between those presently available on the web (a review of our implementation is in [6], a list of our publications is at *www.biocomp.unibo.it*).

5. Modelling of difficult proteins: is it feasible?

In many cases, functional considerations can help in finding the correct fold for a protein. However below the limit of 30% of sequence identity, when entering the so called "twilight" zone, using a template with low sequence homology to the target is questionable and other procedures are necessary. In particular it is possible to take advantage of some experimental findings in order to characterize the relationship between structure and function; this allows posing constraints to the alignment method and to develop basically an expert-driven threading procedure. The strategies that can be applied are:

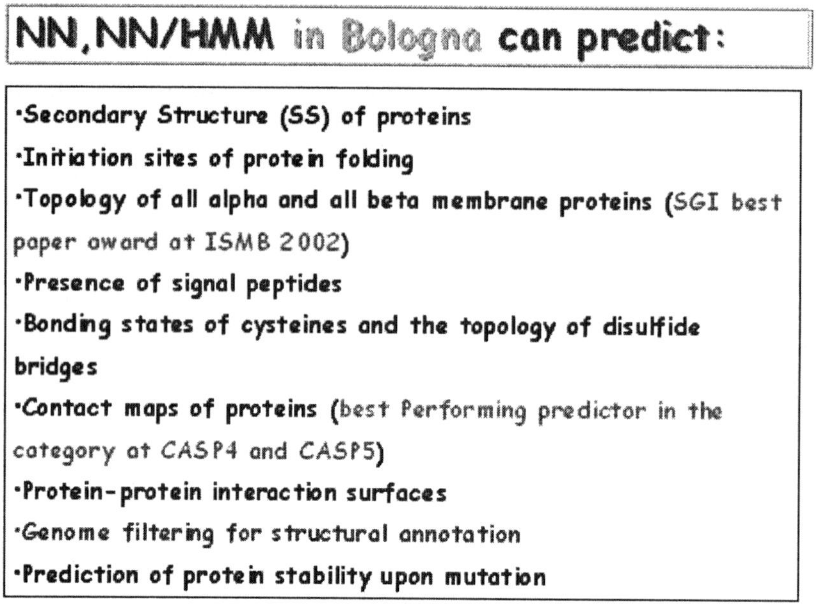

NN, NN/HMM in Bologna can predict:

- Secondary Structure (SS) of proteins
- Initiation sites of protein folding
- Topology of all alpha and all beta membrane proteins (SGI best paper award at ISMB 2002)
- Presence of signal peptides
- Bonding states of cysteines and the topology of disulfide bridges
- Contact maps of proteins (best performing predictor in the category at CASP4 and CASP5)
- Protein-protein interaction surfaces
- Genome filtering for structural annotation
- Prediction of protein stability upon mutation

Fig. 3. Typical problems that can be addressed with machine learning based approaches at www.biocomp.unibo.it

(i) *Multiple sequence alignment of sequences sharing the same function*: the multiple sequence alignment between the target sequence and all the sequences sharing the same function (are their structure or not resolved at atomic resolution) highlights the most conserved residues playing a fundamental role for the stability of the structure.

(ii) *Prediction of structural features starting from the target sequence*: given the target sequence, several structural features can be predicted by means of sequence analysis tools, publicly available, mainly based on machine learning approaches. The predicted features of the target can be compared with the structural features of the template computed from its structure, improving the alignment for modelling.

(iii) *Iterative procedure*: Different models can be evaluated with computational procedures and validated with specifically designed experiments. Then the alignment can be refined and new models can be computed.

5.1. A test case of low homology modelling: the alcohol dehydrogenase from Sulfolobus solfataricus

Alcohol dehydrogenase from Sulfolobus solfataricus (SsADH) is a NAD-dependent metalloenzyme that catalyses the reversible oxidation reaction of alcohols to their corresponding aldehydes or ketones. SsADH contains two zinc atoms per subunit, with a catalytic and a structural function, respectively. In this respect SsADH is similar to the mesophilic dimeric two-zinc containing horse liver enzyme (HLADH), although only 25 % sequentially identical. It is also known that SsADH has a tetrameric organisation and is similar in this respect to the two tetrameric one-zinc containing ADHs from Thermoanaerobacter brockii and Clostridium beijerinckii (CbADH) that are 23-24% sequentially identical to SsADH.

A key feature of our modelling procedure stems out of the following considerations: the target is a two-zinc containing protein with low sequence identity (< 25%) to all the other ADH sequences of known 3D structure; the functional unit of the target is a homotetramer. In this respect, one should consider that the PDB data base contained 31 atomic resolved structures of ADHs, corresponding to only 8 different sequences from different species; 28 of these structures (6 sequences) are two-zinc containing dimeric ADHs, while the remaining 3 are one-zinc containing tetrameric ADHs. There is no two-zinc tetrameric ADH structure available. The ADH monomers have a rather well conserved structure (root mean square deviation (RSMD)< 0.18 nm) irrespectively of the level of sequence identity of the different species, number of zinc ions and aggregation state of the monomeric unit. The observation makes likely that the monomer of the target will adopt a similar backbone conformation. Furthermore, if we require that the template structure has two zinc ions we are forced to adopt only HLADH as a template. However the aggregation state of HLADH is dimeric, while we know from experimental observations that our target is tetrameric and presumably with inter-monomer interactions different from those of the dimer. Therefore for monomer aggregation we should adopt different targets, with a tetrameric aggregation state. A solution to this problem can be to search the ADH database of sequence and structures to find residues in the target, which are conserved both in the two-zinc containing and in the tetrameric enzymes. This would constraint threading of the target to the templates.

In order to cope with our requirements 87 ADH sequences containing two zinc ions were selected from the SwissProt database. Multiple sequence alignment highlights that 38 residues are conserved in more than 90% of the 87. Cys38, His67 and Cys154 (numbering according to SsADH) constitute the binding site of the catalytic zinc. Glu98, Cys101, 104 and 112 are the residues involved in the binding of the structural zinc atom. Glu98 is substituted in all the other sequences with Cys. On the overall, 28 of the 38 highly conserved residues are found in the SsADH sequence; 11 of them are glycines that can be markers of the presence of a loop in the structure. This first step constrains the residues involved in binding both the structural and catalytic zinc ions.

A second alignment is at order to constrain inter-monomer interactions. If the selection among the ADHs in the SwissProt data base is made considering those sequences that are found to aggregate as tetramers, 24 chains are selected, independently of the number of zinc ions present in the monomer. The multiple sequence alignment of the 24 tetrameric ADHs indicates 27 highly conserved residues. These markers can be used to constrain the alignment of our target with the one-zinc containing monomers of the tetrameric structures.

The results described above prompted us to adopt two template structures; we considered as prototypes the structure of the dimeric HLADH (2OHX) and the structure of the tetrameric TbADH (1YFK). Structural alignment between the two sets of templates indicates that the main difference between HLADH and the two bacterial enzyme structures is the conformation of the loop co-ordinating the structural zinc ion, present only in HLADH.

In order to align the target structure with the templates we first predicted the secondary structure of the target and the solvent accessibility (*www.biocomp.unibo.it*). The target sequence was then aligned with the structural alignment of the templates taking into consideration the information derived from the multiple sequence alignments described above and from the predictions. This procedure is essentially an expertise-driven one, satisfying the constraints of the two-zinc binding sites and those of the tetrameric form. The low-resolution model that we obtained is the monomer unit, which comprises two domains separated by a deep cleft (where the catalytic zinc atom is bound). In the assembled tetramer, the four catalytic sites are at the vertexes of a tetrahedron and approximately 4,5 nm distant. The elevated number of ion pairs suggests that SsADH retains its enzymatic activity at higher temperatures because of greater stability of subunit interaction in the tetramer [10].

The structure of SsADH was later solved at 0.185 nm resolution with X-ray diffraction [11]. Superimposing the model to the experimentally determined structure gives a root mean square deviation of the two backbones (RSMD) equal to 0.25 nm (Figure 4). The high level of superimposition proves that the expert-driven procedure can lead to a quite accurate model, even when the level of identity between the target and the template is below the critical value of 30%.

6. Conclusions

In this paper we highlight a strategy that has proven successful in building a low resolution model of a protein with low sequence identity to a putative template in the PDB data base. Our results suggest that building by homology can be adopted also when the target and the template have very low sequence identity, provided that in these cases the alignment is computed taking into consideration all possible constraints that can be derived both using predictive methods and/or experimental characteristics. Ultimately this suggests that difficult cases of protein structure prediction can be solved with strategies different from typical threading.

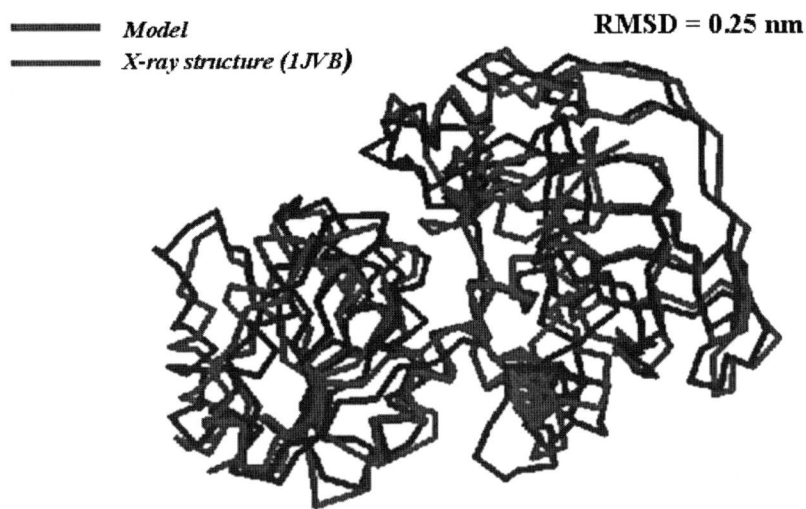

Fig. 4. The prediction of a difficult protein: the alcohol dehydrogenase from Sulfolobus solfataricus. The computed model is compared to the template (1JVB), the functional counterpart in Escherichia coli (sequence identity between the template and the target¡17%)

7. Acknowledgements

This work was supported by grants from the Italian Ministry for University and Research (in particular PRIN 2002 and 2003), FIRB 2001-FIRB 2003 projects devoted to Bioinformatics, and BIOSAPIENS, EU network of excellence. GT and EC and are the recipients of fellowships from a Functional Genomic Project and a FISR 2002 project, respectively. IR acknowledges the Spinner consortium of the Regione Emilia-Romagna for assistance and financial support to Biodec.com starting-up.

References

1. Saccone C. Pesole G (2003) Handbook of Comparative Genomics. Wiley-Liss, USA.
2. Whisstock JC, Lesk AM (2003). Prediction of protein function from protein sequence and structure. *Q Rev Biophys.* 36:307-40.
3. Lesk AM (2004). Introduction to Protein Science. Oxford University Press, London.
4. Kuhlman B, Dantas G, Ireton GC, Varani G, Stoddard BL, Baker D (2003) Design of a novel globular protein fold with atomic level accuracy. Science 302:1364-1368.
5. Baldi P, Brunak S (2001) Bioinformatics: the machine learning approach. The MIT Press, Cambridge.

6. Casadio R., Compiani M., Fariselli P., Jacoboni I. and Martelli P.L (2000). Neural Networks predict protein folding and structure: artificial intelligence faces biomolecular complexity. *SAR and QSAR in Env Res* 11: 149-182.
7. Durbin R, Eddy S, Krogh A, Mitchinson G (1998). Biological sequence analysis: probabilistic models of proteins and nucleic acids. Cambridge Univ. Press, Cambridge.
8. Martelli PL, Fariselli P, Krogh A, Casadio R (2002).A sequence-profile-based HMM for predicting and discriminating beta barrel membrane proteins. *Bioinformatics* 18: S46-S53.
9. Martelli PL, Fariselli P, Malaguti L, Casadio R (2002). Prediction of the disulfide bonding state of cysteines in proteins with hidden neural networks. *Protein Eng.* 15:951-953.
10. Casadio R, Martelli PL, Giordano A, Rossi M, Raia CA (2002). A low-resolution 3D model of the tetrameric alcohol dehydrogenase from Sulfolobus solfataricus. *Protein Eng* 15:215-223
11. Esposito L, Sica F, Raia CA, Giordano A, Rossi M, Mazzarella L, Zagari A (2002). Crystal Structure of Alcohol Dehydrogenase from the Hyperthermophilic Archaeon Sulfolobus Solfataricus at 1.85 Angstrom Resolution. *J Mol Biol* 318:463-475.

Efficient and Robust Global Amino Acid Sequence Alignment with Uncertain Evolutionary Distance

Matthias C. M. Troffaes [1]

SYSTeMS Research Group, Universiteit Gent
Technologiepark Zwijnaarde 914, 9052 Zwijnaarde, Belgium

Abstract

When aligning genetic sequences, we have to rely on estimates of evolutionary distance between sequences and their closest common ancestor. In practice, many alignments are performed on short sequences, and unfortunately, for such sequences it is well-known that estimation of evolutionary distance is subject to serious errors. Without additional information about the sequences, it is hardly possible to improve existing estimators. This paper addresses how imprecise probability theory allows us to substantially weaken assumptions about the evolutionary distance, by using an interval rather than a point estimate. It is shown how under these weaker assumptions a good alignment still can be found, through a generalisation of the well-known Needleman-Wunsch algorithm. In doing so, we rely on an extension of dynamic programming to the case where the gain is described by an imprecise probability model. Our approach also identifies those cases in which insufficient information is available in order to construct a good alignment.

Key words: bioinformatics, imprecise probabilities, Needleman-Wunsch algorithm, substitution matrix, molecular evolution, dynamic programming, sensitivity analysis

---

[1] E-mail: matthias.troffaes@gmail.com

1. Introduction

Aligning genetic sequences is a very widely used and important technique in bioinformatics [1]. To give a few examples, through sequence alignment we can determine evolutionary relationships among species, and in particular, we can reconstruct phylogenetic trees. An alignment may also reveal functional regions in genetic sequences. Such information may for example lead to the discovery of new or improved drug treatments, or may help in deciding what treatment is best fitted for a particular patient genotype. Sequence alignment is also a handy tool in predicting structural and biochemical properties of sequences.

The alignment problem is usually formulated as an *optimisation problem*. Basically, positive scores are assigned to matches, and negative scores are assigned to mismatches and gaps. These scores are summarised in what is called a *score matrix*. We aim to find the alignment with the highest total score. This approach has two benefits: (i) it allows us to characterise the optimal ("best") alignment from all possible alignments in an objective way, and (ii) the highest score, corresponding to the best alignment, provides us with an objective measure of the quality of this alignment. Moreover, an efficient algorithm to calculate the optimal alignment of a small number of sequences (say, two or three sequences) can be constructed through dynamic programming [2]. In this article, we will focus on *pair-wise* sequence alignment, that is, the alignment of only two sequences.

Clearly, aligning genetic sequences relies heavily on the choice of the score matrix: how should we reward matches, and how should punish gaps and mismatches? In practice, a large number of score matrices are being used, and precise choice of the score matrix relies on additional assumptions about the sequences under study. For example, when using PAM score matrices [3], on which we will focus in this paper, the following assumptions are made: [2]
- evolutionary distance of the sequences to their closest common ancestor is known,
- evolution is in an equilibrium point,
- in this equilibrium point, there is evolutionary reversibility—any point mutation is as probable as its reverse,
- point mutations at different locations in the sequence are i.i.d., and
- point mutations at different times are i.i.d.

Different evolutionary distances induce different score matrices. These matrices are denoted by PAM(T), where T denotes the evolutionary distance between the sequences under study and their closest common ancestor.

Obtaining this evolutionary distance is a major issue in molecular evolution, especially when comparing short sequences. Indeed, 'estimation bias usually occurs when the sequence length is short so that stochastic effects are strong' [4]. In many cases, one can only rely on the sequences under study to estimate evolutionary distance—no additional information is available.

---

[2] This is not meant to summarize the current state of the art. A lot of research in molecular evolution is on generalising these assumptions.

One approach is somehow to guess the evolutionary distance from the similarity of the two sequences. Typically, PAM250 is chosen if the sequences are 20% similar, PAM120 if they are 40% similar, PAM60 if they are 60% similar, etc. It is however not entirely clear how in general similarity percentages can be derived from two sequences, prior to alignment.

Another approach to solve the optimisation problem not for one, but for a set of PAM matrices, or even with different other methods, and then choose the method that returns the highest optimal score. The performance of different alignment methods has been studied, and one of the interesting results that have come out of such studies is that 'for different pairs many different methods create the best alignments', and hence, that 'if a method that could select the best alignment method for each pair existed, a significant improvement of the alignment quality could be gained' [5]. However, in practice it is computationally unfeasible to try out a large numbers of methods and to tune all parameters (such as evolutionary distance, gap penalty, etc.) for each one of them.

In this paper, it is investigated whether a bias in the evolutionary distance also leads to a bias in the optimal alignment: a generalisation of the well-known Needleman-Wunsch algorithm [2] is proposed in order to determine whether an alignment, or parts of it, are insensitive to the evolutionary distance in an interval. We rely on an extension of the dynamic programming formalism to the case where the gain is described by an imprecise probability model [6].

The paper is organised as follows. Section 2 discusses the standard approach to sequence alignment, using score matrices, gap penalties, and dynamic programming. In Section 3 we introduce and motivate a robustified notion of sequence alignment, based on a simple imprecise probability model for evolutionary distance. Section 4 deals with generalising the dynamical programming approach for finding a robust optimal alignment. The main conclusions are summarized in Section 5.

2. Optimal Sequence Alignment

2.1. What is Sequence Alignment?

A sequence alignment consists of writing two (or more) sequences in rows, and writing similar characters in the same column. In doing so, one is allowed to introduce so-called *gaps*, denoted by a dash '-' in either one of the sequences. Assuming that the sequences are derived from a common ancestor sequence, matches correspond to conserved regions, mismatches correspond to mutations and gaps correspond to deletions or insertions, briefly called *indels*, in either one of the sequences. Figure 1 gives an example of an amino acid alignment.

It is convenient to represent alignments in a grid, as depicted in Figure 2. All paths from the upper left corner to the lower right corner represent possible alignments. The path drawn in Figure 2 corresponds to the alignment given in Figure 1. A diagonal move introduces no gaps, a downwards move introduces a gap in the

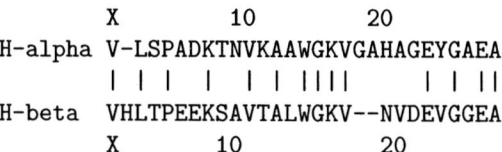

Fig. 1. An extract from a possible alignment of hemoglobin alpha and beta chains [7].

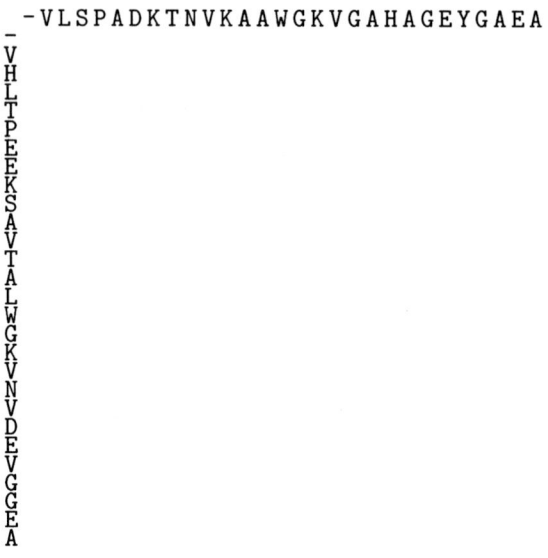

Fig. 2. Alignments can be conveniently represented in a grid.

upper sequence, a rightwards move introduces a gap in the lower sequence.

When trying to explain evolutionary relationships between sequences, we should identify the alignment that has the highest chance of being the result of evolution, and as such identifying the result of evolution from a common ancestor. We first show how evolutionary dynamics can be described on the level of genetic sequences. Then we show how a score matrix is obtained from these dynamics, and how the resulting optimisation problem indeed identifies the alignment that has the highest chance of being the result of evolution from a common ancestor.

2.2. *Evolutionary Sequence Dynamics*

The PAM ('point accepted mutation') matrices are widely accepted as the standard scoring system when looking for evolutionary relationships in protein sequences. They are related to the evolution of amino acid sequences described by a Markov model for amino acid substitution [3]. Indels, which introduce alignment gaps, are not modelled by PAM and are treated separately. We will only give a very brief description of the basic ideas underlying the dynamics; see [3,8–10] for a more extensive discussion and improvements of this approach.

Let $A_t(i)$ denote the amino acid at site i at (discrete) time t of a sequence of length N. It is first assumed that amino acids mutate independently at each site of the sequence. This implies that the probability of the sequence A_t to evolve to the sequence A_{t+s} is equal to

$$P[A_{t+s}|A_t] = \prod_{i=1}^{N} P[A_{t+s}(i)|A_t(i)]. \tag{1}$$

Hence, it suffices to know only the probabilities $P[A_{t+s}(i)|A_t(i)]$ at each site i of the sequence. It is also assumed that amino acids mutate independently in time,

$$P[A_{t+s}(i)|A_t(i)] = \prod_{r=t}^{t+s-1} P[A_{r+1}(i)|A_r(i)]. \tag{2}$$

We thus only need to know the probabilities $P[A_{r+1}(i)|A_r(i)]$ at each site i and time r.

Finally, assuming that the transition probabilities are identically distributed in time and space, $P[A_{r+1}(i)|A_r(i)]$ does not depend on the actual values of r and i, but only on the amino acids $A_r(i)$ and $A_{r+1}(i)$. Hence, if we know for any pair (a,b) of amino acids the probability $P[b|a]$ of a being substituted by b after one unit of time, then we also know the probability of any sequence A_t evolving to A_{t+s}, through Eqs. (1) and (2). Under the assumptions made so far, this establishes that we can model evolution of amino acid sequences through a Markov model.

It is convenient to assume that evolution from ancestors to descendants is modelled by the same Markov process as the evolution from descendants to ancestors, that is, that the Markov process is *time-reversible*. Assuming $P[b|a] > 0$ for all amino acid pairs (a,b), the Markov process attains a stationary distribution π after a sufficient long time. Moreover, π is independent of the initial distribution, and is the unique solution of $\sum_a P[b|a]\pi[a] = \pi[b]$. In this case, the process is time-reversible if and only if $P[b|a]\pi[a] = P[a|b]\pi[b]$ (see for instance [11]).

Consider two amino acid sequences, B and C, that have evolved from a common ancestor A in t time units. Assuming time-reversibility, and assuming that all amino acids in A are i.i.d. according to the stationary distribution π, evolution from A to B and C in t time units is equivalent to evolution from B to A in t time units, and then from A to C in t time units. But this is equivalent to evolution from B to C in $2t$ time units. Hence, we can calculate the probability of B and C having evolved from a common ancestor in t time units simply by calculating the probability of C having evolved from B in $2t$ time units.

In practice, the transition probabilities $P[b|a]$ of the Markov model are estimated using a large dataset of sequences that are already aligned (originally, sequences from closely related species were considered, that is, sequences of at least 85% similarity). Many generalisations of this model have been developed, dropping stationarity, allowing different transition probabilities on different sites, etc.

2.3. *A Log Likelihood Ratio Scoring*

Using the Markov model for amino acid evolution, a scoring matrix is derived that has the interpretation of a log likelihood ratio. The entries of the matrix are roughly given by (up to a normalisation factor)

$$s_t(a,b) = \log \frac{L_{\text{evol}}[a,b](t)}{L_{\text{rand}}[a,b]}, \tag{3}$$

that is, the logarithm of the likelihood that a and b are aligned as a consequence of the evolutionary Markov process from a common ancestor t time units ago, divided by the likelihood that a and b are aligned 'by chance', that is, as a consequence of a multinomial process, where amino acid frequencies are obtained from the same data used to construct the Markov model. A positive score $s_t(a,b)$ means that a and b are more likely to be aligned by evolution than by chance, a negative score means the opposite. Remark that $s_t(a,b) = s_t(b,a)$.

To obtain a score for sequences, recall that we assumed different sites on sequences to be independent. Hence, the log likelihood ratio of two aligned sequences B and C—of equal length and without gaps—is obtained by adding the log likelihood ratios at each site of the sequences:

$$S_t(B,C) = \sum_{i=1}^{N} s_t(B(i), C(i)) \tag{4}$$

2.4. Gap Scoring

More general, let B be a sequence of length N, and let C be a sequence of length M. Consider any alignment u of B and C, and denote the characters (amino acids or gaps) at site i in the alignment by $B_u(i)$ and $C_u(i)$. The score of the alignment is given by

$$S_t(B,C)(u) = \sum_{i=1}^{K} s_t(B_u(i), C_u(i)), \tag{5}$$

where K is the length of the alignment. If both $B_u(i)$ and $C_u(i)$ are amino acids, the $s_t(B_u(i), C_u(i))$ is given by the log likelihood ratio (Eq. (3)). If either one of them, say $B_u(i)$, is a gap, then the score is given by minus the *gap opening penalty* g if $B_u(i-1)$ is not a gap, and by minus the *gap extension penalty* r if $B_u(i-1)$ is a gap (g and r are positive).

2.5. Choice of Score Matrix and Gap Penalties

As argued before, the score for a pair of amino acids is given by Eq. (3). This score rewards alignments that are more likely by evolution than 'by chance', and punishes alignments that are less likely by evolution than 'by chance'.

Gap openings are less likely than gap extensions, and therefore the gap opening penalty g is chosen substantially higher than the gap extension penalty r. The gap penalties should also be chosen relative to the range of scores in the score matrix. If the gap penalty is too high, gaps will never appear in the optimal alignment. And if it is too low, too many gaps will appear in the optimal alignment.

Much research has been devoted to analysing how the score matrix and gap penalties should be chosen. The choice of the score matrix is based mainly on the evolutionary dynamical model and estimates of the evolutionary distance. Through statistical analysis, appropriate gap opening and extension penalties have been motivated for various score matrices (see for instance [12]).

One result is that a good choice for the score matrix, and consequently also a good choice for the gap penalties, can be made based on the evolutionary distance between sequences and their closest common ancestor.

2.6. Needleman-Wunsch Algorithm

Finding the optimal alignment is at first sight an extremely hard computational task. The number of possible alignments of two sequences of length N grows exponentially with N. Even for sequences of modest length, computing power is far from able to compare that many sequences in a reasonable amount of time.

Dynamic programming provides a method for exponentially reducing the number of alignments that need to be considered in order to find the optimal one [2]. Due to lack of space the original algorithm is not discussed here. A generalised version of the algorithm will be discussed in Section 4 further on.

3. An Imprecise Probability Model for Evolutionary Distance

In Section 2, it was argued that a good choice of the score matrix and the gap penalties can be made based on the evolutionary distance between the sequences under study and their closest common ancestor. Unfortunately, for short sequences, estimation of evolutionary distance is subject to serious bias due to stochastic effects [4]. Instead of somehow trying to improve evolutionary distance estimates between short sequences by reducing stochastic effects—this may well be impossible—we propose a different approach.

Instead, does a bias in the evolutionary distance also leads to a bias in the optimal alignment? Or, how sensitive is the alignment to the evolutionary distance? It is well-known that optimal alignment is quite sensitive to the choice of the score matrix, especially for long sequences [5]. But for short sequences, this does not need to be the case. To give an extreme example: if we would find that the optimal alignment is independent of the evolutionary distance, we also should not have to worry about it. Recent developments in imprecise probability theory provide the perfect tool for performing such analysis. Let us briefly touch upon those results and apply them to the alignment problem.

Let $\mathcal{T} = \{t \in \mathbb{R} : t \geq 0\}$ be the space of possible evolutionary distances t between two sequences B and C and their closest common ancestor. Assume that the only information we have about $t \in \mathcal{T}$ is that it takes a value in the interval $[t_1, t_2]$, for some $t_1 \leq t_2$. In imprecise probability theory, this information can be used in order to construct a partial preference ordering on alignments [13]:

Definition 1 (Preference). Let u and v be two alignments (of B and C). Then, u is said to be *strictly preferred to* v, and we write $u >_{[t_1,t_2]} v$, if

$$\inf_{t \in [t_1, t_2]} [S_t(B,C)(u) - S_t(B,C)(v)] > 0. \tag{6}$$

If $u >_{[t_1,t_2]} v$ then there is an $\epsilon > 0$ such that $S_t(B,C)(u) > S_t(B,C)(v) + \epsilon$ for every $t \in [t_1, t_2]$. This means that, independently of the evolutionary distance in $[t_1, t_2]$, u is (uniformly) a strictly better alignment of B and C than v. In such a case, we should of course prefer u over v.

The optimisation problem can now also be restated. Usually, the partial order $>_{[t_1,t_2]}$ will not have a greatest element. Therefore, it makes more sense to look for undominated, or maximal elements.

Definition 1 (Maximality). Say an alignment u is *maximal* with respect to $[t_1, t_2]$ if $v \not>_{[t_1,t_2]} u$, that is, if

$$\sup_{t \in [t_1,t_2]} [S_t(B,C)(u) - S_t(B,C)(v)] \geq 0, \tag{7}$$

for all possible alignments v of B and C.

The idea behind this definition is that, if we do not prefer any other alignment v over u, then we should consider u as a good alignment candidate. The information we have does not allow us to make a better choice than u. An efficient algorithm for finding all maximal alignments will be given in Section 4. But let us first make a few important remarks.

Firstly, the notion of maximality generalises the classical notion of optimality. Indeed, if $t_1 = t_2 = t$ then any maximal alignment actually maximises the score $S_t(B,C)(v)$ over all possible alignments v.

Secondly, it is often argued that it is important to find *the* best alignment. But, when looking for maximal alignments, we do not obtain a single solution, but rather a set of solutions—perhaps even a pretty large set. At first sight, this may seem undesirable. Nevertheless, even a set of best possible alignments can be useful:
- If we obtain a large set, then this simply means that we have insufficient information in order to construct the best alignment.
- We might be lucky and find that there is only one maximal alignment. If that is the case, we actually also know that this alignment is insensitive to assumptions made about evolutionary distance in the interval $[t_1, t_2]$.
- More generally, there may be certain constant patterns in the set of maximal alignments, i.e., it may happen that certain regions are consistently aligned over the whole set of maximal alignments. We then do not only know that these regions are optimally aligned, but also that they are insensitive to assumptions made about evolutionary distance in the interval $[t_1, t_2]$.

4. Finding Maximal Alignments Through Dynamic Programming

Recently, the algorithm of dynamic programming [14] has been generalised in order to find all maximal paths of a dynamical system, including the case in which maximality is defined in the sense of Definition 1 [6]. We briefly discuss how the algorithm is implemented.

Let B be a sequence of length N, and let C be a sequence of length M. First, finding maximal alignments of B and C is restated in terms of finding the maximal paths of a dynamical system. This is done by interpreting alignments as paths of a dynamical system, and scores as gains associated with that path. Figure 2 shows how we can do that. The grid represents the state space. At each point in the grid we can move either rightwards, downwards or diagonal (except at the right and bottom borders). The gain associated with a move from position (i,j) if the previous move was p, is given by

$$G_t(i,j,p,\downarrow) = \begin{cases} r_t, & \text{if } p = \downarrow \\ g_t, & \text{otherwise} \end{cases}$$

$$G_t(i,j,p,\rightarrow) = \begin{cases} r_t, & \text{if } p = \rightarrow \\ g_t, & \text{otherwise} \end{cases}$$

$$G_t(i,j,p,\searrow) = S_t(B(i), C(j))$$

The gain associated with a path is simply the sum of the gains of each move.

The gain depends on the evolutionary distance t. Since the gain also depends on the previous move we must extend the state space with an additional state variable p at each point (i,j) in order to remember our previous move. Otherwise, we cannot apply the dynamical programming formalism.

Let $\mathcal{P}(i,j,p)$ denote the set of all paths from (i,j,p) to the right bottom corner. Observe that p denotes the previous move, $p \in \{\downarrow, \rightarrow, \searrow\}$, which is needed in order to calculate the gain (in order to tell the difference between a gap opening and a gap extension). Let $\mathcal{M}(i,j,p)$ denote the set of maximal paths from (i,j,p) to the bottom right corner, that is,

$$\mathcal{M}(i,j,p) = \max\nolimits_{>[t_1,t_2]} \mathcal{P}(i,j,p) \tag{8}$$

It is convenient to define $\mathcal{M}(i,j,p) = \emptyset$ whenever $i > N$ or $j > M$. Observe that $\mathcal{P}(i,j,p)$ is a finite set for every state (i,j,p). Hence, the compactness condition under which the generalised Bellman equation holds is trivially satisfied [6].

Theorem 2 (generalised Bellman equation). *For any state (i,j,p) the following equality holds:*

$$\mathcal{M}(i,j,p) = \max_{>[t_1,t_2]} (i,j,p;\downarrow) \oplus \mathcal{M}(i+1,j,\downarrow) \tag{9}$$
$$\cup (i,j,p;\rightarrow) \oplus \mathcal{M}(i,j+1,\rightarrow)$$
$$\cup (i,j,p;\searrow) \oplus \mathcal{M}(i+1,j+1,\searrow),$$

where $(i,j,p;\downarrow) \oplus \mathcal{M}(i+1,j,\downarrow)$ denotes the set of all concatenations of the downward move from state (i,j,p), with a maximal path from state $(i+1,j,\downarrow)$, etc.

Eq. (9) yields an efficient recursive algorithm to calculate the set of all maximal paths $\mathcal{M}(0,0,\searrow)$, and hence, all maximal alignments. It solves a global maximisation problem by solving $3MN$ smaller maximisation problems (see Figure 3).

```
        ** initialisation **
        for p=|,-,\
          MAX(N,M,p)={(M,N,p)}
          for i=0 to N
            MAX(i,M+1,p)={}
          next i
          for j=0 to M
            MAX(N+1,j,p)={}
          next j
        next p
        ** dynamic programming **
        for i=N to 0
          for j=M to 0
            for p=|,-,\
              if (i<N) or (j<M)
                ** Bellman **
                MAX(i,j,p)=max{
                  (i,j,p;|)+MAX(i+1,j,|),
                  (i,j,p;-)+MAX(i,j+1,-),
                  (i,j,p;\)+MAX(i+1,j+1,\)
                }
            next p
          next j
        next i
```

Fig. 3. The algorithm for calculating maximal alignments.

5. Discussion and Future Research

We demonstrated one possible way of how imprecise probabilities can be applied in bioinformatics. Imprecise probability theory allows us to substantially weaken assumptions we have to make about data, for instance about the evolutionary distance. In this paper, we did that by means of an interval rather than using a point estimate. It turns out that a good alignment still can be found in an efficient way, through a generalisation of the well-known Needleman-Wunsch algorithm, and relying on an extension of dynamic programming to the case where the gain is described by an imprecise probability model. This generalisation could be particularly useful in cases where the sequences under study are rather short, or other cases where point estimates of evolutionary distance are unreliable or hard to obtain.

Acknowledgements

This paper presents research results of project G.0139.01 of the Fund for Scientific Research, Flanders (Belgium), and of the Belgian Programme on Interuniversity Poles of Attraction initiated by the Belgian state, Prime Minister's Office for Science, Technology and Culture. The scientific responsibility rests with the author.

References

1. D. W. Mount, Bioinformatics. Genome and Sequence Analysis, Cold Spring Harbor Laboratory Press, New York, 2001.
2. S. B. Needleman, C. D. Wunsch, An efficient method applicable to the search for similarities in the amino acid sequences of two proteins., Journal of Molecular Biology 48 (1970) 443–453.
3. M. O. Dayhoff, R. M. Schwartz, B. C. Orcutt, A model of evolutionary change in proteins, in: M. O. Dayhoff (Ed.), Atlas of protein sequence and structure, Vol. 5, National biomedical research foundation, 1978, pp. 345–352.
4. X. Gu, W. H. Li, Estimation of evolutionary distances under stationary and nonstationary models of nucleotide substitution, Proceedings of the National Academy of Sciences of the United States of America 95 (11) (1998) 5899–5905.
5. A. Elofsson, A study on protein sequence alignment quality, Proteins-structure function and genetics 46 (3) (2002) 330–339.
6. G. de Cooman, M. C. M. Troffaes, Dynamic programming for discrete-time systems with uncertain gain, in: J.-M. Bernard, T. Seidenfeld, M. Zaffalon (Eds.), ISIPTA '03 – Proceedings of the Third International Symposium on Imprecise Probabilities and Their Applications, Carleton Scientific, 2003, pp. 162–176.
   URL http://hdl.handle.net/1854/2272
7. C. G. Nevill-Manning, C. N. Huang, D. L. Brutlag, Pairwise protein sequence alignment using Needleman-Wunsch and Smith-Waterman algorithms, personal communication (1997).
8. D. T. Jones, W. R. Taylor, J. M. Thornton, The rapid generation of mutation data matrices from protein sequences, Computer Applications in the Biosciences 8 (3) (1992) 275–282.
9. S. A. Benner, M. A. Cohen, G. H. Gonnet, Amino-acid substitution during functionally constrained divergent evolution of protein sequences, Protein Engineering 7 (11) (1994) 1323–1332.
10. M. Tobias, V. Martin, Modeling amino acid replacement, Journal of Computational Biology 7 (6) (2000) 761–776.
11. S. M. Ross, Stochastic Processes, 2nd Edition, John Wiley & Sons, New York, 1996.
12. W. R. Pearson, Empirical statistical estimates for sequence similarity searches, Journal of Molecular Biology 276 (1) (1998) 71–84.
13. P. Wallcy, Statistical Reasoning with Imprecise Probabilities, Chapman and Hall, London, 1991.
14. R. Bellman, Dynamic Programming, Princeton University Press, Princeton, 1957.

Classifying Biomedical Spectra Using Stochastic Feature Selection and Parallelized Multi-Layer Perceptrons

N. J. Pizzi [a,b,1] R. L. Somorjai [a] W. Pedrycz [c,1]

[a] Institute for Biodiagnostics, National Research Council of Canada,
Winnipeg MB, R3B 1Y6, Canada
[b] Department of Computer Science, University of Manitoba,
Winnipeg MB, R3T 2N2, Canada
[c] Department of Electrical and Computer Engineering, University of Alberta,
Edmonton AB, T6G 2V4, Canada

Abstract

Feature selection is a useful preprocessing strategy for classifying high-dimensional biomedical data especially when the sample size is small. A parallel classification technique is presented where a set of multi-layer perceptrons is trained on randomly selected feature subsets of varying cardinality. This technique is tested using data acquired from a magnetic resonance spectrometer. The results are benchmarked against a conventional multi-layer perceptron and linear discriminant analysis. The new technique produced fewer classification errors than either benchmark.

Key words: Biomedical data classification, feature selection, parallel computing, artificial neural network, , multi-layer perceptron

1. Introduction

Magnetic resonance (MR) spectroscopy [1], which exploits the interaction between an external homogenous magnetic field and a nucleus that possesses spin, is

---

Email address: pizzi@nrc-cnrc.gc.ca (N. J. Pizzi).
[1] Partially supported by the Natural Sciences and Engineering Research Council of Canada.

a reliable and versatile spectroscopic modality. Coupled with robust multivariate discrimination strategies, it is especially useful in the classification and interpretation of high-dimensional biomedical spectra of tissues and biofluids [2], for instance, spectra of yeast species [3]. However, the sample to feature ratio of these data is typically low; the feature space dimensionality is O(1000–10000) while the sample size is O(10–100). This "curse of dimensionality" is a serious challenge for the discrimination of class-labeled biomedical spectra: the excess degrees of freedom tend to cause overfitting, which affects the reliability of the chosen classifier.

Feature selection is a typical preprocessing strategy for attenuating the effects of the curse of dimensionality by reducing the size of the feature space. Formally, consider a c-class classification problem in which $X = \{(x_k, \omega_k), k = 1, 2, \ldots, N\}$ is a set of N class-labeled samples where $x_k \in \Re^n$ and $\omega_k \in \Omega, \Omega = 1, 2, \ldots, c$. Feature selection involves finding a mapping $f : X \to X'$, where $X' \subseteq \Re^m (m \ll n)$ is the reduced feature space. Subsequently, classification involves finding a mapping from the reduced feature space to the space of class labels, $g : X' \to \Omega$.

To this end, a stochastic feature subset selection (SFS) technique is presented [5], implemented via a parallel set of artificial neural networks. Two datasets are presented in Section 3: a synthetic dataset (2 classes, 100 features) with a hyperspherical decision boundary and a set of MR spectra of yeast (5 classes, 1500 features). Section 4 discusses the design of the experiment including a description of the multi-layer perceptron classifier, the linear discriminant analysis benchmark, and some implementation details. Results are presented in Section 5 for both the synthetic and biomedical datasets followed by concluding remarks in Section 6.

2. Stochastic Feature Selection

The initial step for SFS is the random assignment of the samples from the original dataset into a design set and validation set. Once the design phase is complete, the latter set is used to externally validate the classification performance. This validation, coupled with the chance-corrected measure of agreement described in Section 2.4, provides a reliable and conservative measure of the effectiveness of the underlying classifier (classification system). The design set is further divided into training and monitoring sets. During the design phase, the classifier uses the training set to generate classification coefficients and the monitoring set is subsequently used to assess the performance of these coefficients. The overall training and monitoring accuracy is measured taking into account a weighted average across both sets as well across each class. In the case of iterative classifiers, such as artificial neural networks, this approach tends to attenuate overfitting. In the general case, this approach is well-suited to internal cross-validation.

After selecting the minimum and maximum number of feature regions as well as the minimum and maximum feature region size, the general procedure is:
(i) Randomly select a number of regions (satisfying the above constraints) and, for each region, select a random size;

(ii) Prune the features non-selected from the training and monitoring sets;
(iii) Use the training set and classifier to produce classification coefficients;
(iv) Test these coefficients with the monitoring set;
(v) Repeat until accuracy threshold or maximum number of iterations is exceeded;
(vi) Use the best coefficients found and assess performance using validation set.

Fitness functions include: the standard ratio of correctly classified samples to total number of samples; the average accuracy for each class; or chance-corrected measures of agreement. To ensure the reliability of the results, n-fold validation is used between samples in the training and monitoring sets. SFS halts execution if one of two stopping criteria is satisfied: exceeding a specified number of classification tasks; or, exceeding a specified threshold for the selected fitness function. SFS ensures that feature regions are disjoint; however, as an option, they are allowed to overlap. Moreover, transformations may be performed on regions such as computing their averages, variance, or other statistical moments.

2.1. Feature Frequency Histogram

The stochastic nature of this method may be optionally controlled by the feature frequency histogram (Figure 1). During an SFS run, the performance of each classification task is assessed using the selected fitness function. If the fitness exceeds the histogram fitness threshold, which is set to some value less than the fitness threshold stopping criterion, the histogram is incremented at those feature indices corresponding to the regions used by the classification task. This histogram is then used to generate a cumulative distribution function (cdf). Now, when regions are selected for a new classification task, features are randomly selected using the current cdf (rather than randomly selecting the features using a uniform distribution). So, rather than each feature having an equal likelihood of being selected, those features that were used in previous "successful" classification tasks have a greater likelihood of being chosen. A temperature term, $t \in [0,1]$, provides additional control over this process. If $t = 0$, the cdf is used as described but as $t \to 1$ the randomness becomes more uniform (when $t = 1$ a strict uniform distribution is used).

2.2. Quadratic Combination of Features

Stochastic feature selection may exploit the quadratic combination of regions. The intent is that if the original feature space had non-linear boundaries between classes, the new (quadratic) parameter space may have boundaries that are more linear. For example, Figure 2(a) is a plot of a two-feature two-class (grey and dark points) dataset with samples separated by a circular (non-linear) decision boundary. A classifier such as linear discriminant analysis (see Section 4.2) would perform poorly ($\sim$ 50% classification accuracy) with such a dataset as no linear decision boundary (line) can accurately delineate the two classes of points. Figure 2(b) is a plot of the same dataset with the original feature values squared. It is clear that a linear decision boundary now exists that would perfectly delineate the two classes.

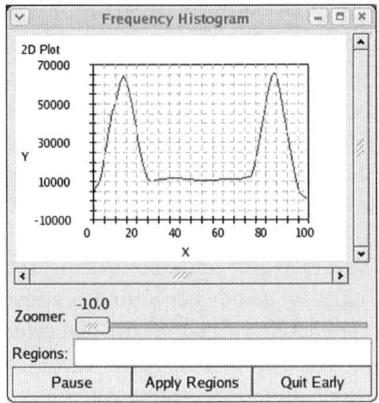

Fig. 1. Feature frequency histogram used in SFS.

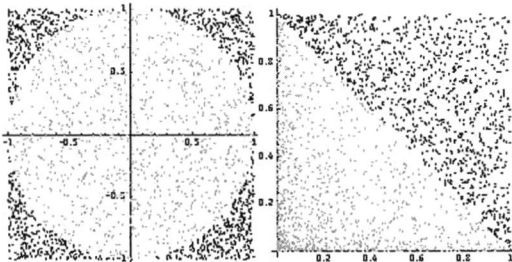

Fig. 2. Two-feature two-class dataset with non-linear (a) and linear (b) boundaries.

SFS has three categories of quadratic combinations: using the original feature region; squaring the feature values for the region; using all pair-wise cross-products of features from two regions. Given the potential combinatorial explosion with the latter category, an upper limit for the region size may be specified. The probabilities of selecting one of these categories must sum to 1.

2.3. Parallelized Classification

SFS takes advantage of parallel computations using the MPI message-passing library specification [6]. A master cluster computer node coordinates distribution of classification tasks and records intermediate performance results. To minimize communication and maximize CPU loads, SFS "bundles" sets of tasks. Furthermore, SFS is strictly deterministic, so, experimental results are perfectly reproducible.

2.4. Measuring Performance

How is the performance of a classifier to be measured given an $n \times n$ confusion matrix of desired versus actual classification outcomes of samples from the validation set? The typical performance measure is the ratio of individuals that lie in regions associated with their corresponding classes to the total number of individuals:

$$P_o = N^{-1} \sum_i n_{ii} (i = 1, \ldots, k) \tag{1}$$

(N is the number of validation samples, and k is the number of classes). However, P_o, does not take into account the agreement that might be due to chance [7]

$$P_c = N^{-2} \sum_i (\sum_j n_{ij} \sum_j n_{ji})(i, j = 1, \ldots, k) \tag{2}$$

A more conservative performance measure is the κ coefficient [8], a chance-corrected measure of agreement between the desired and actual group assignments

$$\kappa = \frac{P_o - P_c}{1 - P_c} \tag{3}$$

If the agreement is due strictly to chance, $\kappa = 0$. If the agreement is greater than chance $\kappa > 0$; $\kappa = 1$ indicates complete agreement. If the agreement is less than chance then $\kappa < 0$ (floor depends upon the marginal distributions).

3. Datasets

3.1. Hyperspherical Decision Boundary

To test the efficacy of SFS, a synthetic 100-feature 2-class dataset was generated with a prescribed 20-dimensional hyperspherical decision boundary (20-dimensional version of Figure 2(a) with values in the range $[-1, 1]$). The first 10 coordinates of the hypersphere are found at feature indices 10-19 and the remaining 10 at indices 70-79. The other 80 features are uniformly distributed random values (noise) in the range $[-1, 1]$. A total of 200 samples were generated (100 points/class) and then evenly divided (at random) into training/monitoring and validation sets.

3.2. Biomedical Magnetic Resonance Spectra

Yeasts are unicellular fungi that use the characteristics of the cell, ascospore and colony. They are found on the skin surfaces and in the intestinal tracts of warm-blooded animals, where they may live symbiotically or as parasites. The common "yeast infection" is typically Candidiasis and is caused by the yeast-like fungus Candida albicans. In addition to being the causative agent in vaginal yeast infections Candida is also a cause of diaper rash and thrush of the mouth and throat [9]. The identification of closely related species of yeasts is problematic.

For this experiment, MR spectra of isolates of five different Candida species were used (their acquisition and description are described in [3]): Candida albicans (A),

Candida parapsilosis (P), Candida krusei (K), Candida tropicalis (T), and Candida glabrata (G). The 1H spectra were acquired on a 360 MHz MR spectrometer. Each of the $N = 444$ (baseline corrected) spectra ($p' = 1500$ features) were divided into five classes, according to the corresponding Candida species: 104 A, 91 G, 81 K, 93 P, and 75 T. Figure 3 are the respective plots of the MR spectra (grey lines) for each class of yeast species as well as the average class spectra (thick black lines). The spectra were divided into three sets: training, monitoring, and validation. A 200 sample training set was randomly selected from the N spectra, containing 40 samples from each class. A 50 sample monitoring set was randomly selected from the remaining $N - 200$ spectra, containing 10 samples from each class. Finally, the validation set comprised the remaining 194 samples (54 A, 41 G, 31 K, 43 P, and 25 T) and were not used during the classifier design phase.

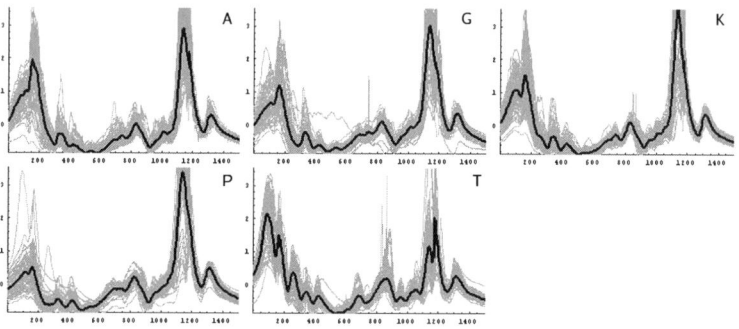

Fig. 3. MR spectra of yeast species by class (with class mean spectra).

4. Experiment Design

4.1. Multi-layer Perceptron

The artificial neural network paradigm has consistently demonstrated its effectiveness as a reliable nonlinear classification technique [10]. The multi-layer perceptron (MLP), a feed-forward supervised neural network often used for data classification, requires the desired class label for each sample (in our case, MR spectrum) in order that it may be compared to the actual output generated by the MLP.

The learning strategy minimizes a global error function, $E = 0.5 \sum_k (d_k - o_k)^2$ (where d_k and o_k are the respective components of the desired and actual outputs), for the set of input data. The MLP uses the back-propagation algorithm to pass this error back throughout the network in a localized, neuron-based, fashion [11]. In general terms, MLP may be considered a non-linear regression system that performs a gradient descent search through the weight space, searching for (local) minima.

In this study, the MLP uses $(1 + e^{-x})^{-1}$ for the transfer function, a learning rate of 0.7, and a momentum rate of 0.05. A regularization (weight decay) parameter of 0.1 is used. The MLP neuron layers included a single hidden layer composed of $\lfloor p/3 \rfloor$ neurons, where p is the cardinality of the subset of randomly selected features, and an input layer for the p features that were randomly selected. The output layer uses 1-of-c encoding, where c is the number of classes. For the output neurons in the MR spectra case, $y_i = [c_1, c_2, c_3, c_4, c_5]$, where $c_i = 1$, if the respective input spectrum belongs to the corresponding class, and $c_i = 0$, otherwise (c_1=A, c_2=G, c_3=K, c_3=P, c_4=T). The synthetic data is encoded in a similar fashion. Finally, rather than randomly initializing the neuron weights, they are initialized so that the slopes of the neurons are randomly placed within the domain of the input spectra.

4.2. Benchmark

SFS was compared against linear discriminant analysis (LDA) [12], a conventional classifier used to determine linear decision boundaries between classes while taking into account between- and within-class variances. If the error distribution for each class is the same, LDA constructs optimal linear decision boundary. In real-world situations, this optimality is seldom achieved since different classes typically give rise to different distributions. Nevertheless, LDA is a useful benchmark classifier to assess the performance of other, more sophisticated, classification systems.

A sample, x, should be allocated to the class for which the probability distribution, $p_i(x)$, is greater than any other distribution, while taking into account known prior probabilities. So, $x \in \omega_i$, if $q_i p_i(x) \geq q_j p_j(x)(j = 1, \ldots, k)$, where q_i is the prior probability of observing x from class, ω_i. Here, we use proportional probabilities, N_i/N, for each ω_i. The discriminant function is $L_i(x) = \log q_i + \mu_i^T W^{-1}(x - 0.5\mu_i)$, where μ_i is the mean for ω_i and W is the covariance matrix. The hyperplane separating ω_i from ω_j is defined by $D_{ij}(x) = L_i(x) - L_j(x) = 0$.

4.3. Implementation

Suitable for the development of extensible classification systems, such as SFS, Scopira (http://scopira.org) is an algorithm development framework, which allows the interconnection of multiple algorithm "modules"[4]. All inter-module data are tightly typed in a hierarchical, object-oriented data type tree. The system of modules may be mapped onto a computer cluster. Modules need not be aware of this parallelism as Scopira transparently provides this service; however, an interface exists for algorithm developers to optionally control parallelism at the intra-module level.

Written in C++, Scopira facilitates the creation of new modules, data types and functions that integrate seamlessly with existing services. The Scopira framework is designed to be modular, portable and distributed. The complete Scopira engine core is compiled into a shared core library. This library exposes an object-oriented interface to module construction and manipulation. This allows C++ developers to embed Scopira in their applications and naturally extends to any language that may call C functions (e.g. Java, Perl, and Python).

The classification tasks ran on a heterogeneous 25-processor Linux Beowulf cluster with a memory range of 256–2048MB. The entire parallelized classification exercise terminated when one of two stopping criteria were satisfied: 1,000,000 MLP classification tasks were completed; or, the fitness threshold of 0.999 was exceeded.

A given MLP classification task continued to iterate until the mean square error was less than 0.001 or 10,000 iterations occurred. With the latter stopping criterion, the MLP was re-initialized with a new set of random weights and the training phase would begin again (if it failed to converge a second time, the task and feature subset were abandoned). In the case of the former stopping criterion, when the training phase converged, the results were reported back to a master recording process, which retained information on the current best MLP classifier and feature subset.

5. Results

5.1. Synthetic Dataset

The SFS parameters used in this analysis: 0.9999 for the fitness threshold; 0.8 for the feature frequency histogram threshold; 0.3 for temperature; and 10-fold cross validation. As it is known that there are 20 discriminatory features divided into two separate regions, we specify that SFS select exactly 2 regions of length 10.

In the first experiment, the quadratic combination categories probabilities were set to 1.0, 0.0, 0.0, respectively, that is, only the original features were used. The poor level of agreement, $\kappa = 0.01 \pm 0.02$, is due to the highly non-linear boundary present in this dataset. The two regions (40–49 and 60–69) selected were noise rather than the discriminatory regions. Table 1(a) lists the validation set confusion matrix of samples inside ($N_I = 100$) and outside ($N_O = 100$) the hypersphere.

In the second experiment, the probabilities for the quadratic combination categories were set to 0.6, 0.3, and 0.1, respectively, with all other parameters unchanged. The feature frequency histogram is shown in Figure 1. The validation set confusion matrix listed in Table 1(b) shows an almost perfect level of agreement, $\kappa = 0.90 \pm 0.01$, which is due to the fact that, while the original feature space had a highly non-linear decision boundary, the new quadratic feature space had a much more linear boundary separating the two classes (analogous to the phenomenon shown in Figure 2). The two regions selected were 9–18 and 69–78 with the values for each region were squared. SFS did not perfectly select the discriminatory regions of 10–19 and 70–79, which accounts for the classification error.

Finally, SFS was compared to LDA using all 100 features. The results were similar to SFS without quadratic features with a slightly lower variance, $\kappa = 0.01 \pm 0.01$.

5.2. Biomedical Dataset

The SFS parameters used in the analysis of this dataset were: 0.9999 for the fitness threshold; 0.8 for the feature frequency histogram threshold; 1–3 feature

Table 1
Confusion matrix for samples bounded by hypersphere without (a) and with (b) quadratic features.

(a) Desired/Actual	In	Out	Class Accuracy	(b) Desired/Actual	In	Out	Class Accuracy
In	51	49	0.51±0.03	In	100	0	1.00±0.00
Out	50	50	0.50±0.02	Out	10	90	0.90±0.01
$\kappa = 0.01 \pm 0.02\ (P_o = 0.51 \pm 0.02)$				$\kappa = 0.90 \pm 0.01\ (P_o = 0.95 \pm 0.01)$			

regions with lengths of 10–50; 0.3 for temperature; 10-fold cross validation; and, the quadratic combination probabilities were 0.6, 0.3, and 0.1, respectively. The mean κ score (for the 10,000 MLP processes) was 0.89 for the training/monitoring sets and 0.81 for the validation set. The best accuracy score, based on the validation set, was $\kappa = 0.93 \pm 0.04$ for an MLP using the following regions: 61–91 (using squared feature values); 103–142 (using squared feature values); and, 1098–1120 (using the original feature values). Only 93 of the original 1500 features were required. The frequency histogram is shown in Figure 4. Less than 0.5% of the MLP processes failed to converge. The validation set ($N = 194$) confusion matrix for the best classifier is listed in Table 2.

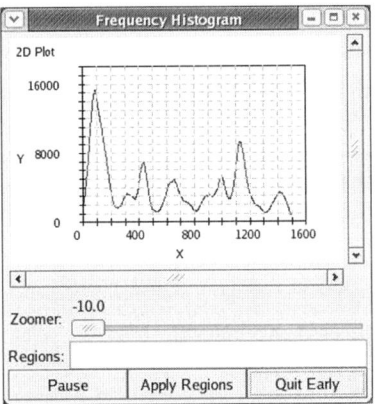

Fig. 4. The feature frequency histogram for the MR spectra.

Table 2
Confusion matrix for the MR spectra using features selected by SFS.

Desired/Actual	A	G	K	P	T	Class Accuracy
A	53	0	0	0	1	0.98±0.04
G	0	39	1	1	0	0.95±0.04
K	0	0	29	1	1	0.94±0.02
P	1	0	0	42	0	0.98±0.05
T	0	1	1	2	21	0.84±0.02
$\kappa = 0.93 \pm 0.04\ (P_o = 0.95 \pm 0.04)$						

5.2.1. LDA Benchmark

With LDA, the overall accuracy using all 1500 features was $\kappa = 0.84 \pm 0.03$ (Table 3(a)), a 10% decrease compared to SFS. Table 3(b) lists the confusion matrix for LDA when an averaging window of 5 was used, producing 300 features. While there was a substantial level of agreement with $\kappa = 0.79 \pm 0.05$, the overall accuracy dropped by 15% (with a higher variance) compared to SFS.

Table 3
Confusion matrices using LDA with 1500 features (a) and 300 averaged features (b).

(a) Des/Act	A	G	K	P	T	Class Accuracy	(b) Des/Act	A	G	K	P	T	Class Accuracy
A	46	1	1	3	3	0.85±0.04	A	46	0	0	3	5	0.85±0.06
G	0	38	3	0	0	0.93±0.03	G	3	36	0	1	1	0.88±0.04
K	0	1	26	2	2	0.84±0.02	K	0	2	24	2	3	0.77±0.05
P	1	0	0	36	6	0.84±0.03	P	1	1	2	36	3	0.84±0.03
T	0	0	0	1	24	0.96±0.02	T	1	0	1	3	20	0.83±0.04
$\kappa = 0.84 \pm 0.03$ ($P_o = 0.88 \pm 0.03$)							$\kappa = 0.79 \pm 0.05$ ($P_o = 0.84 \pm 0.05$)						

5.2.2. MLP Benchmark

SFS was also compared to an MLP (same parameters as previously described) using all 1500 features. The overall MLP accuracy was only $\kappa = 0.86 \pm 0.03$, slighter better than LDA using all 1500 spectral features (Table 4(a)). Table 4(b) lists the confusion matrix for 300 averaged features; overall accuracy dropped to $\kappa = 0.80 \pm 0.03$ (identical results were obtained using 100 averaged features).

Table 4
MLP confusion matrices with 1500 features (a) and 300 averaged features (b).

(a) Des/Act	A	G	K	P	T	Class Accuracy	(b) Des/Act	A	G	K	P	T	Class Accuracy
A	48	0	0	3	5	0.89±0.04	A	47	0	0	3	4	0.87±0.05
G	3	36	0	1	1	0.93±0.04	G	3	36	0	1	1	0.88±0.04
K	0	2	24	2	3	0.97±0.03	K	0	1	27	1	2	0.87±0.05
P	1	1	2	36	3	0.74±0.04	P	1	4	2	32	4	0.74±0.04
T	1	0	1	3	20	0.96±0.02	T	0	0	0	3	22	0.88±0.04
$\kappa = 0.86 \pm 0.03$ ($P_o = 0.89 \pm 0.03$)							$\kappa = 0.80 \pm 0.03$ ($P_o = 0.85 \pm 0.03$)						

6. Conclusion

This paper has demonstrated the efficacy of stochastically selecting feature subsets for presentation to a set of parallelized multi-layer perceptrons for the classification of high-dimensional biomedical magnetic resonance spectra. This technique produced fewer classification errors, on a validation dataset than either benchmark classifier: linear discriminant analysis or a multi-layer perceptron using all of the original features as well as averaged feature sets. Further, this improvement in accuracy was achieved using only a small fraction ($\sim 6\%$) of the original features.

Acknowledgements

We would like to thank Mr. Conrad Wiebe for his programming efforts.

References

1. Friebolin, H., Basic One- and Two-Dimensional NMR Spectroscopy, 3rd Edition, New York, John Wiley and Sons, 1998.
2. Somorjai, R. L., Dolenko, B., Nikulin, A. K., Pizzi, N., Scarth, G., Zhilkin, P., Halliday, W., Fewer, D., Hill, N., Ross, I., West, M., Smith, I. C. P., Donnelly, S. M., Kuesel, A. C., Briere, K. M., Classification of 1H MR spectra of human brain neoplasms: The influence of preprocessing and computerized consensus diagnosis on classification accuracy, J. Magnetic Resonance Imaging, 6, 437-444, 1996.
3. Somorjai, R. L., Baumgartner, R., Ho, T. K., Himmelreich, U., Mountford, C. E., Sorrell, T. C., Comparison of two strategies for classifying biomedical spectra: Genetic algorithm-driven feature extraction vs. the random subspace method, Applied and Environmental Microbiology, 69, 4566-4574, 2003.
4. Pizzi, N. J., Pedrycz, W., Randomized feature selection using Scopira. Proc. North American Fuzzy Information Processing Society, Banff, Canada, June 27-30, 669-674, 2004.
5. Pizzi N.J., Somorjai, R.L., Pedrycz, W., Biomedical data classification using randomized feature selection and parallelized multi-layer perceptrons. Proc. Information Processing and Management of Uncertainty in Knowledge-Based Systems Conf., July 4-9, Perugia, Italy, 1161-1166, 2004.
6. Snir, M., Gropp, W., MPI: The Complete Reference, Cambridge, MIT Press, 1998.
7. Everitt, B. S., Moments of the statistics kappa and weighted kappa, British J. Mathematical and Statistical Psychology, 21, 97-103, 1968.
8. Fleiss, J. L., Measuring agreement between judges on the presence or absence of a trait, Biometrics, 31, 651-659, 1975.
9. Mortimer, R. K., Contopoulou, C. R., King, J. S., Genetic and physical maps of Saccharomyces cerevisiae, Yeast, 8, 817-902, 1992.
10. Ripley, B. D., Neural networks and related methods for classification, J. Royal Statistical Society [B], 56, 409-56, 1994.
11. Hudson, D. L., Cohen, M. E., Neural Networks and Artificial Intelligence for Biomedical Engineering, New York, IEEE Press, 2000.
12. Seber, G., Multivariate Observations, New York, Wiley and Sons, 1984.

On the Sensitivity of Probabilistic Networks to Reliability Characteristics

Linda C. van der Gaag and Silja Renooij

Department of Information and Computing Sciences,
Universiteit Utrecht, The Netherlands [1]

Abstract

Diagnostic reasoning in essence amounts to reasoning about an unobservable condition, based on indirect observations from diagnostic tests. Probabilistic networks that are developed for diagnostic reasoning, typically take the reliability characteristics of the tests employed into consideration to avoid misdiagnosis. In this paper, we demonstrate the effects of inaccuracies in these characteristics by means of a sensitivity analysis of a real-life network in the medical domain.

Key words: probabilistic networks, reliability characteristics, sensitivity analysis

1. Introduction

Since their introduction, probabilistic networks have become increasingly popular for reasoning with uncertainty in a variety of application domains. A probabilistic network in essence is a model of a joint probability distribution over a set of statistical variables [1]. It is comprised of a graphical structure that captures the variables and the influential relationships between them, and an associated set of conditional probability distributions that serve to describe the strengths of these relationships. Since a probabilistic network uniquely defines a joint probability distribution, it allows for computing any probability of interest over its variables. Although probabilistic networks provide for any type of probabilistic reasoning, they are most notably used for diagnostic reasoning, especially in the medical domain. Diagnostic reasoning in general amounts to reasoning about an unobservable condition, based on indirect observations from diagnostic tests. Upon diagnostic

---

[1] e-mail: {linda,silja}@cs.uu.nl

reasoning with a probabilistic network, the available observations are entered and the posterior probability distribution given these observations is established. The most likely value for the main diagnostic variable then is taken for the diagnosis.

In most application domains, the results of diagnostic tests are uncertain to at least some extent. In the medical domain, for example, an X-ray can be difficult to interpret: a physician may easily overlook a small tumour and state a negative result, or state a positive result based upon a phantom image. The uncertainty in the result of a test is captured by its *sensitivity* and *specificity*. The sensitivity is the probability of finding a positive result whenever the condition tested for is present; the specificity is the probability of finding a negative result in the absence of the condition. The reliability characteristics of the various diagnostic tests in use should be taken into consideration in diagnostic reasoning to avoid misdiagnosis. From a study of a real-life probabilistic network in oncology, in fact, we found that taking the uncertainties in the tests' results into account is essential to arrive at clinically acceptable behaviour [2]. These characteristics are typically obtained from literature, from statistical data, or from human experts, however, and inevitably are inaccurate. Since the characteristics are used in diagnostic reasoning, the established diagnosis may be sensitive to the inaccuracies involved and, in fact, may be unreliable.

In this paper, we study the effects of inaccuracies in the reliability characteristics of diagnostic tests by means of a sensitivity analysis of a real-life probabilistic network in the medical domain. Sensitivity analysis is a general technique for studying the robustness of the output of a mathematical model to parameter variation. Within our network, we varied the sensitivity and specificity characteristics of the represented diagnostic tests, and studied whether or not this variation could change the diagnosis established from the network. From the analysis, some distinct patterns of sensitivity emerged, dependent upon the actual test results entered. The paper is organised as follows. In Section 2, we introduce the oesophageal cancer network that we used for our study. In Section 3, we review sensitivity analysis of probabilistic networks in general. In Section 4, we present the results that we obtained from a sensitivity analysis of the oesophageal cancer network and provide some insights to explain them. The paper ends with our concluding observations in Section 5.

2. The oesophageal cancer network

The *oesophageal cancer network* was constructed with the help of two experts in gastrointestinal oncology from the Netherlands Cancer Institute, Antoni van Leeuwenhoekhuis [2]. The network describes the presentation characteristics of an oesophageal tumour, the processes underlying the tumour's invasion into the oesophageal wall and adjacent organs, and the process of its metastasis. The extent of the cancer is summarised in a *stage*, which can be either I, IIA, IIB, III, IVA, or IVB, in the order of advanced disease. The network further models the diagnostic tests that are commonly used to establish the stage of a patient's cancer; these tests range from a gastroscopic examination of the primary tumour to a CT scan of the patient's upper abdomen. The oesophageal cancer network currently includes 42 statistical variables, for which almost 1000 probabilities were specified by the experts. Of the 42 included variables, 23 variables serve to represent test results. For these

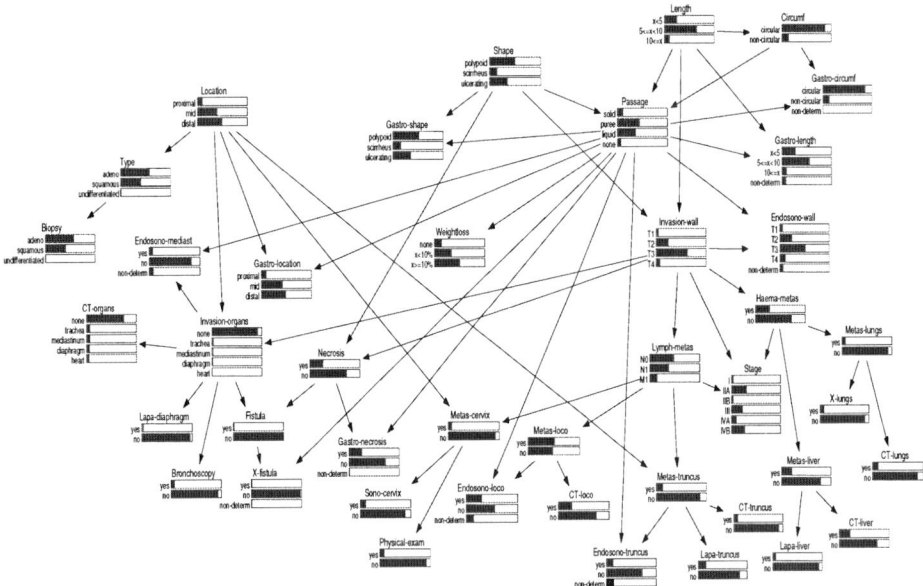

Fig. 1. The oesophageal cancer network.

test variables, between 4 and 25 parameter probabilities are specified, with an average of 8 probabilities per variable. For ease of reference, the network is depicted in Fig. 1, which also shows the prior probability distribution per variable.

To capture the uncertainties in the results of the diagnostic tests employed, the oesophageal cancer network explicitly models the tests' reliability characteristics. These characteristics are defined in terms of two variables. The disease variable D models the presence, indicated by d, or absence, indicated by $\bar{d}$, of the condition under consideration; the test variable T models the result of the test, where a positive result t suggests presence and a negative result $\bar{t}$ suggests absence of the condition. The sensitivity of the test to the condition now is the probability $\Pr(t \mid d)$ that a positive test result is found in a patient who actually has the condition; the specificity of the test is the probability $\Pr(\bar{t} \mid \bar{d})$ that a negative result is found in a patient without the condition [3]. In the network, the characteristics are captured by the probabilities specified for the various test variables. As an example, Fig. 2 shows the probabilities that were specified for an X-ray of a patient's thorax; these

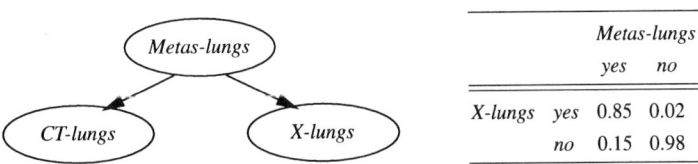

Fig. 2. A fragment of the oesophageal cancer network and some associated parameter probabilities.

are the probabilities of a positive and of a negative test result, respectively, given the actual presence or absence of metastases in the lungs. The X-ray is stated, for example, to have a sensitivity of 0.85 and a specificity of 0.98.

3. Sensitivity analysis

Sensitivity analysis is a general technique for studying the effects of inaccuracies in the parameters of a mathematical model on its output. In a sensitivity analysis of a probabilistic network, for each parameter probability x, a *sensitivity function* $f(x)$ is established that expresses the output probability of interest in terms of x. If, upon varying x, the other parameter probabilities from the same conditional distribution are co-varied proportionally, such a sensitivity function is a quotient of two linear functions [4], that is,

$$f(x) = \frac{a \cdot x + b}{c \cdot x + d}$$

where the constants a, b, c, d are built from the parameter probabilities that are not being varied. These constants can be established by computing the output probability of interest from the network for a small number of values for the parameter probability under study and solving the resulting system of linear equations.

In general, a sensitivity function takes the shape of an orthogonal *hyperbola*

$$f(x) = \frac{r}{x - s} + t, \quad \text{where } r = \frac{b \cdot c - a \cdot d}{c^2}, \quad s = -\frac{d}{c}, \quad \text{and } t = \frac{a}{c}$$

The hyperbola has two asymptotes, parallel to the x- and y-axes; these asymptotes are $y = t$ and $x = s$, respectively. The hyperbola further has two branches; for ease of reference, Fig. 3 depicts such a branch. The values of the four constants a, b, c, d of the sensitivity function now determine the actual shape of the hyperbola. For $r > 0$, for example, the hyperbola is composed of two decreasing branches in the first and third quadrants relative to the asymptotes; for $r < 0$, the two branches are increasing and located in the second and fourth quadrants. Since the output probability of interest exists for any value of the

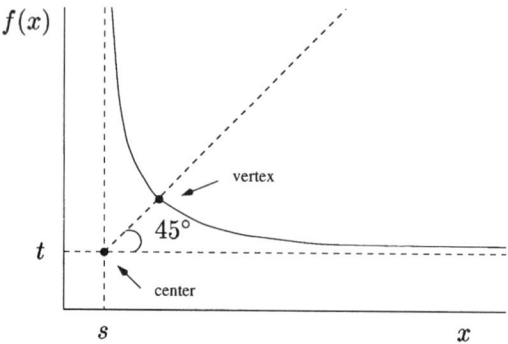

Fig. 3. A branch of an orthogonal hyperbola, located in the first quadrant relative to the asymptotes.

parameter probability x, the sensitivity function $f(x)$ that expresses this output probability is well-defined on the interval $[0, 1]$. We therefore have that a sensitivity function is a fragment of just a single branch of a hyperbola. We further have that the asymptote $x = s$ cannot be located within the interval $[0, 1]$: we have that either $s < 0$, in which case the sensitivity function is a fragment of a branch in the first or fourth quadrant, or $s > 1$, in which case the sensitivity function is a fragment of a branch in the second or third quadrant.

A sensitivity function serves to express some output probability of interest in terms of a specific parameter probability, and therefore provides for studying the effect of varying this parameter probability on that particular output probability. In diagnostic applications, however, we are not so much interested in the effect of parameter variation on a single output probability. Rather, we are interested in the effect on the diagnosis established from the network. To study this effect, we have to consider the sensitivity functions for the various possible values of the main diagnostic variable simultaneously and investigate whether or not parameter variation can change the most likely value of this variable. For an output variable D with the possible values $d_1, \ldots, d_n$, $n \geq 1$, we thus have to study the n sensitivity functions $f_i(x)$, $i = 1, \ldots, n$, that express the probability of the value d_i in terms of the parameter probability x. With the parameter's original value x_0, the most likely value of the output variable is a value d_j for which $f_j(x_0) \geq f_i(x_0)$ for all $i \neq j$. Now, if the sensitivity function $f_j(x)$ intersects with the sensitivity function $f_i(x)$ for some value d_i, then the most likely value for D may change from d_j to d_i upon varying x. The intersections of the function $f_j(x)$ with the other sensitivity functions, therefore, reveal the effects of parameter variation on the diagnosis.

From the intersections of the various sensitivity functions for an output variable of interest, we now compute a pair (α, β) that captures the deviation to smaller values and to larger values than the original value x_0 of the parameter probability under study, respectively, that are maximally possible without inducing a change in the most likely value of the output variable. Such a pair is called an *admissible deviation* [5]. We note that an admissible deviation (α, β) defines the range $(x_0 - \alpha; x_0 + \beta)$ within which the parameter probability can be varied without inducing a change in the most likely value of the output variable. In the sequel, we will use the symbols $\leftarrow$ and $\rightarrow$ to denote that a parameter probability can be varied to the left and to the right boundary of the probability interval, respectively.

4. Experimental results

To study the possible effects of inaccuracies in the reliability characteristics of diagnostic tests, we conducted a sensitivity analysis of the oesophageal cancer network. In this analysis, we varied the parameter probabilities of all test variables discerned and studied the effects of their variation on the most likely stage computed from the network. Because the patterns of sensitivity exhibited by a network typically vary with evidence, we used in our study the medical records from 185 patients diagnosed with cancer of the oesophagus, available from the Antoni van Leeuwenhoekhuis. The analysis revealed various distinct patterns of sensitivity. In this section, we discuss some of these patterns, focusing on the parameter probabilities of a small number of test variables.

4.1. Statistics on induced changes

We consider the four diagnostic tests that serve to give insight in the presence or absence of haematogenous metastases, or secondary tumours, in a patient's liver and lungs. These tests are a CT scan of the upper abdomen and a laparoscopy of the liver, to establish the presence or absence of metastases in the liver, and an X-ray and a CT scan of the thorax, to establish the presence or absence of metastases in the patient's lungs. For each of the associated test variables, four parameter probabilities are specified that correspond with the test's sensitivity and specificity and their complements. Tables 1 and 2 summarise the results that we obtained from varying these parameter probabilities.

Table 1 describes, for each of the four test variables under consideration, the effects of varying its parameter probabilities on the most likely stage computed for patients for whom a negative result from the test is available. For example, for 89 of the 91 patients for whom a negative result from a CT scan of the upper abdomen was found, varying the test's specificity resulted in a change in the most likely stage computed from the network; for just 3 patients, the complement of the test's sensitivity resulted in such a change. In general, we observe that, with the exception of a small number of patients, varying the specificities of the tests induces a change in the most likely stage computed for a patient under study; the complements of the sensitivities tend not to induce such a change.

The pattern of sensitivity that emerges from Table 1 can be readily explained by studying the predictive value of a negative test result. The *predictive value of a negative result* is defined as the probability of the condition under study indeed being absent in a negatively-tested patient [3]. For the four tests under consideration, these predictive values can be summarised by the abstractly stated probability $\Pr(\mathit{Metas} = no \mid \mathit{Test} = no)$ of the absence of metastases given a negative result from the test. This probability can be written as

$$\Pr(\mathit{Metas} = no \mid \mathit{Test} = no) = \frac{g \cdot (1-n)}{g \cdot (1-n) + h \cdot n}$$

where

$$g = p(\mathit{Test} = no \mid \mathit{Metas} = no)$$
$$h = p(\mathit{Test} = no \mid \mathit{Metas} = yes)$$
$$n = \Pr(\mathit{Metas} = yes)$$

From the predictive value of a negative test result, we now observe that, if the probability n of the presence of haematogenous metastases is relatively small, then the term $h \cdot n$ will be small. Varying the complement h of the test's sensitivity will then have little effect on the predictive value: the most likely value of the main diagnostic variable is expected to remain unchanged. Variation of the test's specificity g then is expected to result in a change in this most likely value. If n is extremely small, however, we have that the predictive value equals almost 1: varying g will then also show little effect.

Now, for oesophageal cancer, the prior probability n of haematogenous metastases being present (which coincides with a stage IVB cancer), is relatively small. Upon diagnostic reasoning, moreover, it will not increase unless there is some strong evidence of metastases

Table 1
The number of induced changes in the most likely stage given negative test results: 91 patients have *CT-liver* = *no*; 15 patients have *Lapa-liver* = *no*; 127 patients have *X-lungs* = *no*; 109 patients have *CT-lungs* = *no*.

parameter	induced changes	
$p(\textit{Lapa-liver} = no \mid \textit{Metas-liver} = yes)$	0	(0%)
$p(\textit{Lapa-liver} = no \mid \textit{Metas-liver} = no)$	15	(100%)
$p(\textit{CT-liver} = no \mid \textit{Metas-liver} = yes)$	3	(3%)
$p(\textit{CT-liver} = no \mid \textit{Metas-liver} = no)$	89	(98%)
$p(\textit{X-lungs} = no \mid \textit{Metas-lungs} = yes)$	2	(2%)
$p(\textit{X-lungs} = no \mid \textit{Metas-lungs} = no)$	122	(95%)
$p(\textit{CT-lungs} = no \mid \textit{Metas-lungs} = yes)$	1	(1%)
$p(\textit{CT-lungs} = no \mid \textit{Metas-lungs} = no)$	102	(94%)

in a patient's liver or lungs. From the above observations, we would therefore expect that varying the complement h of the sensitivity of a diagnostic test from which a negative result is available, will not induce a change in the most likely stage computed for a patient. The specificity g of the test is expected to do cause such a change upon variation. Figure 4 serves to corroborate these expectations by showing the effects of varying the two parameter probabilities for a CT scan of the upper abdomen for patient 94-2326 in whom all test results point to the absence of haematogenous metastases.

From Table 1, we observe that the expected pattern of sensitivity shows for most patients. For a small number of patients, however, the specificities of the four tests under study are not influential upon variation; for a small number of patients, moreover, the complements of the tests' sensitivities do induce a change in the most likely stage computed from the network. To explain these findings, we consider again the predictive value of a negative test result. We observe that, if the probability n of the presence of haematogenous metastases increases as a consequence of one or more positive results from the other tests, then the term $h \cdot n$ increases. Variation of the complement h of the sensitivity of the test from

Table 2
The number of induced changes in the most likely stage given positive test results; 4 patients have *Lapa-liver* = *yes*; 7 patients have *CT-liver* = *yes*; 9 patients have *X-lungs* = *yes*; 6 patients have *CT-lungs* = *yes*.

parameter	induced changes
$p(\textit{Lapa-liver} = yes \mid \textit{Metas-liver} = yes)$	3 (75%)
$p(\textit{Lapa-liver} = yes \mid \textit{Metas-liver} = no)$	3 (75%)
$p(\textit{CT-liver} = yes \mid \textit{Metas-liver} = yes)$	6 (86%)
$p(\textit{CT-liver} = yes \mid \textit{Metas-liver} = no)$	6 (86%)
$p(\textit{X-lungs} = yes \mid \textit{Metas-lungs} = yes)$	5 (56%)
$p(\textit{X-lungs} = yes \mid \textit{Metas-lungs} = no)$	6 (67%)
$p(\textit{CT-lungs} = yes \mid \textit{Metas-lungs} = yes)$	2 (33%)
$p(\textit{CT-lungs} = yes \mid \textit{Metas-lungs} = no)$	2 (33%)

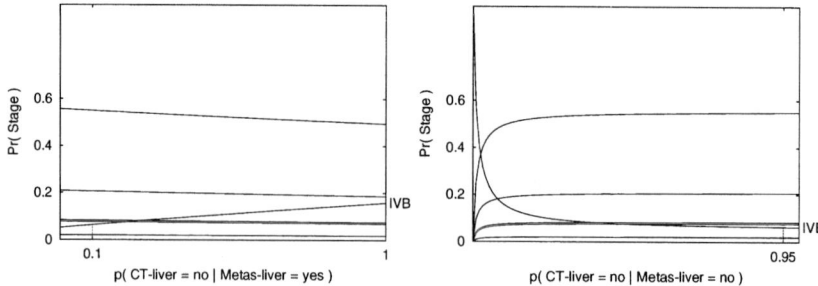

Fig. 4. The effects of varying the parameter probabilities for a CT scan of the upper abdomen for patient 94-2326, for whom all test results pertaining to haematogenous metastases are negative.

which a negative result is available, can then affect the predictive value and thereby induce a change in the most likely value of the diagnostic variable. The test's specificity g will have similar effects upon variation, unless the probability of metastases being present has become very large: if n is quite large, we have that $g \cdot (1 - n)$ is rather small and varying g can no longer affect the predictive value.

As mentioned before, the prior probability of metastases in a patient's liver or lungs is rather small. This probability increases substantially, however, as soon as one or more positive results from the four tests under study are obtained. For patient 95-1554, for example, a positive result is available from a laparoscopic examination of the liver. From the above observations, we expect for this patient that varying the complement of the sensitivity of a CT scan of the upper abdomen will induce a change in the most likely stage computed from the network. Figure 5, showing the effects of varying the parameter probabilities for the CT scan for this patient, serves to corroborate this expectation. For patient 94-1496, to conclude, positive results are available from two of the four tests under study. These results substantially increase the probability of the presence of metastases. Figure 6 now shows that the large probability of stage IVB serves to suppress the effects of varying the parameter probabilities for the X-ray of the thorax from which a negative result is available.

Where Table 1 pertains to negative test results, Table 2 describes the effects of varying the parameter probabilities for the tests from which a positive result is available. As the number of patients with positive test results is rather limited, the patterns of sensitivity

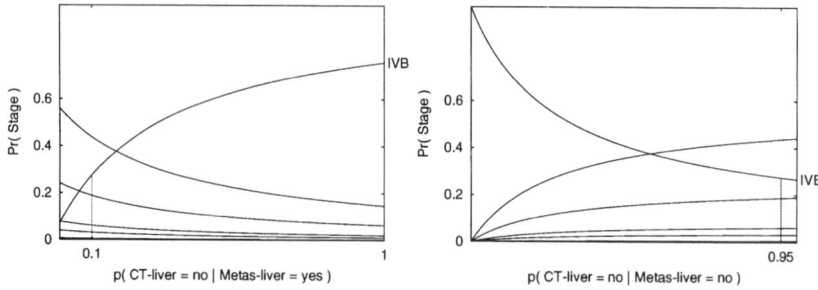

Fig. 5. The effects of varying the parameter probabilities for a CT scan of the upper abdomen for patient 95-1554, for whom a single positive test result pertaining to haematogenous metastases is available.

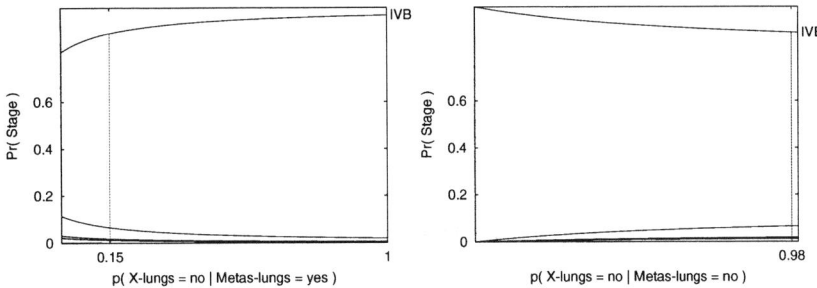

Fig. 6. The effects of varying the parameter probabilities for an X-ray of the thorax for patient 94-1496, for whom two positive test results pertaining to haematogenous metastases are available.

observed are less clear. Roughly stated, upon variation both the sensitivities and the complements of the specificities of the four tests tend to induce a change in the most likely stage computed for a patient. This observation again is readily explained by studying the predictive value $\Pr(\textit{Metas} = \textit{yes} \mid \textit{Test} = \textit{yes})$ of a positive test result.

4.2. Statistics on admissible deviations

If varying a parameter probability induces a change in the most likely value of the main diagnostic variable of a network, then inaccuracies in this parameter are likely to affect the network's diagnosis. The extent to which such inaccuracies can be influential, is expressed by the admissible deviation for the parameter probability under study. In this section, we review the admissible deviations that we found in the analysis of the oesophageal cancer network. In doing so, we focus once again on the reliability characteristics of the four diagnostic tests that we discussed above. Tables 3 and 4 summarise the admissible deviations for the parameter probabilities of the associated test variables; the reported averages are computed over the admissible deviations that we found for the patients for whom varying

Table 3
The average admissible deviations given negative test results; in the order of presentation, the original values of the parameters are 0.75, 0.98, 0.10, 0.95, 0.15, 0.98, 0.10, and 0.95.

parameter	admissible deviation
$p(\textit{Lapa-liver} = no \mid \textit{Metas-liver} = yes)$	–
$p(\textit{Lapa-liver} = no \mid \textit{Metas-liver} = no)$	$(0.8610, \rightarrow)$
$p(\textit{CT-liver} = no \mid \textit{Metas-liver} = yes)$	$(\leftarrow, 0.3043)$
$p(\textit{CT-liver} = no \mid \textit{Metas-liver} = no)$	$(0.8992, \rightarrow)$
$p(\textit{X-lungs} = no \mid \textit{Metas-lungs} = yes)$	$(\leftarrow, 0.8054)$
$p(\textit{X-lungs} = no \mid \textit{Metas-lungs} = no)$	$(0.9683, \rightarrow)$
$p(\textit{CT-lungs} = no \mid \textit{Metas-lungs} = yes)$	$(\leftarrow, 0.2009)$
$p(\textit{CT-lungs} = no \mid \textit{Metas-lungs} = no)$	$(0.9456, \rightarrow)$

Table 4
The average admissible deviations given positive test results; in the order of presentation, the original values of the parameters are 0.25, 0.02, 0.90, 0.05, 0.85, 0.02, 0.90, and 0.05.

parameter	admissible deviations
$p(\textit{Lapa-liver} = yes \mid \textit{Metas-liver} = yes)$	$(0.1875, \rightarrow), (\leftarrow, 0.2033)$
$p(\textit{Lapa-liver} = yes \mid \textit{Metas-liver} = no)$	$(0.0090, \rightarrow), (\leftarrow, 0.0600)$
$p(\textit{CT-liver} = yes \mid \textit{Metas-liver} = yes)$	$(0.7900, \rightarrow)$
$p(\textit{CT-liver} = yes \mid \textit{Metas-liver} = no)$	$(\leftarrow, 0.4150)$
$p(\textit{X-lungs} = yes \mid \textit{Metas-lungs} = yes)$	$(0.5658, \rightarrow)$
$p(\textit{X-lungs} = yes \mid \textit{Metas-lungs} = no)$	$(0.0150, \rightarrow), (\leftarrow, 0.2017)$
$p(\textit{CT-lungs} = yes \mid \textit{Metas-lungs} = yes)$	$(0.8839, \rightarrow)$
$p(\textit{CT-lungs} = yes \mid \textit{Metas-lungs} = no)$	$(0.0461, \rightarrow), (\leftarrow, 0.0422)$

the parameter under study induced a change in the most likely stage. Table 3 reports the average admissible deviations for the parameter probabilities of the diagnostic tests from which a negative result is available. For example, for the 89 patients for whom varying the specificity of a CT scan of the upper abdomen induced a change in the most likely stage, the specificity could be varied from its original value 0.95 to roughly 0.05 on average before the change occurred; for all these patients, moreover, the specificity could be varied to 1.00 without inducing any change in the stage computed from the network. Table 4 similarly reports the average admissible deviations for the parameter probabilities of the tests from which a positive result is available.

From Table 3, we observe that, while originally close to 1.00, the specificities of all four tests, given a negative result, can be varied to almost 0 before a change in the most likely stage is induced. Figure 7 shows, as an example, the distribution of the admissible deviations found for the specificity of a CT scan of the upper abdomen; similar distributions were found for the specificities of the other tests. This distribution of admissible deviations can be explained by studying the shapes of the sensitivity functions concerned. We recall from Section 3 that the sensitivity function yielded by varying a parameter probability x, in essence is a branch of an orthogonal hyperbola. We argued that for the vertical asymptote $x = s$ of this hyperbola, either $s < 0$ or $s > 1$ holds. Now, the denominator $c \cdot x + d$

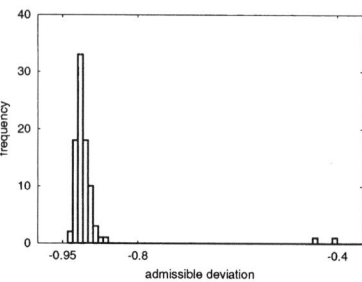

Fig. 7. The distribution of admissible deviations to smaller values, indicated by a negative value, for the parameter probability $p(\textit{CT-liver} = no \mid \textit{Metas-liver} = no)$, given a negative test result from the scan.

of the sensitivity function in essence is a probability [4]. We thus have that $0 < c \cdot x + d \leq 1$ with $0 < d \leq 1$ and $-1 \leq c \leq 1$. Upon varying the parameter probability x, a negative value for c can only arise from co-variation of the other probabilities from the same distribution. Since in our experiments x is a probability associated with a test variable whose value has been observed, these other probabilities do not partake in the sensitivity function. From this observation, we have that $c > 0$. From $s = -\frac{d}{c}$, we conclude that $s < 0$. The shoulder of the sensitivity function thus lies to the left, in the region of the smaller x-coordinates. Note that Figures 4, 5 and 6 support these observations. From the shapes of the resulting functions, we thus have that the various functions are more likely to intersect for the smaller values of the parameter probability under study. Parameter probabilities with a large original value thus are expected to have a large admissible deviation to smaller values; parameter probabilities with a small original value are expected to have a smaller admissible deviation. The results reported in Table 3 corroborate these expectations.

5. Conclusions

To study the effects of inaccuracies in the reliability characteristics of diagnostic tests, we conducted a sensitivity analysis of a real-life probabilistic network. The patterns of sensitivity that emerged from the analysis suggest that, while it is important to explicitly model the possibility of test results being erroneous, most of the reliability characteristics involved need not be very accurately specified. As we could explain the patterns of sensitivity found from fundamental insights independent of the network under study, similar patterns are expected also for other probabilistic networks for diagnostic applications.

Acknowledgement
This research has been supported by the Netherlands Organisation for Scientific Research (NWO). We are most grateful to Arend Jan de Groote for his implementation work.

References

1. F.V. Jensen. *Bayesian Networks and Decision Graphs*. Springer-Verlag, New York, 2001.
2. L.C. van der Gaag, C.L.M. Witteman, S. Renooij, M. Egmont-Petersen. The effects of disregarding test-characteristics in probabilistic networks. In: S. Quaglini, P. Barahona, S. Andreassen (editors). *Artificial Intelligence in Medicine*, LNAI 2102, Springer-Verlag, Berlin, 2001, pp. 188 – 198.
3. H.C. Sox, M.A. Blatt, M.C. Higgins, K.I. Marton. *Medical Decision Making*, Butterworth-Heinemann, 1988.
4. V.M.H. Coupé, L.C. van der Gaag. Properties of sensitivity analysis of Bayesian belief networks. *Annals of Mathematics and Artificial Intelligence*, **36**, 2002, pp. 323 – 356.
5. L.C. van der Gaag, S. Renooij. Analysing sensitivity data. In: J. Breese, D. Koller (editors). *Proceedings of the Seventeenth Conference on Uncertainty in Artificial Intelligence*, Morgan Kaufmann, San Francisco, 2001, pp. 530 – 537.

Dominance of recognition of words presented on right or left eye
-Comparison of Kanji and Hiragana-

Takahiro Yamanoi [a], Toshimasa Yamazaki [b],
Jean-Louis Vercher [c], Elie Sanchez [d] and Michio Sugeno [e]

[a]Faculty of Engineering, Hokkai-Gakuen University,
Sapporo, Japan
[b]Bio-IT Business Promotion Center, NEC Corporation,
Tokyo, Japan
[c]Laboratory of Perception & Sports, University of the Mediterranean,
Marseille, France
[d]LIF, Laboratory of Medical Informatics, Faculty of Medicine, University of the Mediterranean,
Marseille, France
[e]Faculty of Culture and Information Science, Doshisha University,
Kyoto, Japan

Abstract

The authors recorded nineteen-channel event-related potentials (ERPs) during recognition of two types of Japanese characters; Kanji (Chinese characters) and Hiragana (one type of phonetic characters). By field-sequential stereoscopic 3D display with liquid crystal shutter, a word and a non-word were simultaneously and independently presented to the left (right) eye and right (left) one, respectively. Each word consists of two Kanji or three Hiragana characters. Three subjects were instructed to press a button when understanding the meaning of the visual stimuli after 3000 ms poststimulus. Equivalent current dipole source localization (ECDL) with three unconstrained ECD was applied to the ERPs. For both Kanji and Hiragana, the ECDs were localized to the occipital, lingual and inferior temporal gyri at 200 – 350ms, and those at Wernicke's area at 350 – 600ms. The latter ECD for one left-handed subject was located at Wernicke's homologue. The Kanji recognition revealed the activation of the fusiform and supramarginal gyri which may reflect binocular rivalry and spatial working memory. During the Hiragana recognition task, one of the ECDs was located at the angular gyrus which is related to phonological processing. For one left-handed subject, the inferior parietal ECDs were localized contralaterally to those of right-handed subjects.

Key words: Visual processing, Cerebral laterality, Equivalent current dipole source localization, Japanese characters

1. Introduction

The laterality of the human brain is a well-known fact. This paper deals with the laterality of recognition of Japanese words presented to the right eye or left eye. The authors designed a stimulus presentation system with liquid crystal glasses, by which each stimulus is presented independently to the right and the left eye. Then, event related potentials (ERPs) during recognition of words were measured, and analyzed by equivalent current dipole source localization (ECDL).

In 1861, the French anthropologist-physician, Pierre-Paul Broca provided the first clear evidence of functional laterality of the cerebral cortex when he studied a patient who had lost his ability to speak. Broca discovered that the man had a large pathological softening in the left frontal lobe, which Broca identified as the source of his speech problem. The central focus of the lesion was the posterior part of the inferior frontal gyrus, which is now referred to as Broca's area. The left hemisphere is dominant for speech and language functions. It is also dominant for motor planning and skills. The right hemisphere, on the other hand, is dominant for spatial abilities and for some aspects of music. There is also some evidence that it is more involved in various aspects of emotional behavior than the left hemisphere.

Binocular disparity detection for stereopsis has been discovered at V1 and V2 from neurophysiological research. Yamanoi et al. have elucidated the process of stereopsis, after a subject received visual stimuli, especially after V1, by observing ERPs. Some of the present authors have used the same methodology: by presenting fuzzy and crisp calculations to the subjects, the authors recorded ERPs during these calculations. ERPs had been recorded during the subject's fuzzy and crisp calculations. Adding these ERPs during fuzzy and crisp calculations respectively, They subtracted these two ERPs to get the essential difference in ERPs between fuzzy and crisp calculations[1]. From this point of view, in the present study, each potential of components in ERP is detected and analyzed by the ECDL method at that peak latency.

2. Experiments

2.1 Experimental Apparatus and Method

Subjects are three university students from 21 to 22 years old and have normal visual acuity. The subjects put on an electrode cap and watched the 21inch CRT at 30cm in front of them. Their heads were fixed on a chin rest on the table. Each word was displayed on the CRT by stereoscopic display system with field-sequential liquid crystal glasses. The system consists of a personal computer (PC), vertical synchronizer (Solidlay) and field-sequential liquid crystal glasses. This enables to control the simultaneous signals by infrared. With the system, a word (or non-word) to the left eye and a non-word (or word) to the right eye are displayed separately.

Words to be displayed had been stored on the disk of PC (Equium, Windows NT 4.0, Toshiba) as a file and they were presented at random. Electrodes on the cap were followed to the International 10-20 system and two electrodes were fixed on the upper and lower eyelids for eye movement monitoring. Impedances were adjusted to the range from 2 to 5kΩ. Reference electrodes were put on both earlobes and the ground electrode was on the base of the nose. Electroencephalograms (EEGs) were recorded on the digital EEG measuring system (Japan GE Marquette, Synafit EE2500); the amplitude rate is 5μV/V, the frequency band is between 0.5 and 60Hz. Analog outputs were sampled at a rate of 1kHz and stored on a hard disk in a PC (PC-9821Xt, NEC).

2.2 Stimulus Conditions and Presentations

Words composed of Kanji or Hiragana characters were presented to the subjects. We gave two types of words simultaneously to a subject's eyes. One type is a real word composed of Kanji or Hiragana. The other is a non-word that was made in a nonsense order, rearranging characters of the real word. By field-sequential stereoscopic 3D display with liquid crystal shutter, a word and a non-word were simultaneously and independently presented to the left (right) eye and right (left) eye, respectively. All the words are presented in vertical writing.

Stimulus presentation and EEG recording were done for 3 seconds, then a prompt mark "?" was presented in 2 seconds. When the subjects understand the meaning of words, they press the enter key after the prompt, in order to prevent from the involvement of the movement readiness potentials. After input of the answer, the prompt disappeared and it was followed by an inter-stimulus interval of 5 seconds, and then the next stimulus appeared. The above run was repeated for the subject in a few days (Fig.1).

We have analyzed EEGs during the Kanji and Hiragana recognitions; both data were summed and averaged. EDCL analysis[2] was applied to the data. Because the number of the recording electrodes was 19, three ECDs at most were estimated by a PC-based ECDL analysis software "SynaPointPro[3]" (Japan GE Marquette).

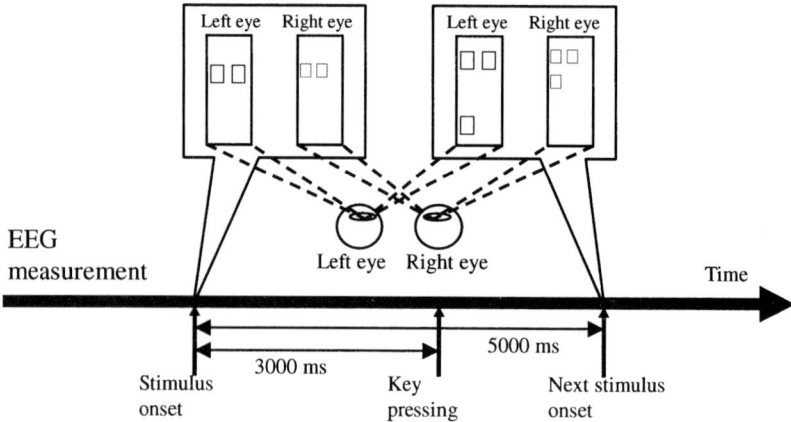

Fig.1 Stimulus presentation and EEG measurement

3. Results

3.1 Results of Obtained ERPs

We have analyzed EEGs during the Kanji and Hiragana recognitions; both data were summed and averaged..

The grand averages of three subjects for Kanji and Hiragana are shown in Fig.2 (a) and (b), respectively. Large negative components occur after the latency at 200ms. The negative waves continue to 400ms, gradually attenuating to 1000ms and disappear in both cases.

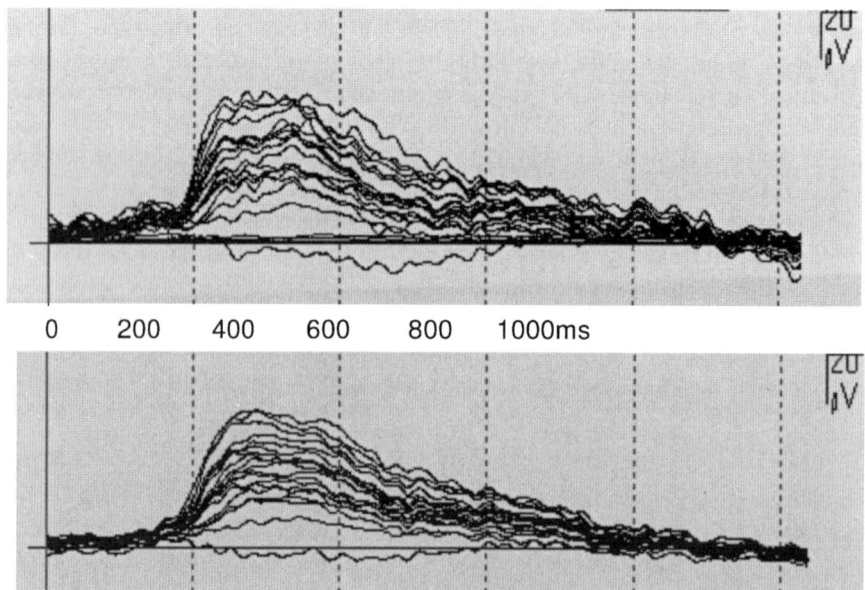

Fig.2 Grand average of the EEG for three subjects. Upper: (a) Kanji, Lower: (b) Hiragana

3.2 Results of ECDL Analysis for Kanji

At latencies from 200ms to 350ms, ECDs were localized to the occipital gyrus, the lingual gyrus, the fusiform gyrus and the inferior temporal gyrus for all the subjects. An example of ECD localized to the fusiform gyrus is shown in Fig.3.

At latencies from 350ms to 600ms, ECDs were localized to the supramarginal gyrus and the posterior superior temporal gyrus for all the subjects. For right-handed subjects, ECDs were localized to the right supramarginal gyrus and the left posterior superior temporal gyrus. However, for a left-handed subject, ECDs were localized to the left supramarginal gyrus and the right posterior superior temporal gyrus, both of which were contralateral to those of right-handed subjects. These examples for a left-handed are shown in Fig.4 and Fig.5.

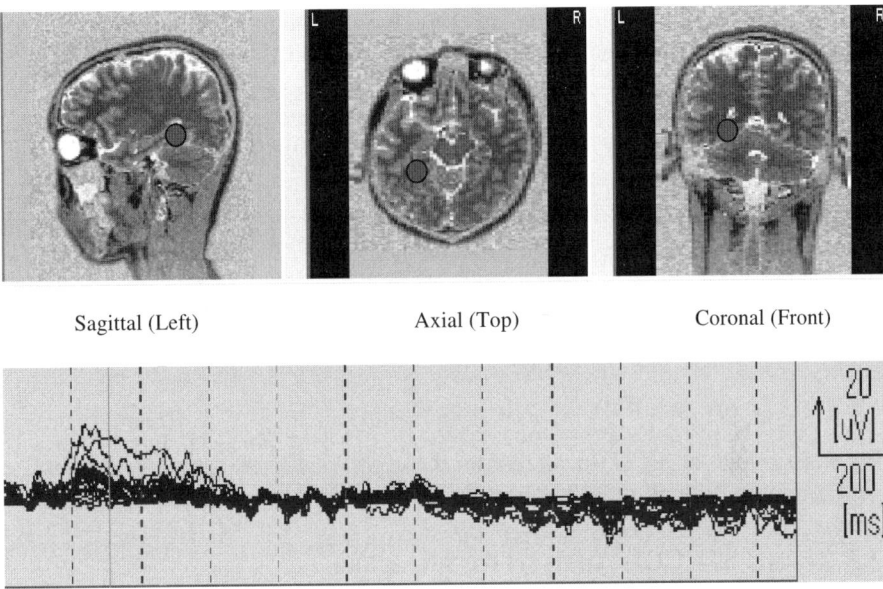

Sagittal (Left)   Axial (Top)   Coronal (Front)

Fig.3 Example of ECD locarized to the fusiform gyrus, superimposed on individual MR images (indicated by dots): Upper and the oroginal EEG: Lower.

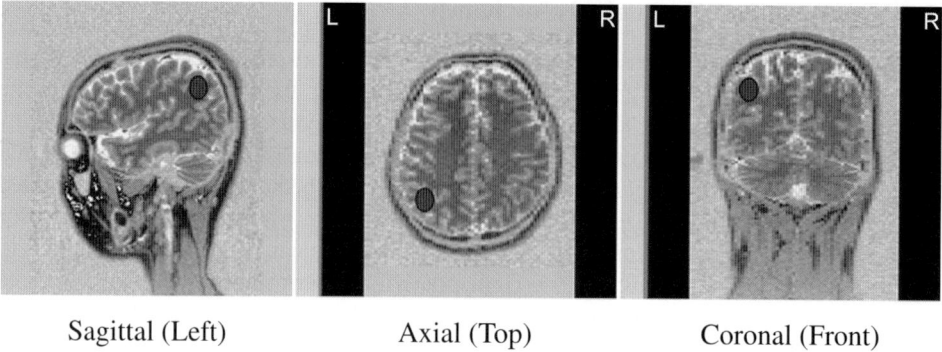

Sagittal (Left)　　　　　　Axial (Top)　　　　　　Coronal (Front)

Fig.4 Example of ECD localized to the left supramarginal gyrus, superimposed on individual MR images (indicated by dots), Subject MT

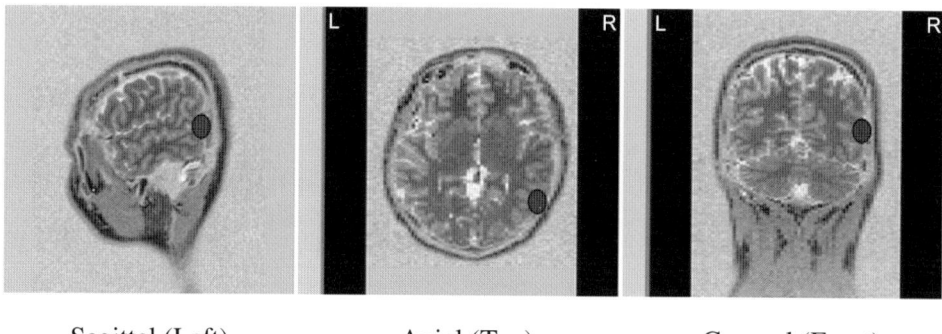

Sagittal (Left)　　　　　　Axial (Top)　　　　　　Coronal (Front)

Fig.5 Example of ECD localized to the right posterior superior temporal gyrus, superimposed on individual MR images (indicated by dots), Subject MT

3.3 Results of ECDL Analysis for Hiragana

At the latencies from 200ms to 350ms, ECDs were localized to the occipital gyrus, the lingual gyrus, and the inferior temporal gyrus for all the subjects. An example of ECD localized to the lingual gyrus is shown in Fig.6.

At the latencies from 350ms to 600ms, ECDs were localized to the angular gyrus and the posterior superior temporal gyrus for all the subjects. These examples are shown in Fig.7 and Fig.8. However, for a left-handed subject, ECDs were localized to the right angular gyrus and the right posterior superior temporal gyrus, both of which were contralateral to the those of right-handed subjects.

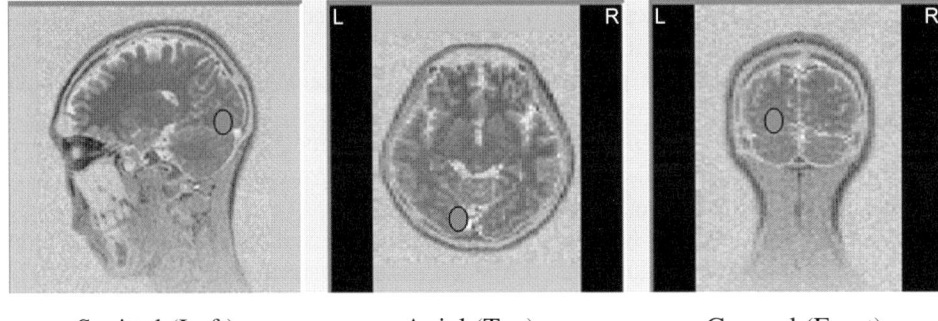

Sagittal (Left)   Axial (Top)   Coronal (Front)

Fig.6 Example of ECD localized to the lingual gyrus, superimposed on individual MR images (indicated by dots), Subject NS

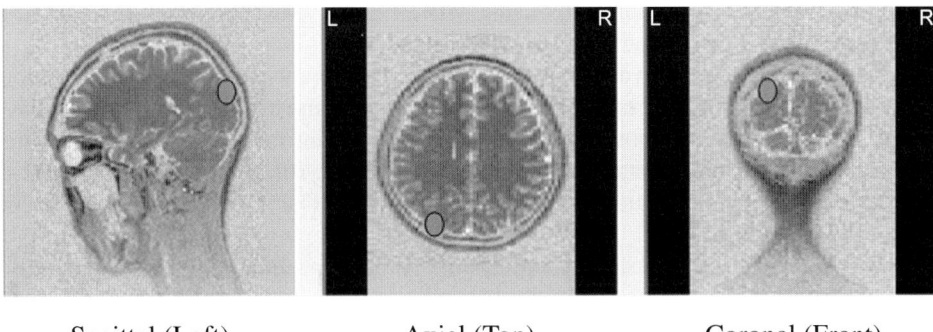

Sagittal (Left)   Axial (Top)   Coronal (Front)

Fig.7 Example of ECD localized to the angular gyrus, superimposed on individual MR images (indicated by dots), Subject NS

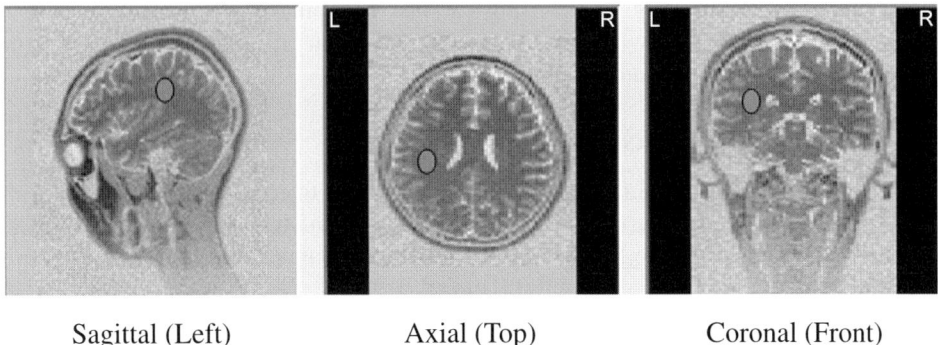

Sagittal (Left)   Axial (Top)   Coronal (Front)

Fig.8 Example of ECD localized to the posterior superior temporal gyrus, superimposed on individual MR images (indicated by dots), Subject NS

4. Discussion

At latencies of 200ms-350ms, ECDs for both Kanji and Hiragana were commonly localized to the occipital gyrus, the lingual gyrus, and the inferior temporal gyrus for all the subjects. It is known that pure alexia (the patient can see a word but not read it) is often the result of damage at the lingual gyrus[4]. An investigation on PET has detected that this area is activated by a visually presented word and or pronounceable non-word[5]. Related activation of the posterior inferior temporal area by pronunciation of visually presented Kanji and Hiragana is detected by the same method[6][7].

The difference between the Kanji and Hiragana recognitions at the latencies of 200ms-350ms is that ECDs are localized to the fusiform gyrus only for Kanji in all subjects. This will be discussed later.

At latencies of 350ms-600ms, ECDs for both Kanji and Hiragana in right-handed subjects were commonly localized to the left posterior superior temporal gyrus. This area is supposed to be the Wernicke's area. During various recognition tasks of a word represented visually, such as sub-vocal reading for Kanji or Hiragana[6][7], discrimination of word or non-word[8], phonetic comparison of Hiragana[9] and judgment of phoneme or category of meaning[10], activities of the Wernicke or its homologue have been reported by using MEG, PET or fMRI. We have also localized to the Wernicke homologue in a case of left-hander.

Stimulation to each eye in our experiment is different from that in the previous studies in terms of binocular rivalry. In order to understand Kanji under these conditions, presentation positions of Kanji are important for the subjects. Activation at the right inferior parietal lobule or the fusiform gyrus is known in the case of binocular rivalry or spatial working memory[11-13]. Our results on Kanji reflect activities on these areas.

On the other hand, understanding of Hiragana, phonological translation of visually presented stimulus and reference of memories is necessary. The center for phonological translation is supposed to be the angular gyrus[14]. A lesion at the left angular gyrus and the posterior inferior temporal gyrus causes alexia and agraphia in the case of Japanese. In particular with lesion at angular gyrus, reading malfunction is stronger for Hiragana and writing malfunction is stronger for Kanji, and malfunction is remarkable for reading and writing for one Hiragana character. In the case of discrimination task for word or non-word, activation at left angular gyrus were localized both for Kanji and Hiragana.

5. Concluding remarks

Both for Kanji and Hiragana, we localized ECDs from early components of the ERPs on the occipital gyrus, the lingual gyrus and inferior temporal gyrus, ECDs from later components are localized to the Wernicke's area. These support the results on MEG, PET or fMRI. From left-handed subjects, ECDs are localized to the homologue of Wernicke. The difference is that ECDs are localized to the fusiform gyrus and the supramarginal gyrus for Kanji, and to the angular gyrus for Hiragana. This suggests that the present ERPs are related to binocular rivalry, spatial working memory and phonological translation. Restricting the binocular rivalry, the results for Kanji might have been similar to those for Hiragana. Generally, the right-handed subject is dominant in the left hemisphere as before, the left -handed is dominant in the right hemisphere. The relationship between the left-handed or the right-handed persons and the dominance of the function on the hemisphere should be investigated further.

Acknowledgment

This research is supported by the project of the High-tech Research Center of Hokkai-Gakuen University by the grant-in-aide from Japanese Ministry of Education, Culture, Sports, Science and Technology.

References

1. T. Yamanoi, M. Saito, M. Sugeno and E. Sanchez: Difference in Areas of the Brain for Fuzzy and Crisp Calculation, Journal of Advanced Computational Intelligence, Vol.6 No.1, 51/55 (2001).
2. J.C. Mosher, P.S. Lewis and R.M. Leahy: Multiple dipole modeling and localization from spatio-temporal MEG data, IEEE Trans. Biomed. Eng., 39, 541/557(1992).
3. T. Yamazaki: Equivalent Current Dipole Localization by 32 channels electro cap, CLIN. NEUROSC., 18-2, 186/190 (2000).
4. A.R. Damasio and H. Damasio: The anatomic basis of pure alexia, Neurology, 33, 1573/1583 (1983).
5. S.E. Petersen, P.T. Fox, A.Z. Snyder and M.E. Raichle: Activation of extrastriate and frontal cortical areas by visual words and word-like stimuli, Science, 249, 1041/1044 (1990).
6. Y. Sakurai, T. Momose, M. Iwata, T. Watanabe, T. Ishikawa, K. Takeda and I. Kanazawa: Kanji word reading process analysed by positron emission tomography, NeuroReport, 3-5, 445/448 (1992).
7. Y. Sakurai, T. Momose, M. Iwata, T. Watanabe, T. Ishikawa and I. Kanazawa: Semantic process in kana word reading: activation studies with positron emission tomography, NeuroReport, 4-3, 327/330 (1993).
8. M. Kawakatsu and M. Kotani: MEG during understanding Kana word, IECEJ, Ser. C, 116-6, 669/675 (1996).
9. S. Kuriki, Y. Hirata, N. Fujimaki and T. Kobayashi: Magnetoencephalographic study on the cerebral neural activities related to the processing of visually presented characters, Cognitive Brain Research, 4, 185/199 (1996).
10. K.R. Pugh, B.A. Shaywitz, S.E. Shaywitz, R.T. Constable, P. Skudlarski, R.K. Fullbright, R.A. Bronen, D.P. Shankweiter, L. Katz, J.M. Fletcher and J.C. Gore: Cerebral organization of component processes in reading, Brain, 119, 1221/1238 (1996).
11. E.D. Lumer, K.J. Friston and G. Rees: Neural correlates of perceptual rivalry in the human brain, Science, 280, 1930/1934 (1998).
12. J. Jonides, E.E. Smith, R.A. Koeppe, E. Awh, S. Minoshima and M.A. Mintun: Spatial working memory in humans as revealed by PET, Nature, 363, 623/625 (1993).
13. J.D. Cohen, W.M. Perlstein, T.S. Braver, L.E. Nystrom, D.C. Noll, J. Jonides and E.E. Smith: Temporal dynamics of brain activation during a working memory task, Nature, 386, 604/608 (1997).

14. N. Geschwind: Specializations of the human brain, Scientific Amer., 241, 158/168 (1979).

Hand posture recognition with the fuzzy glove

T. Allevard, E. Benoit and L. Foulloy

LISTIC-ESIA, Université de Savoie,
B.P. 806, 74016 Annecy, France

Abstract

This paper presents the application of rule-based aggregation techniques for the modelling of human perception of static hand gestures (i.e. hand postures). Acquisition of gestures is made by the Cyberglove® device. This device provides a numerical description of the configurations of the fingers that is converted into a linguistic description corresponding to human perception. Hand postures can then be recognized by fuzzy rules from this linguistic description. This system is used in process control applications and more generally in sign recognition applications.

Keywords: fuzzy systems, data glove, gesture recognition

1. Introduction

Gesture recognition is an active research field which tries to integrate the gestural channel in Human Computer Interaction. It has applications in virtual environment control [1], but also in sign language translation [2], robot remote control [3] or musical creation [4].

Recognition of human gestures comes within the more general framework of pattern recognition. In this framework, systems consist of two processes: the representation and the decision processes. The representation process converts the raw numerical data into a form adapted to the decision process which then classifies the data (see Figure 1).

Gesture recognition systems inherit this structure and have two more processes: the acquisition process, which converts the physical gesture to numerical data, and the interpretation process, which gives the meaning of the symbol series coming from the decision process.

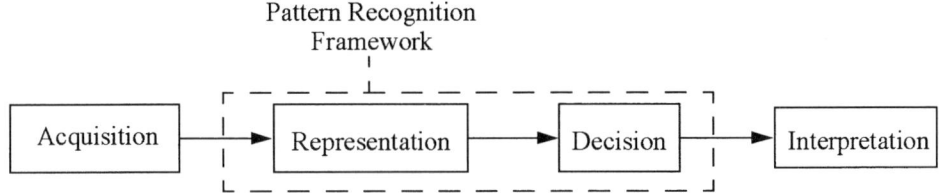

Figure 1: General structure of a gesture recognition system.

It is generally accepted that any hand gesture is made up of four elements [5]: the hand configuration, movement, orientation and location. A crude classification of gestures can also be made by separating the static gestures, which are called hand postures, and the dynamic gestures which are sequences of hand postures.

Two main families of gesture acquisition systems, device-based and vision-based, can be considered. In device-based systems, the acquisition of gestures is made by a physical device that directly measures some characteristics of the gesture, generally the different joint bending angles. A good review of device-based inputs is given in [6]. In vision-based systems, the gesture is captured by a camera. The main advantage of the vision-based approach is its unconstrained nature. It allows a natural execution of a gesture by the user as long as he/she stays in the camera field. Its main drawbacks are the complexity of processings which makes it unsuitable for real-time applications as well as the fact that the user must stay in the camera field. Device-based methods, on the opposite, are fast and robust. They are often criticized because of the constraint of wearing a glove linked to the computer by wires. However, the advent of wireless data gloves makes it possible to imagine embedded sign recognition systems that could be used anywhere, in the streets as well as in laboratories.

The goal of this paper is to use the fuzzy set theory and rule-based aggregation to build a simple model of human perception of the hand. This model is then utilized to recognize gestures. In this model, a hand posture is described linguistically, by giving the configuration each finger takes in this particular posture. Finger configurations are in turn described with linguistic terms.

Such a recognition system has two main advantages. The first one is that it is not a black box system: the recognition process is intuitive and so it is reliable and easily maintainable. The second advantage is that it is the representation process that is trained and not the decision process as is usually the case. The representation process is only trained once to recognize the finger configurations correctly. Then the recognition process can recognize any hand posture if the rule describing it is well defined.

This system is applied to the recognition of hand postures corresponding to control actions for a small robot (see Figure 11). It is shown that it can also be applied to the recognition of more complex hand postures like those of the French Sign Language alphabet (see Figure 14).

After a brief review of related works in the next section, the general structure of the recognition system is presented in section 3. Section 4 gives detailed explanations on the linguistic description of the hand. The recognition of hand postures from this description is given in section 5. Section 6 describes the two applications of this system before conclusion in section 7.

2. Related Works

Recognition of hand postures using a data glove has been widely studied in the literature and some efficient systems have already been designed. Many different approaches have been applied to the classification of data in the decision process. Only rule-based systems are described here, a more complete review of the classification of gesture data is given in [5][7][8].

The TalkingGlove® of Kramer [7] recognizes the 36 signs of the American fingerspelling, the most of which are static signs. It utilizes a binary decision tree based recognition process. The decision boundary at each node of the tree takes the form of a hyperplane. The tree and its hyperplanes are designed by a neural network. Su [9] achieves good recognition rates of postures of the Taiwanese Sign Language (TSL) using a glove-based system. For each sign, a set of hyperrectangles is defined, i.e. rectangles of dimension 20 in the raw data space, each of them corresponding to a classifying rule. If a point is located within one of those rectangles, the gesture is classified as the corresponding sign. The hyperrectangles are constructed by a neural network and fuzzified using a similarity relation. Holden [10][11] uses an adaptive fuzzy system to recognize hand postures and motions. The hand joint configurations are described linguistically. The signs are represented by rules transcribing the knowledge about how these signs are performed from the hand joint point of view. The whole system is trained by repeating some signs and modifying the joint angle descriptions automatically.

The training phase of these recognition systems allows to acquire some knowledge about how the classes can be separated. But this knowledge is already available: it is usually possible for anyone to express linguistically what differentiates one posture from another. The recognition process that is presented here contains an intermediary description of fingers which is richer semantically than the simple description of the finger joints used by Holden. It allows to integrate this common sense knowledge in an automated recognition system.

3. Fuzzy glove

In this paper, the acquisition of gestures is made with a data glove. The Cyberglove® developed by Kramer [7] has been chosen because it gives accurate and independent measurements of the different joint angles. It is made of 18 bending sensors (see Figure 2). The wrist yaw and pitch sensors are useful for hand orientation measurements and are not utilized here. The palm arch sensor measures the cupping of the hand near the pinkie finger, a piece of information which is not used in our model of visual perception of the hand.

The general structure of the recognition system is given in Figure 3. Numerical data is entered in a numerical to linguistic converter which gives the linguistic descriptions of the finger configurations. This corresponds to the representation process. The association of this numerical to linguistic converter with the Cyberglove® will be called the fuzzy glove.

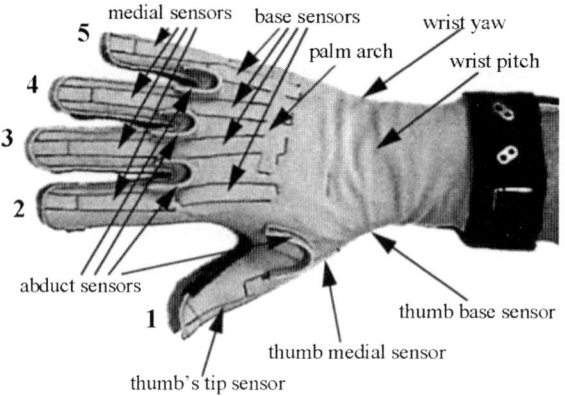

Figure 2: the Cyberglove® and finger numbering.

Whereas the Cyberglove® returns the numerical values associated with a hand posture, the aim of the fuzzy glove is to provide a linguistic description of the same hand posture. This linguistic description is based on the fuzzy description and meaning formalism introduced by Zadeh [12]. This formalism allows to define a connection between a numerical space as the one containing the Cyberglove's measures and a lexical set containing terms of the everyday language like *straight* or *folded*. The semantics of a term is formally defined by its fuzzy meaning which is a fuzzy set of the numerical space. A numerical value can then be described using the lexical set by its fuzzy description which is a fuzzy subset of terms. A fuzzy description is the dual concept of fuzzy meanings. A variable taking fuzzy descriptions as values is called a linguistic variable. In this paper, fuzzy meanings are chosen to meet some characteristics of fuzzy sensors [13] and they form a strict fuzzy partition[1] of the numerical space.

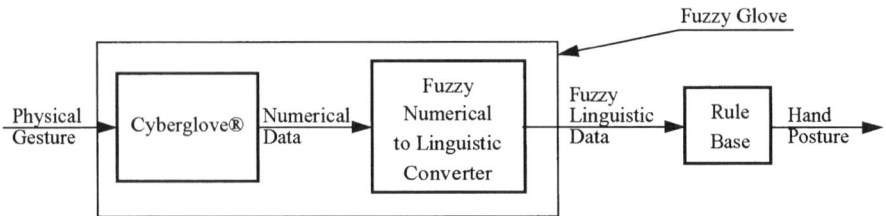

Figure 3: Structure of the fuzzy glove

The lexical sets are chosen to have simple and easily understandable descriptions. This means that given the linguistic description of a hand posture, anyone should be able to understand its shape or to realize it. The terms used in this description are then used to elaborate the rules defining the signs to be recognized.

---

[1] The set of meanings of a lexical set $L = \{l_1, l_2, ..., l_k\}$ forms a strict fuzzy partition of the numerical space U iff $\forall u \in U, \sum_{l \in L} \mu_{M(l)}(u) = 1$, where $M(l)$ is the fuzzy meaning of the term l.

4. Linguistic description of the hand

The hand configuration will be defined by nine linguistic variables. Two variables are used for the thumb description: the *thumbConfiguration* describes the stretching of the thumb and the *thumbOrientation* describes its orientation in the hand reference frame. Four variables are used for the description of the other fingers called the long fingers: the *finger$_i$Configuration* ($i = 2,...,5$). They describe the shape of the corresponding long finger and are also named *index, middle, ring* and *pinkie*. The last three variables are used for the description of the relative spacing of fingers 2/3, 4/3 and 5/4. They are respectively named *fingerAbduct$_i$* ($i = 2,...,4$) or *indexAbduct, ringAbduct* and *pinkieAbduct*.

4.1. Lexical sets

Preliminary studies led to the following choices:

The *thumbConfiguration* variable takes its values in the lexical set $L_{thumbConfiguration} = \{folded, straight\}$.

The *thumbOrientation* variable takes its values in the lexical set $L_{thumbOrientation} = \{external, aside, internal\_below, internal\_above, ahead\}$. These orientations are illustrated in Figure 4.

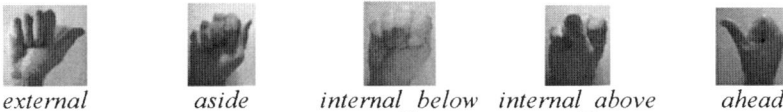

external　　*aside*　　*internal_below*　*internal_above*　　*ahead*

Figure 4: The five orientations of the thumb.

The four *finger$_i$Configuration* variables take their values in the lexical set $L_{fingerConfiguration} = \{folded, square, round, claw, straight\}$. These configurations are illustrated in Figure 5.

folded　　　*square*　　　*round*　　　*claw*　　　*straight*

Figure 5: The five configurations of a long finger.

The three *fingerAbduct$_i$* variables take their values in the lexical set $L_{fingerAbduct} = \{separated, together\}$.

4.2. Linguistic conversion

Numerical measurements of finger spacings are directly given by the corresponding abduct sensors (see Figure 2). A fuzzy partition of the universe of discourse of each of these sensors is defined by taking two sets of characteristic values corresponding to the terms *separated* and *together*. These characteristic values are the core of the fuzzy meanings of the terms. The remainder of these fuzzy meanings is calculated by linear interpolation. The linguistic description of a finger spacing is then deduced from its numerical measurement, using the fuzzy partition of the corresponding sensor (see Figure 6).

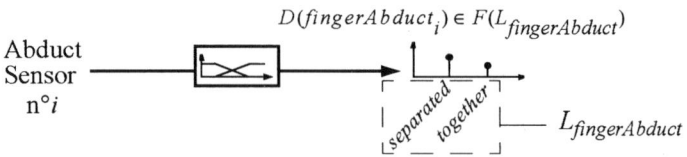

Figure 6 Spacing of the fingers ($i = 2, 3$ or 4).

To qualify the configuration of a finger linguistically, two sensors are used: the finger base sensor and finger medial one. The base sensor axis is partitioned into two fuzzy subsets $L_{baseIndex}$ = {*folded, straight*} and the medial sensor into three fuzzy subsets $L_{medialIndex}$ = {*folded, half-folded, straight*}. The linguistic description of the finger is then deduced from these sensor descriptions by the rule base given in Figure 7

		Base Sensor	
		straight	folded
Medial Sensor	folded	claw	folded
	half-folded	round	round
	straight	straight	square

Figure 7: Rule Base for the description of a finger.

This rule base transcribes our knowledge of the appearance of a finger from the appearance of its joints.

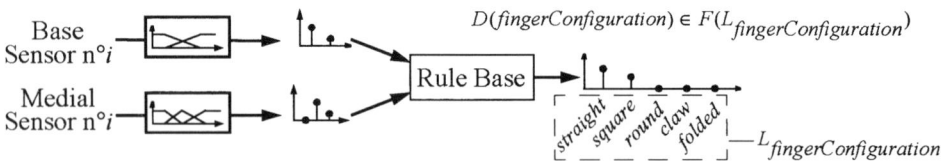

Figure 8 Description of the fingers ($i = 2, 3, 4$ or 5).

The linguistic description of the thumb configuration is deduced from the numerical values provided by the tip sensor. The linguistic description of its orientation is calculated from the values given by the corresponding base, medial and abduct sensors. But first, these numerical values have to be projected on two numerical axes. These two axes have been found from a discriminant component analysis of experimental data. The first of these axes measures the lateral position of the thumb, i.e. its position in the palm plane, it is partitioned in three fuzzy meanings: *M(internal)*, *M(intermediate)* or *M(external)*. The second axis measures its frontal position, i.e. its position perpendicularly to the palm plane. It can either be *ahead* or *inPalmPlane*. The description of the thumb orientation is induced from the descriptions of these two axes by a rule base, in a similar way to the finger description.

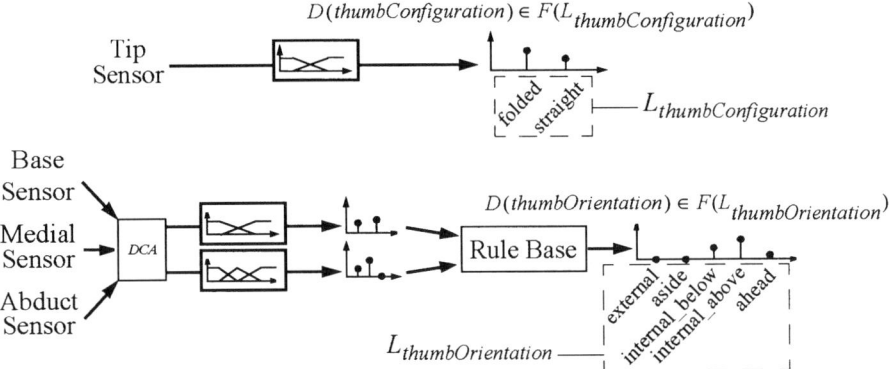

Figure 9 Description of the thumb (two linguistic variables).

The inferences of the rules used for the description of the thumb orientation and of the finger configurations are made using the product and bounded sum operators. These operators ensure that the meanings of the consequent terms form a strict fuzzy partition of the numerical space because the rule bases are complete [13].

Finally, the fuzzy glove provides a linguistic description of the current hand posture given by nine linguistic variables. Each linguistic variable takes values which are fuzzy subsets of its lexical set. These linguistic descriptions can now be used to recognize hand postures.

5. Posture recognition

A hand posture to be recognized is called a sign. A sign is defined linguistically by giving the value each linguistic variable takes in this particular posture. For example, the *Y* sign of French Sign Language (see Figure 14), is defined by the rule:

> **IF** *thumbConfiguration* **is** *straight* **AND** *thumbOrientation* **is** *external*
> **AND** *index* **is** *folded* **AND** *middle* **is** *folded* **AND** *ring* **is** *folded*
> **AND** *pinkie* **is** *(straight or square)* **AND** *indexAbduct* **is** *whatever*   (1)
> **AND** *ringAbduct* **is** *whatever* **AND** *pinkieAbduct* **is** *whatever*
> **THEN** *currentPosture* **is** *Y*

A *whatever* keyword is used in this rule. It allows to have some conditions whose satisfaction degree is always equal to one, which means there is no condition at all. The inference, made conjunctively using the product and bounded sum operators, provides the recognition degree of each sign (see Figure 10). The choice of the bounded sum has the following consequence: if, in the rule (1), the pinkie finger is *straight* with a degree of 0.8 and *square* with a degree of 0.2, then the condition *pinkie* **is** *(straight or square)* will have a satisfaction degree equal to one.

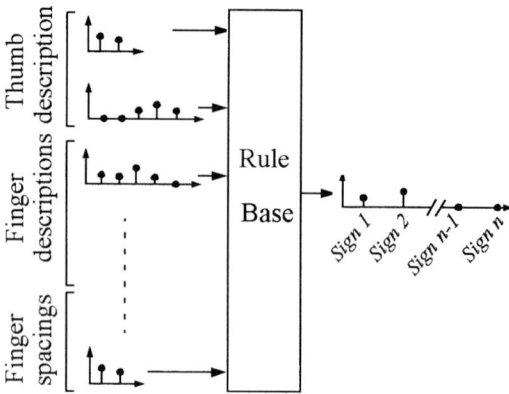

Figure 10: Recognition of signs from the linguistic descriptions given by the fuzzy glove.

6. Applications

6.1. Robot control

This system is applied for the control of a small robot. There are ten control actions for this robot. A sign is associated to each action (see Figure 11).

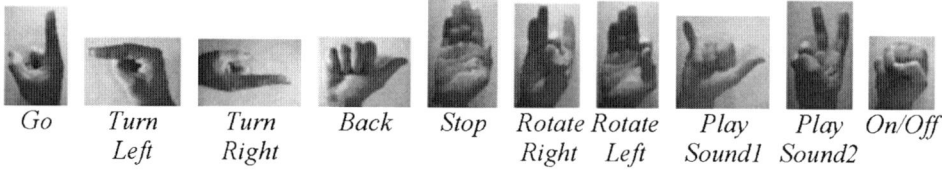

Go   Turn Left   Turn Right   Back   Stop   Rotate Right   Rotate Left   Play Sound1   Play Sound2   On/Off

Figure 11: Signs for the command of a robot.

In this application, the user performs gestures continuously. The fuzzy glove provides a continuous flow of nine fuzzy descriptions which are converted into ten continuous flows of sign recognition rates. This continuous flow has to be segmented, which means it must be detected when a sign is performed. This is done by a simple thresholding procedure. When one of the recognition rates gets above a fixed threshold, the corresponding sign is said to be recognized. Several signs can be recognized simultaneously, the one with the highest recognition rate is selected and the corresponding command is executed.

This procedure is illustrated on an example. A trajectory is represented on Figure 12 with the signs to be executed. A recording of the robot following this trajectory is also represented. Only five actions are necessary: *Go, Turn Left, Turn Right, Stop* and *On/Off*. The recognition rates of the corresponding signs have been recorded during the command period and are represented in Figure 13. The recognition threshold is chosen equal to *0.1* and is represented on each graph. In the last graph, all recognition rates are overwritten. There are eight time points ($t_0, t_1, ..., t_7$) corresponding to the recognition of a new sign and the execution of a control action. It can be noted that these actions are executed before the recognition rates reach their maximum values. Hence the thresholding segmentation procedure induces an anticipation of the signs and a very good reactivity of the system.

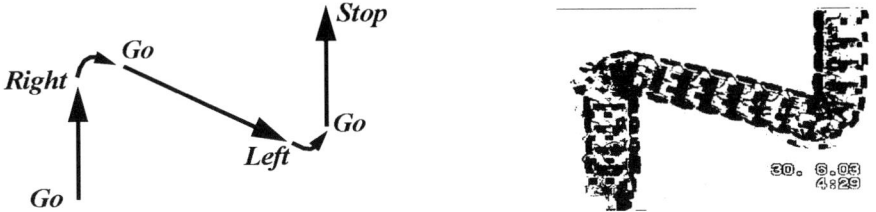

Figure 12: Trajectory to be followed by the robot

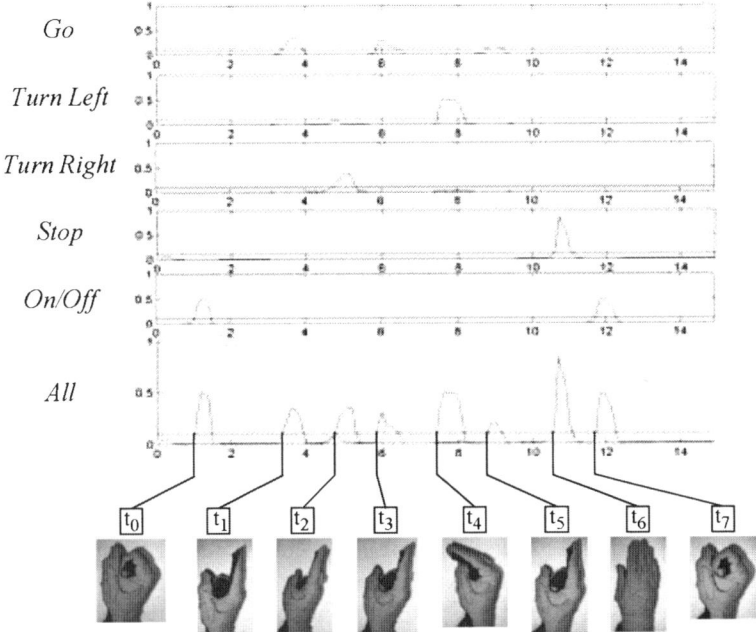

Figure 13. Recognition rates of the hand postures

This first application shows that sign recognition can be performed in real time from the linguistic descriptions provided by the fuzzy glove. Only binary actions have been considered here, but the linguistic descriptions are gradual. This graduality could be used in order to generate proportional actions. For example, the robot speed could be controlled by the index finger: the robot would then accelerate proportionally to the bending of this finger. This problem will be addressed in future works.

6.2. French fingerspelling recognition.

The French Sign Language alphabet consists of 26 signs (see Figure 14). Because only the hand configuration is considered here, some signs cannot be identified by our system.

This is the case for the signs J/Y and K/P that have the same configuration but a different movement. The signs B/M, D/Q and N/U are also differentiated by their orientation only and the sensors of the Cyberglove® cannot discriminate the R and U signs. Finally 20 different hand postures have to be recognized.

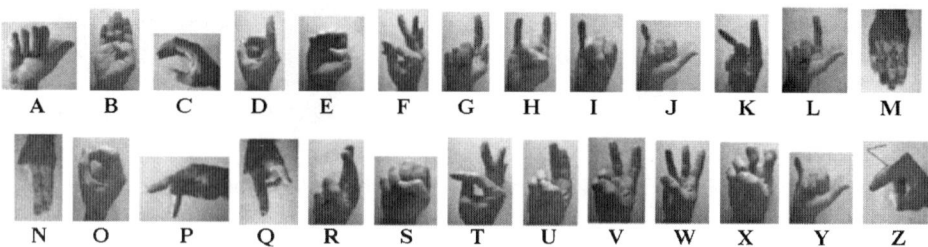

Figure 14. French Sign Language alphabet.

In this experiment, the signs are presented one by one to the system and the sign with the highest recognition rate is selected as the recognized one. The system recognizes every posture successfully. It must be stressed that if the set of signs was chosen specifically in order to achieve high recognition rates, a larger number of hand postures could be recognized. The choice of the French Sign Language alphabet has not been made in this perspective, but in order to work on a set of postures familiar to the gesture litterature.

7. Conclusion

The fuzzy subset theory has been created to model human knowledge and perception. According to Dubois et Al. [14], the fuzzy logic specificity is its capability of bridging the gap between articulated linguistic descriptions and numerical models of systems. It is precisely what is being done in the case studied here.

Apart from its efficiency to recognize hand postures, this method has several advantages compared to other posture recognition systems. It is in conformity with human perception and hence easily usable, maintainable and very reliable. It provides a real-time symbolic representation of the hand configuration at two semantic levels: the finger description level and the posture level. These representations are independent from the measurement system: the terms of the lexical sets have been chosen from the visual appearance of the hand and not from the data format of the Cyberglove. Moreover, these representations are gradual so they still possess a dynamic which could be used to generate gradual actions. This possibility will be studied in future works.

In this paper, no relation has been considered on the lexical sets appart from the equality relation. But usually, more elaborate relations, as proximity relations for example, can be defined between the different terms. Taking into account such relations on the lexical sets for the processing of linguistic descriptions will be the subject of future investigations.

References

1. Bolt R.A., "Put-That-There: voice and gesture at the graphic interface", *Computer*

Graphics, vol. 14, no. 3, pp. 262-270, 1980.
2. Fels S.S., Hinton G.E., "Glove-Talk: A neural network interface between a data glove and a speech synthesizer", *IEEE Trans. on Neural Networks*, vol.4, no.1, pp. 2-8, 1993.
3. Yeasin M., Chaudhuri S., "Visual understanding of dynamic hand gestures", *Pattern Recognition*, vol.33, pp.1805-1817, 2000.
4. Arfib D., Kessous L., "Gestural control of sound synthesis and processing algorithms", *Proc. Fourth Int. Gesture Workshop*, London, *2001*, pp. 28-295.
5. Braffort A., "Gesture recognition and comprehension, implementation for sign language" ("Reconnaissance et compréhension de gestes, application à la langue des signes"), PhD dissertation, LIMSI, Université Paris-XI, Paris, France, June 1996.
6. Sturman D.J., Zeltzer D., "A survey of glove-based input", *IEEE Computer Graphics and Applications*, vol. 14, no. 1, pp. 30-39, 1994.
7. Kramer J.F., *The Talking Glove: hand-gesture-to-speech using an instrumented glove and a tree-structured neural classifying vector Quantizer*, PhD Thesis, Stanford University, 1996.
8. Huang T.S., Pavlovic V.I., "Hand gesture Modelling, Analysis and Synthesis", *Proc. First IEEE Int.Workshop on Automatic Face and Gesture Recognition*, Zurich, 1995, pp. 73 - 79.
9. Su M.C., "A fuzzy rule based approach to spatio-temporal hand gesture recognition", *IEEE Trans. on Syst., Man, and Cybern. C*, vol.30, no.2, pp.276-281, 2000.
10. Holden E.J., Owens R., Roy G.G., "An adaptive fuzzy expert system for 3D hand motion understanding", *Proc. of the IASTED Int. Conf. on Signal and Image Processing*, Las Vegas, Nevada, 2000, pp.141-146.
11. Holden E.J., Owens R., G.G. Roy, "Hand movement classification using an adaptive fuzzy expert system", *Int. Jour. of Expert Systems*, vol.9, no.4, pp.465-480, 1996.
12. Zadeh L.A., "Quantitative fuzzy semantics", *Information Sciences*, vol. 3, pp.159-176, 1971
13. Mauris G., Benoit E., Foulloy L., "fuzzy symbolic sensors: from concept to applications", *Measurement*, vol. 12, no. 4, pp. 357-384, 1994.
14. Dubois D., Nguyen H.T., Prade H., Sugeno M., "The real contribution of fuzzy systems", in: *Fuzzy systems: Modelling and control*, H.T. Nguyen and M. Sugeno Eds., Boston, Kluwer, 1998, pp. 8-10.

Image retrieval by composition of regions

J.F. Omhover and M. Detyniecki

LIP6 – Pole IA
8, rue du Capitaine Scott
75015 Paris, France

Abstract

We present an image retrieval system called "STRICT". Its design is based on a formulation of fuzzy similarity measures that is derived from psychological considerations and that leads to an intuitive formulation of the similarity. We use these measure to evaluate a region to region visual similarity score. Then, we aggregate these scores in different ways depending on the purpose of the request. By aggregating basic scores such as region to region similarity values we form various kinds of composite regional queries. These queries can cover several different user needs such as scene retrieval, multiple aspects retrieval and object filtering.

Key words: Image Retrieval, Segmentation, Fuzzy Similarity Measures, Aggregation

1. Introduction

In the last decade, there has been an increasing interest in image retrieval systems. The idea is to let a user query an image database for a specific image content. Unfortunately, this common goal has not been achieved yet [5].
To find images in large multimedia databases, the challenge is to avoid the use of textual annotations. In fact, they can only be obtained by a time and human consuming process. That is why the image retrieval community has focused on the automatic extraction and comparison of image features. These features gather different visual information contained in an image such as colour, texture and shape. It is then possible to measure the similarity of two images or parts of images in this feature space.
To run a query in a database of images described by visual features, the community

has found a new paradigm: the query by examples. The example (an image) is given by the user and is supposed to express his need. Then the system tries to find images that are similar to this example in terms of visual features. As a response, the user gets a list of images which are found most similar to his request.

Many different feature spaces and many systems have been developed to compute the similarities involved in those queries, among them we can point out QBIC [6] and VisualSEEk [12]. But the use of such description spaces raises an important issue : the comparison in the visual feature space may provide results that do not reflect any intuitive comparison in terms of content. Two images may be similar in terms of color, texture of shape but may depict totally different scenes.

To overcome this drawback, new propositions have been made such as region-based approaches. By using an automatical segmentation algorithm [4], images can be segmented in regions, roughly corresponding to objects in the image. These objects are then automatically described by visual features. These new regional features focus the search on a more semantically meaningful part of the image. They avoid drowning the visual information in a single global feature vector. But in the same time, new querying processes have to be found in order to run regional queries.

For the moment, only a few image retrieval systems follow this approach. For instance, Blobworld [2] proposes its segmentation tool to the user, who specifies the request by selecting one single region of interest. The retrieval then consists in comparing pairs of regions. The returned images are those in which a region can be found that is strongly similar to the requested region. These results fulfil only a limited need: when the user wants to find a single given object.

Simplicity [7,3], another system, extends this to image-to-image comparison. It compares images globally by aggregating the region-to-region similarities. Unfortunately, its scheme does not include the spatial configuration of the regions, though it tries to match regions of the request to regions of each image. This approach corresponds to a global request in terms of objects. It does reflect an objective content but does not take into account several other needs such as those studied in the following.

In this paper we introduce a system called "STRICT". Its design is based on a formulation of fuzzy similarity measures that is derived from psychological considerations and that leads to an intuitive formulation of the similarity. We use these measure to evaluate a region to region visual similarity score. Then, we aggregate these scores in different ways depending on the purpose of the request. By aggregating basic scores such as region to region similarity values, we form various kinds of composite regional queries. These queries can cover several different user needs such as scene retrieval, concept retrieval and object filtering.

We will first show how the system extracts regions from images and compares pairs of regions by means of fuzzy similarity measures 2. In the second section, we will show how these region-to-region similarity measures can be aggregated to form four interesting types of composite queries 3, some of them illustrated by examples requests (for a quantative evaluation of the system's retrieval capabilities, report to [8]). In the third section, we will explain how the system lets the user express his query, and how the underlying architecture of the system carries them out 4.

2. Comparing pairs of visual regions by using fuzzy similarity measures

From an image, a segmentation algorithm extracts regions complying with a given homogeneity criteria. This criterion is usually based on colours: the algorithm tends to isolate regions of connected pixels, which present similar colours. Those regions roughly correspond to the objects present in each image. A similarity measure based on those regions can reflect an objective similarity of the content.
In order to build a semantic similarity between images, we developed a similarity measure for regions based on the similarities of colour, shape, and position. Here we first briefly present the segmentation algorithm used to extract objects from images (section 2.1), then we introduce the definition of fuzzy similarity measures (section 2.2), and finally, we explain which region features we chose to extract and how these features are compared using fuzzy similarities (section 2.3).

Fig. 1. Segmentation in regions

2.1. *Segmentation*

For the segmentation of an image in regions, many different approaches exist [4]. They have been developed for thirty years and applied to various application fields. They all aim at building a crisp partition of the image, based on vectors computed from the pixels: color, texture coefficients, edge orientation.
Our algorithm provides good results (see figure 1) in a very short computation time. It follows the merge approach: each pixel is first considered as an isolated region, then fusions are operated to merge connected pixels of similar colors, until there is no more possible fusion. This occurs when all the connected regions are dissimilar enough.

2.2. *Fuzzy Similarity Measures*

A definition of fuzzy similarity measures [1] has been derived from Tversky's contrast model, a psychological framework for similarity measurement. As shown in [11], these measures provide an intuitive measurement of similarity. They are also independent of the scale of the fuzzy sets. In this scheme, the similarity between two fuzzy subsets A, B of feature space F can be calculated by a function S, with three variables:

- $M(A \cap B)$ the area of the fuzzy intersection of A and B, which measures *the common features* of fuzzy sets A an B.
- $M(A-B)$, the area of the fuzzy difference of A by B, which measures *the features that are only present in A*.
- $M(B-A)$, the area of the fuzzy difference of B by A, which measures *the features that are only present in B*.

These areas correspond to the following sums, calculated based on the membership functions μ_A, μ_B of A, B:

$$M(A \cap B) = \sum_{x \in F} min(\mu_A(x), \mu_B(x)),$$

$$M(A - B) = \sum_{x \in F} max(\mu_A(x) - \mu_B(x), 0),$$

$$M(B - A) = \sum_{x \in F} max(\mu_B(x) - \mu_A(x), 0)$$

This expression of fuzzy similarity measures falls within Tversky's contrast model [13]. Based on this general framework, different particular measures were derived. We chose to implement only four of them as region similarity measures: Jaccard, Dice and Ochiai [10]. With $X = M(A \cap B)$, $Y = M(A - B)$, $Z = M(B - A)$, we have:

$$S_{jaccard}(X, Y, Z) = \frac{X}{X+Y+Z}$$

$$S_{dice}(X, Y, Z) = \frac{2X}{2X+Y+Z}$$

$$S_{ochiai}(X, Y, Z) = \frac{X}{\sqrt{X+Y}\sqrt{X+Z}}$$

Considering different measures enable us to investigate their properties. In particular, we show in [9] that the ranking in the list provided by an information retrieval system using these measures is conserved between some of them.

2.3. *Region Fuzzy Similarity using color, shape and position*

To measure the similarity of two regions, we consider two aspects: color and shape. For each of these aspects, a region is represented as a vector. But since these two description vectors belong to different spaces, and cannot be related one to the other, the similarity has to rely on two different measures.
For two regions $R(i)$ and $I(j)$, extracted respectively from the image request R and from an image database entry I, we define the region similarity S_{reg} as a weighted mean of these two "sub-measures". With $\lambda_c + \lambda_s = 1$:

$$S_{reg}(R(i), I(j)) = \lambda_c . S_{reg|color}(R(i), I(j))$$
$$+ \lambda_s . S_{reg|shape}(R(i), I(j))$$

In our experiments, we set the weights of these two measures to $\lambda_c = 0.7$, $\lambda_s = 0.3$.

Our *Fuzzy Region Color Similarity* $S_{reg|color}$ is based on the color histograms of the regions. To compare the regional color histograms, we use measures presented in section 2.2.

Our *Fuzzy Shape Similarity* $S_{reg|shape}$ is based on the centered binary masks of the regions. A mask is the matrix $K_{R(i)}$ of $\{0,1\}$ that represents the crisp membership of each pixel of the image R to the region $R(i)$. $K_{R(i)}$ is centered so that its central point gives the membership of the geometric center of $R(i)$. To compare the two shapes of regions $R(i), I(j)$, we compute their common and distinctive pixels, and apply the similarity measures of section 2.2.

3. Semantically oriented composite queries

In this section, we show how we form composite queries from basic regional similarity measures. The first step to do that is to build a simple query type (see 3.1), then to aggregate different simple queries in a composite fusion schema. This schema will depend on the meaning of the request in terms of visual content.
By doing that, and thanks to the underlying system's architecture, we can achieve the following goals :
– we can easily extend a single-example query to a many-examples query (see 3.2)
– the user is not limited in the choice of the examples : he can, in fact, choose the examples in different images (see 3.3)
– we can exploit the variety of (see 3.4).
– he has the opportunity to indicate regions that he *wants* to find as well as regions that he *does not want* to find (that may be useful in a filtering perspective, see 3.5).

3.1. *The most simple query type*

To form a composite query, we first introduce a simple query type which is the classical single region query. This simple query type gives the user the opportunity to retrieve images containing a region that is similar to one specified region.

As shown in the section 2, we have a similarity measure $S_{reg}(R_i, I_j)$ that can compute the visual similarity between one given request region R_i and a region I_j of an inspected image I of the database. If we maximise this similarity on each region I_j of I, we obtain the following measure :

$$S_{reg}(R_i, I) = \text{Max}_{I_j \in I}(S_{reg}(R_i, I_j))$$

This *region to image* similarity measure $S_{reg}(R_i, I)$ indicates the truth value of the proposition : "there is a region in I that is similar to R_i". To find images that contain a specified region R_i, we just have to maximise $S_{reg}(R_i, I)$ on all the images I of the database. The images that maximise this score are those that contain one region that is strongly similar to R_i, which is the seek of the request.

Now, we can compose more complex queries by aggregating the different scores obtained by the different simple queries in the same way as when we aggregate truth values with fusion operators.

3.2. Scene retrieval

In a large database, a user may want to find images that contain a given scene. For an image, we define a scene as being the composition of several different regions: for example a house, a tree and some grass. In this case, the system has to find the specified regions *together* in one single result images. It is then no longer possible to just propose the single region query paradigm: we have to propose a multiple-examples query type.

For a scene composed of different regions $R_1, ..., R_q$ of an image R, we have to find images I that present a set of regions that is similar to the specified set $\{R_1, ..., R_q\}$. All the regions R_i of the set have to be found in I. This can be performed by the following measure :

$$S_{scene}(\{R_1, ..., R_q\}, I) = \text{Min}(S_{reg}(R_1, I), ..., S_{reg}(R_q, I)) \tag{1}$$

As pointed out previously, $S_{reg}(R_1, I)$ indicates the truth value of the proposition "there is a region in I that is similar to R_1". Then, $S_{scene}(\{R_1, ..., R_q\}, I)$, as a conjunction of the $S_{reg}(R_i, I)$, indicates the truth value of a conjunctive proposition : "there is a region in I that is similar to R_1, *and* a region that is similar to R_2, *and* ... (so on)". That is the goal we wanted to achieve : the images I of the database that maximise $S_{scene}(\{R_1, ..., R_q\}, I)$ will present all the regions R_i together.

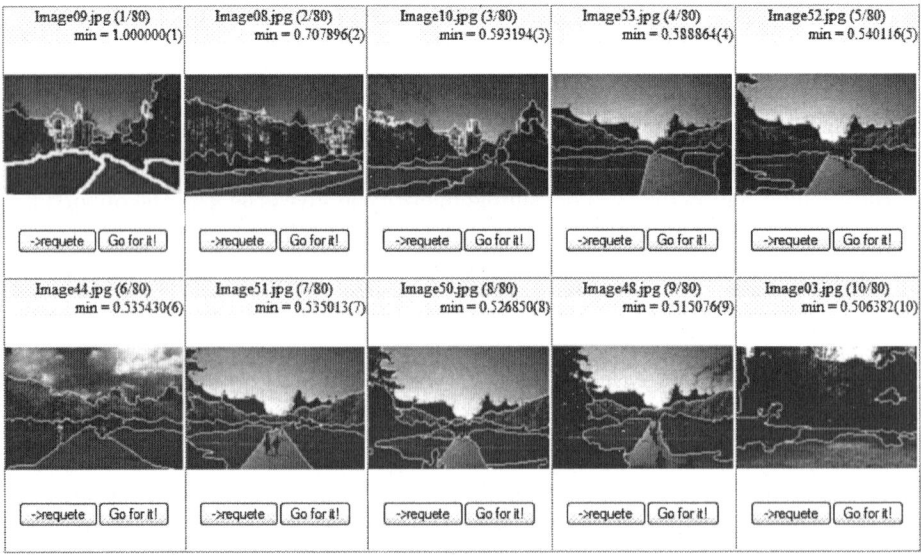

Fig. 2. Retrieval of a scene, the request regions are enhanced in the image on the left upper corner

On figure 2 we show some example request of this kind. In this case, we have found the regions enhanced in the request together (when it was possible) in the following images. As we can notice here, this goal has been achieved just by aggregating scores of different similarity measures (measures that compare I to different regions R_i). In the following, we will use this idea to build different multiple-examples query types by using different aggregation operators.

3.3. *Retrieval of a schema of regions*

The fact that we can perform multiple-examples queries is yet interesting, but it indicates a flaw in the query by example paradigm : why would the user want to retrieve images containing a scene if he already has this scene in the request image ? To be really useful, a system would have to give the opportunity to the user to build a scene from different pieces of content that are not already together.
In this case, the user may in fact "pick" regions in some image, then pick some other regions in another image and indicate to the system that he wants to retrieve all of these. The manufactured request may be assimilated to a schema : the user has built a request from different pieces picked from different sources and put together.

Our choice of aggregating scores from different simple queries enables us to give this handle this type of queries. In fact, by looking at the similarity measure $S_{scene}(\{R_1, ..., R_q\}, I)$ we can notice that the aggregation operator used (in this case, the minimum) is independant on the measures $S_{reg}(R_i, I)$ it aggregates. As a matter of fact, the regions R_i may as well be chosen in different images: the result would not be any different. So, giving the opportunity to the user to form queries based on regions picked in different images is only - in our framework - an issue concerning the system's interface (and our system's interface enables the user to do that (see 4)).

Although, in this case, one has to give a particular care to the aggregation operator used to combine the different similarity measures. For a given set of regions $R_1, ..., R_q$ chosen by the user from different images to form a schema, one can not be sure that these regions can really be found *together* in other images. If any of the regions $R_1, ..., R_q$ can not be found in an image I, the aggregated score $S_{scene}(\{R_1, ..., R_q\}, I)$ will severely decrease. This is because we use the minimum to aggregate the different scores $S_{reg}(R_i, I)$. We should in fact fusion operators different from the minimum:

$$S_{schema}(\{R_1, ..., R_q\}, I) = \mathrm{Agg}(S_{reg}(R_1, I), ..., S_{reg}(R_q, I))$$

In the case of a schema, we should in fact not use a fuzzy logic T-norm but a smoother conjunctive operator such as an average. This would allow to retrieve images that contain some of the regions R_i. A much better choice would be to use the ordered weighted average operator that would lead to the retrieval of images containing a majority of them, or something between "all of them" and "some of them" depending on the choice of the parameters of the OWA operator. As we will see in section 4, our system lets the expert user build a broad variety of operators from basic mathematical operations.

3.4. *Retrieving different aspects of a same object*

In a large database of images, a same object may appear several times in different positions, colours or shapes. In practice, the user may be interested in retrieving images containing a given object and not specifically one aspect of this object. So, we have to propose a way for him to retrieve an object that may be presented in different ways.

This is something we can simply do by changing the fusion operator that is used to aggregate the different similarity measures corresponding to the regions specified by the user. For a given set of examples $\{R_1, ..., R_q\}$ depicting a same object in different aspects (that would surely be taken from different images), we have to retrieve images that contain *one of these* aspects. As in 3.3, by aggregating the similarity measures $S_{reg}(R_i, I)$ (corresponding to the different regions R_i) by the maximum, we obtain the following measure :

$$S_{concept}(\{R_1, ..., R_q\}, I) = \text{Max}(S_{reg}(R_1, I), ..., S_{reg}(R_q, I))$$

This evaluates the truth value of the proposition : "the images I contains a region that is similar to R_1, *or* a region that is similar to R_2, *or*... (and so on)". So images I that maximise $S_{concept}(\{R_1, ..., R_q\}, I)$ will contain one of the aspects depicted by the regions $R_1, ..., R_q$.

On figure 2 we show some example request of this kind. In this case, we have found the regions enhanced in the request together (when it was possible) in the following images.

As we can see now, the use of aggregation operators on simple regional similarity measures enables us to propose different queries that answer to different needs of visual information retrieval. In fact here, the *type* of request is defined by the aggregation operator and not by the similarity measures used to compare the images. This is a powerful property of the framework designed here: it means that we can extend it to any visual similarity measures.

3.5. *Filtering query*

The same framework can be oriented through the exploitation of negative constraints. As an example, the user could be interested in finding an image that depicts a given object and not another specific one : it may be an object he does not want to see, or, given a first result, a filtering constraint he wants to apply to the result list (to eliminate non relevant images).

Again, this can easily be done by choosing the appropriate aggregation operator. As a matter of fact, just as the similarity measure $S_{reg}(R_i, I)$ indicates the truth value of the proposition "there is a region in I that is similar to R_i", the negation of this, namely $1 - S_{reg}(R_i, I)$ indicates the truth value of "there is no region in I

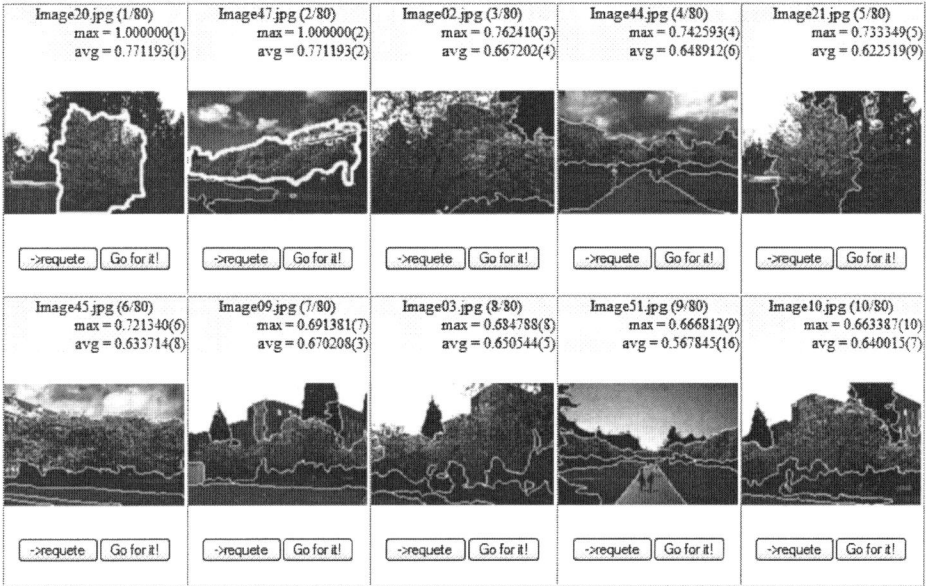

Fig. 3. Retrieval of different aspects, they are enhanced in the two first images on the top left corner

that is similar to R_i".

So, from a *positive* regional example R_+ and a *negative* example R_-, we compute by:

$$S((R_+, R_-), I) = \text{Agg}(S_{reg}(R_+, I), 1 - S_{reg}(R_-, I))$$

a similarity measure that indicates if the image I contains a region like R_+ but no region like R_-. The choice of the operator Agg can simply point out how these two constraints must be fulfilled within I: by choosing the minimum we indicate that these two must absolutely be verified, by averaging the two similarity measures we obtained a "relaxed" tool that tries to maximize both.

4. STRICT Image Retrieval Platform

As we have seen in section 3 we can form various query types by just defining visual similarity measures on regions and aggregating them by various operators. This is basically what our image retrieval is capable of.

This system is called STRICT ("System for Testing Retrieval by Image ContenT"). Its main assets are its dynamic web interface, and its open computation engine. From the interface, the user can formulate an aggretation operator with basic mathematical operations. Using the minimum, the maximum, the negation, the addition and the product, he can define his own operator, specify its entries within the available similarity measures, and then test this newly aggregated similarity against the

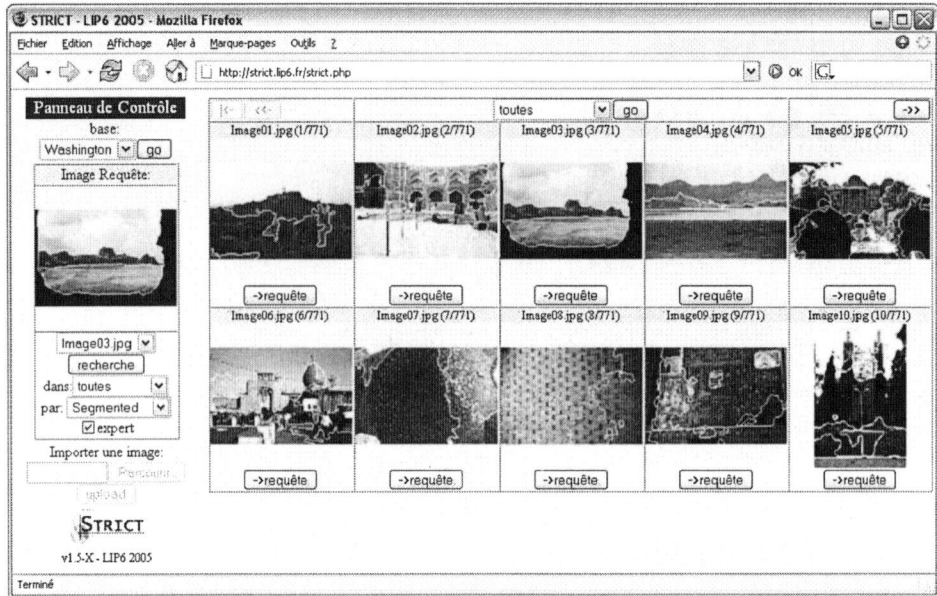

Fig. 4. The interface of STRICT

images. The basic operators programmed in this application let us build most of the known aggregation operators.

So, to form a query like those pointed out in section 3, the user has to :
- specify a given amount of regions choosen from the images of the database. He can do that with no restriction on the source of the regions : they can be choosen in different images.
- specify a similarity measure for each regions and set their parameters. Basically, the similarity measure is always the same (the visual similarity measure explicited in 2 and 3.1), but several similarity measures can be defined in the system in order to be employed by the user simultaneously.
- build an aggregation operator to fit his need. This can be done easily from the interface.

The dynamic interface of our system (see figure 4) is a practical tool to test all of the four query types proposed in this paper. With simple actions, an expert user can simulate one of these four requests, specify its parameters, and compose an aggregator to fulfill its needs. No current CBIR system offers all of these features.

5. Conclusion

Our image retrieval system uses a regional representation of images, built using a segmentation algorithm. This solution, currently investigated in the field, has been implemented in STRICT to let the user specify his visual interest in the request. For the expert, our system proposes features that enables him to modify parameters, build complex requests, and compare their results in a dynamic and easy to use interface.

The requests that can be built using this system extend the use of regional features to multiple example queries. We can now retrieve images containing a given scene, or some object defined by its many possible aspects. We can also built schemas of scenes by picking regions in different images and finally filter the results by adding negative constraints to the similarity measures.

References

1. B. Bouchon-Meunier, M. Rifqi, and S. Bothorel. Towards general measures of comparison of objects. *Fuzzy Sets and Systems*, 84(2):143–153, 1996.
2. Chad Carson, Megan Thomas, Serge Belongie, Joseph M. Hellerstein, and Jitendra Malik. Blobworld: A system for region-based image indexing and retrieval. In *Third International Conference on Visual Information Systems*. Springer, 1999.
3. Y. Chen and J.Z. Wang. A region-based fuzzy feature matching approach to content-based image retrieval. *IEEE Trans. On Pattern Analysis and Machine Intelligence*, 24(9), 2002.
4. H.D. Cheng, X.H. Jiang, Y. Sun, and J. Wang. Color image segmentation: advances and prospects. *Pattern Recognition*, 34:2259–2281, 2001.
5. J.P. Eakins. Towards intelligent image retrieval. *Pattern Recognition*, 35:3–14, 2002.
6. M.D. Flickner, H. Sawhney, W. Niblack, J. Ashley, Q. Huang, B. Dom, M. Gorkani, J. Hafner, D. Lee, D. Petkovic, D. Steele, and P. Yanker. Query by image and video content: The qbic system. *Computer*, 28(9):23–32, September 1995.
7. J. Li, J.Z. Wang, and G. Wiederhold. Irm: Integrated region matching for image retrieval. In *8th ACM Int. Conf. on Multimedia*, pages 147–156, 2000.
8. J.F. Omhover and M. Detyniecki. Strict: an image retrieval platform for queries based on regional content. In *Proc. of the Int. Conf. on Image and Video Retrieval - CIVR (LNCS 3115)*, pages 473–482, Dublin, Ireland, Aout, 2004.
9. J.F. Omhover, M. Detyniecki, M. Rifqi, and B. Bouchon-Meunier. Image retrieval using fuzzy similarity : Measure equivalence based on invariance in ranking. In *Proc. of the IEEE Int. Conf. on Fuzzy Systems - Fuzz-IEEE*, pages 1367–1372, Budapest, Hungary, Juillet, 2004.
10. M. Rifqi, M. Detyniecki, and B. Bouchon-Meunier. Discrimination power of measures of resemblance. In *IFSA'03*, Istanbul, Turkey, 2003.
11. S. Santini and R. Jain. Similarity measures. *IEEE Transactions on Pattern Analysis and Machine Intelligence*, 21(9):871–883, 1999.
12. J.R. Smith and S.F. Chang. Visualseek: a fully automated content-based image query system. In *ACM Multimedia '96*, November, 1996.
13. Amos Tversky. Features of similarity. *Psychological Review*, 84:327–352, 1977.

Blind Image Restoration from Multiple Views by IMAP Estimation

Monia Discepoli, Ivan Gerace and Roberta Pandolfi

Dipartimento di Matematica e Informatica
Università degli Studi di Perugia
Via Vanvitelli, 1 – I-06123 Perugia

Abstract

In this paper we deal with the problem of the blind image restoration starting from several images obtained by applied different blur operators to the same image. We call this problem blind multiple images restoration. We attempt to reconstruct the original image using the IMAP (Indirect Maximum A Priori) estimation. The obtained results confirm the goodness of this technique.

Key words: Blind Image Restoration, Bayesian Estimation, Markov Random Fields, Simulated Annealing Algorithm, Graduated Non-Convex Algorithm.

1. The problem of the blind multiple images restoration

In many cases it is possible to have different images of some object corrupted and degraded by different operators. The observed images are affected from degradation and noise, introduced by the imaging system that we assume to be variable during the time.

In several scientific fields, like astronomy, medicine, robotic etc..., this kind of images have to be elaborated and understood. For this reason, we deal with the problem of estimating the original image from the multiple degraded images. In the applications, the different blur operators are not explicitly and exactly known. Thus it is necessary to elaborate methods that allow to estimate both these operators and the original image, using information about the observed data and the known properties of the true image.

Let N be a positive number, $N > 1$. The direct problem can be formulated as

$$y^{(t)} = A^{(t)}x + n^{(t)}, \qquad t = 1, \ldots, N, \tag{1}$$

where $y^{(t)} \in \mathbb{R}^{n^2}$ are the corrupted and blurred images, $x \in \mathbb{R}^{n^2}$ is the original image, $A^{(t)} \in \mathbb{R}^{n^2 \times n^2}$ are the linear blur operators and $n^{(t)} \in \mathbb{R}^{n^2}$ are the additive Gaussian independent noise with zero mean and known variance σ^2.

To each matrix $A^{(t)}$ is associated a positive matrix $M^{(t)} \in \mathbb{R}^{q \times q}$ ($q = 2h+1$), called *blur mask*, from which the entries of $A^{(t)}$ can be defined as

$$a_{(i,j),(i+w,j+v)} = \begin{cases} \dfrac{m_{h+1+w,h+1+v}}{\nu_{i,j}}, & \text{if } |w|, |v| \le h, \\ 0, & \text{otherwise,} \end{cases}$$

where $\nu_{i,j} = \sum_{i=\kappa}^{\eta} \sum_{j=\ell}^{\delta} m_{i,j}$, $\kappa = \max\{1, i-2h+1\}$, $\eta = \min\{n, i+2h+1\}$, $\ell = \max\{1, j-2h+1\}$ and $\delta = \min\{n, j+2h+1\}$. Here, in lexicographic notation, the generic index $((i,j),(h,l))$ of matrix A is supposed to be equal to $((j-1)n+i, (l-1)n+h)$.

The *blind multiple images restoration problem* consists in estimating both the original image x and the linear blur operator $\{A^{(t)}\}_t$ from the degraded images $\{y^{(t)}\}_t$, $t = 1, \ldots, N$, using partial information about the imaging system and the properties of the true image.

2. Bayesian approach

In this paper we formulate the problem of blind images restoration within a Bayesian framework based on MRF (*Markov Random Field*) models [1,?,?].

Let $Q_n = ([1,n] \cap \mathbb{N}) \times ([1,n] \cap \mathbb{N})$ for every $n \in \mathbb{N}$. A *clique* is the set of points of Q_n on which the finite difference of first order is defined. We indicate with the symbol C the set of all cliques and we denote the finite difference operator on the vector x associated with the clique c by $D_c x$.

A *line variable* b_c associated to clique c is a Boolean variable. If b_c assumes the one value this corresponds to a discontinuity of our involved image in c. The vector b is the set of all components b_c. By the notation $c - 1$ we denote the clique that precedes c in the order $\preceq$ defined as follows:

$$\{(i,j),(i-1,j)\} \preceq \{(h,j),(h-1,j)\} \Leftrightarrow i \le h,$$

and

$$\{(i,j),(i,j-1)\} \preceq \{(i,h),(i,h-1)\} \Leftrightarrow j \le h.$$

In this way the original image is modelled using two coupled MRFs: a continuos-values, x, where $x_{i,j}$ represents the intensity values of the pixel (i,j), and a binary one associated to the vector b.

The *a posteriori probability distribution*, according to the Bayes theorem, can be defined as

$$P(x, b, \{A^{(t)}\}_t | \{y^{(t)}\}_t) = \frac{P(\{y^{(t)}\}_t | x, b, \{A^{(t)}\}_t) P(x, b, \{A^{(t)}\}_t)}{P(\{y^{(t)}\}_t)} \quad (2)$$

where $P(\{y^{(t)}\}_t | x, b, \{A^{(t)}\}_t)$ is called *likelihood function*, $P(x, b, \{A^{(t)}\}_t)$ is the *a priori probability distribution* of the solution and $P(\{y^{(t)}\}_t)$ is constant due to the fact that $\{y^{(t)}\}_t$ are known data.

By the independence of $\{y^{(t)}\}_t$ and by (1) one has

$$P(\{y^{(t)}\}_t | x, b, \{A^{(t)}\}_t = \prod_{t=1}^{N} P(\{y^{(t)}\}_t | x, b, \{A^{(t)}\}_t) = \prod_{t=1}^{N} P(y^{(t)} | x, b, A^t).$$

Taking the common assumption that the noise is Gaussian uncorrelated with zero mean and variance σ^2, we have that

$$P(y^{(t)} | x, b, A^{(t)}) = (2\pi\sigma^2)^{-\frac{n^2}{2}} \exp\left[-\frac{\|y^{(t)} - A^{(t)} x\|^2}{2\sigma^2}\right].$$

Assuming that $\{A^{(t)}\}_t$ are independent to x and b, we have that

$$P(x, b, \{A^{(t)}\}_t) = P(x, b) P(\{A^{(t)}\}_t).$$

Both $P(x, b)$ and $P(\{A^{(t)}\}_t)$ can be modelled by MRFs. An MRF has the property that the conditional probability of an element with respect to all other element actually depends only on the configuration of elements associated to sites in a prescribed neighborhood. The Clifford-Hammersley theorem [7] establishes that the joint probability of an MRF can be expressed in the form of a Gibbs distribution:

$$P(x, b) = \frac{1}{Z} \exp\left[-U(x, b)\right],$$

$$U(x, b) = \sum_{c \in C} V_c(x, b),$$

where Z is the normalizing constant, or *partition function* and $V_c(x, b)$ is the vector of the *clique potential functions*. The potential functions, in this case, are the following

$$V_c(x, b) = \frac{1}{2\sigma^2} \left[\lambda^2 (D_c x)^2 (1 - b_c) + \alpha b_c + \varepsilon\, b_c\, b_{c-1}\right].$$

Here λ^2, called *regularization parameter*, permits to regulate an appropriate degree of smoothing in the solution. The parameter α is positive and is used in order to avoid to have too many discontinuities in the restored image. The last term is introduced in order to have suitable geometric features of discontinuities in the restored image. In particular here we impose that it should not exist parallel close discontinuities. The parameter ε has to be greater or equal to zero.

In the same way we have that

$$P(A^{(t)}) = \frac{1}{\tilde{Z}} \exp\left[-\tilde{U}(x, b)\right],$$

where
$$\tilde{U}(A^{(t)}) = \frac{\mu}{2\sigma^2} \sum_{i,j} \sum_{t=1}^{N-1} \left(m_{i,j}^{(t)} - m_{i,j}^{(t+1)}\right)^2.$$

In this way we impose that the blur masks slowly change one each others and μ is a positive parameter that enforces this constraint.

The solution of the blind multiple images restoration problem can be defined as the set composed by x, b and $\{A^{(t)}\}_t$ that maximizes the a posteriori probability distribution as in (2), or, equivalently that minimizes the following *primal energy function*

$$E(x, b, \{A^{(t)}\}_t) = \sum_{t=1}^{N} \|y^{(t)} - A^{(t)}x\|^2 + \sum_{c \in C} \left[\lambda^2 (D_c x)^2 (1 - b_c) + \alpha b_c\right]$$

$$+ \sum_{c \in C} \varepsilon b_c b_{c-1} + \mu \sum_{i,j} \sum_{t=1}^{N-1} \left(m_{i,j}^{(t)} - m_{i,j}^{(t+1)}\right)^2.$$

To minimize the primal energy function, it is possible to minimize it first with respect to all line variables b_c. The obtained *dual energy function* is defined as follows [1,5,6,8,10]:

$$E_d(x, \{A^{(t)}\}_t) = \inf_b E(x, b, \{A^{(t)}\}_t).$$

When the parameter ε is strictly greater than zero it is difficult to compute explicitly the duality energy function. In this case a good approximation of the dual energy function is the following [1,2,10]:

$$E_d(x, \{A^{(t)}\}_t) = \sum_{t=1}^{N} \|y^{(t)} - A^{(t)}x\|^2 + \sum_{c \in C} \psi(D_c(x), D_{c-1}(x)) \qquad (3)$$

$$+ \mu \sum_{i,j} \sum_{t=1}^{N-1} \left(m_{i,j}^{(t)} - m_{i,j}^{(t-1)}\right)^2,$$

where

$$\psi(t_1, t_2) = \begin{cases} \begin{cases} \lambda^2 t_1^2 & \text{if } |t_1| < s \\ & \text{if } |t_2| < s \\ \alpha & \text{if } |t_1| \geq s \end{cases} \\ \begin{cases} \lambda^2 t_1^2 & \text{if } |t_1| < \bar{s} \\ & \text{if } |t_2| \geq s. \\ \alpha + \varepsilon & \text{if } |t_1| \geq \bar{s} \end{cases} \end{cases}$$

The quantity $s = \sqrt{\alpha}/\lambda$ has the meaning of a *threshold* for creating a discontinuity, while $\bar{s} = \sqrt{\alpha + \varepsilon}/\lambda$ is a *suprathreshold* for creating a close parallel discontinuity.

3. IMAP estimation

A classic estimation of the solution of the blind image restoration problem is the MAP-ML (*Maximum A Posteriori-Maximum Likelihood*) estimation [4,11,13,14]. This is an iterative technique where are alternatively computed a MAP (*Maximum A Posteriori*) and a ML (*Maximum Likelihood*) estimation.

An alternative estimation of the solution of the blind image restoration problem, called IMAP (*Indirect Maximum A Priori*), was proposed by Gerace, Pandolfi and Pucci in [9]. In this paper we extend the use of IMAP estimation to the blind multiple images restoration problem.

Let $\bar{E}_d$ be the term associated to the a priori knowledge in the dual energy (3), that is

$$\bar{E}_d(\boldsymbol{x}, \{A^{(t)}\}) = \sum_{c \in C} \psi(D_c(\boldsymbol{x}), D_{c-1}(\boldsymbol{x})) + \mu \sum_{i,j} \sum_{t=1}^{N-1} \left(m_{i,j}^{(t)} - m_{i,j}^{(t+1)}\right)^2,$$

where the function ψ is as in (2). Moreover let

$$\boldsymbol{x}(\{A^{(t)}\}_t) = \arg \min_{\boldsymbol{x}} E_d(\boldsymbol{x}, \{A^{(t)}\}_t),$$

namely, the image that minimizes the dual energy when the matrices $\{A^{(t)}\}_t$ are fixed.

The IMAP estimation of the solution of the blind multiple images restoration problem can be defined as:

$$\{A^{(t)}\}_t = \arg \min_{\{A^{(t)}\}_t} \bar{E}_d(\boldsymbol{x}(\{A^{(t)}\}_t), \{A^{(t)}\}_t), \tag{4}$$

$$\boldsymbol{x} = \boldsymbol{x}(\{A^{(t)}\}_t). \tag{5}$$

That is, we look for the blur matrix, that used as known in the restoration of a image, permits to obtain the image that better fits our a priori knowledge of the ideal image.

To decrease the computational cost of the algorithm, a deterministic algorithm can be used to compute $\boldsymbol{x}(\{A^{(t)}\})_t$. Indeed, deterministic algorithms can give faster estimations of the solution than the ones obtained by stochastic algorithms [5].

A classical deterministic technique for minimizing the dual energy function, in the case of single image restoration, is the GNC (*Graduated Non-Convexity*) algorithm (see, [2,3,5,6,10,12]). Given a finite family of approximating functions $\{E_d^{(p)}\}_p$, such that the first one is convex and the last one is the original dual energy function, the GNC algorithm is defined as follows

initialize $\boldsymbol{x}$;

while $E_d^{(p)} \neq E_d$ do
- find the minimum of the function $E_d^{(p)}$ starting from the initial point $\boldsymbol{x}$;
- $\boldsymbol{x} = \arg \min E_d^{(p)}$;
- update the parameter p.

The first GNC algorithm was proposed by Blake and Zisserman [5,6], who approximate the dual energy with $A = I$, the identity matrix, and $\varepsilon = 0$. Bedini, Gerace and Tonazzini [2] proposed an extension of GNC algorithm, called E-GNC (*Extended Graduated Non-Convexity*) in which ε can assume values greater or equal to zero. Moreover, Nikolova [12] approximated a dual energy where $\varepsilon = 0$, but A can be arbitrary blur matrix. Finally, Gerace et al. [10] proposed the CATILED (*Convex Approximation Technique for Interacting Line Elements Deblurring*) algorithm, in which both ε and A can be arbitrary.

In particular, we use an extension of CATILED algorithm to compute $x(\{A^{(t)}\})_t$ and a SA (*Simulated Annealing*) algorithm [1,7,8,14] to perform (4).

4. Experimental results

The IMAP estimation algorithm was implemented in C language on a serial computer, and it was tested both on real images and on synthetic piecewise smooth ones.

We assume that the entries of the blur masks satisfy appropriated conditions. Given the elements $m_{i,j}^{(t)}$ and $m_{k,l}^{(t)}$, we impose that

a) the value of $m_{i,j}^{(t)}$ is equal to the one of $m_{k,l}^{(t)}$ if $[i - (h+1)]^2 + [j - (h+1)]^2 = [k - (h+1)]^2 + [l - (h+1)]^2$, that is, if the distance between the positions of two elements of a blur mask and the position of the middle element is the same then the entries of the two elements are equal;

b) the value of $m_{i,j}^{(t)}$ is greater or equal to the one of $m_{k,l}^{(t)}$ if $[i-(h+1)]^2+[j-(h+1)]^2 < [k - (h+1)]^2 + [l - (h+1)]^2$, that is, the values of elements of a blur mask closer to the middle element, are greater or equal with respect to the others.

These conditions are satisfied if the blur masks have a Gaussian shape. This is the case in most of the applications. In our experimental results we fixed $N = 4$. In Figure 1 the first synthetic considered 128×128 image is shown. We refer to this image as LINE. LINE was degraded by the following four blur masks:

$$M_1 = \begin{pmatrix} 1 & 1 & 1 & 1 & 1 \\ 1 & 1 & 1 & 1 & 1 \\ 1 & 1 & 1 & 1 & 1 \\ 1 & 1 & 1 & 1 & 1 \\ 1 & 1 & 1 & 1 & 1 \end{pmatrix}, \quad M_2 = \begin{pmatrix} 1 & 1 & 1 & 1 & 1 \\ 1 & 1 & 1 & 1 & 1 \\ 1 & 1 & 2 & 1 & 1 \\ 1 & 1 & 1 & 1 & 1 \\ 1 & 1 & 1 & 1 & 1 \end{pmatrix}, \quad (6)$$

$$M_3 = \begin{pmatrix} 1 & 1 & 1 & 1 & 1 \\ 1 & 1 & 2 & 1 & 1 \\ 1 & 2 & 3 & 2 & 1 \\ 1 & 1 & 2 & 1 & 1 \\ 1 & 1 & 1 & 1 & 1 \end{pmatrix}, \qquad M_4 = \begin{pmatrix} 1 & 1 & 1 & 1 & 1 \\ 1 & 1 & 2 & 1 & 1 \\ 1 & 2 & 4 & 2 & 1 \\ 1 & 1 & 2 & 1 & 1 \\ 1 & 1 & 1 & 1 & 1 \end{pmatrix}.$$

Fig. 1. Image LINE.

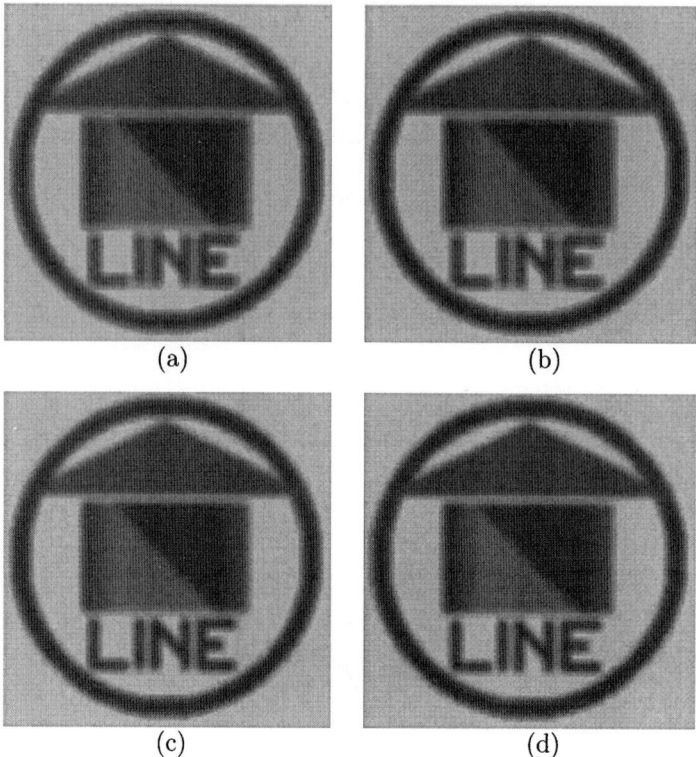

Fig. 2. (a) LINE blurred by mask M_1; (b) LINE blurred by mask M_2; (c) LINE blurred by mask M_3; (d) LINE blurred by mask M_4.

Fig. 3. IMAP estimation of LINE from the images in Figure 2 with $\lambda = 0.5$, $\alpha = 10$, $\varepsilon = 10$ and $\mu = 10$.

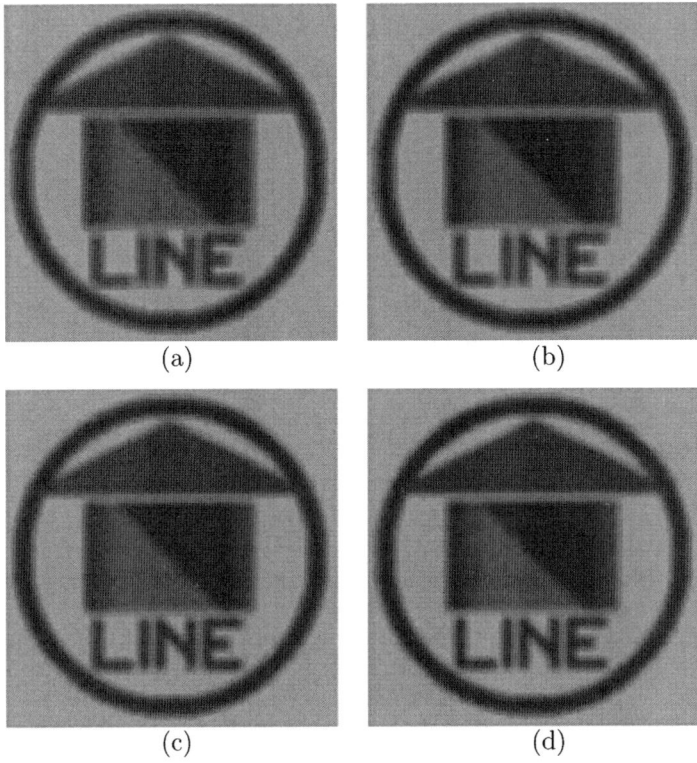

Fig. 4. (a) LINE blurred by mask M_1 and corrupted by noise ($\sigma^2 = 100$); (b) LINE blurred by mask M_2 and corrupted by noise ($\sigma^2 = 100$); (c) LINE blurred by mask M_3 and corrupted by noise ($\sigma^2 = 100$); (d) LINE blurred by mask M_4 and corrupted by noise ($\sigma^2 = 100$).

Fig. 5. IMAP estimation of LINE from the images in Figure 4 with $\lambda = 4$, $\alpha = 2000$, $\varepsilon = 2000$ and $\mu = 2000$.

Fig. 6. Image LENA.

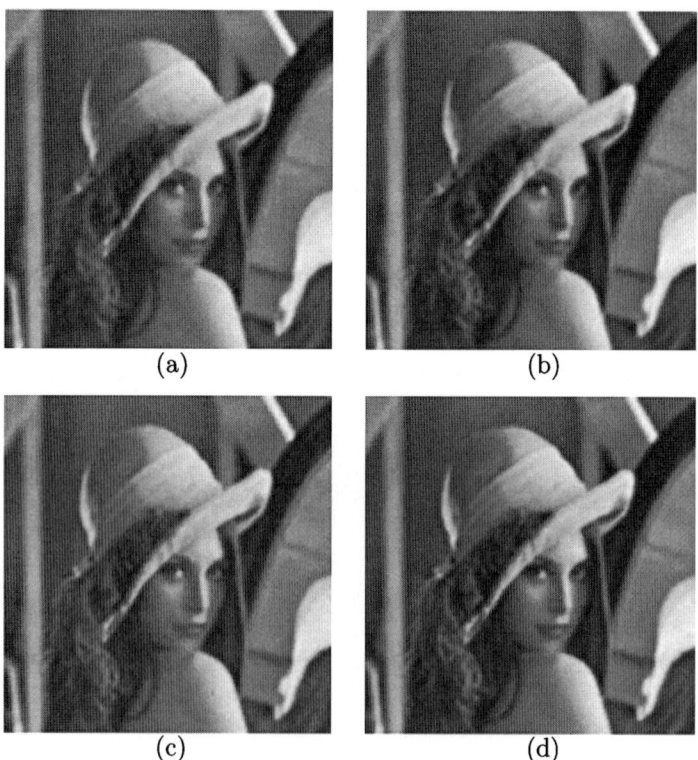

Fig. 7. (a) LENA blurred by mask M_1; (b) LENA blurred by mask M_2; (c) LENA blurred by mask M_3; (d) LENA blurred by mask M_4.

Fig. 8. IMAP estimation of LENA from the images in Figure 7 with $\lambda = 1$, $\alpha = 10$, $\varepsilon = 10$ and $\mu = 10$.

In Figure 2 there are reported the obtained blurred image. The reconstruction by IMAP estimation of LINE is presented in Figure 3. Such an estimation is obtained by setting $\lambda = 0.5$, $\alpha = 10$, $\varepsilon = 10$ and $\mu = 10$. In Figure 4 we present the image LINE blurred by masks in (6) and corrupted by four different white independent Gaussian noises with variance $\sigma^2 = 100$. The restored image by IMAP is shown in Figure 5. The used parameter are $\lambda = 4$, $\alpha = 2000$, $\varepsilon = 2000$ and $\mu = 2000$. Let consider now the real 256-image LENA given in Figure 6. LENA blurred by masks (6) is presented in Figura 7. The IMAP estimation of LENA with $\lambda = 1$, $\alpha = 10$, $\varepsilon = 10$ and $\mu = 10$ is reported in Figure 8.

References

1. L. Bedini, I. Gerace, E. Salerno and A. Tonazzini (1996). Models and Algorithms for Edge-Preserving Image Reconstruction. In *Advances in Imaging and Electron Physics,* vol. 97, pages 86–189.
2. L. Bedini, I. Gerace and A. Tonazzini (1994). A Deterministic Algorithm for Reconstruction Images with Interacting Discontinuities. In *CVGIP: Graphical Models Image Process.*, Vol 56, pages 109–123.
3. L. Bedini, I. Gerace and A. Tonazzini (1994). A GNC Algorithm for Constrained Images Reconstruction with Continuous-Valued Line Processes. In *Pattern Recogn. Lett.*, Vol. 16, pages 907–914.
4. L. Bedini and A. Tonazzini (2001). Fast Fully Data-Driven Image Restoration by means of Edge-Preserving Regularization. In *Real-Time Imaging, Special Issue on Fast Energy-Minimization-Based Imaging and Vision Techniques*, Vol. 7, no. 1, pages 3–19.
5. A. Blake (1989). Comparison of the Efficiency of Deterministic and Stochastic Algorithms for Visual Reconstruction. In *IEEE Trans. Pattern Anal. Machine Intell.*, Vol. 11, pages 2–12.
6. A. Blake and A. Zisserman (1987). *Visual Reconstruction*, MIT Press, Cambridge, MA, 1987.

7. S. Geman and D. Geman (1984). Stochastic Relaxation, Gibbs Distributions, and the Bayesian Restoration of Images. In *IEEE Trans. Pattern Anal. Machine Intell.*, Vol. 6, pages 721–740.
8. D. Geman and G. Reynolds (1992). Constrained Restoration and the Recovery of Discontinuities. In *IEEE Trans. Pattern Anal. Machine Intell.*, Vol. 14, pages 367–383.
9. I. Gerace, R. Pandolfi and P. Pucci (2003). A New Estimation of Blur in the Blind Restoration Problem. In proceeding of *IEEE International Conference on Image Processing ICIP 2003* September 14–17, 2003, Barcelona, Spain, pages 4.
10. I. Gerace, P. Pucci, A. Boccuto, M. Discepoli and R. Pandolfi (2003). A New Technique for Restoring Blurred Images with Convex First Approximation. *In preparation.*
11. S. Lakshmanan and H. Derin (1989). Simultaneus Parameter Estimation and Segmentation of Gibbs Random Fields using Simulated Annealing. in *IEEE Trans. Pattern Anal. Machine Intell.*, Vol. 11, pages 799–813.
12. M. Nikolova (1999). Markovian Reconstruction Using a GNC Approach. In *IEEE Trans. Image Process.*, Vol. 8, no. 9, pages 1204–1220.
13. A. Tonazzini (2001). Blur Identification Analysis in Blind Image Deconvolution Using Markov Random Fields. In *Pattern Recogn. and Image Analysis*, Vol. 11, no. 4, pages 669–710.
14. A. Tonazzini and L. Bedini (2002). Degradation Identification and Model Parameter Estimation in Discontinuity-Adaptive Visual Reconstruction. In *Advances in Imaging and Electron Physics*, Vol. 120, pages 193-284.

A Combined Feature Extraction Method for an Electronic Nose

I. Hristozov [a], B. Iliev [b], and S. Eskiizmirliler [c]

[a] Center for Applied Autonomous Sensor Systems, Dept. of Technology,
University of Örebro, S-70182 Örebro, Sweden
[b] Center for Applied Autonomous Sensor Systems, Dept. of Technology,
University of Örebro, S-70182 Örebro, Sweden
[c] Universite Paris-VII et INSERM U483 9, Quai Saint Bernard,
75005 Paris, France

Abstract

The aim of this paper is to demonstrate a combined feature extraction approach for electronic nose data. The use of wavelet decomposition technique followed by orthonormalization leads to decreased number of classifier inputs. As a result, the number of these inputs is equal to the number of classes. Linear vector quantization network is used in order to overcome the sensors' drift to a certain degree. Two experiments are presented to demonstrate the procedure.

Key words: Electronic Nose, Wavelet Transformation, Gram-Schmidt Orthonormalization, Linear Vector Quantization

1. Introduction

Designed to mimic the odor recognition processes in biological systems, the electronic noses are a rapidly developing technique used in substance identification. The electronic nose is made using manufactured sensors that react chemically upon

---

[1] E-mail: hristozov@gbg.bg
[2] E-mail: Boyko.Iliev@tech.oru.se
[3] E-mail: selim@ccr.jussieu.fr

exposure to a substance. Therefore, the electronic noses have been widely used for quality testing in the food industry, to ensure a low level of toxicity and as a diagnostic tool in medical applications. The main idea is identification of simple or complex odor based on a gas sensor array and processing of obtained signals with an appropriate pattern recognition technique. Due to the high dimensionality of the signals, a feature extraction method needs to be applied. This is one of the main reasons for the large number of recent studies applying different feature extraction methods in classification of odors using electronic noses. Llobet et al. [4] used both transient and steady-state features as inputs to an artificial network classifier. They noticed that the rise time is strongly dependent on the type of odor being presented for an array of thin oxide sensors. Several feature extraction methods such as parameters extracted from curve fitting derivatives and integrals have been investigated in [11] using only one Pt-MOSFET sensor. All parameters are evaluated with respect to their signal-to-standard deviation ratio, the correlation in principal component analysis (PCA), and parameters ability to predict the concentration levels using an ANN. In [8] a comparative study of, on one hand the classical approaches such as Gram-Schmidt, Fast Fourier Transform and Haar wavelet transform and, on the other hand - Granger-Lynch-Ambros olfactory model, is presented. Consequently, the superiority of the wavelet transform for obtaining patterns that are more informative is shown. In [3] several feature extraction methods have been considered, using both steady state (fractional change, relative, difference and log) and transient response (Fourier and wavelet descriptors, integral and derivatives) information. Feature extraction methods have been validated qualitatively by using PCA and quantitatively by using a RBF neural network for classification. An additional problem arises from the fact that most of the gas sensors do not give stable responses over a long period. This drift causes electronic noses to classify gases incorrectly after some time. Still in 1997, Ratton et al. [8] tested their feature extraction methods on drifted data. The conclusion is that Haar wavelet transform is the most robust to this type of distortion, especially for their type of microsensor. Holmberg et al. [9][10], developed two methods for drift counteraction. The first proposed method is a self-organizing classifier based on the adaptation of a set of prototype vectors, called reference patterns. These patterns are initialized to be equal to the measurement vector of the class before drift and then they are updated in order to become more similar to the measurement vector. The second approach uses Box-Jenkins model for each sensor signal and each gas. The models are then used to predict the signal from sensors and prediction errors are used for gas identification. When the gas has been identified, the model parameters of all sensor models are updated according some rules. Recently, Loutfi et al. [1,2] obtained linguistic description, associating sensor results to human like presentation by linguistic expressions. They applied Principal Component Analysis (PCA) as feature extraction method and proposed two methods for data clustering: Artificial Neural Network (ANN), whose outputs are associated directly to linguistic labels, and fuzzy C-means clustering in combination with Gustafson-Kessel methods. The aim of this paper is to demonstrate a novel, combined approach, for substance classification. The main problem encountered in most of the classification approaches is the large number of features obtained after feature extraction. This makes the training of the classifier difficult and less reliable. The application of our approach, which could be summarized as combining good feature extraction characteristics of wavelet decomposition (see for example [3] and [8]) with orthonormalization, leads to significant decrease of the number of classifier inputs. As a result of the procedure the number of features is equal to the numbers of the classes. In order to overcome the sensors' drift, we use a self-organizing map such as LVQ network as classifier.

2. Electronic Nose (e-nose)

The electronic nose used in this work is developed in the Center for Applied Autonomous Sensor Systems, Department of Technology, Örebro University. It consists of a collection of four metal oxide (Taguchi) gas sensors [5], contained in a partly sealed capsule (Figure 1). A uni-directional passage of air is allowed to flow through the e-nose by means of air pump. Four individual curves, corresponding to four different gas sensors represent the input voltage over time. The testing process with

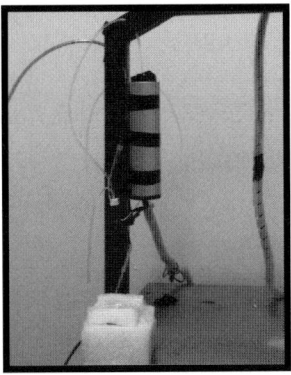

Fig. 1. The e-nose developed in AASS.

this nose has three distinct phases. The first phase, called the calibration phase, records the pre-exposure conditions by measuring the sensor readings for the clean air normally present in the nose. These values are used as a reference steady-state level. The testing phase exposes the sensors to a particular substance for a short time. The length of time is fixed for all the tests to avoid saturation of the sensors, which may require an extended recovery period. The final phase is the recovery phase where the substance is removed and the sensors are slowly flushed with clean air. The desired result is for the sensor value to return to the initial steady-state value during the recovery phase, but unfortunately, due to the presence of drift, the sensor value does not return to the initial steady-state value. During measurement, 8800 readings are collected for each sensor at regular intervals over a period of 270 seconds. In order to remove some of the noise and redundant information from the data, the sequence of readings of each sensor is divided into subset of 40 readings and each subset is replaced by its mean value. Thus the final data from one sensor contains approximately 220 readings.

3. Signal Processing Issues

3.1. Wavelet transform

Over the past few years, wavelets have been used extensively in many signal processing applications such as signal and image analysis, filtering, compression, decomposition and system identification [7]. The wavelet transform does have many similarities with the Fourier transform, but instead of projecting the signal over cosine or sine waves, the wavelet transform projects the signal over wavelets. This property is very useful when the measured signal is non-stationary. In this case the wavelet transform is localized both in the time- and frequency domain, while the Fourier transform is not. In this way, the wavelet transform provides means for overcoming the limitations of Fourier analysis.

The wavelet transform analyzes data at different resolution levels, which means that the signal appears on multiple scales simultaneously. This multi-resolution approach slices the measurement space into nested sequences of subspaces, where each resolution is a subset of a subset of a higher resolution.

Let us consider the basic function $\psi(t)$, called a *mother-wavelet*. If scaling and translation operations are performed on $\psi(t)$, a family of scaled and translated versions of the mother wavelet function can be created:

$$\psi_{a,b}(t) = \frac{1}{\sqrt{|a|}} \psi\left(\frac{t-b}{a}\right) \tag{1}$$

where a and b are the scaling and translation parameters. In the discrete case of wavelet transformation, time-scale parameters are discretized as $a = 2^j$ and $b = k \cdot 2^j$. The family of wavelets $\{\psi_{j,k}(t)\}$ is given by:

$$\psi_{j,k}(t) = 2^{j/2} \psi\left(2^{-j}t - k\right) \quad j, k \in Z,$$

The discrete version of the wavelet transform (DWT) of function $f(t)$ is:

$$DWT_f(j,k) = 2^{j/2} \int_{-\infty}^{+\infty} f(t) \psi\left(2^{-j}t - k\right) dt \tag{2}$$

The method used to compute the discrete wavelet decomposition and reconstruction is the so-called *Mallats pyramid algorithm* [7]. This algorithm is a classical scheme of two-channel subband coder using conjugate quadrature filters. The Mallats algorithm uses two filters to perform wavelet decomposition: a low-pass filter (LPF) and a high-pass filter (HPF). The signal is convoluted with LPF and HPF. After downsampling of the filtered signal, the approximation coefficients (a_1) and the detail coefficients (d_1) from first decomposition level are derived. Coefficients for each of the following decomposition level ($a_2, d_2, \ldots, a_K, d_K$) are derived from the convolution of the two filters and the approximation coefficients of previous level, followed again by downsampling. After the wavelet transform, the number of wavelet coefficients is the same as the number of variables in the original signal.

All operations of convolution and downsampling can be represented as a multiplication of the signal with two matrices W_K and V_K. The approximation coefficients a_1 and the detail coefficients d_1 from the first decomposition level can be respectively achieved by:

$$a_1 = V_1.f \qquad (3)$$
$$d_1 = W_1.f$$

where f is a data vector. For each of the next decomposition levels k, the approximation coefficients a_k and the detail coefficients d_k are obtained as

$$a_k = V_k.a_{k-1} \qquad (4)$$
$$d_k = W_k.a_{k-1}$$

In order to obtain a reconstruction of the signal, the approximation A_k has to be calculated for the last decomposition level, while the details D_k for each level. Due to the orthonormality of wavelet function, A_k and D_k could be obtained as follows:

$$A_k = (V_k \cdot V_{k-1} \cdot \ldots \cdot V_1)^T .a_k \qquad (5)$$
$$D_k = (W_k \cdot V_{k-1} \cdot \ldots \cdot V_1)^T .d_k$$

Then, the reconstructed signal after K levels of decomposition can be obtained by

$$f_r = A_K + D_K + D_{K-1} + \ldots + D_1 \qquad (6)$$

If we denote the energy of the signal with

$$\varepsilon_f = \sum_{i=1}^{N} f(i)^2 \qquad (7)$$

and the coefficients' energy of the Kth decomposition level with

$$\varepsilon_{(a_K|d_K|d_{K-1}|\ldots|d_1)} = \sum_{i=1}^{N_K} a_K(i) + \sum_{j=1}^{K}\sum_{i=1}^{N_j} d_j(i) \qquad (8)$$

it could be shown [7] that

$$\varepsilon_f = \varepsilon_{(a_K|d_K|d_{K-1}|\ldots|d_1)} \qquad (9)$$

This property of wavelet transform is called *conservation of the energy*. Furthermore, it could be shown that large percentage of the signal energy is accounted in the approximation coefficients a_K:

$$\varepsilon_{a_K} = \sum_{i=1}^{N_K} a_K(i) \approx \varepsilon_f \tag{10}$$

This property is called *compaction of energy*. Due to these two properties, a compression of the signal can be achieved by keeping only the coefficients with highest absolute value, since they account for the most percentage of signal energy, and setting the rest to zero. In this way, one can achieve very high level of compression, because with the increase of the number of decomposition levels the most percentage of signal energy is concentrated in less and less number of coefficients. As a control criterion, the closeness between the reconstructed and the original signal could be used.

3.2. Data orthonormalization

The data vectors $q_1, \ldots, q_k$ are orthonormal if they satisfy the conditions

$$q_i^T q_j = \begin{cases} 0 & \text{whenever } i \neq j \\ 1 & \text{whenever } i = j \end{cases} \tag{11}$$

The first condition is connected with the orthogonality while the second one gives normalization. Gram-Schmidt orthonormalization approach is used in this paper. The Gram-Schmidt process [6] starts with independent vectors $a_1, \ldots, a_n$ and ends with orthonormal vectors $q_1, \ldots, q_n$. At the first step q_1 is obtained as a division of the vector a_1 and its length:

$$q_1 = \frac{a_1}{\|a_1\|} \tag{12}$$

At the step j we subtract from a_j its components in the directions that are already settled:

$$a'_j = a_j - \left(q_1^T a_j\right) q_1 - \ldots - \left(q_{j-1}^T a_j\right) q_{j-1} \tag{13}$$

Then q_j is a unit vector:

$$q_j = \frac{a'_j}{\|a'_j\|} \tag{14}$$

In the end of the process, the following matrix of orthonormal columns is obtained

$$Q = [q_1, \ldots, q_n] \tag{15}$$

The projection matrix is usually $Q \left(Q^T Q\right)^{-1} Q^T$, but here it is simplified to

$$T = QQ^T \tag{16}$$

3.3. Linear Vector Quantization

A Linear Vector Quantization network has two layers-a first, competitive layer and a second, linear layer. The competitive layer learns to classify input vectors, and the linear layer transforms the competitive layer's classes into target classifications defined by the user. The classes learned by the competitive layer are referred to as subclasses and the classes of the linear layer as target classes. Different from the perceptrons, LVQ networks can classify any set of input vectors, not just linearly separable sets of input vectors. The only requirement is that the competitive layer must have enough neurons, and each class must be assigned enough competitive neurons.

4. Method

The method consists of six steps.
1. The input data consists of M sets of measurements performed with C different substances. L data sets contain the responses from S sensors of the nose. From each measurement, we take a data matrices F_m, $m \in 1 \div M$ of dimension $S \times N$, where $N = R.2^K$ is the number of readings per sensor.
2. A K-level wavelet transform (described in (4) and (5)) is applied to the signal of each sensor (each row of the data matrices F_m, $m \in 1 \div M$). In this way, for each measurement m we obtain S sets of wavelet coefficients vectors of the form

$$[a_{K,m,s}, d_{K,m,s}, d_{K-1,m.s}, \ldots, d_{1,m,s}], \ m \in 1 \div M, \ s \in 1 \div S.$$

All approximation coefficients from a measurement are arranged in *features vector* $v_m = [a_{K,m,1}, \ldots, a_{K,m,S}]$, $m \in 1 \div M$. The next steps are performed on these vectors.

3. A basis $q_{c,s}$ is obtained by orthonormalization of features' vector of the substance c and the sensor s using the Gram-Schmidt procedure [11], shown in (12)-(14). Each basis has a length of $R.S$. Applying the simplified projection matrix C projection matrices T_c, $c \in 1 \div C$, of dimension $R \cdot S \times R \cdot S$, are constructed.

4. The features' vector v_m of each measurement is projected onto the C bases

$$p_{c,m} = T_c.v_m, \ c \in 1 \div C, \ m \in 1 \div M \qquad (17)$$

That is, C projection vectors $p_{1,m} \ldots p_{C,m}$ with length $R.S$ are obtained for each measurement.

5. For each projection the standard deviation is calculated by

$$d_{c,m} = \sqrt{\frac{1}{R.S-1} \sum_{r=1}^{R.S} \left(p_{c,m}^r - \frac{1}{R.S} \sum_{r=1}^{R.S} p_{c,m}^r \right)}, \ c \in 1 \div C, \ m \in 1 \div M \qquad (18)$$

6. The values of $d_{c,m}$ are used as inputs to the LVQ-network mentioned above. Note that the network has C inputs and C outputs, where C is the number of classes.

5. Experimental Results and Discussion

The method was tested on the measurement data sets of three substances - lavender, vinegar and yogurt. For each substance, 17 measurement data sets were available. Eleven of them were used for network training and the other 6 for network testing. Each measurement data set captures the signals from four sensors. The typical e-nose sensor response for a substance (lavender) is shown on Figure 2.

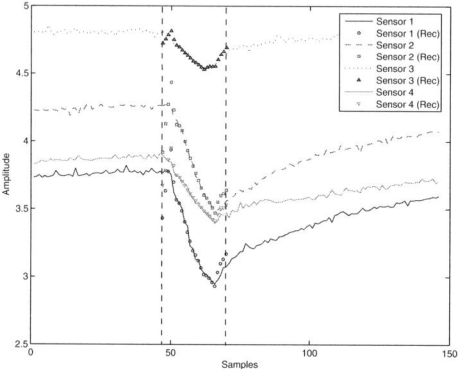

Fig. 2. Sensors data and reconstructed signal (Lavender).

In the first experiment, we take 28 samples from the decreasing phase of each sensor response (see Figure 2).

In this paper, a wavelet function, called Daubichies-2, is used. Daubichies-2 has the form, shown in Figure 3 and its LPF and HPF are represented by four coefficients (Table 1).

Fig. 3. Daubichies-2 wavelet function.

c_1	c_2	c_3	c_4
$\frac{1+\sqrt{3}}{4\sqrt{2}}$	$\frac{3+\sqrt{3}}{4\sqrt{2}}$	$\frac{3-\sqrt{3}}{4\sqrt{2}}$	$\frac{1-\sqrt{3}}{4\sqrt{2}}$

Table 1
Daubichies-2 coefficients.

The two matrices W_k and V_k mentioned in (4)-(6), in the case of Daubichies-2 have the following forms:

$$V_k = \begin{bmatrix} c_1 & c_2 & c_3 & c_4 & 0 & & \cdots & & 0 \\ 0 & 0 & c_1 & c_2 & c_3 & c_4 & 0 & \cdots & 0 \\ \vdots & & & & & & & & \vdots \\ c_3 & c_4 & 0 & & \cdots & & 0 & c_1 & c_2 \end{bmatrix}_{(N_k/2 \times N_k)} W_k = \begin{bmatrix} c_4 & -c_3 & c_2 & -c_1 & 0 & & \cdots & & 0 \\ 0 & 0 & c_4 & -c_3 & c_2 & -c_1 & 0 & \cdots & 0 \\ \vdots & & & & & & & & \vdots \\ c_2 & -c_1 & 0 & & \cdots & & 0 & c_4 & -c_3 \end{bmatrix}_{(N_k/2 \times N_k)}$$

where k is the number of current decomposition level, $N_k = N/2^{k-1}$ and N is data length. Hence, 2-level Daubichie-2 wavelet decomposition was applied on each sequence. Figure 4 shows some typical coefficients obtained from the wavelet decomposition (in this case for lavender). The features' vector of each measurement is constructed from the 6 approximation coefficients of the four sensors. Figure 2 shows comparison between the original and the reconstructed signals, accomplished only on the base of approximation coefficients. The features' vector from first measurement of each of the three substances is used to construct, using orthonormalization, a basis and a projection matrix for corresponding substance. The three bases obtained in this way are shown in figure 5. Each features' vector of training data sets is projected onto these bases (see Figures 6 and 7).

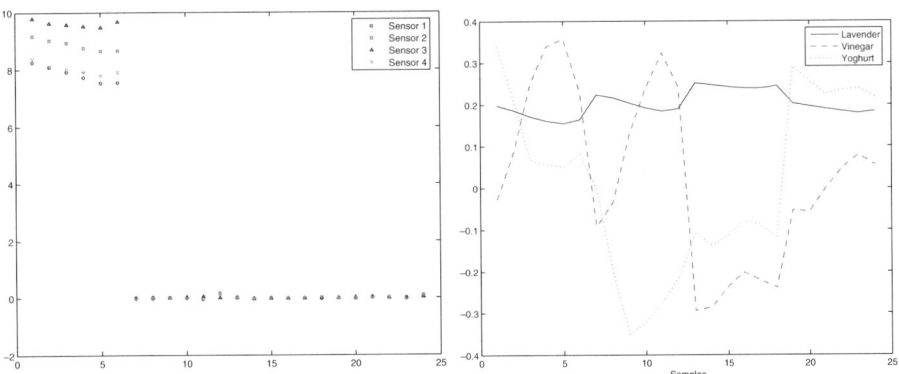

Fig. 4. Wavelet coefficients from 2 level decomposition with Daubichies-2 (Vinegar).

Fig. 5. Gram-Schmidt bases

The standard deviations of the three projections for each measurement are obtained (Figures 8 and 9). These values for 33 measurements are used as inputs to train the LVQ neural network. A perfect learning (0% error) is achieved after two steps. In network test phase, performed with 18 unseen examples (6 measurements for each of the 3 substances), 11.11% prediction error was registered, that means two measurements were misclassified.

The second experiment was performed on 56 samples from each sensor. In this case, the rising phase of the signal (see Figure 10) was also included in feature extraction procedure.

Three-level Daubichies-2 wavelet decomposition was applied on the selected sequences. Seven approximation coefficients (Figure 11) for each sensor were obtained. They were used to construct the features' vector for the measurements.

462 I. Hristozov et al.

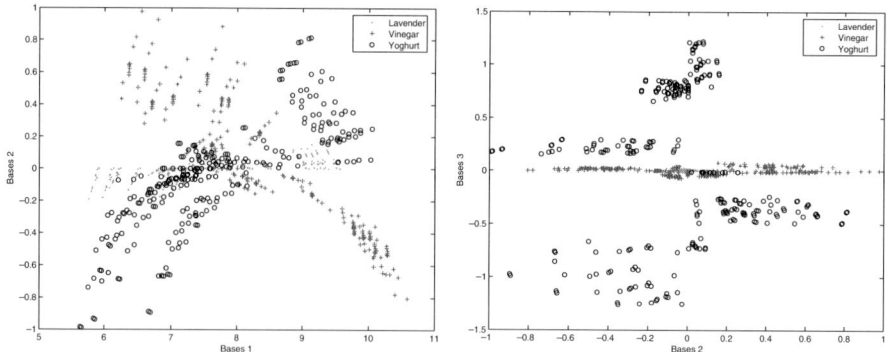

Fig. 6. Projections of features' vectors on bases 1 and 2.

Fig. 7. Projections of features' vectors on bases 2 and 3.

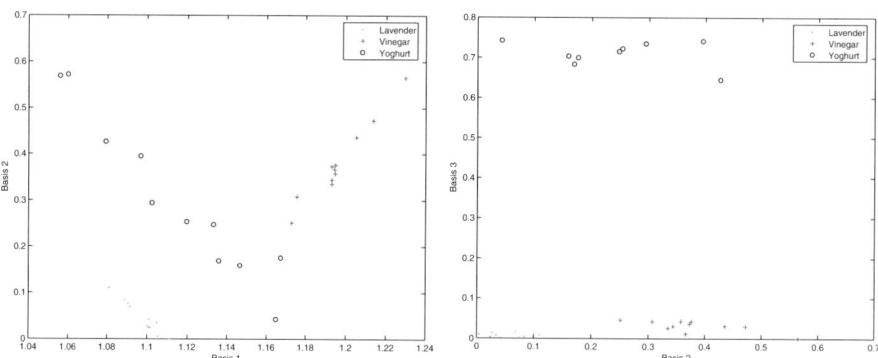

Fig. 8. Standard deviations of projections.

Fig. 9. Standard deviations of projections.

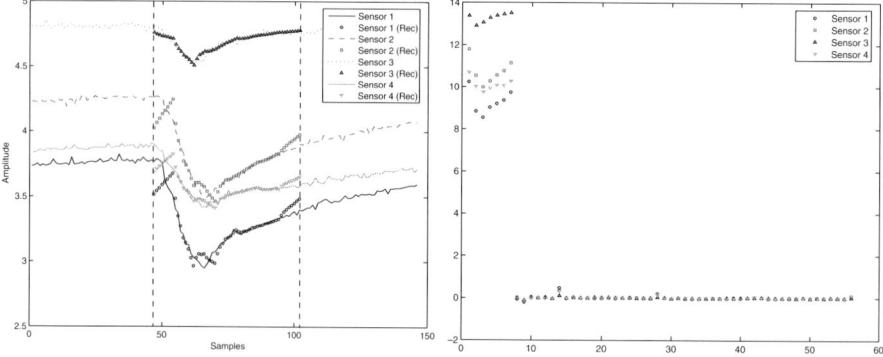

Fig. 10. Sensors data and reconstructed signals.

Fig. 11. Wavelet coefficients from 3 level decomposition wits Daubichies-2 (Lavender).

The same steps as in the previous experiment were performed. The obtained bases are shown on Figure 12.

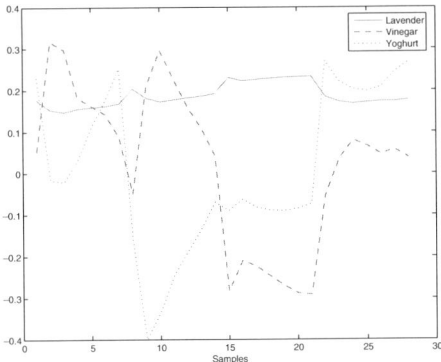

Fig. 12. Gram-Schmidt bases.

Figures 13 and 14 present the projections of measurements features vectors on the bases, and Figures 15 and 16 their standard deviations.

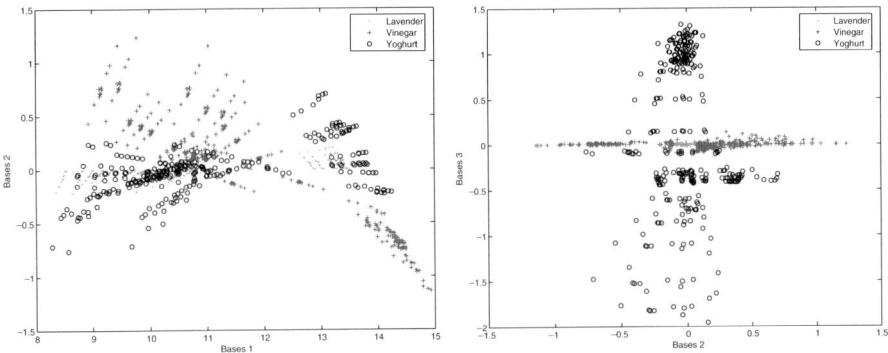

Fig. 13. Projections of features' vectors on bases 1 and 2.

Fig. 14. Projections of features' vectors on bases 2 and 3.

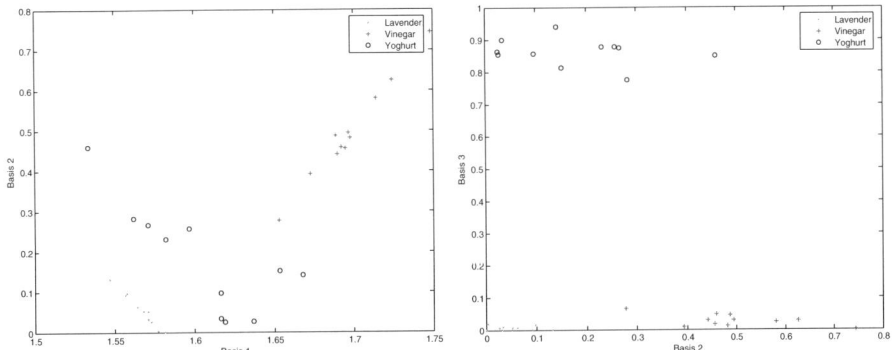

Fig. 15. Standard deviations of projections.

Fig. 16. Standard deviations of projections.

Thirty-three measurement features vectors for three different substances were used for network training and the other 18 - for network testing. The prediction error decreased to 5.56%, that means one measurement was misclassified.

6. Conclusions

It was originally planned to investigate wavelet decomposition as an alternative approach to feature extraction for odor classification purposes. The idea was to use the approximation coefficients as inputs to a classifier. The main obstacle here was the tradeoff between huge number of coefficients, respectively computational difficulties, and loss of information, respectively bad classification. This has led us to look for techniques for additional feature reduction. Gram-Schmidt orthonormalization was used for this purpose. This combined approach produced to very good results the number of features was reduced to the number of odors.

The second problem was the drift in electronic nose sensors. In order to counteract it, a self-organizing map, in this instance linear vector quantization, was used as a classifier. The idea is to obtain a classifier having a self-training character during the work process. The good results from the first experiments show the efficiency of the procedure. Better results from the second experiment have also confirmed the observations of other authors [3] that the information for substance is carried from both the decreasing and increasing parts of the signal.

7. Acknowledgements

This work has been performed as a part of Marie Curie Fellowship contract reference: HPMT-CT-2001-00249

References

1. Loutfi, A., Wide P., To Appear in Inf. Proc. and Management of Uncertainty, 1, 2002, 222-234
2. Loutfi, A., Coradeschi, S., Wide, P., IEEE Instr. and Meas. Techn. Conf., USA, Anchorage AK, May 21-23, 2002
3. Distante, C., Leo, M., Siciliano, P., Persaud, K., Sens. and Act. B, 87, 2002, 274-288
4. Llobet, E., Brezmes, J., Vilanova, X., Sueiras, J. E., Correig, X., Sens. and Act. B, 41, 1997, 13-21
5. Figaro gas sensor: Technical reference, http://www.figarosensor.com, 1992
6. Strang, G., Linear Algebra and its Applications, Harcourt College Publishers, 1988
7. Walker, J., A Primer on Wavelets and their Scientific Applications, Chapman & Hall, CRC Press LLC, 1999

8. Ratton, L., Kunt, T., McAvoy, T., Fuja, T., Cavicchi, R., Semancik, S., Sens. and Act. B, volume 41, 1997, 185-194
9. Holmberg, M., Davide, F. A. M., DiNatale, C., DAmico, A., Winquist, F., Lunstrom, I., Sens. and Act. B, 42, 1997, 185-194
10. Holmberg, M., Winquist, F., Lunstrom, I., Davide, F., DiNatale, C., DAmico A., Sens. and Act. B, 3536, 1996, 528-535
11. Eklov, T., Martensson, P., Lunstrom, I., Anal. Chim. Acta, 353, 1997, 291-300

Author Index

Aczél J 3	Foulloy L 417
Allevard T 417	García Lapresta J-L 87
Andre-Obrécht R 255	Gerace I 441
Angryk R A 171	Giordani P 195
Baioletti M 73	Guo X 333
Baudrit C 37	Gutiérrez J 55
Ben Amor N 159	Guyonnet D 37
Benferhat S 159	Hallez A 321
Benoit E 415	Herrera F 121
Bonissone P 147	Herrera-Viedma E 121
Bosc P 309	Hristozov I 453
Burstein F 269	Hunter A 345
Calabrese R 359	Iliev B 453
Capotorti A 73, 133	Kyburg H E 61
Capriotti E 359	Lamma E 207
Casadio R 359	Lesot M J 183
Ceberio M 281	Liétard L 309
Chen G 333	Lin L 333
Chiclana F 121	Liu J 295
Cholvy L 245	Liu W 345
Churilov L 269	Marani P 359
Coletti G 25	Martelli P L 359
Compiani M 359	Martínez L 295
Coppi R 195	Modave M 281
D`Urso P 195	Montanucci L 359
Daniel M 49	Montero J 87
De Baets B 99	Montes S 99
De Tré G 320	Omhove J F 429
Detyniecki M 429	Ovchinnikov S 111
Díaz S 99	Pandolfi R 441
Discepoli M 441	Pedrycs W 383
Dubois D 37	Petry F E 171
Elouedi Z 159	Pizzi N J 383
Eskiizmirliler S 453	Prez L G 295
Fargier H 37	Renooij S 395
Fariselli P 359	Riguzzi F 207
Formisano A 133	Ristic B 11

Rouas J-L	255
Rolland	231
Rossi I	359
San Pedro J	269
Sanchez E	407
Smets P	11
Somorjai R L	383
Storari S	207
Sugeno M	407
Tasco G	359
Teng C M	61
Troffaes M	371
Tulipani S	73
van der Gaag L C	395
Vantaggi B	25
Vercher J-L	407
Verstraete J	321
Wasserthei J	269
Yager R R	221
Yamanoi T	407
Yamazaki T	405
Yang J B	295